THE JOINT

THE JOINT

LANGUAGE AND CULTURE IN A MAXIMUM SECURITY PRISON

By

INEZ CARDOZO-FREEMAN, Ph.D.

The Ohio State University

In Collaboration With

EUGENE P. DELORME

With the Technical Assistance of

David W. Maurer, Ph.D., and Robert A. Freeman

With a Foreword by

Simon Dinitz, Ph.D.
The Ohio State University

CHARLES C THOMAS • PUBLISHER
Springfield • Illinois • U.S.A.

Published and Distributed Throughout the World by

CHARLES C THOMAS • PUBLISHER

2600 South First Street

Springfield, Illinois 62717

© *1984 by* Inez Cardozo-Freeman

ISBN 0-398-04911-4

Library of Congress Catalog Card Number: 83-9266

With THOMAS BOOKS *careful attention is given to all details of manufacturing and
design. It is the Publisher's desire to present books that are satisfactory as to their physical
qualities and artistic possibilities and appropriate for their particular use.* THOMAS
BOOKS *will be true to those laws of quality that assure a good name and good will.*

Printed in the United States of America

SC-R-3

Library of Congress Cataloging in Publication Data

Cardozo-Freeman, Inez.
    The joint : language and culture in a maximum
security prison.

    Bibliography: p.
    Includes index.
    1. Washington State Penitentiary.   2. Prisoners—
Washington (State)—Language.   3. Prisoners—Washington
(State)—Attitudes.   4. Prison psychology.   I. Delorme,
Eugene P.   II. Title.
HV9475.W22W373   1984   365'.6'0979748   83-9266
ISBN   0-398-04911-4

For our beloved friends, Marion and Robert Gatrell

FOREWORD

Walla Walla is a prison, a place, and an image. Located on a knoll in the rolling countryside of southeastern Washington, hard by the Oregon border, the 500-acre Washington State Penitentiary is tucked away so inconspicuously that it does nothing to mar the terrain or the small community of the same name. The grayish granite walls and depressing towers testify to the fact that the Washington State Penitentiary was built before the turn of the century. Before the recently completed twenty million dollar interior face lift, this ancient fortress, west of the Rockies and east of the Cascades, was an ugly and compact complex of eight cellblock buildings and enough ancillary facilities to accommodate up to 1600 inmates on only fifteen of the 500 acres. The most prominent inside-the-perimeter feature, to a visitor at least, is a long breezeway, a promenade of sorts, which is the collecting point of the institution. Men stroll back and forth, mostly in groups of twos and threes, gossiping, telling tall tales, conspiring, and dealing with their boredom. Despite the Big Sky, or maybe because of it, one leaves this ugly and depressing place with a sense of relief, of liberation.

The community of Walla Walla takes the prison for granted. Although a major employer and an important source of revenue for the community, the prison receives little media coverage in town and, except in special circles, is generally dismissed as a necessary if undesirable neighbor. In any case, short of a disturbance within the walls, the Washington State Penitentiary is tolerated by the community, whose citizens seem more concerned with leisure pursuits and coping with the everyday problems of living than with penal reform. The prison is a pocketbook and not an ideological issue, and as long as the perimeter remains secure, the staff safe, and the interior noise level low, the two

vii

worlds coexist by ignoring each other—one by choice, the other
by lack of choice.

The Washington State Penitentiary is also an image—a blurry
procession of events, of lockdowns and shakedowns, of riots and
murder, of stability, innovation, and change. Walla Walla is to Big
Houses what Watts, Detroit, and Newark are to street riots, what
Kent State and Jackson State are to the student protest of the late
1960s and early 1970s. Walla Walla is even more. It is a prison that
experienced unprecedented innovation, restructuring, and subse-
quent failure in which a psychiatrist and lawyer team in Olympia
sought to create a "just society," based on participatory democracy
by the prisoners, and a therapeutic environment and were totally
discredited in these efforts. Not since the Howard Gill experiment
at Norfolk Prison in Massachusetts were expectations raised to
such heights or dashed as painfully. The Walla Walla experiment,
like Norfolk and like the abolition of juvenile facilities in Massachusetts by Jerome Miller, will be studied for years to come by
penal experts.

Inez Cardozo-Freeman is acutely aware of Walla Walla as a
prison, a place, and a symbol, but rather than deal with macrolevel
transformations, she has written an ethnography of life inside the
walls focusing, as did her intellectual mentor, David Maurer, on
language as the key to sharing and portraying the thoughts, feelings,
worries, aspirations, defeats, and fleeting moments of joy of the
men inside the untidy and brutish world of this maximum security prison. A folklorist by profession, a penal reformer in the
hallowed tradition of that term, Dr. Cardozo-Freeman has successfully captured the standard lingo of the convicts in all its
richness and subtleties (over 800 words and expressions of which
only a handful are required for successful interaction and hardly
any of which are acceptable media words or phrases). But she
has done more. She has successfully penetrated the minds and
souls of her subjects, speaking their thoughts as though they
are her own. We feel (understand) with her what it means to be
transported from the classification center or the courts on a rick-
ety bus in chains across the mountains to Walla Walla. We feel
(*verstehen*) the fear of debarking, the uncertainty of these men
condemned to long terms of imprisonment under conditions of

personal and psychological degradation few of us can truly imagine. We recoil in horror as we realize that these men are being measured for sexual exploitation and victimization, for gang recruitment, even as they debark.

Inez Cardozo-Freeman leads them from the bus through their socialization or prisonization as she describes the adventures and misadventures of her convicts: the dreariness of daily life; the inverted values so highly esteemed in the world of powerless men; the loneliness, exploitation, even insanity, of her charges and wards; the intergroup struggles between rival groups, especially but not exclusively, the infamous Bikers, Lifers, and the small group of native Americans. She carries us with her as she explores the worlds of the *punks* and *queens*, the *good people* and those less so, the *fried brains*, the connivers and racketeers, and the inmate self-government types. Even the coldest among us become less certain that the Walla Wallas in this country do anything well except inflict the "pains of punishment" on inmates as we read the most touching and sometimes contradictory voices of the inmates describing, through the author, their feelings to and about their *Ladies*. Inez Cardozo-Freeman makes it easy to forget that some of these men have committed the most heinous offenses as she watches them *slip and slide* through their terms or retreat, as in "The Great Escape" into fantasy, drugs, and unreality.

Eugene Delorme, native American, prisoner, leader, *good people*—a man predestined for Walla Walla as his autobiography attests—did most of the interviews within the walls with nearly every type of inmate and on nearly all imaginable subjects. Dr. Cardozo-Freeman wanted more, always more, as she asked her collaborator to open new subjects, expand on others, probe the worldview of his colleagues, friends, and enemies. I have listened to some of the tapes, read the transcripts of others, and found them true to what I had seen and heard in my own research in this facility. Painstakingly edited, utilizing her own insights from the days spent interviewing inmates and sitting in observation in the visiting room at Walla Walla, I believe Dr. Cardozo-Freeman has written a brilliant ethnography that only a folklorist of her accomplishment could achieve. This may not be the Walla Walla of the administrators or the corrections officers or even the treatment people. It is, indisputably, the Walla Walla of most of the inmates. And this Walla Walla begs improvement. The reader will not again be able to confront the issue of imprisonment as "just deserts," as reformative, or even as a warehouse for losers with equanimity after reading *The Joint: Language and Culture in a Maximum Security Prison.*

Simon Dinitz
The Ohio State University

INTRODUCTION

This book, which attempts to bring together some elements of language and selected aspects of the social structure of a maximum security prison, grew out of field work conducted at the Washington State Penitentiary in Walla Walla from June, 1978, through December, 1980, by Eugene Delorme, who was then an inmate, and myself. It is a study that focuses on how, in the process of describing life in prison, prisoners reveal their worldview through the language they use and is premised on linguist Benjamin Lee Whorf's hypothesis that language shapes and in turn is shaped by culture. Inherent in the worldview of the men is a severe condemnation of the "system" and all that supports or perpetuates it. Although the book is directed to students, scholars, and interested lay readers, it has particular relevance to those who study or work with prisoners. It is a book that, while critical of prisons and their often dehumanizing and repressive operations, recognizes the efforts of those persons in all areas of corrections, in particular those who serve "on the line" as guards, who try to deal justly and therefore humanely with prisoners despite the often trying circumstances.

From the inception of this study, David W. Maurer, a pioneer in the field of sociolinguistics and the foremost authority on criminal argot and subcultures, served as consultant and technical advisor. His work and wisdom had great impact in shaping the direction of this book. It was on his advice that the body of carefully edited data presented here—representing only about one-fourth of all the data collected—remain as free as possible from theoretical opinion so as not to detract from the power and freshness of the material contributed by the men. An attempt has been made to present the story of the men simply and directly, focusing on how the language, in particular its connotative aspects, reveals the worldview of prisoners.

One of the problems in describing a prison culture is that generally the point of view of everyone except the prisoner is presented—prison staff, guards, officials, researchers, and so on. Since a prison culture is largely determined by the prisoners themselves and not by society as represented by the prison authorities or others, this has not always been a satisfactory way of accurately describing a prison culture. What is presented here, however, is the description of a prison culture as seen from the perspective of the prisoners themselves. I have selected from a gigantic *corpus* of material what can be considered to be a representative sampling of the prison culture. The language of the prisoners is correlated with their behavior. The prisoners have been allowed to interpret this correlation and have determined their own terminology. I have tried to avoid putting thoughts in their minds or words in their mouths. My interest has been in learning about how the men view their life in prison, what they have to say about it, and what they mean about what they say about it. My chief function then has been to correlate the life patterns of the prisoners (as described by the prisoners) with the language (used by the prisoners) along with the meaning of the vocabulary (as expressed by the prisoners). I have attempted to bring these three aspects together and define them in the prisoners' terms, not in the language of the conventional lexicographer.

Since my goal has been to present the views the prisoners have of life in prison—what they say about it, as well as what they mean about what they say—I have not focused on what other persons in the dominant culture think prisoners ought to mean about what they say, nor have I focused on what others believe about how prisoners ought to live, ought to think, or ought to talk. Although it is impossible to be completely objective, I have made every effort to present a *corpus* as free from outside interpretation as possible. To the best of my ability I have tried to set down what the prisoners mean, not what I think they mean. For example, the metaphor of the *Chain* in the chapter that begins the prisoners' description of their lives is drawn from their experience and is expressed in language defined by them in terms of their own culture.

No researcher can produce a completely objective *corpus* of material. As James P. Spradley and David W. McCurdy point out, "the 'objective observer' who is detached from his subject matter, who refrains from allowing his values to influence his observations, is a myth."[1] Throughout, I have tried to identify and move beyond my own values and biases, dealing respectfully with prisoner values and biases in an effort to better understand and present their cultural view. My perspective has been determined to a great extent by the nature of my goal: when accurately describing the worldview of a culture, one must of necessity present what Erving Goffman calls a "partisan view."[2]

Gresham Sykes warns in his book, *The Society of Captives*, that there are two serious problems a researcher confronts when attempting to study a prison culture. The first is "the peril of being 'conned' by highly articulate, glib prisoners who seek some personal advantage," and the second is the danger of becoming "partisan" consciously or unconsciously [and that it is] "only by remaining firmly neutral in one's sympathies [that] a valid picture of prison life [can] be uncovered."[3] I disregarded both these warnings; indeed, I believe that being partisan was not only the key to not being conned but also the reason I was able to uncover a valid picture of prison life. In my field, one trusts those who give information about their lives; after all, they are the only people who truly know and understand their culture.[4]

The first step toward realizing my research goal was to collect the folk speech in its natural context. In order to do this it was necessary to find men who were clever with the language and who wanted to tell people in the free world what life in prison was like for them. What was needed, therefore, were "highly articulate, glib men who were seeking personal advantage." The personal advantage each man sought in this instance was a legitimate and worthy one—a chance to tell his side of a much told story usually described by people outside the walls of a prison looking in. My approach to the study demanded that none of the language be altered or censored and that the men should determine what they wanted to talk about, since I realized that what was important for them would certainly be described vividly in the *lingo* of the prison.

Research for this study began after I was granted permission to enter the Washington State Penitentiary to interview inmates in order to select one or more to assist me with the field work. Using a glossary of argot and slang collected in the mid-1950s by Robert A. Freeman, then Associate Superintendent of Treatment at the prison, eight inmates known for their facility in using *con-lingo* met with me for a week, reviewing the 1950s collection, pointing out changes between the languages of the 1950s and the 1970s, and discussing with me methods on how best to achieve my goal of collecting the current language in its natural context. This first field trip brought to my attention which of the eight men I had met with were most interested in working with me. Two men, one of them Eugene Delorme, agreed to work together after I left the prison, to discuss on tape the language still current from the 1950s list in order to give me some idea of how and when it was used. In the process they agreed to add the new language that had replaced the old in the glossary that had disappeared from usage in the prison, describing in the process the circumstances that elicited the language. This initial step produced fifteen hours of taped conversations between the two men and was done over a period of about six weeks. After returning to my duties at the university, Delorme and I were in constant communication, and by the time the fifteen tapes were completed he had agreed to work with me to conduct the field work in the prison.

Eugene Delorme was thirty-nine years old when I first met him. An Isantee Sioux who had been in and out of the prison since 1962 for theft and parole violations, he was highly respected and trusted by the prison population. Several of the inmates whom I spoke to referred to him as *good people*, a term used to describe a small number of men in the prison who are leaders exercizing a positive influence in the population. They are *old timers* who know intimately the workings of the prison to whom other men sometimes turn for help in problem solving. Two guards also referred to Delorme as *good people*. The inmates knew that he was compiling information on life and language in the prison, and they were willing to talk to him about themselves and their situation. Some men helped him collect material. He was able to interview or talk to men from every important group in the prison—black, white, native

American, and Chicano. Delorme describes his methodology:

"I need to mention how I picked my interviewees. The first thing I will say is that I did not do the tapes at random. I took great pains to balance the interviews with the ratio of different ethnic groups in the prison. I also made sure I interviewed new men as well as old timers. I think the contrast of opinions is obvious. It is also very important that the reader note how a man's impression of the prison and his attitudes will change and he will adopt the attitudes of the older cons if just for his own safety. A man can often become almost frantic in his efforts to fit in. It doesn't take long to discover that street attitudes, or square John opinions, can get you into trouble. Again, this doesn't apply to everyone. It would be a cinch if everything could be generalized. It was very important for me to get the majority opinion. Very few of my interviews were with offbeat cons. I interviewed dings, fruits, murderers, punks, rats, squares, good people, bad people, nuts, Indians, Chicanos, blacks, whites, cowboys, hippies, dopers, college students, pimps, psychos, idiots, and brilliant cons. The majority group which I interviewed were white. Blacks comprise a large portion of the interviews since they are the second largest group in the pen. The Mexicans are the smallest group, but even so, they are well represented. The Indians contributed a small portion of the total interviews. The guys I interviewed were typical, including me."

Everyone interviewed knew how the material collected was going to be used. The men approved and were cooperative and generous in their contribution. "Conning" did not occur. The men simply told about life as they lived it in the prison.

I entered the prison convinced that trust was central to the success of my field work, and this leads to the second warning by Gresham Sykes—not to be partisan. Being partisan, it must be emphasized, was a major part of my methodology. No fieldworker in folklore succeeds without being sympathetically interested in his or her subjects. In the course of our work together, Eugene Delorme and I became trusted friends. In turn, the men who cooperated with him to help me realize my goal trusted him. Without this important dimension, nothing productive would have resulted. Eugene Delorme and I have both benefited from our collaboration, each learning from the other's world, each growing in the process.

As the results of his field work began to arrive, I realized that what Delorme was producing added a new dimension to the study, which needed to be recognized as unique. What he was doing was a folk ethnography, an extensive description of life in a maximum security prison as seen through the eyes of the "folk" and told in their words. Their efforts grew out of their desire to change their existential situation through making others outside the prison aware of their condition. What Spradley and McCurdy call "strategic ethnography" became in this instance strategic folk ethnography.[5]

The decision for structuring the content of this study was carefully worked out in consultation with Eugene Delorme and David W. Maurer. Although each chapter focuses in some depth on one particular part of the prison cultural scene the men believe important, it would be impossible and misleading to isolate one specific cultural aspect of the prison from the totality of the experience; therefore, each chapter brings out facets of life in general in the prison. But since it is important to focus in some depth on certain areas that stand out in their significance and impact on the lives of the men, these particular topics have been selected for chapters; however, care has been taken to see that the totality of the material covers all the important elements of the culture — interaction, association, subsistence, bisexuality, territoriality, temporality, education, recreation, defense, and exploitation of resources — the ten indices of culture developed by George L. Trager.[6]

One hundred and fifty-two hours of taped conversations and interviews were made during the two and one-half years the field work was in progress — some two thousand pages of transcribed narrative material. Many conversations between Delorme and myself were taped; several included other prisoners, as well. In addition, I spent several days observing family visits and talking with the wives and sweethearts of the men.

Approximately one-fourth of the total *corpus* collected was used in this study. The selection of narratives was determined by the degree to which they represented the majority view of life in prison as described by the men who were interviewed, the use of the argot, and the liveliness of the language. Overall, the best narrators were chosen. In order to determine whether the views expressed in the completed study were representative of the prison population, I returned to the prison in June, 1982, after the manuscript was completed. Ten prisoners—five white, three black, one Chicano, and one native American—who had been in the prison prior to June, 1978, were selected randomly from the population to read the manuscript for me and critique on tape its representative qualities with respect to prisoner worldview: all agreed that the story of life in the prison as described by the men speaking in the narratives was accurate and that the perspective presented represented the views of most of the men in the prison.

Throughout this study, Delorme is presented as "everyman" who is a prisoner. As an archetype, his life, opinions, and insights are constantly presented in order to show how one man came to be confined to prison and how he resisted and fought the experience almost to the point of self-destruction and finally how he discovered within the hated system something (the college program) he could use positively and of his own free will to help him escape into a new life of dignity and promise. Today (1982) Delorme is a senior at the University of Washington majoring in Society and Justice. His story is a hopeful one for those imprisoned, as it makes a statement about how one man led himself, after many failures and a great sense of despair, up and out of the depths of hell, using as his guide human reason and wisdom. His story is important because it demonstrates the ability of a man to find what is best in himself in the midst of his prison experience and it tells of a prison that, despite its indignities, horror, and oppression, provided within it the opportunity for positive transformation.

NOTES

[1]*Conformity and Conflict: Readings in Cultural Anthropology* (Boston: Little, Brown and Company, 1974), p. 6.

[2]"The world view of a group functions to sustain its members and expectedly provides them with a self-justifying definition of their own situation and a prejudiced view of non-members. . . . " *Asylums* (Garden City, N.Y.: Anchor Books, 1961), Preface, x.

[3]*The Society of Captives* (Princeton: Princeton University Press, 1958), pp. 135–136.

[4]The term "informant," commonly used by researchers in such fields as anthropology, sociology, and folkloristics should not, for obvious reasons, be used in prison research.

[5]*The Cultural Scene: Ethnography in Complex Society* (Chicago: Science Research Associates, Inc., 1975), p. 5.

[6]*Encyclopedia Britannica*, 1955.

ACKNOWLEDGMENTS

I owe thanks to many in the creation of this book. First, Robert A. Freeman, who gave me the 1950s' glossary and arranged for me to enter the prison to conduct my field work, and second, David W. Maurer, my beloved teacher and friend, who guided, scolded and advised me. I miss him dearly and hope that wherever he is, he knows and approves of what I have done.

Heartfelt thanks to the many prisoners at Walla Walla who so generously contributed their experiences and words for the good of "our" book. All their narratives are quoted with permission. Especially, thanks to inmates Kashif Abdul-Aziz (Smith), David Bo Bailey, John D. Canaday, John Carothers, Ron Staley, Willis L. Stanmore, D. L. Velasquez, and George Walks-on-Top for reading the completed manuscript and for putting their stamp of approval upon our book. Thanks also to those two readers who did not wish to be identified.

We thank the officials at the Washington State Penitentiary for allowing us absolute freedom to conduct the field work and in allowing me complete access not only to every staff person and prisoner and all prison records but to every part of the prison. In particular, thanks to Eric Gabrielson for reading some of the chapters and making helpful comments (and for running such a superb educational department at the Joint!) And thanks to all the correctional officers who so generously took time from their busy schedules to describe on tape what it is like to be on-the-line at Walla Walla. Their words are also used with permission.

My sincere thanks to Simon Dinitz, The Ohio State University, William Gealy, Northwestern University, and Allan Futrell, who read with care and commented constructively upon the book while it was taking shape. Although I take full responsibility for the final product, their helpful comments and advice play an important role in the direction that it took.

Deepest appreciation and thanks to Deither Haenicke and Ann Reynolds of The Ohio State University who not only read parts of the manuscript while it was in progress and enthusiastically supported it, but saw to it that traveling funds and professional leave were mine when needed. Thanks, also, to the Graduate School, the College of Humanities, and the Newark Campus Research Fund of The Ohio State University for their financial assistance.

My thanks to Barbara Walker, typist par excellence and friend, who helped transcribe the many tapes and type the manuscript. Her skill, accuracy and deep interest in our work made her a treasured jewel.

Last, we thank our gentle and beloved friends, Marion and Robert Gatrell, who supported and encouraged us through our work, read our manuscript, including the heavy lingo and, best of all, understood and approved.

CONTENTS

THE JOINT

Chapter 1

THE JOINT

E rving Goffman identifies prisons as "total institutions" whose "encompassing or total character is symbolized by the barrier to social intercourse with the outside and to departure that is often built right into the physical plant, such as locked doors, high walls, barbed wires . . . [and is] organized to protect the community against what are felt to be intentional dangers to it, with the welfare of the persons thus sequestered not the immediate issue. . . . "[1] In describing total institutions, Goffman writes that "all aspects of life are conducted in the same place and each under the single authority, [that] each phase of the member's daily activity is carried on in the immediate company of a large batch of others, all of whom are treated alike and are required to do the same thing together, [that] all phases of the day's activities are tightly scheduled, with one activity leading at a prearranged time to the next, the whole sequence of activities being imposed from above by a system of explicit formal rulings and a body of officials and finally, [that] the various enforced activities are brought together into a single rational plan purportedly designed to fulfill the official aims of the institution."[2] Although the Washington State Penitentiary is indeed a total institution, only the first aspect of Goffman's description fits the penitentiary described in these pages, which makes for a very distinct kind of total institution, indeed.

Simon Dinitz, distinguished sociologist and experienced prison observer once told me that the Washington State Penitentiary was "unique," that "no other prison in the United States is quite like it."[3] The circumstances that brought about this uniqueness began in the early 1970s. Originally, the prison was just another "big house" like Menard in southern Illinois, studied by Donald Clemmer in the 1930s,[4] or the New Jersey State Prison described by Gresham Sykes in the 1950s.[5] Later, it began to move toward the "correctional institution" model. What transpired in the decade of the 1970s caused it to be called a "mad house" not only by many prison observers but by some Walla Walla prisoners, as well.

Before the Washington State Penitentiary at Walla Walla was built, all felons in the state were contracted out to work for private groups who profited from their slave labor. They lived in strap-iron cells in a wooden prison at Seatco, now called Bucota, just seventeen miles from Olympia. In one of the official brochures describing this early prison, a former guard recalls "the terrible chains riveted to the ankles of the prisoners." These "Rindquist boots" were never removed day or night and allowed the prison to function with a minimum of guards. The Washington State Penitentiary at Walla Walla opened in 1887. Although men no longer were punished by having their teeth pulled out for talking, as they had at Seatco, shaved heads, striped suits, and the silent system were the order of the day.[6]

In 1893, J. H. Coblentz became warden. Using convict labor he "added a new hospital, built a prison stockyard and packaging plant, improved the water supply, landscaped the grounds, doubled production in the prison jute mill, and in an unprecedented move, supplied the luxury of underwear to the members of the outside work gang."[7]

By 1926, the prison had added a 160-acre farm, twenty-three enclosed acres, and five cell houses with 460 cells on three tiers providing space for more than 900 prisoners. Instead of hammocks, the men now slept in beds with straw-filled mattresses. No plumbing was provided. In 1929, the prison held 1100 prisoners in 460 cells, a vastly overcrowded situation.[8] In the 1930s, the National Society of Penal Information criticized the penitentiary for its "overcrowding, lack of industries and its rigid and repressive discipline," adding that "in few prisons in the nation is the overcrowding more serious and in none of them is less done to reduce the evils inherent in such a condition."[9]

By 1942, the Osborne Society (formerly the National Society of Penal Information) reported that three more cell houses had been added, for a total of eight, and that there were now 780 cells housing 1630 men. The society, warning that overcrowding was still a serious problem, strongly urged the building of single cells, the abolition of the silent system in the mess hall, higher pay for staff, the upgrading of staff recruitment policies, and "the organization of an inmate advisory council."[10]

In 1953, a riot brought national attention to the penitentiary. Preceding the riot was a two-day sitdown and hunger strike, which brought a representative from the governor's office in Olympia to Walla Walla to listen to prisoners who demanded that Warden Larry Delmore be replaced and that parole board policy be liberalized. No action by officials was taken. Then an explosion and fire occurred in the license plate factory. Scattered incidents of violence broke out that caused between 2 and 3 million dollars in damages. Again ignoring prisoner demands, officials hired more guards. This was followed by a massive riot in which hostages were taken and riot leaders ran the prison for two days.[11] At this point, negotiations began with the State Director of Institutions, Dr. Thomas Harris.[12] In 1955, a reporter for the *Seattle Post Intelligencer* wrote, "Picture yourself in a steel ceiling tank 5×7 feet. I literally mean a steel tank. It has steel walls, a steel ceiling and a steel floor. Your view is a steel-slatted floor . . . a bucket beside your bunk serves as a toilet. . . . Picture yourself in that tank for twenty-four hours a day!"[13]

In 1956, Merle Schneckloth became warden. When he returned to California that same year, he was replaced by B. J. Rhay.[14] B. J. Rhay, who assumed the leadership of a traditional, poorly equipped, and antiquated warehouse prison, presided over its transformation into one of the most open maximum-security facilities in the nation and finally led the return to a custody-oriented institution.[15] In an official report published during his first year as superintendent, he stated, "Cell blocks four and five at the Penitentiary were built in the 1880s. . . . There are no plumbing facilities in the cells [and] twice a day the inmates empty buckets into an open sewer outside the cell block building. . . . During the hot weather if the cells are kept closed the odor is unendurable."[16]

Between 1957 and 1966, the Washington State Correctional Central Office was under the leadership of Dr. Garet Heyns. During his tenure, he bureaucratized the Department of Institutions

(Corrections) unifying the autonomous institutions across the state into a central system. New programs were developed and old ones were upgraded or modernized. He was highly respected by the administration and staff of the prison at Walla Walla.[17] His policy with respect to maximum security left discipline and punishment up to the discretion of the superintendent of each institution in the state. As a consequence, men placed in solitary confinement at Walla Walla sometimes stayed for months and even years for infractions.[18] The institution was tightly run in the manner of the old Big House. Inmates needed passes to move from one area to another, and although many men were idle, some had jobs and some went to school.

The restrictions on movement about the penitentiary provided a measure of safety for the men serving sentences in the prison during this time; consequently there were fewer killings and fewer inmates preying on those in the population who were weaker. It was during this period that Robert A. Freeman developed a two-year college program for the inmates, which later expanded into a four-year program. Still in operation, prisoners today regard it as the most positive program in the penitentiary.

In 1966, Dr. Heyns was succeeded by Dr. William Conte, a psychiatrist by profession. His leadership, from 1966 to 1971, provoked a revolution in the corrections program of the state.[19] While Heyns had been highly respected, Conte was regarded as an outsider, one who, in Rhay's words, had "never walked the line."[20] Conte, aware that he was regarded as an unqualified intruder and that his philosophy for treatment was unwelcome, resigned July 1, 1971, but not before his reforms had been set into motion. Later he made this statement about the situation at the Washington State Penitentiary:

> When I raised questions about the reason for the strip cell and/or when I spoke about the human aspect of the treatment endeavor. . . . I was told by many staff at all levels of the organization that the men in prison were animals and that this was the only kind of treatment they could understand. Of course I was being told I did not know anything about prisons. . . . There is no way I could have described the prison as an arena for treatment or rehabilitation. It was not even a place where a man might expect civil treatment.[21]

Rhay, an authoritarian warden of the old school, carried out Conte's reforms, despite his reservations. At a press conference in 1970, Conte set forth a series of reform measures that included "the abolition of censorship; the extension of telephone and visiting privileges; the easing of disciplinary methods (the final demise of the strip cell) [actually still in existence today] and, the most far-reaching and controversial, the promise of forming a resident government council, to embody the principle of inmate self-government."[22] In addition, Conte announced his policy of stepping up work-training release programs, instituting furloughs, and expanding educational programs (both in and out of the prison) for the prisoners.[23]

The new policies and programs were not viewed with favor by prison personnel or administration. Indeed, "they blamed the reforms . . . for the demoralization, violence, and confusion which followed."[24] The sudden switch from a traditional custody-oriented philosophy to one that focused on treatment created enormous resistance at all levels.[25] Even some of the more traditional prisoners objected.

The prison staff and administration stated that these changes had been imposed without proper preparation of the prison staff, which in turn created considerable misunderstanding as well as strong resistance.[26] Particularly disliked was the Resident Government Council (RGC), because it gave the inmates a say in their own destiny, something that threatened the institutional staff who saw it as a power shift placing them at great disadvantage in the management of the institution. In particular, it removed power from the superintendent. The prison authorities charged that the leaders of the RGC "did not necessarily reflect the will of the majority but that of a verbally aggressive minority. Their main object was to extend inmate authority vis-à-vis the custodial staff. A massive effort to bust the boundaries of prison rules and regulations was launched by the Resident Government Council. . . . A focus on inmate rights rather than on inmate obligations and duties came to be a rallying point in the power struggle."[27]

Stastny and Tyrnauer brilliantly document the institution and demise of the RGC, prisoner self-government at the Washington State Penitentiary.[28]

Through a peculiar series of circumstances W.S.P. became, in the early
1970s, a laboratory for one of the boldest experiments in recent penal
history. Along with many other maximum-security prisons during the
1950s and 1960s, it had been evolving toward a type of prison we have
called "interactive." This development was related to broad social trends
which have undermined the absolutist character of the prison regime.
One of the most important of these is the bureaucratic model of
correctional management, which, in the years following World War II,
came to supplant the autocratic rule of the warden. This change took
place at varying rates in different institutions. At Washington State
Penitentiary, it did not overtake the Rhay regime until the early 1970s.
The onset of this trend was usually marked by the creation of a Department of Corrections, which undermined the local and personalized rule
of the warden. Neither humanitarian reforms nor commitment to rehabilitation and the introduction of a professional treatment staff had
succeeded in eliminating prison absolutism at W.S.P. The preeminence
of custody and the autocratic rule of the warden remained a reality until
the early 1970s.[29]

Conte's reforms began to be instituted in December, 1970, when
a sit-down strike was called by radical prisoners who sought a
liberalization of hair regulations. This protest shut the penitentiary down for ten days and ended on New Years Day, 1971, with
the agreement that all of Conte's reforms would be instituted, with
the exception of self-government.[30] Self-government began with
the election and institution of the first Resident Government
Council on April 24 and 25, 1971. By agreement of the staff and
residents, the first RGC was to be a dry-run for full-scale self-
government.[31] Rhay described the concept as "a fifty-fifty partner-
ship" in which "the guards were to pull back 50 percent and the inmates were supposed to come forward 50 percent in responsibility."[32]
Stastny and Tyrnauer point out that there was general agreement
that "a significant degree of power redistribution had taken place
[that] for better or worse, the old patterns of control had been
drastically shaken by the theory and practice of 'self-government'
as introduced by the reformers in Olympia."[33] A "top-level evaluation team" after visiting W.S.P. in June, 1971, warned that as long
as "many of the staff see themselves as being short-circuited out of
the action," the program had "little chance" in the long run, but
"to retreat from these advances now could well be disastrous."[34]

According to inmates, the first council established an image of considerable power in contrast to the inmate committees, which had previously functioned in a liaison capacity, and succeeded in solving a considerable number of problems that the prisoners viewed as contributing to low morale and inaugurated proposals for participation in classification and adjustment committees in order "to get a vote and be able to support some of the men who had a good claim."[35]

On March 20, 1971, a young white prisoner struck an older black inmate in the prison auditorium over a TV viewing disagreement. This led to fighting among blacks and whites, which continued sporadically throughout the prison for the next twenty-four hours. According to Stastny and Tyrnauer, blacks, who represented only 20 percent of the population, felt most threatened, as hundreds of angry white inmates gathered in the auditorium armed with clubs. Guards beat a hasty retreat, abandoning their posts. Presumably, they anticipated a massacre. What followed was documented by a prisoner:

> Several inmates, blacks and whites alike, mounted the stage of the theatre and acted as a catalyst, and managed to calm the confused and hostile crowd of would-be combatants. Appeals were made by several inmate leaders not to proceed with the hostilities but to unite and combine the strength of the races against the system which had encouraged and fostered racial distance and which had tacitly sanctioned a near-massacre. The crowd who only a moment before were ready to kill each other responded with a spontaneous sigh of relief, weapons were discarded, and thus began a racial unity and harmony that continues to baffle the most cynical observer of prison behavior.[36]

It was at this point that inmates formed the Race Relations Committee (RRC), which played an important role in avoiding and settling interracial conflicts.[37]

On April 24 and 25, 1971, the first RGC elections were held. Stastny and Tyrnauer describe the events leading up to this new epoch in Washington State Corrections as remarkable:

> Even given the trends generated by the pressures for change in America's warehouse prisons, which had been accumulating over recent decades, W.S.P. had appeared to lag behind. It was a typically tough maximum-security custodial fortress, operating in a plant nearly a century old, when suddenly it was transformed. Inmate organizations and clubs rang-

ing from the ethnic native American, Chicano, and black formations to
the "Lifers with Hope" sprang up and received formal recognition. And
the tough convicts became legislators, policy makers, with a government
of their own, the Resident Government Council [RGC] representing the
inmate body as a whole.[38]

The president of the guard's union reflected the point of view
the corrections staff took of this momentous shift in power: "Now
this program was dropped in, just dropped in. The residents and
staff didn't know exactly what to do with it. As it happened, the
residents organized first and better. They took advantage of the
staff and the staff found themselves backed into a wall. The residents could call them names for just doing their job, you know, as
it was done before."[39]

During the early period—what Statsny and Tyrnauer refer to as
"the hopeful years, 1971–1973"—the inmates looked upon self-
government as extremely positive. One former RGC officer gave
his views on the role this early council played: "The RGC had
distinctive voting rights and priviledges, we could call Olympia
[the state capital], we could set up our own press conferences. We
could call in reporters when we wanted to. We could take pictures,
we could, you know, write out what we wanted to write out, we
could send out, we could write out our own newspaper. We had all
those discretionary situations that the former [advisory] councils
never had. . . . "[40]

In 1973, a new Division of Adult Corrections was formed out of
two areas within the Department of Social and Health Services.
Milton Burdman, a correctional expert from California, became
deputy secretary of the division. L. N. Patterson, a former California prison superintendent, was brought in to reorganize adult
corrections in the state. Patterson, who was not a supporter of
Conte's reforms, called them a farce. Officials in the new division
determined that the power given inmates should be retracted.
"The dilemma that this posed was how to pull in the reins without
precipitating an explosion."[41]

The development of inmate clubs gave rise to new power groups
within the population, which tended to weaken the RGC. In 1973,
eleven demands drafted by the RGC were presented to the administration. "These included due-process reforms in disciplinary

hearings, introduction of a drug-rehabilitation program, and removal of an unpopular hospital physician."[42] A struggle developed between Rhay and RGC leaders over the results of an informal poll of the population soliciting support by the RGC for a work stoppage. "Rhay questioned the authenticity of the poll, put the penitentiary on 'deadlock' keeping the inmates locked in their cells for ten days—and then proceeded to conduct his own poll in an effort to demonstrate the shallowness of the support for the RGC's current leadership. . . . Rhay was able to exploit divisions among the inmate clubs and their leaders, some of whom disapproved of the work stoppage. The RGC president resigned, announcing that only a faction of the Council backed the strike."[43]

In December, 1974, an outbreak of violence in the prison hospital (involving a small number of prisoners who took thirteen hostages and injured two nurses) and a take-over in Eight-Wing (a separate incident) sealed the fate of the RGC. The guards and Rhay believed that the incidents had been instigated by RGC leaders. One inmate who was interviewed claimed, however, that these outbreaks had been spontaneous: "Some couple of guys who were drug users, who have been abused by the system, primarily, went to the hospital and flipped out, went to get their stuff. Spontaneous as all get out. You know, two spontaneously, totally isolated incidences, which connected together to make it seem as though Walla Walla's going to explode."[44]

Rhay charged that members of the RGC had used their power for personal gain.[45] Three months later, the Resident Council (RC) came into being, replacing the RGC and signaling the end to inmate self-government at Walla Walla. The final authority, Rhay stated, "is and will be the Superintendent." The demise of the RGC saw the ascendency of the Bikers Club, who, as Rhay claimed, had helped calm the population down after these disturbances.[46]

Further complicating the situation at Walla Walla in addition to the RGC and the emergence of clubs—the administration called them "gangs"—was a prisoner's union called FUSE (Felons United for Self Endeavor) with a dues-paying membership of some 400 men with lobbyists in Olympia, the state capitol. All of these groups lessened the control and power of prison officials and were an immense threat to the custodial staff.

Accompanying the revolutionary reforms instituted by Conte at Walla Walla was the new awareness of prisoners with respect to their rights. This new rise in consciousness was part of a national movement acknowledging the rights of all people in the United States, not only in prisons but in free society as well. This began in the 1950s with the Civil Rights Movement led by Dr. Martin Luther King, Jr., and crested with the anti-Vietnam War Movement in the 1960s and early 1970s. Participatory democracy became a hallmark of these movements; everyone had a right to participate in the determination of his destiny. It was inevitable that such ideas would filter into the penal institutions of the country.[47] Conte's reforms were in the spirit of the times.

When Superintendent B. J. Rhay resigned in 1977, Douglas Vinzant, former head of juvenile rehabilitation, was appointed to replace him. Vinzant was liked by the inmates because his policy—rehabilitation through self-help programs—allowed them unprecedented freedoms. Although his policies were humane, his procedures in implementing them were disastrous. His gravest error was ignoring the custodial staff and appearing to favor inmates over them. This intensified the already great hostility the guards had for the inmates. Another error was failing to recognize that not all of the men were able to handle the freedom and responsibilities he granted them. Some, of course, were ready and responded with responsibility, imagination, and a new-found sense of hope; for example Lifers with Hope teams, who repaired and insulated the homes of the poor and elderly in Walla Walla, and Black Prisoners' Forum Unlimited (BPFU), who ran a program for juvenile offenders in the western part of the state similar to "Scared Straight" at Rahway in New Jersey. However, some abused and misused their rights, and the prison staff focused on these failures. Eventually, violence provoked a great outcry from guards and powerful critics in the legislature and elsewhere, which doomed the program. Nicholas Genokos, whose philosophy was similar to Vinzant's, briefly served as superintendent when Vinzant assumed full-time directorship of Adult Corrections for the state. Both men were removed by Governor Dixie Lee Ray when violence erupted in 1978.[48]

Although critics of Conte's reforms charged that his radical changes had accounted for the upswing of violence in the prison, other important factors contributed heavily to this phenomenon. Among these were the increase in racial tensions introduced by the rise in the prison population of minority groups (Chicanos, blacks, and native Americans), the introduction of drugs brought in by the "new inmate" of the 1960s, and a very important factor — the new worldview introduced from the streets by these groups.

A new spirit of lawlessness seemed to prevail if one looks at the statistics. Between January, 1972, and November, 1978, for example, seventeen inmates were murdered and twelve committed suicide.[49] It was evident that an upswing in killings and inmate-on-inmate violence had occurred. Alarmed observers of the prison, officials, and some of the more traditional inmates believed that these new freedoms were gained at great sacrifice to the safety, both physical and psychological, of the inmates and custodial staff. One inmate compared the prison to a "bombed city ravaged by gangs of marauding scavengers preying on the weak and infirm." The animosity the guards felt towards the inmates, in part engendered by the dangers faced by them in trying to carry out their duties in such a dangerous environment, eventually exploded in tragic consequences.

Several factors accounted for the upswing in violence at Walla Walla. Between June, 1978, and December, 1980 — the period during which all the material for this book was collected — violence among prisoners and then violence against the guards brought about a dramatic change in the leadership and policies of the penitentiary. In August, 1978, a bomb that two guards were attempting to dismantle exploded, killing one and seriously injuring the other. All the inmates were placed on a twenty-hour lockdown, and it was at this point that Genokos and Vinzant were fired by Governor Dixie Lee Ray. Guards, who were unionized, threatened to strike, demanding that power be taken back from the inmates. James Spalding, who had at one time been a guard at Walla Walla, was appointed superintendent.

Guards were happier with Spalding but urged him to "take back power" from the inmates. It was under his leadership that almost all of Conte's reforms were halted. Prisoners, most of whom voiced their opinion through the leaders of the Resident Council and the

more prestigious clubs, were disturbed when Spalding dismantled
their self-help programs, limiting furloughs to only those men in
the Minimum Security Building outside the walls of the prison.
They warned that possibilities of violent outbreaks had greatly
increased because Spalding's actions had "taken hope from them."
The institution was extremely tense; according to news reporters
allowed inside the walls during this period, the prisoners and not
the administration or the guards were "keeping the lid on."[50]

In June, 1979, Chicanos murdered a native American. On the
day native Americans were preparing a traditional funeral ritual
for their murdered brother feelings were running high, and one
guard who came to the assistance of another guard (who had
approached one of the prisoners for a weapon's search) was killed.
The entire population was immediately placed on a lockdown that
lasted for over four months—an unprecedented period of time for
this prison—during which time all clubs and self-help programs
including the Resident Council were disbanded by order of the
officials.[51] During the lockdown some of the inmates in Eight
Wing, a large cellblock holding 408 men, protesting the destruction of their personal property by guards and the intolerable
conditions of being confined four men to a cell 10 x 12 in the dead
heat of summer without showers or exercise, rebelled, tearing out
the plumbing fixtures in their cells. Most of the men in Eight
Wing were transferred into the Big Yard where they remained for
forty-three days. Many class action suits were filed by the men as a
result of these incidents. In 1979, the state legislature approved 13
million dollars for architectural changes in the prison to make the
penitentiary "safer and more manageable." It is in this context
that the men tell their story of life in this prison.

THE PRISON SETTING

The Washington State Penitentiary is located on the edge of
Walla Walla, a small community of about 25,000 people. A conservative and prosperous community surrounded by rich wheat lands,
it is located in the extreme southeastern part of the state. The
prison complex is situated on 500 acres of land, only sixty of which
are used for the prison, its surrounding buildings, and service areas.

The main unit of the prison is enclosed by granite walls. The area inside the walls takes up 15.2 acres, with 4.6 acres serving as recreation area and yard. Included inside the walls are an inside administration facility, educational facilities including a library, a hospital, a kitchen and two dining areas, a gymnasium and inmate recreation area, an inmate canteen, an auditorium, miscellaneous inmate services, a chapel, and maximum and close custody housing in six cellblocks—the Admissions and Security Unit, and cellblocks 4, 5, 6, 7, and 8—called "wings." With the exception of eight strip cells, which have nothing in them but a hole in the floor, all other cells have toilets and wash basins. Six and Eight Wings hold the largest number of men—102 four-men cells 127.5 sq. ft. and 130 sq. ft. respectively, in three stacked tiers for a total of 408 men in each wing. Four and Five Wings are one-man cells each 48.8 sq. ft., a total of 256 cells. Seven Wing has 54 four-men cells each 102.5 sq. ft., a total of 116 men, and 30 one-man cells each 68.5 sq. ft. There are a total of 1488 beds exclusive of health care beds within the walls. The Minimum Security Building (MSB), which is located outside the walls and is self-sufficient, holds 297 beds. Outside the walls immediately adjacent is the industries building, which houses the laundry, inmate intake and clothing areas, plant engineering, and industries shops. The oldest building—inside administration and recreation—dates from 1888 and was remodeled in 1957–71. The newest building is the new power plant built in 1967–68. The alterations to create a safer prison will drastically alter the present layout of the prison.

POPULATION CHARACTERISTICS OF PRISONERS

Ethnic groups, in particular blacks, Chicanos, and native Americans, are found in the prison in numbers out of proportion to their numbers in the general population of the state of Washington. A report of a study by Frank Dunbaugh, prepared with the assistance of the National Institute of Corrections, released to the press in December, 1980, revealed that although blacks constitute only three percent of the state's population, 21 percent of Washington's prisoners are black. Dunbaugh compared prison statistics with 1976 population figures of each state and found that Washington state incarcerated more than twice the national average—1342 black inmates for each 100,000 of black population, as compared to the national average of 544 inmates for each 100,000 blacks.[52]

The quarterly publication, *Client Characteristics & Population Movement Report* issued by the state of Washington, Department of Social and Health Services, Division of Adult Corrections, listed 1621 men in the Washington State Penitentiary for April–June, 1979. Racial characteristics are as follows:

Racial Characteristics at WSP—April–June, 1979

White	1097 men representing 67.7 percent
Black	368 men representing 22.7 percent
Chicano	66 men representing 4.1 percent
Native American	62 men representing 3.8 percent
Asian	6 men representing 0.4 percent
Not Reported	2 men representing 0.1 percent
Other	19 men representing 1.2 percent

Age distribution of the men in the prison for the period of April–June, 1979, showed the following:

Age Distribution of Men at WSP—April–June, 1979

18–20 years old	10 men	45–47 years old	85 men
21–23 years old	69 men	48–50 years old	59 men
24–26 years old	184 men	51–53 years old	44 men
27–29 years old	295 men	54–56 years old	44 men
30–32 years old	269 men	57–59 years old	24 men
33–35 years old	181 men	60–62 years old	17 men
36–38 years old	141 men	63–64 years old	4 men
39–41 years old	119 men	65+ years old	15 men
42–44 years old	85 men		

Felony violations in the state are classified into five categories: (1) Person Offenses—first and second degree murder, manslaughter, vehicular manslaughter, robbery, first and second degree assault, rape, statutory rape, indecent liberties, and other sex crimes; (2) Property Offenses—first and second degree burglary, theft, auto theft, forgery, welfare fraud, and other property offenses; (3) Drug Violation; (4) Parole Violation; and (5) Other Crimes that do not fit the above categories.

The *Report* on program needs of inmates in the Washington

state prison system covering the period for March 1, 1979, to April 30, 1980, published a breakdown of crimes committed by the men at WSP as follows:[53]

Types of Offenses at Walla Walla

Person Offenses	837	(56.6 percent)
Property Offenses	292	(19.7 percent)
Drug Offenses	56	(3.8 percent)
Other	68	(4.6 percent)
Parole Violations	226	(15.3 percent)

As the statistics point out, a high number of men are parole violators. According to statistics in *Client Characteristics and Population Report*, first and second degree assault (Person Offense) and first and second degree burglary (Property Offense) are the crimes most commonly committed in the state. According to the inmates, most person and property crimes are drug related. *The Analyses of Programs Needs Report* reveals that 25 percent of the men at Walla Walla had attended a community college prior to their last arrest.[54] Length of stay for inmates during this period at Walla Walla was reported in the Analysis as follows:

Length of Stay at Walla Walla

0–5 months	192 men	12.7 percent
6–11 months	269 men	17.9 percent
12–23 months	375 men	24.9 percent
24–35 months	245 men	16.3 percent
36+ months	425 men	28.2 percent

The statistics point out that more than half of the men at Walla Walla are in prison for violence against persons and that more than a quarter of the men are serving very long sentences, two characteristics that, it can be hypothesized, contribute to high inmate-on-inmate violence in the prison.

The brochure, *Washington State Penitentiary*,[55] an official publication, describes the system:

COURTS: After a suspected felon has been found guilty by the judge or jury, a maximum term of confinement is set in accordance with state law and the individual is granted probation—or, is sent to the RECEPTION UNIT at the Washington Corrections Center in Shelton. After thorough testing and evaluation, the offender meets the Parole Board which then sets a minimum term—using the information compiled on him as the basis for this decision. If he is a repeat offender—or guilty of a capital crime, the offender may be sent to the STATE PENITENTIARY which houses mostly "repeaters" or the more criminally sophisticated first offenders. Here the Classification Committee evaluates the recommendations from Shelton, studies the individual, and assigns jobs, housing, training, individual program and custody—usually starting with CLOSE CUSTODY which is composed of three forms of housing—"isolation" for offenders who have committed offenses while in the institution; "special segregation" for those who request protection—or, are unable to live in the general population; and "close" for the bulk of the population who live in the regular housing wings until their behavior and attitude warrant MEDIUM CUSTODY. If the offender's Counselor recommends it, the resident goes before the Classification Committee who again evaluate his performance since his entrance into the institution and grant him "medium"—if he meets the minimum criterion of favorable recommendation, good institutional adjustment—and, his remaining sentence approximates two years or less, he might be given MINIMUM CUSTODY and assigned to the Minimum Security Building outside the walls where more freedom exists. If he has learned a trade—or, has a usable skill, he might be placed on WORK RELEASE, an innovative program under which the individual leaves the institution in the morning, goes into the community and works a full shift with a local employer, and returns to the Minimum Security Building after work. Others in MSB may be participating in a program called TRAINING RELEASE under which residents attend the Community College in Walla Walla. After a day of classes they return to Minimum Security. The Classification Committee also sends some men direct from MSB to CAMP where the men clear timber and snags, build roads and fight fires. The camps are operated in conjunction with the Department of Natural Resources. Wherever he is staying, the Parole Board annually reviews the man's progress and if it appears that he is adjusting and becoming more knowledgeable in the skills needed to stay free from the criminal behavior, it can reduce his length of sentence and readjust the date of PAROLE. When the man leaves the institution he has an obligation to work with Field Parole Officers who evaluate his readjustment to society. As the offender has some conditions of parole (parole being a privilege) these must be followed; if the conditions are not met he can be returned to the institution. Upon the completion of his original sentence; or, if his adjustment is rapid and he petitions the Governor, he may be given his final RELEASE, once again a free man with full restoration of civil rights.

LANGUAGE AND CULTURE

As stated in the Introduction, the goal of this study is twofold: to have the prisoners describe their life in prison and to analyze how the language they use to tell their story reflects their worldview—the beliefs, attitudes, and values they hold about their existential condition.

To fulfill the first goal, presented here are those narratives, dialogues, and conversations collected from the prisoners believed most accurately to describe life in this particular prison as it was during the early 1960s through December, 1980, when our field work ended.

Anthropologists view culture as a "cognitive map" that people use to understand their world in order to act meaningfully or purposefully within it. Culture, the underlying "rules" for interpreting and constructing behavior, is learned by people from others around them.[56] It is "a meaning system by which people design their own actions and interpret the behavior of others."[57] This study, in part, is a description of culture in a maximum security men's prison. It is an ethnography, or folk-ethnography, conducted in the main by the prisoners themselves. Presented is a revelation of the system of values that exists beneath the patterns of behavior that occur in the prison. What is revealed may help bridge the vast abyss of misunderstanding and lack of communication that exists between those who are imprisoned and those who imprison. There is ample evidence that prisons (and juvenile institutions) are "gladiator schools," which often turn ambivalent offenders into *stone* criminals. This approach to the study of prisoner worldview suggests that those concerned with prisons should listen to what prisoners themselves say about their situation.

The second goal—analyzing how the language the prisoners use to describe their existential condition reflects their worldview—is premised on the Whorfian (or Sapir-Whorfian) hypothesis that language reflects and is in turn reflected by culture.

The language a community speaks is a sociocultural index of that community. The language records the speakers' experiences through time. It has its own unique vocabulary and terminology (lexicon), its own kinds of words that serve to classify, identify, modify, and indicate action (morphology), and its own particular way of arranging words (syntactical structure). These qualities, which together make up the form of any language, are unique to the particular speech community. Joyce Hertzler writes that "each language has its own 'spirit,' 'psyche,' 'ethos,' 'style,' 'inner form,' 'genius,' 'individuality,' or 'idiosyncracy,' which is an expression of the 'cultural particularity' and the 'spiritual personality' of the speakers of the language."[58]

The language of a given speech community encircles or holds the speech community within itself. Language enslaves people: it gives the speech community its cultural style and determines its thoughts and acts. People fit unconsciously into the institution of a language system. They react, observe, and express themselves through the instrument of the given language, expressing in the process their worldview, their interpretation of reality without knowing it.[59] "Language 'marks off' for its speakers all their 'working' interpretations of reality—their interpretation of what they comprehend as essences, things, forms, processes, actions, time and temporal sequences, space and distance, qualities and quantities, and the manner in which they comprehend. . . . [Language] provides its speakers with what they are aware of, what they imagine, believe, and feel, their ideas—in short what they think about the way they think. It carries for its speakers their connotations and interpretations of what is existential, important and valuable in the universe."[60] Benjamin Lee Whorf wrote, "We are inclined to think of language simply as a technique of expression, and not to realize that language first of all is a classification and arrangement of the stream of sensory experience which results in a certain world-order, a certain segment of the world that is easily expressible by the type of symbolic means that language employs. In other words, language does in a cruder but also in a broader and more versatile way the same thing science does."[61]

Language not only contains the worldview of a speech community but it tends to structure the experience and overt behavior of the community. In other words, language serves as a "lens" by which a group views the world.

The relationship of language to culture has been termed *metalinguistics*, or superlinguistics. Metalinguistics is defined by George L. Trager and Henry L. Smith, Jr.:

> Metalinguistics is the over-all relation of the linguistic system to the cultural totality.... Metalinguistics includes the various matters often referred to as "ethnolinguistics," but is far more inclusive. Not only does it deal with WHAT people talk about and WHY, but also considers HOW they use the linguistic system, and how they react to its use. This leads further to the consideration of how the linguistic system affects the behavior, both conscious and unconscious, and the world-view of the speaker, and governs or influences the interactions between individuals and between groups. Linguistic behavior is, by definition, part of the overt culture, but the study of it as metalinguistics shows it to be not only a guide to the covert culture, but, in large part, the structural framework of the covert or sentiment structure.[62]

In 1929, Edward Sapir presented the important elements of the metalinguistic position in his work, "The Status of Linguistics as Science." He stated, "We see and hear and otherwise experience as we do because the language habits of our community predispose certain choices of interpretation."[63] Benjamin Lee Whorf, a brilliant student of Sapir, however, is the chief advocate of the metalinguistic hypothesis. His conclusions are primarily based on comparative studies he conducted on North and South American Indian languages. The important aspects of his hypothesis appeared in his article, "Science and Linguistics," published in 1930, and can be summed up in this quotation from his work:

> We dissect nature along lines laid down by our native languages. The categories and types that we isolate from the world of phenomena we do not find there because they stare every observer in the face; on the contrary, the world is presented in a kaleidoscopic flux of impressions which has to be organized by our minds—and this means largely by the linguistic systems in our minds. We cut nature up, organize it into concepts, and ascribe significance as we do, largely because we are parties to an agreement to organize it in this way—an agreement that holds throughout our speech community, and is codified in the patterns of our language. The agreement is, of course, an implicit and unstated one, *but its terms are absolutely obligatory;* we cannot talk at all except by subscribing to the organization and classification of data which the agreement decrees.[64]

In 1939, Whorf wrote that "the cue to a certain line of behavior is often given by the analogies of the linguistic formula in which the situation is spoken of, and by which to some degree it is analyzed, classified, and alloted its place in the world, which is to large extent unconsciously built up on the language habits of the group."[65] David W. Maurer, who has researched extensively on criminal subcultures, points out that there is some evidence that such cultures are "language-generated." He writes, "Criminal sub-cultures seem to evolve about [their] specialized body of language; in fact, the more I observe the nature of criminal sub-cultures, the more I tend toward the opinion that they are, at least in several significant respects, language-generated."[66]

The Sapir-Whorf hypothesis is not accepted as conclusive evidence of a causal relation between language and thought because it is so difficult to prove. Although it remains an unproven theory, it provides a foundation for investigations on language and culture by those who believe in it. Max Black writes that "on the whole, the verdict of competent anthropologists and linguists upon Whorf's suggestive ideas is that until some other 'near-genius,' with a talent for exact thought, succeeds in deriving some reasonably precise hypothesis, there is little scope for profitable argument."[67]

The implications for society and culture based on the metalinguistic hypothesis are profound. If we wish to understand a culture, we must understand what the language of the culture *means to the people who speak it* — to know a person is to know how he thinks and how he interprets himself, his group, and his world in his particular societal and cultural context, "which is revealed in and determined and limited by his language."[68] Language organizes and controls behavior; in turn, behavior determines the meaning of language. Since language carries within it the values, beliefs, attitudes, and ideas of a group, anyone speaking the language participates in the "world-stance" represented by the language. Worldview, then, is the way in which a culture views and describes its relationship to the world that surrounds it. A human being perceives what his culture (and culture includes language) trains him to see.

In *The Cultural Experience*, Spradley and McCurdy write that "agreed-on cultural definitions enable people to coordinate their behavior and make sense out of their shared experience."[69] In order to understand the cultural scene of a prison community, it is necessary to become aware of the frame of reference around which cultural knowledge is organized for the prisoner. This must be done by exploring the underlying patterns upon which the frame of reference stands. In other words, culture is structurally organized around patterns of ideas, values, beliefs, and attitudes—what Spradley and McCurdy refer to as "symbolic-meaningful systems."[70] By studying the language of prisoners, in particular, metaphor, we discover the patterns of shared ideas, values, beliefs, and attitudes that reveal the cultural worldview. Language, although not the exclusive revealer or carrier of these patterns, is the most important means by which they are shared and communicated. Central to this study is metaphor, its function and meaning in prisoner worldview.

Kenneth Burke wrote that "every perspective requires a metaphor implicit or explicit, for its organizational base."[71] In metaphor, an applied analogy unexpectedly and imaginatively connects one concept with another; for example, men are fish. The attributes and emotional qualities of the one is ascribed to the other. Metaphor is ofted used by a group as a way of symbolically revealing a truth that cannot be communicated any other way. Metaphor connotes that a word means far more than its initial meaning.

In *The Social Uses of Metaphor*, J. David Sapir and J. Christopher Crocker point out that man uses language in a symbolic way to try to control his existential situation. Citing the work of Kenneth Burke—who obviously respects the Sapir-Whorfian hypothesis—Crocker examines the social use of language, stating that it is "based on the premise that all human action involves purpose, or motive in the full, classical sense of *action*," that in the Burkian view, "language itself is action."[72] Further, he writes, "symbolic activity does more than merely express reality: it actively structures experience."[73] Through figurative language, "actors attempt to provide some linguistic truth about a social situation which summarizes its moral essence in such ways as to define possible actions."[74]

This study, then, is concerned with worldview as it presents itself through the language (and the behavior described by the language) of men in prison. A prison culture—actually a parasitic subculture dependent, although reluctantly, upon free society — is a folk group. Barre Toelken defines a folk group as, "any group of people who share informal communal contacts that become the basis for expressive culture-based communications . . . the group will have maintained itself through its dynamics for a considerable time . . . [and] the expressive communications [of the group] have become the educative matrix in which newcomers are brought up. . . ."[75] Sociolinguists call such a group a "speech community." Toelken points out that "the evocative powers of connotation are commonly used consciously by succeeding generations of tradition bearers," and refers to such language usage as "word-play."[76] "The possibilities for connotative richness are enormous in folk groups, where closely associated members are in constant touch with one another, sharing continual references, attitudes, and information. Among such groups the most basic statement or performance may elicit a tremendous depth of meaning."[77]

Neither the language nor the culture of the prison is presented in its totality. Furthermore, much has not been captured that is current, as both language and culture are dynamic and therefore in constant flux. What is presented is only a part of a whole that was culturally and linguistically vital between June, 1978, and December, 1980. In studying the language, only its semantic and lexical elements are considered, with particular emphasis placed on the connotative meaning of the language.

A prison is a folk community by every definition: it is a culture by which the values, beliefs, attitudes, and traditions of the group are passed on by word of mouth or by imitation from one person to another and from one generation to the next. Like all folk groups, it experiences changes that gradually bring about alterations in its folkways and beliefs. Traditions that no longer serve a purpose disappear and new ones arise to fill the needs of the group. The changes in the language between 1950 and 1980 is a prime example of this. Old traditions may become altered, yet they preserve the core of their functionality within that alteration if they are still useful. In general, it can be said that a folk culture holds to those expressive forms that help it survive and define its existential situation, while at the same time expressing its beliefs, values, and attitudes: in short, its worldview.

A major change has undergone prisons today because a new kind of prisoner has invaded this once highly traditional folk culture, bringing with him his own folkways, values, and beliefs. His worldview has invaded this prison, and his language has captured and subdued the old. His influence is strong because the home base from which he draws his values outside the walls of the prison is strong—the drug– and countercultures of the streets. He is a rebel, angry and defiant, opposing everything that the "establishment" values, and his influence has had a profound impact upon prisons everywhere in the country.

UNDERGROUND LANGUAGE IN THE PRISON—A RATIONALE

Certain taboo words and phrases in polite society, which I refer to as "underground language," are used—*ad nauseum* to conventional ears—by prisoners. Although all such language is quite common today in free society since WW II when returning GIs brought their everyday battle language home with them,[78] its usage is greatly intensified in a prison community. Why? It is important to explore why this language is used so much, as it represents an important category of folk speech in prison that serves many functions, most of which help the prisoner cope with his existential condition.

John Ciardi has insightfully pointed out that obscenity ("dirty" words describing "dirty" things) offends Protestant sensibilities, whereas profanity or blasphemy (profaning the Lord's name) offends Catholic sensibilities. Offending Protestant sensibilities seems to be most evident in prisoner underground language usage.[79] *Fuck, motherfucker* (the greatest offender of conventional sensibilities), *pissed off* (originally an army expression), *cocksucker, sonovabitch, bastard, goddam* (the Catholic taboo word most often heard), and *shit* (the prize winner in usage in this prison, which, believe it or not, even surpasses the much loved *motherfucker*, and which is a street term used for just about anything) are the most commonly used expressions.[80]

Profanity and obscenity in language permeates all aspects of daily existence in prison, from the most tragic to the most mundane. Underground language expresses all situations, not only those that reflect the negative aspects of the prisoner's life and world. The language is used to express every feeling or emotion, concept or idea. Expressions of love, concern, and affection are carried out in the language. "Where in hell have you been, you *goddam motherfucker?* I thought some *fuckin ding* had *dusted* your *ass!*" The greater the release of tension caused by anxiety, the greater the sense of relief that nothing awful has happened to a friend, the more the underground language. Humor also appears in these moments after experiencing episodes of violence from guards; for example, the men joke about getting the *"fuckin barnacles knocked off"* their heads by the *"fuckin pigs."*

Underground language serves very importantly as a safety valve release, not only for the psychological well-being of the prisoner but also for the physical safety of those who guard him. The use of abusive language lessens the likelihood of physical abuse. Men in solitary confinement who shout obscenities at the guards are venting their rage and frustration at their helplessness. Guards who are experienced and sensitized to this through proper training do not take offense so easily or become hostile under such abuse since they recognize what it means. However, poorly trained guards do not understand and take the language as personal insult and react by physically punishing the prisoner. Hurling abusive language at guards is the only thing a man has left to protect his sense of manhood. If he does not defend it, he will despise himself. Psychologically, this is very important for the prisoner.[81]

Underground language is also used as a weapon by imprisoned men. The prisoner in the *hole* releases his feelings of bitterness, his sense of outrage at the injustice he feels is being perpetuated against him. He also expresses his helplessness in the face of the overwhelming power that is used against him. Very often, men resist physically when taken to the *hole*. If a man is spirited, he will resort to using underground language as a weapon. When people are pushed to the wall, their language often becomes abusive. This reveals their inability to act. But language can be devastating: the children's chant, "Sticks and stones will break my bones but names will never harm me," is grossly untrue. When abusive language is hurled at guards, they become scapegoats in the eyes of the imprisoned men for the powerful system whose bidding they do without question. The guard, in such circumstances, is viewed as a wooden puppet or robot in his seemingly blind and emotionless obedience to higher ups. Under trying conditions, some guards treat the men in their power cruelly; a spirited prisoner will respond with abusive language as a retaliatory weapon against them since he has no other weapon at this disposal. Such language use is a kind of "magic" and is employed to try to take control of the situation.[82] Sometimes prisoners in the *hole* hurl feces and urine along with abusive language at guards, who then may bring physical punishment down on them in retribution. Under such stress, even properly trained guards may lose their composure and return in kind, hurling abusive language in the same wounding way. Use of such language as a weapon is a man's way of defending himself under circumstances where his dignity has been stripped from him, whether abused prisoner or abused guard.

Underground language is sometimes used to express the unhappiness, sadness, and regret that a man feels for his intolerable circumstance. It is a kind of reverse crying, a prisoner-approved manner for lament. Since the prison culture mandates that a man should not cry, he must "cry out" his sadness and anguish in this approved manner.

Underground language expresses symbolically the reality of the prisoner's existential condition. Prison is obscene, profane, violent, terrifying, grim, cruel, inhumane, impersonal, ruthless, and dehumanizing. Underground language reflects all these conditions. It is also used to call out to others to recognize their condition. In this instance, it is used to stun, to wound, and to shock the conventional, straight sensibilities of guards and others with whom they interact in an effort to point out their life condition. Related to this is their desire to affirm their existence, to insist that their presence is felt, since they live constantly with the dread that they have been buried and forgotten. Prisoners believe that civil death is very close to physical death.

Underground language is used to express fear, even terror. The prisoner is sometimes frightened and traumatized by what happens to him in particular circumstances. Terror is a companion to the prisoner who each morning when he awakens wonders whether or not he will live through the day. Anger, fear, and hatred are closely related and are all expressed in the prisoner's language.

According to Delorme, one function of underground language used in the prison is to fight off feelings of guilt over the killings, rapes, and beatings that go on regularly in the prison. The code that demands for each man to *do his own time* forbids reporting prisoners who victimize other prisoners. Some men feel great guilt over this. Watching one man murder another is a horrible experience. The first reaction is to put a stop to it, but peer pressure forbids it. Any man who reports it is a *snitch* and is placed in immediate danger of losing his life. If a young man is raped, for example, and reports it, he must seek protective custody because he is in danger of being murdered by the *wolf* (or *wolves*) who raped him or by friends of the *wolf*. When the men talk about such prisoner-on-prisoner violence, they sometimes joke, using much profanity in describing the particular incident. The joking stance and the language are, perhaps, reflections of the guilt the men may feel for not getting involved, for not helping the man in distress.

Prisoners are realists about their situation, therefore their language is often used as a statement of that reality. In some ways their language serves as a model for directness and honesty in language usage. A prisoner calling a spade a spade oftentimes stands in sharp contrast to conventional society's tendency to coat or hide a reality that is uncomfortable or offends delicate sensibilities. Conventional etiquette does not allow for certain awful truths to be dealt with directly and honestly; there is a strong tendency for people to describe certain uncomfortable aspects of reality in euphemistic terms. Prisoners do not do this. They strip language down to its bare bones, revealing it in all its rawness. In these instances, prisoners are truth tellers, stripping away all hypocrisy and patina from meaning in language. Often their language, shocking as it may be, more truthfully reveals the human condition than does much of conventional, proper language usage. Because their daily existence is filled with ugliness, they do not fear ugly language. Prisoners tell the ugly truth because for them the truth is ugly, whereas most people in conventional society tend to hide the awful truths from themselves through euphemistic language in order to protect themselves. But it takes ugly words to accurately reflect ugly truths. The prisoner's condition is violent, obscene, and offensive, and so is much of his language. When in hell, one uses hellish language.

A considerable effort is made presenting an apology for prisoner's use of underground language in order to make the point that such usage is extremely useful, indeed, beneficial for the prisoner. Those who wish to understand the experience of prisoners must recognize the important role that this language plays in helping the prisoner survive his existential condition.

NOTES

[1]Erving Goffman, *Asylums* (New York: Anchor Books, 1961), pp. 4–5.

[2]*Asylums*, p. 6.

[3]Between December 1980 and June 1982, dramatic architectural and policy changes completely altered the prison and the living environment of the inmates. In "What Went Wrong at Walla Walla," Gabrielle Tyrnauer pointed out that between 1970–74, "the Washington State Penitentiary was a laboratory for what some observers consider the boldest experiment in recent penal history. The experiment was an exercise in inmate self-government, and the Resident Government Council (RGC) was its centerpiece and symbol." *Corrections Magazine*, June, 1981, p. 37.

[4]*The Prison Community* (New York: Holt, Rinehart and Winston, 1958).

[5]*The Society of Captives* (Princeton University Press, 1958). For information on the history of prisons in the U.S. see David J. Rothman, *Discovery of the Asylum* (Boston: Little, Brown and Company, 1971) and *Conscience and Convenience* (Boston: Little, Brown and Company, 1980).

[6]*Washington State Penitentiary, Walla Walla, Washington*, State of Washington, Department of Institutions, Division of Adult Corrections Brochure, n.d.

[7]Charles Stastny and Gabrielle Tyrnauer, *Who Rules the Joint?* (Lexington, Mass.: Lexington Books of D.C. Heath and Company, 1982), p. 15. Stastny and Tyrnauer present an excellent survey history of the Washington State Penitentiary on pp. 77–129. All quotes reprinted by permission of the publisher.

[8]*Ibid.*, p. 80.

[9]*Washington State Penitentiary, Walla Walla, Washington*.

[10]*Who Rules the Joint?*, p. 80.

[11]*Ibid.*, p. 81.

[12]*Ibid.*, p. 82.

[13]*Washington State Penitentiary, Walla Walla, Washington*.

[14]*Who Rules the Joint?*, p. 82.

[15]*Ibid.*, p. 82.

[16]*Ibid.*, p. 82.

[17]Israel Leonard Barak (Glantz), "Punishment to Protection: Solitary Confinement in the Washington State Penitentiary, 1966–1975." Unpublished Ph.D. Dissertation, The Ohio State University, 1978, p. 105.

[18]*Ibid.*, p. 105.

[19]*Ibid.*, p. 107.

[20]*Who Rules the Joint?*, p. 84.

[21]*Ibid.*, pp. 84–85.

[22]*Ibid.*, p. 86.

[23]*Ibid.*

[24]*Ibid.*

[25]*Ibid.*

[26]Stastny and Tyrnauer point out, however, that Conte went to considerable effort to "educate" B. J. Rhay, even sending him to visit correctional institutions in Europe (England, France, the Netherlands, Denmark, Norway and Sweden), and to talk with correctional authorities there: "Rhay was impressed by such features as short sentences, small prison populations, high levels of staff training, intensive involvement of the parole officer with the prisoner throughout the term of incarceration, use of community sponsors and advisory groups, furloughs, and the role of the ombudsman. The ideas that he found most compelling were those related to democratization and decriminalization." *Who Rules the Joint?*, p. 85.

[27]"Punishment to Protection: Solitary Confinement in the Washington State Penitentiary," pp. 107–108.

[28]*Who Rules the Joint?*, See pp. 87–129; 151–188.

[29]*Ibid.*, p. 151.

[30]*Ibid.*, pp. 87–88.

[31]*Ibid.*, p. 89.

[32]*Ibid.*

[33]*Ibid.*, p. 90.

[34]*Ibid.*, p. 91.

[35]*Ibid.*, p. 92.

[36]Lloyd Allen Weeks, "The Background of Penal Democratization," in Resident Government Council (WSP), Institute I: "A Search for the Prison of Tomorrow," (January 10, 1972), p. vi–xvii. Quoted in *Who Rules the Joint?*, p. 88.

[37]*Ibid.*, p. 89.

[38]*Ibid.*

[39]Sgt. Robin Moses, quoted in "Walla Walla," KING (Seattle) television documentary (1971), produced by Emory Bundy. Quoted in *Who Rules the Joint?*, p. 90.

[40]Interview, April, 1978. Quoted in *Who Rules the Joint?*, p. 92.

[41]*Who Rules the Joint?*, p. 96.

[42]*Ibid.*, p. 97.

[43]*Ibid.*

[44]*Ibid.*, p. 99.

[45]*Ibid.*, pp. 99–100.

[46]*Ibid.*, p. 101.

[17]John Irwin describes the important influence of this movement in prisons, particularly in the California system in *Prisons in Turmoil*, Chaps 2-3.

[18]Stastny and Tyrnauer describe this period, 1977–78, on pp. 105–108 of *Who Rules the Joint?*

[19]*Seattle Post-Intelligencer*, Nov. 21, 1978.

[50]*Ibid.*, Nov. 19, 1978.

[51]Eventually some of the clubs were reinstated but with limited privileges.

[52]*Seattle Post-Intelligencer*, Dec. 10, 1980.

[53]*An Analysis of Program Needs of Prison Inmates in Washington State* (Olympia: State of Washington, Department of Social and Health Services, April, 1980), p. 129.

[54]*Ibid.*, p. 75.

[55]*Washington State Penitentiary, Walla Walla, Washington.*

[56]James P. Spradley and David W. McCurdy, Editors, *Conformity and Conflict: Readings in Cultural Anthropology* (Boston: Little, Brown and Company, 1974), p. 2.

[57]*Ibid.*, p. 3.

[58]*A Sociology of Language* (New York: Random House, 1965), p. 117.

[59]*Ibid.*, p. 118.

[60]*Ibid.*

[61]John B. Carroll, Editor, Language, *Thought and Reality: Selected Writings of Benjamin Lee Whorf* (Cambridge: The Technology Press of M.I.T. and New York: Wiley and Sons, 1956), p. 55.

[62]*An Outline of English Structure* (Washington: American Council of Learned Societies, 1956), pp. 81–82.

[63]"The Status of Linguistics as a Science," *Language*, Vol. 5 (1929), pp. 209–210.

[64]*Language, Thought and Reality*, p. 214.

[65]*Ibid.*, pp. 134–139.

[66]"The Laying of the Note or You Can Cheat an Honest Man," *Studies in Linguistics*, M. Estellie Smith, Editor (The Hague, Netherlands: Mouton and Company, n.v. Publ., 1972), pp. 324–343.

[67]*The Labyrinth of Language* (New York: Frederick A. Praeger, 1968), p. 75.

[68]*A Sociology of Language*, p. 126.

[69]*The Cultural Experience: Ethnography in Complex Society*, p. 60.

[70]*Ibid.*, p. 59.

[71]*The Philosophy of Literary Form* (New York: Vintage Press, 1957), p. 132.

[72]*The Social Uses of Metaphor* (Philadelphia: University of Pennsylvania Press, 1977), p. 33.

[73]*Ibid.*, p. 34.

[74]*Ibid.*, p. 37.

[75]*The Dynamics of Folklore* (Boston: Houghton Mifflin, 1979), p. 51.

[76]*Ibid.*, pp. 206–209.

[77]*Ibid.*, p. 206.

[78]"Wide Armed Forces use during WW II, and the general loosening of moral restrictions and taboos has encouraged such language usage among all strata of

the population." *Dictionary of American Slang*, Second Supplement, Edited and Compiled by Harold Wentworth and Stuart Berg Flexner (New York: Thomas Y. Crowell Company, 1975), p. 204–468.

[79]Dante Alighiere, *The Inferno*. Translated by John Ciardi (New York: Mentor Books, 1954), pp. 187–188.

[80]Images of violence are very much evident in the underground language of our society. The English language, unlike European languages like French or Spanish, reveals no tenderness, no sense of the aesthetic in sexual language. All the language related to sex that is nontechnical holds images of violence within it. The most notorious phrase that can be hurled at a person is "fuck you." Such usage implies the desire to harm the recipient of such a verbal missile. "To get fucked," "to fuck over," and the closely related "to screw," "to get screwed," are metaphorical concepts for certain business tactics in our society. What happens in a society is reflected unconsciously in its language. Maurer states that "fuck," which has been in print since about 1200, comes from the Latin *pugno*, which means dagger; to strike, to stab with a weapon. Quoted with permission from correspondence, June 18, 1979.

[81]Cervantes, the great sixteenth century Spanish writer who himself spent considerable time in prison, understood this need for prisoners to use vituperative language in order to help maintain self-respect: "The sergeant raised his staff to strike [the prisoner] in return for his threats but Don Quixote interposed and begged him not to ill treat him, for it is no great matter if a man who has his hands tied let his tongue free a little." Miguel de Cervantes Saavedra, *The Adventures of Don Quixote*, translated by J. M. Cohen (New York: Penquin Books, 1976), pp. 171–181.

[82]Hertzler points out that "the essence of word magic in the control of reality lies in the mysterious identity of the verbal symbol and the nonverbal fact." The word is much more than "a mere piece of verbiage; it carries vast power. The power of the specific word derives from the qualities, good and evil, that are believed to inhere in the relevant aspects of the world to which the word refers." *A Sociology of Language*, p. 270.

Chapter 2

THE CHAIN

One unique and important characteristic that sets a prison folk group off from other folk groups is that its members are captive. The group does not select its own members; rather, new members are "born" against their wills into it learning, in the process of acquiring the new worldview, how to survive. They are not a natural born group but rather are created artificially or synthetically by society. New members bring with them their former cultural and linguistic identities that in turn influence the development of their new worldview. Furthermore, the "universe" into which they are thrust and the actions of the "god" who holds them captive play an important role in the formation of their reality. Language usage in the prison is a constant reminder of that reality. Inherent in the language is a statement or message to themselves and to outsiders manifested through the use of metaphor. The reality the state imposes upon its prisoners and out of which they must create a worldview of their own includes not only individual and cultural dimensions but spatial and temporal ones as well. Much in the worldview of prisoners is an angry response to their involuntary condition. The prison is a captive universe, the subjects of which despise their "god" upon whom they are absolutely dependent; "he" has created for them an inferno in which to dwell where the ultimate desire is release from hell (captivity) into paradise (freedom).

THE METAPHOR OF THE CHAIN

The Chain is the name of the bus that carries convicted felons from the jails to the state's reception center and then to the prisons in the state to which they are sentenced to serve their time. Before boarding the bus each man is chained. All the men being trans-

33

ported on a given day are bound to each other by a long connecting chain and placed, ten men to a chain, on the bus.[1] Transporting the prisoners, some of whom are desperate or dangerous, is made easier by chaining them together so they cannot escape or take over the bus. Chaining also makes it possible for the state to handle its captives with the least amount of inconvenience as they are transported from one prison destination to another. Feelings of vulnerability and helplessness attack the men as they ride on the Chain; within their minds, the Chain, that is, the actual bus itself, becomes a metaphor for their captivity in all its dimensions.

Chains are powerful symbols that have been used for centuries throughout the world to humiliate and reduce the enemy to a condition of impotence and bondage. A symbol of absolute physical restraint, chains are the iron straitjacket of centuries past and present. The men despise all that the Chain represents. Metaphorically, it connotes a powerful image both conscious and unconscious in their minds. It is the symbol of enslavement, defeat, and impotence of both physical strength and the will. It is not, however, an image of spiritual defeat or subjugation.

The Chain symbolically connotes an extension of the jails and prisons to and from which the men are transported. They are reminded that they are imprisoned just as securely on the Chain as they are behind the walls and bars of the prisons and jails. The Chain is an overarching symbol for their entire experience of imprisonment, as it represents the state's punishment for transgressions of the law now and in their future experience in prison. It represents the state's power not only to perpetuate the captive group within the prison but also to determine its living environment in all its dimensions. Connected to the image of the Chain is the concept of law and order. The state, recognizing that the willful and defiant question and therefore threaten to undermine its authority, responds with a display of power that overstates; the Chain in all its dimensions, both figuratively and realistically, is overstatement.

THE CAPTIVES

Imagine that twenty-five felons are on the Chain bound for Walla Walla where the maximum security prison of the state is situated. The ride is long and tiring—six hours of bumping across the Cascade Mountains to the southeastern-most corner of the state. (In winter it is extremely cold on the bus, as it is not heated and there is much snow in the mountains.) Hard wooden seats remind the men that their discomfort is only beginning. Who are they and how has the state prepared them for their prison experience? Of the twenty-five, seventeen are white; six are black; one is Chicano; one is native American. The youngest is eighteen and the oldest is perhaps forty-five. Most are between the ages of twenty-two and twenty-seven. Six are parole violators returning to the prison for some infraction of their parole generally not related to committing a crime. One parole violator, Eugene Delorme, is returning for the sixth time. Eleven men have been sentenced for committing person offenses, mainly first and second degree assault. Two of these are murderers. Six of the men have been convicted for first and second degree burglary. Another two have been sentenced for drug violation. Except for the six parole violators, none have served sentences in this particular prison, although several have been in the state reformatory at Monroe or the juvenile detention centers of the state. Two have never served sentences anywhere before. Of the twenty-five, only one comes from the middle class. He is white. All the rest are from the poorer classes— white, black, Chicano, and native American. What experiences in the state's chaining process have the men gone through so far? What do they think and feel about these experiences? As they ride on the imaginary bus bound for Walla Walla, the captives define their reality of *the Chain* and all it represents for them.[2]

THE PRIMAL CONTEXT: THE JAILS

The fashioning of the prisoner's worldview begins when he enters a city or county jail for the first time. For the first offender,

a novice thrust into the new world, the impact of the jail and
everything that happens to him while he is there begins to im-
print strongly upon his mind. The primal context begins to shape
and form his new worldview. Very few felons are initially committed exclusively to deviant behavior. As John Irwin points out,
most have participated in both conventional and criminal systems
and even "criminals," to some extent, are ambivalent, to begin
with, about their identities.[3] However, the experience of *the Chain*
in all its dimensions impacts in such a negative manner that
probably most turn away from conventional behavior toward a
deviant identity. A foreshadowing of the state's policies can be
seen in this first narrative, central to which is the lack of concern
for the physical and psychological welfare of those who at this
stage have neither been tried nor convicted for a crime. This
prisoner returning to Walla Walla on *the Chain*, a recidivist now
forty-two with many years experience as a captive of the state,
recalls the jail experience in the King County Jail in Seattle and
emphasizes the danger that young men, in particular, face. Survival takes on an urgency never before experienced. The initial
impact of the chaining process is overwhelming.

"The guys are put into a tank. The cell block tank used in King
County Jail would handle on the average of forty men. Every time
that I have been in the King County Jail, young white males that
would come in were subject to predatory-type sexual acts. They
want to get down with the kid and turn him out if he's young and if
they can't turn him out by finesse, they will rape him. The things
that go down in the city and county jails by not separating the
different groups is frustrating and dehumanizing. While waiting
for his court date, the guy has to go through all the survival-type
techniques that he never knew before. If you're big enough to take
care of yourself, you learn to survive."

In addition to the very real threat of homosexual rape in the
city and county jails, other experiences the new captive goes
through in the chaining process of the criminal justice system
begin to shape his reality. The narrative continues with the prisoner reflecting upon the bitter memories he holds of the beginnings of the state's chaining process, recalling those aspects that

made the deepest impression. His concept of reality has been strongly influenced by this early perception.

"The person gets to the county or city jail where they either have tanks or single cells. Sometimes you're able to make a phone call, and sometimes you're not, to try to make bail or try to contact somebody to let them know you're in jail.[4] You go back to either the cell tank or the single cell and you lay there and all of a sudden you start flashing back to the streets to what was going on there and what happened, and here you are in jail again.

"For a repeater, but also for a first timer, I want to express explicitly the demeaning, dehumanizing effect. People look down on the prisoner. Usually, he's given a pair of coveralls in the city and county jail. In Seattle, some are red. Bright red. Usually they're different colors in different county and city jails. From this time on the person is subjected to the guards who dominate with unprofessional techniques and tactics.

"The person goes on through the court process. There's usually a preliminary hearing to see if they're going to bind him over to the superior court and here you go with a chain, a group of prisoners chained together, mostly with everybody with their heads down, ashamed, walking through the hallways of the courthouse going to the courtroom to be arraigned to have bail set or to have a hearing. They take you before the presiding judge or whoever's going to bind you over. The prosecutor at this time has got reports on you from the police department, so what they do is tell the judge that this person was picked up on such and such and charged with burglary, robbery, and here's the facts. And here's the judge sitting on this high-type of pedestal and here you are in this very demeaning and very low and emotional and traumatic time.

"All of a sudden here you are in the city or county jail—the bars, the steel, the doors are clanging; homosexual acts going down by force or by finesse. The ever increasing domination and rape of young offenders in city and county jails is outstanding. It's one of the most terrible things you can imagine. If you could imagine a woman being raped...a man being raped is worse because it's in a more sensitive area. You can imagine the trauma of a man being raped by men. It usually happens to the young

Orientals or Caucasians, or whoever is young. The wolves are there waiting like vultures for somebody to come into the tank so they can shoot the shot. The tank has anywhere from forty to a hundred men in it and the way these jails are overcrowded with people sleeping on the floor, it's really out of line.

"I can't say enough words about the cruel and unusual punishment a person goes through to be put through the criminal justice process. When he gets a court date set, he goes through the process of waiting and waiting and waiting, having visits usually once a week through a glass cage on a telephone. Every time anybody comes up to see him, he can't touch them. There's no contact and it's the most crucial time in a person's life when he's taken from off the street from a loved one or somebody very close. And they're not able to even come close enough to give a kiss or to hold close or to give some assurance.

"I got married in 1969 and my son was born in 1970. I got busted in 1971 and my ex-wife, who I have been divorced from now for ten years, brought my son up to see me through this glass cage and I couldn't touch him and hold him and he would be trying to get through to me and I went through some very bad times. I was unable to see my family or touch or hold my baby and it affected me very bad.

"The whole system is geared toward the lowering of the self-image. All at once this person sees himself as a low person. If the person is going on through bargain type of sessions, the pressure, if he's got multiple charges can be almost unbearable. I don't know how many people are listening to this, Inez, but the public defenders and the different deals and processes and the prosecutors and all the ways that there are of dealing in and trading human flesh are terrible. They make all kinds of deals with people to make the cop, to lower the charges in order to further up the system so everybody don't get a jury trial and it doesn't plug up the system. How the defense lawyer or public defender has to go through so many changes when he believes somebody's innocent and everything goes against him.

"A person is usually given a public defender who is like a medical intern. He's a guy who is usually just out of law school a very short period of time. He's not up on criminal law to the extent to where he is even capable of going in to a jury trial. Or they will appoint a dump truck, a regular one that is in private practice.

"But going through the jury trial is a very different and traumatic experience. They say you're supposed to be judged by your peers but I noticed that there weren't any ex-convicts on that jury. There weren't any street people. They were all professional people who were taxpayers, which is the jury system. That's the way it goes down."

Central to this man's response to this experience is the lowering of his self-esteem and his belief that this is a deliberate part of the state's chaining process. "The whole system," he states, "is geared toward the lowering of the self-image." The internalization of the self as unworthy becomes a part of the new worldview developing for the captive. In the midst of strangers—captors who ignore his pleas and captives like himself, many of whom threaten his well-being—he struggles to keep his personality from disintegrating while his world turns upside down. The physical surroundings are ugly, hostile, and foreboding. Coping with living in such a restricted environment is made even more difficult because so many share his space. The steel bars and clanging doors register the harshness and rigidity of the state's hand upon him. No one seems to care. The prisoner feels shattered. Irwin writes that "one's identity, one's personality system, one's coherent thinking about himself depend upon a relatively familiar continuous, and predictable stream of events. In the Kafkaesque world of the book room, the jail cell, the interrogation room, and the visiting room, the boundaries of the self collapse."[5]

Looking at one's family through glass is a particularly disquieting experience. The captive is forbidden to touch those whom he loves and who love him during a period he describes as "the most crucial time in a person's life." Irwin's description of this world as Kafkaesque is extremely meaningful. The captive is like a specimen under glass who may be looked upon but not touched. He begins to incorporate into his worldview the idea that he has metamorphosed into an animal, an insect. He uses these words to describe his situation: demeaning, dehumanizing, traumatic, emotional, cruel, unjust, and unbearable. It can be hypothesized that part of the reason for this prisoner's return to prison over and over again is his refusal to join the world of his captors out of hatred for their chaining policies.

THE PRIMAL CONTEXT: THE RECEPTION CENTER

The next step of the chaining process occurs when the captive is taken after conviction to the reception center at Shelton. Shelton is where "for approximately six weeks the prisoners are held for indoctrination and diagnostic study [and] where the staff seeks to individually classify offenders, test aptitudes, do vocational counseling, and recommend programs and [the] institution for confinement."[6] From the perspective of the men, indoctrination is central to the statement of purpose of the state's reception center. *Brainwash* is what the prisoners call it. In the worldview of the prisoner, the chaining process involves a deliberate policy to prepare a man to live in an enclosure like an animal. In order for him to accept this he must question his identity as a human being. This is very threatening to him. This prisoner speaks of self-hatred brought about by the chaining policies of the state.

"I always felt hate when the pigs came to take me to Shelton, being shuffled around like cattle, standing naked while I waited for my turn to bend over so the pig can look up my asshole. That type of skin search is the very last thread of self-respect going down the drain. They do it knowing they are not really looking for anything except a small show of resistance from one of us, and when it does come it is pitiful and embarrassing for everyone except the pigs. They love it and pile on the man with fists and clubs.

"There is something about being naked that makes you just a piece of meat, even less than an animal. That's when the inner hate begins and it doesn't go away because being a fish at Shelton is a constant stream of abuse and disrespect. It is six weeks of brainwash designed to internalize your embarrassment and disrespect for yourself at letting men treat you like shit without doing anything to hit back even though it is physically impossible to do anything. The slightest resistance results in punishment all the way down the line to Walla Walla or other joints."

Prisoner belief that the state deliberately aims to destroy self-respect in its chaining process is reinforced by this man's narrative.

The "inner hate begins and does not go away" because the captive allows the captors to treat him inhumanely without defending himself against such treatment despite the odds. Within the prisoner's worldview, the image of the self as less than a man continues to build. The awesome powers of the state juxtaposed against the impotence of the prisoner produces anger, frustration, and self-hatred. Does the state believe that by lowering the self-estimation of the captive this will benefit the state or the captive? Evidence is to the contrary. Hatred directed inward eventually spills outward. Although most men acknowledge that they have broken the laws of the state, the treatment they receive during the beginning stages of their chaining experience turns their thoughts away from the injustice of their behavior and towards the injustices the criminal justice system perpetuates against them. Where they could be helped to learn new and more successful ways of living, they are instead taught hatred and resentment of the system and the society that condones the tactics and methods the criminal justice system uses.[7] It is perhaps at this point that a recidivist is being formed—out of the ingredients of rage, self-hatred, insult, and the desire for revenge—all of which cloud the rational mind of the captive and prevent him from controlling the destructiveness of his emotions not only while he is in prison but once he is released.

The reception center at Shelton is regarded by the men as more punitive than the maximum security prison at Walla Walla. At Shelton, captives are separated from their identities by having their hair cut off and by being forced to wear "baggy clown coveralls," whereas at Walla Walla, they may wear their hair any length and are allowed to wear their own clothes if they wish, although state-issued clothing is given them. The following description of "basic training" at Shelton brings out aspects of the chaining process the men see as dehumanizing. Delorme compares the similarity of his experience to that of the Jews in the Nazi concentration camps being prepared for the gas chamber. Although his analogy is based on the process of dehumanization, the comparison to the Jews who were systematically exterminated as an unwanted race also reminds him of what has happened to his own people, since he is native American.

"If you've never been through it before, it's a bitch and it just gets progressively worse.[8] You get to Shelton and there you become part of the herd; you really disappear into the number stage. At Shelton they run you through their grind for six weeks. The whole process of those places after your arrest—county jail and Shelton—is like basic training. It just softens you up, I guess.

"The new fish gets on the Chain, goes to Shelton, gets off the Chain, and the bulls come march you on in and they start unchaining you. There you sit on a bunch of wooden benches. They've got a bunch of little empty boxes sitting around. Everybody gets a little box and they say, 'Put your clothes in it if you want to send them home.' Otherwise, they'll give them away to Goodwill. They got a great big box in the middle for everybody to throw their stuff into like Jews in concentration camps. I always relate everything about this experience to Jews because when I see films about what happened to them, it reminds me in the worst way of Shelton. You all stand around naked with the bulls shouting at you. It's a dehumanizing process.

"While you're at Shelton, they give you all dark blue coveralls and they're all different sizes. You might get one that's too little; you might get one that's just huge. Then you go to the barber chair and they cut your hair off. A dumb haircut. You know how hair is to most of the guys. That, I wipe out of my mind so it won't bother me before I even get there. I'm always ready for haircuts so I won't get mad. I cut my own hair rather than give them the satisfaction of cutting my hair. Even though I might want to grow my hair, I don't. So that's something you can do on your own. But new people don't do that. They don't know. Or they might say, 'I'm not letting them cut my hair.' You hear that all the time but you know in your mind what's going to happen. But if they don't want their hair cut, they run everybody out of the room and run in and grab the guy and force him into the chair and handcuff him to it and then they really cut his hair off with big splotches sticking out all over.[9] And so he gets his hair cut anyway.

"After you get through the haircut you got all this hair down your neck. After a shower everyone gets sprayed with a stinging spray of some kind. Then they give you a bag of lunch because you spend your whole afternoon in there while they're processing you, writing down your name, writing down all your tatoos and things like that. They've done it a hundred times to some people, taking their history. They take your picture and they fingerprint you, then you all pick up this little roll with blankets and sheets and stuff in it and you go down these long underground tunnels. Makes you feel like you're in a science fiction movie. It's because you're underground and it's really cold in the tunnel.

"Shelton is way over on the coast, the rainy part of the state. Every place you go is underground from one building to another. The tunnels go down and come up, see. They're a real trip. You can't help but holler in them cause if you do and wait, then the sound comes back to you. When you're walking down the tunnels and you snap your fingers, it's always echoing and you can hear people whispering in the tunnel clean from here to the end. You can hear their conversations. The tunnels branch off and the cops watch you and holler if you try to stop and talk to someone. That's Shelton."

Another prisoner continues describing Shelton, pointing out that it is so crowded it is difficult to carry out programs.

"Guys who are returning to prison on parole violations generally spend thirty days. There are no more tests or interviews for them. They just sit for a month dead time then head out on the Chain for the Walls.

"For new people supposedly, they have orientation. They talk to sociologists and they talk to the nut doctor if they need it, and they spend time doing a work-up on them for the Parole Board, and they make a recommendation. They also recommend where to send them from Shelton [whether to] keep them at Shelton, send them to Monroe [the state reformatory for men] or send them here [Walla Walla]. Or they might get intensive parole, which might happen for one out of a hundred guys if he's a first timer, but with conditions in this state, Shelton's purpose and what they actually do is two different things. It's so crowded that they haven't got a choice, really, where to send a person. So if there's an opening here at the Joint, you go here. That's why your first timer and your youngsters end up here because they've filled the other places. So it's not where you should be, but who can take you. As a consequence of that, the sociologists and whoever else works there feel,

'What's the use?' Nothing they say makes any difference anyway.

"Right now they have men in Shelton who have been sitting in those small empty cells for ten months waiting for a prison to go to. This is because of the overcrowding all over the state. Last October [1980] was the first uprising ever in the reception units at Shelton.

"Shelton is also a regular institution but half of the place is the state's reception unit for the fish. This is three large cell blocks all sitting side by side connected by one long breezeway. The blocks are called 'R Units.' R-1 holds men going to the Joint for the most part. R-2 is a mixture, but mostly younger men headed for Monroe Reformatory or Shelton itself. R-3 is designed to hold guys that they think might make it on intensive parole programs. It also holds rats that have come in with a reputation either from the county jails or even other joints.

"It's a fucking ugly place. Even us hard-core old timers hate the trip through Shelton and the torture and indignity of the Chain. We dread it and talk about it with hate and disgust years after we have passed through."

The physical setting and architectural design of the reception center have a disquieting effect upon the captive, which contributes to the picture forming in his mind of losing his identity and being pulled further and further into a new reality. Located in an area of the state where almost continuous rainfall forbids sunshine, the reception center creates a depressing and foreboding primal context for the new worldview taking shape. Being herded through labyrinthine underground tunnels when moving from one building to the next disorients the men and contributes to their impression that every point of reference that was previously meaningful no longer is valid. Furthermore, testing and evaluating contribute to the growing impression that one is constantly under scrutiny by an enemy, not a benefactor. Distortion becomes part of the worldview. The impersonal enemy is everywhere.

Cardozo-Freeman: "In your experience as a young person, a *fish* at Shelton, were there any people there who really were kind and understanding toward you?"

Delorme: "Not that they seem deliberate in their actions but you give up after a couple of days expecting even a decent answer from anybody, so you don't ask and they have a way of looking at you so you don't ask anybody."

Cardozo-Freeman: "Impersonal?"

Delorme: "Yeah. Everywhere you go everything is a shout or a growl. They just turn you away automatically so you're not going to ask anything. You go to your caseworker and he'll talk to you, but the cops, it's like they've got a herd of animals, and it's really hard for people to accept that."

The next prisoner to speak struggles to maintain his connection to his former world, realizing that the privilege of seeing his people is dependent upon his submission to the chaining policies of the state. He talks about his reaction to "letting go of the outside world" and the difficulty of adjusting to his imprisonment.

"We will put up with almost anything to protect that one hour visit we can have after we are there two weeks. That visit somehow makes everything easier to take. You can sit and stare with love through the glass at your Lady and tell her she is so beautiful, even if she isn't. You kinda maybe hold your hand against the glass and she'll hold her hand up there, too. You can laugh at your shaved head and joke at the cut of your baggy clown coveralls. It makes it easier when your sweetheart says those magic words, 'I'll wait for you.' That warms your whole body up and you can walk back to that bleak cell with a smile.

"The biggest thing that helps us to endure our treatment besides that short visit are the letters. You will even say a prayer for a letter. 'Please, Lord, let her write me today. Please let there be a letter on my bed today when I come back from the yard.' I can't say enough about the total depression that no letter can bring. It doesn't matter quite so much as the months go by and you move out to other places, but it just takes weeks to adjust and to begin to let go of the outside world.

"Shelton is where you meet shock, hopelessness, helplessness, fear, depression, hate, extreme sadness, coldness. It all hits like a freight train and no one can help you. Some men cry; some men commit suicide; some try to comfort others; some tease the man that cries; maybe it somehow helps them to deal with their situation."

Getting the prisoner to let go of the outside world is part of the plan of the state's chaining policy. Is this why the prisoner resists it so desperately? Does he believe he is letting go of some important quality within himself? Why is the state so intent on removing so much from the prisoner that defines him as a human being, as a man, in his own eyes? The stated policy with respect to prisoners in the state is rehabilitation. In the sociological sense, rehabilitation means to restore to a state of physical, mental, and moral health through treatment and training. So much occurs in the chaining process that attacks the dignity and manliness of the captive, it is difficult not to conclude that this attack is part of "treatment and training" for rehabilitation. The struggle of the prisoner, however, to maintain physical, mental, and moral health under such treatment and training is almost impossible. The previous narrative speaks of "hopelessness, helplessness, fear, depression, hate, extreme sadness, and coldness" as part of the captive's reality in his new environment of rehabilitation. A new captive worldview is beginning to replace the worldview the prisoner had before he became a captive. A profound sense of injustice develops.[10] An attitude begins to evolve that manifests itself in the language of the captive as well as in his actions. This is characterized by toughness, cynicism, and hardheartedness as a response to his existential condition. But before these qualities take hold firmly, another process occurs—mourning—which is a response to the sadness and depression which the captive feels.

"Shelton is where you hear people cryin. And that's where you start that other mean process. There's absolutely no compassion there because the fish are already practicing to be tough. I've cried, too, even as many times as I've been through there.

"The last time I was at Shelton I cried because one night I was just sittin there thinkin about G. and that got to me cause I had promised her that I would never go back, and here I am again. It really got to me.

"But people hear that and some guys, they're young and the whole thing just breaks them down. Some of em will cry in the visiting room and make their people feel miserable, but because they're not gettin beat up, they should be able to take it. So even though the other fish might want to try to comfort the guy, they don't do it. The other guys say, 'You baby,' and call em names and make it worse for em. But that's their idea of tryin to get ready for what's ahead for em so you can't blame em, you know.

"If you try to talk to a man that's feelin that bad, he's gonna get to you. It'll spread to you cause you're feelin that way, too. Shelton would be an ideal place to have a little privacy so you could kind of get those feelings out where other people couldn't see or hear you. You're not gonna get out but you got feelings that have to come out and then you have to shut them off for a long time, probably."

Certainly, the mourning that manifests itself in crying is an important coping mechanism. It is also evidence of the ambivalence the captive feels about his criminal-noncriminal identity. Those prisoners who taunt the men who cry recognize, however, that toughness must replace vulnerability if they are to survive their experience in prison.

Monotony, boredom, and repetition of the indoctrination routine make the captives anxious to leave the reception center; they look forward ambivalently to their prison assignments, as though jumping from the frying pan into the fire might be a relief. This may be part of the state's intent in the chaining process so that the men will want to go to the penitentiary. This prisoner points out that going to Walla Walla has an advantage—the college program.

"By the time six weeks is up you're anxious to go somewhere. You are and you aren't, but you know you're going so you're in a hurry to get the hell out of there because all you do is stay in the cells at Shelton. They get you used to staying in your cells. There's no radios or TV or anything like that to kill the time and the only thing you have to do after being put in cells is they take you out for chow. They have their own dining halls.

"There's three buildings they put the guys in. Each unit has eighty individual cells. You go to meals three times a day and you have your yard exercise once a day for an hour and that's your routine. The rest of the time you're in your cell.

"You go to a classification committee and you go to the Parole Board, hopefully, and you get your time and then the classification committee says, 'We've studied this and we think that you would do good at Monroe and we recommend that you go get some vocational training,' and things like that.

"Monroe doesn't have a college program like we got here. We're lucky here at Walla Walla. They decide what might help you but if

you've been in a penitentiary or any place like that once, then
they're done with you. Then it's the Joint, the end of the line and
all that. But what's happening now is there's so many people
coming into Shelton that they place you wherever there's a spot.
That's why it's so good that they have a college program at the
Joint because if you get these younger guys in college, man, it
might save em.

"Anyway, Tuesdays will be a Monroe Chain and Wednesdays are
the Walla Walla Chain. So you wait til the following Wednesday
and in the morning right after breakfast they call the guys out that
are going on the Chain and you go right out."

THE CHAIN BUS

The twenty-five men on the imaginary bus, having experienced
the deliberate cell-training process imposed at the diagnostic center,
presumably are now accustomed to the treatment they will receive
as prison inmates at the maximum security prison of the state, but
they never become accustomed to the actual chaining process
itself. Delorme describes his feelings about this.

"The thing you'll always remember is the chains. They have
heavy chains almost like a tow chain and it wraps around your
waist twice and they've all got these padlocks and it's got a big ring
in front, a big silver ring and they've got handcuffs through that.
Then your hand goes through here and they're handcuffed to the
ring. Then after everybody is chained up like that, they've got
another ring on the side and they run another long chain through
all that so you're all kind of close together and they make ten-man
chains and put you on the bus. All the time you're on the bus
you're scared that the bus driver is going to have a heart attack and
go in the river or the bus will catch fire. You see, anytime you're
helpless, all those thoughts come to your mind.

"When they come and take you off on the Chain, you make sure
that your people don't know when you're leavin because it's not
something that you want them to see. You wouldn't want your
people to see you cause you hide this stuff from people that you
love, anyway. You don't tell em what's goin on too much. It's bad
enough for me bein in jail. Hell, she'll freak out if she sees me all

chained up. She'll think that's the way I've got to run around all the time and besides, I can't give her a little wave. I'd just rather go because it's just a short while that you're chained and then you're unchained again.

"It's the reason I didn't go to my dad's funeral [while at Walla Walla]. They took us out front and then they started with the chain business and I just said, 'No, I don't want to go.' They said you had to wear the chains in church and everywhere, so I passed on it. What the hell. But chains, you know, there's just something about em. Only men are chained in this fashion anywhere in the world. Animals are on a leash or halter, or maybe guided or herded, but seldom chained.

"When I go to the hospital down here in Walla Walla, the strangers, I don't care if they look at me, but not my family when my legs are chained. There's no use bein ashamed of it. The chains aren't going to go away. Right? So you kind of start playin the role they expect you to play, givin everybody dirty looks and things like that. They can tell where you come from and you know what they're thinkin about you so you just kind of fall into it and maybe it's the same way we do when we get out of prison a lot of times; we play the role we're expected to play. And we do play it. I did that last time they took me down to the hospital. I got off on it a little bit because I couldn't hide the chains. People were lookin at me."

Cardozo-Freeman: "So you played the tough guy?"

Delorme: "Yeah. Scared the little old ladies. Actually, the little old ladies were the only ones that would talk to me. One minute you want to say, 'I won't hurt you.' You want to explain about your chains, but you don't have to with two guards standin there. This whole play takes place in silence. The only sound in the carpeted waiting room is the muted rattle of my leg chain and handcuffs. Everyone seems uneasy and most people try not to stare.

"The last time I made the run to the local clinic I was standin in the waiting room lookin at the people. There were a few empty chairs but the looks on the faces were hopin I wouldn't sit down. Finally, a lady asked me to a chair beside her. She was one of the two little old ladies in the room. I spent the entire ride down tellin myself not to be embarrassed and not to fight the chains so I wouldn't trip and fall flat on my face. If you do trip and fall you have a very hard time gettin up because your hands are not only cuffed, but a waist chain holds the arms and hands close to your waist. No balance. You have to be picked up and put back on your feet if you fall. That can be embarrassing. There is something special about the way a person walks in chains. It is a slow, even shuffling pace, so the guards are always waitin for you to catch up."

Chaining disturbs the men deeply because it is a powerful, age-old symbol of enslavement, degradation, and surrender. The state invokes this awful symbol of *the Chain*, fully realizing what a terrible effect it has upon the men.

The captives introduced earlier are bound for "hell" on *the Chain*, the infernal bus piloted across the Cascade Mountains by a driver, not unlike Charon of Greek mythology who rowed the damned across the River Acheron to Hades. In this instance, the damned are prisoners of the state of Washington chained and manacled together, bound for the maximum security prison at Walla Walla. And like Charon, who dumps the damned at the Gate of Hell, the driver of *the Chain* dumps the prisoners at the back gate of the penitentiary. Delorme describes the final journey from the reception center to Walla Walla.

"No one ever looks forward to a ride on the Chain. Chain day is always a bummer. Everyone is generally quiet, withdrawn, deep within their thoughts. It's time for some real chainin and trainin, a time to look at nagging fears we have been able to ignore and push to the back of our minds for six weeks.

"It all comes crashing down on Chain day. All the small bits of hope we had nursed looking for that one miracle that would some-how put us back on the streets is all gone up in smoke when you hear your name called and hear the rattle of your set of chains and locks. This is it. Deep inside you scream the words that will follow you throughout your stay: 'Why me? How could I do this to myself?'

"The process of being chained, cuffed and driven to the pen or reformatory seems to be so automatic it is done without your paying attention most of the time; pretending you don't give a damn. They ask you to turn this way or that; maybe they will nudge you and you turn just enough so they can get the locks locked and the cuffs cuffed. If you are interested in what they are doing with you, you will watch the other men being chained.

There isn't any thought of fighting; even the meanest ones accept the chains quietly. It's a time for training, kicking out all the bad thoughts of freedom which hours ago were good thoughts.

"The ride itself amounts to six hours of uncomfortable boredom sitting on hard wooden seats and wishing for a smoke. When the trip begins there's generally a lot of rapping, some nervous laughter and a lot of sightseeing through dirty windows. We strain to catch a last glimpse of familiar landmarks in each town or city we pass through. I'm lucky, or unlucky, because my mother's house can be seen from the freeway. I dread looking out but I can't help but sneak a peak to see if I can see her car. I swallow hard and I'm glad I didn't see it.

"We are well guarded and secure on the Chain. There won't be any fights on this ride. All that garbage comes later.

"After we leave the Seattle area, the ride becomes quiet. There isn't anything to look at and we have talked all we want to talk. The new men, fish, are full of questions but they won't ask the important ones. They all want to know just one thing: 'What's going to happen to me?'

"After what seems like weeks of driving, the bus rounds the last corner and the men strain to see the Joint from the freeway. It's evil and it's saying to me, 'I'll break your ass this time, motherfucker.' And I'm smiling now and thinking right back, 'No you won't. I'll die first.' So the fight begins.

"We pull up in front of the Administration Building where some packages are unloaded. Tickets, or papers for each man, are taken inside for processing and we are officially added to the daily count. The guards step out to stretch their legs and joke with old friends who are coming off the shift. We all take this time to stand up and stretch. Asses are sore. Itches are scratched by a buddy and you return the favor.

"This is the last leg, the final wait before we are clear to come on in. We are thankful it isn't summer because the bus becomes an oven during this waiting period in the hot months. We will sit here anywhere from half an hour to two hours. By the time they return we are all anxious to get inside and get started with whatever. Minds are made up. Plans are made. Someone shouts, 'Let's go, motherfucker!' And we're off to the races.

"The fish on arriving at the back gate get their first look at the infamous Walla Walla convicts who are waiting and watching. They all are looking for old friends so they can welcome them and shout out a cell number, or tell them which chow hall to eat in. They have care packages and street clothes ready for their friends, their brothers. Some who are there waiting are checking for new punks, queens, and known rats."

What do the prisoners reveal in describing the reality they experience as a result of the state's chaining process? Central to the formation of their worldview is the *way* the power of the state is used against transgressors of the law. The prisoners view the policies of the criminal justice system in preparing them for prison as calculated and deliberate procedures aimed at dehumanization. Instead of beginning a process of restoring a man to physical, mental, and moral health, rehabilitation dismantles him, tears him apart, and leaves him without help to put the pieces of himself back together again. The sense of alienation from the self is so great that for many the rebuilding produces a human being who is far more disoriented and fragmented and therefore more dangerous to society than before he entered the criminal justice system in the first place. This prisoner sums up what the men believe.

"The system in this state is supposed to be tryin to make straight people out of us. Right? Instead, it treats us like dogs in cages. No, not as good as dogs cause the SPCA don't allow dogs to be treated the way we are. Hell, the repeater rates are so goddam high, they run a revolving door operation in this state. Guys are constantly comin back into the system. I'm tellin you, man, you can't take a guy and reduce him to an ole animal and expect him to come back out lovin society, cause he sure ain't gettin no lovin in the system; you know what I mean? They're supposed to be teachin us not to break the rules on the streets; instead, they're teachin us to hate em so much that we want revenge when we get out. They're crazy, man. They don't make no sense!"

Central to the state's failure is its lack of sensitivity to the feelings of the captives. One man remarks that "you've got to be lacking in humanity in order to take it away from others. How we feel about all this can't be recognized by them since they think of us as 'things' and everybody knows that 'things' don't have feelings."

Several of the men point out that the state's chaining policies are set for the convenience of the authorities and not to help them overcome the problems that cause them to be caught up in the criminal justice system in the first place. One example that shows how the state operates out of convenience for itself and not out of concern for the rehabilitation of the men is the policy in the jails and at Shelton of keeping the men from physical contact with their families and sweethearts. The men believe, as did the prisoner who described his efforts and those of his little son to reach out and touch one another, that these are cruel, calculated, and unnecessary procedures aimed not at rehabilitation but rather at punishment through removing the men from personal contact with those whom they know would best give them hope and strength to survive their ordeal. They point out that it is simply a procedure designed "for the convenience of the keeper of the caged." Skin searches of the men after visits would eliminate any possibility of passing of weapons or other contraband.

Ignoring the way prisoners feel in the chaining process defeats the state's purpose. All the effort and money spent to discourage criminal identity and behavior only intensifies and increases both. Central to this failure is not recognizing the power of the spirit; a power that cannot be controlled by chains of any kind. Delorme, riding on *the Chain*, illustrates this power of the spirit to insist on freedom at any cost when he holds an imaginary conversation with the prison as it comes into sight. "It's evil and it's saying to me, 'I'll break your smart ass this time, motherfucker.' And I'm smiling now and thinking right back, 'No you won't. I'll die first.' So the fight begins." I asked Delorme to explain what lay behind this attitude.

"You wanted me to expand on coming in on the Chain and seeing that big ugly pile of bricks waiting like a man-eating monster. It really is a man-eater in every respect.

"I have developed a feeling through the years that this whole prison trip was sort of a personal fight between me and the state or the system. It's been my belief that the 'powers' want to break me down and make a mindless robot out of me. But first they have to defeat me. Kick my ass until I scream for mercy; fuck with my head until I can't hang on anymore.

"What I try to hang on to is the beliefs I had. Right or wrong, I was stuck with them and I defended them. Only *I* will let those beliefs, attitudes, and bad habits go, and only when *I* decide to do it.

"The major point was that I thought I couldn't let my real self be seen while under 'their' control or it would show weakness and giving in to what 'they' wanted. Each time I came to prison I was sad, completely burned out and feeling like, 'Aw, fuck everything.' I wanted to just let go and ride with the current, even if it meant following their rules, heaven forbid. But once we came around that last bend in the road and the Joint sprang into sight, every cell in my body said, 'Here we go. Get your shit together now or forever hold your peace.' I would say to myself, 'Fuck this. I'll make it again, no matter what comes down.'

"The Joint had a mind of its own to me. It was built to destroy people like me, and I took real pride in having ridden through so many times untouched, unchanged, and still saying, 'Fuck the world.' I was afraid to let go because I didn't know any other way. I hadn't learned enough about life to even imagine that I could begin to take control in a different way. I was fully institutionalized and thought I had this tiny bit of freedom to hate, and to think my own thoughts. So I moved my world to my head and somehow was able to be happy in the thought that I was free mentally. I never saw the wall or the towers after a week or so. I wasn't crazy, of course, but I took satisfaction in the thought that I was holding on to something 'they' hated and wanted—my ability to smile and think my own thoughts. That is what the price would be—I would lose these if I let the Joint break my ass."

The work of running prisons is complicated by the irrepressible need of the human spirit for dignity and freedom. Working with the needs of the human spirit, rather than against them would produce a different response from the captives. This is what the prisoners reveal about their view of *the Chain* and all that it represents for them. Despite the awesome power of the state, it cannot chain, defeat, imprison, or subjugate the spirits of its captives. *The Chain,* symbol of the absolute power of the state to subdue, humiliate, and reduce the "enemy" to a condition of impotence and slavery, in the final analysis, fails. It fails because it looks upon its captives as mere physical entities, just so many bodies to warehouse out of sight. It fails because it does not attempt to "capture" the minds and spirits of its prisoners although it could do so by using humane procedures. Formulating chaining policies that consider the humanity, hence the right to dignity of every offender, would turn away from a life of crime those who initially are ambivalent about their criminal identities. These could be salvaged by such a chaining process. This is the message the prisoners reveal of *the Chain*.[11]

NOTES

[1]Today, two-man chains are used.

[2]The profile for the men riding on the imaginary *Chain* is compiled from the statistics presented in *Report: An Analysis of Program Needs of Prison Inmates in Washington State*, compiled by Thomas M. Sykes, Robert L. Riccolo and Joann K. Thompson, published by the Analysis and Information Services Division of the Washington State Department of Social and Health Services, Olympia, Washington, April, 1980.

[3]John Irwin, *The Felon* (Englewood Cliffs, N.J.: Prentice-Hall, Inc., 1970), p. 36. Irwin is quoted extensively in this chapter because his research in the California penal system reveals many similarities with the Washington corrections system. An outstanding researcher and scholar in the field, he spent five years in the California prison system as a felon. His insight and understanding of prisoner worldview is both outstanding and authentic. All quotes reprinted by permission of the publisher.

[4]" . . . the suspect's most importunate entreaties go unnoticed, or harshly repulsed. To gain permission to make a single telephone call, as is his legal right, often takes considerable persistence on the part of the prisoner. . . . 30, 40, 60, or possibly 120 days pass by slowly. . . . These experiences—arrest, trial, and conviction—threaten the structure of his personal life in two separate ways. First, the disjointed experience of being suddenly extracted from a relatively orderly and familiar routine and cast into a completely unfamiliar and seemingly chaotic one where the ordering of events is completely out of his control has a shattering impact upon his personality structure." *The Felon*, pp. 38–39.

[5]*The Felon*, p. 39.

[6]Taken from the description of the procedures at Shelton from the brochure, *Adult Corrections in Washington State*, Department of Social & Health Services, Olympia, Washington, 1973.

[7]"Instead of furthering the 'treatment' of the felon, in many cases classification and sentencing actually promote self-disorganization, a sense of injustice, and increased commitment to criminal values and beliefs. . . . Official agents approach these tasks from a position of ignorance, insensitivity, or intolerance of the

experiences and perspectives of the felons they are attempting to correct." *The Felon*, p. 36.

[8]"The first day he is stripped, bathed, reclothed, fingerprinted, and photographed. In the ensuing days he is examined, interviewed, and tested. All this takes place while he is facing the foreign, possibly hostile prison world. Furthermore, he is embarking on a prison term of indeterminate length. In the first weeks at the reception center he is being observed almost constantly by people who will make an evaluation of him, an evaluation which will be influential in determining the course of his prison life. . . . The investigations conducted . . . may have an important impact upon his struggle to reconstruct his identity." *The Felon*, p. 41.

[9]Because of legal action by inmates, today the men receive only conventional haircuts at Shelton.

[10]Irwin writes that "adult criminals have felt some sense of injustice for various reasons for many years. This feeling stemmed, first, from their perception of the inequality in the social circumstances in which they were born, grew up, and competed as adults. Second, they perceived inequality and unfairness because of corruption and class bias in the way they were handled by law enforcement agencies and the courts. . . . Formerly, criminals tended to accept the inequality of their social circumstances because it was consistent with their worldview. . . . Presently, convicts . . . are acquiring a basically more critical perspective on society and some of its institutions and organizations. This shift in perspective has produced a new profound sense of injustice." *The Felon*, p. 51. The new awareness is what Paulo Freire calls *conscientizaço*, the "perception of social, political and economic contradictions, and the desire to take action against the oppressive elements in reality." *Pedagogy of the Oppressed*, Trans. by Myra Bergman Ramos (New York: Seabury Press, 1968), p. 19.

[11]Prisoners critiquing this chapter pointed out that the colors of the coveralls worn in King County Jail depend upon what part of the jail one is housed. Blue and gold are the most common colors, with red designated for a particular area of the jail.

Chapter 3

THE FISH

It is agreed by men in prisons and jails that *fish* connotes a certain kind or category of prisoner. *Fish* is an "agreed-on cultural definition" of a man coming into a captive community for the first time. Behind the term *fish* lies a poetic metaphor that is extended in its meaning. Within the poetic meaning is a statement or observation about the reality of life lived by prisoners. That statement is ironic and bitter and reveals a paradox. Behind the connotative wordplay on the human condition of captives is a "message." In *fish* and its metaphor we have an excellent example of a paradigm that reveals an important aspect of the cultural worldview of prisoners.

GENESIS OF FISH

According to Maurer, the genesis of *fish* is *sucker*, a term dating to before the 1900s connoting a person easily deceived or duped. It is used in the underworld to identify someone from the dominant culture who becomes a *mark*, a victim of a criminal act centering upon any kind of theft from extortion to pickpocketing. In *Whiz Mob*, Maurer writes that amateur adult criminals are looked upon with contempt by professional criminals, as just another species of *sucker*.[1] Professional criminals seldom go to jail or prison because they maintain connections with police and political figures in the community, which allows them to operate relatively unhampered in exchange for payoffs. Amateur criminals, however, have no such ties; when they are caught they are thrown into jail like so many "suckers" who have been "taken."

For a professional criminal, a *sucker* from the dominant culture happens to be in the wrong place at the right time; he is unaware, naive, and therefore at the mercy of the skill of the professional criminal. The *sucker* (amateur criminal) who is caught by the police also happens to be in the wrong place at the right time; he is unable to avoid a downfall because he, too, is unsophisticated and unaware and so is outmaneuvered by the superior skill of his captor. There is an analogy between professional criminals and law enforcement agents: the professional criminal catches *suckers* from the dominant culture who are dumb enough to get caught, and the police capture *suckers* from the underworld who are dumb enough to get *hooked.* Successful criminals are fishers of men; successful law enforcement agents are also fishers of men. The *sucker* is the bread and butter of the professional criminal; the *sucker* caught by the police is the bread and butter of the criminal justice system.

Among freshwater fish, the Sucker is a species that feeds off river and lake bottoms. It is regarded by fishermen as the least desirable of species, a scavenger that sucks up leftovers and scraps rejected by other fish. It is from the Sucker, literally a garbage fish, that the criminal underworld draws its poetic analogy. Such a derogatory term used to describe someone in the dominant culture who is victimized by the professional criminal is an indication of the contempt with which the professional criminal holds the dominant culture from which he makes his living. The *sucker*, the amateur criminal, caught and thrown into jail becomes the *fish* in the *fish tank*, regarded also with contempt by those who make their living by catching him. He is so much garbage from the river and lake bottoms; that is, the slums, *barrios*, and ghettos of the community.

THE METAPHOR OF THE FISH

The term *fish*, meaning new men in jails and prisons, has been in use since before 1915.[2] The term and all that it connotes has moved beyond its original source, *sucker*, and while it still retains its original sense of someone who is gullible or stupid, it has taken on a broader connotation that reflects the condition of newly imprisoned men.

Delorme remarks in this chapter that *fish* "either learn to swim or they sink." How are newly imprisoned men like fish swimming or sinking in a tank? A fish tank is an aquarium where fish are kept and where care must be taken by the keeper to create a living environment that assures that the fish survive. The temperature[3] must be carefully regulated, as must the population of the fish, since they will not survive if the water of the tank is too warm or too cold or if their numbers are too dense. Care must be taken, also, to see that the right amount of oxygen flows into the water in which the fish swim. Furthermore, fish that are dangerous to others are placed in separate tanks. Prisoners quite rationally compare themselves to fish in an unnatural environment. The irony of the image—fish in a carefully maintained aquarium, juxtaposed against the reality of what actually happens to *fish* in prisons and jails—serves to heighten awareness of the fate of imprisoned men.

THE FISH WHO SWIM IN THE TANK

Once the men disembark from the *Chain*, once they have arrived at the Washington State Penitentiary, they pass through the back gate and begin their descent into the inferno of the prison where new dangers and anxieties, real and imagined, await them. The welcoming reception they receive from the guards and the inmates already there remains stamped indelibly in their memories, as does their initial impression of the prison.

Terror is the initial response of men coming to Walla Walla for the first time. Although all have been in jail and Shelton's reception center and some have served sentences in Monroe Reformatory, the other adult prison, the *Joint* has such a terrible reputation it frightens all but the toughest recidivists who regard returning to Walla Walla as just another *pit-stop*. The frequent newspaper headlines of trouble and violence at Walla Walla are reinforced by stories, some of which reach almost legendary proportions, told by men who have *done time* there. Gang rapes, hijacks, and stabbings are only some of the subjects dealt with in the tales passed on in oral tradition by men in other prisons and jails in the state. This prisoner describes his initial response to Walla Walla as "fear and trembling."

"There's three gates that you drive through before they get you inside the prison. They drive you in and they open this great big iron gate that rolls up into its own area. It's supposed to be unbreakable, a super tough gate, anyway, made of steel slats or some damn thing, and they wrap like venetian blinds. The Chain drives on inside with you. You say, 'Man, this fuckin joint is ugly!' It looks like it's ready to fall down. It really does.

"You get inside and by then the first thing you see is a lot of people standin around. Guys come out on Wednesday just to watch the Chain. They can't get close; they have to stand way back, but they can watch from there and holler and shout.

"I remember when I first came through, I was really nervous and scared. I didn't know what was gonna happen. I knew I was in the state penitentiary. Even though I came over from another one, it didn't make any difference cause they're all different. You get used to one and then you go to the next one, that's all. Each one you hear stories about and you pretty much go along with the stories you keep hearin.

"All you hear about this joint is people killin each other, fuckin each other in the butt, rippin off the youngsters, crazy people over here, and all that shit, so you got a whole busload of people that are mighty goddam nervous, awful sad. You have no idea what you're gonna do, and the worst thing in the world is you don't know whether you're gonna live. You don't know what anything looks like; you're just walkin into the unknown.

"When I first came in here, I got off the Chain and they were unchainin us and I was just shakin, you know, and it pissed me off that I was shakin. I just couldn't stop shakin. It was embarrassing and I was hoping nobody else noticed it. Course, since that time I've seen that again and again and again. People just can't help it sometimes. It goes away in a little while, a few minutes. But it's a terrible feelin, anyway. I just wished to God that something would happen, that I could leave or something."

The "keeper" does not prepare the *fish* ahead of time for the ordeal that awaits them in the *tank*; consequently, anxiety is extremely high when they first come in. As the previous narrative points out, the men walk into the unknown unprepared, without knowing whether or not they are going to survive. Because of this they become disoriented and frightened, therefore, extremely vulnerable to the real dangers awaiting them. The next narrative, a description of the physical layout of the prison and the procedures the men go through in getting settled ends with foreboding — the distinct possibility that some of the new *fish* who do not learn immediately how to *swim* will undergo a devastating initiation rite.

"The building they take you into to process you is the oldest building in the Joint. It's the power house building, just a big empty place. They made a clothing room out of it and put in counters and this and that, but it's really ugly. They take you in there after they unchain everybody.

"You all stand around in little groups while they're taking your chains off. Some of the guys are yelling and talking to friends that they see over there in the crowd; others are trying to keep their backs to them cause they don't want to look at them, or they don't know anybody. And you just mill around. You stick close to each other, and, of course, you try to talk but you're so scared, looking around wondering what's going to happen next.

"What you can see from right there is the big powerhouse and right behind that is the smokestack a mile high. Off to your left is a little building which I used to call the Dodge City Jail. What it turned out to be was the coke shack and inmate store (canteen), but it's just a little one-story building with barred windows on it and a solid iron door with bars, so it looked like an old time western jail to me. Next to that is the end of Big Red. The other end of it stretches further down. There are two wings to it.

"When you first come in, that's one of the first buildings they tell you about. This end is Segregation and the other end is Admissions. If somebody asks you and you say, 'I just got out of Big Red,' you're saying, 'I just got out of the Hole.' But if you say, 'I live in Admissions,' then you live in the other end of the building and not in the Hole, which is what is meant when you say Big Red.

"There's four decks over there in Segregation — ABCD. A Deck is the Hole — there's segregations units, holding cells, and Death Row down on the end of A Deck — about six cells.

"You can see part of the kitchen, also, when you first come in the back gate. It's just another one of the newer buildings which is rcd brick. That's the view you have when you first come in.

"Oh yeah, the one tower is looking down on you. They unload you underneath the tower. There's a bull up there standing with a rifle, trying to impress everybody, and he does. I think there's eight guard towers.

"So anyway, they take you in and get your coveralls off you and issue you all the clothes you got coming, which is two pair of jeans, tee shirts, work boots, a pair of tennis shoes to kick around in, shorts, socks, sheets, blankets, pillowcase. They give you a bag that's got some tobacco in it, got a toothbrush in it, toothpowder in it, a utility razor, just an old fashioned screw together razor, double edge. Then if there's some cons there to talk to you, they pretty much tell you what's going to be your routine for the rest of the day. They tell you what you're going to have to do the next day, like going over to the clothing room and take your clothes over there and get them all marked and go pick up some more stuff.

"Let's take it from when I came in. The next day you had to go and see your caseworker for what they call the initial interview and that would be the last time you see him for months and months unless something come up. That night you'd go from there to your wing. The guards tell everybody where they're going and they stand them in groups. Six Wing over here; Eight Wing over there. That's about the only two places you go to. If anybody's going to PC, the sergeant takes them over there. It's in Big Red. All the blacks they always automatically go to Six Wing. The rest of us pick our stuff up.

"We used to have to carry a mattress and I sure hated that cause that's a lot of stuff to carry. You got a big clothing bag with all your junk in it. You're pretty weak by the time you get here cause we just been laying around in Shelton without any exercise, so you really struggle. And a guard takes us to Eight Wing and you follow him.

"You don't look around much while you're heading over there. Not much to see, anyway — People's Park and Lifer's Park — that's about it. There's a short part of the Breezeway from Seven Wing down past Big Red. You pass in front of the kitchen as you go to Eight Wing, then you go down the sidewalk and you look over to the right and you see Seven Wing, so you get some idea what the outside of the wings look like right away. They're just big buildings with high windows and you can't see anything from them. They'll tell you it's Seven Wing if you ask but you're not asking by then cause you're just concentrating on getting that load they put on your ass over to Eight Wing.

"When you get into Eight Wing they tell you what cell you're going to. You go inside the wing and you look up and it's just huge, man, three tiers stacked on top of each other, and then you look down to the end at all those cells. It looks huge, I'm telling you! Everything's ugly in prison, you know. And there's some more guys standing around in there looking at you. 'Oh, here's the fish. Here's the fish. I get this one. I get that one.' That scares you right there. Mostly, that's just joking around there, though, but you don't know that and it scares the hell out of you."

INITIATION RITES

The "initiation rite," rape, is a tradition common to jails and prisons everywhere in this country. The original tradition still very much alive involves a young man (*kid*) being *turned out* by an older man (*wolf*) through verbal seduction (*finesse*) or force. The young man then becomes a *punk*, a very low species in the prison, and receives protection from his *daddy* in exchange for his sexual favors. A variant has evolved from this tradition—gang rape. Groups of two or more men lure or isolate an unsuspecting *fish* into a secluded area and overcome him by force. This next narrative is from a *fish* who learned very quickly how to defend himself against such encounters. He was also fortunate to have friends nearby to help him. This young man, now twenty-five, has been in the prison since 1976. Although it is not brought out in this narrative, he survives his prison experience by staying high on drugs. It is, he says, the only way he can cope with prison life—a very common response for many men.

Jim: "Describe the prison and how you felt when you first come in."

Bill: "I was confused on what was really happening. I was really high. They brought you in and unloaded you and just kicked you off and didn't say a word to you about where you was at or what."

Jim: "Did they give you anything from Central Supply like clothing issue and stuff?"

Bill: "They didn't give us anything. We was here for three days before they give us anything, then they give us a blanket and kicked us right out to the Yard. That was during the hostage takeover in 1976."

Jim: "Kinda describe those first few days of the struggle of gettin around the prison grounds seein as how they were under hostage conditions being held at the time. How was it?"

Bill: "I was just lost. Nobody says nothing to ya."

Jim: "Did you find your own way around? Did you ask questions of others?"

Bill: "No, I didn't ask no questions. I wandered around and found where I was goin by myself."

Jim: "Did you find people that was considerate of you as a new fish or did they just kinda brush you off?"

Bill: "Yeah, they brushed you off cause they weren't considerate at all. There was a few guys that helped. And playin games. . . . "

Jim: "Yeah, that's my next question. Did a lot of people play tricks on you?"

Bill: "Oh yeah."

Jim: "Like send you to the wrong wing or somethin like that?"

Bill: "No, it was more serious—homosexual games."

Jim: "You mean when you cut that guy for playin homosexual games with ya?"

Bill: "Yeah, that started right the day I come in. Cockaminy games. It was like a very foolish person done found another foolish person to play games on."

Jim: "About that knifing; what exactly came down on that?"

Bill: "It was just two guys runnin around hasslin new fish and one of em hit on me and the other said, 'You better give it up,' and then they jammed me up against the wall on that. And it come down to a fight and one of the guys I moved in with stepped up on these two guys and helped me, so I dealt with this one guy and the next guy came along and by that time I was done fightin him."

Jim: "You got yourself a shank and cut him up?"

Bill: "Yeah. It wasn't planned or anything. It just kinda happened. But it stopped [attacks from others]."

Jim: "Yeah, I know. It stopped instantly, didn't it."

Bill: "Yeah."

Jim: "Who helped you the most during the first few weeks and how was that help offered?"

Bill: "Just a friend of mine. He told me what to watch out for. I would never a made it at all, but he was there."

Jim: "He was there when you needed him. Did the guards ever assist you when you first come in or did they actually put up blockades for you?"

Bill: "They was in a trick bag."

Jim: "Yeah, that's what I ran across, too. Describe what kinda actions the guards had after they took you off the Chain."

Bill: "Smart asses."

Jim: "Smart asses?"

Bill: " 'Alright, punk, you're here.' "

Jim: "How long did it take before you felt you were no longer a fish?"

Bill: "About a year."

Jim: "One of my cell partners told me, he says, after you been here the first two years, you know the system a little bit, then you do another two years and you think you know it, but then you do five or six years and you finally do know it. Actually, you are a fish for at least the first two years, not really knowing where to go or what to do."

So many dangerous sharks swim in the tank, the new *fish* become partially paralyzed. Some new men become so frightened by the threat of rape or other violence that they sleep with their clothes on and often refuse to come out of their cells. Furthermore, they fear taking showers since the *carwash*, as it is called, is a very common place for attack. Terror shapes the worldview of the new *fish* coming into the *tank*.

Although gang rape is common among all groups, blacks are known in the prison for carrying out this tradition against young whites coming in for the first time. They refer to this as "the game." When the Chain arrives on Wednesdays, groups of prisoners watch for unsuspecting white fish to initiate. The following narrative describes a technique used to disarm the unsuspecting fish.

Bill: "I used to sit and watch the Chain come in and the blacks lying off to the kids who come in and rape em. They'd say, 'Come into the house and smoke a joint.' And once you get in that house, you ain't goin nowhere."

Jim: "Unhuh. Yeah . . . I seen that happen several times. Yeah, I sure have. I seen that happen right next door to the house where I was livin. Over there, man, they were just constantly pickin up some young kid and draggin him off into the house and fuckin him. One of the guys is down here right now [in the Minimum Security Building]. Stayed in that one house. They drug him in there off the Chain and he stayed in that house three years that I know of, just constantly gettin abused every day and he never once tried to do anything about gettin out of the situation cause he was scared shitless. But they gave him a break for awhile; they drug some other kid in there and kept him for about six months."

Some imprisoned blacks turn on young whites as scapegoats in prisons and jails out of revenge for what has happened to them in white society. Kenneth Divons and Larry West quote Billy Robinson—a black inmate regarded by them as a writer comparable to Eldridge Cleaver—as saying that the white man must pay through sexual assault for the injustices they have suffered: " . . . in prison, the black dudes have a little masculinity game they play. It has no name, really, although I call it whump or fuck a white boy. . . . The black dudes go out of their way to make faggots out of them. . . . "[4] Some black leaders in the prison strongly disapprove of and have tried to discourage this game among their brothers, as evidenced in the following narrative by Zack, a black inmate leader who explains why he helped the new fish coming off the Chain each Wednesday.

Delorme: "But you'd operate in that capacity yourself after awhile with the new guys, wouldn't you?"

Zack: "Definitely. And I found that it was a need. I had to do it. I had to get up there and see em because if I didn't see the new guys, they were goin to walk around the institution, there were goin to get caught up in somethin that was wrong. They were goin to get their lives wasted by gettin caught up in a beef that might lead em right down Death Row. It's really simple to be caught up, to be led down to Death Row in this kind of an institution.

"I see so many guys who come in here on the Chain. You know yourself; you used to sit around and wait for the Chain and say, 'Hum, I wonder if that kid will be a turn-out. I wonder if he'll be a nice little punk in about a month.' You find guys standin around doin that all day long. You have to get some group here that goes over there to them and says, 'Hey, just because this little guy's a little man here, he wants to be a man. He doesn't want to be a punk. Leave him alone.' That's kind of the reason I did it."

Other kinds of predators who terrorize the new fish also swim in the waters. This inmate, fortunate to have good friends already in the prison to help him through the first crucial weeks, brings out other dangers for the fish.

Cal: "When I first came here I was petrified. Scared to death and they dumped us off at the back gate and they raised the gate and we walked through and we went to Central Supply, got our bedroll and clothes and here I am, I don't wear underwear and they say, 'Strip out of your coveralls,' and I'm just standin around in the middle of winter bare-assed naked, snow up to my ankles and I'm just standin there dancin, and I'm freezin to death and they're passin out clothes.

"Then they took us and said, 'O.K., we're gonna call your name and you show up here, or there, or wherever.' So they ran us into Six Wing first. I went to Six Wing. I knew somebody there and it so happened I ended up in the same cell with the guy. I was really lucky. I didn't get dumped off into no strange cell or anything.

"All them buildings looked real drab, real old to me. I was thinkin to myself, 'Oh, my God, what have I gotten myself into this time?' Over the years, though, it's become more or less like a home to me. The outside, the streets, seem strange to me now in comparison, cause I have been here now quite a few years.

"They walked us into the wing and we got in the door and the whole block was locked down for count time. They got us off into our cells and when I got in our cell there wasn't a mattress in there and I went back out to get one and the guards told me to get in my cell, that they didn't give a fuck if I didn't have a mattress, to get in my cell now and they'd get me one later. And I'm sayin, 'Hey, you people are uncouth.' So I went in. It looked pretty ugly. It had paint splattered on the walls, dye and stuff from people havin their hobbies and crafts. Graffiti on the walls and shit, real shit on the wall!

"Don was there, man, and just made everything right. We sit down and he give me a cup of coffee and we waited for count to clear and we had a recount, so we had to sit there until about seven o'clock before we got to go out and eat.

"Don and Joe both told me, 'Don't talk to any fuckin body around here because they will know you're a fish even though you been around here a month.' "

Delorme: "You got short hair and all those snazzy new clothes and you smell like ink."

Cal: "Yeah. So they said, 'They'll know you're a fuckin fish, anyway, so just don't talk to anybody or you'll get in trouble.' So I listened to them and tried to keep my mouth shut, but still ended up gettin in some scrapes the first couple years.

"They'd say, 'Don't go over to that side of the dining room and sit down because that's the Bike Shop's area. Don't talk to those guys, no matter what because they're all trouble. They'll rat pack you in a second.' And then later I ran into some Bikers that had quit the shop and found out that they'll rat pack even their own. They're real animals. I don't know why they're so different than anybody else in prison but they are. And also I was told, 'Don't go anywhere near BPFU. They'll drag you off and butt-fuck you.' And I said, 'Oh, my God!' And so I stayed away from there. And then they said, 'If you want to go into the Lifer's or Indian Club, always stop at the door and holler for an escort.' "

Delorme contributes his impressions of learning to swim during the first week.

"When I was new it was much worse. You are not only lost when you come through the back gate, you stay lost like some idiot for a week.

"It all looks the same, the people all look alike. Pigs look like they come from one pig mold; cons from one con mold. It's confusing, frightening, frustrating, and an overall feeling of hopelessness sinks straight to your bones.

"The clothes don't fit. Everything smells of printer's ink. You're cellies don't like you. The pigs have no patience with you. All your worldly belongings are packed into a white mesh laundry bag, and right now you would sell your saintly mother for a good friend.

"Somehow, someway, you survive the first few days. You haven't had your ass kicked or even had a challenge; no one has hit on you. Your cellies haven't killed you or even tossed your mattress and personal stuff out of their house. You discover that they were just upset at having a full house, which left everyone with no place to put anything. The bunk you're sleeping on was the cell storage place for a couple weeks before you came. They had all kept their fingers crossed each Chain day hoping that they wouldn't be stuck with a fourth new fish. 'Please, God, at least let it be a guy that knows his way around, a violator.'

"Your cellies have been kind. They have had patience with you and you pay attention to all they tell you each day. These guys know what slippin and slidin is all about. They will tell you but one time and if you fuck it off and get your stupid fish ass in a sling, then you're on your own.

"'Don't bring no heat on our house, man.' 'Don't be starin at people and don't be askin dumb ass questions.' 'Don't do this, don't do that.'

"It's really a bitch to get everything down. No matter what you do you're branded with a fucked-up short haircut which says, 'This is a stupid fish. Don't rap to the motherfucker until we know more about him.'"

Some initiation traditions are lighthearted and humorous. Common games are giving wrong directions, and sending *fish* to get something that is either unattainable or nonexistent, a kind of prison snipe hunt. The following trick was played after this inmate had been in the prison for a few weeks.

Delorme: "Anybody play any tricks on you? Got any stories?"

Hal: "One guy did. He sent me up to Jane and he says, 'Go ask her for a pair of her pantyhose for me because when I'm out runnin and I'm cold, my tee shirt rubs my titties and they get all chapped. I need a pair of pantyhose so I can cut the legs out of it and wear it up around my chest.' I says, 'O.K. I'll go ask her for ya.'

"So I go in there and I ask her and she turns all different colors of red, every shade in the book, and then it finally dawns on me, you know; the guy quacked me. He quacked me good. And I said, 'Aw forget it, Jane.' And I turned around and walked out of her

office and I'm totally ticked at myself. And then I see Ron later
and I say, 'Hey, you really did me wrong.' And he says, 'No, I
didn't,' he says, 'I really wanted those.' And I says, 'Yeah, so here we
are in a men's prison with forty million men around and one
woman and I'm there talkin to her and sayin, hey, I want a pair of
pantyhose.' Yeah, sure."

Delorme: "Jane was pretty new then."

Hal: "And the only reason that the whole thing got over without Jane gettin ticked off at me or me bein tagged for bein a
pervert or somethin was that Betty and me had grown up together."

Delorme: "If that had been somebody else they probably would
have had you thrown in the Hole."

Hal: "If that had been one of the other female teachers that
didn't know me, I know that's what would have happened."

Another tradition called *Joe the Grinder*[5] is seriocomic in dimension. Older men torment a new *fish* about his wife, suggesting that
Joe the Grinder is now "taking care of her." *Joe the Grinder* is a
legendary character, a former convict who is a killer with the
ladies, and when he leaves the prison, he promptly "fills in" for
the husband, a former "friend" still in the prison. *Fish* are made
miserable by this merciless teasing.

Duane: "O.K., what have you done with those two kids you got in
your house since they been here? How have you tormented them?"

Gene: "Teachin em the rules and regulations of the house."

Duane: "What about their personal life? Tell em about Joe the
Grinder?"

Gene: "I tell em about how much time they gotta do and how
they should think about it realistically."

Duane: "And about Joe the Grinder?"

Gene: "Joe the Grinder, I tell em he's fuckin their wives and
that's just a fact of life. What they don't know won't hurt em."

Duane: "You're laughin all the time you told em."

Gene: "No. I'm serious. I'm deadly serious."

Duane: "Not right now you're not."

Gene: "I don't want em to think I'm jokin, you know what I
mean? I told the guy, 'I don't know what the fuck your trip is but
you talkin about goin back to Monroe, man, you can't keep any
closer eye on her over there than you can here.' "

Duane: "Why don't you tell him to write home and ask his Old Lady who Joe the Grinder is?"

Gene: "I thought about it. If he don't get a letter tomorrow, when he's really burnin, then I'm goin to say, 'Well, maybe the old fuckin jock won't let her get out of bed long enough to write a letter.' That other fish is just as bad, worryin all the time about his Old Lady. I'm tellin you, all them stupid fish are alike."

Prior to the mid-sixties a separate living unit and an orientation program was maintained to help the men adjust to the prison. This was discontinued when Shelton opened its facilities. The absence of these programs complicates the adjustment of the new men who need a safe environment initially to calm their panic and learn how best to avoid the hazards and perils of the prison. Many prisoners believe that the officials do not maintain a separate living unit because of overcrowding—more men come into the prison each month than are released—and because "they just don't give a damn about what happens to us around here." Inmates in positions of leadership in the clubs and Resident Council recognized the problem this created for the new men and brought their special needs to the attention of the administration, but they received no support for a separate unit. They then instituted their own orientation program called *babysitting*. Delorme, a member of the inmate Resident Council and former chief, or president, of the Indian Club, brings out the attitudes of the men toward the officials for not providing a separate unit for new men entering the prison.

Cardozo-Freeman: "How does a young man first coming into the prison get along? Does a process take place in which he is educated by the older men?"

Delorme: "People look out for them. They see them standing around out there like dummies. When he first comes in there's things he has to do and you know he's lost, so you go tell him, 'You guys supposed to get your clothes today or what?' The guy says, 'I think so.' You tell him, 'Well, you go down the stairway right there,' and so on. Little things like that. If they don't know any better than to go in when everybody else goes in, you tell them about it."

Cardozo-Freeman: "Don't the officials see that the men are not just thrown in here without information?"

Delorme: "No. It's right straight into the wing. That's the worst thing you can do to them."

Cardozo-Freeman: "Shouldn't there be something to help the new men? The older men who might help?"

Delorme: "That's what we call babysitting and I used to do a lot of babysitting. They'd bitch and holler about it but they'd do it. I'd say, 'You take this guy for a couple of days. I'll take this guy for a couple of days.' And we'd just babysit em. You show em where to go, show em how to get their phone calls and take em to chow. Might take em to a movie. All this time that you're doin this there's all this conversation goin on and he's just like a little kid. He's just full of questions until it just about drives me crazy."

Cardozo-Freeman: "Learning how to *slip and slide?*"

Delorme: "Yeah. And you can cut him loose when the next bunch comes in the following Wednesday. It's hard to keep older guys doing that. They get tired of it."

Cardozo-Freeman: "Was this something that the inmates did on their own or did the administration ask you to do it?"

Delorme: "No. We've been askin them, we're always askin em all the time; every year it comes up more than once, 'You got to do something about the new guys. You got to give em a place. You can't just keep pushin them in the cells with guys cause they're gettin beat up, raped. They're scared to death.' And we'd take that to the administration, explain it, lay it out, give em a plan, tell em we'd take care of it but for them, to give em a place where they can stay by themselves for at least a week, just even one week. It's a tough go, anyway, that first to third week. They got to have a safe place to go to at night to think it over and not worry about nothin. But they [administration] never went for it. They don't have nothin. They don't tell em anything when they come in. They leave it up to us. They leave all these things up to us, then they complain that we're controllin the Joint. Those are the kinds of things that they call controllin the Joint, but it's their idea in the first place.

"Years ago the prison did have such programs for the new guys and overcrowding, I guess, they can blame it on that. But they can make room. Just like the tier I'm on; there's twenty-five cells; they can give em one of those tiers and just keep it for em. Nothing should push those fish out of there. They had it in 1962, 1963, and somewhere in the middle sixties they quit it. They don't orient them at Shelton, either, so they don't do anything. But it causes a lot of problems."[6]

Delorme describes the procedures he and other Resident Council members used when meeting the *Chain* each Wednesday. Every effort was made to insure that no informers were placed in the general population since their lives would be in danger. The irresponsible role that police, prosecuting attorneys, and other officials of the law play in encouraging informing as part of plea bargaining, for example, sometimes results in death for those who turn state's evidence, as these informers often end up in the same prison as those they testified against. Maurer points out that narcotics addiction, which is very high among some criminals, makes them "less resistant to police pressure, and more likely to talk when faced with the terrible abstinence syndrome in jail."[7] Although Maurer is talking specifically about pickpockets, his statement is applicable to the circumstances we are describing: " . . . the immunity granted thieves of this type is usually limited, for detectives can use a thief as a stoolpigeon only as long as he is not suspected in informing; once he is known, his usefulness ends, and the very detectives who protected him are often instrumental in sending him off to prison where he may continue his informing activities in a fresh environment. His chances of getting killed in either location are good."[8]

"When they get off the Chain, Bob and I are there and so we start watching. First off, we ask the cop that brought them over if any of them are stool pigeons and if the sergeant knows anything about any of them he should tell us. Then we go talk to the guy and tell him to check into PC. We generally advise him to check in. And we ask the guys one at a time if they got anybody after them, if they expect any problems with anybody, and if they do, maybe we can help if it's an old beef. Maybe we know the guy and we can talk him out of it.

"But mostly, we try to tell them to give themselves a chance with the population before they run off to PC because once they go into PC, even if they haven't done anything other than to just be scared, they've bought it for themselves. They can't come back

out because if they do, everybody knows where they've been so
they're stigmatized; they're marked. And that's what we try to tell
them. 'It doesn't mean a shit what you go in for. If it's known, then
you're a coward, a dirty lowlife punk; you're a snake, a snitch, so
don't go. Tough it out for a day or two and then if things are just
too rough for you, let's talk again, but don't go to PC.' But a lot of
them still go. Maybe they did something and they don't feel they
can ride it out."

Cardozo-Freeman: "Maybe they're just young and afraid?"

Delorme: "It's not necessarily the youngsters that do it. A lot of
older guys do it for whatever reasons. They usually won't talk to
anybody when they step off the Chain. They unchain the guys and
soon we spot them. They edge up to the guards and whisper
something. You know he's up to something."

Although the *babysitters* warn the new men not to choose protective custody unless they absolutely must, occasionally someone
can safely move into the population after being in *PC*, but it takes
a certain procedure involving action on the part of certain big *fish*
in the *tank*. Delorme explains.

"Someone respected by the population decides to go in and
bring a guy out of PC. The population will respect a judgment or
decision by a few people, leaders who are respected, so if people
question why the guy is back out of PC, all they have to do is find
out who supported his coming out. You're like a sponsor for the
guy and can vouch for his character. These people can then make
it in main population because a lot of leg work has been done to
clear the way for them."

Delorme continues describing the *babysitting* procedures for the
new "baby" *fish* who have been placed in the *tank*.

"So we tell the rest of them about the wings. We don't know
where they're going to go for sure but we tell them what the
different wings are like before they get there. We tell them a little
bit about four men in a cell and we make sure that they know in
their minds that they don't have to stay where they're put. They
can make a choice to go elsewhere.

"If the guys jump them or ... well, you don't say that either,
cause it will scare them, but 'If you get a little nervous or things
don't look cool, you don't even have to stay there tonight if you

don't want to. Come out of the cell at chow time or the first opportunity you get. Don't scream at the guard and say, let me out of this cell. These guys are picking on me! That's dead action cause they can nail your shit before that guard can open the door, so you just don't do that. You tell when you come out of the cell and when you go to chow. Go to the Control Room or come over to the RC office and we'll go with you and get you a cell change.'

"And we have a list of guys that we keep and we'll go around the Joint and we talk to older guys. We talk to guys that we know are good people and we get them on a list and those guys agree to try to keep a bunk open for a new guy if he really needs it. In some cases a guy will go so far as to move out of his cell temporarily just so that new guy can come in for a week or two and they'll just go somewhere else, cause they know their way around. Then they'll come back to their house later on after the new guy finds a place he feels safe in.

"So if the guy will come over to the RC office and talk, they can go over there and tell one of the RC members why they're there. 'I need a cell change. Guys in the cell are looking at me funny.' Or 'They're threatening me. They took my coffee and they took my cigarettes.' Course, that's to be expected. If a guy can't get past that, he's in trouble. I mean, if he can't lose a few little personal items without getting up in the air . . . it's kind of a test, anyway, to see what kind of an asshole you are. You're not supposed to go freaky just because a guy stole your pack of cigarettes.

"But if a guy comes over to the RC, then they call one of us and we come over and go with the guy. First off, we'll go over and see where he was and the RRC [Race Relations Committee, a group within the Resident Council serving as a problem solver between men or groups of men] will go talk to those guys in the cell and if I can't talk to them I refer them back to the RC and the RRC will go over and talk to them. If that don't do it, I don't know . . . the RRC don't generally get too violent, you know, but they will. [The RRC has been known to follow 'an eye for an eye' policy in meting out justice.]"

Cardozo-Freeman: "Who were the people who thought that these new men needed orientation?"

Delorme: "Guys just like myself who have been through it and remember how it was. Everybody remembers how it was. Some don't care but a lot of people do care. The babysitting goes on for a couple of days. Goes on that afternoon, that night, and we babysit them for the next morning. We'll try to get out there on time, those of us who don't sleep all morning. We try to get out there while they're out waiting for their clothes and wondering where the hell to go.

"They're not too hard to spot cause they're all wearing big old baggy coveralls and their eyes are about this big and they're all clumped up like little baby ducks, you know. So you go over and tell them where to get their clothes so they'll look half human. And they've got little short haircuts and they follow like ducks, too. Yeah, they follow you around, 'Come on, let's go.' Take em here, take em there, 'quack, quack, quack,' and people hollering, 'Hey, babysitting today, huh?' 'Yeah, shit!'

"So then you take em over and show em where the phone rooms are and tell em how to phone home. By then, they should know where to eat."

Cardozo-Freeman: "Do you warn them about these other types that prey upon them?"

Delorme: "Well, we tour around and point out a few people here and there, kind of on the sneak, though. The guy ain't gonna like you pointing him out either, so you really don't do it out in the open like 'Stay away from that asshole.'

"It's all tough but most fish will swim and do alright. Those that sink do so in a hurry. Some fish are unable to make it into population. The hotter it gets in here the more fish will decide they can't make it while they are on the Chain. And these go straight to the guards and ask for protective custody."

Three *fish* who have learned how to *swim* compare Monroe to Walla Walla. Their callous attitude toward the daily occurrences that are horrifying is an indication that they have survived their ordeal in the dangerous *fish tank* through developing very tough *fish* "scales" to protect themselves.

Steve: "I just got transferred up here from Monroe about a couple months ago, and I might tell you some of the comparisons right now between here and Monroe.

"Over there they talk about killing people and stabbing them when they owe money and over here they do it. That's the difference. Over there the cons got the run of the institution and over here the guards run the institution. I always thought it was vice versa but over there it's the guards that got almost no say in any action that comes down there, and over here they've got ultimate domain, imminent domain. Yeah, they control everything. Every guard's got that at Monroe but over here they take full advantage of it.

"But here, you got to fend for yourself. They consider them kids at Monroe but here we're men. The whole thing is, over here we're in a penitentiary and over there it's a reformatory."

Tom: "Yeah, the only thing I don't like is the difference, man; they classify us here as penitentiary people."

Bob: "Your reform days is done. You just sit and make do now. Do your time the best you can, man."

Tom: "We go back to being like gangs in a bombed out city, taking food away from other people, taking what you can get, stealing what clothes you can get, preying on the weak. They had us down for that, too. It's not as bad as it used to be in here, really. They quit giving us coats and things and you just had to get what you could get, you know. It was big hijack time all the way."

Bob: "That's why the leather coats went [were forbidden] for one thing. Anything nice and a guy would kill somebody to take his coat away, beat him up. Fuckin ole dings didn't have nothin. They were really tattered. They was like beggars from the Far East or somewhere, man. If you did get a watch, you got to look at it for one hour and that was about it. If they made it through the whole hour without losing their watch they was doin alright. A lot of em didn't come out of their cells, for chrissake, they was so scared."

Steve: "That's what they get for sportin the damn thing."

Bob: "They used to terrorize the motherfuckers. That was a few years ago, though. I think it's pretty mellow now. The shit and things that go on at Monroe goes on here but me and you don't notice it. But everyday it's goin on here. Robberies and hijacks and shit like that. Throwing these fuckin dings up against the wall when they see they got a watch on. They won't say nothin, you know; they're scared."

Steve: "Over at Monroe if a new guy come in, like you say, his people send him his clothes and stuff; that's dead action, especially if he lets anybody know it. The first thing you do is just go in his house and take it all."

Tom: "Yeah. He ain't gonna do nothin. Tell him it's a joint rule and if he's brand new he don't know no better."

Bob: "Give him a couple years, though; he ain't gonna forget you. But that's the things we got to deal with in this damn joint."

Delorme refers to the protective *fish* scales as "psychological toughness." Those *fish* who survive the initial shock of the *fish tank* and have learned how to *swim* in the dangerous waters build psychological barriers between themselves and their treacherous environment. They never drop their guard, as they intuitively realize they are in mortal danger, not only physically but psychically. Much of this toughness begins to build early in their lives — in juvenile institutions, in jails, and during the six weeks they spend at Shelton. This psychological toughness manifests itself outwardly in callousness, in attitudes of cynicism, in a biting, grim humor disparaging everyone and everything connected with their damnation, in a bravado "fuck the world" attitude, and in an apparent lack of concern for the pain that others around them experience. They also suppress their own suffering, refusing to feel pity for themselves or for their fellow inmates, often making ruthless jokes about their existential condition. In actuality, the psychological armor, despite its drawbacks, and there are many, that these strong *fish* manifest is the best adaptation they can make to this man-killing environment. To respond otherwise would end in disaster — a broken spirit, madness, the destruction of the inner self. Paradoxically, psychological toughness for survival in these dangerous waters cannot be adapted for survival in the mainstream waters of free society. Shedding the protective scales, readapting to living in waters that are not life-threatening, is extremely painful and oftentimes unsuccessful. Delorme's "die first" attitude exhibited in the previous chapter is a manifestation of this psychological toughness. All those who survive the prison experience possess this quality. They become hardened and experienced warriors, veterans doing battle in the depths of hell against the demonic forces of the prison. Under siege is their humanity, and they battle fiercely to protect it despite the great wounds and scars they acquire in the process. Some of these wounds never heal. Delorme, in his long experience behind the walls of this prison, briefly discusses the price that is paid for psychological toughness.

"The fish that enter this prison are on their own. Those men that are able to adapt, adjust or swim have to be admired because they are tough. You just fall in here from Shelton on the Chain and they dump you out into the population and that's it. You make your way from there. You either make it or break it. So if you're not about half tough—maybe not physically so much anymore, but mentally—then God help you if you can't adjust and get through the first three or four weeks and make it so you can see nobody's going to jump you. Some of the kids they got coming into this place today ... it's just ridiculous. But you do the best you can. You don't get any help in here from the officials."

LIFE IN A FOUR-MAN CELL

Those fish who swim are fortunate if the cell assignment given them by the guards when they first come in to the prison is satisfactory. Some men try two or three situations before they find cellmates who are accommodating and not threatening to them. Once a *house* is found, the men cheer up noticeably.

There is a thriving real estate business in the prison involving ownership of individual four-man cells. A man can own a cell and decide who will live with him, as well as control everything else that goes on in the cell. Prices vary, depending on the desirability of the cell, its location and condition. As high as three hundred dollars has been paid for a house and higher prices have been considered. Although it is illegal to own, buy, or sell a house, officials have not been able to eliminate the practice as great secrecy surrounds it. Two inmates discuss the real estate business.

Tim: "Did you ever buy a house? Did you ever ask to buy one?"

Al: "No. I've had people come to me that want to sell one, though."

Tim: "How much would you have been willing to pay for a house?"

Al: "About 300 dollars."

Tim: "That's strange cause my partner and I, we took and built our house real nice. We had a street sink in it, a street toilet and had cupboards built on both sides of the room and we had places to hang our clothes. Had it built real nice. In fact it was the only house in the whole Six Wing block, man, that had a tile floor. We put a tile floor down and we put Formica® down around the sink. We had Formica cabinets around it. It was really nice. We had a medicine chest and all that. But we never did sell the damn thing. And we been approached many times by guys comin around sayin they wanted to buy it but we'd have to have about a thousand dollars for it, which just automatically drove everybody away."

Al: "Well, I was in a three hundred dollar house. We had a nice place."

Four men in a cell makes for a very difficult living situation. The men must carefully adapt and restrain their behavior in order to make life tolerable in such close circumstances. Several of the narratives collected about living together in four-man cells reveal strong views on the negative aspects of this situation.

Tom: "Well, you know in this business with our cell partners, we kinda have to put up with some funny actions by some of those guys. Like spitting out on the tier drives me crazy. You hear a guy sit in a cell and go 'Harrughoom,' and you hear it hit the tier then he walks off. It just makes me sick, you know. H.T. used to be so terrible about that shit. Spittin over the tier and never lookin to see if anybody's down there and if he hit somebody he wouldn't apologize. He'd just say, 'Aw, fuck you,' and all that shit and laugh, 'ho, ho, ho.'"

Gary: "Not too many people give H.T. any shit back, either."

Tom: "Every morning I listen to my cell mate sittin there and hack for about half an hour."

Gary: "Light a cigarette and then start coughin?"

Tom: "No. He opens his eyes and he starts coughin, then he lights a cigarette. I mean the coughin lasts for about a half hour. Aw jeez."

Gary: "That can be pretty irritating."

Overcrowding—four men to a cell approximately $12' \times 10'$— presents grave problems. In *The Hidden Dimension*, Hall describes studies made of distance regulation and spacing mechanisms in animals. These studies can be applied to the situation of imprisoned men. Hall speaks of "flight distance" and "critical distance" in referring to different species' meeting each other.[9] "All animals have a minimum space requirement, without which survival is impossible. This is the 'critical space' of the organism. When the population has built up so greatly that the critical space is no longer available, a 'critical situation' develops."[10] "A wild animal will allow a man or other potential enemy to approach only up to a given distance before it flees. . . . Flight is the basic mechanism of survival for mobile creatures. In domesticating other animals man has had to eliminate or radically reduce the flight reaction. In zoos it is essential to modify the flight reaction enough so that the captive animal can move about, sleep, and eat without being panicked by men."[11]

Four men sharing a 10' x 12' space allows for no "flight distance," which is particularly crucial if some of the men who share the space are predators. There is no way to flee from the danger since no flight distance is allowed in such confining space, and therefore since a man has no way of maintaining "crucial distance" he reverts to attack to protect himself. "Crucial distance," defined by Hall as "encompassing the narrow zone separating flight distance from attack distance" is "present wherever and whenever there is a flight reaction. . . . " "A lion in a cage will flee from an approaching man until it meets an insurmountable barrier. If the man continues the approach, he soon penetrates the lion's critical distance, at which point the cornered lion reverses direction and begins . . . to stalk the man."[12]

Getting in your face is the expression used by the men in this prison to describe breaking this critical distance taboo. Fights break out between men when someone *gets in someone else's face*. It is not only a spatial violation but a temporal one as well, as the men state that anyone who *gets in your face* is *doing your time for you*. One of the important commandments in the prison is *do your own time*. The maintaining of critical distance is complicated by overcrowding, not only in cells but within the prison.

Apparently critical distance goes beyond the physical to the spiritual. Hall writes that "certain types of schizophrenics . . . apparently experience something very similar to flight reaction. When approached too closely, [they] panic in much the same way as an animal recently locked up in a zoo. In describing their feelings, such patients refer to anything that happens within their 'flight distance' as taking place literally *inside themselves*. That is, the boundaries of the self *extend beyond the body*" [italics added].[13] The potential for conflict and violence is greatly enhanced by overcrowding in the prison, as critical distance or boundaries cannot be adequately maintained between one man and another. Hall states that proper spacing for animals is maintained by an invisible bubble that surrounds each individual.[14] Presumably, man also is surrounded by this invisible bubble, which serves as a protective spatial device for the personality. Schizophrenics who are often seers, understanding far more about the truth of existence than normal people, sense this special quality in themselves; therefore, in their great sensitivity react strongly to anyone who breaks past this protective spatial boundary of the spirit. The angry reaction of imprisoned men when anyone *gets in their face* (gets in their *space*) must certainly be an indication that they, too, realize that their person is in danger of invasion. Rape is the ultimate act of invading someone else's space.

This prisoner describes some of the less serious problems that occur while trying to maintain critical distance in a four-man cell.

"In cells like this, any place that has two guys living together is like being married. You have to learn to accept each other's personal habits. You may not agree with their ideas or they may be irritating.

"Some guys you just know that you can't live with. No way. You'll know if you spend over five or ten minutes with a guy. He might sniff his nose too much, or cough or clear his throat too much, or spit too much, or spit all the time. He may be real fidgety, a real nervous person. You can stand out in the Breezeway talking to a guy and you know how he's going to act in the house. You have to decide whether you can handle that or not. If some guy's real nervous, the sonovabitch is going to be up and running in and out of the cell a thousand times a day. He'll be screaming and hollering to get the door open. He's going to be a smart ass or he's going to pace back and forth in the cell and drive you crazy.

"When you're trying to study or read or watch TV, there's nothing worse than a walker, somebody that has to walk back and forth, back and forth in the cell. God, there's a lot of guys like that. I've had my share and I've kicked them out of my house. I don't care if the guy's a good guy or not. I've just got to ask him to leave. He's doing my time. That gets old fast. It causes fights, man. I tell the sonovabitch, 'Why don't you sit down?' Chrissake, it comes out in an outburst. He's bugging you so much that you finally say something about it. It's not going to come out good, you can bet on that.

"I'm very conscious of the things I say and do because a place like this where you have the real estate business and every cell has an owner, you always feel like you are in somebody else's house or you're company if you don't own a house.

"After you live here long enough, if you get real tight, if you can accept each other, then you can get along. Whoever the guy is that's the owner feels that he can say or do what he wants but still all in all, in your own mind, I know what I don't like about cell partners.

"My best friend, I don't like to live with him. He's got too many personal habits that I can't stand. He talks too much and he tries to explain things to me that I already know and a lot of little things like that. I like him; he's my best friend, but he's pretty restless. He's a foot shaker. If you slept on the top bunk over him, you'd have to have a lot of patience because he's the kind of person that lays down there when he's reading or even when he's sleeping, he'll be shaking his foot, wiggling it all the time. It bugs the hell out of me. Those are mind busters. But that's part of cell life."

In order to get out of a cell the men put signs out through the bars. First they shout to the guard, "Key up on F Deck," and the guard shouts back, "Put your sign out." The men put their signs out, which have the numbers of their cells on them. Some men make very elaborate signs for this door-opening procedure; for example, colored lights that flash their cell number off and on.

Praise for a guard is reported in this narrative.

"We get along pretty good, the guys in our cell. The youngest guy that is in the house, he's only been here two weeks. He's a young kid. He's in with a life sentence and he's only eighteen or nineteen. His brother is with him now; he finally came in on the Chain. This is Friday and his brother came in on Wednesday, so they moved him with two other youngsters up on E Deck.

"Lt. C., the assignment lieutenant, he knows where everybody lives. Boy, it would be chaos around here if Lt. C. left and they put somebody else in here. Nobody can be as familiar with names and houses as him. Who owns what, who lives with who—he knows it all. He's been here so long that he even knows what kind of cell partners can live together and who can't.

"Before he'd put a new guy in my house, he'd make sure that guy has a chance to stay here, so it's pretty neat that way. He's one of the most important cogs in the administration. His job is important, but his experience is priceless. Like I said, guys like myself, he knows me and he goes by that before he puts a new guy in my house. He also will put a lot of the younger guys in my house because he knows that I won't bother them. He knows that I'm not going to . . . he knows that I'm not a fruitcake and I don't have no weirdos living with me. If he has somebody that he was worried about in here, he'd put him in my house and I'd just naturally, goddamit, end up babysitting and taking care of him until he got settled and sort of able to go out on his own. I don't mind that.

"I got good cell partners and none of them are nutty or nothing like that. They got concerns other than this prison. I usually try to keep an empty bunk for a new brother that comes in and so I've got an empty now since Hank left and there will be another guy that fills it. But that's the way we run these cells.

"We got some rules on the wall. What they say are, 'take care of yourself and I expect you to share expenses, share gear and things like that and coffee. Things that we all use. If you can't get any money then that's O.K., too, but if one or two guys buys all the coffee then when another one comes in and he gets money, he goes out and buys dope, that won't work. That might work in another house but it doesn't work in this house.'

"Got another rule—'keep your sniveling to yourself. We don't want to hear about your wife. We don't want to hear about your child. We got troubles of our own.' A guy's got to snivel once in awhile. We all got a snivel coming, for chrissake. You got nobody else to talk to so we talk to each other. That rule is just kind of a joke, you know. We don't pay any attention to it.

" 'Don't let any strangers come in the house. Don't lend stuff out unless it's your own. If you're going to run around this joint and run up debts, things that you don't intend to pay,' the sign says clearly to 'move out to some other cell. You don't belong here.'

" 'If you smoke dope, go ahead and smoke it; that's alright, too, but if you start selling dope or something like that, move in with somebody else or get your own place, cause that's heat, man. If you're tryin to get your shit together, as we say, you can't be doing that. You've got to hit the road.' It's possible to avoid that problem but you can't avoid it if somebody's in your pad, man, that's sellin dope on the side because then you got all those creeps hangin around and hittin on you all day long up to your door and the cops can see that and they're no dummies. They know what the hell's going on. All the cops have to do is sit on the Joint awhile and watch. They can detect that play in a hurry."

THE FISH WHO SINK

A considerable number of the new men are unable to deal with the stress and danger of the prison. Some of these men are already mentally ill when they enter the prison. Often their problems are precipitated or exacerbated by their jail or Shelton experience. Mental illness is a growing problem in prisons and jails across the country today.[15] The narratives that follow reveal that this prison is, as states Dr. Alvin Groupe of the California Medical Facility at Vacaville, a "breeder of psychoses." Hall, citing the research on stress by Hans Selye, points out that animals under constant stress die from shock. "Any increased demand on the organism must be met by the addition of energy. In mammals this source of energy is blood sugar. If repeated demands exhaust the supply of sugar available, the animal goes into shock."[16] Delorme's perceptive observations of what happens to new fish points out that what happens to animals under extreme stress also happens to men; he believes that fear paralyzes the new men, making them susceptible to psychological damage.

"It's not just psychological. It's a temporary weakness which hits them most of the time. Just the shock of this place is what really drops the guard of these new guys and sometimes they can't keep up their little fronts for a while. When that happens you get a peek at them. You see what they really are and they can be nailed, see. The Joint just tears their guard down and they're just wide open."

It is as if a severe blow has been dealt the new fish, not only psychologically, but psychically, so that they are temporarily stunned and therefore unable to protect themselves from the predators and other dangers lurking in the perilous waters that surround them. Shelton has not identified them, and guards, unfortunately, are not trained to recognize them when they come in on the Chain. Some of them retreat into madness. Many, but not all, end up on the *Third Floor*, the psychiatric unit. There are no psychologists or psychiatrists on the prison staff. Delorme and Zack both point out that inmates meeting the Chain are able to identify those fish who are not going to survive.

Delorme: "You got to be awful damn strong to see your way through it."

Zack: "So many of em come in on that Chain and they sit there. That's one of the sad things."

Delorme: "You look at those new guys and feel sorry for some of em cause you can see right off the bat they're dead guys. They ain't gonna make it. They're like wounded animals or something."

Zack: "Yeah. I was with a guy, I came in on the Chain with him. He was a nice youngster. He looked like he could have been anything. He looked like he got caught up in the times, maybe drugs or somethin, and he got himself in this problem. O.K. He was on the Chain and he kept sayin, 'I'm really scared.' He was really scared and nervous and I kept sayin, 'You've got to be cool, man, you've got to take it easy. It's not as hard as you think. It'll be alright.' But he kept sayin, 'I just can't make it. I can't make it.' And I knew when he kept sayin that he was gonna lose his mind, man. It wasn't a week before he was on the Third Floor. And he was socked full of Thorazine®.

"He walked around on the Breezeway after that for two years. Completed his sentence, then did another two years because he'd been C.I.'d, criminally insane, I guess. I don't know what they do to you when they put you on the Third Floor but they have to judge them some way, don't they?"

Delorme: "It's not legal, whatever they do cause they got no professionals up there. They just keep you."

Zack: "He was over his time. I think he had a year or a year and a half that they gave him. But he did four years. And he just left three weeks ago. And you can imagine how much time he did over his time if he's been here for four years and he only had two to do in the first place."

Delorme: "I don't know either because my partner did the same thing. He had ten and he ended up doin about fourteen. He was on Third Floor.

Zack: "And you know, the bad thing about it is I wrote to the guy's mother and told her he had this nervous breakdown, this mental breakdown and his mother didn't want him to parole home anymore."

Delorme: "I wrote, too, and I told em to come and get him, to do something and they came down. They were pretty upset, broken-hearted when they looked at him."

Zack: "Well, he was a fortunate person, but most of the people, their families cut em loose when they get up there on the Third Floor, man. You know, they call home, they're a little bit warped in the head. They might say anything and all of a sudden they lose contact with their families and therefore the institution just keeps em."

Delorme: "I don't think the institution helps. They probably advise em, 'Better let us care for em. He's dangerous.'"

Zack: "That's what they did with Jimmy A's brother. He's five years over his release date. He walks around here, they call him Butter Man. They make jokes about him and stuff; say he's a nut.

"Why don't they do something about the nuts? You know yourself we fought that with the administration. We been fightin that for a long time. And then when these guys come off the Chain, man, guards can't recognize something's wrong. They aren't trained to recognize the symptoms of these people who are goin to lose it. But then, we can spot em."

Delorme: "Spot em a mile away."

Zack: "They're walkin around and we say, 'This guy's goin.'"

Delorme: "Fuckin eyes are big and round and they're shakin and they tell you right off the bat they can't make it."

Zack: "They're nervous and they're scared and they don't want to be here and they get put in a cell with three people that they don't know and the guards say, 'Hey, you're supposed to make it.' They walk in there and the guys kick em out of the cell."

Delorme: "Yeah, kicks em out right off the bat."

Zack: "And as soon as they get kicked out the pigs say, 'O.K., if you can't make it in the cells, we'll put you in Big Red,' and they throw em in Big Red, put more pressure on em and the next thing you know, man, the next step is the Third Floor and they're zonked full of that dangerous drug. The drug that you can't get back from. I've never seen a person yet come back from Thorazine."

Delorme: "They were speculatin about brain damage from Thorazine about ten years back."

Zack: "There's no way you can get back from that. Six months of that and you're probably done for. It tears the body down; they lose shape. Mentally, they're like kids. I think it's terrible."

According to the men, the keeper of the *fish tank* does not properly provide for those *fish* who are mentally ill. Horror stories about treatment on *Third Floor* are profuse. Tim, who suffers from mental illness, discusses why he dreaded being placed in the psychiatric unit on the third floor of the hospital.

Delorme: "How did you feel emotionally the first week?"

Tim: "Chaotic mass of confusion in my head, really. My feelins and my emotions were just at wit's end. I didn't know which way to go or what to do or anything."

Delorme: "Were you still havin problems from the streets, yet? What about that nut bag? Were you worryin about that?"

Tim: "When I first went through Shelton they said they was goin to put me on the Third Floor when I got here and when I got here, they didn't. So I was pushed into that nut bag."

Delorme: "Inez, I'm sure you understand we don't have a lot of sympathy for each other, so we make jokes about things like this. Just like we call guys with one leg 'flat tires.' My man here has a little touch of manic depressive but he deals with it real good."

Tim: "Try to."

Delorme: "Tries to. Got him a little trouble a few years ago but he's worked his way through it."

Tim: "They was goin to put me on the Third Floor when I first come here and they didn't and I was pushin all that crazy stuff in the background and tryin to keep it there cause I didn't want to go on the Third Floor from some of the stories I'd heard."

Delorme: "You woulda been a basket case by now."

Tim: "Some of the stories I heard were about **guys** that they'd feed em with a baby bottle and make em **wear diapers** and then they'd come around and the guy would knock the baby bottle on the floor off his bed or off the nightstand and they'd jerk his diapers off him and they'd fuck him in the hospital! And I'm thinkin, oh my God! This whole place is sick. Everybody wants to fuck everybody in the ass."

Delorme: "Well it was all those guys up there who were attendants."

Tim: "They had these guys in diapers!"

Delorme: "That was when they had Dr. G. up there. He said, if you act like a fuckin baby, I'll treat you like a baby. When you quit actin like it and deal with problems, he'd put your pampers away and let's go back to reality. It worked for a few guys but some guys liked it and stayed that way."

Tim: "Well, I couldn't have dealt with it. I would have whipped all the way out on that one because that was sick. But I really suppressed all those manic depressive moods, or tried to. I didn't suppress them all; they come back out but then finally, I've gotten good medication for it. I'm dealin with it pretty good now."

One of the narratives that follow points out that there is not enough room on the *Third Floor* to hold all the men who are mentally ill, so consequently, they are placed on drugs and left to fend for themselves in the general population. These procedures are reported in other prisons across the country.[17] Inmates at Walla Walla call the men who behave strangely *dings* and *nuts*. Other inmates are threatened by their often bizarre behavior and may attack and beat them, not realizing they are ill.[18] Delorme and Zack continue discussing the situation of the *fish* who sink to the bottom of the *fish tank*.

Zack: "A lot of em that are here, they shouldn't be here. We got guys in here that are eighteen to nineteen years old. They shouldn't be in here."

"I know a guy, I think he just turned twenty. He snatched a purse and they gave him twenty years. First time he's ever been in trouble, and now he's an idiot in here; he's a damn fool. I don't look for him to ever get out unless somebody kills him. They give him all kinda pills, give him all kind of medication because that's the easiest way for them to handle him, to handle the problem.

"All them little funny pills. The Thorazine shuffle, the Stelazine® shuffle. You see guys how they walk, all of em. The penitentiary is full of em. They're in population. There's only room for about thirty guys on the Third Floor. The guys don't bother nobody but they are in a little danger cause if you lookin at one of these guys that's full of that shit, and they get around you, you be watchin him and if he be makin some kinda odd move, you might hurt him, not knowin what he gonna do. I seen incidents where that's happened.

"A guy just runs up, a brother, now he was a nut. He would never bother anybody but he would run up to you and you'd be walkin down the Breezeway and all of a sudden here's this guy runnin up to you. A sudden move like that in the penitentiary will get you hurt. And he just run up and stand there lookin at you then turn around and go away. They ain't nobody know what they doin. Somebody's got to go explain. 'Hey, this guy's a nut. Ain't gonna harm you.' They just run up on people like that."

Delorme: "There's a guy who will just come up and look at you like this, and he'll sit down and stare at you and the guy sittin there will tell his partners that don't know about him. 'Don't pay no attention; don't tease him cause that makes him paranoid.' He'll come right up to your table, he'll be shufflin past, and man, you're ready to jump in his face."

Zack: "He don't say anything and he walks away kinda smug and probably in his mind he's cussin at you. He turned out not to be a bad guy.

"One day I give him some weed to smoke. You don't understand what he be talkin about but he's not a bad guy. He is dangerous, though, if you get him started, but he don't bother anybody except stare at you if you leave him alone. I know that he was O.K. when he first come in and then it was just downhill, and they started givin him pills. See, a lot of guys . . . you fight a lot, get in a lot of fights. They'll take and give em pills to control you."

Wilson reported in *Corrections Magazine* that "many prison medical staff members admit that medication is used as much for custody purposes as for therapy purposes," and that in 1979, thirteen federal penitentiary inmates at Leavenworth complained to U.S. Representative Robert W. Kastenmeier that "the prison authorities utilize widespread forced drugging for completely inappropriate reasons; [that] it could be fairly viewed as a preventative detention measure utilizing chemical strait jackets." When observers were sent to the prison to check the allegation, the staff denied that there was any wrongdoing.[19] Similar charges against the hospital staff at Walla Walla have met with the same response.

Delorme: "When I was first here, I was on Thorazine half the time. They'd take me up to the hospital and give me a shot of that shit. They tricked me, tellin me it was dope and stuff."

Zack: "They say they don't do it but I wouldn't put it past em."

Delorme: "Convicts took me over by the arms."

Further horror tales in the prison involve the use of inmates from Protective Custody to "care" for inmates on the *Third Floor*.

Zack: "They got so-called convicts used to run Third Floor. When they feel like doin somethin they come in there and beat you up, fuck you. The guys they had workin up there, they were all from PC. They would take their hostilities out on the guys on the Third Floor."

Delorme: "The nurses were there; they didn't care. They'd deny it if someone said something had happened. 'Never happened on my shift.' But when you seem em later, they say, 'I can't say nothin.'"

Cardozo-Freeman: "Do you have any ideas of how you could stop that sort of thing from happening?"

Zack: "Yeah, we always have a lockdown. We sit down on a strike."

Cardozo-Freeman: "If you were running a prison?"

Zack: "All you got to do is keep checkin and make sure that people are carrying out your orders. If you're runnin the show then you're supposed to check. If you say, 'Gene, I want such and such a thing did,' well, Gene knows that I'm not gonna come checkin on him so he don't have to do it if he don't want to. But if he knows there's a possibility I'm gonna come through and check on him, you know he's gonna do it."

Delorme: "Make the leaders accountable for their responsibility. In a sense, they're foolish not to because when the shit comes down, it's their heads. Right?"

According to Zack, only the native Americans watch out for their brothers who are mentally ill. Delorme states that only when they become violent towards others do they allow them to be placed on Third Floor.

Zack: "Black guys, Chicano guys, white guys, we got these guys walkin around here, dings, and nobody associates with em, don't want em around, but I seen the Indian guys lookin out for their guys. They know this guy's a ding, they look out for him. I don't see it anywhere else. They explain to you 'This guy's a ding. Shine him on. He don't mean no harm.' They look out for em."

Delorme: "We got Merton out here; he gets off doin this for awhile and nobody knows what he's doin so you have to go around and tell people in front not to pay no attention. 'He ain't gonna hurt you none.' Merton don't know you're doin it but you're doin it all the time."

Cardozo-Freeman: "Has this always been a tradition with the Indian guys?"

Delorme: "Yeah. You tell people to keep an eye on Merton or this guy or that guy, watch out for em. You make sure he always comes up [to the Indian Club] and you try to get him involved in things, treat him like everybody else. I talk to him, even if he doesn't talk right. I still talk to him and let him be in the group, let him be in on the [Indian] dancing. Don't stare at him, treat him like he needs to be treated."

Zack: "Don't treat him like he's a dog. A lot of times I think that's all those guys need. But they don't get treated right by the administration or from them hospitals. I go up on the Third Floor every now and then but I can't stand it. Them guys, they not gettin any help up there. They don't get no love up there. They gettin more help from their own people than they can get up there."

Delorme: "They can be too much of a job for us, too. Then we might have to let em stay on Third Floor when they're violent with the other Indians. We can't have the guys fightin all the time. But ordinarily, we don't let our brothers up on Third Floor."

Language is the means by which a speech community interprets reality, shapes comprehension of its environment, and supplies definitions and categories for all that is experienced. The language of a culture carries within it the definitions of all conditions and situations. The term *fish* is an indicator for the experience of a particular member of the imprisoned group. All members in the society known of as *fish* belong to this category, which represents a unique and particular life circumstance in the reality of prisoners; it represents the babyhood of prison life, the beginnings of the cultural experience. *Fish* denotes a particular level of development in prison culture; it serves to determine and is determined by the prisoners' reaction to their cultural, social, and physical environment. *Fish* is an important marker or indicator of prisoner worldview; it is an agreed-on cultural definition that enables prisoners to coordinate their behavior and make sense out of their shared experience. Prisoner frame of reference is partially structured and organized around the symbolic meaning inherent in the word *fish*.

The metaphor of the *fish* connotes ironic truth dependent upon a paradoxical turn: things are not what they should be in the keeper's *fish tank*. The metaphor reveals that the existential condition of men in prisons and jails in this country is tragically absurd. A new prisoner thrust into a prison environment lives in a constant state of panic, of fear and trembling, of dread, of unbearable psychic and emotional pain and trauma. His older brothers, who have suffered through the same experience and survived, laugh at him and call him *fish*; they stamp an absurd tragicomic label on him, which he carries until he becomes so experienced and knowledgeable about his circumstance, he sheds the label for a new one. His babyhood in "fishdom" may last anywhere from one to two years. It is very hard to grow up in the *tank* that is the prison environment. Some babies never make it, sinking to the bottom. Survivors become tough "hard-scaled" *fish* who swim cautiously and defensively through the highly populated and dangerous waters of the *tank*. These are the regular *cons*, the older and more experienced *fish* in the *tank*, who joke and make fun of the "stupid *fish*," yet they *babysit* him, worry about his situation, and are relieved when he finally learns how to maneuver through the treacherous waters. Whatever oxygen (care and concern) the baby *fish* receives comes from those older, wiser *fish* whose scales are not so thick that they have forgotten what it is like to be newly caught up in these grim waters; they empathize because they, too, have shared the experience but, miraculously, have not lost their humanity. In *fish* we have an excellent example of an important underlying pattern upon which the frame of reference for prisoner worldview is built. *Fish* speaks not only in its metaphorical meaning to imprisoned men but also to those who swim in the free waters of mainstream society.

NOTES

[1]David W. Maurer, *Whiz Mob* (New Haven, Conn.: College and University Press, 1955), p. 30.

[2]*Dictionary of American Slang*, Second Supplement Edition. Edited by Harold Wentworth and Stuart Berg Flexner (New York: Thomas Y. Crowell, 1975).

[3]Officials of the prison, when seeking information on the mood of the prisoners, often ask, "What's the temperature of the Joint?"

[4]Kenneth Divons and Larry M. West, "Prison or Slavery," *The Black Scholar* (1971), p. 29.

[5]Bruce Jackson reports a narrative poem, "Jody the Grinder," presumably a black toast, in his prison research. See Bruce Jackson, "Prison Folklore," *Journal of American Folklore*, 78 (1965), pp. 317–329.

[6]Sometime in late 1980, the administration reinstituted a place on the Admissions tier for the new men to stay for a few days.

[7]*Whiz Mob*, p. 34.

[8]*Ibid.*, p. 33.

[9]Edward T. Hall, *The Hidden Dimension* (Garden City, N.Y.: Anchor Books, 1969), p. 10. All quotes reprinted by permission of the publisher.

[10]*Ibid.*, p. 16.

[11]*Ibid.*, p. 11.

[12]*Ibid.*, p. 12.

[13]*Ibid.*, pp. 11–12.

[14]*Ibid.*, p. 13.

[15]Dr. Alvin Groupe, Chief Psychiatrist at the California Medical Facility at Vacaville believes that "prisons breed psychoses," and Dr. Dennis Zurczak, Medical Director of the Michigan Department of Corrections, claims that 20 percent of Michigan's 14,000 inmates have some serious mental disorders and that at any time one-third of those are in an "acute" episode "requiring intensive treatment." Rob Wilson, "The Mentally Ill Offender: A Growing Debate Over the 'Mad and Bad,'" *Corrections Magazine*, (1980), pp. 5–17.

[16]*The Hidden Dimension*, p. 34. See also, Hans Selye, *The Stress of Life* (New York: McGraw-Hill, 1956).

[17]"The Mentally Ill Offender: A Growing Debate Over the 'Mad and Bad,'"
p. 11.

[18]In 1978, Eric Nalder of the Seattle *Post-Intelligencer* wrote, "The prison's mental health ward, with a capacity of 24 prisoners, is overflowing. Men who are mentally unbalanced, must be put in the general population. . . . Examples are a man who howls at the moon and another who doesn't know he's in prison. . . . "

[19]"The Mentally Ill Offender: A Growing Debate Over the 'Mad and Bad,'"
p. 11.

Chapter 4

THE CONS

One of the primary functions of language is naming or labeling. Everything must be identified if it is to have meaning.[1] Through labeling, what is experienced becomes reality. By naming we order what is important in our world. As with all speech communities, prisoners have labels by which they categorize themselves. This process of naming or classifying helps them order and organize their precarious existential situation, bringing into it some degree of predictability, stability, and safety. Only those groups considered important are identified and labeled by the men. As Nathan Kantrowitz points out, "The lack of a name indicates that a phenomenon is unimportant or non-existent."[2] Each label by which the prisoners identify themselves denotes a particular kind of experience; each possesses distinct qualities and attributes separate from the others. In addition, each label carries with it a particular status in the hierarchy of the prisoner's world.

Since survival is the top priority in the prisoner's world, those in his culture whom he identifies as playing an important role in his survival hold very high status, those who threaten or complicate his survival hold very low status, and those who neither assure nor threaten or complicate his survival hold neutral status. Qualities or characteristics that high status types possess are courage, high intelligence, positive leadership ability, charismatic power, long prison experience, political skill, trustworthiness, loyalty, ability to stand up to as well as communicate with prison authorities, capacity and willingness to use physical or brute power, and the ability to intimidate the prison population through ruthless recourse to assassination, when necessary, to keep the peace. With the exception of courage, which all high status types possess, these characteristics are not equally shared; indeed, the talent of one type may not be found at all in another. Together all the characteristics represent those talents necessary in the culture to assure the prisoner's survival. Those with low status either threaten in some way, or make troublesome, the daily life of the prisoner. Some of the qualities found in these categories include low intelligence, emotional instability or insanity, eccentric or parasitic behavior, and treachery.

THE CONS—ALL-INCLUSIVE CATEGORY

All the prisoners refer to themselves as *cons*. *Con* is therefore the major category for self-identification, an agreed-on cultural definition under which all other self-naming in the culture can be included. *Cons* may be classed into two distinct types—"real" *cons* and "inmates." Real *cons* order their lives in varying degrees by the old convict code, whereas inmates do not. Real *cons* include those men who entered the prison before the 1960s and those since that time who have adapted the old code as a survival tactic. The new prisoner includes all those who entered the prison since the 1960s. About 90 percent of the population are identified by the men as *street people*. All those coming from urban areas since the 1960s fit this category. Exceptions are the very old *cons* who were in the prison prior to the 1960s, *cowboys*, who come from rural areas and small towns in the state, and *square* or *straight johns*, who represent those few men whose values and worldview come from the majority culture. In a general way, status in the prison from the highest category to the lowest is as follows: high status includes *good people*, who are at the pinnacle, "intelligent" *killers, Joint politicians, Joint tough guys, old timers;* middle or neutral status includes *hustlers*, state-raised youth, *cowboys, dopers, straight johns, wolves* (*daddies* and *pimps*); low status includes *youngsters* and *fish, biblebacks, Breezeway bums, dings, nuts, fruits* (*queens* and *punks*), *rapos*, and *snitches*. Since inclusion appears to be a universal principle in the organization of knowledge in a culture, the study of categories related by inclusion—what anthropologists call "typology" —is therefore an important approach to understanding prisoner worldview.[3]

Among the first lessons the newly arrived *fish* begins to learn is that he stands at the bottom of the prisoner hierarchy because he is new, therefore untried or unproven. He is interested in discovering who all the other prisoners are as he realizes that the more he knows about the social situation in which he finds himself, the more secure he will feel and the better he will be able to make sense out of his new reality. He begins with the all-inclusive label, *con*.

"The first thing I want to say is the cons in the Joint are no different than those in any state or federal prison. If you were to do a breakdown of the population, you will find that every crime that constitutes a felony is represented, including hijacking. Drug related crimes are not classed as a drug beef—sales of narcotics, possession of drugs, transportation and distribution of dangerous drugs are some of the classifications that the dopers are doing time on. Use of drugs is not a crime unless the user happens to be on parole.

"Murder, rape, robbery, arson, burglary, theft—which can be anything from a car to a bail of wire—is classed as theft one or two. Sex crimes seem to be on the increase; crimes against children are well represented.

"Embezzlers, forgers [paper hangers]—there are very few real con men [confidence men]; I mean the good slick con-men that hustle the old ladies out of their drawers. I have met a few men that considered themselves to be professional at what they do, but they are few and far between. It is awful hard to find a good safe-cracker in here.

"The largest bunch in this prison, I would guess, are the murderers. You see so damned many people in here for homicide and armed robbery and that percentage went up, doubled, since they brought back the death penalty.

"A lot of people in here are on dope-related crimes. Most of the armed robberies are for drugs, too, so it's hard to distinguish those two, but armed robbery is a special crime in itself because it takes a little planning.

"About 90 percent of the guys that are in here come from the urban areas, I'd say. We all hate Walla Walla. There are people in here from seventeen to ninety-eight. Old Pop—we celebrated his birthday down here—he was ninety-eight. He ain't no poor old guy; he's a tough old bastard. Man, I never seen anybody that runs so much and so long and does as much work in the Joint. He works

for the RC [Resident Council]. All day he runs tryin to track guys
down for visits all over this joint. Pop will turn 100 in here."

Although all prisoners recognize that they hold in common the
label, *con*—they have all been convicted and are therefore convicts—
there are differences within this all-inclusive cover term. There
are *cons* and *cons*. Generally, it takes years of experience to acquire
real *con* status. According to Delorme, some *cons* are only inmates.

"You can go through county jail, juvenile, reformatory and still
it doesn't make you a convict—not in respect to the way cons use
the term. It has a special meaning for em.

"When you're doin time, kickin around the Joint with everybody else, if you can't get out and you know you're going to have to
sit here half your life, or the rest of your life or whatever it takes,
and you know you're gonna keep gamin and caperin, then actually
the Joint is pretty much the only thing you think about. It's your
life and so you think about how you can do better in it; how you
can get more things; how you can get a good reputation; how you
can get people to like you; how you can get people to not fuck with
you. It takes you so long to do that. You have to keep pluggin,
slippin and slidin and doin things right.

"It might not seem right to the square johns but if you see some
dude get wasted or something—he might be a snitch, a stool
pigeon, or just a fuckin no-good—if you're a real con, you hope
like hell that the motherfucker don't get caught who did it, so you
ain't gonna tell. And if the people that did it get busted right away,
somebody told on em, and that casts a bad shadow when everybody
finds out who could have possibly seen it happen. Anyway, you've
got to watch little tricks like that. It takes a long time to learn, so
when the old timers decide that you're a convict, then that really
means something in the fuckin Joint.

"You can stay a fish forever sometimes in some cases. Somebody
who ain't been around that much might say, 'That guy's a pretty
good con there,' and another guy standin around who's a real con
might look at him like he's crazy and say, 'What the fuck you mean
he's a convict? That punk ain't no convict; he ain't nothing. He's
got a big mouth. He sure as hell ain't no convict; he's a stinkin
inmate and that's that.'

"To be called an inmate ain't the coolest thing in the world in here cause that means you ain't trustworthy yet. You don't know about nothin; you just think you do. You got a big mouth and talk shit; you ain't proved yourself in any way. You might hustle a little dope, be a typical ole punk hustler and you might call yourself a convict and you just ain't; not in their eyes cause you ain't done shit.

"The old cons, they wear that name like a badge of honor. And yet there's old cons in Walla Walla, those sonovabitches, they may have fifteen to twenty years in the goddam Joint and they ain't convicts. 'They can't make a pimple on a convict's ass,' that's what they say about em. They hide around in their fuckin house, snitch once in awhile to get somethin, think nobody knows about it, but they ain't no convict, 'He's a fuckin ole inmate.' In the army, just because you put on a uniform and you march, walk that walk and talk that talk, that don't mean you're a soldier. Not to the old buck sergeants and the combat veterans, the officers and the men that have been through the wars; you're a rooky. The guy can be in the army three-four-five years but he ain't no soldier. You see the relationship? To outside observers, everybody in the army is a soldier, but if you're in the army, everybody ain't no soldier. You got to prove yourself somehow; *then* you're a soldier. 'That man's a soldier!' That means he'll back your play; he ain't scared to shoot; he ain't scared to stick his head up, fire up, and do this; do that.

"Course, the younger cops in the Joint, the younger fish-bulls, they call everybody a con. To them everybody's a con if you're behind the wall, but you talk to those bulls that have been here ten years, or six-seven years . . . Big P., the bull who took you on that tour, he can pinpoint a convict in a minute. He'd say, 'That's a punk; he ain't no convict.' See, them cops talk the same way. He'd say, 'He can't do his own time . . . big mouth; he ain't shit; he ain't no convict.'

"But technically, we are all cons. Anybody gets sent to the Joint is a con. And there's guys inside the prison, they get busted, they go through the whole routine, they come to Walla Walla and no way in the world do they want to be known as a convict. They refuse to act like a convict, and it hurts their feelings to be called a convict. They ain't done no time at all, and they're not worried about their image in here; they want to keep their street image; that's what they're tryin to hang on to.

"You'd think everybody in the Lifer's was convicts but that ain't so, either. You know the Lifers is the guys doin the most time. But it takes a long time before they're real convicts and, of course, there's a hell of a lot of em just never make it. Course, a lot of em don't attempt to make it cause they don't plan on bein here the rest of their lives, so they don't care if they're a convict or not. All they want to do is get out, so they do the best they can. They're just inmates tryin to get out. Bein a convict doesn't mean you don't want out . . . it means you want to make the best of a bad situation cause you're here to stay.

"When I first came to Walla Walla in 1962, one of the first things I found out was I was definitely not a convict. Regardless of the fact I had done good time all four years I was at Monroe. I played the game; I walked that walk, talked that talk at Monroe; made sure I followed all the convict rules; I don't mean cop rules. But I had a long way to go and a rough row to hoe. Jeez, I had to work at it. I had to watch my every move. During them early years I couldn't be friendly with no fuckin bulls or any shit like that. It was strictly con-types, man. You stayed the fuck away from them cops. 'Fuck them rules, fuck them good attitudes; fuck the work; fuck all that shit!' That's a real convict you're talkin about.

"Whereas an inmate, he'd be bustin his ass to see that he always acts right when the pigs are lookin at him; makin sure they don't think he's got a bad attitude; that he's gettin con-wise. That's what inmates worry about all the time. 'I don't want the motherfucker to see me fuckin off. He'll be thinkin I like this place.' A convict don't give a damn about that; they don't give a shit about what the guards think."

Street People—Major Subcategory

Street people differ radically from the old prisoner in the prison before the 1960s. Their values, beliefs, and attitudes, all of which are revealed in their language, which is so evident in this prison, have invaded the prison, coloring and influencing all aspects of life. Despite this, however, the old code has held firm and continues to play an important though somewhat altered role in the prison. Many of the older *street people* have incorporated much of the philosophy of the old code into their worldview, while at the same time holding on to much that identifies them as *street people*. This has occurred in varying degrees with the different groups who identify themselves as *street people*. *Street people* from the early 1960s and *street people* from the late 1970s in the prison differ somewhat from each other. Many of the newer *street people* are labeled *youngsters* by the older *cons*. *Street people* of the 1960s — now identified as *old timers* in the prison — point out that these *youngsters* are not only younger than they were on first entering the prison, but also they are beginners in the criminal experience and do not share with the older *street people* their long history of repeated offenses and previous sentences in other prisons in the state. These *youngsters*, they believe, are also more violence prone, disruptive, and anarchic in their behavior. Crowded conditions in the state's prison system is one of the reasons why *youngsters* who are *first timers* are sent to this maximum security prison, which is supposed to be reserved for only the most experienced criminals in the state.

Political awareness and activism have been hallmarks of the street experience since the early 1960s across the country.[4] Many *street people* in the prison are highly aware politically, outspoken in the opposition to repression in the country and in the prison, and knowledgeable about the legal aspects of prisoner rights. Some *street people* are well educated and widely read; they know what is going on in the world. By comparison, the prisoner before the 1960s was poorly educated and politically unaware. He accepted unquestioningly repressive authoritarian control and assumed that he had no rights, submitting with very little resistance to the stern and heavy hand of prison authority and policy.[5] The following narrative raises the disturbing thought that the 1980s may well see even greater violence and unrest in prisons across the country, given the characteristics of *street people* in prison, since the mood of the country is toward a decidedly more repressive, punitive, and authoritarian response to law breaking. A prisoner, a 1960s street person identified as *good people* in the prison, describes the "new prisoner."

"A lot of the guys, especially the young group — what I consider to be the street people of the sixties — are a whole different breed in this institution, and probably all the institutions across the United States. The officials don't understand that it's a whole new ball game. They're used to the old time prisoner, being able to manipulate him by using the leaders to keep them in line. But it won't go now; we're in a whole different era. This is 1979, almost 1980, and people who are in here have come through different type things on the streets. It's different on the streets, too, you know. Outside there's something going on all the time. People are aware; they have some very strong feelings and some very strong commitments and causes and it's different than the old traditional prisoner. That went out when they was able to keep em under control. They can't dominate, use the silent system; they can't take your dignity away. You know the people from the sixties, they're becoming our lawyers, our judges, and they're becoming our politicians today. Some of our rowdiest convicts, too, they've been fighting ever since they were young against the system. They can at least see how a police state is coming to the United States. How the economy is all fucked up, how everything is coming down. You just don't have the passive convict you had in the 1930s and 1940s. You got a whole younger type of element to deal with. The old prisoner, they had him conditioned; they had everybody bottled up. When they said, 'You peon,' there was no resistance. The street people, they're a whole different class. They seen the police brutality go down on the streets; they seen the National Guard whack people. They come in here and you can't say that they're amoral or anti-everything, but they're not for authoritatian rules and regulations, and they're not afraid."

The prisoner speaking in the next narrative takes a dim view of middle-class *street people* in the prison. He does not understand why they, who have had every economic advantage, should choose to share his condition. Although he and others like him attached themselves to demonstrations on the streets during the 1960s, which were carried out by middle-class protesters, he lacked their political awareness and moral conviction. Nevertheless, the reason he joined them — to "get at the pigs" — represents an elementary understanding of what the larger issues of protest were all about.

"Everybody in here is street people. The guys who were in here in the 1940s and 1950s are almost all dead and gone. The old prison of the 1950s and back just isn't here anymore. All of that old language [used before the 1960s] isn't hardly happening anymore; maybe one out of a hundred guys knows some of that language, that's all. The guys that are in here now are the same guys that were out there demonstrating.

"A lot of us traveled around demonstrating just for the fun of throwing rocks. We didn't know what the whole thing was about; it was a chance for us to get at the pigs. There's a lot of guys that did that. But you fight. You learn to fight. It gets to be a regular war. These people are in here right now; they're not passive and they're not gonna be passive.

"Some of em are from the middle class. I call em brats. They piss me off because when I see pictures of their families and homes, you say, 'You little bastard. What are you in here for? You're sittin in this stupid cell and here are your people out there that have tried to give you things all your life and you don't know what the hell you want.'

"There's a lot of guys like that in here. They act in here the same as they do on the streets—smart-assed—they're against everything. They're antilife, I guess. They don't know what the hell they want. They're just chasing their tails around in circles. Why some of em have fun bein in this sonovabitch!

"It's really the middle class in here that act like prison is nothin. Usually their crimes are drug related—it can be murder, burglary, robbery, whatever they might a had to do to get what they needed [drugs] and just dealin [in drugs]; they got busted dealin. But there's street people in here that aren't drug addicts. They use drugs in here, of course, although not as much as you hear.

"But that's what we got in here. The flower children of the 1960s and up. Now those are the street people. They're the ones who took the antiwar, anti-everything attitude. Their economic situation, it seems to be more from the middle class than from the lower class. Course, a lot of poor kids from the streets are in here, too."

Many *street people* do not make good prisoners in the traditional old convict sense. For this reason, the convict code is not as important to them. Their values—antimaterialism, resistance, anarchy, and their protest ritual (drugs)—are adversaries of the values centered around the old criminal code, which so strongly structured prisoner worldview before the 1960s. Today, the new structure, which is seeking to impose itself upon the old, is deliberately antistructure. It is against rules and regulations, against order. In the following narrative, Delorme reveals that he is an *old timer* who still believes somewhat in the old code ordering prisoner worldview and behavior. Those like him in the prison view the values and behavior of *street people* with a certain distrust and apprehension. He, too, is a *street person*, but his youth was partially spent in juvenile detention centers and his prisoner point of view is, therefore, more traditional and conservative.

"Nothing's valuable to these people. Clothing ain't valuable, jewelry ain't valuable; everything seems to be to trade. They have good clothes but they wear garbage.

"I don't trust none of them in here because they gossip too much. I see it. Guys have told stuff . . . they come and blab stuff out loud about somebody else. I say, 'Geez, do you know what that guy told me? He had no business tellin me somebody else's business.' Or I hear em say out loud, 'Who's got some weed?' Cop's right down on the bottom of the tier. You know he can run over and get the guy if he wants. They're loose, see. And if the bull comes and the guy gets caught, they say, 'Oh, man, I didn't think. I didn't think.' They're bright enough; it's just that they say, 'To hell with the system.'

"They want to live outside the system and whatever the system's values are. A lot of em seem to watch TV to find out what not to value. Check with their friends on the street on what they should like and shouldn't like. 'What's in today? What's out? Should I spit on the flag or should I salute today?' Go by the hippy newspaper before you make a move. Remember it started out to be 'do your own thing.' But you have to spend a lot of money to look like everybody else . . . to buy those leather vests and everything . . . well, they got it now to an extent that a guy don't feel right if he doesn't have a raggedy old jacket and if his jeans ain't raggedy enough and patched, he takes a new pair of jeans and does something to em, patch em up, see. This was an idea that began up at the top with the well-to-do and it just filtered down to the poor. Their brains must look like their jeans—full of patches and not wrapped too tight.

"They don't show a lot of fear in here, but maybe it's not so much that . . . you gotta look into it a little bit . . . put yourself in the position where you're gonna get beaten up by the cops and you know it before you do it. You know when everybody keeps doing it and they get beat up and come back and do it again, you think, 'Well, he ain't scared of nothing.' But when I talk to em—which I have—the guy says, 'Man, I was never so scared in my life!' I say, 'You don't act like you're scared, man. When you're callin the goddamned cop names and spittin on him, you know what he's gonna do to you.' 'I didn't know they was gonna do that to me.' That's what I've been hearing ever since. 'I never thought they'd do that.' A lot of people told em what the cops are gonna do. I said, 'You can only push people so far. You're gonna be in the Big Yard, gonna be naked, probably get the shit beat out of you. Lucky if you don't get killed.' 'Aw, they don't dare do stuff like that to us. That's only in the movies.' 'It ain't in the movies, friend.'

"These guys, they run around like kids in a day-care center. They don't snap to where in the hell they're at. It isn't real. They're havin fun and some guys like it in here. 'Oh man, free food! I can eat better here than I could on the streets.' You know, shit like that. They got so long to live, that little bit of time they're doin doesn't mean anything to em. That's the way they think. It doesn't mean anything to em and so raisin hell and gettin cops mad all the time, that seems to be their big thing in here, keepin cops mad. In a way, they're hopin that the guards will get so mad they'll quit. These are poor kids, not so poor kids, college kids, and a lot of veterans.

"The veterans have been ruined. They're tryin to catch up somewhere along the line the shit they missed, so that's a mistake right off the bat. They get out of the service and especially if they've seen some action, and they come back with one thought in their mind and that's to catch up on what they missed. That's a dream; you never catch up on anything. You don't know what you missed in the first place. Guys were ruined on drugs. Those people keep sayin, 'My life's shot because I took drugs in Vietnam.'

"There's a friction between all these kinds of people and guys like myself, old timers, but it's under cover. It's a culture clash.

Older guys say, 'You better stay away from those punks; they don't know how to do their time.' "

Disorder and turmoil as a value brought in by *street people* in the 1960s seems to be intensifying in the prison, in part, a reflection of what is going on on the streets today. The younger prisoners who are being sent to the prison are carriers of this intensified anarchy from the street into the prison. Many prisoners, themselves rebels of the early 1960s, are concerned by the impact these *youngsters* are having on the general prison population. Attitudes of the public toward hippies is viewed as one reason for harsh sentencing policies against young offenders by the state's criminal justice system. Another important reason is that more serious crimes are being committed by younger people.

Delorme: "There's a lot of first timers in this joint right here, which is one of the things we scream about. This is supposed to be a penitentiary; it's not supposed to be a reform school.

"When you start having a bunch of kids seventeen to eighteen years old, first time in prison, and in this particular penitentiary, it's sick, and even us older cons start bitching about it to the administration. That has always been one of our complaints, but they keep putting first timers in the Joint; they keep putting youngsters in this place. And it just destroys them. We know that. We all agree that it's wrong. Those are the people that we're talking about. There's other things that can be done with them. Nobody's tried to work with those kids."

Cardozo-Freeman: "Why are they being placed here?"

Delorme: "It's the political attitude, I think. They don't like hippies. They don't like anyone who's anti-anything and so when they get in front of the judge, you know, that's one of their values — to be themselves — that gets them maximum sentences.

"There are kids here who haven't done anything serious, lots of them. If they're really lucky they . . . well, they can't get through this pressure without going on ahead and saying, 'Aw, hell with it. I'm taking what I can get out of life and that's it.' And that's the attitude they'll go out of here with. So in the meantime they'll find other things to do.

"Without even trying you learn other crimes. You learn that burglary isn't anything; you should get a gun. If this is what they're going to do, you, the kid decides, 'Well, I am what I am. This state's going to keep me in prison all my life so I'd better not be a burglar, better to be an armed robber.' That's the decision he makes and he's a first timer, second timer. You can be a third and fourth timer and still be a first timer. You never learn a damn thing in here. It's surprising."

Resistance as a value of the *youngsters* coming in off the streets is brought out in the next narrative. Certain older *cons* who agree with and encourage the tactics of these *youngsters* contribute to the unrest and upheaval which occurs in the prison.

"The kids in prison these days are many years younger than when I first went in. They are constantly bored and so they will do anything to liven things up. They actually enjoy all the turmoil and can't wait to heal their bruises and start some more shit with the pigs. Those who were beaten and left to suffer for well over a month in the Big Yard after that riot [in 1979] were proud of it and many stood up to the guns and spit at the pigs. They were back at it just as soon as they were let back into the wing.

"The last time I was in that wing it was worse than before the riot—dirty, dangerous—doors were open and the pigs were almost under a state of siege in their little cages, and that was during a normal day when nothing was going on! It isn't the older cons who take part in this shit. It isn't the old timers, although there are exceptions and some old timers do spend all their time trying to stir people up, which is easy."

The power and leadership that certain older radical prisoners exert over *street people* in the prison is hinted at in this next narrative. This prisoner reveals that he longs for the "old days and old ways" in the prison, which were calmer and more ordered. The younger prisoner, he says, adapts the convict code to suit himself. This accounts in part for the partial eroding of this important structuring principle in the prison.

"The people that are coming into prison these days are different. I don't see the self-control that some of the old time convicts had and the age has really dropped on the average for a state prison. We are full of the people that really belong in the reformatory and somehow this place brings out the worst in their personalities.

"One important factor is the fact that the younger convict thinks that the older convict is too mellow so he isn't inclined to follow his lead. The younger prisoner sets his own pace and method of doing time in here and if he looks up to anyone, it is the violent prisoners that will become his model. About the only thing that he wants to learn from the older convict is the rules of the convict code and even that ends up being changed to fit every different situation that comes up."

Antiorder, antiestablishment, anarchy, and seeming purposelessness are hallmarks of the behavior of *street people* in the prison. But their style of operation—apparent mindlessness—is deliberate. It is a powerful resistance mechanism for confounding and defying the "enemy." They represent a powerful antistructure compounding the problems that officials have in running prisons today. The central value of *street people* is drugs. Since the majority of the inmates in this prison are *street people*, drugs are central to their lives. It is the *dis*organizing principle upon which their culture is based.

Dopers—Important Subcategory

Closely related to the major subcategory *street people* are *dopers* or *dope fiends*. Although all prisoners do not use drugs, the culture of drugs is highly evident and plays an important role, mostly negative, in the daily life of the prison.

"We have dope fiends or dopers in here. We don't call em heads, although it means the same thing. It sort of depends on where you come from. Spacemen are acid heads in here. Of course, speed will space a guy out pretty good, also. When we refer to someone as being 'spacey,' 'spaceman,' 'spaced,' or 'in the O-Zone,' it means the ding done blew his brain on acid or speed.

"The dopers make up a large portion of the population. In using the term 'dopers' you can cover every type of knick-knacker and hard core dope fiends. Some dope fiends do manage to keep habits going in here although the habit wouldn't be near as bad as it would be on the street where drugs are not so hard to cop.

"Hard core dope fiends, dyed-in-the-wool junkies, whatever you choose to label them, these guys are the ones who live, breathe, eat, and dream about getting high. They do whatever drugs they can hustle in here and as soon as the outfit or rig is put back in its secret stash they are on the move again. This is a daily ritual.

"The best days of the year for a dope fiend are the days when a good load of dope comes in and there is enough around so that he or his small group of friends can score enough to have a 'wake-up' hit in the morning. That is really a good feeling knowing you have some dope to start the next day. I say from personal experience that under these circumstances it truly is a good feeling.

"I'm talking about good dope. I'm not talking about weed. Good dope would be any class A narcotic 'drug store dope.' All the way from morphine to codeine. Heroin is the ideal high and it is used a lot, but the quality of street heroin is bad so that the quality of Joint smack is twice as bad, because whoever receives the dope inside is going to make additional cuts so that he can double the volume. This cutting process, which is generally done with milk sugar, is called 'stepping.' Two-step dope is good; three-step dope is worse and so on.

"Anyway, Joint heroin is never good dope, but people buy it at super inflated prices. For example—a twenty-five dollar quarter ounce packet would go for fifty dollars or more in the Joint—plus it will be stepped on at least once again so the dope is no good. This explains what I said earlier about the habit not being so bad. It can't be because the dope you're hooked on just isn't strong enough to really get a grip on you. A Joint habit is 99 percent psychological. The come-down is more like a bad hangover or a case of the flu.

"Weed is available at all times inside the Walls. If a pig does decide to earn some extra cash by packing, he will bring weed. Good dope isn't available to the guards or very many other people in Walla Walla. Of course, you can always have a friend, brother, or wife bring heroin over from Seattle to pass on to a guard if he will take it inside, but generally, it is just as easy or easier to bring it in some other way. Weed doesn't cost much so it is used by just about everyone who plays with drugs.

"Most of the potheads learned to smoke in school before they ever came to the Joint. Just like in college, everyone just seems to have it. There isn't any major source of drugs inside the Walls.

"Just about everyone who uses hard drugs either has or is

working to get his 'connect' going. Once you develop a reliable connect [connection] then life becomes much more interesting and the days are not so grey. He will try to score some extra to sell [deal] so that there will be money enough to pay for the next drop. This type of connect could be a wife, friend, or other family member who is on the visiting list, so generally there has to be money enough to help pay the cost of gas. With the inflated prices that Joint dope commands, it isn't hard to sell enough to cover all expenses. Out on the streets a junkie can hustle the money by stealing, boosting articles and returning them for cash refund, burglary, robbery. But inside the Walls the hustles are limited.

"A lot of effort goes into hustling people on the street through the mail or by phone. There isn't much to sell inside — some of the things that are sold would be personal items like clothes, radios, rings, watches, hobby work such as quality leatherwork, woodwork. It isn't easy to sell a radio that has been stolen from someone else's cell because the personal items like watches and radios are marked and registered when they enter the institution. That's not to say that these items are not stolen and sold.

"Some groups try on a regular basis to take over a particular area of the drug trade. Weed is widespread so it remains pretty much open to competition. The Bikers have had their extortion racket going and they not only sold dope but offered to protect the interests of those parties who were into the business of dealing heroin and other drugs. This included ripping off and putting out of business other guys who tried to make some bucks from their own stuff.

"Killing a guy wasn't unusual. A case in point: One day in one of the wings during the noon break in the visits, a fellow came back to his cell with a load of dope that his wife brought. He was in his house alone when three cons drove on him and told him to give up his shit [dope]. He said he didn't have anything. They began to beat him, then finished by stabbing him to death. They also found the dope. His wife was still waiting in the lobby for the afternoon visit when they took his body out in a canvas bag.

"The main reason for this killing was to put him out of business, or in his case, not to even let him get started. At that time a small group controlled the heavy dope. These were all white dudes.

"One interesting thing about this is that the same interference does not apply to other ethnic groups. Blacks find and deal their own dope among themselves; the same goes for the Chicanos.

" 'If you don't want trouble, keep your nose out of the dope.' This is one of the first warnings that the fish receive. They are told exactly what can and probably will happen if they are dumb enough to get involved. After that it's up to them.

"Dopers as a group of people in a community either inside the walls of a prison or on the streets have as their uppermost goal getting high just as quick as possible, and for as long as possible, and as loaded as possible. This is what they value, respect, love, and lust for. There isn't any friction with the rest of the population because they are on a different course, like trains in a large yard. Pick your course and stick to it and you won't crash into others.

"It's a game, just as everything in prison is a game. Play the game right and you'll win. At the very least, you'll live. We are *all* losers or we wouldn't be in the Joint. The law won. We can accept that and vow to not make the same mistake next time. I don't mean get religion or go straight; I mean change our game and play our hand better next time—wear a mask or wear gloves, eliminate those fool moves that got us in.

"Dopers don't hang around in groups and talk about drugs. Neither do they function like a recognized group, although some are much more visible than others. Most dopers don't even know each other; however, dealing and getting high can be a good socializer.

"Dopers keep the guards busy; actually it can take pressure off other small hustles. Even a good escape plan has a better chance of success if guards are preoccupied with the drug business.

"An increase in drugs inside the walls means an increase in violence, increase in drug busts, heat on the visiting room, more fights; the hustling and noise levels go up in the wings; people stay up later at night; people get sick; the pill line doubles; use of money orders doubles, which means more regulations on use of money orders; the amount of white money inside the Walls goes up to dangerous levels. Dangerous for the guy or guys who are holding onto a thousand bucks. Activity increases all over the Joint when a large load of speed [meth tabs] comes in; the Breezeway and tiers are like beehives. Everyone is either hustling money for more, a rig to fix what they have, or coffee because they will be rapping and dinging out on speed all night. These are some of the outward effects of the Joint dopers.

"Many grow tired of the hustle; some get killed; some just get paroled to continue the same game starting with the hundred bucks gate money. Most come back before a year passes."

High Status Cons

Good People

The traditional thief, the elite of prison population of years past, the man skilled in his craft with a strong honor code by which he ordered his life, is greatly diminished in numbers in this prison, although some of his values still persist.

"If I'm talkin about a good thief, I mean a heel and toe man, a guy that's a good booster. He's a good con man [confidence man]; he's a good pickpocket; he's got skill. He can jump behind counters in [drug] stores and get things without being seen and grab a drawer of drugs. That's a good thief. Very few guys, maybe about 20 percent are thieves in that sense in here. The rest of us are dings . . . just guys who did dumb stuff that got us in prison. I used to want to be a good thief and I got pretty good at boosting. I picked up TV's and just walked out the door, but it's just luck that nobody saw anything. They thought I owned it or something, but that's not bein a good thief. Most of the guys in here are guys that goofed, got caught."

The thief's tradition of honor is still carried on by some of the older *cons* in the prison despite the drastic changes that have occurred in population characteristics over the past twenty years. Although radical changes may occur in a culture, traditions do not necessarily disappear, particularly if they still serve important functions. They may become altered, however. The convict code, for example, adapted from the thief's tradition that he brought into the prison from the underworld,[6] is still a useful point of reference and an important ordering principle for some of the older, more traditionally oriented *cons*. Loyalty to fellow prisoners, dignity and courage, coolness, never betraying others—hallmarks of the thief's style—still persist in this prison. Many of these qualities admired in the old thief are qualities that *good people* possess. *Good people* are the elite of this prison.[7] They represent a small group of highly influential leaders who are respected by the population for their dignity, decency, courage, coolness, and positive leadership. They represent the best in personal character and conduct, which paradoxically very closely resembles the ideal good man in mainstream society. The efforts of *good people* to help individual prisoners with problems and to forestall racial conflicts, inmate-on-inmate violence, outbreaks over misunderstandings with guards or the administration, or repressive treatment or policies within the prison make them a much admired group. *Doing your own time* and not *snitching* on other inmates are traditions inherited from the thief's code, which *good people* uphold. The commandment of the old thief not to interact with guards or others in the population who are not thieves, however, is not strictly observed in this prison. In fact, *good people* work closely with those guards, who are also acknowledged and accepted by many in the population as *good people*, to help solve problems. Although *good people* are the elite, they are not, as were thieves in the old prison culture, elitist. In some respects, *good people* resemble the "real man" described in Gresham Sykes' *Society of Captives*. Like the real man, a prisoner at Walla Walla who is identified as *good people* "confronts his captors with neither subservience or aggression" and "endures the rigors of imprisonment with dignity," serving as a "hero" for the population.[8] Delorme describes some of the characteristics of prison leaders who are *good people*:

Delorme: "Status in here has nothin to do with the crime you committed. We got good people in here; they're at the top of the status list. They're good people; they get along with everybody. They rap to dings; they rap to anybody. They take a little more effort to try not to put people down. They treat other people with a little respect. None of em are ever involved in cruelty. A person always feels that they can go to that person for help. Not that he's going to jump out and fight for em but he's going to try to find a way to help em. It's how you get along in here. Even though a person might not want to be that way themselves, the population tends to respect these guys."

Cardozo-Freeman: "In a situation where so many terrible things happen, decency is admired, respected?"

Delorme: "That's true. The good people are not one group. They're all different groups in the institution. I'm not talkin just about clubs. These people may be found among all groups.

"One name comes to mind—a Chicano—and he doesn't even belong to the Chicano Club anymore. He used to be the president but, anyway, he's just an all-round good people. Things that happen in here hurt him and he doesn't like that, but he's not down on anyone or anything. It would take an awful lot of pushin to get him to fight but he would if he had to. But he'd do all that he could not to, and the Chicanos look to him to help them even though he's not in the club anymore. The guys that need help and need advice, they come over here and get him; they haul him off the tier."

Cardozo-Freeman: "I notice that's the way you are with your Indian brothers."

Delorme: "And it gets me into trouble. I won't stop, but it's irritating. In some situations it's either me go down and tell those guys to stop, try to get em to stop or they're going to the Hole, and they just come out of the Hole, you know. The Hole's going to end up killin em. But you gotta live with yourself, so you gotta help when you can."

Some *good people* were disruptive lawbreakers in the prison in their younger days but have mellowed, an indication, perhaps, of wisdom gained through maturation and experience. Delorme, who is an example of this metamorphosis, continues describing *good people*:

"Good people don't have to be big guys physically, but they're big in their heads; they're good-minded. They're good leaders. It doesn't depend on physical size. One of em I can think of is Little Man Johnson. He knows how to shoot a little shit, too. He's a little blonde man, looks like a teenager.

"Inmate leaders are generally good people. The only time you use the term 'good people' is when somebody asks you about somebody specifically. You say, 'He's good people.'

"Cops can be good people, too. That guy standing down there on the tier and that other guy next to him; they're good people.

They don't bother people. They just do whatever the job is and they smile and they're normal, so they're good people."

Killers

There are a small number of leaders who are respected by the population not only because they are excellent leaders and advocates for prisoner rights, but because they are feared. They are known killers in the population. Generally, these are *Lifers* who hold in common their high intelligence, outstanding leadership qualities, and ruthless recourse to murdering their fellow prisoners when they are endangering the rest of the population. A very few of these men are true revolutionaries. Courageous and in many ways altruistic in fighting for prisoner rights, these men are recognized as powerful adversaries by the prison authorities, since through their charismatic leadership they can easily persuade the population to riot and rebellion. Sometimes these "intelligent" *killers*, as Delorme calls them, are well educated; some come from the middle class; all are extremely aware politically. They can be connected, philosophically at least, to resistance movements throughout the world that employ terrorist tactics against "repressive enemies" in power. Delorme describes some of the attributes of "intelligent" *killers*:

"We got different kinds of leaders. We got guys here that are the leaders at the top of the hierarchy who are looked at as dangerous in that they kill people, other convicts or whatever. Generally, they've murdered on the streets and they've gotten into positions of power in here. They're intelligent and they do good things, but they also lead the bad things. They'll try to keep riots down.

"If we got people in prison that will rob other people, you tell these guys about the guy and they'll go to that guy and they've got their little group and you know what's gonna happen. The guy isn't gonna get talked to, you know. They're the ones who take him in and they break his hands with a hammer, tell him 'bad boy,' and next time he does it, they break his head with a hammer. They're well respected by the population because of fear. Some of em are tough guys, and they don't stand out in a crowd or anything.

"I've known R.D. for a long time. He's a pretty nice guy. I've worked with him on that RRC thing [Race Relations Committee].

He was chairman and I was vice chairman. That was the crew that was runnin around killin people, torturin people. I dropped out when I realized what they was doin.

"When they formed the RRC there was a lot of trouble in here, and it was gettin worse and worse. Blacks and whites, blacks and Indians, Indians and Chicanos. So the administration sanctioned the committee. It was the Lifers who thought it up, but nobody knew they were goin to kill people.

"And we had guys robbin older guys, dings, and robbin the fish. A couple of em that were into that shit were Indians and we [Indians] were ashamed. We weren't able to control the little bastards. We never thought of beatin em up cause they were our brothers.

"Anyway, a week or so later I heard that the RRC wiped out somebody. The guy got his hands broke up with a hammer. 'Who'd do a thing like that?' They said, 'The Race Relations Committee did it; caught the guy stealin.' 'Good for them,' and all that shit and nobody got mad at that. 'That's a good sentence,' they thought. 'If you steal, break their hands.' I'm tellin you, the [Parole] Board should be so tough! Goddam! Seems like any time it's left to the cons to determine the sentence, it's rough; it's always physical. Something they'll remember. And it works, too. It didn't work for the Indians but it worked for these guys. I said, 'I didn't know that we was going to be administering punishment. Are you sure it was the RRC?' They said, 'Yeah, they had them red badges on. They took the guy up to the Lifers Club and put his hands on a cement block and broke em with a hammer.' I said, 'Who did that?' They said, 'R.D. and a couple of their guys. F. was one of em.' The two worst suckers in the Joint right there. And that's their idea of a let off. That was a slap on the hand there. The next one was death. 'The next time we'll bring you up and kill you.' That's what they told him. But anyway we found out what was goin on and we quit.

"Those two guys on that committee were a couple of killers. They had no patience with anybody who was causing problems in the population. We'd sit in committee meetings and we'd say, 'Let's just bring him in for counsel,' and they'd say, 'Let's just kill the sonovabitch.'

"In a way you keep these guys on the committee because it scares the population, so it's a whole power trip. You understand power and you understand threats. When you're tryin to deal with each other and hold the line, that's about the only way it works inside the walls—bigger versus littler. But you keep these guys in check by puttin them in positions of leadership. That keeps them out of the real bad cliques cause it makes em feel important. And they are important because they do have a lot of influence through fear.

"R.D. and F. are very intelligent, real intelligent but cold. Something really lacking. You can deal with em on a brother basis, be as friendly as you want, but by the same token, if you do something wrong, you wouldn't count for nothin then.

"When I'm talkin to a guy like that I don't feel like I'm dealin with a human being. Inside it's not like talkin to a person. It's like talkin to a zombie or something.

"Three of em that I know have similar personalities. They are the nicest guys. I really like em, except I stop short. If I really got to know em, I'd really like em cause they are bright and they really smile easy, go out of their way to help you. They got nice lookin girl friends and dedicated mothers out there helpin em all the time. They got good positive ideas all the time. They're always on the move, always doin something, comin up with ideas all the time. They're just like competent children, their traits. You can spot em a mile away, but by the same token, there don't seem to be any boundaries on what they'll do and won't do. They're fun to be around.

"Like F., I didn't like to go to big meetings unless he had the chair because he could just keep it goin; everything he said was right. And he would just get everybody mad, or keep everybody sad or whatever he wanted to do. He could do it with a crowd and he's just a youngster.

"But there's always that one thing there—they kill people too easy. That's their solution to people that get in their way, that irritate them too much or pose a threat in any way. They just eliminate em. Everytime we send one of those guys somewhere a riot's happened. We've got our fair share of those guys here. You only need about one of em in every prison and we got a dozen of em in here. Those guys were all here during that riot [1979] and they sent em all out over the country but they're almost all back now."

Other killers exist among the population. Although not of the caliber of the intelligent *killers*, they are begrudgingly respected since the population fears their easy recourse to murder. Generally, they are not leaders. If they assume leadership, it lacks the altruistic dimension of the intelligent killers.

"There are other guys in here that are killers, too. Lifers have good leaders but sometimes they have real crazy leaders; then the whole club goes crazy. You can always tell that by how many guys quit the club. If the guy that comes into office is a maniac—homicidal maniacs, I call half of em—they'll just turn around and kill another convict. He's more than a murderer. Sometimes they get voted in as president of the clubs and the clubs turn into cliques and gangs, and they don't give a damn about the membership and the membership quits. The good people quit, the people who want to do things other than have trouble once in awhile. Guys like that are way down on the hierarchy."

Joint Politicians

Joint politicians enjoy the limelight and run for office to serve on the Resident Council. Each year they announce their candidacy and run on certain platforms that draw votes from the population. They campaign, make speeches, put up posters, and talk to individual prisoners to further the success of their campaign. Today's *Joint politician* differs from the "politician" identified by Clarence Schrag in this prison in the 1940s.[9] The status of *Joint politicians* is in the upper levels of the prisoner hierarchy since they perform a useful function for the population.

Delorme: "Joint politicians are certain guys that like to get involved in prison government or anything to do with buggin the cops or tryin to get some rules changed or bitchin about something the administration's done; just bein a spokesman for the others' complaints. In most cases most people don't want to say nothin, like bein a troublemaker. You hafta make a decision either to keep a low profile or step out in front. I was involved in a lot of things but I was never considered a Joint politician because a lot of the things I was doin I was expected to do as a club leader, [Indian]—part of the job. Real Joint politicians are always the ones runnin for office."

Cardozo-Freeman: "Are they Lifers?"

Delorme: "Usually but not always. There are so many Lifers they always step forward on serious things because they have to do a lot of time. About half are really interested. You have to be on the RC or the administration won't deal with em. The RC is a club in its own right. It's separate from the clubs but it has club backing. The guys are elected to office. They put up posters, run around talkin to other guys, pick a concern, make that their platform, run once a year. The Arbitration Committee is a group of guys from the clubs that watchdogs to see that the guys on the RC don't fuck up. There are advantages and disadvantages to bein a Joint politician. If you've got too big a mouth, you get in trouble with the administration, unless you play it real smart, then you're in danger of becoming a real 'yes' man."

Joint Tough Guys

Joint tough guys are next in the prisoner hierarchy. These are men who are respected because they "hold muscle power." They do not, however, resort to murder. There are two classes of *Joint tough guys*—those who under the guise of altruism employ physical violence and those who are only bent on satisfying their own selfish interests. Only those who use their power to help others have a high status.

"Joint tough guys are the next group down on the hierarchy simply because they hold muscle power, but they're not really jumpin on people. They're big guys with a lot of muscle who have been known to be tough in a physical way. They're respected for their courage, I guess. These guys are bullies but don't want to look like bullies. If they see a little guy gettin beat up, they'll beat the shit out of the other guy. And guys go to him to be rescued, but his real reason is not to help them so much as to beat somebody up. At least he uses it [his physical power] through good channels. This guy don't go around rapin people.

"We've got another guy in here though that just stands out cause he's just too goddamned tough to do anything about. All he wants to do is get things for himself. He wants drugs and if he's been in here awhile, probably he's goin to play the game and use some little kid. He'll talk him out of it, or if he can't, if he gets frustrated, if he wants the kid, he'll slap him around a little bit and if that don't do it, he might rape him. These guys are also called wolves."

Middle or Neutral Status Cons

Hustlers

In this prison the label *hustler* applies to any man who *hustles* within the prison itself. Many whites, Chicanos, and native Americans, as well as blacks, are prison hustlers. A good prison hustler is respected for his intelligence and ability to use language to exploit others.[10]

Delorme: "We got hustlers in here, guys who wheel and deal. Hustlers are pretty high on the status list. People have respect for his intelligence and because he's a good hustler. They know how to beat people out of stuff, talk em out of stuff. I used to think, 'How come I can't fast talk like this guy?' This guy knows he's gettin beat and I'm watchin Dan standing there talkin him out of something and the guy he's talkin to is supposed to be half sharp."

Cardozo-Freeman: "A snake-oil salesman?"

Delorme: "Yeah. Actually, there are plenty of white, Indian, and Chicano hustlers. All are pretty much the same. Most of the good hustlers I know both in Walla Walla and on the streets are white. I will say that 'hustler' in Walla Walla applies to every race equally. A hustler hustles. He is always workin to get white money [real currency], dope to buy and sell; he's after the profit. It's a game that he gets hooked on and he's at it day and night.

"A lot of guys learn to hustle while they are in here. They learn to get out and deal dope for others when they haven't got any of their own; they sell clothes; they go out and cop a lid of grass for others and in turn get a cut or a couple joints or numbers. A hit or joint of weed is also called a doo-be. They sell white money. Ten dollars is worth fifteen dollars Joint scrip. [$7.50 scrip is worth $5.00 real currency] Ten dollars is worth fifteen dollars Joint scrip. Twenty for thirty, and so on. I used to get a twenty from W. now and then just so I could trade it for thirty dollars worth of scrip. A Joint hustler generally can't make a dime on the streets. A good street hustler will talk him out of his shorts."

State-Raised Youth

Some of the men recognize an important group in the population known as 'state-raised youth.' Although this is not an agreed-on cultural definition, it represents an important group of men in the prison.[11] State-raised youth, Delorme states, are easily identified in this prison. They are comfortable and secure in their environment since prison (and the juvenile centers in which they grew up) are the only homes they ever had. Delorme identifies himself as a state-raised youth.

"We live just like kids in a foster home. To me the state of Washington has always been my mother, really. The state has been my parents and the big concrete fortress prison has been my home. I have picked my attitudes up in prison from other prisoners and from the guards. All my habits, all my models have been convicts, killers, rapists; you name it. There are so damned many of us like that in here, and we continue to live like kids until we decide we have had enough.

"You can tell the guys that have been in the different juvenile joints and other joints in the state. I can pretty much spot people that have been in Greenhill; I spot em if they've been in Monroe, and I can tell the ones that have been under the state's hand for years, raised by the state. They're like spoiled brats, spoiled kids. There's no discipline. There's no respect for anything or anybody. There's no respect for rules. It's all just a game, a real game.

"You don't see em runnin around cryin . . . well, they do snivel a lot, but they only snivel when they want something, or if some rule change affects em, they snivel. But they don't really snivel because they're in here. All their cryin is always because they want something. And they don't run around and look depressed. They're not sad all the time. They're not beatin their heads against the wall. They skip and hop around in here, play games, find things to do. They find a lot of hustles. They're the ones that are always gettin the best jobs. They can get information or they can steal and make some money, somehow. I don't mean an eight hour payin job; I mean stealin-type money. They can steal things out of the kitchen and sell it for money. The other money is there but they can make more by hustlin.

"So the person that has pretty much been raised in institutions wants everything now, and you're used to havin all your basic needs met. If you want shoes, you want em now; you don't want to wait. You take it for granted that you're gonna have all the clothes you need. You're gonna have all your food. All you ever do is listen to the radio, look at TV, and play games until it's time to get out again.

"I'm a state-raised youth. I been through everything again and again and again. Oh, it's tough. Course, I'm workin on it. I'm still tryin to figure it out myself. I think I'm luckier than most because I'm gettin a little grip on myself. I'm gettin a little understanding and so I'll pull myself out of the rat race. I'm here and I'm not here."

State-raised youth have trouble growing up. The state, through institutionalization of young offenders, fosters dependency; consequently immaturity is one of the strong identifying characteristics of this group.[12] Delorme discusses this inability to assume responsibility with another *old timer*:

Old Timer: "I call them institutional cripples. Most of them are state-raised and they don't learn anything positive. They gripe and the bulls treated them kind of mean when they were kids cause they wanted to boss them around, and they become real resentful and they never grow out of it. It seems like they just stay and get hung up in the teenage bracket. You come in real young in here; you're still feeling like a teenager and being hostile and angry and resentful like a damned kid when suddenly you find yourself to be thirty-five or thirty-six years old."

Delorme: "They got no patience, no tolerance. Refuse to understand or look at two sides of a thing. No thinkin; they react. And they just act like ten-year-old kids that are spoiled. It's always gimme, gimme, gimme.

" 'You're a friend, so gimme a cigarette, gimme your book, gimme your shirt.' In the case of minorities like the Indians, it's 'Brother this, and brother that.' Used to drive me up the wall, man. 'Oh yeah? Now it's brother cause I got a job. If I had to go along with you guys I'd be totally poverty stricken.' Can't have anything for myself. And no offer to pay stuff back. Oh no. Never thought of that, apparently."

Old Timer: "That's the convict 'we' and it don't work in society. There, they call them 'bums.'"

Delorme: "Yeah. They got no sense of responsibility. As a man grows up, the institutions do all their thinking for em. They're not responsible for anything and if they make a mistake it's always someone else's fault. And they tell us we're responsible but we're not accountable.

"Responsibility and accountability goes together, otherwise, if a man isn't accountable for his actions, why responsibility means nothing. If I'm responsible for something and you're accountable for it, why should I care? You'll take the rap. That's why they pass it off.

"It's the prison system. It teaches a person, especially when they're juveniles right up through, that they don't have to be responsible. All their thinking is done for em. They say, 'So what?' They go to the Hole ten days, it's all done; they go right back and do it again, whatever it is. They're not accountable."

Old Timers

Anyone who has been in the prison for at least ten years is considered an old timer. Some old *Lifers* who date back to the 1930s and 1940s live strictly by the old convict code of Big House days and still speak the *lingo* that was used in the prison during that period. The more recent *old timers* are generally *street people* of the 1960s. *Old timers* are respected for their experience. They are prison-wise. Delorme explains:

"I'm an old timer because I have been in the Joint several times, plus my age, I guess.

"The guys I know consider an old timer a guy with at least ten years behind the Walls. He doesn't have to ask questions anymore, that's for sure.

"Old timers generally don't run with other people. They may go to a show or eat with other old timers, but they avoid the politics and hustle of the Joint. They are dangerous because they have no patience for dings, bums, or Joint tough guys. They don't sit still for threats and will kill an asshole faster than most. So old timers run and do their thing as if they had a small wall around them. You just learn who they are in a hurry so you will be careful of them. Even the old timers who are dings have the population's respect.

"The really old convicts in here, some of them are loners. You can't sit down and carry on a decent conversation with em because it is mumbo jumbo, and they're either falling off into that old slang or they won't say names; they won't say places; they won't even say a town where this robbery was committed, or whatever. When they talk about crime they bring their voice to a whisper like somebody's listening and it's weird. You can't say to him that there's anything decent or honest, or you believe in the system, or this guard is halfway decent. That's the old convict and his code."

Senior Citizens

Some *old timers* are identified as *senior citizens*. The population changes of the 1960s disturbed the status and safety of these oldest prisoners.

"Senior citizens constitute a small percentage of the prison; however, their contributions far outweigh their numbers. For many years, the older convicts stayed out of the mainstream of the prison life and would find a safe niche to do their time in peace and quiet. The administration during the 50s and 60s obliged this desire by providing housing to fit their individual needs. This generally consisted of lower level cells in the large wings and singles in the wings built for single housing. Many of these men managed to make a permanent home in the hospital. Of course, the Joint was not overcrowded during those years. Single cells were a priority item and were almost exclusively reserved for the older inmate if he requested it. Work has always been scarce at Walla Walla, so the factory jobs went to the younger cons. Gardening, kitchen work or porters' jobs [cleaning] in the wings were generally filled by the old timers.

"During the early years the old timers commanded a certain amount of respect from the rest of the population and were able to do their time at a more leisurely pace with little or no hassle from the other men in the prison. The older convicts' lot in the prison changed radically with the changes brought about by Dr. Conte in the 70s so that he no longer found it easy to do his own time. As the prison rapidly changed from a slow-moving, disciplined prison to a fast-paced mad house, virtually free of rules and suddenly run by the inmates, the old timers found that they were being pushed out of the comfort of the single cells and being forced to get out and hustle like everyone else if they were to have a cell at all. The overcrowding seemed to come all of a sudden during the early 1970s and there was no room left for special housing. Even seating became a prized item in the dining room and the movies, or any other event, for that matter. The seniors found that they were becoming a mark for the younger con rather than someone to look up to. His safety was no longer assured and he found that he also had to get out and hustle if he was to survive in his new prison.

"The senior citizens were the last group to organize. A series of beatings and robberies finally provided the incentive for them to come together and form a tight-knit group aptly named "Senior Citizens Club." This club began operations in the midseventies and provided a comfortable place for its members to meet, drink coffee, watch TV, and find safety in numbers just the same as the other groups in the prison.

"The seniors went a step ahead of most clubs and established a well managed gift shop in their club area. This shop provided a much needed service to the rest of the population by offering quality greeting cards and attractive handmade gifts which could be mailed to loved ones at home. All members benefited from the proceeds of these sales. The old timer had always been a source of advice and with the advent of self-government, he slowly began to offer his experience and knowledge to the rest of the population through the RGC [Resident Government Council]. Politics was his hole card and consequently, some of the most constructive leadership in the prison came from the senior citizens.

"The senior citizens took special advantage of the opportunity to pool their resources by using their money to hire or pay for protection when it was needed, consequently, younger cons soon discovered that it was extremely dangerous to rob, beat, or harass any of the senior citizens in the prison."

Cowboys

Cowboys, who come from the small towns and rural areas of the state, are generally respected by the prison community. Recog-

nized as individuals who *do their own time* quietly and unobtrusively,
all *cowboys* are white.

"Guys who like cowboy music and wear cowboy boots and hats;
those are the ones we call cowboys in here. They like to identify
with anything western. Most of the cowboys play guitars and are
from the small towns on the eastern side of the mountains which
are western oriented because of the ranch style living and work. A
lot have roots from Tennessee, Oklahoma, Texas, and so on. They
stay together pretty much.

"There are a few loners in all groups. A lot of club members are
considered loners even though they come to meetings and do club
things. The majority of their time is spent in their houses or if
you see them anywhere, they will be alone.

"Cowboys are nonviolent. They don't have fights like other
clubs. Generally, we know them as pretty mellow, easy going
people and they get along with all the clubs and cliques. For the
most part they are pretty decent people."

Straight or Square Johns

Straight johns (square johns) generally hold a relatively neutral
status in the prison. Others are wary of them because they do not
understand or follow the convict code. They come from the
majority culture, hence, their values are different from the rest of
the prisoners.

"Straight johns are kind of down on the list. It's not because
they're snitches. You get along fine with em but people will tell
you if they seen you running around with one guy all the time
that they know he's not a criminal, really. Your friends might tell
you to be careful because he doesn't know the game; he doesn't
know the code. He's normal. He's got more humanity in him than
anything else. He's not going to have any loyalty toward us, so
he'll tell on us what he saw. Be careful what you talk about to this
guy because he'll blab, not necessarily because he wants to be a
snitch but because he has no loyalties. If he comes across a murder
or something like that, he might just run straight to the bulls. And
he's scared. He has normal values and that makes him dangerous.
Very dangerous. But he's still liked.

"He just kind of floats around in the middle, status-wise. He

goes around and is almost invisible. He can do whatever he wants
and nobody pays him any mind. He's so insignificant he doesn't
even have a title. Just straight john. He's just watched. Other
people, sure, they know who he is.

"And the straight johns, they stick together but they don't run in
groups. He usually ends up being friends with another straight
john. Might take him weeks or months to find another one but it'll
be another guy just like him. Not many straight johns in here but
they're here."

Lower Status Cons

Some important labels identifying groups in the prison reflect
extreme disapproval in the community. These categories include
bibleback, Breezeway bums, dings, nuts, fruits (queens and *punks), rapos,*
and *snitches. Punks, rapos,* and *snitches* are the very low-status *cons.*
Those given derogatory labels do not live up to the standards of
the prison community and therefore exist at the bottom or near
bottom of the social hierarchy. Their label implies rejection,
contempt, disdain, and even hatred. The very intention of such
labeling is to humiliate, degrade, and deprecate, to hurt the bearer
of the label not only socially but psychologically as well, Name-
calling attempts to control the social situation, also, by marking
off the untouchables of the population. Implicit also in the name-
calling is the admonition or warning that those so labeled should
somehow change or behave differently. *Greaser, nigger, blanket ass,
honky,* or *redneck* are common terms found in the prison. Like
conventional society, the prison society exhibits little tolerance
for racial or cultural differences.

Although much of this naming appears in the prison, it is important to point out that what often appears to be derogatory
name-calling is actually an indication of humor and affectionate
acceptance. A black inmate calling a native American friend a
fucking warhoop or a white prisoner greeting a black friend with
the name *spear chucker* are indications of friendliness and mutual
acceptance. It all depends on the contextual situation and the
individuals involved. Delormes explains, "If you really like a guy
you call him the worst name in the book. It's kind of a challenge to

see what he comes up with for you."[13] Open or direct expressions of affection are not approved in prison culture; however, much evidence of caring exists, but it is always displayed in this ritualistic and stylized manner. Certain guards who have the respect and affection of the prisoners will sometimes refer to the men as *assholes*. This is recognized by the men as the particular guard's way — the prisoner-approved way — of communicating concern for them as human beings. I personally witnessed such name-calling. Delorme points out that "if a guard can call an inmate an 'asshole' and get away with it, that's a sign that he's really good people." Sometimes "false" labeling occurs. This is referred to as *putting a jacket on* someone and is done deliberately to harm or break down another inmate. *Putting a jacket on* a young *fish* by calling him a *punk* and spreading this false rumor, for example, can be devastating because other prisoners will begin to believe this and *shine him on*, ignore or snub him.

Prisoners occupying the lowest status in the population have the distinction of being pariahs in a community of pariahs, since convicts are a stigmatized group in the eyes of conventional society. The prisoner with a low-status label cannot, unfortunately, "alienate himself from the community which upholds the norm, or refrain from developing an attachment to the community in the first place," as Erving Goffman advocates, since control of the situation is impossible.[14] In the following description of low-status cons, homosexuals and pseudo-homosexuals are omitted since they are described in Chapter 8.

Delorme: "Guys that hang around the Chapel all the time are called biblebacks. They have fellowship meetings and just hang around. Most are punks or other assorted creeps and sickos. A small percentage are serious minded, I think. I don't know what else I can say about this group, but they are a distinctive category and every prison has them. I suppose they join for safety, and how much trouble can you get into in the Chapel?

"A ding isn't always a nut or a dummy. Some of the dings are the smartest people in the Joint but they are too dumb to do things right inside the Walls. One thing that marks off a ding is that he is naive as hell; hasn't done much in his life so he is not prison-wise. He does things that would get a regular guy in here beat in the head. But if he's a known ding, then people will let a lot of his stupid shit slide.

"Only a ding would sit in someone elses' seat in the movie or the chow hall when everyone around knows that the chair belongs to Joe Blow, and only a ding will miss the obvious fact that all the Bikers are sitting in the same place and so you just don't plop down and eat there. Only a ding will take a job on the garbage crew. Dings dress like bums for the most part. Dings don't comb their hair right, and dings generally have dingy wives and dingy kids. Dings are crazy, stupid, smart, naive, ugly, not cool, dirty, and if you run around with a ding, you must be a fuckin ding yourself. What can you say about the dings. They do their time and leave. No one knows who they were, when they came, or when they left, and no one cares. A ding can't help or do anything for anyone so no one bothers with them.

"I'll tell you one thing. It wouldn't be very cool to hurt or kill a ding unless he's a rat. That would cost you whatever respect you may have for yourself. Others would put you down for doing it. I would never live down hurting some ding; might even lose some friends in the process. I'm supposed to be tough so I don't have to prove it on some poor ding who doesn't stand a chance in a fight. You can shoo him away or give him a push, but you don't punch him out. Most nuts are dings for sure.

"A Breezeway bum, sometimes called a Breezeway ding, is a bum anywhere in the Joint. The only difference is he doesn't like to do cell time so he spends much more time on the Breezeway, even in the cold and rain. Every time you go anywhere you'll see the same bums and dings hanging around the Breezeway, just standing or walking back and forth, so they get to be called Breezeway bums. They stand around and bum smokes or anything else they can. He never has any money. People catch on to the regular bums in a hurry and most guys just tell him to 'fuck off' if he asks for anything.

"A Breezeway bum isn't always a ding, although nuts or dings, or just dings do bum a lot. Others are just regular people. Some are even part of the regular crowd and belong to a pretty good group but they just bum all the time. It is sort of a hustle to them but, in fact, it's no way to hustle.

"We got guys in here who are insane. They're not dings. We call em loose. 'See that cat over there? Sit here and watch him. He's loose, I'm tellin you.' They're really not named anything, really. But there's a lot of disturbed people in this prison. Some of em are up on Third Floor. Most of the nuts are invisible in the population. The ones that stand out are dangerous. They have their own little dustball world, usually grubby. Don't comb their hair and so on.

"We don't ask a guy what he's done on the streets. We don't use that to determine if we're going to like him, except for sex crimes. Guys in here hate rapos. It's a disgusting crime and guys who commit it are creeps. You watch these guys and see what sickos they are and if you've got family you think about it. We know that could happen to our people. Everybody has disgust or hate for sex criminals. There's way more than there used to be in here. Every year it's increased, almost doubled. I don't know why. Funny thing, there's a lot of rapos out in population and they get along fine."

Cardozo-Freeman: "Why are the guys down on men who rape women but not down on raping men in here?"

Delorme: "They're down on it but they don't say anything about it or they might get raped. It's kind of a part of life in here, I guess, an ugly part that you don't want to have happen to you. Actually, snitch is at the bottom of the list. That's the most unforgivable sin in here. Punks are below the rapo."

Gresham Sykes points out that the label "rat" or "squealer" is never applied lightheartedly or jokingly, as are many other derogatory labels in prison because it represents the breaking of the most serious taboo in prison culture. The *snitch* performs the supreme act of disloyalty by participating in the game of divide and conquer with the officials against his own group.[15]

THE CLUBS

Clubs are an organizing principle in the prison that serves important functions for the prisoners. Those with similar interests or who share cultural or racial identities in common, group together for fellowship and protection. Most of the clubs are positive and peaceful support systems. A few—the "big five"—are recognized as political forces exercising considerable power both positive and negative. Individuals do not hold power in this prison; clubs do. All leaders are connected to clubs. Of the twenty-eight clubs officially recognized by the administration, the five with the greatest power and influence are Lifers, BPFU (Black Prisoners Forum Unlimited), Chicano, Indian, and Bikers Club. Although the smaller clubs are not political forces, they often align themselves with these powerful groups for protection when the "temperature rises" in the prison.[16] Most large-scale problems between prisoners center around racial and cultural clashes and misunderstandings. Most of the "wars" that go on are racial between the blacks, Chicanos, and Indians.

"Clubs are the controlling force in here. Only the major groups hold the power—Lifers, Bikers, and the ethnic groups. All the small clubs are more social and try not to get involved with politics and fighting. They avoid taking sides in any beefs. For instance, whenever the Indians get into it with the blacks, the Bikers and Lifers will join forces with the Indians. The Bikers and Indians have had a long-standing pact to help each other in any beefs with the blacks.

"We got twenty-eight clubs and just one club alone—the Lifers—has 300 members or better. You can figure that the Bikers have about sixty to seventy members, we [Indian Club] are about sixty to seventy; Chicanos have about the same; BPFU has about 300 to 400. Right there, you're talkin about a lot of power. So clubs are the majority.

"And you have all those other little clubs like the Jaycees. They're a pretty big club. They're all white. The AA's are a pretty big club, mostly all white; you see a black face once in awhile. Chess Club, Bridge Club, Senior Citizen Club, the Kitchen Club; they call themselves the Kitchen Workers. They got their own wing and everything. Even have their own basketball team. There's MAS [gay club], and even the church is a club. The church people that work in the Chapel. There's guys that are in the choir that have a fellowship.

"When people come together long enough in here they start getting invited to these club meetings cause we see that they represent a fair faction, you know, more than ten people. Clubs are a good thing except when the beefs come down, then the big clubs can turn into gangs."

Lifers Club

Lifers wield the greatest influence among the big five clubs. Since they are serving longer sentences than the other prisoners, they have an interest in improving conditions in the prison and in keeping the peace.

"I ain't never counted but it seems to me like the biggest part of the Lifers are made up of guys that haven't been convicted of killing anybody. Like my friend, Speedy—he's a Lifer. He hasn't killed anybody. It's just the habitual criminal laws in Washington. They're rousted for three or four beefs and then they take you down and bitch you. Then you've got a life sentence. I don't know what percentage have actually killed somebody.

"I'd say the Lifers are the number one influence in the penitentiary. They got more brains, it seems like—a whole conglomeration of brain power. They have a real mixture of people—black, white, Chicano, Indian, cowboys. You can branch off, belong to another club, but as a rule they don't. For example, Indians that are committed for murder, since you do have your own club, you stay with it, but you have a go-ahead. You can come and go in the Lifers Club, whereas somebody else can't come and go.

"The majority of the time the Lifers are a pretty positive outfit. They're about one of the only groups, other than the Jaycees, that try to concentrate on doing community projects. They always have little businesses. They got a good head for business.

"Most politicians are in the Lifers because everything that goes on in the Joint is more important to them. They have to stay here so they keep a close watch on everybody. They keep pretty close tabs on what you're doing. They don't like to be in an uproar all the time. When it starts gettin bad, they form some kind of committee or something and start calming things down. So everybody pretty much looks to them for advice or leadership in certain situations.

"Most of the other clubs are not really willing or anxious to take that kind of leadership over the main population. We're all concerned with our own group of people and that's it. Sometimes, however, you're forced to when the RC is really fucking things up, then you get a coalition of club leaders that come together. They make a decision to do something and it's done. You're talkin about a lot of power there and there's not too much you can't do when you get your forces together, but as a rule we always let the Lifers take the lead cause they usually got a cool head and they have a helluva lot more topside supporters, outside help. The Lifers have contact with legislators, senators, and everything else that they have established through the years. So when they really want to get something done, they can really do it."

BPFU Club

Willis, a black inmate, briefly describes the beginning of *BPFU* (*Black Prisoners Forum Unlimited*).

"The group started January, 1970, after the ten-day lockdown. Of course it was against the rules to meet as a group. The first meetings were held in the weight room. The administration always had the shift lieutenant and an officer or two in the area. There was always a side-arm [pistol] on display by the officer. Now the formation of the BUF was formed out of survival for the black resident. Black United Forum was changed to BPFU when the group was finally accepted by the administration on March, 1970. There was less than 100 blacks in the institution at the time, and about 65 or 70 percent attended these meetings. This was the first recognized group by residents in the Joint.

"After holding meetings, in spite of the administration telling us to stop, we were given the go ahead. We were placed on the call sheet and given meeting space. The administration also found funds for travel for our sponsor, Wally Webster. It was now summer of 1970, and the number of black prisoners was beginning to swell. Self-government was in office and since the blacks and lifers had the only recognized groups, they had all the power. They were able to dominate the elections, putting their people in key positions, elective and otherwise. So the power these groups held [Lifers and BPFU] was generated by the recognition of these groups by the administration. They had the ear, and held regular meetings with the superintendent and other administrative staff.

"BPFU was started because of the racism in the joint. They were able to get jobs in areas where blacks were usually excluded. They also gained respect, something that did not exist prior to the formation of the group."

A black prisoner describes how his club helps provide support for its members. Clubs, particularly those of the minority groups, serve as "family," offering help and emotional security that otherwise might not be found in the prison. Despite the problems that develop when the clubs "war" against each other, the positive contribution they make far outweighs their negative aspects.

Hank: "I'll give you some idea about BPFU. The power of the clubs has been taken away so they don't have as much freedom or power to do the things they was doing before. At one time we had our own building and we'd hold classes.

"A lot of blacks that come to the Joint, in my opinion, a lot of the people's problems start with the inability to communicate. A lot of the guys didn't get very far in school. Some don't read very well or write very well and can't communicate very well and that causes a lot of problems; so the thing I was interested in was teachin some of the guys verbal skills and things like basic English and reading and how to write."

Cardozo-Freeman: "Do you have programs that help the *fish* that come in?"

Hank: "We have outreach programs for the new guys that come in, an orientation-type deal where we take em around and show them how to do everything, you know, the simple things that you have to learn, like where to send your kites, if you want a job, how to get a job, how to get enrolled in school. Most guys that come in on the Chain don't have any cigarettes so we have a fund to loan them cigarettes until they can get on their feet or get a job. Also, in a crowded situation, . . . we used to have guys that come in on the Chain . . . the cell situation is quite unusual. You can get put in a cell with guys who can throw you over the tier and say, 'Beat it.' So we have a little deal where we try to move guys into cells where we know they will be compatible.

"Some of the guys coming off the Chain don't know anyone, but most guys comin in off the Chain are repeaters and quite naturally they know someone here that are from the same walk of life, but in case they don't, we try and find a place that's compatible for them.

"We have drama workshops. Each of the instructors are guys

that were involved in that type thing on the streets. So we have a drama workshop and teach drama skills and put on plays.

"BPFU is also a place where you can sort of socialize with your own people. In other words, stay off the Breezeway. Keep you out of danger; keep you out of trouble. If you're hangin around the Breezeway, there's no way in the world you're going to keep from getting into any trouble."

Cardozo-Freeman: "How is the club supportive, help you make it through the prison experience?"

Hank: "It's supportive in many different ways. It brings you in contact with people on the outside. Once a year we have a celebration on June 19. People come from outside and we put on plays and have music and eat good food for a change. All the people bring in food and everybody has a good time.

"It's also supportive in so far as getting into trouble. A lot of times the guys won't know the ropes of what's happening at the Joint and they'll get in trouble, or they'll get into debt or someone will get into your debt. Also it acts as a buffer between two warring factions to make sure a whole lot of bloodshed doesn't come down."

Cardozo-Freeman: "How about emotional or psychological support?"

Hank: "Well, it's always better if you can find one corner on this earth where you can go and be surrounded by your peers. It's a feeling of release. At one time BPFU was a place where the black people could relax from the tension of being locked up. They took all clubs away and now the guys meet in the auditorium. All we have now is a plain office and you can't get all the blacks you have at Walla Walla to congregate in that little office. We got over 400 blacks here. Now when we have a meeting we use the auditorium. Before we had our own building. It was called the Walter Carter Hall in memory of a brother that was hung by the police a long time ago. Well, they said it was suicide but a lot of times that just isn't true.

"So anyway, we also are involved in a juvenile offender-type program. It was wrote up a few years ago. We just finally got it implemented. It's interracial, blacks, whites, Indian, Chicanos; but BPFU wrote the proposal.

"Some of the problems come about when you have a power

struggle between the clubs. All our wars start behind two people. That's all it takes. Say an Indian peels a black. O.K., sneaks up on him and peels his head, and he's been active in the BPFU and he's a regular brother and everybody likes him. So he comes over and he says, 'Hey, that guy peeled my head. He's claiming he'll kill me. I need some brother to come and help me straighten this out.' So really there would be no alternative but for a group of brothers to get together and straighten it out, and that way wars break out.

"Anytime you have that many groups, everyone either belongs to some club or some clique. It's a matter of survival, protection in numbers. You have the Bikers, the Indians have their club; the Chicanos. You even have a couple Aryan Brotherhoods. They don't call it KKK, but they're pretty under cover. They came out in the open once after the guys. 'Well, we're going to make sure all the young white boys that get off the Chain won't experience any trouble.' But it turned into a Nazi-type organization and they had to disband it. Anyway it's there but it's undercover.

"It's amazing that people with so many different backgrounds can get along. It's really no rampant racism so far as the inmates are concerned. I mean they all feel like 'We're in this together and we got to survive.' But Walla Walla is a lot better than most other joints as far as the races getting along. Matter of fact, I cell with a white dude. Three of us in a cell, another black guy and a white dude and it's cool and everybody gets along."

The Muslims

The Islamic community at Walla Walla (The American Muslim Brotherhood) is a religious organization. Although not one of the big five clubs, its role in the prison has been both important and influential. Initially, prison administrations across the country feared the rise of the Black Muslim organization believing that they were a threat to security. Muslims, who are highly disciplined and dedicated to the teachings of Allah, however, never initiate violence. Aziz, a member of the Muslim Brotherhood, talks about the organization at Walla Walla.

"The Muslim Brotherhood was instrumental in changing institutional policy, acting as advisors for many clubs; and as an example of unity, we often sponsored club head dinners. We provided a peaceful area whereby everyone could settle their disputes in an intelligent and respectful manner. There was two brothers by the name of Harold X and George X who exercised tact, diplomacy, and wisdom in resolving disputes.

"In the 70s Muslims were considered militants preaching racism instead of adherence to the Islamic teachings. We policed and checked our members and settled our own problems. Many external problems were avoided because a Muslim is never the aggressor in word or action. If a Believer lost his life simply because he was a Muslim, we would avenge his death by taking the lives of ten of their [whatever club] best.

"Inez, please don't misunderstand me! We were not in the category of punks, breezeway bums, biblepushers, snitches, and those on the bottom rung of the prison hierarchy. Muslims have a greater respect for decency and authority. Muslims have a direction and good sound principles that will not allow us to follow emotional and irrational prison leaders.

"Survival for the Muslim in this unnatural environment is much greater than the hustler slippin and slidin or the snitch constantly looking over his shoulder or the doper looking for another hit or a rig. A Muslim must put his righteousness on front street every day, and people laugh at him. They think it stupid of him to object to smoking, abusive language, smut, drugs, etc.; abstaining from all those things that lead him away from worshiping the one true god [Allah].

"The Islamic Community is one of the few groups really trying to do positive things that will benefit the inmates as well as the prison officials. The pervasive theme of Al-Islam signifies 'peace,' which can be readily seen in the deeds and actions of the Muslim. Our intention was to lessen the possibility of conflict between inmate versus inmate or inmates versus administration, and to unite under one banner or support one common cause for the good of everyone. We didn't have the last word in anything but we had an equal voice in every issue. I believe the prison administration recognized this and, therefore, allowed us to sponsor club head dinners. These dinners were usually held in the Steward's department. A representative from every club or organization would be in attendance. The purpose of these dinner meetings was to provide a peaceful area whereby everyone could settle their disputes intelligently and in a respectful manner, and to dispel all rumors by confronting one another face to face. The bottom line is 'to want for your *brother* what you want for *yourself.*' "

Chicano Club

The Chicanos represent a little more than four percent of the prison population. Three distinct subgroups exist within the one group—the city-bred *vato loco*, who hails from Los Angeles or other large cities in the Southwest; the small-town Mexican-American who has migrated north and settled in small communities in Washington; and the immigrant from Mexico who speaks little or no English. The Mexican Mafia and La Nuestra Familia, two factions who war against each other in the California prison system, do not exist in the Washington prison system, although some of the Chicano prisoners in the prison who come from California have been members of these groups.[17] The Chicano identified earlier by Delorme as *good people* describes the Chicano population in the prison and some of the problems they have. Approximately one-third of the men, according to one Chicano prisoner, speak little or no English.

"We have three factions of Chicanos. We have guys from Mexico who speak very little English and once in awhile we bump into a guy who's got some understanding of both languages. There's the guys from the suburban areas, not from the big cities but from Sunnyvale or Walla Walla, and these types of Chicanos, they're not gang-oriented or nothing like that. They're like family people who have hot tempers or they booze once in awhile and they catch a fight or they might shoot somebody. Sometimes these people come from cities.

"The people from Mexico in here, most of them who have come over here are simply down-to-earth people. They're real naive. They ain't hip to how to play the game or manipulation. They ain't been indoctrinated to the city life up here in America, so they come up here for one purpose—to make money and try to support their families, but they get up here and they get caught up in this fast life and they don't know how to adapt to it and they end up catching a beef. Then on catching a beef, they come in here and life's even faster here than out there.

"The survival part, the communicating department—how'd you like to feel being caught in China somewhere and you speak American and very few people in there speak American? Everybody is speaking Chinese so that you're confused. You don't know what's going on. You're scared and you're vulnerable.[18] Just all those little different feelings that can be created in a person takes away any kind of self-worth that they've got. And they gotta count on this person for something. They gotta depend on that person to interpret. All we had was white counselors. Now what's a white counselor . . . how's a white counselor gonna interpret? As president of the Chicano Center, I could go to a counselor with a Mexican from Mexico, interpret for him, then the Classification people wouldn't know nothing about where this guy's coming from since they wasn't there when the person was communicating for the guy, so when the Mexican goes to Classification he's going to get the short end of the stick cause he can't explain his situation.

"Anyway, we got another group, the *vato locos*, the guys who grew up in the big cities like L.A. They know how to play the game.

"So we got these three factions. They can be pulled together by the right leader. When I was down there as president, I knew all those Chicanos from Mexico. I knew all the ones they call 'foreigners' and I knew all the *vatos locos*. They all know me. They all respect me. I get along with them and I tell them, 'You know, man, you're brown and I'm brown. That's our common denominator. We all like beans. We all like tortillas. We all got families out there.' And these are the things that they stop and look at. And as long as you can get some kind of hook to work with and get them to see, then they start treating each other right.

"But when you come from different backgrounds and different cultures, it's hard. It's just like you get a guy from Alabama. He comes up with 'you all.' He has that real accent. Well, he gets around guys from Colorado and the accent sounds funny. If these people don't have an understanding [of what they share in common] well then they talk about them or laugh at them [the men from Mexico]. These things build up complexes and

stuff. It causes trouble within the group. So we have conflicts in
identity.

"Another thing, we're far away from where the majority of our
people are. We're decentralized. We're a minority in this area, so
they tend to seek each other out cause there's only a few. Where we
come from we comprise the majority [Southwest]."

Indian Club

The Indian Club attempts to serve as a support system for two
groups—reservation Indians and urban Indians. Reservation
Indians, in particular, suffer greatly from prison confinement and
often retreat into alcohol or sniffing glue to escape their condition
in prison. Officials have recognized the need to allow native Americans to practice their religion, and a sweat lodge is maintained;
however, prejudice and misunderstanding of the function of the
sweat lodge by some guards causes much bad feeling. Native
Americans are greatly feared by the population, particularly when
they go on the "warpath." Delorme talks about the situation of his
people in the prison.

"Reservation Indians are very quiet and don't mix with the
population. They are slow to make friends and are drawn toward
each other. These guys are defensive and generally uneducated,
seldom reaching the eighth grade. Their beliefs clash with urban
values. One of the things they have in common is booze. Reservations are very isolated places. Some places have electricity, although some don't; but they do see TV. Their view of the world
comes from TV, or the advice and stories from the old people. So
it must be very confusing. Reservation Indians come in for violent
crimes like murder. Seldom sophisticated crimes like paper hanging or armed robbery. Murder, committed either in a tavern or at
a party while blind drunk, is the usual story.

"Their religious beliefs run from none to very traditional.
Indian religion is kept quiet and is practiced almost at the drop of
a hat. The ceremonies are not elaborate—a pipe, a drum, and
eagle feathers are the tools. The Medicine Man is for special
occasions.

"Indians pray together more than just Sundays. Indians pray

alone in their houses while holding the eagle feathers. They speak to the Grandfathers, the ancestors. They praise the Mother Earth. They honor the four spirits of the earth—wind, earth, sun, north for the land of the Snow People; the eagle, the four-leggeds, the winged people, the fish people, all the animal brothers and sisters.

"These beliefs are somewhat removed by the forced attempt at assimilation into the white culture that the urban Indian goes through. We [urban Indians] relearn our truths from the traditionals, but we do not live the way our religion teaches. The Indian path is one of beauty; not one of death and destruction.

"The urban Indians are on that fast track and move too fast for our reservation brothers in the prison. The reservation Indian suffers more from the closeness of the prison; he does not accept the prison and resists the rules just as all Indians have fought control and genocide by the white man in power. We learn from each other, but more often than not we lead each other into the jaws of the monster.

"The reservation Indian is so far removed from education that his learning ability is affected. It is a very hard chore for him to enter the completely white-oriented school in this prison and make any progress. When he tries to work in the industries or the vocational school, he will get into trouble because he will discover that there are chemicals that when put on a rag and inhaled will eliminate the pressures of the institution and the world. He will discover that he can see visions if he continues. The Indian believes that these visions are not only of the gods, but very often since they are a product of the self-conscious, they will carry a man back to the plains, the buffalo, a war party, buckskins, and blue sky. So he is hooked.

"The urban Indian also searches for these visions, so both groups are constantly in trouble with 'sniffing glue,' as it is called. It is seldom glue, but that's what is always written on the tag [for infractions]. Both groups are very proud, or at least they try to be. Very sensitive and defensive as hell.

"The Indian is not very far removed from the violence of the old days, in my observation. It takes very little booze or chemical to eliminate what small bit of control there is."

Bikers Club

Bikers are a particularly interesting category in the prison. Tough and eccentric, they are viewed with fear and fascination by much of the population. They are the "barbarians" of the culture. Membership rituals of Bikers strongly resemble college fraternity initiation rites.

"When the Bikers first began to show up at Walla Walla, they were few in numbers. Three California gang members, all Hell's Angels, came in after a bust in Seattle for one thing or another. These were the first that I ever noticed. Actually it was during a period of the 1960s when their particular club was in the limelight all across the nation. It was also during that period when we were all building clubs.

"They hung out together and, of course, they had many good stories to tell about fights, rapes, robberies, drinking, fucking, riding around the country on their hogs, or choppers. Anyway, other guys were attracted and they began to build a club of their own, since there wasn't any opposition from the administration. They also started to wear the uniform of the Biker—dirty Levi jackets with sleeves cut off at the shoulder, dirty jeans, the dirtier the better, long hair, sunglasses, motorcycle boots, chains hanging off the belt, pins, flags, emblems, club colors with Hell's Angels death head badge sewn on the jacket. Other members of other clubs—like the Banditos from Texas, now from Washington state, the Gypsy Jokers from Portland, the Comancheros from Washington [an Indian club], these guys started recruiting from the population.

"A lot of members had never even been close to a motorcycle. The new members had to go through a series of trials and tribulations to earn their badge [colors]. They had to be what is called a 'prospect' during this stage, which lasted a couple months. They must do whatever is asked of them—like running around waiting on the tables of the regular members, washing clothes, cleaning the houses of the Bikers' tier in Eight Wing. I don't think they are required to give head or anything like that since the Bikers always have punks hanging around just for that purpose.

"The Bike Club never was into anything social. They are super clannish and do outrageous things whenever they get a chance, like hugging and kissing whenever they get a notion. The overall appearance is strange to most guys in here.

"Not everyone, but some people are outraged by the sight of homosexuals, Bikers, hippies. We have a larger than normal share of square johns and rednecks among the cons, unlike a California joint where everyone is conditioned to creeps everywhere you turn on the streets of L.A. or San Francisco. Their strangeness comes from the attention-grabbing acts they fall into, the sloppy way they dress and live, and the supposed lack of concern for anyone or anything but their own brothers. It's all a game. Guys tire of it and move on to better things.

"The real clubs on the streets haven't got respect for the prison Bikers, except for their own members. They are very seldom welcome to come out and ride with a club.

"The Joint Bike Club fucked things off by not being careful about who they let join. They let punks get into their ranks, men in the Joint who were meek as hell and didn't have friends until they joined the Bike Club. They were involved in a lot of violence and gained their reputation through force, which was their intention.

"Bikers never have had the power in the Joint, but they did rule the Breezeway through fear for a couple of years. Bikers like to run the dope game, also extortions and protection. They would be ashamed to be known as do-gooders. So their social contacts are strictly with outside bike clubs. They had a shop where they fixed motorcycles and painted bikes. That was their business.

"They party more than anyone else in here and a hell of a lot of them are doing big time. That is what seems strange to a lot of guys—no visible efforts towards programming, or playing for the gate like a sane person would do. Peer pressure stops that kind of foolishness on the part of the members."

Although each category defines a particular experience and status, all men fit into more than one category. A *hustler*, for example, might be *doper*, a Biker, and a *Joint tough guy*. It is unlikely, however, that a *rapo, punk,* or *fish* would be identified as *good people*.

Considerable information about prisoner worldview is gained through an analysis of the status given to the different categories. To begin with, the all inclusive label *con* breaks down into real *cons* and inmates and reveals the tenacity of the old values ordered around the convict code. Some men after serving a difficult and demanding apprenticeship are admitted to the "profession" of the real *con*, thus signifying that they have earned the respect of their peers. The real *con* is compared to the professional soldier; he, too, has been tested and proven genuine. Inmates, on the other hand, never acquire this prized status in the prison hierarchy because they are not able to learn, or choose not to learn, to "walk that walk and talk that talk." Such values about personal conduct and behavior imply that a certain kind of manliness, stamina, and attitude is necessary to survive in an atmosphere of constant battle and battle preparedness. Like professional soldiers, professional, or real, *cons* are skilled on the prison battlefield. Values such as these reflecting the reality of prison life give further credence to the belief that the code, although it may develop variations, will not disappear despite the dramatic changes taking place in prisoner characteristics.

The important subcategory *street people* identifies the new worldview that entered into the prison beginning in the early 1960s. The tension between the old prisoner, the real *con*, and the new prisoner reflects this culture clash, which has been taking place for two decades. The two worldviews battle daily with each other, an indication of the prisoner's world in transition. Despite the strength of the antiorder, antistructure point of view of the new inmate, the survival value of the old code held by the real *cons* will insure against its demise. Some kind of order has to be imposed in the midst of the often confusing and disruptive circumstances of daily existence in the prison caused, in part, by the new antiorder point of view, since chaos coupled with intense physical danger in such close quarters makes life intolerable. New official policy changes—more restrictions on the prisoners—will also impact upon the new worldview in process.

The impact and importance of the new worldview should not be underestimated. Many *street people* react to their imprisonment with defiance aimed particularly at guards who "do the work of the enemy." This behavior is not a recent phenomenon in prisons, although the number of men who are reacting to their imprisonment in this manner is greatly increased. Verbal abuse and obscenities, taunts, spitting at guards, and hurling urine and feces at them when locked up in the *Hole* are common tactics of defiance, which always bring down severe retribution from outraged guards. Gresham Sykes identifies a category named by prisoners in the 1950s in the New Jersey Maximum Security Prison as "ball busters." Possessing a "certain Promethean quality; they refuse to come to terms with their helplessness, their loss of autonomy, and... continue to shout their defiance despite the ultimate hopelessness of their position."[19] Defiant *street people* of the 1960s and 1970s in this prison personify this Promethean stance.

The status given to the different categories in the prisoner's hierarchy reflects a realistic adaptation to prison existence, as well as the importance and strength in prison of traditional values carried over from mainstream society. At the top of the hierarchy stand two opposite types, both of whom are leaders. Both are intelligent and both act in the interests of the population as a whole; both are highly respected, although for different reasons. One is *good people*; the other is intelligent *killers*. The prisoner, despite his alleged amoral point of view, values and respects decency in human behavior and character. *Good people* represent the preservation of this ideal in the prison. However, the prisoner is a realist, also. He recognizes that he is not living in the Garden of Eden but rather that his world is full of violent and desperate men who do not play by gentlemen's rules. Violence met by violence is understood as an important tactic in such a world. For this reason, intelligent *killers* are valued. When necessary they can be called upon to bring an uneasy peace into the prisoner's environment. Men possessing two kinds of power—moral power and the power to instill fear—stand highest in the prisoner's hierarchy because both are recognized as needed in the community. Both perform valuable functions which help the prisoner to survive.

Politicians and *Joint tough guys* hold high status because both also serve useful functions in the prison community. The *Joint politician* speaks up for prisoner needs with the prison administration, and the *Joint tough guy* can be called upon to beat up individuals in the population who are bullying others. Intelligence and verbal facility coupled with courage in one and brute physical power and courage in the other are recognized as qualities in certain pris-

oners that are useful. Again, this is evidence of a sensible accommodation to the realities of prison life. Someone has to "face up to
the Man," and someone is needed to discourage the predators who
if left unchecked contribute to considerable unrest in the community.
Intelligent *killers* and *Joint tough guys* operate as policemen, in a
sense, keeping order through fear. *Good people* and *Joint politicians*
serve as statesmen, using reason and persuasion to keep order.
The prisoner's world in many ways resembles the world beyond
the walls of the prison.

The attitudes toward those prisoners given derogatory labels
and low status strongly reflects values, attitudes, and prejudices
that come from mainstream society. None of the people holding
low status are viewed as contributing anything of value to the
prison culture; some contribute to violence and unrest; others are
regarded as nuisance; a few are involved in behavior that is viewed
as reprehensible, and the behavior of one group—*snitches*—is
intolerable. A few, *punks* and *queens*, in particular, often face daily
humiliation from the population. Like conventional society, the
prison values those in its culture who make a positive contribution to its survival and holds in low esteem those who do not.
Those whom the prisoners regard as threats to their situation are
dealt with in ways similar to those employed in the majority
culture—indifference, ostracism, contempt, ridicule, harrassment,
severe physical punishment, and death.

The prisoner's world, in many ways, is a microcosm of the
society that holds him captive. Because his world is compressed,
what occurs is intensified, less subtle, more direct, and at times,
distorted. The model for building his prisoner world, however,
comes in great part from the world beyond the walls of the prison.
In attempting to cope with and survive in his dangerous captive
domain, the prisoner manifests much of the same social behavior
and assumes many of the same values and attitudes as the society
from which he came.

The clubs serve the very important function of providing safety
and identification for the various groups. Such identification is
particularly important for the minority or ethnic groups in the
prison. The role of the "big five" is similar to that of "super
powers" in the prisoner's world, which, in times of danger, form

alliances with each other (and with smaller clubs) to maintain a balance of power in order that peace reign. In this respect the prison resembles a little world of its own with "countries" and "armies," and even a "United Nations"—the Resident Council. On the whole, the "big five super powers" operate in a positive manner, except when "war" breaks out between the racial groups, not unlike what happens in the outside world.

The prisoner makes the best of a precarious situation. Using his talents and those of his fellow prisoners, he faces his situation realistically. Through the process of naming or labeling he assumes a considerable degree of control over his experience, thus making the reality of his condition more manageable. The ordering of his world manifests a firm grasp of reality and a respect for those qualities that make survival under dangerous circumstances possible.

NOTES

[1]Delorme is doing most of the "performing" in this chapter. I specifically sought this information from him on one of my field trips to the prison.

[2]Nathan Kantrowitz, "The Vocabulary of Race Relations in Prisons," *Publications of the American Dialect Society*, Vol. 51, 1969, pp. 23–24. Nathan Kantrowitz and Joanne S. Kantrowitz have written an important study on prisons called *Stateville Names: A Prison Vocabulary*, based on research data collected from inmates at Joliet Penitentiary in Illinois.

[3]James P. Spradley and David W. McCurdy, *The Cultural Scene: Ethnography in Complex Society*, p. 63.

[4]See Theodore Roszak, *The Making of a Counter Culture* (Garden City, N.Y.: Anchor Books, 1969); Roger Lewis, *Outlaws of America: The Underground Press and its Context* (Middlesex, England: Penguin Books, Ltd., 1972); and Kenneth Leech, *Youth Quake* (Totowa, N.J.: Littlefield, Adams & Company, 1977).

[5]See Donald Clemmer, *The Prison Community* (New York: Holt, Rinehart and Winston, 1958); and Gresham Sykes, *The Society of Captives* (Princeton, N.J.: Princeton University Press, 1958). Both of these important studies deal with the world of the prisoner before the 1960s. John Irwin's research in the California prison system is most relevant to this study since he covers the 1960s and 1970s, and because the Washington prison system in many ways patterns itself after the California system. See John Irwin, *Prisons in Turmoil* (Boston: Little, Brown & Company, 1980).

[6]See David W. Maurer, *Whiz Mob* (New Haven, Conn.: College & University Press, 1964), pp. 181–199. Also Edwin H. Sutherland, *The Professional Thief* (Chicago: The University of Chicago Press, 1937), pp. 197–228.

[7]In "The Lingo of the Good-People," published in 1935, David W. Maurer wrote, "To the modern gangster an old-timer is good people. . . . Even as the countless generations of criminals who preceded them, the good-people were criminal Dapper Dans, their lingo was the last word in linguistic nobbiness. . . . " *American Speech*, Vol. X (1935), pp. 10–23. Good-people were "old-timers or professionals who had *packed the racket in*." The word then, as now, was used both in the singular and plural, as for example, "Gene is good people." Maurer's research was done among men serving life sentences in large penitentiaries. In a letter to me, dated May 25, 1981, Maurer wrote about the label *good-people*: "I think it is interesting to note that this not only verifies your finding the words in current usage, but also that it goes back at least 100 years since I was interviewing people 70 years of age when I wrote that original article. This goes perhaps even further back in human memory to establish a 'new' word, which is only new because the dictionary makers have not found it in print. This term must have been well established when these *old-timers turned out on the racket* as young men, so that its history must go well beyond 100 years."

[8]*Society of Captives*, p. 102.

[9]Although the politician or Joint politician thrives today at Walla Walla, he does not exactly fit Clarence Schrag's description. Schrag's "politician" was a confidence man in society who in prison continued to utilize his high-powered personality to connive and manipulate the inmates, guards and administration. He belongs to the underworld category of criminals whose intelligence, skill, and talent with the "fix" seldom brought him behind the walls of a prison. Maurer's research on these fascinating elite underground figures is extensive. See David W. Maurer, *The American Confidence Man* (Springfield, Ill.: Charles C Thomas, Publisher, 1973). Clarence Schrag identifies five important social types in the Washington State Penitentiary in the 1940s. These were "right guys," "outlaws," "politicians," "square johns," and "dings." The term "right guy" has given way in most instances to "good people," and "outlaw" is almost never used. "Outlaws," in some respects resemble "state-raised youth" and *Joint tough guys*, while some of the qualities of "right guys" fit *good people* in the prison today. See Clarence Clyde Schrag, "Social Types in a Prison Community," a thesis submitted for the Degree of Master of Arts, University of Washington, 1944.

[10]The *Dictionary of American Slang* defines anyone who *hustles* as "one who earns a living by illegal means; a petty criminal," and dates this definition to around 1930. The term dates back to 1891 with respect to begging, and to around 1915 with respect to stealing. *Dictionary of American Slang*, Compiled by Harold Wentworth and Stuart Berg Flexner. Second Supplemental Edition (New York: Thomas Y. Crowell Company, 1975), pp. 277–278. Although it has become strongly identified with blacks, the term *hustle* did not originate with them. John Irwin identifies the *hustler* as the black inmate in the California prison system. He describes *hustling* as thievery adapted by blacks from the "short con" of the white "flim-flammers" who invaded the South in the 19th and early 20th centuries. "In general, hustling meant making money through one's wit and conversation such as 'greasy pig,' 'three card monte,' 'the pigeon drop' [and] rackets such as the numbers and

pimping." John Irwin, *Prisons in Turmoil*, p. 53. Julius Hudson describes the world of the black *hustler* in "The Hustling Ethic," in *Rappin' and Stylin' Out*, Edited by Thomas Kochman (Urbana: University of Illinois Press, 1972), pp. 410–424.

[11]John Irwin describes this group as "tough," with clique-forming propensity and a "tendency to use violence in settling disputes." For them the "streets are a place where [they] temporarily sojourn and engage in wild, abandoned pleasuring," seldom staying out of prison for very long." See John Irwin, *The Felon* (Englewood Cliffs, N.J.: Prentice-Hall, Inc., 1970), pp. 27–29.

[12]Gresham Sykes writes that "the frustration of the prisoner's ability to make choices and the frequent refusals to provide an explanation for the regulations and commands descending from the bureaucratic staff involve a profound threat to the prisoner's self-image because they reduce the prisoner to the weak helpless, dependent status of childhood . . . men under guard stand in constant danger of losing their identification with the normal definition of an adult and the imprisoned criminal finds his picture of himself as a self-determining individual being destroyed by the regime of custodians." See Gresham Sykes, *The Society of Captives* (Princeton, N.J.: Princeton University Press, 1958), pp. 75–76.

[13]This prison tradition of name-calling somewhat resembles the black tradition of "sounding," a "game of verbal insult known in the past as 'playing the dozens.' . . . " See "Toward an Ethnography of Black American Speech Behavior" by Thomas Kochman in *Rappin' an Stylin' Out: Communication in Urban Black America*, Thomas Kochman, Editor (Urbana: University of Illinois Press, 1972), pp. 241–264.

[14]Erving Goffman, *Stigma: Notes on the Management of Spoiled Identity* (Englewood Cliffs, N.J.: Prentice-Hall, Inc., 1965), p. 87.

[15]*The Society of Captives*, p. 87.

[16]This is an expression used by the officials that implies that tension is building in the population.

[17]See John Irwin, *Prisons in Turmoil*, pp. 189–190.

[18]Don Pedro, age 56, imprisoned for the first time in his life for killing one of four men who beat and robbed him, speaks and understands almost no English. In a taped conversation he told me that during an outbreak of violence in 1979, guards rushed into the kitchen where he worked and issued orders for all prisoners to go immediately to the Big Yard, then hurled tear gas at them. Don Pedro, confused and frightened, thought the guards were ordering the men to go to their cellblocks so he rushed to his wing, only to be beaten by guards for disobeying orders which he did not comprehend. In Hispanic culture, the label *don* is bestowed only upon a man who is highly respected for his decency and honorable behavior. All the Chicanos whom I spoke to at the prison believed that Don Pedro should never have been sent to prison for what he did; since he was defending his life and property and because he had lived such an exemplary life, respected by those who knew him.

[19]*The Society of Captives*, pp. 99–100.

Chapter 5

SLIPPING AND SLIDING

In describing the behavior of *Dopers* in the previous chapter, Delorme states, "It's a game, just as everything in prison is a game. Play the game right and you'll win; at the very least you'll survive." To an outsider, this seems to be an inappropriate procedure for accommodating to prison existence.[1] By definition, a game is a form of play, an amusement involving competition under specific rules with the goal as victory, or winning. To play a game well requires skill, endurance, and courage. In every game, the risk of losing is involved; the gambling element, taking a chance, is always present.

Johann Huizinga, the Dutch cultural historian recognized by anthropoligists for his contribution to the study of play,[2] defines play "as a voluntary activity or occupation executed within certain fixed limits of time or place, according to rules freely accepted and absolutely binding, having its aim in itself and accompanied by a feeling of tension, joy and the consciousness that it is 'different' from 'ordinary' life."[3]

Many of the elements Huizinga defines as play are evident in the "games" played by the prisoners at Walla Walla. First of all, the games are survival games. The prisoner chooses of his own volition those games by which he will *do his time* while he is locked within the confines of the prison. Although he is free to choose which of the games he will play, he *must* choose, since his survival depends upon it. One has to play survival games in prison. Both time and place for playing the game are fixed within certain limits. The period of time he plays the game is the length of his sentence, and the playground is bounded by or restricted to the space marked off by the walls of the prison. It is a temporary world in which he plays, and within this arena exists a particular and unique order that determines how he will play his game. He

153

understands that the rules are binding; he knows the rules for playing and the consequences should he fail. The aim of the game is in itself—that is, winning or surviving. Because the outcome is never certain and the stakes are high, the game he plays is filled with excitement or tension. Success at playing brings him a certain sense of exhilaration, perhaps even joy. He recognizes that the game he plays is different from the ordinary games of life that people play. The prison game is an extension of a larger survival game played on the streets.[4] The player, whether inside or outside the walls of the prison, recognizing that his game is out of the ordinary, is constantly aware of the consequences should he fail to make the right moves. He plays, using all his intelligence, skill, strength, and cunning, testing himself against his opponent, sometimes frauding him in the process. Through his playing the game, he expresses his interpretation, his view of life, and his world. Although an outsider might focus with disapproval on the sometimes fraudulent aspects of his game, the prisoner does not look upon what he does as fraud. He does what he must do in order to survive, using every game he knows to accomplish this end.

Placing Delorme's statement that "everything in prison is a game" into the framework of Huizinga's concept of play, it can be demonstrated that the prisoner plays a war game, a game of survival against an "enemy." Although "war games" in today's world are pretend games in which soldiers practice at pretend war and where the "dead" do not really die but rather return to life to repeat their performance on the battlefield the next day, in archaic cultures, as Huizinga points out, *actual* war was a game. Men went out on a *real* battlefield and played for keeps. Dying was not pretend. "Ever since words existed for fighting and playing, men have been wont to call war a game. . . . The two ideas often seem to blend absolutely in the archaic mind. Indeed, fighting that is bound by rules bear the formal characteristics of play by that very limitation."[5] The prisoner plays, as do the warriors in archaic culture, using "bodily strength or force of arms . . . reason . . . fists . . . big words, boasting, vituperation . . . cunning and deceit."[6] Sometimes the antagonists are not the prison authorities but other prisoners, as for example, when two clubs "go to war" against each other over a disagreement. The game is a play of survival against the forces of the prison, its authorities and policies, and against the forces within the prison population that threaten the survival of the prisoners. *Slipping and sliding* is the expression used to identify this game of survival played by the men in the prison.

METAPHOR FOR SURVIVAL

In pointing out that play is involved in all the "great archetypal activities of human society," including language, Huizinga writes that "behind every abstract expression there lies the boldest of metaphors, and *every metaphor is a play upon words*" [italics added].[7] The phrase *slipping and sliding*, which is the metaphor for survival in the prison, aptly pictures the point of view that the prisoner carries with him of "playing a game." In actuality, "playing a game" is a metaphor that precedes *slipping and sliding*. The prisoner looks at survival as *if* he were playing a game. This is not to say that the one is equal to the other. Survival is *not* a game; rather, looking upon survival *as if* it were a game helps the prisoner deal with his precarious situation in such a manner as to make his existential condition both more tolerable and manageable. He attaches the connotation of play or playfulness to his tense and life-threatening condition because this "as if" makes possible his survivability. By playing down the seriousness of the situation, it becomes manageable in his mind.

There is much in the language of the prisoner that connects survival to play: a con *makes a play for the gate*; the prison is a *play pen*, a *day-care center*, a *country club*, or is referred to as *fun and games*. When describing some action, it is *running a game down*. One prisoner asks another to *back his play* or *back his move*. Some *play games with the pigs*; others *play the queens*. *Coming in for a pit-stop* implies that the men are involved in a contest or race. *Conning* and "playing games" are often synonymous for the men.[8]

The phrase *slipping and sliding* defines and holds within it many images, which although applicable in the conventional sense correctly picture the point of view the prisoner carries with him in his game of survival. Some of these images are to move without attracting attention, to go swiftly and safely, to escape, to slip one's bonds or to break free of the restrictions of the situation, to give the slip or to slip one over, and to trick or hoodwink. Implicit in the expression also is the possibility of taking a fall, of making a mistake, or of slipping and "sliding" into trouble or disaster. In black speech, the term *slipping and sliding* means moving around quietly and secretively, as in the lyrics, "slippin' and a slidin', peepin' and a hidin', been such a long time ago. . . . " In the argot of the underworld, David Maurer points out that the term *slip* goes way back and was originally, at least in one sense, a type of counterfeit coin: thus to give someone a *slip* was to give him something false, which eventually came to mean a false departure; that is, a sneaky one. *Slide* also has an interesting history in the *lingo* of the underworld. The *slide* is a type of short change maneuver that used to be popular at carnivals and circuses. A vender would give someone the *slide* by counting out change, especially one-dollar bills, with one or more of the bills folded so the person receiving the change could not detect the shortage. Since this was done in front of a group of people and usually in a hurry, the person cheated had little recourse when he discovered he had been *fleeced*. He would complain, but with so many witnesses the *con man* had a perfect defense.[9]

Another expression sometimes used instead of *slipping and sliding*, which holds somewhat the same meaning for the men, is *ducking and dodging*. The images this phrase projects are to dive or plunge, to bend or turn so as to avoid a blow, and to move quickly. *Ducking and dodging* images the avoidance of violence or danger and adds the dimension of evasiveness, or devising clever plans to outwit. To *play the dodge* is an old term in the underworld and means to hide out, whereas *duck* in the underworld means more or less to look out. Although Delorme states that *slip and slide* and *duck and dodge* both deal with survival, there are differences in their meaning, as demonstrated in their usage in the narratives. One may *slip and slide* in a rather cool and unobtrusive way in the prison, whereas, one must *duck and dodge* in a much more open, harsh manner.[10]

Placing the important daily preoccupation with staying alive into the realm of play can, on one level, give the prison the appearance of being a "stage" on which the play of survival is enacted or performed.[11] The prisoners and guards are both "actors" and "audience." The play can be comic, fun, monotonous or boring, exciting, absurd, suspenseful, dangerous, horrifying, cruel, and tragic. Death often plays a leading role on the stage, as does fraud and brutality. When an "actor" is killed, the "audience" experiences a cathartic sense of relief that they are not the "role." Aristotle's *Poetics* applies to the tragic aspects of the prison drama. Oftentimes comedy, the theatre of the absurd, and the theatre of cruelty prevail, also.

SLIPPING AND SLIDING—PART I—ROUTINE SURVIVAL GAMES

Hard Time—Easy Time

Since survival is the foremost preoccupation of the prisoner, the manner in which he chooses to *do his time* plays an important role in the structuring of his worldview. If he looks upon his incarceration with self-pity, blaming society for his predicament, he is a poor loser and his attitude becomes colored by this point of view. He *snivels* all the time, blaming everyone else for his situation. He lacks a sense of humor; anger and bitterness are his constant companions. His preoccupation with this stance keeps him from concentrating on learning all the ways that are available to him to make his predicament less painful, and he increases his chances of getting into trouble with both the guards and other prisoners. He refuses, in other words, to learn to play the *slipping and sliding* game. The prisoner who chooses this style of life in prison does *hard time*.

Delorme: "It helps a lot if you look at survival as a game. You're not bitchin and hollerin all the time. You know what you have to do to get out. You don't have to wonder about it or beat your head against the wall every day tryin to find ways to get out; writin letters, screamin and hollerin 'bum beef' and this and that. You just do what you gotta do cause in the end they ain't gonna let you out until they want to anyway.

"The law won the first round. That's why you're in the Joint in the first place. Just by the fact of your bein here you know you're the loser. You accept that right off the bat and learn from that. Sometimes you don't learn a damn thing. Guys like me never learned anything. You learn how to survive in here but you don't learn nothin to keep you out. I don't know if you just can't learn, or you refuse to learn, or you just want to hang on to your own rules."

Cardozo-Freeman: "Maybe some guys enjoy playing the game; enjoy playing cops and robbers."

Delorme: "Well, that's part of it, too. When you're younger it seems like the years they give you don't seem that hard. It seems like you're never gonna hit thirty, so you can do the time. I've been comin in here for pit-stops for so many years — in and out, in and out. Sometimes I'm only in here for three or four months."

Cardozo-Freeman: "*Pit-stop* — it's like you're in a fast car racing around a speedway."

Delorme: "Yeah, you come in to get healthy. Get some good meals and some sleep and go out and try it again.

"But guys who can slip and slide in here have a lot easier time. A lot easier. They cut things loose. There's some things you can only worry about so long — your wife, love, and all that kind of stuff. You have to deal with that, let go of it or you're miserable. That's part of the game, too. Learnin how to do that."

Learning how to avoid *hard time* is important for survival. *Hard time* distracts the prisoner, keeping his thoughts constantly on what he has lost — the life that he had on the outside.

"A guy that's doin hard time, the first thing he's doin hard time over is generally his wife. That's the biggest problem. A guy can come in here, the court can give him a lousy little year, which is like goin to sleep tonight and gettin up tomorrow as far as I'm concerned, and I'll be damned if he won't cry about it every day that he's here. He does hard time. He doesn't trust his wife; obviously they have problems. He's got a face like a hound dog every day he's here because of it. He does hard time. He can't cut the strings loose.

"You've gotta cut these problems loose from the outside or you can't make it in here. You got a family and you got a beautiful little daughter and you got people you love. You still got em but you can't care too much and you gotta push em to the back of your mind where they belong. You write em once in awhile and if they got problems, so what? You got problems, too, and sometimes your people send you their problems, which is fine, but not if they're bankin on you to help em because what the hell can you do?

"If a guy can't cut his family loose, then he's gonna do hard time. He wants to see em. He wants to help em. He wants to send em money and there's nothin you can do about it. Every day is filled with that and he probably will even get sick. Won't eat right. Can't cut his thinking loose long enough to go outside and exercise, play ball or something like that.

"So if your friends are doin that you try to get em interested in things. You take him out to a ball game or you talk him into goin to the movie.

"How you do your time is awful important in here. It's the difference between suicide or becoming a stone criminal. Gettin out of here half decent or becomin a criminal one-hundred percent. Sayin, 'To hell with it.'"

The prisoner who chooses to view his predicament as a continuation of a larger game in which he was participating outside the prison looks upon his incarceration simply as an indication that for the moment, at least, he has lost the game. As Delorme states, "We are all losers or we wouldn't be in the Joint: the Law won. We can accept that and vow not to make the same mistake next time." This prisoner's viewpoint helps him deal with his situation with considerable imagination and skill. He often looks upon his predicament with irony and humor. His language clearly reveals this. He has a tendency to laugh at himself, no matter what happens, and he takes great pleasure in acquiring the skills necessary to play the prison game. He is able to shake the moments of despair, which from time to time overwhelm him because of his situation. This prisoner becomes expert at *slipping and sliding* and does *easy time* in prison. Guards and other prisoners will acknowledge that he is *con-wise*; he knows "the game." Because of his view of his situation he spends no time in self-pity, wastes little time *sniveling*, and very importantly, he does not view the guards with the degree of hostility that the other prisoner does. To him the guards are simply worthy adversaries whom he tries to outwit, often with considerable success. Achieving such skill, however, does not happen overnight; it takes considerable time and practice. Obviously the game this prisoner plays often involves trying to put something over on *the Man*. Delorme describes this important aspect of the survival game.

Slipping and Sliding as Comedy— Winning the Game

Cardozo-Freeman: "Do most of the men regard prison as a game?"

Delorme: "Well, it takes awhile. When you first come in it ain't no game. It's torture. You have to figure it out. After awhile you figure out there's a lot of rules to go by. You learn on the outside that the law is a game with two sides. Just watchin television will tell you that. In prison it's a two-sided game, too. The same thing. You gotta learn how the Law works in here, too. What the rules are. You gotta learn how you can twist the rules. What the penalties are. What they're serious about; what they're not serious about. Same as they got laws outside the Walls that they don't go by much. Like they got blue laws and other kinds of laws. The rules like that inside the Joint, too, you just ignore. But there are certain things in certain areas that you have to be pretty cool in. You don't step out of bounds. You learn all the boundaries."

Cardozo-Freeman: "Is there a term in here that relates to street-wise?"

Delorme: "Yeah. Con-wise. If you know how to slip and slide, you're con-wise. I'm as con-wise as they come, which is supposed to be bad because it means you're institutionalized. They say, 'This guy's con-wise.' Con-wise to the Parole Board and to the cops means they don't trust you. It means you've learned to bullshit your way through everything so you're not to be trusted on anything you say because it's probably a lie. You hate to be termed con-wise with the Parole Board cause you know as soon as you open your mouth they're not goin to believe you so you're down, man. When they got you in that bag it's hard."

Cardozo-Freeman: "Can you give me some examples of slipping and sliding?"

Delorme: "I was tellin you about my bro. I'd say, 'Man, why don't you slide out of that kitchen tonight with some tenderloins.' He'd say, 'O.K. I'll try and see if I can do it.' And he would, too.

"He'd slip out of there with that baby, man, a whole tenderloin steak down in his belt. Blood might be comin off it . . . Yuk . . .

but it was good that night. We'd stoke the ole fire, barbeque that baby.

"The thing with the steaks, that's one form of slippin and slidin. You gotta slide past five or six bulls to get that steak out of the kitchen into the wing. So you be slippin and you do be slidin.

"I guess you can see that just about anything that you can slide by the Man would fit into that category. That includes bringin in all that sniffin glue, that cleanin fluid from the furniture area. Those guys are slippin and slidin past shakedowns and everything with that stuff to get it inside here so they can get loaded on it.

"They used to bring it inside in empty tubes like Prell® tubes and sell em for a buck apiece. It's a paint remover, varnish remover, a liquid stripper that they use in the furniture factory. They'd bring it in in small tubes and you'd get smashed. You don't drink it; you sniff it. Just turn into a dummy.

"There's several ways to bring it in. They used to throw it over the wall. Somebody would say, 'Man, where you gonna be?' I'd say, '390.' They'd say, 'O.K.' and have the spot marked inside and outside the wall, '390.' There was a great big white '390' painted on the wall. It's the same thing as a ball park on the streets. You know how they have the back walls painted 450, 300, or whatever. That's how far that wall is from home plate. We used to have a hard ball field out here so it's an old number. This guy would come out on the back dock of the furniture factory and as soon as the bulls weren't lookin, he'd check the tower guards and if they weren't lookin, he'd fire that tube, or a shampoo bottle that would fill up many tubes, over the wall and then you'd be sittin out in the Yard on the other side of the wall and so you would be there when it came over and snatch it up and slide on by the gate, slide on into the wing with it, see, and distribute it.

"Those kinds of games are just natural slippin and slidin games. You learn all the different ways to pack that stuff in. That includes knives, homemade shanks. A guy might make four or five good knife blades out there in the machine shop or one of the factories, on a grinder, using files or using strips of stainless steel, and he would rough em out, meanin he would just cut em out in blade shape and put a rough edge on em because they could be finished inside with a file. Also a handle could be put on inside. Generally they made the handle out of wood. If it was goin to get fancy, you might put a little leather on it and you'd tape all those together. No use makin just one.

"I know the last bunch of shanks I picked up, there was four taped together and they damn near killed me. I was duckin and dodgin, I'm tellin you, seein them babies come in like a fireball out of heaven. They're heavy, too. Those were all stainless steel and they were stilettos, big ones. So I picked em up real quick. They were all wrapped in masking tape. There was a little somethin in it for me, a tube of 201 for me pickin the blades up and movin em across the Yard. Then I dug a hole and buried em along the wall. I just sat on the bench and then as I sat there I just kinda swung my legs on the bench and as I swung my legs I'd dig out dirt with the toe of my shoe and when the hole was deep enough, I dropped the blades in it and then covered em back up, stomped it down and then walked in. Marked it on the wall where it was. Course, I came out and showed the guy that night where I put em and then he took em from there.

"I'm not tellin you anything the guards don't already know. We've played that game with em for a lot of years tryin to catch em not lookin, but they catch us about half the damn time. Kind of over now; don't work no more. Things change. Times change. You have to go to another game, another way to slide by."

Slipping and sliding often involves game maneuvers, which Erving Goffman calls "strategic interaction."[12] Strategic interaction involves rational decision-planning; that is, assessing a situation from every possible angle, then choosing from among the possible moves that action or play most advantageous to the party or player, despite the uncertainty or risk that may be involved.[13] The following narrative is an example of two actions or plays involving strategic interaction in prison. The first play in an absolute bust; the second is a winner. This is a continuation of Delorme's description of *slipping and sliding*.

"I made me a knife one time to sell it. I figured it would probably bring me ten bucks and I really made it nice, a double edge stiletto, real sharp on both sides. Then I cut out a wooden handle and I put the handle on it and wrapped the handle in leather. It was really nice. I made a sheath for it, and I'll be a dirty sonovabitch; I got busted. The pig ran into me on the tier.

"I was walkin down talkin to some of my partners and they were all loaded in the house. They were gettin down with the 201 and I had a couple little snorts, of course. I was kind of actin like a fool on the tier, you know, rowdy and carryin on, and this pig waved to me to come up to the end of the tier. Wanted to shake me down. So I tell him, 'Aw, fuck off.' I just kept on talkin, see. I didn't move.

"My cell was right next door and I kept rappin and I had that shank in my belt. I'd been carryin it around like a dum-dum, but we was havin some tough times in here so I started packin it for awhile, but I should have known better. And so he kept hollerin at me and finally this pig starts trottin down the tier and I says, 'Oh, shit. The motherfucker's gonna try to roust me, man. He's gonna put the arm on me.' So I took the knife out of my belt and I shoved it through the bars and these guys are all freaked out on the juice, old joy juice. We used to call it 'moon juice,' too. It really sends you to the moon. I ain't bullshittin.

"So the pig's trottin down the tier. He's got an eye on me and I tried to slide the shank into the cell and when it went in, nobody saw it. I did it so fast it just fell onto the floor in there . . . Klank! And one of the guys freaked out and kicked it back out of the cell and the sonovabitch came and landed right back in between my legs.

"And here comes the cop. Oh shit, he caught me cold. So he run back down to the desk and he called the ole goon squad over and man, I'm tryin to get my goddam head cleared up enough so I can come up with a fuckin story real quick. And there wasn't too much of a story I could use. I mean, what can you say? A fuckin shank. A shank's a shank and this was monstrous.

"So here come the ole gooners. They come on down, man, gaffeled me up, and put the cuffs on my hands. Away I went. Then they shook my house down and they found the knife's sheath layin right on my bed. Then they went to the back of my cell and found another tube of that goddam sniffer, that son of a gun. Whew! I thought I was in trouble.

"But as luck would have it, I put out a good story, man. I just had time to tell my partner what I was goin to say so he could run around real quick and tell the other guys to back my play. I told em I had picked that knife up intentionally from some guys in the cell that were loaded and I talked em out of it cause we didn't want anyone gettin hurt and in the process I got caught with it.

"So people were screamin and hollerin after I went to the hole. They went right over to Control, several guys, and they were screamin and hollerin, puttin the story down. I had told the same story when they took me in so I was out the next morning. I was tagged but I was out. I got a reprimand and warning for a thirteen inch shank, which was pretty phenomenal!

"But anyway, jeez, I never played that fuckin game again. I stayed strictly away from those knives since I really don't want to use one. I mean, hell, why carry it? But I'm tellin you, I wasn't slippin and slidin too cool that night. That time the pig slid up on me and got my ass."

Delorme is party, player, and pawn in these two scenarios of strategic interaction. In the first scenario, Delorme has succeeded in *slipping* into the wing *packing a shank* but makes the wrong play by stopping in front of his friends' *house* to sniff some *moon juice*. This causes him to become rowdy and draws the attention of the guard. As a party, he wants to avoid the discovery by the guard that he is *packing*. He quickly assesses the situation and moves to slide the *shank* into the cell. The move fails because his friends have not been forewarned and are themselves on a *trip to the moon*. One of them reacts to the arrival of the knife by kicking it right back out of the *house* and between his legs. Delorme, the pawn, now is in real trouble. In fact, he loses the game; he is caught with the goods. He fails in this first scenario because his rational decision-making powers have been clouded by the *moon juice*. The next scenario is more successful. He manages to make the best of a temporary defeat because he succeeds in clearing his head and is able to rationally assess his situation from every angle. Recognizing that the guard's *play* will be to summon the *goon squad*, he quickly moves to gather his own resources, his friends, who all collaborate with him in his fraudulent explanation of why he possessed a *shank*. Although he spends a night in the *hole*, he is released with a mere warning or *tag* for an extremely serious offense. Despite Delorme's comment that he wasn't *slipping and sliding* very well, he managed to turn a potential loss or disaster into a respectable win. Delorme proves himself immanently game-worthy. In Goffman's words, he possesses among other qualities, "the intellectual proclivity to assess all possible courses of action and their consequences ... the ability to think and act under pressure without becoming either flustered or transparent ... [and] the ability and willingness to dissemble about anything."[14] Delorme is a master gamesman. He continues:

"I'm wonderin if I'm giving you the general idea of the game. In the penitentiary it's a way of life to be able to learn the ropes; learn how to get by; how to survive; how to get around shakedowns. How to break rules without gettin tagged; how to break rules, get tagged and still get out of it; developing daily routines that slide you past all the troubles, slip you past the bulls when you're packin all the time. You might be packin a knife, packin contraband. Might be packin food out of the kitchen, which is contraband. So you have to slide easy when you're packin. It's a way of life in here.

"I slip and slide on the streets all the time. I use that term when I'm out, too, but it's not a well-known term on the streets. Seems like it applies more when I have a lot of heat on me out there. Then I have to really tighten my game up. Then slippin and slidin really applies from the time I get up in the morning til the time I go to sleep at night if I'm still free. If I'm still out of jail I haven't done too bad, cause they got every cop in town lookin for me. If I managed to slip and slide without them puttin the arm on me, then I've done pretty good.

"By the same token, if I get up in the morning in here, I go through the day; I break a few rules; pack a little contraband; I avoid a few hassles. Then I've slipped and slid through the day, did O.K. and that's because I know my way around.

"I know who can be beat and I know who can't be beat. I know what bulls to stay away from. I might start to go up to the club and I look up and see a certain two pigs that are always out to shake you down for no reason, then I don't go to the club. Whereas a dummy will come by carryin a knife. Hasn't even learned really what bulls do what and he just walks right off into it. Bam, he's busted. They pull him aside and he's busted. But three times out of the week, I'll start up there, I'll see those cops; I'll turn around. I won't go by there, you see. Simple as that. So I don't get caught.

"I might want to bring something into the wing but there's

certain days that there's certain cops on that tier [that] aren't goin to turn their heads. They're not gonna let me pack any lumber in, or pack this or that, so I don't even try. I know when they're on duty and when they're not on duty. I know what cops give less than a fuck what I do. All they want to do is be left alone. They'll open your door. They'll let you in, let you out. They're not gonna hassle you; not gonna shake you down; not gonna ask you what you're carryin; not gonna look in the box that you walk in with to see what's in it. Then those guys that keep their eye on those kinds of things and know their way around, they pack every goddam thing in the Joint in — typewriters, radios, boards, lumber, tools — walk right in with the stuff. Don't even try to be slick half the time. Don't have to be. We slip and slide; we know how to get by. We got our shit together.

"Then you got the motherfucker that don't learn the game. Every goddam time you turn around he's gettin shook down. He's gettin caught. He's gettin tagged. He's in fights; gets in the wrong people's face; gettin busted; gettin stabbed; gettin fucked.

"Some people just have a natural talent for slippin and slidin. They've slipped and slid from town to town; just part of their nature in here to watch things, to observe, to look at people before they make a move; to look at doorways to make sure there ain't a cop sittin on the other side, man, to watch the door to make sure it's not gonna close behind you and lock when you go through.

"You time the gates in here. You time everything in here. You know when you can come and go; when you can't come and go. When you're gonna walk through a door where you get stuck there for three hours, you don't go through. But not the dum-dum. The dum-dum goes on in and then he's raisin hell, screamin and hollerin because he can't get back in. 'Oh, man, I just went in to get my radio.' 'I just wanted to talk to this guy.' Cop will tell him the same thing: 'When the goddam gate's up, you know you can't go back out there until three,' see. He didn't have to get himself locked in there. All he had to do was learn the times; learn the gates, when he can go through and when he can't go through, cause once you're through you're like bein in some kind of trap. You can't turn around and come back out until somebody lets you out.

"Slippin and slidin, both names, they're also used individually. It can be just a slang term for walkin. For example, 'I'm gonna slide over to the hospital and hit the pillow.' 'Man, I'm gonna slide on down to the movie.' 'I'm gonna slide over to the chow hall.' Slip can also be used that way. It's kinda versatile.

"Slippin and slidin is survivin, gettin by without gettin tagged; gettin by without gettin stabbed, without gettin killed. Course sometimes you lose no matter how slick you are. But we never stop that slippin and slidin. A man has to do that. He has to keep learnin new ways as the Joint changes, as the cops change. There's always new ways to do it."

Life in prison is made up of a series of little games, all of which are part of the larger game of *slipping and sliding*. Learning all the games is challenging, often filled with tension and excitement, and all-consuming—a way of *doing time*. The aim of the game is survival, *easy time*, and a *fast play for the gate*. In other words, the aim of the game is to win. For some, the game will be continued in another dimension on the streets. Both in and out of the prison the rules of the game are acknowledged as absolutely binding. If you lose the game on the streets, you "go to jail." If you lose the game in *the Joint*, other fates await you.

Delorme: "It's harder to slip and slide when you're new and then if you don't learn, there's a place for you. There's four places for you—the hole, P.C., Third Floor, and Nine Wing. Nine Wing is the graveyard. That's the nickname for the graveyard. Everybody don't know that.

"I went through the whole Joint one day asking. I said, 'Let's see how many people still remember what that means.' And we asked guys and we got so damned many different answers. 'It's up on the hospital floor.' 'It's right behind the gym.' 'Let's see, I think it's over at the end of Seven and Eight Wings.' 'I never heard of Nine Wing.' 'Isn't that MSB?' That one was pretty close cause the little graveyard is up behind the hog ranch."

Cardozo-Freeman: "Does it have little tombstones?"

Delorme: "No, it don't have no tombstones. Doesn't even say when you died. Just has your number on it."

Cardozo-Freeman: "This was not a person; this was a number?"

Delorme: "Yeah. That's life."

Little Games for Doing Time

The more a new *fish* learns about what goes on in the prison the more he will be able to determine how he will *do his time* and the better he will be able to assume some control over his destiny. Many little games for *doing time* are played on *the Breezeway*, the "skid row" of the prison. Some men spend their entire day "shooting the breeze" on *the Breezeway*. Idleness is a profession for many but not always by choice since jobs are scarce in the prison. Hanging out on *the Breezeway* is a way of *doing time* but is a dangerous way of *slipping and sliding*, as violent confrontations may occur out there.

"The Breezeway, it's sort of the skid row of the Joint, the center, I guess, for extracurricular activities where the hustle and bustle goes on; where everybody's out there either tryin to cop dope or sell dope. Guys who are into heroin, it's an all day hustle. You're either buyin, sellin, or shootin, or on the phone trying to get money. Keeps their minds occupied. Their whole intent is to keep loaded. They're really happy when they score. It's also a way of keeping out of the hassle; their way of slippin and slidin. Anyway, they got marijuana, they got heroin.

"Anything that's around you're goin to find out there on the Breezeway. It stays crowded all the time. A lot of people come out of their houses and they just hang around there all day long until nine o'clock at night. Take a break for chow and go back there again. And you can buy anything from nickel weed to a shirt, a pair of pants.

"Everything's for sale in here. Everything, including people, so there's nothin you can't buy. The prices for a little itty bitty pinch of marijuana wrapped up in a little triangle of paper is called a 'nickel,' so you just say, 'You got any nickels, man?' That's a little teeny pinch of weed. Makes about two skinny little joints. So that's the main thing out there.

"A lot of times you come out, even if you're not buyin dope or sellin dope. You just go out there and sit around and you wait for somethin to happen, I guess. Waitin for someone to stab each other, or wait for someone to beat each other up. Anything to break up the boredom, for chrissake. The sidewalk that goes down to Big Red or the kitchens or the shops runs right over to the

Breezeway, so if you sit there long enough you're gonna see someone get hauled off to the hole or see the gurney go by with somebody's carcass on it bleedin. It's that kind of thing.

"Same reason kids hang out at certain parkin lots or drive-ins. They just sit there all night like a bunch of idiots in their cars. Well, these guys are all doin the same thing; just standin around here all day like birds on a telephone line. That's the Breezeway, and to some people it's damn near a profession, you know. I mean that's all they want to do. They get a thrill out of it, a little excitement, seein what they can come up with; what they can turn over.

"A guy that never has any money, he might end up hustlin on the Breezeway sellin a little bit of weed for somebody else and he makes a few cents, so he's got a little dough. It's the same thing for certain streets in the cities where all the action is. Skid row street is where everybody hangs out who wants to buy dope. Where all the taverns are. It's that kind of a deal.

"The Breezeway was just a covered sidewalk when they started it. It had chain-linked fences on both sides so we asked for it to be covered cause we'd get soaking wet every time we came out of the wing to go anywhere in the winter time, so they made it and covered it. Put a roof over us. Every time it rained we had someplace to stay out of the rain. So pretty soon more and more people just kind of started hangin around because it's in an area where everybody has to pass you, so you see if you hang out there long enough, somebody's goin to come along that you know and pretty soon things started happenin out there.

"The guys comin back from the pill line would end up on the Breezeway sellin their pills. That's where the dope thing got started. Everybody bought from the pill line. It's kind of stupid dope, but it's dope, I guess. Tranquilizers, they used to give out a lot of tranquilizers. That used to be pretty good dope years back.

"Anyway, you pick up on all the news on the Breezeway. Somebody will come up and say, 'Man, have you heard any good rumors lately.' You say, 'No.' Well, they'll start one or something. We'd start rumors for fun and then see how long it takes to get back to you and how much it changes. It's only a matter of a couple of hours. 'They're movin forty guys out of here. Sendin em to Leavenworth.' Things like that. Or you tell em that you just came from hearin the radio. If it's a crowd in the kitchen where they don't have a radio, you run over and you say, 'I just came from the wing, man, and I saw on the TV that the Board is cutting out 500 people.' And then you walk away. A lot of rumors are started on the Breezeway. There's nothin to do and it's part of the entertainment.

"It didn't take long for the Breezeway bums to be named. Actually some guys aren't really on the bum, but others, that's the best way for em to get cigarettes and they just kind of bum all day like those guys on the streets. They bum cigarettes. They bum scrip. 'Hey, man,, you got a nickel?' They're playin the ole nickel game. They got a pocket full of nickels. Everybody gives em nickels. 'Got any spare change, man?'

"There's all kinds of people out there on the Breezeway. Like this dude down here with his wheelchair. He might wheel out there for an hour. There's several guys that are crippled. See that black guy there? Well there's another black dude on the tier that takes care of him and makes sure he gets carried up and down the stairs and things. But he'll say, 'Take me out to the Breezeway for awhile.' And he'll just shoot him on out there and he'll hang around for two or three hours. He gets a chance to see people and say hello and everybody sees that he's alive. He may not come out again for a week or so, see. So he comes out to get the news and people might hand him some smokes or whatever.

"Anyway, you buy clothes on the Breezeway; you trade stuff; you check on the dope; buy it; buy booze; trade things. You can trade anything in here. They're standing around tradin watches, this and that. Got clothes hangin up on the fence to sell, bunch of shirts, a couple of rugs, bunch of magazines. The ole garage sale, you know. They got a little chair sittin there and they have a bunch of candy bars and cigarettes they might be sellin. They set up a little street store. Once in awhile they hawk their wares. I've heard em callin out if things don't move, but generally they just sit there and you come by and check it out.

"They trade punks out there. The queens are out there flirtin, floozin it up. They're just swishin around. Got their hair all fixed up. They don't try to hustle on the Breezeway. They don't say anything to anybody. They don't talk to guys that don't talk to them first.

"If anything's going to come down, it happens at one end or the other of the Breezeway. Those are the places where murders take place."

Going to school or holding a job are safer and more constructive little games for *doing time*. Any activity that keeps the prisoner away from trouble is regarded as a good way of *slipping and sliding*.

"Even goin to school is a form of slippin and slidin. It's a way of gettin through. It's a way of doin time. You're not only gettin an education, you've got your head off the choppin block most of the time. You're up out of the population where you're probably not gonna be in the middle of any gunfire or anything. That's a way of slippin and slidin. That's a part of findin a way to do your time. Findin a way to stay out of trouble; findin a way to be in a position or place that makes you feel good."

Clubs are another choice that men have for occupying their time. Each of the clubs have their own activities. BPFU, for example, holds classes in Standard English for some of its members and the Chicano Club helps Mexican nationals learn English. All the clubs hold activities that help keep the men occupied and away from the trouble areas of the prison. Some men spend their whole day in their club.[15]

Slipping and sliding also involves little games for "making a living" in prison. Although "room and board" is provided by the state along with basic necessities, all those items prisoners consider luxuries or necessities that help them to do *easy time* cannot be acquired without money. What Virgil Williams and Mary Fish call a "sub rosa economy" thrives in the prison.[16] Some ways of making money, however, are perfectly legitimate. There are many money-making games in the prison. Although legal currency is forbidden, some of it floats around in the prison. Scrip is used in the prison as currency; five dollars in the outside world is equal to seven dollars and fifty cents in scrip.

Cardozo-Freeman: "Talk about how guys make money around here."

Al: "I'll tell you the ways we make money. The state pays a slave wage out in the furniture factory and in the engineering department, metal plant, the license plates. The guys that clean the buildings, the tier porters."

Gene: "Everybody that works on the school floor gets paid more because the college pays us. Guys that work in the kitchen get paid about twenty-five to thirty-five dollars a month, wouldn't you say?"

Al: "Guys work in industry like upholstery and making furniture, their top rate is maybe a hundred a month. The others make fifty-sixty dollars and they work up to a higher wage. Then there's guys in here that make a pretty steady income selling marijuana."

Cardozo-Freeman: "What else?"

Al: "A lot of people do hobby work. They make leather purses and sell those and there's places that they can sell them, like in Seattle. There's a store there that handles nothing but prison made handicrafts on consignment. The Mexicans sell their tortillas."

Gene: "That's Commie food, we call it. Anything's that foreign is Commie in here."

Al: "The Chicanos make good dough selling tortillas, though. There are guys in here who always have enough scrip or whatever to do what they want with it. I bought a TV for seventy-five bucks and I paid for it in scrip."

Gene: "That was seventy bucks more than you're supposed to have legally."

Al: "I had two hundred."

Gene: "What did you do? Hide it?"

Al: "I had other people carrying it for me. That's just scrip I made selling things and I won some bets. The biggest thing I won was sixty dollars on a football game and it cost me a dollar to buy the ticket."

Gene: "That goes on during football season."

Al: "People might clean rugs or clothes. People type for other people. They make money typing your schoolwork for you. Generally those guys work in the law office, library, or school where they've got access to the electric typewriters and plenty of paper, if they don't have a typewriter in their house. But a lot of guys have them in their cells, as you know. They've got a little business going steady typing."

Gene: "Some guys type TV guide where they sell them for fifty cents and they deliver every week. They buy one *TV Guide* and then they copy everything and they throw out what we can't get on our set anyway."

Al: "You hate to try to figure out what's local, so they do it for you and sell it."

Gene: "I used to like their TV guide better than the regular one."

Al: "There was another guy that came around the cells and installed the things to hook your TV on. Remember? It was angle iron and they'd drill holes in the wall with an electric drill. They charged you three bucks for that."

Gene: "I think it was the same guys that put out the TV guide."

Al: "Yeah. They had a going business. Some guys in the kitchen make sandwiches and they run around selling them. They steal food out of the kitchen."

Gene: "I can go into the kitchen and pay a guy to serve me fried potatoes and steak at night and when I come in to eat, everybody gets the beans and I run over to the table and my tray is already there with steak and potatoes."

Al: "The food used to be the biggest thing a few years back. We'd sell everything. In the butcher shop you buy steak. You can buy a whole tenderloin there like this for five bucks."

Gene: "Yeah, then you cut it up and fry it in the house."

Perhaps the most lucrative little game for doing time is money-lending. Most "bankers" are also involved in the drug enterprise. As do good capitalists, the money-lenders believe in usury, charging exorbitant interest for loaning money, mainly to buyers of drugs. Those who do not pay their debts are dealt with harshly as money-lenders hire tough inmates to collect for them.

Duane: "The majority of the money-lenders in the Joint, man, is people that have got their money through dope and they're goin to loan it out because they know the money is goin to be used to buy dope; therefore, they loan a ten dollar bill out, say maybe for twenty bucks and they get their ten dollar bill back."

Gene: "How many money-lenders we got in here?"

Duane: "You always see em come out when the dope bag's in."

Gene: "Then that's their sole business? Just to lend money?"

Duane: "It may not be their only business; their business is supplyin dope, too. I loan you twenty dollars. I got the bag. I got somebody else frontin the dope off for me. Let's say I got the bag. I give it to Slick to deal. You come to me, you say, 'Hey, man, Slick's got some Dilaudid®. Twenty dollars to deal. Loan me twenty dollars for a money order.' And you sell me. What do you do? You send me out for a forty dollar money order for a twenty dollar bill in which you turn around and buy a tap of Dilaudid and still get the twenty back, therefore, I made sixty on twenty, or forty on top of the twenty, plus I got the twenty back, which I can loan out again for another twenty; another twenty for forty."

Gene: "He's a loan shark, you know."

Duane: "He's only tryin to support himself. He's loaning out money so you can come back and buy off my man. In actuality he's makin sixty dollars a tap."

Gene: "Which ain't a bad profit."

Duane: "Loan sharks out on the streets are doin good to make twenty percent a week."

Gene: "A lot of people in here that are buyin the dope and shit out on the streets when they're dealin just for convicts, they're cleanin up, too. Really cleanin up on just marijuana alone. A lot of guys are sendin out a lot of money."

Duane: "The grass you get in here, I could jump down and buy a lid in here for sixty-five dollars. I suppose I'd get about two hundred and fifty dollars worth of nickel bags. A nickel bag is the corner of an envelope. You cut the corner out of an envelope."

Gene: "Three-fourths of an inch, wouldn't you say?"

Duane: "Yeah. Cut diagonally across the envelop to approximately the same size as the other side. Give it two folds and you got yourself a nickel bag. A lid in here is about one-half ounce."

Gene: "I might send Inez one. Cut that nickel size corner off an envelope and let her see it. That's worth five dollars."

Duane: "Yeah, that's five dollars; seven-fifty scrip in here or fifteen dollars money order."

Gene: "Isn't that ridiculous?"

Duane: "Fantastic prices. The bag in here is just like the amphetamines. The amphetamines go. I don't understand why amphetamines go so good in the Joint. You would think they would respond more to a downer like Dilaudid, morphine, heroin, or goofers, or trackwisers like Valium®."

Gene: "Those are the guys you was talkin about; they'll just take anything."

Duane: "It's what you call a knicknacker, a thrill seeker."

Gene: "Half of em just want to go around tellin em, 'Hey, I'm loaded.' Just youngsters. Shit."

Duane: "Yeah. Just like the guy who sells next door to you. That's his big bag; just to let you know."

Gene: "Boy, he lets the whole Joint know it, too. You can always tell when he's smoked a joint or did anything."

Duane: "I'll tell you one. Now there's the type of person out there that's probably never been loaded every day in his life until he come to this Joint. Now he's one of those guys that can really hustle in a Joint, you know, but can't do a damn thing on the streets outside. There's a lot of em in here that are good Joint hustlers but no play on the street."

Gene: "You'd think that game would carry over a little bit, man."

Duane: "Well, there's a lot of difference."

The most dangerous money-making game to play is supplying drugs and marijuana in the prison. Although a great deal of money can be made, successful drug distribution requires much skill, important friends, connections, and protection from the powerful.

Gene: "Have you ever dealt dope in here?"

Bill: "Yeah. A few times off and on but it's not worth the hassle, really."

Gene: "What I was curious about was some of the hassles connected with it."

Bill: "The hassles that go along with it is you gotta think of the amount of scrip that is comin in per week. You gotta look at that. You gotta get to know people that use a lot of dope or a lotta grass. You gotta look at em, you gotta get to know em. By that I mean financial-wise. I check to see if the guy's got money. I check, also, I get to talkin to people and say, 'O.K., is he good or do you know?' And I'll put it on the one to ten scale sayin. 'Is he good on his word? One to ten scale.' They give me a number, you know. If he's about a five, I might deal with him. If he's above seven, I know I'll deal with him."

Gene: "I wish business was run like that. I'd get credit every-where."

Bill: "I try to look at these things and the amount of scrip that's comin in a week and if he's workin I might go with him on a monthly basis.

"I try to keep away from people that are goin to burn me and if they do burn me, why I just give that amount to a collector, then he goes out and he can collect. There's really very few people that I've dealt with that still owe me. I don't say nothin to em, you know, but I just want em to feel guilty and teach em something. They come up to me again and say, 'Well, do you got anything?' I'll say, 'Hey, buddy, I've got something but I can't give it to you.' I ain't gonna give em anything.

As far as dealin goes, it's a hassle, really, and I won't deal with those guys at all. I got a way to get some dope in here but I just don't want to go through the hassle. If I do go, it's gonna go on a percentage basis to a guy that I really trust and can work with. I'm goin to say, 'O.K., you get nothin but grass.' I'll give em an ounce and out of an ounce he can expect eighty nickels and I'll tell him, 'Every five you sell, out of every five you keep one.' I think that's a pretty good deal. That way, he'll push for the money. I'll give him twenty nickels of weed and I'll take out four. "So when you got those sold I'll give you these four.'

Gene: "What do you do with the money? I know you must collect a lot of money."

Bill: "With the scrip I'll buy white money with it. If I get white, I'll send it out for more weed, and if I get ahead, a lot of that goes to my family or somebody I know that I can trust out there to bank it."

Gene: "Guys make thousands, don't they."

Bill: "Yeah. You could if you're dealin in the right stuff. If you've got quality stuff. Like grass on the one to ten scale. If you've got a number eight or nine grass—you always get above seven—then you're always goin to make some bucks. But if you get some bum shit that people have been pushin you're not goin to get anything. You try to push off three nickels for seven and a half of the bum stuff, nobody's goin to buy it. You probably have to pay the guy to take it."

Gene: "The collecting business was a pretty thriving business around here for awhile, wasn't it."

Bill: "Still is. If you can get into it. Say that you wanna get into it, it's a good business."

Gene: "What will you give the collector? What does he get out of it? Half or something?"

Bill: "If I don't really care for the guy that owes me, I'll just give him [the collector] the whole fuckin thing and say, 'Here's the whole thing.' Say like he owes me fifty [dollars] and he ain't come across, I'll say, 'Here, you take this whole fifty. I want that guy roughed up. I want him to remember it. Just drop it. Just tell him it's from me and if he's got a bone to pick with me he can come to me.' The next time you know he's gonna think about burnin somebody. Some people get half; some people get one-third for collecting purposes, and he could stay in new clothes, new TV if he's in that kind of business."

Gene: "That was sort of a club thing, wasn't it?"

Bill: "Yeah. I know a couple of free-lancers; they don't belong to any club. They just do it on their own, mainly because they're too damn lazy to work."

Gene: "It's just a regular living for em, a regular business. Do you think the administration as far as the dope issue . . . if you feel uncomfortable about it you don't have to talk about it . . . I'll just give you my viewpoint on what I think—that they'll never take it out because there's a need for that, too, at this time, to keep the guys kinda mellow and you know you got the grass culture in here, the marijuana culture in here."

Bill: "I used to be pretty heavy into drugs. I had two habits at the time. I was drinkin heavy and dopin heavy out on the streets but I had to make a choice of which one I wanted and drop one, and so I stuck to drinkin, but the last year or so I went back into smokin grass and the reason I smoke it is because it mellows me out and mainly because I want to get away from thinkin about this life sentence and how much time I might have to do and it just takes me away from all this. I don't think that they'll take it away or keep it out because it does mellow a lot of guys out. Mellows a lot of their hard cases out. There's always ways of gettin it in. You can never stop gettin dope in here."

Gene: "Yeah. I saw one of these guys up in the visitor's room. Course, I'm naive and after all that time I thought, well, that's gonna put the heat on him, but I didn't see no changes. I see more dope in here than ever before. Comes in in packages, visitors bring it in. Bulls bring it in."

Bill: "If you got a good horse packin for you, or you got a good pipeline . . . I used to send it in when I was out in the Building [MSB]. I sent it in with a caseworker once. I've known four different ways it comes in from the Building. To my knowledge none of these ways have been known to us in here and I've known about it for about four years. I get notices when shipments come in from the Building. You just know by who's got back from the visiting room. They walk around like a neon sign."

Gene: "And they look like that — falling down, droolin all over the place. And then they'll pick somebody else's skin to shake up. I watch that shit."

Bill: "If a person wants to keep a low profile in the penitentiary, like I do, I try to keep to myself. I do a little bit of cell time, work, go over and if you gotta talk to the heat, do it some place where the Man ain't gonna see you. If you're doin some dealin, keep em away from the house. Get a middleman. I try to keep a low profile."

Gene: "How could you avoid this gang of people at your house all the fuckin time while you're dealin, botherin you all day and night, like the guy next door to me down there? It's obvious what he's doin, cause it's just a steady fuckin stream of people in his fuckin house. On the streets, that's how they bust you. The neighbors see that shit and they call the cops and say he must be dealin dope over there."

Bill: "I got a friend or two that I know that's on the Breezeway and they won't burn you. You do em good, you know. I try to do em good so they don't burn me. If they do burn me I tell what's gonna happen, then I tell em, 'O.K., well here it is. Get out there on the Breezeway. Don't tell em who it is [supplying]; who it's comin from or anything. Just keep it up. I don't want no traffic in front of my house. At the first sign of traffic in front of my house, there'll be no more supply for you.' I'll get one or two guys to work the Breezeway. And if I wanna work another wing, I get a guy in that wing. That'll take the heat off."

Gene: "How much can you make?"

Bill: "On a lid of grass I can make, oh, about four hundred dollars a lid."

Gene: "Just on a lid? I didn't know that."

Bill: "I pay any place from sixty to one hundred and twenty-five dollars an ounce."

Gene: "What's a lid, an ounce?"

Bill: "Yeah. You get eighty nickels out of a lid."

Gene: "What would the lid cost you on the street?"

Bill: "Sixty dollars, dependin on what the quality is. Say like you got some good Hawaiian, why that's goin to run you some money. You got some good Colombian, it's gonna run you some money."

Gene: "So the people on the street, you're payin em as much as you're payin for the grass just to get it. Right?"

Bill: "Yeah. You gotta figure in order to get it here you've gotta have a good pipeline or a good horse. You're payin him. You pay your horse to pack it in; you pay your middleman to push it on the Breezeway, so you figure that out of all that you're makin about one hundred-seventy-five to two hundred dollars a lid. That's not much over but you figure if you're got some good stuff, you've got about four or five ounces of it, you're gonna come out ahead. So I'll just come straight across with my middlemen. I'll tell em, 'You guys divide that up and give the rest to me.' And after they give me the rest, then I give it to the man who's packin for me, give him his share, and I send the rest out for another order."

Gene: "Like you say, if the fuckin hassle wasn't so involved, would a guy stay in the business forever? Get used to it? Or just go for a shot and make a little bundle and pull out of it?"

Bill: "I think if a guy had a good thing goin; a good go on it and is pretty tight with some people in here, they could make a livin at it."

Gene: "You gotta get busted eventually. Somebody's gonna tell."

Bill: "Yeah. That's one thing you always gotta remember, that if you deal in here, you'll get busted eventually. But if you work it right long enough where you can keep your middleman out there and all he gives you is the money, your chances of gettin busted are a lot slimmer than you goin out there doin it. That's how come I always try to keep a middleman."

Gene: "Any club or any people try to run you out of business? Ever threaten you or tell you to stop? That that's their fuckin racket?"

Bill: "Nobody has ever done that to me but I've known a couple people that have been pressured into quittin."

Gene: "Recently that's happened to a couple guys I know."

Bill: "I think the main reason that it hasn't happened to me is because I guess you could say the friends I've got, the old timers here that I've done time with, some of these Lifers here. If I get pressured and I needed some help, then I can go to these people and say, 'Well, I'm gettin some pressure from over here. Help me out. Let's talk to em."

Gene: "What would the pressure be? Different types?"

Bill: "Like if your quality of grass was pretty good and you're makin your nickels a little bit bigger—that's one reason that they push you out because you're sellin quality stuff and givin em a little bit more."

Gene: "That's the same on the street, isn't it."

Bill: "Just the same. And say like we're pushin pills it's the same thing. You can give more for the same price and quality and stuff. That's what a lot of these guys don't want in here. They get some bum shit in here like alfalfa or something and they try to push it."

Gene: "The people that do get run out. Do they come right out and get beat up? Get threatened or do they demand a percent of their profits that are so heavy that it don't make it practical to keep tryin to deal? I remember the Bikers used to run up on a guy and say, 'We're takin twenty percent of your shit.'"

Bill: "They used to but the way I heard it now, they're just plain old tellin em not to deal and if they do, they get a percent. From what I heard it's a sixty-forty bit."

Gene: "That's a tough percent."

Bill: "Nobody'd go for it. Jeez, you'd go out of business. Quit."

Gene: "You get a guy that gets grass in once or twice a year; they ain't gonna bother with him cause he ain't that big a threat. I guess that's our only . . . what would you call the dope thing here, the source of most of our troubles? I mean in the form of violence. Dope doesn't bother us otherwise, the guys that are gettin down. The guys that are gettin killed, the guys that supposedly are on the hit list that some people say is real and some guys say ain't real, but it is real, really. But with most of the guys around here it means some pretty bad burns. Or is there some stool pigeons from somewhere else?"

Bill: "That's the individual's fault that he feels that he can outdo em, outsmart em by burnin the con, you know, then checkin into PC. That's his own fault because if he's a real up and up dude, he won't do this. If a guy's on the hit list, I don't pity him at all because he put himself there."

SLIPPING AND SLIDING—PART II—WATCHING YOUR BACK

Although the men *slip and slide* through each day playing their routine survival games, they are always aware of the possibility of a mood change or a change of scenes in which death may step to the center of the stage. Because of this, they never drop their guard. They refer to this as *watching your back.*

"I'm constantly looking over my shoulder. I don't like anybody sneaking up behind me, and whenever I sit down to meals I always look around to see who's sittin by us and then my partners always look out behind me and then I always watch out behind them when we're eating. In case a stranger walks toward us or has his hands in his pocket or he's got a coat over his arm, if that's the case I stand up and holler, warn everybody at the table. So we watch for things like that. If we've had a beef with somebody, he usually doesn't sit in our area of the chow hall and if we see him sittin there all of a sudden, we'll keep a close eye on him. That's our defense. It's like standing back to back.

"We constantly check on each other wherever we are at and if we do have a beef or something, we make sure the others know about it. The others I'm talking about is whoever your closest friends are. With me it's Speedy and a couple other guys in school. I let them know. I might even let G. know cause he seems to be pretty good at keeping things to himself, not letting my name come out in anything and if I'm havin troubles he maybe watches my door while I'm workin, cause he can see my door from his office all the time, so he can kind of keep an eye out. We do that; that's ongoing daily. So it's kinda our defense.

"We don't carry a knife but I like to always check and see that I've got a weapon, a natural object if I'm caught, salt, pepper shakers, coffee cup. If I'm at work, there's things that I can use if I needed it, things that are close by, things that are heavy. I don't carry a weapon. I might carry pepper once in awhile. I might carry a little ammonia if I can get it. You put ammonia in a squeeze bottle, Mennen's After Shave® bottle, it's a little plastic bottle. If I had a hot argument going with somebody I don't trust, I would fill it up with ammonia and that'd stop anybody. It's like tear gas, you know. That's defense hazards and everybody does pretty much the same. A lot of people still carry knives, of course; other people carry rocks. They put a rock in a sock, the ole rock in a sock trick, things like that, wear sharp rings."

Watching your back is one of the most important commandments for survival in the prison. For some, the stress of trying to protect themselves is intolerable. Men who have *done time* in more conventional prisons in particular resent the danger. A prisoner, now fifty-four, formerly from the Illinois prison system, describes his reaction to this prison:

"I was born and raised in Mississippi. I left when I was quite young and went to Chicago when I was fifteen and I got into trouble. I didn't spend too much time in Chicago; I spent most of my time in prison. I got put in when I was seventeen and didn't get out until I was thirty-six.

"Back there you know where you stood at all times. You can't do your time in here. That's one of the reasons I like this job out here. [He was in MSB outside the prison walls.]

"I went to Pontiac when I was seventeen. Pontiac is for youngsters in Illinois. I left there and went to Stateville. I done most of my time in Stateville and Joliet. In 1959, I went down to Menard, come back to Joliet and got out in 1967. I started out with sixty-five years. This is my first time at Walla Walla. My first and last, I hope.

"But I'll tell you, man, I been to quite a few penitentiaries and I ain't never seen a penitentiary like this in all my born days! What's so bad about this place . . . it's not the time; it's how you have to do your time here! You don't know from one day to the next what the hell it's gonna be. I bet I aged ten years the year and a half I was behind the wall. You couldn't go nowhere and rest in peace. You couldn't go to the movies. I couldn't feel comfortable. The only time I would feel comfortable was when I was in the dining room, workin."

Violent and nonviolent share the same space, and everyone except those in protective custody or in segregation has complete freedom of movement during the day. Closeness heightens the possibilities for violence, making survival for even the most skillful exceedingly stressful. Those regarded as dangerous killers roam freely throughout the population, compounding the conditions that set the stage for tragedy. Their ominous presence makes the rest of the population extremely tense. At times, however, prison officials ship these dangerous men to other institutions in order to relieve the situation.

Gene: "What do you work on most in here? What's most important to you?"

Les: "Well, number one is acceptance so you're able to walk around this motherfucker. You want to make sure that there's no one lookin at your back. I always make sure of that. I might be a little paranoid."

Gene: "O.K., that's survival."

Les: "It's not easy, to hurt someone's feelings in this motherfucker and then expect to walk around and not have some dude try to stab you in the back or some fuckin thing. That's what's so rank about it. That's what I hate. That's the hardest thing in this damned place."

Gene: "You got to learn the steps, what to look out for."

Les: "Yeah. That's definitely what you gotta do."

Gene: "Who to look out for. The look on people's faces."

Les: "If I was sittin here and some new guy come in and he never been around, I'd tell him, 'Whatever you do, don't go around askin questions. Just feel things out. If things look bad, go some place where you can find another mood. There's things you can get into. You can get into a club. You can get into school, into vocational training. Course to get into that, you gotta be here awhile and know somebody and every other damn thing to get in line, but if you're having problems, if you got any questions at all, ask the counselor. Don't ask another con because once they realize you don't know it, man, that's their next move. Just walk slow. Don't walk paranoid cause that's a dumb thing to do. It's hard to live that way. If a guy has to live paranoid, he might as well check into PC. You just got to be in the middle; give a little, take a little and just walk it.' "

Gene: "This is one of the places where you say, 'Just because you're paranoid, it don't mean somebody ain't after you.' "

Les: "A guy's got to do his own trip. I try to do my own and I expect every guy to do the same. You know what I mean? Get off of mine; this is mine. I'm doin this one. But the powers-that-be in here . . . well, they're gone now, but the reason they were the powers-that-be was because they were the ones that could stand up; only what they were standin up for I don't think was really as good a thing as it could have been. It could have been standin up for a lot of things other than the size of the bag [drugs]. And they would kill for it. You see, there's a lot of paranoia that runs around this Yard because we got ten guys come out and they're all transmittin death. You just automatically know it because you been directly involved in it before and for that reason I'm tryin to be perceptive to what's goin on around me at all times because defense is the best offense.

"Before the apes shipped out you could step out of your cell and look around and see the tenseness. After they left then you could see how much people started relaxing and the tenseness went away.

"I don't understand why they put guys like me that got no violence on em in here with violent people. That surprises me—why they take and put these people together like that and then they tell em not to be violent. I mean, they tell you, 'If you get violent you're goin to get all this time added on.' And they got these guys over here, man, they give em so much time that they can't even look at the gate and they gotta exist in here and they have their moody days and they're gonna get into bullshit. And then they got these guys over here, they're lookin at the gate [they have short sentences] and both these type guys are walkin the same tier and they're both gonna have their moody days and they're both gonna have their conflicts. Then they're [officials] tellin em, 'Any violence, man, and you're gonna get this and that.' But the thing is, man, the only one it hurts is the one that's lookin at the gate. But then they keep both here in the same institution. They don't keep em apart. It don't make no sense."

How some prisoners try to survive in prison is described in this conversation with an inmate from Six Wing.

Gene: "O.K., let's go back to this survival thing. How do you deal with that problem personally? Do you compare it to slippin and slidin through a war?"

Wes: "Yeah. And there's so much pressure bein locked up all the time. Even in the free world you can't seem to do what you want to do."

Gene: "What pressures do you feel?"

Wes: "You get up in the morning here and you may not really make plans but you got to figure that you know in your mind after you're here awhile, you've got to duck and dodge and slip and slide and make sure you survive. There are certain characters in here you don't even want to bump into on the Breezeway because with them it is a fight, you know. Certain guys you stay away from because they have such a fuckin asshole attitude about everything. That is basically what we're talkin about. That goes with the themes of an institution.

"You have violence. Violence is our culture here. We've all got our little plans and schedules and the way we conduct ourselves, the way we handle these things and the way we avoid them. Number one is avoiding hassles. We put ourselves in other areas of the institution when we know something is going to come down on our side of the Joint. We just make it a point to be on the other side of the Joint; then we are not hooked up with it.

"If I could do this on the streets like I'm doing in here. In here I'm a very private person. I really don't like to stick by myself but still I know everyone in here has so much problems and I have enough of my own. Hopefully, I can work some of them out somehow and be able to get out of here and do things which the society wants to be done.

"So how do I go about just bein an A-1 citizen? I am constantly thinkin about how I can do it and what I can do. They say, 'You can't.' You have to be careful not to overemphasize it, your anger, which can happen easily just through resentment. You hate the system and you hate them. You start actin like they expect you to; you act like in them cops and robber movies.

"There might be certain steps and procedures that you can allow yourself to do but you know where you're at at all times. If that is what it takes to get out of here [rules and regulations] there is no loss of pride. It doesn't take weakness. It takes strength to do these things and hang on to your own identity. Play the game and use the system as a tool to get out of here. You see that some people can't do that and finally, they are defeated by the system.

"This is what they're doin to me now. I'm not here for hardly anything actually. I'm just in here for breakin one of the rules [violating parole]. Not the law — a rule. This is frustrating me day in and day out. What did I really do? I didn't hurt nobody or anything. Lousy no-good rules that they have that they want me to follow. This tryin to change me to be like them, that really bugs me. 'O.K., let's do this; let's do that.' Seven days a week. Nights are a little different cause we can relax."

Gene: "Tell me what you know you have to do to get through each of those seven days."

Wes: "It's a lot of repeating. It becomes a habit without realizing. That's the way it is with me now. I just wake up in the morning and put on my clothes and walk out the door like a monkey, not really having anything on my mind."

Gene: "Is there particular people that you know you are going to avoid that day? Like if there's friction between two clubs, on that day do you make it a point, as long as that is going on, to stay away from certain groups?"

Wes: "I think that is why I like to stay in the house a lot."

Gene: "All of those frustrations out there and hard feelings I associate with em."

Wes: "I like to stay out of their way if they stay out of mine."

Gene: "Are you prepared to stay with your club, your brothers?"

Wes: "Oh yes. You darn right."

Gene: "I want to stay away from all of those things but I'm always ready, on guard, for whatever might happen with another fellow inmate."

Wes: "This is a bad feeling with me, you know. I am constantly on my guard."

Gene: "Are you mentally tired? Tired physically?"

Wes: "Yes, and I don't like that."

Gene: "Just being in here is a lot of punishment alone without havin to be punished, too, and so where do you turn?"

Wes: "I just stay to myself in order to avoid all of these hassles. Just about everywhere you go, you step up to a group and all that you hear are bad things, you know, bad feelings, bad hurts. Everywhere you go in here, bad, bad, bad, and so I stay a lot to myself. It's not that I want to. I don't like to be by myself."

Gene: "What would you say is the best part of your day?"

Wes: "The best part of my day is when that door is locked behind me. The door is locked at night and you know that there isn't a goddam sonavabitch from any club coming through the door."

Knowing about certain blind areas in the prison where assassinations are most likely to occur and avoiding them unless accompanied by trusted friends who can watch your back is an important tactic for survival in the prison. Being mistaken for someone else is a distinct possibility, since murders often occur in places where illumination is poor. Blood Alley, the theatre, and the *carwash* are examples of dangerous territories.

Gene: "What's Blood Alley mean to you?"

Tim: "Nothin except a lot of people get stabbed and cut up and killed in Blood Alley. It's a place where you don't even want to walk."

Gene: "They run it all the way down here but it used to start farther down and go down from the end of the movie. You used to never want to go down that thing if you didn't have to. Me and you walk down it but the majority of people didn't want to go down that end. It was a dead end."

Tim: "The only place you could get to at the dead end was the theatre and it was locked and the doors going into Four and Five Wings were locked."

Gene: "Once you got a guy runnin down there it was like a slaughterhouse for cattle. You run em down the chute."

Tim: "Guards wouldn't open the door for them."

Gene: "Couldn't see em. You see they couldn't shout or scream. When they closed that off they brought that same type of bullshit out here to this part of the Breezeway. Well then they knocked that down and it always has been the worst part about it, bein trapped like that. They took down that fence. Now chumps can't jump you.

You can get away but before you was just like a cow goin down that ramp. You couldn't go either way."

Tim: "They came up behind you and blocked you off. They just followed you down to the end."

Gene: "My partner got stuck, got stabbed by accident. The guy stabbed him then apologized. My partner cussed the fuck out of him, mistaken identity"

Tim: "I'll be damned."

Gene: "Yeah, stabbed him right in the chest. Lucky he was tough. But tough isn't worth a fuck if he'd a went far enough and got his heart or lungs."

Many men decline to go to the theatre because it is such dangerous territory. Even if a person is completely surrounded by his friends, he continues to watch his back in the theatre, seldom able to settle down and completely give his attention to what is showing on the screen.

"It's nice and dark in the movies. I'd say two-thirds of the stabbings probably take place in the movies. Most stabbings will occur in the movie if they catch a guy there. If a guy's in trouble, he's goin to avoid goin to the movies. If you see two guys walkin up and down the aisle lookin down the rows, you get suspicious then. You really get suspicious if two or three guys run in with towels wrapped around their faces. Then you know something's up, too. The sucker better not be there. You try to keep your eye out on it.

"You make sure where you sit. You sit with your brothers so that you have a brother behind you and brothers in front of you, brothers on the side of you. It gives you the creeps when somebody's behind you that you don't know. I've sat in the movie and tried not to turn around but you hear a noise behind you or anything, man, after the movie starts, when somebody starts down the row behind you, you just can't help but watch him, see what he's up to. Has he come to watch the movie? Has he mistook you for someone else in the dark? Is he goin to stab the guy behind you? You want to get out if something's goin to come down, so it's really hard, man. It's so hard not to look around."

Sometimes dangerous territories must be entered alone. A good example is the carwash, the shower in Eight Wing, notorious for

unexpected attacks. It is particularly dangerous when racial misunderstandings create hostilities. At such times, life is in jeopardy
for even the most skilled at *slipping and sliding*.

"This morning was the worst shower that I've ever taken. Three
Mexicans came in and I was there alone. That is just plain stupid
on my part but there wasn't any Indians around when I went down
to the carwash and my cellies were asleep.

"There is a reason for this feeling and I'm sure you want to
know what it is. Right? We are sort of on the verge of a war with
the Mexicans right now so every one either has a shank on him or
stays with someone who does. One of our brothers cut a Chicano
last week and they made statements to the effect that they were
going to retaliate. It would be stupid on their part since we have
just as many crazy Indians who just look for a chance to put steel
in someone.

"The shower is a favorite place to trap a guy because it's out of
sight and sits way down at the end of the cellblock and it has just
one door leading out. So you can understand my discomfort.

"I was busy washing my hair and trying to keep my eyes open at
the same time, which isn't easy—try it sometime—when in comes
three of the worst of the lot. I almost let out a groan that they
could hear. It was sort of a resigned, 'Oh, shit. Why me?' They
weren't carrying any towels and that is always a good sign. I was
determined to fight to the death though and I did have a good
weapon at hand. I had deliberately taken in a squeegee sponge
mop with me—you know like you use to clean the shower. And I
sat it in the corner right by me, and I hurried up gettin the soap
outta my hair. Then the Mexicans went down to the other end of
the carwash so I just finished up real quick and hit the road. So
there was no fight or anything but I was ready. I had a good
weapon.

"I'll try to explain the carwash for you. It is one big room and
the first impression I always get is a walk-in meat locker. When the
shower is full of bodies I always think about the Jews being led
into the showers by the Germans. It is dark and dingy with the
only light coming in from some tiny, dirty broken windows down
at the end. As a rule these same windows are broken so that during
the winter months it can get cold as hell. For us Indians it could be

compared to the sweat lodge where we sweat and then jump into an icy stream, but it isn't a sweat lodge even though it stays full of steam. In this case the steam is there to cover the business going on in the back end of the shower and the back ends of the girls, for that matter. No one really cares one way or another about what they're doing but it's just uncomfortable to be in there when beefs are coming down. Of course, I stay, no matter what. I need the shower."

A dangerous episode, even for an expert in the survival game, may occur when a prisoner participates or takes the lead in overriding decisions made by powerful club leaders after outbreaks of violence lead to hostilities with the guards. This narrative was taped February 20, 1979.

"We are on the verge of another lockdown. There is talk now of killing a few pigs so it will be a constant fight to hold things down. I have been in half a dozen club head meetings in the last two days. I still speak for the Indian prisoners. I voted 'No' on any violence on lockdown. Since I opposed the Lifers, I kept a close eye on all of them when I left the room to go to the shitter. My reason for the 'No' was that I won't put any Indians out under the guns without some rational planning for a change. I want to see an attempt to deal with these problems through the courts for a change. I'm sick of the gut feelings. That's how every major decision is made in here, or else the stronger groups are able to bulldog the smaller groups into going along with all their crazy shit. The blacks were with me in the voting. Our two clubs together were able to turn the vote last night."

Gladiators and Warriors

There is an ugly aspect of *slipping and sliding* with which each prisoner must come to terms—the possibility that in order to protect his own life he must kill another, even though he may abhor the idea. Making peace with this has a profound effect, and living so close to being either the recipient or deliverer of death undoubtedly affects everyone. Certainly most prisoners are not murderers. Guards suffer as well from the anxiety produced by closeness to death. It is impossible to remain "normal" under such stress. Prisoners are very much aware that the life they live is "different" from "ordinary life" and that the game they must play in prison in order to "win" must not be played in the "real" world outside the prison, and they worry about what this game of survival does to them.[17] A man has got to be prepared to be a killer if he lives and plays out his life in an arena as dangerous as this one. He has no choice but to be a *gladiator*. The rules of the game inevitably are kill or be killed.

"Our culture is—I guess I should ask people what they think our culture is—most of the answers you would get would be that we have a culture like a tribe of savages or something. We are right on the verge of chaos all the time—temper tantrums, wild animals, lunatics, and just the savage part of a man, survival instincts—maybe that's what makes you so goddam ready to strike out at people all the time.

"There's not that much of an attempt to hold back, you know. Everybody is so damned defensive. Cops yell at you; tempers flare. Our sports is a joke. We watch intramural sports because we watch fights. We watch and we snivel. They play sports like a bunch of little kids. They fight. They scratch. They argue. They holler. They pick on the referee. They pick on each other; lose their tempers or they flip out. It's a real carnival. They take forever to get to a goddam softball game out here because every goddam play and every call they argue and argue, regardless. If it's obviously wrong, they'll still argue or complain. It comes out as a fist fight. The fist fight will go on to something else. It will get to be a stabbing. We're just on guard.

"My cell partner said it pretty good one morning. He got ready to go to breakfast and he said, 'Wish me luck. Here I go.' And then at the end of the day when the door was closed behind us he took off his coat and the first thing he said was, and he breathed a sigh of relief, 'Ah, I made it. Safe for another day.' It is sad but true.

"Sometimes I feel I understand it. I wish somebody would change it. But in order to do it, you have to change the whole philosophy and the whole direction of the prison system all over.

"People have to be concerned, people on the streets. We know what is happening to us and we know it's happening to others in here. People out there just have to realize that ninety-nine percent of us guys are coming back out of here in just a few years. Not a

long time and no matter what you do, you're gonna be worse when
you come out.

"Eventually if you are not a violent criminal, you're going to be
a violent type of criminal, because every day you spend in a
prison like this, that is run like this where you have to fight to
survive, you have to learn all the tricks, you have to accept the
thought of maybe having to kill somebody. I haven't been in
combat in the army but just to me it's always been like Vietnam.
You have to be ready to kill somebody and you have to live with it.

"You realize the fact that conscience, what people say is stopping people from killing other people; if your conscience is
bothering you, you find out for a fact your conscience isn't shit.
There is no such thing as a conscience. Some people in here,
instead of their conscience bothering them, it does just the opposite.
And that's a fact that I have found out from being in here.

"Some people like to kill in here. You find out that a human life
isn't worth anything. Nevertheless, it's worth something to you.
You are a living, breathing, laughing person, but just as quick you
can be a dumb ole carcass laying on the ground. You have to
accept that in your mind because you have to go all the way in
order to protect yourself. You come to the point where you accept
that as a fact and you live with it and then you know how you are
going to do it and you know how you are going to defend yourself.
All that remains is for that person, for that situation, to come
around.

"They all know how they are going to act; what they are going
to use to do it with. They just hope they can get in the first punch
or stab, but you know you live in back of a play and you laugh
constantly with these men that have killed again and again. They
have killed convicts and people on the streets. You look in their
eyes and you see they are just like anybody else, laughing and
joking. There's no sign of conscience. If you ask them if it bothers
them, hell no; it doesn't bother them. They'll sit and tell you
about every goddam detail of the crime or murder. They glory in
it. They don't mind talking about it. Hell, they're proud of it.

"You see what the system is turning out? All you can do is just
keep stressing the fact that for the first few months or a year that
the guy is in here he will remain fairly normal and make an effort

to hang on to what he has. He'll try if he doesn't have years to do. If he has years to do, he immediately starts getting rid of all those controls, readjusting to be a tough ready-to-kill convict because he has to be here for several years and that is what he has to be in order to survive.

"You can't run around here trying to be a normal human being. I guess society's viewpoint, society's conscience and things like that, he can't do it. He'll be whooped. He'll be stripped. A month is a rough go in here. Sometimes you don't have to give a guy years, for chrissake.

"You hear about this place being a country club. That's bullshit. That is the most ridiculous thing I have ever heard in my life.

"I want to change myself and that's what I'm trying to do but I could very easily go the other way with this life sentence. Just flip out over it and say, 'To hell with it. I'm goin to kill a couple of sonovabitches.' I can do that, too, or I can take my sentence out on all the guards that work here and be an asshole, make their job as tough as I can. I can do that, and of course, there are a lot of people that are getting a lot of satisfaction from doing that, but I'm free to choose not to and I choose not to.

"A culture of violence; a culture of savagery, no hope; a culture of sadness. There are no social controls in here. Our social norm is survive any way you can. Violence is our norm. Thievery, treating others with disrespect, and existing in a war culture; that's our norm. Obeying laws is definitely not a norm in here."

Many situations contribute to the potential for violent confrontations between the men in the prison: overcrowding; the anxiety and stress of living in such a close and dangerous circumstance where no escape from tension is possible; the pent-up anger the men may feel about their imprisonment; *machismo,* or the need to maintain self-respect, dignity, and pride; peer pressure to live up to the "tough guy" image; the need to be tough when responding to an affront in order to protect the self from harrassment by others who may interpret your leniency toward those who offend you as a sign of weakness; unpaid debts; problems that arise from living in a one-sex society; racial prejudices and hostilities; misunderstandings caused by cultural differences; misdirected hostilities meant for unjust guards; drugs, alcohol, and the inhalation of chemicals, which can trigger violent behavior; and so on. Possibilities for disaster are almost limitless; everyone is dangerous to everybody else. Consequently, men arm themselves just in case war breaks out. A vicious cycle is perpetuated. No one wins; no one can relax.

Delorme: "We start out tryin to build on psychological defense. Damn lucky if we can get one goin in time and once it's gone, I don't know where you get any strength from, but it's a constant thing and that's what sometimes makes me wonder.

"I thought about it last night; how long can you go without ever bein able to rest? To be able to drop your guard? I wonder, when will I rest? When I'm sleeping? That's when you go into your house and your door's locked. The only time you can rest is if you're in a single cell. That's why this doubling up really gets to you after awhile.

"The psychological defense is important. I spot it in different guys. It takes different forms. When I get really mad, I try to cool it back cause when that happens my defense goes. You gotta stay cool in a place like this. I'm still a little bit fast on the trigger. I pop off and drop back down to everybody's level cause I don't want to argue. If somebody calls me a name I think to myself, 'You nervous sonovabitch.' That's the part that's gotta go. I'm ready to fight and I don't like that. I don't like bein like that. We should be able to have some conversation [disagreements] in here. People on the outside don't do that.

"I notice that a lot of guys in here have bad tempers. When guys get into fights they don't have anyone break it up; they let em fight. It never lasts long—two or three blows and it's usually over. In sports, it generally doesn't go any further than that. Cops will break it up. If somebody sees the cops comin, they'll break it up, otherwise the guys probably let em fight for awhile just for something to watch.

"We used to do that. We'd say, 'Let's go watch basketball. The Chicanos are playin' or 'The Indians are goin to play the blacks.' You know there's gonna be some fights; when those two teams play they fight. And everybody's generally loaded. Everybody comes over just to watch, plus we come over with our knives to protect our players just in case, so it gets a little more serious.

"I might see a couple Indians that I know that are the ones that like to carry knives. I tell em, 'Hey, the team's playin. Gotta get over there. They're playin with the blacks.' 'Oh, O.K. I'll be there just in case something happens.' If nothing happens they leave, but just in case, they've got their own security.

"We've got our warrior society in our club, too. Six or seven guys that always pack knives, so these are the guys you pick that you know don't mind stabbin people. So their job is to protect other guys that don't want to pack knives, and they take care of any beefs that come down and that's all they do.

"At least one of em hangs around the club during the day when big groups aren't there and other guys are in there playin dominoes by the hour, watching TV. We got our own share of dings we got to look out for. Quiet little guys, a little goofy and shit. We don't let em go up to the nutward. We take care of em ourselves, see. So you gotta protect em and they're up in the club by themselves during the day when nobody's there so that way we protect em. The warriors check on people. Don't let nobody up there in the club that don't belong there."

Cardozo-Freeman: "What would happen if none of you guys carried knives?"

Delorme: "We'd probably get beat up all the time. As long as they know you do, you'll be able to slide for two or three months without doin it because they think you're packin. Every now and then you let em know you're carryin a knife. It's just simply the world you live in. You've gotta be armed to protect yourself.

"It's like out there beyond the Walls. If I get in an argument, people are more careful because they know I've got these guys around somewhere who are carryin. I don't have to fight and I don't want to fight. It's like Russia and the U.S. It's a power thing. It relates to the world. The blacks have their own warrior group. They always practice karate. The Chicanos have the same thing, although they're sneakier. I don't even know who their guys are who carry. Ours are pretty much out in the open. I mean people know our guys pack but they don't know who's packin."

Cardozo-Freeman: "Do the whites have warriors protecting them?"

Delorme: "No. They haven't got any except for the Lifers; they carry. And Senior Citizens hire the youngsters to protect em. But we protect ourselves from each other. All our fights are with each other; not with the whites."

Cardozo-Freeman: "Tell me why this only happens between the minorities; why do they always fight with each other?"

Delorme: "Well, we always seem to be threatened by somebody. First and foremost we say nobody likes Indians. And we all know that the blacks don't like anybody and we all know the Chicanos don't speak any English. Right? The Chicanos and Indians are always startin a lot of trouble."

Psychological defenses involve such protective devices as masking fear with an outward show of toughness.

Gene: "I see guys in here that don't adjust to this routine, or lack of routine. About half of em sink. The other half swim."

Steve: "That's true."

Gene: "They may be a fairly decent person when they come in but they have to pick a direction to go."

Steve: "Some of em don't know how."

Gene: "They fall in with these other groups and maybe they're convinced that tryin to be a tough guy is the way to go, you know, so that's the way they go."

Steve: "That's fear. That's fear when you put up that front."

Gene: "Yeah. That's fear."

Steve: "Tough, rough guys. Everybody in here has that fear but they're always saying, 'Well, man, I ain't scared of anybody.' "

Gene: "But they're scared of everybody around em."

Steve: "They don't want to admit it. I'm scared every day I step out that door. I try to put up a front without voicin it. I walk around lookin mean and hard. That's my fear. And I know I can be hurt just as well as the next guy and I can hurt somebody just as much."

Gene: "How old are you?"

Steve: "I'm forty."

Gene: "You been in here a long time, haven't you."

Steve: "Yeah. A long time and I'll never get used to it."

Slipping and Sliding as Tragedy—Losing the Game

Sometimes a game player fails to learn the game properly or in a careless moment drops his guard, *slips* and makes a wrong *play*, and *slides* into disaster. The stage is then set for tragedy. The greatest danger is being murdered by fellow prisoners. Every man lives constantly with this thought. No one is immune to death, not even the most skilled at *the game*. Each killing, as it was pointed out, greatly increases the possibility for further violence because the men become so tense and fearful for their own survival. The following conversation was taped right after a killing took place in Eight Wing. Delorme and his cell partners express concern for a *fish*, Joe, sharing their *house* who had not let them know of his whereabouts. The conversation reflects the tension felt by everyone in the wing.

[Incredible noise, screaming. The man in the cell next to Delorme screams at guard: "Open the goddam door, you goddam sonovabitch! Don't make me mad or I'll break the fuckin door!"]

Gene: "Here's some sounds of lockup. Lockup time in the ole penitentiary. It's nine o'clock. Time for everybody to go in. We had a killing today in Eight Wing. They're all rootin around the tiers now ready to lock you up for the night. The maniacs next door are makin all the noise. [To cell partner] Well, they got us pretty much locked in, I think."

Bill: "Yeah. You ain't bullshittin. They all got dope or something."

Tom: "Yeah. He's loaded tonight. He got hold of some heroin or something."

Gene: "People are fuckin wired! Everybody thinks we're gettin locked down. They're havin a meeting about it and all that bullshit. They caught those jokers that escaped out of here. They caught those motherfuckers after they kidnapped a kid or something. Another life motherfuckin beef. I don't know why people do that kind of shit, man."

Tom: "Where they get the escapees at?"

Gene: "I don't know."

Bill: "I heard the name of the town but I can't remember it."

Tom: "You say he grabbed a hostage afterward?"

Gene: "Yeah. A young kid. [To Joe who has just come in.] Where'd you disappear to so goddam fast? You had a visitor?"

Joe: "Huh? No."

Gene: "You just split, man. You didn't come back for the count

and then you hit the road. Man, I thought you went out and got
knifed or something. I asked people if they'd seen you."

Joe: "I ate early and then I went back."

Gene: "You can't be doin that shit, Joe. You got to let us know
where in the fuck you're goin around here, man, or we can't keep
an eye on you if you don't."

Tom: "Gene was already cleaning out the cell."

Gene: "Sure. I already told Fatback he might move in here,
man, as soon as I checked on you. A man came in on the Chain
yesterday. No, tonight."

Bill: "I think the guy that came in on the Chain was a good guy,
too, from Yakima. They said he was a pretty good guy. He didn't
mention his name or nothin. We're goin to get another guy in here
sooner or later."

Gene: "Well, we'll wait. When they move somebody we'll trade
the guy, man. What they got to boost to go along with this deal?
'Here, you take this one. Make a little profit from the body.' . . .
Somebody talked with K. this afternoon and he said that if we had
a lockdown he'll resign. In other words, they wasn't even talkin
about a lockdown."

Tom: "It's the Lifers spreadin that shit, man. Why can't they just
fuckin lay low and let it blow over?"

Gene: "They like to cause this excitement shit, man. They
really whisper all over the place."

Bill: "So they got three guys locked up over the killing?"

Gene: "That's what Fatback says. Three of em. With those kinds
of vibrations goin around here, somebody's goin to get knifed
again in the next day or two, probably. Yeah, cause I seen some
damn near get down at least three times today. Different people
bumpin into each other just accidentally. One guy bumped into
another guy. It fuckin almost went all the way to a knife beef right
there. Thought this guy was goin to get his shiv after him. The
guy tried to apologize. It was a white and a black. 'What you think
you doin, white boy?' They went on and on and the guy says, 'Hey,
just the fuckin hang around. I'll be right back. I gotta go get a shiv,
man.' And his partner's goin, 'Hey, let it go, man.' Nobody gives
a fuck. It's a cold, cold world, man. You wonder does anybody give a
fuck about anything."

Bill: "They'll take a life just like that."

Gene: "Yeah. I was in here and they told us, 'Hey the guy who left here just got killed.' I missed my class and all that shit. I was sick, man, and I didn't even know the guy."

Tom: "So what you goin to do, man? You can't get involved or the same thing will happen to you. Guess that's what your life is worth in here, man."

Gene: "Ain't worth two cents. You don't like to see yourself gettin that way but how else you goin to be? You gotta be that way. You can't give a fuck about anything."

Tom: "See, Joe? You know now if you get killed around here, Gene ain't goin to worry. He's goin to wonder who in hell to put in that bed."

Gene: "I was already talkin to that guy. I said, 'I ain't seen my cell partner for hours, man. I may have this bottom bed for you tomorrow. I'll tell you tomorrow. He might of checked in. I think he's either dead or went to PC. The sonovabitch dropped the count. Never said he was goin to be out for chow. Never left me a fuckin note.' "

Joe: "Well, I didn't know until I got over there what had happened . . . "

Tom: "I started to think last night. I wonder if the guys out there did the killing?" [the escapees]

Gene: "I don't think so. They're all from Seven Wing. That don't mean they couldn't get in this wing. Eight Wing is easy to get in. You can't get in Seven Wing. I was over there the other night to see Fatback. They don't run around on the tiers over there or nothin. Nobody out of their cells in Seven Wing."

There are circumstances that touch off killings in prison that on the surface appear to be absolutely absurd. The episode of the killing described in the next narrative took place because of a dispute over spaghetti in the chow hall. A closer look at what occurred, however, reveals that something far more important was involved—a man's sense of his own dignity. One man asks another for a helping of spaghetti and is snubbed. The insulted man is so outraged he turns to powerful allies who ambush and stab the other man to death and wound his friend. The insulted man is a known *punk* who has become a member of the tough Bikers Club.

He is regarded as notorious for his troublemaking and the fact that he always turns the "dirty work" over to his Biker friends once the trouble starts. *Punks* are regarded with the utmost contempt by the population, as they are viewed as men who sell out their manhood out of cowardice and play the woman's role in the prison. The anger and hatred that a *punk* must feel toward the heterosexual men who revile and insult him in the prison can only be imagined. But, if a *punk* has been able to align himself with a group as ruthless and tough as the Bikers, he can set about exacting his revenge upon the self-righteous population. The man whom the *punk fingered* for assassination was a Lifer, a member of the elite club in the prison. In such a context, cruel and unjust as it is, a killing over spaghetti does not seem quite so irrational. This killing took place September 27, 1978, and the taping of what took place was made immediately after. The dialogue reflects the anger and helplessness many of the men felt after the violent episode.

Gene: "There's been two fights and a stabbing tonight so the Joint is in an uproar right at the moment. I just came in. There's guys outside the wing right now refusing to come in so it remains to be seen what happens here. As the evening wears on here I'll tell you what happens. If they refuse to come in, there's going to be a lot more trouble out there and it looks like we're goin to be locked up for a few days. We'll get that squared away. So that's the latest of the latest. Hasn't even hit the radio yet. Course, they'll know it before you do. It's lockup time so we shall see. I see some of the guys comin in for lockup. They're comin in slowly here, slowly but surely they're filtering in. As soon as something pops, I'll let you know. There's no big noise or screaming. If there was I'd put it on the tape so you could hear it. Believe me, it gets loud, banging these bars with tin cans, throwing stuff and screaming. It does get loud. I don't know about what happened down here yet. I watched the fight from in front of the chow hall [speaking to cell partner who just came in]."

Steve: "A few guys come over to the Lifers' table. When the guy was leavin he was at the end of the line and they grabbed him. He stabbed him."

Gene: "The rest of em took off?"

Steve: "Yeah. The other guys, those motherfuckers left him for dead."

Gene: "He was dead?"

Steve: "Well, he wasn't dead when they brought him back up to the. . . ."

Gene: "Did you see him go by? That long stringy haired punk?"

Steve: "Yeah."

Gene: "He's always throwin shit around in the chow hall. Thinks he's tough because he's got all those guys with him. He starts lots of fights. He ain't never fought alone yet."

Tom: "I ain't never seen him do nothin more than start the fight then back off and the rest of em jump the guys. They kick you all over the fuckin head and all that shit so you can't get a blow in."

Gene: "Like I was telling you, that's the way they do it. There's several of those Bikers I knew from years ago that are nothin but Joint punks. Now they feel like they got a little protection, you know. So that's what happened to em, man. They start doin that.

"Like they pulled that shit on that Lifer and they could have went one-on-one cause their guy wasn't fucked either. It would have been equal and it would have been over with, but not when they pull that shit. They sit around the door and wait for the other guy to come out. There was that little punk started hittin him and that was all he hit was once, then the rest of em jumped on him and started kickin him on the head and the Lifer had a buddy with him. He had nothin to do with it and they beat him up, too, kickin him around. Shit.

"I was sittin there watchin em. I knew they were waitin for him cause they had the door blocked off so he couldn't run or nothin when he come out. Well if I'd a known the guy was a Lifer, I'd a told Dan or somebody so that before the guy come out of the chow hall they'd a got a few Lifers down there to help him. If it was an Indian guy it wouldn't have happened either cause we was all out there. We'd a got him out. They thought they had that guy alone."

Tom: "So it died off?"

Gene: "Well, we'll find out when Ted comes in. I got that all down on tape for little ole Inez. I meant to tell her how it started. When they were goin through the chow hall on my side, I was

sittin there watchin and they ran out of spaghetti on our side. So
them other guys were still goin through on the other side. They
still had spaghetti. Well this dude, this Lifer, he was goin through
on the other side servin himself and that other asshole slammed
his tray over and said, 'Hey, man, put some on this tray.' The guy
told him to fuck off and walked away. That's all. It was over right
there. And the guy got pissed off and started screamin and hollerin
and he went on over to the fuckin guy [Lifer] and told him, 'Hey,
you better not come to the movie tonight,' and all that shit. Then
he went back over and started stirrin his buddies up, you know.
'That guy wouldn't give me any spaghetti.' And when it was over
he got his spaghetti and some knives, too.

"I was watchin him doin his fuckin cycle act, man [Biker act]. I
couldn't believe it. He wears glasses, plain rimmed glasses. This
guy I'm talkin about that started the whole thing has stringy blond
hair about this long, Levi jacket and everything. The whole Biker
trip. And he has a blond goatee. Oh, he wouldn't be as tall as me, I
don't think. Maybe with his boots on he might. So anyway when
they got done eatin, the guy [Lifer] was still eatin over there and
the Bikers went outside.

"When I walked out of the chow hall I seen the Bikers standin
around so I knew they were waitin for him. They got a trick. They
block this way and then they block that way and then they stand
right in front so the guy can't make a dash. They nail you either
way. They just kinda surround the door. Then when the Lifer
came out, man, the punk fingered him right there and they started
a fight and then they got him down on the ground an they started
kickin him and shit like that. His buddy tried to do something and
they got him down, too, and somebody kicked him in the head
before he could move."

Tom: "A lot of things are like for benefits. Workin for benefits."

Gene: "Yeah. I was goin to tell Inez about one of the things she
wants to know about—the power structure in this prison. You can
see this prison is different because it's groups; not individuals that
have the power. Those guys could never be leaders in here [Bikers].
They could never be constructive leaders in here because all they
care about is themselves and bein tough. They put that tough
thing on, push people. All the time pushin people. It's gotta

turn on em. The whole population, that whole club is like that."

The Lifers have got a helluva lot more of the population than they've got. There's like 300–400 Lifers in this joint. If those guys got mad about it, the Bikers wouldn't stand a chance. They wouldn't have a club. They wouldn't have nothin. They'd be killin everyone of em off."

Tom: "I'm gonna see what else I can find out about this. . . . "

Gene: "Played funeral music for the brother that was killed tonight. . . . I'm back. We had a meeting about this fracas. One guy stabbed seven-eight times. He died. Another guy stabbed in the hand. He's in the hospital downtown. They said they're not goin to lock us up so we'll be out tomorrow. They called us all out to a meeting to talk about it about 10:30–11:00 o'clock. [club leaders]

"I just got back in. It's about one o'clock [AM] We had to go to all the wings and tell everybody everything's cool. Tell em not to worry about gettin jumped. There won't be no gang war between the clubs. That was the main thing—to see what happens now to the guys that were involved. That's gonna come out later on. I don't know too much about it myself yet. I know the whole thing started over some spaghetti, if you can believe that. Just some spaghetti. One man dead. Another man in the hospital with a crippled hand. He got all the tendons cut in his hand. . . .

"This is Sunday morning. Everything came out alright. Nobody dead today. Nobody wounded. Anymore, it's a miracle to get through the day and not lose somebody. All we can do is keep workin at it. Keep tryin. It's all gangs when this happens. It's supposed to be clubs but with the atmosphere in here it kind of looks that way at times. The idea is [for the clubs] to serve as protection, security for the members, safety, so in that respect it looks more like a gang thing because if somebody gets hurt, you'd have a gang fight with some other club. It's not supposed to be that way. When positive vibes go on then you have better programming, but now it's at an all time low, really. We just survive from day to day the best we can, each guy lookin out for himself. If you're lucky, somebody else is lookin out for you if you belong to a club. And anybody that doesn't belong has no protection."

One of the most painful experiences in prison is witnessing the murder of another man. Each man connects the violent death of another to his own end and reacts intensely to the traumatic experience. Viewing an assassination causes enormous psychological suffering, not only because a killing is horrible to witness but because the viewer may be overwhelmed with feelings of guilt for having stood by and done nothing to stop it. The code demands a *do your own time* policy, and anyone who tries to stop a killing is likely to be murdered himself later on.

"This past week I witnessed a killing right outside my wing. Made me mad, sick, depressed; you name it. This was the second one in less than a year for me. I wish the tower guard would have killed all three of the guys who did it.

"I was coming back from supper and I was walking towards the wing when I saw a group struggling up ahead. They were stabbing the guy in the front and back. Someone also cut his throat during the scuffle. I hung back til they let him go. They turned and ran into the Lifers Park but they weren't Lifers. The guy that they stabbed staggered into the wing door and tried to get in but the pig wouldn't open the door—scared. The blood was squirting all over the place.

"I just stood and watched. I didn't feel anything for him at the time and that's what really bothers me now. There isn't anything to be done. He was dead on his feet. I knew he was dead. I'm sure he knew he was a dead man. The guard knew he was dead. All that was left was for him to lay down and die, which he did. There was so much blood that it seemed like someone slaughtered a cow instead of a man. I looked at his eyes. They were glassy and he quit moving pretty quick. It was still a while before the stretcher came to pick up the 'carcass'—that's what you're called when your game is up; just another carcass to haul away.

"The convict code stinks. It's so wrong I can't tell you. I hate it and it makes me feel subhuman. I don't agree with it in any way, but still I've changed. I can remember when I thought it was right. But I know now it's not right. I have investigated it. I have watched it and seen it work and it's the horriblest goddam thing I have ever seen. It makes you feel like an animal. It makes you feel subhuman. It drains you.

"I never had a part in a killing but I still feel guilty. These killings make me feel rotten. I want to stop it somehow and I feel like somehow I have participated in it. I know that I haven't, you know, but just being here and being a good convict, I guess it makes me partially to blame. These things happen. I do what I can to change things in here to stop it but it is just a losing battle.

"This system works hard to turn us all into monsters. This prison is a jungle and makes good men turn back into savages just to survive. Society, free society, sets controls and a man works to become civilized because he has to be civilized to keep from becoming an outcast. In a place like this it works just the opposite. I fight it constantly. I always have.

"There have been times in here when my own thoughts have turned to murder as the only way to deal with someone who I didn't like or who I thought did me wrong. Those times were hard for me. I fought with everything I had to understand and cool my temper. It scared me because my rage would be so hot and when I aimed it all at one person it became almost uncontrollable.

"The wrongs done me never amounted to much—it would be something like a watch I bought once and it didn't keep the right time. It became super important to keep the guy who sold it to me from thinking he put one over on me. I made some pretty gory plans for him. I had a knife, but I also had my brother to stop me when things became serious. I sat and brooded over that watch for a couple weeks till I thought everyone was laughing, then I felt I had to do it or everyone would think I was a punk. Needless to say, I also didn't want to do it either. I realized at the time that it was this place working to turn me into a monster like some of the others in here.

"I always call these people monsters, the people I know who have killed another inside or outside the prison. I tried to explain the evil in here to close friends but it seems like I'm alone most of the time or others don't really care.

"Speaking about culture, I often picture us like in scenes in movies I've seen that show groups of people roaming around a bombed out city after a nuclear war taking food from other groups, no laws, every man for himself, killing people who have something you want. That's my picture of this place. I don't know about other prisons but I believe that most American prisons are run the same—the strongest survive, prey on the weak.

"Sometimes I despise the weak ones and other times I wish I had the power to sort them out and take care of them. I think mostly I walk around and try not to see them but I'm fascinated by the way they accept their condition and move out of people's way or duck and dodge and run, which saves them from a beating most of the time, because it's funny to see a grown man scamper off yelling for help—there isn't any help—so tempers cool fast. I wonder if they know this or if they are acting on impulse.

"It's hard to explain why there is such little regard for human life in here. I can see that it isn't any different on the streets and that's the way it is in here. I'm talking about the criminal element and drug culture. They are always at each other's throats on the streets. This attitude is brought inside. It's a sign of the times—every man for himself. Do your thing and fuck anyone who gets in the way. If a guy burns you for some dope once, dust him so he can't beat you twice.

"In a closed culture like the Joint every move you make is like being on a stage—all eyes are on you so that even if you don't want to hurt someone over a petty debt, the pressure is on to deal strongly with the problem or your ass will be fair game for everyone else. You'll lose all respect if you let anyone slide. It is easier if the guy is smaller, but you can't take any chances on not kicking some ass because the prison culture is a deadly culture—we want revenge for insults and a life for an ass-kicking. The attitude says, 'No one has to take any shit from *anyone* in prison.' No man is bad enough to withstand a knife in the heart.

"All men want to have respect in prison. Respect does not come easy and it never comes from letting people fuck you over. Nice guys can't win, although in extreme cases you can be both tough and nice and charm the skin off the snake so he can't slip no more."

The episode that brought about a four-month *lockdown* and gave the officials the opportunity to "take back power" occurred in June, 1979. It began with the killing of a native American by Chicanos over a bad debt in drug dealing and ended with the killing of a guard. This example of wrong moves made in *slipping and sliding* brought about a revolutionary change in the running of the prison. The curtain came down on an era that had lasted for nearly ten years.

Delorme: "In the case of those guys that killed Broncho, those guys were killin people for money, for dope money. And the guys I was tellin you about, the killers, they wanted to get rid of the guys that killed Broncho. They put those guys down as not even human because of what they was doin to people in here, so it was nothin to kill em. So when Broncho got killed that was the last straw and the guys came to me and they knew my feelings about it. Those were the three guys I was tellin you about.

"Like I told you we got guys in here who sort of take care of everybody. They spot a cancer in the population. They spot two guys that are dangerous to everybody, then they consider these guys, how much time they're doin and so on. These guys, they figure should die for what they've done because they've killed two or three people and they're gonna do it again over the dope game. All this affects the morale and the mood of the institution. It affects these guys lives, too, because they have to live in here.

"But anyway they came to me and they said, 'We want to kill the guys that killed Broncho. We'll do it for you if you want us to do it.' "

Cardozo-Freeman: "Was Broncho an Indian?"

Delorme: "Yeah. So they said, 'We'll do it. This is it. This is the last person they're gonna kill in here.' So I said, 'Wait. Give me a chance,' cause I wasn't positive who did it to Broncho. I was still tryin to find out some names and everybody knew but I wasn't sure. They didn't even want any dough for doin it. But that put me on the spot there. Hell, I'm not goin to be the one to tell em to go do it. The real danger is gettin the wrong guy cause when you're that mad. Don Pedro, that old guy you was talkin to, would die if he walked by because he was Mexican, see. That was the attitude of everybody. 'Fuck who did it. We don't care who did it. Get any Mexican.' "

Cardozo-Freeman: "Was it a Chicano that killed Broncho?"

Gene: "Four of em. Four of em and one white guy."

Cardozo-Freeman: "What caused the trouble between the Mexicans and the Indians? Why did they kill Broncho?"

Gene: "A lot of your favorite subject—cultural differences. They constantly was arguin about it. The Mexicans kept talkin that respect shit and their macho bullshit. And the Indians didn't give a shit about their respect. Don't give a fuck about their macho bullshit and actually chide em. They say, 'We're more man than you guys are anyway.' "

Cardozo-Freeman: "Are you saying that Indians aren't concerned with this?"

Delorme: "It isn't first and foremost on their mind."

Cardozo-Freeman: "But it is first and foremost for Hispanic men."

Delorme: "Yeah. It's not that important to Indians."

Cardozo-Freeman: "So the Indians didn't know that what they were doing was tampering with something that could get them killed? 'If you insult my sense of my manhood, I'm willing to kill you and to die for it.' "

Delorme: "The Indians didn't weigh that."

Cardozo-Freeman: "That's a traditional Hispanic view."

Delorme: "Some people you just don't come up and threaten to kill. Well, they went up to Broncho. They were hasslin. They were arguin. There was lies goin back and forth. Broncho owed one of em twenty-five or thirty dollars. So something happened and his check didn't get here and he had to put it off a couple of times.

"And then we had a little Indian that was a liar in the group that was an instigator. A lyin little bastard—Fire Necklace. And they sent him over from Monroe for causin trouble over there and we knew this and was warned in advance that he was gonna cause trouble if we listened to him cause he was always lyin. He was real young. So he come runnin to Broncho.

"Broncho was real dangerous, too, only he didn't like nobody to bother him and he's self-righteous. Like when this Indian got in a fight one day he thought we should go stab the other guy and all that shit. That's a pride thing, too, but when it's the Indians, it isn't simply an individual thing like it is with the Mexicans. The Indians seem to be protecting their whole race from gettin killed or 'You can't do that to Indians.' But it isn't an individual *macho* trip."

Cardozo-Freeman: "It might avoid confrontations if the guys understood their cultural differences. There should be an understanding for the respect aspect, which is so important to the Chicanos."

Delorme: "Yeah. You're right. Anyway, one of them Chicanos came over and Fire Necklace happened to be alone in the house. The Chicano said, 'Man, somebody's got to take care of this debt or there's just goin to be trouble.' Which is what you would say cause everything in here leads to trouble when there's debts. And so he left and then the guys came back to the cell, the Indian brothers, and they were all loaded. Not on pot; they were loaded on that sniffin glue, cause that's all we ever used to do in there. And they're still doin that. They're just real crazy all the time.

"And Fire Necklace said, 'Them Mexicans came over and threatened me. They came over and threatened me and they said they're gonna kill a bunch of Indians.' Actually, only one guy came over. They didn't all come over. He said they came over and threatened to kill a bunch of Indians, which we found out after this was all over it was a goddam lie. So they said, 'Well, who in the hell do they think they are comin over here and threatenin us?'

"So they all got their knives and they went around the corner of the tier over to those Mexicans' cells. And they said, 'You want to kill us? Come out right now and let's get the shit on now.' The Chicanos didn't have their knives and shit then. They didn't know what the hell they were talkin about anyway. The Indians were all standing there like this sniffin with them rags and crazy, and the other three guys [Chicanos] didn't even know what the hell had gone down. But they were gettin called every kind of creep, greasy punk in the world.

"The Indians said, 'Come on out here. Let's get it on.' But the Mexicans wouldn't come out and fight, see. So that was a little stab at the ole pride right there, you know, to get put down like that. But they had sense enough not to open the door. So it snowballed from there. They got madder and madder about that and nothin happened.

"That happened one week. Another week or two went by and nothin happened. I lost track of it and pretty soon one day Broncho was goin over to go call his sister to send him the dough, but in the meantime Fire Necklace and another guy were still instigatin and they started threatenin each other more [the Indians and Chicanos]. Broncho started bein Fire Necklace's protector.

"The Chicano group were gonna kill Fire Necklace; not Broncho.

They were gonna kill Fire Necklace because they knew who started it. So Broncho decided he was gonna protect Fire Necklace cause he believed him. So Broncho ended up gettin killed.

"He took his knife and went over there to the phone room. There was five Mexicans over there. Broncho took his knife and he didn't tell any of us because if he would of, it wouldn't have happened cause the guys woulda went with him."

Cardozo-Freeman: "Was he independent of the other Indians?"

Delorme: "Yeah. He didn't like people fighting his fights for him. Broncho was *macho* in that respect. He didn't like anybody interferin in his fights. He figured he could handle them himself, and he could. So he'd walk into any crowd.

"Anyway he didn't see em when he went to the phone room. He went in and they caught him goin out around the corner and jumped him in the phone room. A great big guy pulled him out of the phone booth and held his arms while the other ones stabbed him in the belly. Then after they finished stabbing him they let him go. He fell to the floor and died. He was screamin, 'They're killin me!' Nobody helped. Everybody ran away. So he never even got his knife out.

"But he didn't let nobody know what was happenin. I guess he didn't really know that they were there cause they were hidin in the RC office. But somehow they knew he was goin to be there. Oh, I know; one of em came over to Broncho's cell right after breakfast; that's how they knew. The white guy came to Broncho's cell."

Cardozo-Freeman: "A white guy was involved?"

Delorme: "Yeah. They shipped him to Idaho after that."

Cardozo-Freeman: "What was he doing with the Chicanos?"

Delorme: "Oh they always have a couple white guys with em and they have one Indian."

Cardozo-Freeman: "Guys who are on their side?"

Delorme: "Well that guy was because . . . well, that's natural; whoever sells dope has the most friends and that's all those guys did was sell dope, so they had two or three white guys, and this guy spoke Mexican. He was probably from California. Guys that come down from California get along better with em than other guys do because they speak Mexican, or if they've been in Quentin or somewhere, or if you've been in Colorado [in prison]."

Cardozo-Freeman: "How did that explode into a general confrontation?"

Delorme: "Oh well, shit, word was flyin all over the place. Guys that seen it happen came runnin, beatin a path over to Eight Wing to alert everybody that the shit was on, that they had just killed an Indian. And so Sam came up and told me. This was the beginning of June. Sam was standin there and then a couple more guys came and told me so I got up and put on my coat and went over there to see who it was and what it was about. I couldn't get any info other than I could see him laying there around the corner, but I couldn't get in. So I was checkin all the faces and takin names to get back later to who was hangin around there."

Cardozo-Freeman: "Could you have avoided this disaster?"

Delorme: "Yeah. If he wouldn't a went alone. If he had some help with him it wouldn't have happened then."

Cardozo-Freeman: "Was there anything after the murder took place that you could have done to calm things down? What caused the lockdown?"

Delorme: "We helped calm things down. We went to two lieutenants and let em know who did it. Let em know what was gonna happen if they didn't do something about it and they didn't do nothin. They wouldn't."

Cardozo-Freeman: "What did they say to you?"

Delorme: "They didn't say nothin to me cause I didn't talk to em personally. I went through E. and listened on the phone while he told em. The whole population knew who did it. They [the lieutenants] said, 'Yeah, yeah. We know. We'll handle it.' And then three-four days later they still hadn't done anything. They still hadn't taken knives away from anybody."

Cardozo-Freeman: "Should they have locked those guys up?"

Delorme: "Yeah. They should have put em in segregation. They should have shaken our clubs down; took our knives away. They sent me and D.G. out there to try to cool things down. You couldn't cool nothin down."

Cardozo-Freeman: "The guys were still in population? The killers?"

Delorme: "Yeah."

Cardozo-Freeman: "So the problem was that the Indians were going to get the Mexicans?"

Delorme: "The problem was the administration for not lockin em up and anybody else that wanted to get their nose into it."

Cardozo-Freeman: "Just like a war. People taking sides as if they were lining up two armies to battle each other."

Delorme: "Yeah. By the time the Indians had their list together of who they were gonna off, number one on the list was an Indian who was in the Lifers Club. He was president. They were gonna kill him first. Then they were gonna kill that white guy. Then there was another white guy that had somethin to do with it somewhere along the line just distantly. They put him on the list. And then they had five Mexicans on the list plus fire bombs for their club rooms. That's what was gonna happen that day that the guard got killed, so actually he saved a lot of lives."

Cardozo-Freeman: "How did that happen?"

Delorme: "Oh, he was just a dirty racist dog and he'd been always fightin with the Indians, harrassin em anytime he could and the sweat lodge was out behind Eight Wing by the kitchen and so they needed some wood to get the fire goin for the sweat that day. And the sweat was a memorial for Broncho who just got killed, so you know emotions were pretty high.

"So they were out there breakin up some old boxes and wood they found behind the kitchen and the sergeant come runnin out and told em to get the hell away from there and took it away from em, carried it, runnin over and being smart all the whole time, so then that night in the chow hall after everybody was pissed off at him anyway, and after the shift lieutenants told all the guards, him included, not to bother the Indians and Mexicans, leave em alone and let this shit calm down or something. Actually, they wanted a war to start. But he had the information along with everybody else to leave em alone. He walked up to one of the Indians and tried to shake him down."

Cardozo-Freeman: "Was he a new guard?"

Delorme: "Fuck, no. He'd been here years. Well-hated. Been here quite awhile. He was a stinkin racist. Anybody that wasn't pure white, and as far as that goes, anyone who wasn't raised in Walla Walla. To him we're all Commies, hippies, and radicals. So any chance he got to run over to make you mad—he thought he was protected by God or someone—he would do it. Like grabbin stuff out of your hands and things like that. Rude all the time. Snotty.

"So he went up to those two Indian brothers that night after chow and told em to stand for a shakedown, so they just spit in his face. Then when he tried to grab hold of one of em, he started drillin him with a knife and the other brother reached out and stabbed him. Then there was another cop standin there so somebody punched him, knocked him down and that was it. But they weren't out there to kill no cops. They weren't out there to kill Mexicans either that night. They were gonna take the guards hostage in Eight Wing at nine o'clock after lockup. Some Indians were gonna stay out and take the guards hostage and tie em up and open the cells and go down and take care of that hit list."

In *Homo Ludens*, Huizinga writes extensively about the characteristics of archaic culture. Many of the values, attitudes, and behaviors of men in such societies can be recogned in the prison culture. In some ways a prison culture resembles the archaic, although in a sunken form.

Several characteristics attributed by Huizinga to archaic culture are found at Walla Walla; for example, the concept of honor is firmly grounded in *superbia*, or pride.[18] Similarly, pride is extremely evident in prison culture—a man is often willing to die defending his honor or the honor of his people and is quick to kill another man for insulting him. The narratives on the murders of the Lifer and Broncho clearly demonstrate this. *Machismo* is simply a continuation, though in a lower form, of archaic behavior. Courage and honor are uppermost in archaic culture; the same is true in prison culture.[19] Archaic culture is a "shame" culture; that is, how one looks in the eyes of one's peers is uppermost. Similarly in prison, to lose respect or esteem, to be shamed in the eyes of fellow prisoners is unacceptable. Again, the murders of the Lifer and Broncho demonstrate this need for respect.

In archaic society every win for an individual in a battle was a win for society as a whole. The same is so in a prison culture. The "feeling of being 'apart together' in an exceptional situation, of sharing something important, of mutually withdrawing from the rest of the world and rejecting the usual norms"[20] gives the prisoners participating together in the game of survival a sense of unity. In prison, as in archaic society, every victory "realizes for the victor the triumph of the good powers over the bad."[21]

Huizinga points out that heroic and agonistic elements were very strong in such societies; indeed, archaic society was built upon contest.[22] These elements can also be recognized as very important aspects of prison culture. In archaic times virtue meant "manly courage," and a man received respect and was honored by his peers by demonstrating that he possessed manly courage. He proved that he possessed "virtue" by contending on the battlefield in games of war. In prison the same is true: manly courage *is* virtue. As Delorme states, "All men want in prison is respect." And respect in prison is won through demonstrating manly courage through battle savvy. Respect comes to the man who knows how to contest successfully, how to contend in all ways, including on the prison battlefield. This is how he proves himself.[23] Taking risks, tolerating uncertainty, and enduring tension are all connected to the agonistic aspects of having to play the game. Agonistic activities involve mental and physical hardship. Such activities are "agonizing." The Greek word for contest originally meant "death struggle" and "fear."[24] Contest is connected to struggle, exercise, endurance, suffering, and exertion.[25] All of these agonistic aspects are experienced by the prisoner in his game of *slipping and sliding*. Pitting himself against all the odds that confront him on the prison battlefield, the contender contests, endures, suffers, and struggles to win.

Huizinga acknowledged that although higher civilizations do not approve of cheating in game playing archaic cultures employed trickery as a means of winning.[26] The same approach to winning is used by the men in prison. *Conning* is a very important aspect of the game the prisoner plays, as demonstrated by Delorme's narrative describing his apprehension by the guard for *packing a shank*.

Huizinga states that men in archaic culture prove themselves through "noble strife" and that "chivalry, loyalty, courage and self-control" contributed much to the archaic cultures that pursued these ideals.[27] While "noble" may be the incorrect adjective to use in describing "strife" in a prison culture, the pursuit of loyalty, courage, and self-control is often evident. Those men who are most respected demonstrate these qualities.

Loyalty was paramount in the "agonistic warrior-life of archaic times."[28] Loyalty is defined as "surrender of the self to a person, cause or idea without arguing the reason for this surrender or doubting the lasting nature of it."[29] Central to the convict code, in itself a kind of warrior code, is the concept of unquestioned loyalty. The code is also grounded in the premise that the prisoner is at war with prison authorities. In studying the many narratives collected from prisoners at Walla Walla, I have often noticed how much a prison culture resembles a war camp under siege and how often prisoners' behavior resembles the behavior of warriors in combat. The analogy of a prison with archaic culture is justified.[30]

There is irony in the perception that survival in prison is "play." Play is not supposed to be serious, yet this play is very serious indeed. Wrong moves can be fatal, as the last few narratives have demonstrated. Thomas Szasz and Eric Berne both point out that people play games in an attempt to take control of difficult life situations.[31] Certainly this is what the prisoners are attempting to do—take control of an unpredictable and dangerous life circumstance. In addition, *slipping and sliding* allows the men some degree of control over the concept of time, speeding it up, making it pass unnoticed, making it less monotonous, even interesting at times, and certainly making it less dangerous. Furthermore, mastering the skills of survival helps the men assume not only a degree of mastery over the tyrant, time, but also over the territory or space within which they play their game. Through understanding the layout of the "playground," a player is careful about when and where he makes his moves. Skilled players manipulate and use both time and space to their advantage. Placing survival into the context of play not only lightens the gravity and danger of the situation but also relieves the boredom and routine that so often engulfs the prisoner in his world. Viewing survival in prison as a game is not, after all, an inappropriate procedure for accommodation to prison existence, but rather it is a wise accommodation. Such a stance assures the greatest possibility for successfully confronting and dealing with the difficulties of prison existence. Of course, no one is ever assured of winning every game, as has been demonstrated.[32]

NOTES

[1]John Aron Grayzel has written on play and the play motif in a state penitentiary. Grayzel noticed how the prisoners manipulated the concept of play through an awareness that symbols that indicate play are symbols, which therefore can be manipulated to suit their purposes. He points out that the prisoners viewed much of their activity as "play" and spoke of it as such. For example, both the prisoners and the staff looked upon "programming: as 'playing a game.' " "Playing" for the men was the same as "not being serious in what one was doing." This was in contrast to the concept of "gaming," a "serious pursuit of a goal, such as obtaining an early release date." No mention of play as a game for survival is brought out in Grayzel's study. "The Functions of Play and the Play Motif at a State Penitentiary," in *Play: Anthropological Perspectives*, Michael A. Salter, Editor (West Point, N.Y.: Leisure Press, 1978), pp. 94–103.

[2]Although anthropologists recognize Huizinga's contribution to their field, they do not agree with his definition of culture. Alyce Taylor Cheska points out that current research on play focuses on, "developing theoretical paradigms of anthropology: psychobiological orientation, cultural ecology, and structural analysis," and that future research "may polarize around symbolism and structure, bio-cultural phenomenon, and adaptive potentiation." "Theoretical Contributions to the Study of Play," in *Play: Anthropological Perspectives*, p. 29.

[3]*Homo Ludens: A Study of the Play Element in Culture* (Boston: Beacon Press, 1950), p. 23.

[4]Maurer's work reveals that in almost all the subcultures of the underworld, the members refer to themselves as "players" and the connotation goes beyond the obvious meaning of playing in a game. They feel that they are the only true people, and while they realize that other people exist, they set up a social distance between themselves and others as a strategic way of rationalizing their acts against others. I am endebted to Allan Futrell for pointing this out to me in a correspondence of June 27, 1981.

[5]*Homo Ludens*, p. 89.

[6]*Homo Ludens*, p. 52.

[7]*Homo Ludens*, p. 4.

[8]*Conning*, in this sense, is derived from the word "convict" and is not to be confused with the professional maneuvers of confidence men in the underworld rackets described by David Maurer.

[9]Quoted from a correspondence concerning Maurer's work with Allan Futrell, June 27, 1981.

[10]Correspondence, Futrell, June 27, 1981.

[11]Bruay Heading states that the analogy of the theatre with the relationship between the social structure and the individual, inspired the development of role analyses. Malcolm Bradbury, Bruay Heading, and Martin Hollis, "The Man and the Mask: A Discussion of Role Theory," in *Role*, J. A. Jackson, Editor (London: Cambridge University Press, 1972), p. 43. Erving Goffman has written on the dramatic aspects of cultural and social transactions. He views society as a stage

where individuals play their parts assuming masks for each role. *The Presentation of Self in Everyday Life* (Garden City, N.Y.: Doubleday Anchor Books, 1959), and *Encounters: Two Studies in the Sociology of Interaction* (Indianapolis, Indiana: Bobbs-Merrill Company, 1961).

[12]Erving Goffman, *Strategic Interaction* (Philadelphia: University of Pennsylvania Press, 1969), pp. 100–101. The conditions for strategic interaction are defined by Goffman as follows: "Two or more parties must find themselves in a well-structured situation of mutual impingement where each party must make a move and where every possible move carries fateful implications for all the parties. In this situation, each player must influence his own decision by knowing that the other players are likely to dope out his decision in advance, and may even appreciate that he knows this is likely. Courses of action or moves will then be made in the light of one's thoughts about the other's thoughts about oneself. An exchange of moves made on the basis of this kind of orientation to self and others can be called strategic interaction."

[13]*Strategic Interaction*, pp. 85–86.

[14]*Strategic Interaction*, pp. 96–97.

[15]The long *lockdown* of 1979, which caused the officials to disband and then reinstate the clubs in an altered form, has profoundly affected their usefulness, while at the same time alleviated some of their dangers. Before the *lockdown*, each club had its own meeting place, whereas today all clubs hold meetings in the auditorium during scheduled times.

[16]*Convicts, Codes and Contraband* (Cambridge: Ballinger Publishing Co., 1974).

[17]A tragic example of mixing signals and confusing prison survival games with street survival games can be demonstrated in the experience of Jack Henry Abbott, author of the compelling book on prison life, *In the Belly of the Beast* (New York: Random House, 1981), who when released from prison after spending most of his life there, responded to a personal confrontation on the street in the only manner he knew: kill or be killed. Had authorities responsible for releasing him recognized the enormous difficulty he faced in making the transition from the world of "kill or be killed" to the world of "Thou shalt not kill" and tried to "deprogram" him, he may not have been returned to prison for murdering a man.

[18]*Homo Ludens*, p. 100.

[19]In contemporary American society, honor and courage are pursued, or made manifest, through less dangerous avenues such as spectator sports and commerce.

[20]*Homo Ludens*, p. 12.

[21]*Homo Ludens*, p. 56.

[22]*Homo Ludens*, pp. 46–75.

[23]In archaic culture, honor *is* virtue. Virtue, which comes from the Latin *virtus*, originally meant "manly courage." "Virile" comes from *virtus*. (Since the time of the Greeks and Romans, "virtue" has changed in its meaning assuming under Christian influence an ethical-religious dimension.) Men in archaic times sought honor or virtue through agon, or contest—that is, war play. It was through play on the battlefield that Greek warriors, for example, achieved glory through

excellence in their exploits in battle, and hence gained honor and respect from their peers. *Homo Ludens*, p. 64.

[24]*Homo Ludens*, p. 51.

[25]*Homo Ludens*, p. 51.

[26]*Homo Ludens*, p. 52.

[27]*Homo Ludens*, p. 102.

[28]*Homo Ludens*, p. 104.

[29]*Homo Ludens*, p. 104.

[30]The more "archaic" the prisoner's perspective, the more he adheres to the prisoner honor code; whereas, the more convinced he becomes that he would prefer to join the "civilized" majority culture, the more he distains the code. The change in Delorme's attitude is an example.

[31]Thomas S. Szasz, *The Myth of Mental Illness* (New York: Harper & Row, 1974); Eric Berne, *Games People Play* (New York: Grove Press, 1964).

[32]In the killing of the guard by the native Americans, prisoners who critiqued this chapter pointed out that the guard that was killed had come to the assistance of a younger and more inexperienced guard who had attempted to *shake down* the native American.

Chapter 6

THE BULLS

Control of reality is realized through identifying and defining what is perceived in it. If something or someone is viewed as threatening, the identifying label reveals this. Derogatory naming is, in a sense, a form of exorcism, a neutralizing of the malevolent powers that are perceived. In such circumstances, words assume magical power. In prison, language sometimes takes on this magical dimension. Derogatory naming is used by prisoners and sometimes guards to identify, define, and place each other into perspective. Such name calling flourishes in the prison and becomes particularly intense during periods of extreme tension or when confrontations between guards and prisoners develop. Ordinarily, guards do not call prisoners names to their faces, and they are forbidden to do so, but under extreme stress, some guards "lose it" and resort to the same verbal behavior as the prisoners. Fear and hatred are always the basis for such invective. Derogatory naming functions in this respect as defensive action against the "enemy," with both prisoner and guard using language in a magical sense to ward off the malevolent powers of the other.

METAPHORS FOR EXORCISING POWER

The derogatory labels the prisoners at Walla Walla use to identify guards manifest a particular quality in common: they signal that the prisoners view the guards as nonhuman, as *bulls, dogs, pigs, goons, robots,* and *silons*. In part, this is a coping mechanism, as it helps the prisoners deal with the power the guards hold over them. An attempt is made to neutralize the guards' power by reducing them to something less than they are. Such a method for dealing with people who are threatening is also commonly used beyond the prison. It is especially prevalent in instances of racial

219

prejudice, ethnocentrism, chauvinism, and so on.[1] Disapproval
and uneasiness, as well as fear is implicit in the images the labels
convey: stampeding bulls and mad dogs, for example, or armies of
robots and silons relentlessly closing in. Such animals, monsters,
or mechanical creatures can create havoc when their powers are
wantonly unleashed on caged or cornered human beings. When
the guards choose to exercise this threatening power, they, in the
view of the prisoners, are the ones who should be caged, since
when they behave inhumanely, they are dangerous and damaging.

Bulls, dogs, and *pigs,* the derogatory labels most commonly used
by the men, have long been used to designate policemen. *Bull* has
been in existence since before 1800. It originated in England and
may have been borrowed there from Spanish gypsy usage since *bul*
is Spanish slang for policeman.[2] In English, the word images the
aggressive and brutal physical strength of the most *macho* of animals.
Bull-dog, meaning a sheriff's officer or bailiff, was in use in England
before 1698.[3] *Bull,* commonly used in the American underworld,
has assumed many variations; for example, a *cinder bull* is a private detective or policeman employed by the railroad,[4] a *fly-bull* is
a policeman assigned to special duty,[5] a *harness bull* is a uniformed
policeman,[6] and a *yard bull* is a prison or railroad guard.[7] *Fish-bull,*
a common term at Walla Walla, identifies young, new, and inexperienced guards. Although *pig,* designating policeman, may have
originated in the U.S. during the late 1950s or early 1960s, its use
in England dates back to before 1785.[8] In London, a Bow Street
Officer was called a China Street *pig.*[9] In the *lingo* spoken at Walla
Walla, the *pigs* often "root around" and "trot down" the tiers. *Dog,*
which identifies a particularly bad guard, is a contemptuous term
for man that has been used since before 1703.[10] Today, the term is
commonly used in the majority culture to identify anyone or
anything considered inferior. Dogberry, denoting a stupid constable or magistrate, appears in Shakespeare's *Much Ado About
Nothing.* As demonstrated, the prisoners carry on a very old
tradition by identifying policemen as *bulls, pigs,* and *dogs.*

More recent labels—*goon, robot,* and *silon*—reflect modern times,
however. The label *goon squad,* designating groups of guards all
chosen for their great size, who are sent to break up fights or take
offenders to Segregation or the *Hole,* may have been borrowed

from the Labor Movement in the U.S., as "goon squads" were groups of thugs employed to break strikes. The label dates to around 1935. Alice the Goon in "Popeye," the comic strip created by Elzie Segar, may in all likelihood account for the use of the term *goon*.[11] The identification of guards as *robots* and *silons* is a recent phenomenon in the prison. The men connect the ominous appearance and behavior of the riot squads during times of serious confrontation to these nonhuman creations. Presumably, the men see these detached and depersonalized creatures as man-made specifically by the state to tyrannize and intimidate them into submission.

OTHER LABELS

Despite the derogatory naming and the fear, hatred, and contempt their use reveals, the prisoners have other labels for guards that demonstrate that they are not always viewed as nonhuman. Terms that may be defined as neutral or friendly are frequently used. Under certain conditions, some guards and prisoners respect one another and may develop positive, personal, and supportive relationships. It all depends on the particular people involved, the circumstances, and the conditions in the prison, as some of the narratives presented here reveal.

Neutral terms used by the prisoners are "guards," "officers," and *cops*. *Cops*, designating policemen, dates to before 1848 and is an abbreviation of the British *copper*. Copper refers to the buttons on the English policeman's uniform.[12] Although *copper*, a term commonly used in the American underworld is derogatory, *cop*, as used in the prison is not.[13] *The Man*, although sometimes used to identify guards, is a term that also identifies higher ups in power both in the prison and society. *Asshole* is a term popular with both prisoners and guards, a term that everyone calls everyone else (a curious phenomenon). *Good people* is, on rare occasions, a name bestowed upon certain guards who have proven their fairness. Bestowing such a title on those who are traditionally viewed with suspicion, hostility, and contempt reveals an appreciation for decency and fairness among the prisoners despite the often negative encounters and the milieu of prison existence, which militates against positive communication, attitudes, and behavior between keeper and kept.

Cardozo-Freeman: "You were saying there's a difference between the *Goon Squad* and the Riot Squad."

Delorme: "They have certain people that they call when they have a situation in the wings. It's not necessarily a riot-type of thing but a drunken party or something like that, and they like to send the big people, oversized. They always have their biggest guards as part of the goon squad so when they have to go and take guys to the Hole or something, they call these guys and get them all together. They might be sergeants; they might be nobodies; they might be lieutenants, too. Just so they're big. They go together and arrest somebody, or just their physical presence [settles the situation]; that kind of thing. That's the Goon Squad."

Cardozo-Freeman: "Why do they call them *goons?*"

Delorme: "Well, just because they look like goons. Big ole hulking dummies, gorilla-type suckers. That's a goon. The Riot Squad is everybody. Every cop in the Joint is on the Riot Squad. They have helmets, plastic-faced shields, and they have blue overalls. I don't know what's special about em, if they're waterproof or fireproof or what. They have pockets in em and all kinds of zippers. And they grab their clubs and their Mace® and all their gear and come trompin in. They all wear gloves. They used to use gloves with lead in em. I don't know if they still do. They don't leave any marks when they hit you. Those are the guys that John referred to as silons. They all march around like robots. They're pretty ominous looking with all their sticks and shotguns."

Cardozo-Freeman: "Have you ever thought about why so many names have to do with animals?"

Delorme: "No. There's no difference between bulls and pigs. A dog just does things to bug people. Silon comes out of *Star Wars.* However you feel at the moment [determines] what you call him. If the guy hurts your feelings, if he got you in trouble, he's a dog sonovabitch, to you, anyway. He might get along with somebody else. A lot of the cops that I get along with real good, everybody else might hate em because something happened."

Cardozo-Freeman: "Do you ever call them *bulls* and *pigs* to their faces?"

Delorme: "Sure, all the time."

Cardozo-Freeman: "In a friendly or unfriendly way?"

Delorme: "Either way. It doesn't make any difference. They're used to the names, too. You don't call em 'officer.' I might call em cops or guards. Other guys might do that, too. It's a habit you gotta get into. Moods change. You get pissed off at people. If you want something you might even call him an 'officer.' 'Officer, can I get out for a phone call?' If he says no, you say, 'Fuck you, you dog sonovabitch.' He'll say, 'Oh, now I'm a dog, huh?' 'You fuckin right, you asshole.' Dogs are the most common term you use. Asshole's a real popular term, too. Assholes and dogs are the same thing. They're both real rotten. They like to fuck with people's minds. They keep you pissed off all the time. They seem to enjoy that. Asshole is used for cons, too."

Cardozo-Freeman: "Have you heard these terms of *silon, robots,* and *clones* from people other than John?"

Delorme: "Oh, they just started that. It's only been a couple years since they had that. They bought all that riot gear and shit. I've only heard John use the term, 'clone.' A silon and clone would still mean the same thing exactly. Everybody looks alike and everybody acts alike. That's what the silons are. They're just a big group of robots that they used in *Star Wars* marchin around attackin everybody. It's only since those cops have been usin riot gear that we been usin those terms.

"The way I see it, is that an awful lot just depends on how you feel that determines what you call people at the moment; or how you're livin at the time. If you're in trouble all the time, you have a reason to really be hostile. They'll be callin you names, maybe not to your face, but if you're alone they might call you an 'asshole' to your face. At the same time, you're never calmed down enough so that you just internalize that hate towards them cops. As soon as you see that uniform, you just automatically use the worst fuckin name you can think of and then by usin those terms among other people, you're actually trying to show other people what your attitude is toward the pigs. You don't want em to think that you're kissin ass. You don't want people to think you don't hate em by callin em an 'officer.' People will say, 'Who the fuck are you, callin them an officer? What do you mean, officer?' Then in other groups it doesn't make any difference.

"It seems overly important to some guys to make sure that they use the worst term they can in front of other cons. Sometimes you even have to reach for one and correct yourself. Instead of saying 'officer,' you call him a 'pig' instead. That's peer pressure, I suppose, huh? It depends on what group you're with. The guys I'm around all the time are in the Education Department. They're not in trouble all the time. You don't hear those terms. You hear 'cop' or 'officer.' They're more intent in just trying to live their lives and stay out of trouble and not have to deal with all that hate. That hate just kills you. But guards use the same language we use. They call a snitch a snitch, a punk a punk, and so on. They call us cons and whatever."

Cardozo-Freeman: "Do they ever refer to themselves as bulls?"

Delorme: "Yeah. They use the same terms. They even refer to themselves as pigs sometimes. I've heard that. They call each other dogs. They'll call a dog a dog, too. Just like us. They'll call other bulls dogs if they don't like em. It's common. It's just like us. There's a lot of cops they don't like, either. When they sit down in my barbershop and get to talkin, hell, they'll be callin em all kinds of dog assholes, no good sonovabitches, and stuff like that. And they'll be warnin other cops that 'He's a fuckin dog; look out for him.' and all that. They use the same terms to describe certain officers. They know the personalities they have to look out for, too, cause some dog will even write them up, tag em."

Cardozo-Freeman: "Is that right?"

Delorme: "Oh, yeah. It's a military hierarchy. Captain's at the top. New bulls are rookies but the cops call em fish-bulls. They imitate us all the time. They enjoy usin the language. It doesn't take em long. Especially the new guys. They really get off on bein able to use all the terms, even though they use it wrong half the time. A lot of new ones used to ask me what such and such meant. I'd tell it to em or I'd tell em about terms that were important for them to learn, words that I knew, as long as they understood em, would make their adjustment a little easier."

IN DEFENSE OF THE BULLS

"There's very little difference between the inmates' overall conditions and mine. We live side by side in a hovel, hoping that something will happen to rescue us from this nightmare. Sometimes I feel like I'm on sort of a work-release program. If I'm good they'll let me go home at night, and if I really don't rock the boat, they'll give me [time] off for good behavior and let me retire early."[14]

The work of the prison guard is extremely stressful, particularly if he is assigned on a daily basis to work in the cellblocks and is in direct contact with the prisoners. Contrary to popular belief, a prison guard, unless assigned to tower, perimeter, or riot duty, is never armed. At Walla Walla he often sits inside a *cage*, which in itself could become a trap. As Robert J. Wicks points out, a new correction officer may be assigned to one of three duties. He may serve as "watchful killer," if assigned to tower duty, where his responsibility is to prevent escapes or quell riots, killing or wounding prisoners if necessary, or he may serve in a "pressure cooker" locked in with prisoners. His responsibilities may be to open and shut gates and doors (at Walla Walla a cumbersome chore) and deal with all types of prisoners, from the most belligerent and threatening to the most frightened and disoriented. Fights and the possibility of violence are a constant threat under such conditions. All the guard has to protect himself is his experience and his ability to relate to his charges.[15] Finally, he may be assigned to segregation or isolation duty, one of the most trying of assignments, since in such circumstance the unhappiest of men are his charges. The constant verbal abuse that accompanies such an assignment taxes human patience, often beyond endurance. One of two things happens to a man working in such a stressful environment: he either quits or becomes hardened and inured to the suffering of his charges and may even contribute to their brutalization. One cannot guard the deepest hole in hell without becoming corrupted by the horror, cruelty, and ugliness of it all. If prisoners are overwhelmed by the evil of their situation, those charged with the responsibility of guarding them are also profoundly affected by this punishing environment.

The prison guard is charged with doing society's "dirty" work; that is, he is responsible for keeping out of sight and subduing those society despises and wishes to punish harshly. The guard is himself punished and stigmatized by carrying out this responsibility. If he follows through with brutal and overly harsh reactions to prisoner behavior, he is accused of being cruel, when in actuality he is carrying out society's directives. As Wicks points out, there is some credence to the idea that guards are victimized by society, that they are made scapegoats in society's unconscious:

> We live out urges in various people (in this case criminals); we show ourselves and others how much we hate such impulses by punishing these offenders who symbolize the unwanted parts of our unconscious; and finally, we even remove ourselves from, and ultimately deny, this punishment by calling to task the very persons we have forced to do our . . . punishing for us. . . . We live out our unacceptable impulses in inmates. Denial that this is occurring or that "good people" like us have these impulses is proclaimed by showing our disdain for offenders. (This is done through the use of corrections officers, *guards*, whom we recruit, select, train, utilize, and characterize in such a way that they are encouraged to fill punishing roles.) We distance ourselves from this punishing process by turning our backs on the very guards we've instructed and prosecute them for (doing our bidding and) being brutal.[16]

In *The Society of Captives*, Sykes points out that guards and prisoners at the New Jersey State Maximum Security Prison share many of the same beliefs and values, that they possess a "common language and a common historical experience," and that they come from the same cultural milieu.[17] This is not true at Walla Walla. The majority of the guards are drawn from the rural and small town areas where the prison is located, whereas most of the prisoners come from the large urban centers in the northwestern part of the state. Not only do most guards and prisoners not share the same cultural attitudes, beliefs, and values, they literally and figuratively sometimes speak a different language, therefore hold a different worldview. Guards at Walla Walla, the majority of whom are white, tend to hold ultraconservative and traditional cultural values in sharp contrast to prisoners whose values, beliefs, attitudes, and behavior are often shocking to those who guard them. Although efforts are made to recruit whites and minorities from the urban areas to work as guards, it is difficult to convince them, if they come, to stay at Walla Walla. Differences in cultural worldview between guards and prisoners have produced extremely serious confrontations. In particular, a lack of proper training in this area has created misunderstandings with respect to the culture and values of black, Chicano, and native American prisoners, and some of these misunderstandings have contributed to tragic consequences. The killing of the guard in 1979, for example, was in part caused by a lack of understanding of and respect for the religious traditions of native Americans.

THE OFFICIAL POINT OF VIEW

In order to set the prisoner's view of the guards into proper perspective, it is necessary to present the official point of view and objectives of the state with respect to guard-prisoner relationships. The official *Employee's Manual for Men's Correctional Institutions* was published in the early 1970s, during the period when William R. Conte headed the state's corrections program. It presents the philosophy of corrections for the state, as well as sets down the proper relationship the correctional staff should have with the residents, as they are called. Important and relevant aspects of that philosophy and those responsibilities are included here.

> The relationships between staff and residents traditionally have been those of keepers and kept; of superiors to subordinates; and of mutual suspicion and isolation. The basis of the need for change was simple: the traditional relationship simply failed to work. In terms of bringing about lasting change in resident behavior and attitudes within the institutional setting, there is probably no more vital arena of operations than that of relationships between staff and residents....
>
> "Without a constructive and healthy interaction and communication between residents and staff, the resident does nothing with his time but "put it in," awaiting his next release into free society—basically unchanged and still identifying with the criminal culture....
>
> If you want a resident to respect, cooperate, and communicate openly with you, you must be ready to exhibit respect, cooperation, understanding, and a willingness to communicate openly with him....
>
> It takes a mature and secure staff member to "keep his cool" when residents are swearing, name-calling, or the like toward him, and to quietly and firmly continue to get his message across. It is a rare situation, however, that cannot be restored by such behavior on the part of the staff....

If a resident has a problem which he wishes to discuss with you, listen attentively to him, help him in ways you can, and see that he receives additional help as needed from appropriate staff. One can be courteous and show that he cares without being too familiar. . . .

Where actual penalties are attached to infractions, all residents should be made aware of them upon entering the institution. These rules must be fully explained and defined, and the consequences for violation made clear. Careful attention should be given to fairness and "due process" in the administration of these rules. While staff may be somewhat flexible in enforcing rules, new residents should know this flexibility is to enable discipline to be fair according to the situation, and that this flexibility should not be abused. . . .

People do not happily or willingly go to prison. The curtailment of personal freedom, the submission to strange rules, and the separation from family and friends are productive of anger, frustration, and resistance to the forces which placed them there and those who keep them there. As an employee of the institution, you are asked to be aware of the circumstances which are likely to make a resident angry, defiant, and dangerous. Those of you who are Custody Personnel, are in a critical position because you represent the dual function of this institution — custody and treatment. To the resident, you represent the authority of both the institution and society at large. The resident's anger and other negative behavior may be directed at you simply because you are the closest representative of a system which, from his point of view, has caused him to be in a situation that he does not like. If you have been fair in your dealings with him, it is unlikely that his anger and/or aggression are directed at you as an individual. Although it may tax your patience to do so, it is best if you avoid responding to his anger with your own anger. . . .

The actions and attitudes of custody staff can help or hinder progress with a resident. You will be most effective with him if you are able to set a strong and dependable example of patience, consistency, firmness, objectivity, and self-control. Your relationship with the resident is very important and you perform a vital part of the treatment within the institution. If your relationship is constructive, you can do much to enable him to discover a new and more mature attitude toward authority and with society in general. Staff must remember that we cannot expect a person to grow in respect for his obligations as a member of society unless his rights as a member of that society have been upheld. . . .

Given the continuing need for order and security, it remains only to differentiate between order and security which are invoked fairly, consistently, and firmly. If you are fair and open in your contacts with residents, the tensions and frustrations which underlie most dangerous developments in correctional institutions will be greatly lessened. . . .

Institutional personnel will rely on punitive measures only after other avenues of influencing behavior have failed. Punitive measures administered in the correctional system must always be relevant, appropriate, and should employ the least possible force necessary to bring the situation under control. Penalties should never be cruel, unusual, or excessive, and should never be administered in anger. Under no circumstances should you strike a resident, unless it is for your own or another's defense, or when necessary to prevent an escape, or quell a disturbance....

Any institution is faced with the possibility of the persecution of one or more residents by others. This may take such forms as fighting, intimidation, or acts of perversion. These situations tend to break down morale, engender mistrust, or breed an atmosphere of anger. Thus, if you observe such behavior, it is your responsibility to bring it to a halt and report the incident to the appropriate supervisor....

Religion often plays a major role in the treatment process of the residents; thus, regardless of your own religious views, staff should respect the religious convictions and activities of the residents....

Consistent with our over-all philosophy of corrections, any discrimination by any staff member will not be condoned. This includes, but is not limited to, offensive actions, words, or attitudes directed against an individual's race, ethnic background, appearance, abilities, or personal beliefs.[18]

The official position with respect to the responsibilities and obligations of correctional staff advocates a humane policy, combining both custody and treatment as dual responsibilities for those who guard the prisoners. There is considerable evidence that some guards follow the manual conscienciously. There is also considerable evidence that some who work closely with the prisoners completely ignore the philosophy and directives, exhibiting the cynicism that sometimes prevails in such trying and discouraging work.[19] Unfortunately, proper training programs have not accompanied the implementation of this enlightened and humane approach to corrections; consequently, the contrast between the ideal as presented in the manual and what occurs in some instances is startling. New guards coming into the prison suffer as much from shock as do new prisoners. Considering the inadequate preparation for guards, particularly with respect to understanding human relationships and cultural differences, it is astounding that so many survive their initially traumatic introduction to their prison work experience and develop into good guards in the eyes of their charges.

Delorme has observed during his long experience as a prisoner that some corrections personnel at this prison, after a number of years associating with prisoners, tend to be affected by this association in a negative manner, not only in their work but in their personal life as well.

"Sometimes if a guard has worked here for over six years you don't trust him anymore cause you know he's probably picked up too much from us. The inmates don't trust him. Not only that, but we've noticed through the years that some of the guards that work here six years on up start adopting attitudes of convicts and they become dangerous themselves. They become emotionally unstable. They're the ones that are involved in the violence [in the prison]. They get in more trouble downtown. They get murder beefs; they get assaults in taverns. The local cops are afraid of em. They get just like us. 'Fuck you.' And they use the con language. They get more violent; the violent streak starts comin out. They get in much more violent beefs downtown in taverns and they clique up. They drink a lot; they get mean."

Cardozo-Freeman: "Why six years?"

Delorme: "That just seems to be the amount of time it takes to start fallin into it. It just takes that long to see that they're not really doin any good. I don't know what it is. Whatever their ideals was, went out the window in that amount of time. Then if they stay and don't move on, they have nothing in their lives. They have no hopes and dreams. 'This is goin to be it. Stay here.' So then it becomes a sentence for em. They talk just like they're doin time. They act like they're doin time. They talk like it in their language. 'Man, I only got six years to do; flatten out six years and I'll be outta here.' They're talkin about retirement; we're talkin about exactly the same thing only we're talkin about freedom. 'Well, I'm just goin to go up in the tower and do my time today. Just try to stay out of trouble.' I go down past the tower guards and they say, 'What's happenin, Gene?' I wave up and say, 'What's goin on, man?' 'Oh, just doin my time. Tryin to stay out of trouble.' I say, 'Alright,' and go on by. They talk like that all the time."

Those guards who ignore or do not follow the philosophy and precepts for dealing with prisoners as described in the employees' manual either are or have become cynical and hardened toward their charges. These men have a tendency to stick together, and since most of them have been employed at the prison for a considerable period of time, they possess considerable power. Sometimes they are successful in indoctrinating newer guards, imposing on them their views and attitudes towards the prisoners. There are incidents in which prisoners actually try to help "good" guards avoid confrontations with "bad" guards.

"Sometimes the guards have their own beefs. One guard snitches on another one, or one guard helps a convict like Bobby C. and the others will get him, threaten him at home or threaten his family if he helps a con who they don't like. See, they were tryin to get Bobby C. They were tryin to bum beef him on an escape deal. Well, they had him for a couple days but another little guard who was pretty new signed a statement sayin that he was with Bobby C. in Recreation; he knows he wasn't in that tunnel. It was a jokin matter for awhile but then a jeep tried to run over him in a parking lot here and his wife got threatened, and he got threatened and he lasted as a guard another month. They scared him out because he wrote that statement. We didn't do it; the guards did it. He worked at night and he'd be over in the RC office with a bunch of convicts and what are we doin? Tryin to teach him how to survive on the streets. 'Be careful. When you go outa here at night off duty, check the parking lot and watch what cars are parked there. Be careful when you go home. Don't make no stops,' we were tellin him, tryin to protect him against these other guards. They had goon squads runnin around town. It gets that way sometimes."

Some of the differences between good and bad guards are brought out in the following conversations.

"We're not talkin about a lot of guards when we talk about guards. I'm talkin about the guys who don't give a shit except that they get paid. They work like they're workin at the humane society, except there's no control. You can't hit those dogs in the humane society. Those guys don't care what's goin on, that this guy or that guy is gettin hurt. They don't want to be involved in it. You see what I mean? They don't care because they don't consider the cons to be human anyway. They just come here to just do their eight hours and hit the road."

Cardozo-Freeman: "Is there a difference between the decent guards and the guards who are Christian?"

Delorme: "Only in that the guys tell you that they're Christian. They might even read the Bible while they're workin to give em a little boost during the day. You'll be talkin to em and they'll read to you little quotes, and guys listen to em. Some guys like it and some guys don't. But they'll say it anyway because they're tellin you what they believe in, which explains how they operate. We don't cut em no slack, boy, if they say they're Christian. They better stick by the Book; they ain't got no room to be a hypocrite if he's goin to be a Christian and work here. They take a mental whipping from some of the other guards. Some guards tell me they don't trust em. Baloney. You trust them more than any. It makes these other guards nervous or something, havin them around.

"Them Christian guards are serious, sincere people. Most of em that I know, they don't go out of their way to be a good guy. They do their job and irritate people because they do it good. They stick by the institution rules. Just because a guy is Christian doesn't mean he'll let you out of your cell when you're not supposed to get out. They are fair and firm. They don't mistreat you. They don't get smart with you when you ask em something.

"I don't know what it is, they kind of stick together. Some of em are super righteous, of course. They know you committed a crime and should be here, yet at the same time they don't think you should be punished extra while you're in here; bein here is punishment. You're bein punished just by bein here.

"So many small things. Some of the guards that I've been able to talk with have come to me about guys with problems inside the walls. They come up to ask me things; they really go out of their way. They get off duty and come down to see me in the barber shop and say, 'Slim has got this problem and this problem and how can I help him?' One of the Christian guards did that. You met Slim in the chow hall, that fellow with the long black hair."

Cardozo-Freeman: "He's the one you said got beat up by some guards?"

Delorme: "Yeah. He's supposed to be out here [MSB] tomorrow, finally. This guard, had been tryin all year to try to help Slim cause he could see that Slim was changin. Slim wasn't throwin stuff anymore. Slim was startin to talk to people again, and especially, he was answerin guards without cussin em out. And this guard, he seen this and watched it and went out of his way to go down and talk to him and help him and send letters for him to his sister, and write letters to the Parole Board for him, give him good reports, encourage him cause he seen the change. But all the other guards, like he told me, he says, 'Man, I'm gonna keep doin all I can cause Slim is a good person. He's got a lot inside him.' He says, 'These other guys are tellin me I'm crazy, that he's a sonovabitch and leave him alone.' That's what the other guards are tellin him.

"He's an older guy in his fifties, raised a family and he has a lot of insight. And when he first came here, the convicts really helped him. He first come here during the lockdown. He slept in his car. He didn't have any money and he had a family waitin, but he had no money when he came here, and he worked his ass off during the lockdown and the convicts seen it. He was doin all the work, other guards were makin him carry stuff over to the wings. And then he was hungrier than hell himself and the cons would feed him, make sure he ate and stuff like that, and he never forgot that. Never. The cons were offerin to carry stuff for him to help him. It was Jesus carryin the cross, you know that? Really. He never got over the cons helpin him, see? In the midst of all that violence, that happened because they seen him and respected him as good people. They pegged him right off the bat. He was polite; not overly nice but polite and sincere. There isn't a stroke of insincerity in him anywhere. When he asks you a question, he ain't patronizing you none. He likes you as a person. Or if he doesn't like you, he doesn't do anything. He kind of avoids you cause it hurts his feelings if you call him names. But he's a super person and I'm a good friend of his and I'm proud of it. I'd help him anytime. He's just an ole guard."

Cardozo-Freeman: "He hasn't been here very long?"

Delorme: "He got past that six months and that was kind of a good thing because they usually fire guys like that. He was just raggedy, holes in his shoes, but he toughed it out. He's got that family taken care of now. They're here with him now. But he works about sixteen hours. He don't work eight hours. He works double as much as he can work. But there's a lot of guys like him here. I don't know em personally; I don't know their names. I have a couple names that I carry around in my wallet of good guards that got fired. We were sad, they were sad. They told W. that the reason he was fired was because his conduct wasn't professional. He was friendly. He talked too much to the guys. But he was interested; he wanted to hear why people act like they act. And he wasn't inexperienced; he worked in the California system. But if you get past that six months, they can't let you go that easily. But that first six months they watch close. And I don't know how that Christian fellow made it. He kept a low profile somehow and he made it so even the cons were happy for him, if you can imagine that. But it was touch and go.

"We're aware of the attitude you have to show your superiors. We're aware of that six month probation period and we know they'll let him go if he isn't actin the way they want him to. The advice that the cons give him was, 'Just do your work. Don't make no noise, man, just do the job and keep your eyes out on yourself. Don't complain about nothin and you'll get through, maybe. You may even have to write some tags.' He don't like to write no tags. That hurts him. He'll do everything he can before he writes a tag, but he goes out of his way not to. And that's not acceptable behavior. After you're here six months you can do that but before that you have to be careful. If a con's out of line you're supposed to tag him if he breaks a rule. You got a little discretion. If other guards aren't lookin at you and seen that you're supposed to write that tag. It's just like if I got in an argument one-on-one out here with a guy, we don't have to fight. But if I got a lot of my friends around watchin and the guy calls me the wrong names, we can't even talk it out. We're supposed to fight. Same thing happens to the guards. Even a dog will let you go for breakin a rule, but he won't let you go if another guard's standin there. 'I will give you a pass this time,' and walk away, and you're standin there with a joint in your hand wonderin, 'What the hell happened? The guy didn't tag me?' If there was somebody lookin at him, he wouldn't do that. He'd say, 'I gotcha.' "

Few guards, for obvious reasons, relish breaking up a fight between prisoners. Those who do are viewed with incredulous admiration by the prisoners. (When I asked this particular guard, an older man, why he had such a good rapport with the inmates, he replied that he had gotten into trouble with the law when he was young and understood what it was like to be "young and wild," and that since he had grown out of it, he expected many of the young men in this prison would, too.)

Cardozo-Freeman: "What about the guard that isn't afraid to come and break up a fight when it gets started?"

Delorme: "Those are few and far between but it's nice to have somebody like that. P. will do that. Sometimes I wonder if he's just crazy or if he's brave. Whatever it is, it's a quality that's hard to find. Some guys see the comparison. In here your inclination if you're a convict, if there's a big fight goin on — and a fight always makes a lot of noise; things are flyin all over — the convict's inclination, the guys who have been in quite awhile, is to run towards the fight to see what's happening. The guards' inclination is to run away from it because all those convicts are there. You see what I mean? If the cons get out of hand they can turn around and bust those cops up and they're scared to come in there and put a hand on anybody because a knife might come up and get em, or somebody behind em might get em cause they have to step into a bunch of people. You can't blame em. It's a tough one. So the guy who hears that noise and he runs towards it, that's a good guard, a good guy to have around. Very seldom will they do that. P. will do that. There are guys hangin over the tier watchin what's happenin and they'll say, 'Here comes P.! Here comes P.!' They're wonderin if he's crazy, cause even to you it's a little touchy and you're a convict. And he's pushin guys out of the way and he's goin in like that, but it's nice to have him around."

Cardozo-Freeman: "I was very aware of how much the men respected him. They were joking with him about getting his hair done. He's kind of bald. He just lifted up his hat to show them."

Delorme: "He always give me white money when I cut his hair. Yeah, he's a good man. I look for that and other people do, too."

Cardozo-Freeman: "Is he a Christian guard?"

Delorme: "I wouldn't know. I never talked to him that much. But he's a good guard."

In the old days when the prison was much more restrictive and the old convict code was strictly observed, prisoners risked ostracism by their peers if they were friendly with guards. Today this is not so.

Hank: "I remember once if somebody walked up and said 'Hi' to a bull, man, nobody in the rest of the Joint would ever talk to that guy. The system has changed now to where if a bull is going to work here and be in this environment every day, he's going to adapt and adjust to part of it. He's going to get his due if he gives his due. Right? Get respect for giving. Everybody automatically knows who the dogs are. Nobody don't ever talk to em, huh?"

Cal: "Yeah. You see a guard walk up and start talkin to somebody's guests you don't think nothin about it. You're lookin to see who he's talkin to and what he's sayin."

Hank: "I can remember a time when nobody would ever say anything to a bull and we had them on the dummy for years. Now you see the bulls in the cells gettin coffee and stuff from the cons and don't think too much of it one way or another in Eight Wing. Six Wing, too. And the bull leaves that door open. So yeah, they're playin 'get something; give something.' "

Cal: "Tit for tat."

Women have been employed as guards for the past several years. Although most of the male guards disapprove, the opinion of many of the prisoners is that women guards tend to be more sensitive to their situation.

"Well, it's nice to talk to em and just sit by em or something. They're not mean. Feeding time is hell in here [during lockdown]. Guys are usually throwing coffee at the guards. It didn't happen that day, not with her on the tier, it didn't. Women guards will joke and laugh with us like when a woman guard gives me my TV dinner I say, 'Aw man, chicken again?' And she says, 'Well, it's all I could cook tonight.' That kind of bullshit. But when the male guard comes by he just throws it in. You say that and he freezes up on it. Well I've had long talks with guards about women guards and they're just sick of it, man. Most of em want to quit. They get

one here and they treat em like dirt because they're friendly to us.
Mostly women guards haven't got that natural hostility. One woman,
a nice looking girl, came down on our tier passing out mail one
day. Man, it was silent. Nobody insulted her, but she was nice to
them, too. As soon as she left the tier, everybody started shoutin,
'More mail! More mail!' Man, they wanted her to come back
again."

Prisoners complain that officials encourage the men to betray
each other by offering bribes for information. This is an extremely dangerous tactic, since under certain circumstances, prisoners will turn on a *snitch* and kill him. This is one of the reasons
given for the massacre that took place at the New Mexico State
Penitentiary in 1980.[20]

Doc: "Every time it gets formed up into a bunch, they divide
and conquer, see. As long as they keep dividing and conquering,
as long as they keep sayin, 'O.K., here's a guy with eight years.
He's in here and he's in the clique and they're doin that,' whatever
is goin around. They pull this guy up here and say, 'Look here,
man, you can go home tomorrow on parole. You can go home six
months from now when we get enough collaborating evidence to
do this and that.' You do that to three or four guys, you're goin to
break all those structures down. You looked around lately at who
isn't here?"

Robb: "Oh yeah, I watch it."

Doc: "Somebody told me a year ago that that was goin to
happen and that within a year them people walkin around with
eight, nine years would all be goin out on parole. You'd see a big
turnover, a big change. You'll see how they do it. O.K. They came
in and they snatched all them people up and took em out of here.
Sent a couple to Marion, some down to Atlanta. I looked around
and some of the other people that didn't need to go nowhere
[weren't causing problems for the administration] man, they're out
on parole. I don't know how they do that. You see somebody told
me to watch for that in the future and here it is a year later and
that's exactly what's happened."

Robb: "You mean club leaders or you mean guys that seem to
have influence in here?"

Doc: "I'm talkin about how this system has a way of makin stool pigeons out of convicts by holdin that bait out there. 'We give you back your freedom and you can go to your ole lady and go on and mind your business, go on down the road, and we got this and this. To be able to control this place we got to know about this and blah, blah, blah.' So they end up knowin everybody's business and all the different cliques, and they know exactly what's goin on all the time."

Robb: "Yeah, that's pretty obvious."

Doc: "If you had all the cops on the dummy and nobody ever talked to a cop and this place was organized and unified right, they would have no information, but they say, 'Well, who's going to testify against so-and-so? Anybody testifies against him, we give him a parole tomorrow.' And this guy got right up out of Peoples Park and walked right into Control. And he was supposed to be one of the solidest convicts in here. He said, 'Follow me, man. I'll tell you anything you want to know about the guy. All them charges, weed and all that other bullshit.' He says, 'I'll tell you.' Just turned stool pigeon just like that and they let him out. Man, the only way you're goin to be able to circumvent that is to assure that the population keeps control of their power so when that guy goes up there and does that, that guy gets killed. We're talkin about our own hit list we got in here. A guy's got it comin, he gets it. I seen it every day for years. That's the way it used to be."

A few guards are corrupted by the prisoners, cooperating with them in circumventing or breaking prison rules.

Gene: "One of the most common ways they get in trouble is by bringin things into the institution—marijuana, heroin, money. That's about the main three things that they would pack in. Weapons, I don't know. Seems like those guns that show up must of had to come from them but who knows for sure. They do it for money, not friendship cause some of the cons do have a lot of money. So it's not hard to find a guard that needs a few hundred dollars real quick. You can set up the connections for him, and that would be your wife or a friend of yours—and they just meet the guard downtown in a restaurant or something and pass the package over to em. The simpler you make it for the guard and the more you pay him, then it's pretty hard for him to turn it down.

Everybody likes that money. You make sure you tell em different ways they can bring it in without gettin caught.

"Things didn't tighten up on them until the last few years, til a few of em got busted for packin, then pretty soon all the guards, staff, and everybody had to go through shakedowns when they entered the institution, briefcases, everything had to be opened. Teachers had to go through it, too, and that was because of somethin like that. The cons work on em constantly. They're always tryin to get a hook into one of those guards. The new ones are the best ones to hit on. The older ones if they did it when they were newer, they usually quit it later on, cause they know they just got lucky by gettin away with it. They usually won't bother with it later. That's when they're established in their job and probably got some money in the bank. So they're always workin on the new guards tryin to get em to do some little teeny thing. Once you get em to do some little itty bitty thing that probably won't get em in too much trouble, you got em, cause it's all illegal. It doesn't matter what they're packin in; the fact that they did it hooks em up pretty good. It's like bein a dope addict, you know. You kinda use that as a threat so they'll keep packin.[21] And they get paid cash money for whatever they do.

"That guard that worked in the Chicano Club he got paid to turn his back on the little whorehouse they were runnin there. For five bucks you could bring in your ole lady or your girl friend over to their club. They had a little room in there and you could stay for a couple hours and the cop would keep jiggers for em. That was when we could have people comin inside the walls. I'm sure that cop knew what was goin on, and I'm sure they'd protect him. If they did get caught everybody would back him up and say, 'Naw, he didn't know anything about it.' and shit like that. And they'd always give him a cut of the money, or maybe he smoked grass. A lot of these guards smoke weed. A whole lot of em do. They don't do it on the job but they do at home and stuff. They have a lot of weed in Walla Walla but they don't have anything else.

"That one guard in Seven Wing when I was there years ago, he's the one I was sayin got involved in that bogus check deal they had goin on. They used to have a print shop here at Walla Walla and they started printing payroll checks or some kind of checks. It wasn't a welfare check but it was a good check. It looked good. And they'd print em up, fill em out for the amount they needed, sign em and when the bull went off shift he'd take em with him and then he'd mail em from outside to the people, the guys' wives. The wives would get the checks, then they'd endorse it or whatever they needed to do, and they'd send it back to the prison and the prison would cash em right here, put the money on the guy's account. Then the next day the guy would make a money order and send all the money back out to a friend somewhere, so the money would move so damn fast they could never get a handle on it."

Cardozo-Freeman: "The guys were *paper hangers?* Forgers?"

Delorme: "No. Ain't nothing to it if you got the right equipment. The machinery does the work. What they did was they found some plates that used to be used for that stuff because all the state's paperwork used to be printed in the Joint, all the booklets and all that stuff. They took that printing equipment out of the Joint and sent it up to Monroe where they do the work now. But all those pamphlets and things are printed there, so they have all the plates to run that stuff. Somehow the cons dug out an old plate for checks or something here. So they just run it on the press at nighttime so nobody was around. They used to have night shifts at the cannery, the print shop and places like that. They made several thousand dollars before the guard got busted with a load. I think they caught him with some of the checks. They ended up firin him.

"But he was the same one that, when he'd come on the shift (he worked all night long, see), he'd come on about 10:30–11:00 at night and he'd just run around the tiers askin if you wanted back out again. He'd crack your door and everybody's runnin around in the dark. He'd scream if the Lieutenant was comin or something and everybody'd duck or slip into their cells. When the Lieutenant comes around at night and checks the cellblocks he never goes up on the tiers. He just comes in the door, shoots the breeze for a few minutes at the desk, then leaves if it sounds nice and quiet. Then as soon as he left, it would be just like the mice runnin around the house. Everybody would be back out again and he'd be back up in somebody's house eatin sandwiches cause they used to pack in, bring him in steak sandwiches from the kitchen to make sure he ate good. The cons always made sure he had hot coffee. He'd stop in the cell and play poker for an hour or two, win a few bucks and talk shit, and he'd have a con sittin downstairs at the telephone. That was in the sixties. It was a lot tighter then, too, but the bulls and cons had better relationships. People just weren't mad at each other. There wasn't so much violence, really."

Cardozo-Freeman: "Do you think loosening the prison had a lot to do with making people mad at each other?"

Delorme: "I think it created more opportunities to hustle, and bein looser, there was too many ways to get stuff in. Just like hustlin on the streets. People out there who are messin with dope and different things like that, there's fights goin on; people are always rippin people off and doin things like that.

"I really can't say why feelings were better between cons and guards. It was more settled, I suppose. Even though the people you had to deal with were real dogs, harsher; I don't mean all the line guards but some of the higher up guys, like C.S.S. and his regime. You just automatically wasn't goin to get no breaks, no matter what you did. I don't know how much that contributes to anything. There wasn't much goin on, it didn't seem like. There was fights between guards and cons, and there was a lot of fist fights between the cons and there were quite a few knifings but not half as much as later on. But there wasn't so many dope games goin on, not so many hustles. Drugs wasn't such a big deal on the streets then either. The dope contributes an awful lot to the violence. Now the guards are in more danger and then they want people to be treated like they seen in them old movies, the ole hard line."

Charges are sometimes made by guards that the prisoners have control inside the walls of the prison. In one respect, this is true, particularly with regard to the guards themselves. If a guard is unpopular or easily intimidated, the prisoners will do everything they can to drive him out. The men are particularly contemptuous of cowardly or insecure guards, and their harrassment and verbal threats toward them are ways of getting rid of weak links in the security system. Often new guards must go through a period of initiation and testing to see if they can stand up to the prisoners. The men respect guards who do not panic under inmate pressure and can take firm hold of a tense situation. Their self-confident presence lends a degree of stability to the prisoners' precarious environment.

Frank: "They keep talkin about convicts runnin this joint, man.[22] I can't understand what they're talkin about. I ain't never been able to run nothin. I've gotta go to them for every goddam thing and everywhere I go there's some fuckin pig there. What are they talkin about? They run this prison. They run the gates. They run every goddam thing they have twenty-four hours a day. If we were runnin this fuckin prison, them bulls would be on the wall and they'd never come down here. So that's bullshit.

"All you can do is to get the bulls out of here who are afraid. The ones that can hold their cool; they're the ones that should be in here. I mean, prison is prison. Kindest prison in the world is dangerous for a fuckin guard if he's an asshole.

"This prison ain't shit for some of these other guards in here. I mean they can run around here in this wing and the guys will give em coffee and rap with em and do everything in the world and they can work this fuckin wing. Some assholes can't. Like B. He don't hardly dare walk down the tier. Anything scares him like a mouse, the sonovabitch. That bullsey little punk. He'll keep the wing [the men] out in the fuckin cold. We call him names, the creep, he's got to go down to Control to get a key, get a Lieutenant to let us in our fuckin cells. When B. gets scared they take him out and let him have a coffee break for a couple hours. Go off shift early. What a creep! You know, one night someone threatened him when we came back from a fuckin movie. He had the whole fuckin wing standin out in the snow and wouldn't let nobody in. We're freezin to death, kickin at the door, spittin at him."

Hank: "Where do they put him when they open the door?"

Frank: "They had to talk him into opening the door. One of the goon squaders had to."

Hank: "Wasn't goin to open, huh?"

Frank: "Yeah, he wasn't goin to open it. We said, 'Open the goddam door!' And he says, 'Well, clear them guys out.' Chrissake, there's 300 of us standin there! Clear us out? Sonovabitch! Then he had us all promise to leave him alone before we could get in our fuckin cells. The guys were saying, 'Don't say nothin to him. Don't say nothin. We'll never get into our cells.' He keeps comin back in here though so he must have a little heart somewhere.

"I don't know what it is about that guy. He's weird. Hard to understand. He'll be just as friendly as hell to you and tag you, too. Treacherous. Only cop in this fuckin joint that has tagged me friendly as hell. He was friendly as I was goin out the door with the goon squad. He tagged me, had me locked up. I was just lookin at him. I couldn't believe it. I said, 'What did you have to call the fuckin goon squad for, man? I wasn't doin nothin.' I wasn't arguin with anybody. He said I was intimidatin him the way I looked at him or something! Well, I looked at him like he was a snail. I intimidated him. I should have smiled. He kept screamin at me to come down to the end of the tier. He wanted to shake me down."

Hank: "I know there had to be a rule about skin searching. It's crazy. If you're packing you sure as hell don't need all that skin searching."

Frank: "Hell no. You've got to take off runnin, man. Some of these bulls are pretty fleetfooted, too. Them bastards will catch you. I can't outrun these pigs, even the fat ones, man. I'm not too swift. But you see a guy runnin like hell, you know he's packin. They'll try to outrun the bulls. One guy runnin and two cops behind his ass tryin to get around a corner somewhere so he can unload, then he'll slow down and start walkin and let em catch you. All they have to do is to go back and look right behind him right where he stopped runnin and find what he was packin.

"They chased two guys during a lockdown a couple years ago. They chased em around the wing there, it must have been two hours, and they kept runnin around and around. They'd go up the tiers and they were runnin back down. They were out for showering and they just got frisky, you know. God, it was like a football game. It was really funny cause there was so many bulls there when you take showers during lockdown. They must bring fifteen bulls in the wing. A couple of the cons broke and ran screamin and hollerin, naked."

Hank: "Oh, you gotta leave your house naked, huh?"

Frank: "Yeah. The fuckin bulls ran this way and that way but they couldn't step out in the open; they had to run along the bottom, underneath the overhang of the catwalks above, try to reach up and grab these guys. And the guys would be up there spittin down at em, then they'd come down here and they'd say, 'Here they come! Here they come!' And the guys would jump to the next tier. And you'd hear the screamin and hollerin and finally they got tired. They caught em and drug em down there by the fuckin feet. Tired the pigs out, too. They get excited cause you know how noisy the wing would get with something like that. Plenty cheering, man, everybody's cheering. Everybody would keep the bulls from steppin out in the open by throwin shit at em. What happened, some of them pigs were sittin back there laughin like hell, the old timers. They were havin a good time watchin that shit. They sent them young dogs after em so they'd catch em. They would kind of boost each other up over the tiers and the guys were throwing water in their faces."

Hank: "Tie a string out there when they come by."

The guards are constantly faced with the ability of the prisoners to overcome restrictions imposed on them. For every problem the guards solve in the area of security, the men find a way to work around it. Prisoner ingenuity and tenacity seems endless. Constant vigilance is not exactly a tradition among some guards, who have been known to get careless or become intimidated by large groups of prisoners making demands on them. Some attempts at security, which are enormously expensive, only challenge the cleverness of the *cons*; whereas, others only succeed in placing the guards in greater danger than they were in the first place. These men are talking after the *lockdown* of 1979 in which new security changes were made in the prison. Hostility between guards and prisoners as a result of the *lockdown* is evident.

Doc: "This prison's never gonna change. The hard line crew are still here. They refuse to quit because maybe they understand the cycles just like we do, cause we have a tough time; we have an easy time; we have a tough time. But the nature of the penitentiary, I don't worry about the change-over. I don't worry about it because you wear them down. They'll shake you down and everything else. It'll go on for awhile and it's like a new toy for these guards. The nature of this joint is to do things as easy as you can."

John: "They just want to rub their hands on you and a guy can carry anything he wants to through those shakedowns. Carry it in your hands, like a folder, you carry it and they shake your body down and whatever is in your hand they just carry on through."

Hal: "Or carry it under your arm."

Doc: "Yeah, those metal detectors are a big joke. They had them in Folsom, too."

John: "I don't think there's more than one that works in the whole inside of the Joint. They have them off most of the time. Everytime the line gets long they turn it off and then just go back to the old way. Everybody's bitchin and hollerin and callin em idiots. 'Get this goddam line open, you stinkin pig!' "

Doc: "Puts a man in a helluva position just working here. They're intimidated."

John: "They're still so much in the open. That hasn't changed. They're intimidated because they have to go face to face with the lines of convicts."

Doc: "Yeah. They look up and see 200 cons standing there and it's time to turn the machine off cause everybody's standing out in the rain at that time. They're getting wet and calling em all sorts of dirty names."

Hal: "I thought they had changed with such a big turnover of guards, but the old ones got their hooks into them."

Doc: "Yeah, they have."

John: "They got the new ones scared. When they walk in they're scared and some of the old guards keep pounding it into their heads."

Hal: "I pray for a good tunnel escape just to slap it in their faces."

Doc: "Let's analyze that concrete they poured over Lifers Park. O.K. Allegedly, they've had tunnels going out of Lifers Park. Maybe that's true. I don't know. But for the sake of argument, allegedly in the papers they said there was. I've never heard of a tunnel but now all one has to do is start anywhere in that concrete area clear out by Nine Tower if you want and the minute you get under that concrete all you have to do is knock a hole in it, scoop a little out and there's gravel from there on, and you've got a perfect roof over your head. You can bore all over the place."

Hal: "One of the best tunnels there was ever out of the Joint was through concrete. Remember S.P. and them out of Six Wing? Out of the cell floor. That's thicker concrete than Peoples Park."

Doc: "You could bore all over Peoples Park out there under-neath the concrete. It ain't gonna cave in on you."

John: "Perfect shoring, come out of the wings under it."

Doc: "Look at these guard cages that the guards built for them-selves to protect themselves. Look at those goddam death traps. And them guards are steadily goosing the population."

Hal: "Just burn them in there."

Doc: "Of course. You fry them like a bunch of do-dos. Look at the screening devices they got around here, their so-called big shot control devices and metal detectors."

John: "Turned them off the second day we was out of lockdown."

Doc: "All you gotta do is to walk by and hit it in the wings, and man, so many places to kill somebody. I've checked them out since I've been out of Seg. Those security devices that they've put in here are actually blind spots in favor of killings."

Hal: "They stick you up in that hallway up there. You can't see what's happening. They've created danger spots with their own security devices."

Doc: "I see some good bone mesh. Bone mesh ain't gonna upset no metal detector. Look at all that steel laying around. When they tore that stuff out of the fuckin auditorium they took all them iron things that the seats were bolted to. They're a foot long, two foot long. They took all that steel out and just tossed it out there beside the auditorium in Six Wing. Guys walking back and forth there. Five days that steel layed there. The Sergeant of the wing over in Six Wing told Hank that every time that metal detector dings, there's a shank possibly going through there and he says, 'We don't care as long as you guys stick them into each other.' Bulls over in Six Wing are telling some of the blacks, 'Man, a lot of places I worked before, blacks run things. Don't look like you guys run a goddam thing here.' And all the time I'm thinking they're putting the clamps on us over in Eight Wing, driving us up the goddam wall over there. You can cut the tension over there in Eight Wing."

John: "Is that right? I haven't been back in there for a long time?"

Doc: "You just get the shakes when you get in there. There's so much tension in that wing and them pigs are continuously yelling, keeping it going."

Black prisoners believe that provincialism and racism among many white guards intensifies the punishment of their prison experience, and that it is difficult to keep good black guards. This black prisoner expresses his opinion about the prison and the criminal justice system in the state with respect to blacks.

"Racism in here—you won't believe it. The prison is way out in the country. Walla Walla is a farm town. No black people around and your folks have to come across the mountains to visit you. The type of people that are in the area aren't used to being around blacks or Indians or anybody different and they're racist. Double racism once you go to the Joint. The whole state is racist.

"There are very few black guards here. The excuse they use about not having any black guards is there's none to select from, which is true. So we got on them about that so they're recruiting in areas like Portland, Pasco, Seattle, and so on. But the other guards here make it so hard on the black guards. They can't stay very long unless they move to their side.

"There was an incident where a black was a good guard. He was doing a good job but there was another person that wanted his position so they started doing things to him like putting stuff in his briefcase and setting things up on him that got kind of dangerous. Things started blowing up on him and he quit. He was holding a pretty high position for a guard and blacks aren't supposed to hold a job that high.

"As far as prejudice of guards go, it's shown in every aspect of the prison. They call us names, they draw little signs on the blackboard that was meant for leaving messages. Like the most recent was, I guess it was supposed to have been an African with a bone in his hair, rings in his nose, and flies flying all around his head. It was inside of a locked cage so only a guard could get in there to draw it. It had a racial slur over it: 'Inmate No. 0000,' and all that stuff.

"If you get a tag and go to a hearing, if you're black, you receive the stiffest punishment, the stiffest penalties. It goes all the way from the guards, who are really a minor harrassment, it goes all the way up to the Parole Board, and it starts with the court system.

"If you're black you just get ripped off all the way through. Number one, you won't receive as much probation. Washington state, like you say, has more blacks locked up than anywhere else in the country. We got four percent of the population, yet we make up almost half of the population inside the Joint. But it starts with the court system where you won't receive as much probation as anyone else or any programs or anything, and it goes on through to the Parole Board where blacks as a whole do far more time than white inmates for lesser crimes. It follows on through.

"Once you get in here, the guards have never had any contact with blacks and they love to use racial slurs like 'jungle bunny' and 'spear chucker.' They rarely say 'nigger' cause that could cause them a lot of trouble but they use other little racial slurs. And the area where most of the blacks are housed which is Six Wing, they always manage to put in the most racist of guards. They make it a point to put in people who can't communicate with us. It's as simple as that.[23]

"Pigs are not always cut out of the same mold but when you find one that's decent, it's rare. Usually he won't last very long. The other guards get on him, give him hell, or they fire him. All the black guards that were decent human beings, good brothers, they fired them. All those that looked like they couldn't be serious Toms they fired. Also you have the black guards that overcompensate in order to stay by not showing any favoritism to niggers and they get tougher. They're tougher than need be cause they want to show them they're not showing any favoritism to blacks. Now that is one of the stupidist fucking things you ever saw.

"I can relate one incident that happened to me. This was during a lockdown and I got into a verbal argument with a black guard and when I get to arguing, I can get pretty raw and I ran his heritage down to a dog from the beginning. So he got mad and he said, 'Well, nigger, I'm going to get you.' Well, I didn't pay no attention to him. I didn't figure there was any way he could get me. So what happened was that he went and got the Goon Squad and told them that I had assaulted him, reached through the bars during lockdown and assaulted him. And so they came in and they stomped me on the hand [this prisoner only has one arm] and everything and they beat me and all this and took me to the Hole. And all the time I ain't done a motherfucking thing except cuss him out. But what it came down to, I lost ten months good time and spent a month and a half in the Hole and it was all behind that single little incident there. I went to Kangaroo Court and, of course, I was found guilty. No one wins in the Kangaroo Court unless they feel like letting you win. I mean no matter what type of evidence you have or anything. All the blacks that go through, if you get a minor tag, they tack a 701—which is a threat to the orderly running of the prison—to make it more serious.

The following narrative reveals the regret one young guard felt for overreacting to a situation in which an old man was injured. It is an interesting example of the man-to-man interactions between prisoner and guard that sometimes takes place. This incident occurred after the long *lockdown* of 1979.

Scot: "Tell me some good, good *back yard*, some good *back fence* [gossip]."

Ernie: "Alright. I was talking to this guy, he's an officer, saying he was involved in that little incident upstairs with that old man, that hurt that old man. And I said, 'Your name is S., isn't it? I recall your name.' I mentioned Officer B. and he said B. wasn't involved in it and he says, 'Well, I felt sorry for what happened to the old man.' He realized that it could have been handled in a different way and he tried to tell me that the old man was drunk. And I says, 'No way.' O.K., what it come down to finally after we had a little talk sort of, he told me he was going to quit. And he also mentioned something about what's happened in New Mexico [prison riot, 1980]. He feels that it's going to happen here and he feels that his life is threatened and he doesn't like the paranoia which has affected him. He don't like that tension that he feels, that paranoia that somebody is after him. He feels that his life is threatened, that somebody is going to shank him.

"He says, 'I wish there was some other way we could settle this. [The bad feelings between guards and prisoners after the lockdown] I wish you would bring out one of your champions.' And I said, 'Man, this isn't the Thirteenth Century.'

"He said, 'Man, I don't like this. I think I'm gonna quit but I have to give two weeks notice.' And I said, 'Man, that's your choice. If you want to, if you feel that way, fine,' I said, 'There will always be somebody to take your place."

Scot: "Did he get paranoid after that old man thing?"

Ernie: "Yeah, cause he said he didn't mean to hurt him and it was an accident."

Scot: "He did jump him though?"

Ernie: "Yeah, he did jump him. See, the ole man hit his head on the back of that shelf back there."

Scot: "He fell down?"

Ernie: "Yeah. So that tells me a little bit about how a lot of officers feel in here, especially him. He's got that paranoid feeling."

Scot: "You know what they say, 'Just because you're paranoid, don't mean it ain't true! It don't mean somebody ain't after you.' "

Ernie: "Yeah, but I don't think it was that bad the way he put it. The way he expressed himself, he says, 'You know that I only work here eight hours a day and you're here twenty-four hours a day and you have to be on guard all twenty-four.' He says, 'I don't like this eight.' "

Scot: "He don't like eight and he's locked in a little cage. Is he the one that screams for you to lock up?"

Ernie: "Yeah, same one. 'Lock up! Lock up!' "

Scot: "It would be easy to drive him out then, wouldn't it. Just have to scare him for a fuckin minute and walk on by, call him a few names and shit like that."

Ernie: "Well, I can see where he's paranoid. He realizes a lot of this is caused from the July thing."

Scot: "He wasn't here then?"

Ernie: "No. He wasn't here then. But he's paranoid."

Scot: "You should ask him how many of the new ones are, the new guards. It pulls a lot out of you being here."

Ernie: "Oh yeah, definitely. That would change your pattern of behavior."

Scot: "Scared of everybody so you treat everybody wrong."

Ernie: "Yeah, well I told the man, 'There was other ways, other opportunities to handle it.' I said, 'You don't have to use them violent forces and attack somebody like this.' I told him, 'You didn't have to do what you did.' He says, 'I realize that now.' He said he was sorry about it. He didn't mean to hurt the old man. So that's how it came down."

Scot: "Did you get any more reports on how the old man is?"

Ernie: "I heard he's on Third Floor."

Scot: "That would have fucked his head up more than it was. He ain't been botherin nobody, you know. He just goes about doin his little ole thing. Hasn't been payin too much attention to what's been goin on around him. Then he gets jumped by a bunch of fuckin who-dos, man. Somebody will fuck his head up permanently."

Ernie: "Oh he [guard] realized that what he should of done is just close the door and leave the old guy alone."

Scot: "Lock the door. He wasn't drunk."

Ernie: "I guess that's the way they try to excuse what happened. They say he was drunk or something. He wasn't drunk. They're trying to excuse their behavior, their actions. It could have been handled a lot different than it was handled, really. Nobody would have got hurt, especially the old man. He must be about sixty years old."

Friendships sometimes develop between guards and prisoners that carry on when the prisoner leaves the prison. Occasionally friendships may develop between officials and prisoners that may continue when the prisoner leaves to begin a new life. Seeing a man straighten out his life brings satisfaction to the officials. This guard is unusual; despite the unkind treatment he often received from prisoners while serving on the line, he offered to help an inmate who had finished serving a sentence and was leaving the prison.

Doc: "I've had about eighteen, maybe twenty-five offers of help right here in Walla Walla. And some of these ex-bulls, they come up, 'Oh hell, Doc's getting out again. I'll give him a hand.' Just little things like we're talkin about, but they're willing to help and it makes me feel kind of good. There's that B. that we run out of Seven Wing. I called Mikey and Mikey was gonna give me a place to stay over here before the wife got here. B. was drunk at the time. He says, 'Hell, I'll help if he wants to go out on parole or something. I'll sponsor him.' And I called back because sometimes he talks through his hat when he's drunk and I asked him sober. No, he remembered. Yeah, he'd help me in any way."

Hank: "That's a long, long relationship."

Doc: "Yeah, I've known him quite a while, but he was a real dog in Seven Wing. The guys run him out. They didn't want him in the wing but he was willin to help."

Hank: "Was he a dog or was he tough?"

Doc: "He wasn't tough. He was just kind of, he was that short blonde-headed bull that was over in Admissions for awhile."

Hank: "Yeah, I know he had trouble everywhere he went but at that time, too, everybody was actin like spoiled brats."

Doc: "Yeah, you're right."

Hank: "And if you couldn't get the officer to let you do what you wanted to do, then they'd all drive on him and try to get him run out."

Doc: "That's the way it was when he offered help. It surprised me coming from him because the convicts didn't treat him good at all. Run him out of every place he went. The Hospital, Admissions, Seven Wing, but they was drivin on him. Like you said, everybody was actin like a spoiled brat."

MYSTIFYING THE BULLS: SECRET CON-LINGO

Secret languages are a thriving folk tradition constantly used, particularly in Segregation and *the Hole.* They also surface and flourish in the general population during periods when suspicion and mistrust between prisoners and guards is high. Some of these languages date back to before the seventeenth century. Many come from England. Prisons are not the only place where secret languages and codes flourish. When a group of people sharing a common background are surrounded by what they perceive to be the enemy, it often becomes necessary to devise methods of communication to exclude them. In research now in progress, Tobey Blum Dobkin reports that secret languages evolved among the Jews in German concentration camps during WW II, and that the Japanese-Americans placed in internment camps in the U.S. also developed secret codes.

When conditions are *loose* in the prison and the men are free to move around in their cellblocks, they *hit the tiers* moving from one cell to another holding private conversations with their friends without the use of cryptic codes. When security tightens, however, or when the men are confined to their cells during a *lockdown,* they revert to cryptic communications to pass on messages; for example, if a man locked in his cell wants to *borrow a rig to do some dope*, he needs to shout the message down the tier, and in order to keep the guards from knowing what he is saying, he reverts to cryptic slang. The same applies for all contraband activities, whether drugs, alcohol, weapons, food, or anything else that is forbidden. Secret languages differ from the *con-lingo* spoken daily by the men because it is more cryptic and because its purpose is generally restricted to dealing in contraband or other forbidden activities. There are, however, a few secret codes that are used merely as in-group pastimes.

It doesn't take a genius to break prison codes, and the guards pick up on them very quickly if they hear them often enough. In fact, the guards often turn out their own codes when they meet inside the walls and don't want the prisoners to know what they are saying. The prisoners humorously refer to the guards' secret languages as "*pig's Latin*." Delorme explains the use of prisoner codes.

"By using codes which are not understood by the Man, or by other cons who are outside your group, you are able to keep your business off the streets. If your business is out in the open all the time, then the chances of going to the Hole or gettin rousted by the goon squads all the time is hopefully lessened. A small group or clique may deliberately keep their code to themselves and change it on a regular basis if they hear others using it."

The Segregation unit has a language all its own. The men in *Seg* are constantly surrounded by guards and it is assumed that the place is bugged. There are four tiers in Segregation, all of which lead to a control area called the *cage*, and since the tiers are open-ended, except for the bars on the cells, sound carries easily into the control area. In order for the men to have any freedom of communication between cells, a code is a must, and it has to be constantly changing. Key words within the code alphabet must constantly change, also. Names for contraband constitute key words. Contraband in Segregation involves drugs, alcohol, or weapons.

It is possible for the men in Segregation and *the Hole*, which are both located in the same building, to communicate through what they refer to as the *phone system*. *Getting on the line* is actually communicating through the plumbing system by way of the toilet. Large drain pipes run the length of each tier and these pipes carry flushed water. The pipes are large enough so that standing water does not fill them but does leave enough water to carry a man's voice through the system. Water can be dipped from the bowl leaving an *open line* to talk throughout the building, either up- stairs or down. Although this means of communication is not ideal, it eliminates the need for screaming back and forth to get a message to the other side of the building. The guards listen in *on the line* and even attempt to tape the conversations, but when the subject turns to serious business, the English language and the regular *con-lingo* usually heard suddenly disappears and what takes its place is next to impossible to decode even for the other prisoners who are listening in. Delorme continues:

"It takes time to pick up on this lingo and if the other men in Seg don't trust you, then you will stay in the dark while all the heavy stuff goes by. I used to sit and talk with friends while I was in the Hole and during these trips I might bring them up to date on what was happening out in the population, or tell them who came in on the last Chain, and while I and my friends would be talking regular English, all the while the other lingo would be flying back and forth over the same line and neither would bother the other because each is a separate animal unto its own. It's almost effort- less to single out. You grab what belongs to you and let the other slide by without a thought. I have heard up to three and four conversations going at the same time, and all the while people will be helping each other to understand a word from a friend while at the same time carrying on their own rap with someone.

One of the secret languages spoken by the prisoners at Walla Walla is called "Tut" and is what linguists refer to as a "little- language."[24] Tut is one of the many codes invented, presumably by children, for play purposes.[25] It belongs to the same family as pig Latin, also known as dog or hog Latin.[26] Pig Latin is the best known of all the little-languages and although its structure is less complex than Tut, there are similarities. Basically, all little- languages produce language distortion and are formed from "known words by adding specific meaningless sounds or groups of letters at the beginning and end of a word, or more frequently before or after each syllable or before or after consonants or vowels. This may be accompanied by some respelling or reordering of the syllables of a word."[27] Little-languages are handed down in oral tradition by children from generation to generation. Some are very old. Pig Latin, for example, dates to before the 1770s.[28] Most words transposed in little-languages are one and two syllable. Tut and the other little-languages spoken in the prison were brought in by men who have *done time* in juvenile detention centers of the state. Growing up in reformatories, they become adept at speaking these little-languages that they learned, presumably, during their childhood experiences in schools and on playgrounds. Men who are state-raised are often particularly adept at using secret codes like Tut. Most of the play languages they learned as children become deadly serious working codes in this prison, however, particularly in the Segregation unit.[29] In Tut, *mum-a-nun on the tut-ie-rak* = Man on the tier.

A second code used in the prison identified as a little-language in the *Dictionary of American Slang* but which Maurer states was invented by carnival workers is *Ceazarney* or *Carney*,[30] one of the few underworld argots that deliberately seeks to conceal meaning. This language is more difficult to speak and decipher than the simpler forms of little-languages although it is not as difficult as Tut. One of the prisoners, an *old timer* who spent his early life as a carnival worker, discusses *Ceazarney* and its antecedents. Oral tradition places its origins in Europe and Australia.

"Back a couple, two or three, hundred years ago the people who toured with shows and carnivals and that sort of thing all over Europe and Australia and the United States back in the frontier settlements and all, they developed a simple means of communicating among themselves that other people, unless they knew the trick to it, could not understand. And they termed the language 'Carney.' In some places it will be 'Hooker Talk,' depending where you are. Primarily, it came from the traveling shows and this sort of thing in Australia, all over Europe and this country.

"Now what they did—you know what pig Latin is? O.K. Now what the people did, they took the first letter of each word and after the first letter they put 'izz.' You can use complete sentences but primarily what happens is, let's say we're gamblin, shootin crap. We're together as a team and I'm down here and you're the stake, the shill. You're tryin to get these suckers in and so you're over there and you want to tell me how much money this guy's got so we'll know how to hard work him. So you get down with the dice. You're gettin ready to roll the dice and instead of sayin a dice chant like 'seven come eleven' or 'eighter from Decatur,' you might say, 'fissifty in the pizzocket,' meanin, 'This guy's got fifty in his pocket.' Or maybe a hooker will use the language when they're settin up a mark, when they're tryin to talk between one another about which one they're goin to take, whether or not they're goin to charge him twizzenty or dizzouble, double for a double sawbuck [$20]. Remember, Australia was a penal colony. That's where all this stuff developed, in the penal colonies of Australia, and the prisoners came from England so they brought with them the European gypsy, carnival, caravan, hustler, grifter, grafter talk."

There are other secret languages used in the prison, as for example, Agini, Bong-Song, Alfalfa, and Elephant. Some prisoners claim that Agini is street hustler's talk, which they use to *prime the mark* or *set the sucker up for a take*.[31] Generally, the men mix all the languages up when conversing and in order to understand what is going on, one must know all the codes. Delorme continues:

"Secret languages are a very important part of prison life and a combination of con-lingo and made up languages can make the daily rap sessions on the tiers and the Breezeway conversations sound almost foreign to an outsider as well as to the majority of the cons. I really haven't given you any new working codes cause I don't know them. Those currently used in Seg I wouldn't give if I knew.

"Agini is used every day, so you'd say it is a working code. So is Elephant, Alfalfa, and Ceazarney. The Tut is the least used because it takes a little longer to say something so people don't use it too much. Tut is mixed up a lot of times with Agini. You can even throw in pig Latin, too, and another once in awhile called Bong-Song. You might get mixed up with that one. It's just another method [of communication]. I've heard it straight. I've heard it said sing-song. The more you sing-song the Bong-Song, the harder it is. I'm telling you, some of these people I used to hear, I swore to God they were speaking Chinese the way they'd sing-song it. *Gongenonge*, that would be my name. That language, Bong-Song, in particular, is the kind you play with, to have fun with. Of course, you use it when you need it.

"There's certain little groups in here and they catch hold of one particular language and they even kind of claim it as their own sometimes, or they distort and readjust a language like Tut. Or they take Agini and bastardize it so that it's their own special language and that group will stick to it and keep it among their own members so that if they're speaking Agini or something just from close association and daily contact that they have, they may sit and rap it and run it right around your ears and you only pick up about half of what they're saying."

GETTING BUSTED BY THE BULLS: STRIP CELLS, SEG, THE HOLE, AND LOCKDOWN

Within the confines of this maximum security institution exists a prison within a prison where men who break the rules are incarcerated. Located within the Admissions and Security Building (*Big Red*) are eight strip cells, twenty-two isolation cells, and 170 segregation cells. The men refer to the isolation area as *the Hole*, or A Deck, and the segregation area as *Seg*. *Death Row* is also located within *Big Red*. The isolation and strip cells both have double doors that shut out light and sound. Strip cells, normally reserved as extra punishment for those in *Seg* and *the Hole*, is a veritable prison within a prison within a prison. Delorme describes some aspects of life in a strip cell.

"Strip cells don't have anything in em. They're just that—stripped. They don't have a sink or a toilet or a bunk in em. Strip cells don't have anything but a hole in the floor, which is the toilet. You're naked when they put you in there; they strip you. You may or may not get a blanket. It might be two days before they give you a blanket. They can rationalize that by sayin that you were dangerous or something, or you might be a possible suicide, so they couldn't give you any blanket or any clothes.

"If you cause trouble, if you riot over in Seg or you get in a fight with the pigs or something, they either take you to the Hole or throw you back in the strip cell. Whoever's fighting the hardest will usually end up back in the strip cell and they take you from there to the Hole. Strip cells got that hole in the floor. That's where you have to take a crap and about every two or three days they come in and hose it down with a water hose and if they're mad at a guy they just put you right back into it and it's wet and stays wet. If you been in there and you been quiet and haven't said anything or fucked with em, they generally move you out of there or move you to another cell til the other cell dries. They leave the door open after they hose it down so it will dry out. Three days, I think, is about average to be in a strip cell, or should be. Then they either don't take you out; they put you back in Seg or on A Deck, which is the Hole. You might stay down there for a week in the Hole. But they're all connected. I think they use some of the strip cells for Death Row. Death Row used to be over in Seg but they have so damn many people in Seg they didn't have any room so they put em back there. As far as I know they're still usin strip cells."

Many problems develop in the prison over the treatment by some of the guards of the men confined to *Seg* and *the Hole*. The area is locked away and hidden from the general population, but they know when something is wrong because the men confined in Segregation make a great deal of noise, not only in protest to the guards, but also as a way of asking for help from their friends in the general population.

"Down in Segregation, the more those guys scream, the worse they treat em. I heard em screamin in anguish today and it was just a scream of pain. You know, I mean sadness, anguish. The guy had just [lost it] you know, but that's understandable and there ought to be special guards for Segregation. Those men should be very special. They should be sorta the cream of the crop. Aw, they [the guards] go crazy after awhile. I mean, just cause you're a good guard doesn't make the guys in the cells feel any better, either, because they've had good guards down there. The Sergeant worked down there, just about drove him crazy. He tried. He did the best he could but that doesn't change the guys in the cells, you see. They been treated bad too long. Well, it's just too much anger."

Some of the charges made by the prisoners against the treatment received in *Seg* and *the Hole* involve the beating of the men, the use of Mace, blackjacks, and weighted (lead) gloves, the withholding of proper medical care and medication, the confinement of the mentally ill, the lack of religious services, the withholding of materials and rights that have been won through the courts, the lack of access to legal books and materials, and the lack of sufficient exercise. Some men are confined to Segregation because their leadership capacities are regarded by the officials and guards as a threat to the safety of the institution. The men in the general population, through the Resident Council, protest the mistreatment of those confined in *Big Red.* There are always problems between guards and prisoners confined in *Big Red.*

"If you get too out of line then they throw you in Seg. It's another Little Berlin in here that's tucked away out of sight and the guys are down there for a long time. Some for two, three years. Guys who escaped, guys who murder other cons, guys caught drinkin or sniffin, and so on stay down there. They stay in their cells all day except for one hour and ten minutes a day.

"The tier, itself, you wouldn't believe it; it's hip deep in garbage all the time. They haven't got anything to do except to come out and they walk up and down the tier for an hour, for an hour and ten minutes, then it's back in the cell and a couple more guys come out. And they have a TV on the tier. They can look out the bars at it. They eat the same food that we eat only it's trucked over there on those steam carts. They feed off that.

"Seems like they're always on a sit-down strike over there or they're always on a hunger strike, or they're always screamin or hollerin about something. Actually there's a lot of movement that goes on inside that building cause they're always draggin em out and takin em to the Hole for one reason or another.

"Segregation and the Hole has always been a constant source of trouble in the institution, especially in the last five or ten years. The majority of the demonstrations they've had behind the walls is because of the way they treat people in Segregation and the Hole, beatin people and puttin outrageous restrictions on em and takin things away from everybody when they don't have anything anyway and denying em access to law books and things that they won years ago in the courts, and so they send word out about what's happening to em and start off again. The RC would be runnin around trying to change it and then when nothin happens those guys in Segregation—it's centrally located so no matter where you go you always hear em and they're hollerin and bangin on their bars or something, so that always spreads out to the population cause everybody has friends in there, and there's a lot of guys in there that are usually the leaders of clubs and they expect their friends to back em up, back their play, do something for em. That's the only way to get attention. They can't seem to get access to the courts from in there. In there they've really got you wrapped up tight. But in Seg, they sentence you for thirty days, sixty days, ninety days or indefinite and then you could be in there for years.

"But over there, you can have a phone call once a week or more depending on how they feel. They bring you out and take you up to the cage and you get a five-ten minute's call. And they have visits on special nights. I think they visit when PC visits. They go out to the visiting room or they might use an office in the Control Room. They can make limited store orders so they can buy coffee. They can smoke, order cigarettes; they can order writing material. They wear coveralls, same thing you wear in the fishtank when you're in Shelton. They keep a bunch of those coveralls, or they have a big box of old jeans and tee shirts and you find something in there that might fit and you wear that.

"And after thirty days they can let you out or they can keep you in, depending on what you're in there for. If you're in for too much drinkin or too much sniffin or something like that, generally they'll let you out after thirty days if you haven't had any tags while you been in there. Other guys that are in there indefinitely are there for murder or something like that. Them guys just have so much trouble all the time they just have to put em down there and keep em down there. The same thing I might do and get away with, somebody else might get thirty days for. You never know; it depends on your record, how you been doin in the wings and stuff like that. Some guys they just want to keep in there. There are some protective custody people in there, too. They're on another separate tier just because they didn't have any room for em. Sometimes even in PC they like to call each other snitches and threaten each other. Even in PC some guys have to be in special PC. They can't even get along with the other guys. [Protective Custody is a separate area in Four and Five Wings. Men usually request to be placed in PC because they fear living in the general population. It is not punitive but, rather, protective housing.]"

Some men spend more time in *the Hole* than in their regularly assigned cells. Many of these men are spirited and rebellious, manifesting the Promethean spirit that refuses to bow to the rules of the prison or to those who are charged with enforcing its rules. Many confrontations between guards and prisoners in this punitive situation become very personal. For both, maintaining manly pride is uppermost. A man loses self-respect in such humiliating circumstances and automatically turns on those charged with reducing him to a caged animal. In turn, the guards can only stand so much of the language that is used like a sharp weapon against them.[32]

A prisoner who has spent considerable time in *the Hole* describes this home away from home. Strip cells and *the Hole* are similar in that both are designed to shut out light and sound, giving the impression that one is, indeed, in a hole.

"The Hole here and at Monroe, they're the same thing, really. Physically, they look alike, too. They're designed the same, styled the same. Apparently the same assholes built them. The cell itself, I think it's five and a half steps long and about three and a half steps wide. That's how big it is. No, it ain't even five and a half steps long because they've got it blocked off. It's got a bunk in it with a mattress in it. It has a sink and a toilet and they're built as one unit. You can use it as a chair, too. The sink is at the top where the old-time toilets at home would have the water tank. Where the watertank would be is a sink and it has push buttons for the water.

"The extreme outer part of the cell has a solid front. It's like a wall and it has a door on it, a wooden door that has a window on it and it can be opened or it can be closed, depending. When they close it, it's called being put on blackout. They check the lights, shut the lights off in the cell and then they close the outer window on the door and no light gets in the cell; so you're in blackout. If you're talking too loud or you give em a bad time about something, then that's how they get back at you. They put you on blackout for a few days.

"Inside the wood front of the cell, you have a space maybe two feet and then you run into the solid bar front of the cell itself. It's damn near like a little chamber in between there. You come through two doors before you get in the cell. Actually your cell has two doors. One slides open and the one has a key and it opens and swings out. Out here in the wings the bars on the cells are, oh, maybe four inches apart between bars so there's enough room to put your arms through it. If you're in the Hole, there's an extra bar slipped in so that you can't put your hand through. You could put your fingers through and wiggle em around but you can't put your hand through the bars.

"If you tell somebody they've got to do ten days on A Deck, then that means you're goin to do ten days in the Hole. Some joints call it Sleepy Hollow or the Growler, but here it's just the Hole or A Deck. The Hole is on a tier. All the cells are on the same side. It's kind of creepy, really. It's so quiet down there, that's the first thing you notice about it. There's fifteen–twenty guys down there but you don't hear any noise. That's because they're quiet cells. Quiet cells in that no noise comes out of them because of those fronts. They're designed to muffle the sound, so when you're locked into one of the cells it's really quiet. About the only thing you hear is yourself, so you spend all your time talking to yourself. It doesn't take long. I talk to myself anyway so when I get down there, it's just natural. I start right off with a conversation. You sing a lot, too.

"First, you go to Kangaroo Court over in Big Red, then they take you out of there and take you through five barred gates before you walk into your house in the Hole. When you get down there, they give you a pair of coveralls to wear. They take your shoes and all your clothes away. You can't smoke in there. You could conceivably get a paper and pencil and write a letter but there isn't a guarantee it will be mailed. They don't give you any mail while you're down there. You eat regular. They don't withhold food. They do knock off the dessert. You can't have cake or ice cream but you get enough to eat.

"You go into your cell, you take your coveralls and *Bible* and they slam the doors shut and you start doing your time. Immediately you mark off that day. You don't count that day and you don't count the last day that you're going to be there because you generally get out in the morning of the last day. So you start

countin eighteen days from the time you walk in the door. That's
the same way you count your time in the Joint if you get a lot of
time. Some guys don't bother to count the last six months in the
Joint. But anyway, as soon as they slam the door on you, you get
your eyes adjusted so that any bit of light that's in there is enough
to read by. There is a light on the wall. There's two ventilators in
there; one to take the air out; the other to take the air in. That's
about it; that's what's in the Hole. As a rule, one guy might try
shoutin around right away to try to find out who else is in there."

Delorme describes a game he used to play in *the Hole* to pass the
time. Isolation can cause problems for those men who don't know
how to deal with the darkness and silence as will be brought out
later. Bravado sometimes helps men to handle their punishment.

"There's a little trick to gettin used to the silence. You get your
ears used to the silence. Nobody talks much. It's such an effort to
talk and hear each other shoutin because everything muffles the
sound, so you have to scream forty times to understand what the
other guy says so it's not exactly conducive to long conversations.
But there's a little trick to the whole trip.

"In between walkin the floor, singin to yourself, you can do
what I used to do. I used to take toilet paper, get it wet and then
make little balls out of it and if I had a pencil I'd draw a bull's eye
on the wall and I'd just start walkin and everytime I'd walk to one
end of the cell I would deposit one little toilet paper ball on the
bar. I'd set it on the cross bars then walk back down to the other
end of the cell. Then I'd make another one, then walk back over and
I'd set that one on the bar. I'd stack up about thirty or forty of em,
then I'd stand out there and throw em at the bull's eye on the wall
and they'd stick. Then I'd just do the whole trip over and over again.

"Sometimes I'd talk down into the toilet on the phone. You gotta
sit right there on the floor, put your head down in there then
holler down into the toilet, unless you're talkin to your neighbors,
then you don't have to holler too loud and you can hear real good.
I'd get a headache after awhile from the fumes. They're not that
strong but after an hour or so you really begin to notice it. You get
a headache. Once in awhile you hear a voice screamin, 'Anybody
on the line? Anybody on the line? Who are you?' And you yell out
and see what they want. This system works in the Hole and Seg,

too. The Segregation tiers are also hooked into the system so they could also scream and it would come up through the plumbing to one of us in the Hole, and we could hear and pass messages around like that. That was the main way of talkin to people. And another way was to stand up on the side of your sink and talk through the vents, because the vents run from cell to cell so that you could shout through the vents and hear pretty good that way."

Some men become disoriented in *the Hole*, particularly if they have not had the opportunity to prepare themselves for the experience. Delorme describes almost going to pieces in *the Hole*.

"The last time I was in the Hole I did ten days for being in possession of carbon tetrachloride. We'd inhale it. I was a real sniffer for awhile. Anything for a trip. So they used to give out ten-day sentences for that shit and I was always gettin caught. Jeez, I got caught, well, if you're known to do that, they're goin to keep their eye on you.

"So I tried comin back to my house by myself one time. I bought a little bottle of it for two-three packs of cigarettes and I was happy as hell. Boy, and I'd been sneakin back to my house, go in the back, then I'd pull the curtain across, sit back there and turn the radio on and get the rag all set up and pour it into the rag, sit there and start sniffin it. You hold it right up to your mouth and you inhale, so you take it right down. Man! You get loaded. Whew! It really fucks your head up, but it seems like I'd no more get started when the pig would be there. He'd come trottin by and if he asked me a question, I was busted cause I couldn't answer. I wouldn't be able to. I couldn't tell him my name, you know, so they'd take me to the hospital and they'd say, 'This guy is loaded.' I was fucked up. Generally by the time they walked you over to the hospital, your head cleared up a bit. So anyway, it was good for ten days on the shelf, as they call it.

"Well, I had that ten days once. I did it. I hated it. Had me goin crazy the end of the ten days. I was pacin; I was so goddam nervous; wanted out of there, that solitary shit. By the time you come out of there, it's like gettin out of prison and goin home or something. It's a joy to come out here with the livin again. It's like bein in a vault or some damn thing. I just will never get used to it. Oh, you get used to it, say if they just force you to live down there.

Some guys do. Guys have been down there for months and months, even years. But it's nice to come out, I'm tellin you.

"I did that ten days and got out. I got out in the morning. Came staggerin out into the goddam sunlight holdin my eyes and dyin for a cigarette and a cup of coffee. I came back out to the wing and got into my house and had the bull shout up to me, 'Hey, it's good to see you back.' and all that bullshit.

"I said, 'Yeah, that's cool.' and I went down to the house and I wasn't in the house ten minutes and this dude came truckin down the tier and he's a friend of mine. He says, 'Hey, man, you want to get down or what?'

"I says, 'You goddam right.' So he pulls on in and gives me a snort. He gives me another little bottle. He had about half a jug left he was goin to share with me. The same trip. The dirty sonovabitch. I no more than got started and here comes the goddam sergeant. Caught me cold. Got me.

"So away I went. I was back down in the goddam Hole again. I went to court the next day and got ten more days. I said, 'Oh, Lord, give me a break. Let me stay out a day or two at least.'

"They said, 'No, no way.' Ten more fuckin days!

"I said, 'Oh God.' I could do ten days but you got to stay out awhile, two–three days and get your head back in shape and get yourself psyched up, you know, then you can go down and do it, see. They put my ass back into the same cell again, too.

"God, I just had a feelin, I says, 'No, I can't do it.' Course. I should a never said that to myself either. You can't do that to yourself. You gotta right off the bat, immediately when you're caught, you gotta start workin on it, gettin your mind set up, knowin that's what you gotta do and that you *can* do it, no matter what they do. You have to tell yourself, '*I can do it*. It ain't shit. I can do it,' and 'It don't bother me a goddam bit.'

"But I got a little weak. I was pretty disoriented anyway from the sniffin and shit and so I wasn't functioning too good. I thought they were tryin to kill me or drive me crazy and thought they might succeed this time. And so I went down there. That was in the morning.

"They give me ten days in the morning and by one o'clock that afternoon, I was out. I kept tellin the bull when he came down, I

said, 'Hey, you know me. I'm serious, man, serious business, man.
I don't think I can do it.'

"He says, 'Aw, you can do it. Ten days.'

"I says, 'Naw, I'm tellin you. I can't do it. You gotta cut me some
slack.' I says, 'I want to talk to the lieutenant. I want to talk to the
sergeant. I want to talk to somebody.' I says, 'I got claustrophobia.'
Which I do have a little touch of but normally I've always been
able to hold it down and not let it bug me too much. You have to. It
doesn't bother you in a big cell because you can come and go. You
go to chow, you do this and that. I know if I really need to, I can
get out of the cell, so it's completely different. But down there, it
bein the Hole, it kinda brings those things out in you and you lose
it a little bit. It started when I went into the cell and they closed
the door.

"Already my nerves were startin to jump. I was startin to spin in
circles and I thought they turned the air conditioning off and I
kept standin up on the sink checkin the air conditioning. I couldn't
hear any air. I couldn't feel any air, so I thought I was goin to
smother and I started sweatin. I remember that. Sweatin and
walkin the floor and wonderin what the hell I was gonna do. So I
guess they musta took me serious and they notified some people
in the mental health tier or something. And so things worked out
alright.

"Then I asked the cop, 'Will you not close the outer door? My
air vents don't work. At least just leave the outer door open. I
won't scream at nobody or nothin. Just give me a break and leave
the door open for a little bit. I can't go nowhere. My inner door is
closed. The iron door is closed. At least I could peep out of the
crack and feel the air comin in.'

"He said, 'Well, don't worry.' He said, 'Yeah, we're goin to feed
you lunch now. You go ahead and eat and the sergeant's goin to be
down to talk to you and I don't think you're gonna be in here too
long.'

"Oh boy, those were good words to me. Sure enough, about an
hour later the sergeant came down with another cop and they
opened my door and said, 'Come out.'

"And I says, 'Damn, you lettin me out early?'

"They says, 'Yeah, you gotta break this time.' He says, 'We're gonna try something different with you. We're goin to give you up. We're gonna send you over to the recovery tier, the mental health tier, and see what they can do with you.'

"I said, 'That sounds good to me. Let me go. Shit, I fit right in with those nuts.' So I stayed real serious until I got over there then I cut loose. Boy, I was so happy to be out of that fuckin Hole! Whew! I didn't care where they put me just so it wasn't in the Hole."

Drinking alcohol and sniffing carbon tetrachloride are offenses for which many men are confined to *the Hole*. Delorme interviews a friend in an effort to capture on tape the futility and despair some men feel.

"I'm gonna talk to a friend of mine. I'll call him Jimmy. Well, Jimmy is always in trouble. He has a very special attitude. You'll notice it's super negative and him and I are like black and white together, but yet for the last couple years we've been pretty close. And he goes to the Hole all the time. He's always in the Hole for some damn thing, and I try to encourage him to change a little bit, to do a few things right, but it hasn't worked. Imagine he kind of stores it away or something. But I don't know, one of these days he might change. I want to get him on this tape to talk a little bit. And I want to emphasize that this guy is going to speak the words of a lot of people in here and he has the attitude of an awful lot of people—kind of down on everything.

"I'm sure that you're going to be able to sort through this information and really get a look at what this place builds, what it turns people into, or how the negative thing gets into a person in here and just stirs everything up in them so their feelings are so mixed up.

"It pisses me off. I hate to see him go into the fuckin Hole all the time, goddam it! I just, yeah, I've been like a babysitter, for chrissake, and I just get burned out. I don't want that bullshit to start rubbin off on me. I don't want to start thinkin like that again. I've already thought it, so maybe it can't happen again. I don't give up. I don't flip out and start cussin and slammin stuff around and pay em back anymore. You pay em back somehow by throwin all this anger and stuff on some of the pigs that's in the wing. Then I suffer the consequences. That's kind of the way Jimmy would do it.

So that's where his head's at, and I'll try to bring it out on the tape."

Gene: "Have you been in the Hole much?"

Jimmy: "Well, in the last year I've been over there a half a year. They send my mail there before I get it here in the wing."

Gene: "What were most of your beefs for?"

Jimmy: "Just for a minor alcohol situation."

Gene: "Why do you think it is that you get busted so much when you see it goin around and around you all the time? Everybody else doesn't go to the Hole as much as you do."

Jimmy: "Then they got it in for me."

Gene: "That's true in part. Now they're watchin you all the time. You do everything but sign autographs for em. What do you think of this joint?

Jimmy: "This is Disneyland."

Gene: "Compared to?"

Jimmy: "Monroe, Prince Albert, Kingston, Georgeville [Canada]."

Gene: "How old are you?"

Jimmy: "Twenty-nine."

Gene: "Not even thirty years old yet. You've been in five prisons. We're not even countin juvenile bullshit. Every day you got a routine. How are you gonna get through the day and what are you gonna do?"

Jimmy: "I got no routine."

Gene: "You gotta routine. You got places you hit every day. You got things you do; you got little projects; you got hustles. Let's talk about that a little bit. Just start when you get up in the mornin where you come down and invite me to breakfast or whatever."

Jimmy: "I get up in the morning, wash my face, have a cup of coffee, wait for the door to open, check to see if the stash is still there."

Gene: "The stash is pruno?"

Jimmy: "Yeah, I go to chow, have breakfast, go over to the Bridge Club, sit around, go up to the Club, sit around, play cards."

Gene: "You're always on the lookout to see what's happenin, man?"

Jimmy: "Oh, I've always had a scheme on how to get out of here."

Gene: "Now that's a routine. You used to go to school, that would be a routine."

Jimmy: "Oh yeah, that's garbage. School's no good."

Gene: "How long did you plug along on that? The school."

Jimmy: "A year."

Gene: "Did you try to get back in or did you change your mind?"

Jimmy: "Yeah, changed my mind. Whole different attitude. I said, 'Fuck it. I ain't gonna try it.'"

Gene: "How much time are you doin right now with your new two years? You just got two years added on yesterday."

Jimmy: "No, a year yesterday. About another year and a half."

Gene: "What do you think about when you think about gettin out, man? Are you happy about it?"

Jimmy: "I get nervous. Don't know what I'm going to do when I get out."

Gene: "No plans? No dough?"

Jimmy: "No dough. Afraid I'll get out there and I won't know how to act."

Gene: "Yeah, That really bothers you? I mean, not knowing how to act? I think about that, too."

Jimmy: "I don't know. I just think about using people. It's a game. So when I get out now, I want to be that way."

Gene: "Well, some people survive that way. I guess you have to watch that you don't get used, too. How do you use people? Girls?"

Jimmy: "No."

Gene: "Well, you use people in here. How do you use them?"

Jimmy: "Oh, I just manipulate them and get them to do things for me."

Gene: "Pretty standard practice, isn't it? Well, I use people, too. You and I have got along for a long time and we do things different. We think different but we've thought the same. I just changed it along the line is all, so that's why I can understand it and accept it. I think one day you're gonna get tired of it, too. I'm tired of it already but what the hell; it's hard to get goin especially when you establish a reputation in here as a fuck-up, man, a drinker, and all that bullshit. So that's really tough. Tough to get around that one. People wouldn't let you change if you wanted to, really. The bulls, too; the bulls especially. Well, I'm talking to you, man. If you try to straighten up, they think you're gettin slick. Right?"

Jimmy: "Yeah."

Gene: "Then they really think you're up to something. They say, 'Oh, he must of moved up into something big, man. He's tryin to be cool.' How do you get along with the cops in here?"

Jimmy: "I think they're animals. Stupid, ignorant. Can't find another job if they wanted to. They're sick for working here."

Gene: "When you was down in the Hole, man, you always tell me you don't like it. What do you do each day in the Hole? I mean, give me a typical day."

Jimmy: "A typical day, man, you wake up in the morning and wait for breakfast to come by and yell at them a couple of times."

Gene: "Yell what?"

Jimmy: "Anything. Cuss at them."

Gene: "Just let em know you're alive?"

Jimmy: "Yeah."

Gene: "Still kickin and ready to go on. Well, you're always right in the middle of things down there, too, aren't you?"

Jimmy: "Yeah."

Gene: "Tell me about a couple of things that happened while you was down there the last time."

Jimmy: "Last time? Not much."

Gene: "You never fill me in."

Jimmy: "Well, it's not on my mind now."

Gene: "What's on your mind now?"

Jimmy: "Running out of here. Getting off this tape."

Gene: "It's important that I talk to you, man, because a lot of people in here have the same attitude as you. You're kinda stuck, man, in that attitude. A lot of things are pretty bitter, resentful, negative, and it keeps comin back and it's a fuckin wheel you can't get off. That's why it's important. Don't you think?"

Jimmy: "Yeah."

Gene: "I mean everybody ain't able to stay out of trouble."

Jimmy: "Aw, I just get bitter at them because they have me here in the first place and in the second place, they keep picking on me for some rotten ole pruno, lock me up two months at a shot."

Gene: "Five days last time. That wasn't so bad."

Jimmy: "I wasn't drunk, though."

Gene: "What was that for?"

Jimmy: "It was jumping on that pig's back, trying to save his life and that's the thanks I get."

Gene: "What did they say about that in court?"

Jimmy: "They said you're not supposed to touch an officer for any reason whatsoever."

Gene: "What did you tell em?"

Jimmy: "This guy went crazy down here in the chow hall Sunday morning at breakfast and run over at my partner and started throwing hooks and jabs. My partner got up to defend himself and started hitting back. Police came over there and grabbed my partner. Thought he started it, so I grabbed the policeman. This other guy was running at him. I thought maybe this nut might have a shank or something to kill the policeman in front of my friend. I was worrying about the cop. I was trying to protect him. I didn't want him to get hurt."

Gene: "Was the cop there in court?"

Jimmy: "Yeah."

Gene: "What did he say or did he talk funny?"

Jimmy: "Yeah, he said I jumped on his back and started choking him. You know how they all lie."

Gene: "Five funky days, man, that wasn't too bad. I thought you'd get more."

Jimmy: "Me, too."

Gene: "Might knock some more bark off your fuckin head while they had you down there. Every time you get drunk over there, man, you guys have to go out fightin."

Jimmy: "Not me."

Gene: "Bullshit. You ain't never walked outta that cell. You're always upside down, got your arms up behind your back. They're thumpin you on the head and shit. What do you think about this? Last time they didn't bring no small motherfuckers in either. That goon squad, those guys are big, man, like that night one came."

Jimmy: "Yeah. They're all scared of me."

Gene: "Sonovabitches are so big they can hardly get through the door. Most of em are fat."

Jimmy: "They can ask me gently to come along."

Gene: "Why certainly."

Jimmy: "And I can gently tell them to fuck themselves."

Gene: "Did they ever jump you when you were in Segregation? Come in your cell and drag you out for something?"

Jimmy: "No, they came close, though. It was next door. Lucky it was the other fella instead of me. I was ready, though."

Gene: "Did you get a chance to throw any piss on em?"

Jimmy: "Oh yeah."

Gene: "Tell me about that."

Jimmy: "Oh they came down there harassing us, promising us the world, give us a ping-pong table, took it away fifteen minutes later. Didn't even get a chance to play at it. They said it was a weapon. Then they refused this guy his phone call. Guy got mad and threw some piss at them. They came by with the ole goon squad, kinda gave him a thrashing. We wasn't going for that so we started to putting turds in cups and throwing it at them."

Gene: "Do they do that very often down there? I mean do they get down and dirty with a lot of the pigs down there?"

Jimmy: "Well, not anymore. They don't like that piss and shit."

Gene: "They know they can crack that up now. Well, you was livin with a pretty rowdy bunch over there."

Jimmy: "Pretty rowdy? Well, they're a nice bunch of guys. It's just how you look at it."

Gene: "Tell me a little about the Segregation tier there. Like how you're locked in your cell."

Jimmy: "Just an old single cell. Got a little table there, have your books, letters, magazines, cigarettes, coffee."

Gene: "A real home away from home?"

Jimmy: "You know the front yard's kinda messy cause you got about a foot of garbage out there. If you pick through the stuff and get the rotten fruit you can make some pruno."

Gene: "Still able to make some down there, huh?"

Jimmy: "Oh man, every week."

Gene: "Do you get your yeast? Or do you make it?"

Jimmy: "Yeah, you just make yeast."

Gene: "By lettin the bread sit?"

Jimmy: "No, you put the bread in a cup then you put water in there until it's kinda soggy. Then you throw a top on it and let it sit for three-four days until it's got a good top of mold on there. Then you scrape the mold off. All underneath is yeast. And you throw that in there, then you can change the water into wine."

Gene: "Well, you're a pretty good pruno maker, brew master."

Jimmy: "Well, I like to drink."

Gene: "How do you get yard-out on the tier down there? One at a time?"

Jimmy: "Yeah. It was at one time but there was twenty-three guys down there and you get an hour and ten minutes apiece and there wasn't enough hours in the day for everybody. Three or four hours for chow for three different meals. But then they started throwing their food out there and trays and stuff so now they have two people out in the yard at a time."

Gene: "Well, that was a pretty bad move taking this other fuckin yard down."

Jimmy: "Yeah, it was terrible."

Lockdowns are not infrequent at the prison and are instituted when a disaster or threats of impending riot cause officials to order that prisoners be confined to their cells. When murders or other outbreaks occur, the chances of further violence escalate. *Lockdowns* serve the purpose of helping to calm the situation, preventing further trouble, and providing both guards and prisoners a cooling off period of relief and security from the enormous tensions that develop in such situations. The men hate to be placed on *lockdown* since all programming and other activities cease. Although generally quite temporary, lasting no more than a few days to a few weeks at the most, a *lockdown* was ordered in June, 1979, that lasted for over four months. Research for this study was in progress during this period, and since Delorme and other prisoners recorded much of what occurred, it is presented here in considerable depth. In the epilogue at the end of this chapter, several guards respond to the charges of the prisoners.

Although the murder of a guard by two native Americans appears to be the reason why, apparently, so many of the guards behaved so unprofessionally during the *lockdown*, the fuse for the explosion that took place had been burning for many years. The story of the great *lockdown* of 1979, as seen from the perspective of the imprisoned men, is told in the following narratives collected during the time these dramatic events were unfolding. Several of the narratives in this section were taken from a tape made by inmates during a press conference held July 8, 1979. A former vice president of the Resident Council describes the events leading up to June 15 when the guard was killed.

"My name is A.B.. I'm gonna give you a brief presentation of what transpired up to June 15, when a correctional officer was stabbed here in the penitentiary. The present administration has condoned repeated acts of guard harassment of inmates, beatings, et cetera. The administration was openly disrespected by correctional officers, and memorandums that are issued by the administration are overlooked.[33]

"During the months of April, May, and June of this year a battle for control of WSP emerged between the guards' union and the administration. Correctional officers defied orders of the administration when given and purposely engaged in acts of harassment against inmates, inmate clubs, and inmate programs in an effort to promote negative reactions from inmates to better their plans to control the penitentiary. The president of the guards' union has been quoted in the past several months as labeling the superintendent as a 'wolf in sheep's clothing.' With this statement in mind, it is a well-known fact that the superintendent started out in the field of corrections as an officer here at this penitentiary and served on the line himself with numerous officers who were in fact still here when he came back as superintendent. He was to be the final part of the plan, the homecoming of one of their own.

"The Superintendent and Assistant Superintendent of Custody was informed by many inmate club leaders and the Resident Council through our meetings in April, May, and June that the inmate population was being pushed to the limits by correctional officers. Visitors were openly harassed; residents were being subjected to skin searches two and three times daily. Fictitious infraction reports were written on inmates, and the major hearing committee imposed sanctions on inmates on officers' reports alone.[34]

"Practically every form of propaganda has been printed and broadcast by the news media following interviews with the administration and guards' union officials concerning the problem of violence, its causes, and inmates incarcerated at WSP during the past four months. This propaganda has not been the reality of the situation. It was simply utilized by the latter to shield their incompetency, crimes, and to secure their employment.

"On June 12, 1979, an Indian inmate was fatally stabbed in the Resident Council office. As vice president of the Resident Council, I attended a meeting between representatives of the Chicano Center and the Indian Brotherhood. This meeting was held in T.'s office in the Control Room at the request of Shift Lt. G., who stated prior to the start of this meeting that if he wasn't assured by the presidents of the two clubs that there would be no more reprisals involving the matter of the death of inmate Broncho, that he would lock the penitentiary down. He agreed that he would let the presidents of the two clubs talk to their members and a meeting was set up in the Black Prisoners Forum Unlimited club area.

"At 2:30 on June 12, 1979, the presidents of the Chicano Center and Indian Brotherhood, along with L., Minister of the Muslim Brotherhood, and myself met with Shift Lt. H. and Captain B. in the Captain's office. An agreement was made by the two inmate groups that no incidents would transpire between the two inmate groups. We asked Captain B. to pull his officers back and not have any more shakedowns on that thing. He agreed to that and stated that he would tell his officers to back off. Three days later Sergeant C. was fatally stabbed."

Once the men were placed on *lockdown*, the anger of some of the guards at the death of one of their own produced a tremendous upsurge of hatred and a desire for revenge. Some of the men believed that guards wanted to punish the native Americans, since all at this moment were perceived as enemies. Delorme begins the story.

"When they locked everybody up after C. got killed, it was a couple hours before the goon squad went in there to take the S. brothers out. [The two native Americans who were involved in the killing of the guard were brothers.] Actually, they took two cells, seven or eight Indian guys. They took em out to the Hole. But they took two other brothers, not the S. brothers, and took em up to the hospital, put em in an empty room, took all their clothes off of em and just beat the shit out of em with sticks and fists and Mace and left em layin. They stripped em down. And neither one of em had been involved in the killing. They had just made some comment about the treatment the other guys were gettin, you know, so they just grabbed em by the neck and took em along. They threatened to throw em over the tier, too, on the way. Everybody on the wing heard it. I was on the other side. I couldn't hear it but I knew it was goin on. Guys taped it all. I could hear a lot of yellin."

Cardozo-Freeman: "How could they get away with that in the hospital?"

Delorme: "How? Pretty easy. They got control of everything in here. The guards run the fuckin prison. They can do pretty much what they wanna do."

Cardozo-Freeman: "Didn't the nurses protest?"

Delorme: "Them nurses ain't gonna say nothin to nobody. They were scared for their lives. They're about half cop anyway so they absolutely wouldn't say nothin. Anyway, they stripped the rooms bare and left them guys in there for three or four days. Told the nurses not to feed em, not to give em anything. They asked what they'd done and they told em it was none of their goddam business. That's what the guards told the nurses, and threatened them, too, if they did say anything about it. They got nasty with those nurses, so they never said anything after that."[35]

According to the men, native Americans were not the only victims of the guards' wrath. On July 6 and 7, a *shakedown* took place in Eight Wing. Although the administration had ordered the guards to follow specific procedures in searching the cells and removing items, some guards went overboard in their zeal, removing and destroying personal property, such as family photos, which was very important to prisoners. A Chicano prisoner describes conditions in the wing at that time and the treatment that he said he personally received at the hands of the Riot Squad.

"I'm so-and-so and I'm presently a resident in Eight Wing. I'll take it from the day of the lockdown when we were first locked up.

"Well the first three and a half weeks that we were locked up in our cells without showers, we were constantly told that a shower was coming the next day. The attitude of the guards had deteriorated to the point where they weren't even speaking to the men and they weren't even seen. The only way you knew they were there was when they brought the cold TV dinners around. At that point the mail slowed and it virtually stopped for a couple weeks. We were ignored completely. Our cries for showers, and I'll say cries, because at that time the weather was very hot [July].

"We were looking forward to the shakedown so we can get this thing over with cause we were told that after the shakedown things would return to normal. At that point it had not been said the cause of the lockdown was because of the Indians and Chicanos. As A.B. said, that was resolved and there were no acts of violence committed between our particular groups.

"When the shakedown came, a memo was issued that listed the things that would be taken out of our cells and the things we would be able to keep. That was totally disregarded. Everything was taken out of our cells. They came to my cell, they took the four of us out. Myself, Lucero, and a couple other Chicano brothers, and they locked us up in a closet, naked. As we were waiting in there, an hour lapsed. We were taken back to our cell and there was nothing in there but the bunks and the mattress and a blanket. As I stood at the cell bars to look at the things that had been removed, as they were throwing them all on the tier floor, I seen pictures of my daughter, of my wife torn up and on the floor. Members of that particular squad who happened to be shaking down were also loading things into barrels and members of the same squad were also driving them out of the institution, hence so many missing items, so many personal belongings lost, some expensive."

While the riot squad was going through the cells in Eight Wing destroying property, Delorme, waiting for them to arrive at his cell, made a tape.

"Just been kinda sittin here since the lockdown started. Everybody was screamin and hollerin and talkin all morning; kind of burnt out on it right now. Everybody's just kickin back, coolin it. There's about three feet of garbage covering the whole floor downstairs. [Delorme is on the second tier.]

Everything from mattresses to tore-up sheets to, oh, you name it, is layin down there. Pictures and a lot of other things and boards and brooms and shoes; just everything that's loose, that could be thrown out is down there. Made a pretty fair mess myself out there throwin a lot of garbage out. It's nothin that they're not goin to take out anyway cause when they come through it's like, fuck, I don't know; they just go crazy, just take everything out, you know, leave us sittin here pretty bare. So a lot of people just throw it out themselves. What the hell. Kind of fun to throw stuff anyway. Throw it at the windows, at least try to break the windows. Little sonovabitches don't break that easy for some reason.

"I know tomorrow morning they'll, well, maybe not in the morning but tomorrow sometime they'll get to us. They'll start to shakin this side down and I'll get the recorder goin again and you'll hear some screamin and hollerin then, believe me. Bangin and smashin. They're still throwing shit around over there and raisin hell now. You can hear the boards going. I don't know what tier they're on but they're down at the end some damned where, so I'll have a lot of that on here and you'll hear plenty of good shit.

"This one guy down the tier, I'll be able to catch him on here. All he does every day, you hear him screamin, you know. He's talkin about the guard that got killed and he'll just come up out of the blue and start hollerin, 'They spit in his face and they cut his heart out,' and all that shit. It's really weird. The guy's mind snapped or something. He's takin a rest right now. I don't hear him or I'd put it on here. 'They spit in his face and cut his heart out, the rotten sonovabitch.' Just kind of something to bug them guards.

They've been beatin on things over there with hammers all day long. Haven't been able to figure out what the hell it could be. I think it's these supports from these beds. They're made of steel. Beautiful shanks. These are the kinds that would almost make swords, you know what I mean?

"There's a helluva mess down there, man. You can't even walk down on that tier. It's just everything torn up. I'll bet you'd never imagine people puttin a mattress through one of these cell doors, huh, a mattress. They tore it in half and stuffed it out. Tore up all the sheets and tore up all the blankets and stuffed it out. Just craziness, craziness, but that's the way it goes. We're a nuthouse. So what's new? Right?

"One of the biggest worries I have with this lockdown is I'm worried I'll lose my tape deck and my tape recorder. They just act crazy and they're subject to take my tapes and throw em over the tier. Take my tape recorder with em, so that's one reason I wanted to get a couple tapes made if I can.

"You can't help but stay uptight during this and so that has an effect on everything I do. Concentration, especially. So damn many things goin on. I don't have a hell of a lot of time to really concentrate on one thing. Man oh man! I hope nobody throws cigarette butts over the tier. Man, you couldn't throw enough water down there to put out that fire.

[Several hours later] "Well, that was really a trip. They marched us to the end of the tier and locked us in a small mop closet with eight other guys. It was nice walkin down the tier after bein locked up in that cell for so long.

"It seemed like we was in that closet a helluva long time but it was probably more like a half hour to an hour. The house is stripped bare, just like we expected. Our personal stuff is strewn all over the place and some of our pictures are layin in a heap on the tier. It must be our lucky day cause none of us got thumped on the head with the war clubs that the goons are packin. Ah me. Well, one thing nice about the whole thing, our cell was never so clean.

"I lost most of the nice books on Indians you sent me. Maybe I'll keep that a secret so you won't feel bad. Lost half of my tapes, too. It isn't like we haven't gone through this before. In fact, this is a yearly thing around here. One thing is strange about this shakedown; there are four of us in the house. Right? The goons left us two cups and two toothbrushes to use. I guess we have to look at the bright side of things. It sure beats nothin.

"Oh boy, they [guards] look mad, too after the shakedown. We're gettin off on it, see. We already have been through this whippin jag and now we got to watch them take it. We got our whippin and we're kickin back and watchin TV, writin letters. Finally got that shit over with. Them guys are just goin through it.

"It's cold, baby. It's cold blooded. They're just bein . . . they're mean to us. Lord, those coppers are cruel! You wouldn't believe it. Man, they can't treat me like this, can they? Obviously they can. Oh shit! Fun never ends, you know what I mean? Fun never ends.

"I gotta get outa here! The pressure they get on us, the worse it gets, the more I giggle. What are you goin to do? That's a sign, I know it is. That is a bad sign.

"But really, it's pretty relaxed. I could see it a little different, you know. It's easy enough. Slow but sure.

"Right now they're really puttin us through the fuckin grinder. They want to put us through the mill right now. O.K. We got our TV antenna up. We got our clothesline back up. I laid a blanket on the floor. I put all my clothes on when they come through so they wouldn't throw them all out. I got some pretty nice clothes. Now I got em in a pile back there cause they took all our clothes hangers away. Cell's bare but it seems like more room in here anyway. There's more room for the four of us.

"We don't get much to eat. Aw, poor baby. We have two TV dinners and then we have two boxes of cold cereal for breakfast.

"Oh man, I don't like to sound bitter about it but I'm tellin you, the people they hire to work here are really strange! Goddam, they're worse than the people that are doin time in this sonovabitch. Gets a little shaky, you know.

"Right now they're sittin out here callin names to guys in their cells that are locked in. Can't believe it, man, really.

"The state has made a request of the National Corrections Association to send a panel of guys down here to make interviews. They were on the news tonight. They only spent a couple hours looking the Joint over today. They want to talk to prisoners and they want to talk to anybody that wants to talk to em. I don't think the administration is goin to let them talk to prisoners.

"Really spooky this morning. You see the windows out in front of my house here, they stretch about three tiers high and on the outside of the building they dropped some canvas. They covered up the window and all there is to see out there is dirt in the first place. Man, it's really strange. I don't know what the hell they're up to. Oh well, ours is not to question why. But right now nothing surprises me. Curtains on the outside of a building.

"I'll tell you something funny but typical of this population. For the first week of the lockdown, the guards retaliated by starving us, or 'forgetting' to feed the entire Joint except at night. The thing is, that everyone knew what they were doing and none said a word in complaint. Everyone just took the food at night, one very

small TV dinner, and went on watching TV or playing cards or
whatever. But the funny part came this week when they began
feeding us 'lunch.' Everyone started hooting and calling them
weak for selling out and giving us more food! This is from the
guys, me included, that were starving! I even felt some disappoint-
ment in the switch, and joined in the shouting! I did feel a sort of
power from being able to accept anything that they were going to
dish out, and I was ready for the worst. Maybe that is the whole
thing about this game. We know the position that we are in, and
that is *always* the losers spot. So whenever something happens you
never get ready to win any battles. Rather you set yourself to
expect the worst including death or injury at their hands. Starvation,
torture, questions; it all becomes a game, and one thing you
always know is that all the cons living around you are watching or
listening to every move you make whenever the Man comes by the
cell. So, even if the goons come to drag you off to the Hole, you
either go down fighting or you hold your mud and take it like a
man, with a smile or smirk on your face. But *never* do you whine
or beg or snivel in front of the other cons. Maybe after the goons
get you off by yourself you might put in a plea for justice or
something of that order. That is part of the convict code.

"Keep this in your pretty little mind, also, the men in the cells
are polite and friendly to any officer that stops by and treats them
that way. So it's not all the officers, and it's not all the convicts that
are fighting. Rather there is a faction on both sides that just stay at
each other's throats, and the worst thing is the instigators on both
sides."

The *shakedown* of July 6 precipitated the explosion in Eight
Wing on July 7 in which prisoners rioted and tore the plumbing
up in their cells. Not all the men participated in this outburst.
The main reason for the uprising was the response to having
personal belongings destroyed and the unprofessional manner in
which some of the guards went about this wanton destruction.
Considerable evidence gives credence to the charges by the men
that these guards ignored orders given by the higher officials.
Secondary factors for the riot were the extreme heat of the summer,
long confinement of four men to a cell without exercise or relief,
no showers, and, of course, the frustration, anger, and helplessness

the men felt as a result of their treatment by the guards. In their eyes, they were punished unjustly for something they personally had not participated in (the killing of the guard by the two native American prisoners). As one of the previous narratives pointed out, negotiations had taken place between officials and prisoner leaders to assure that no more violence would occur as a result of the problems that had surfaced between the Chicanos and native Americans. The men perceived that the only reason for the *lockdown* was to destroy their programs and return the prison to more restrictive status. When the men rioted, the riot squad removed approximately 245 men from their devastated cells and herded them out to the *Big Yard*. They remained there for forty-seven days. For a period of time, they were without shelter from the sun or the cold of the night. A native American describes what happened to him when he was taken to the *Yard*.

"My name is B.C. and I am a resident of Eight Wing. July 7 after this shakedown incident came down to where they took all our stuff, there was a promise of showers. There's been a lot of things written in the news media about that as the reason we went off in Eight Wing and became destructive. That is not true. We went off in Eight Wing because of the way that they brutalized us and our personal possessions. Things that had meaning to us, that kept us in contact and kept our ties with our people on the streets. Things that had meaning to us.

"At approximately ten o'clock in the evening, July 7, guards came into the wing, fired off a round, they say it was a blank, I don't know, from a shotgun. They proceeded to F tier; they proceeded to take people out of the cells, one cell at a time. There was approximately fifteen–twenty guards in full riot gear. The guards at the bottom of the wing down by the main gate had weapons. People were taken out two-three-four, however many people lived in a cell—one cell at a time. They were beaten. They were knocked to the ground. They were stomped on. They were handcuffed with their hands behind their backs.

"I live on D tier, the last cell on the tier. I listened to all of this coming down from the time they took all of F tier out, then they proceeded to E tier, took all of E tier out, then C and D tiers. When they began on D tier, I noticed the process with a mirror that I stuck out of the bars of my cell.

"As the inmates of each cell was brought out, they were brought out one at a time with their hands on their heads. They were kicked, punched, and hit down to the front of the tier. There they were turned over to another cadre of guards. They were handcuffed behind their backs with a specific type of cuff. It's a plastic cuff with a wire that runs through it that can be cinched up tight. They were slammed into walls.

"I observed these things with my own eyes when they hit my tier. I watched. I was on the last tier so naturally you know how I felt knowing they were getting closer to our cell. They came to our cell. We were all standing there waiting for them. I was in the front. There was four of us living there. I had my hands on my head. They asked me to step aside to see if there was a toilet in the back of our cell. I told them there was no reason to look, there is not a toilet in my cell. So they yelled down and said, 'O.K. Well who are the Blanket Asses in here?' There's two Indians living in the cell; myself and my brother-in-law. One of the guards said, 'Well, that's one and I know who the other one is.' When they opened the cell I was told to step out. When I proceeded to do so, I was punched in the gut with a baton. I had glasses on. The glasses were smashed in my face. I was beat the length of the tier. At the end of the tier I was turned over to an officer called Mr. C. He slammed me into the wall. He weighs about 300 pounds. He slammed me into the wall face first after I was cuffed, ripped my watch off my arm. I was taken down in front of the wing. I was thrown in the dirt in front of the wing on my face. Feet were put on my head. My face was pushed into the dirt. I could hardly breathe. Every time I would try to move to get breath, I was stepped on again. I was kicked.

"I was taken from there with I don't know how many prisoners, fifty–sixty people. We was told to put our heads down and place them in the back of the person in front of us and to get as close to them as we could. We were told to double time from Eight Wing to the Big Yard, which is approximately 600 yards, maybe more than that. If there was any space that ever came between you and the man that was in front of you, you were hit. There was approximately thirty–forty guards on each side of us. I don't know where they all came from. We were hit and we were punched all the way to the Big Yard.

"At the gate of the Big Yard, I was told to strip after the cuffs were cut off me. I was stripped, put into the Big Yard and after I was in the Big Yard, I was told—we were sitting in rows—to sit and hold my knees up to my chest and place my arms around my chest and put my head down between my knees and sit there and not move at the threat of being shot. Lt. E. at that time informed the guards that were on the wall, the SWAT team, that if anyone was to move they was to be shot."

A white prisoner continues describing what took place in the Big Yard.

"While we were laying in the dirt, construction was going on at that time for Eight Wing. It was all just turned over dirt and dust. While we were there, there were certain officers on the wall that were urinating on inmates that were laying on the ground. One of the deputy directors was right behind me. As I was laying down on the ground he was over my left shoulder. His name was Mr. F. He witnessed this entire thing. Mr. H. witnessed it. Mr. G. witnessed it. Mr. J. witnessed it. People were beat.

"There's no way to tell how drunk these guards were. I don't mean drunk through adrenalin. I mean drunk, alcohol. There was no way obviously we could run any analysis or anything on the guards that were involved in this move. But myself, I've had a few pops in my day and I can tell you if a guy's been drinking. I know for a fact they'd been drinking. As they were herding us to the Yard there were even comments between the guards joking that as soon as they get this crew moved into the Yard, they're going to have something else to drink.

"When they skin-searched people going to the Yard, they would take off any jewelry that you had—watches, necklaces, rings—and I don't know where they went. We haven't seen them since. No shoes or socks. The grass had been throughly saturated. It was real wet and it was cold at night. Inmates were beaten and herded into rows.

"Lt. H. at that time ordered them to shoot anyone that moved. When that order was given, the Yard was secure with the State Patrol and riot personnel from the institution. One resident informed the Nine Tower Control that he was going to get up to use the toilet facilities. At that time as we were being moved out an officer by the name of L. stuck a nightstick between an inmate's legs called M., tripping him and at that time Officer L. and Officer N. beat M. until the guy was unconscious. They had to drag him from the Yard.

"We stayed there in the Yard all night long. It was real cold and finally the sun came up and things warmed up a little bit, and that afternoon they gave us some shirts to wear. Sunburns were so bad that people's eyes were swollen shut. People's feet were burned so bad they couldn't walk on them. If they did, it would split them and they would start bleeding. Periodically what they would do then for harassment, they would run what we called the Silons, because they looked a lot like people on television in their riot gear; that's what they looked like. They'd run them in and line us up against the wall under threat of our lives if we didn't move against the wall. They did come in and remove things that were in the Yard. They did this on four–five different occasions. On a couple occasions, shots were fired. They finally passed us out blankets and we used TV dinner trays and stuff to make tents."

A Lifer describes what went on during those forty-seven days in the *Big Yard*. This man, an advocate for prisoner rights, was removed from the *Yard* and placed in Segregation because he and another prisoner spent their time while there documenting what was happening to the men.

Tim: "We got hit on the head with a nightstick, sapped with a sap glove, all bruised up and beat to hell, handcuffed and driven to that Big Yard for forty-seven days. I have never in my entire life seen more madness than I seen out there. They just went insane. Can you imagine the impact on me and Ike when they jerked us out of that Big Yard and slapped us in Segregation for no reason, either, saying that we were a very dangerous threat to the security of the institution."

Hank: "Why did they single you and Ike out for special treatment?"

Tim: "I'll give you for instances that might fall in with your question. When I was brought out of the front of the wing, pigs on the wall made a statement, 'Here comes S. How come you're not smiling now, S.?' My jaws were locked so tight, I was so mad. They was yellin, 'Run' to people and stuff like this. Well, I didn't run but I observed. I looked and I seen most of what was happening and that was my main objective of the whole trip after I got out in the Yard.

"When I first come into the Yard there was already four tiers sittin there. They was lined up by tier. This was just to break it down. The union president was standin behind me underneath the Nine Tower there and he hollered. We was all sittin down on the ground. I never had no shirt on. The only thing I had on was a pair of pants. I was barefooted and no shirt, no undershirt. I damn near froze my butt off, especially that first night, no clothes, no blankets, nothin. He yelled, 'S., stand up!' And I looked over my shoulder and he's tellin me, 'Yeah, you.' He's standin there with a shotgun.

"Well, up to that time the impact on my mind was 'How serious are these people in what they're doin here?' because what I'd already seen them doin was total madness. So what are they capable of now by my being singled out, and told me to stand and put my hands on top of my head, looking over that wall. Lookin at that sunrise, I faced that morning, I said, 'Well, I'm goin to be singled out and they're goin to shoot me as an example. That's the way it's goin to come down.' That's what I thought. But I said, 'Well, what the hell. I'm ready for that.' And I stood waiting for a shotgun blast in my back. Well, it never turned out that way.

"But I've seen people out there do things, man; I seen people eat bugs and worms, grasshoppers, grass, different things that grew out there in the Yard, those little mushrooms they make soup out of that grows in your grass, angleworms. The Bikers were eating angleworms and grasshoppers. And I don't know what all that was for.

"But the same time that you guys were bein fed inside, we was bein fed in that Big Yard. I mean, the real story, the in-depth story of what took place in that Big Yard those forty-seven days has yet to be told. I don't think there's an individual that's competent enough to tell all those stories.

"We had the same food, the same TV dinners and two pieces of bread with a cup of milk as everybody else did but we was out in the elements. We needed more as human beings, more subsistence than they were allowin us. We fought hand and glove to get vitamins. People deteriorated mentally not only from the elements but from the diet. A lot of people that I've talked to lost teeth. I lost three teeth since the lockdown last summer. I attribute that to the diet.

"Take 240 men and stick em in the Big Yard and slam the door. I'm tellin you, they slammed not only the barred gate out there, they slammed the outer gate and then they cut a little slot about six inches long and about a half inch wide so that they could peek through it. They was so afraid and ashamed. I know. I watched em. They was so ashamed and afraid of what they had inside that Big Yard, they didn't even want to look in there. I mean this went on all the time we was out there.

The State Patrol, I know, recorded the whole thing. They took pictures out there every day and night so they've got pictorial coverage of the whole thing. Somebody could just take those stills alone and make a helluva movie out of it. I mean it was so degrading. I have never seen anything like that in my life.

"We had a twenty-by-twenty pool of excrement behind those two toilets that they had. Then they brought three of those rental pottie things and finally they had six rent-a-potties at a time. Well, they let those things completely fill up and overflow. And guys would be walkin in pain. I'm tellin you, in pain. I am a religiously daily toilet goer but out there, man, it was every five days. And you just had to sneak up on those toilets, the urine and excrement, you know. It was terrible. And the flies, there was just a black cloud, you could see em. It was right up in front and ten feet away you'd get your food.

Hank: "Guys ain't gonna forget that."

Tim: "No, that's something that will never go out of anybody's mind. They can't suppress it. They took Ike and I because we were FUSE, because we filed litigation, but I say there was still respect there. There still is respect there today. I don't care what an asshole a cop is or who he is. From the top to the bottom they still respect us. That hasn't got much pay value to some folks but that's the name of the game.

"But bein out in the Big Yard forty-seven days, layin at night and talkin to your friends and watchin the satellites trip over, the stars and the different little trips we went on out there, the bigness of it all after bein locked up in a cell like that, and then returned not to an Eight Wing cell which we came out of. We never had done anything out in the Big Yard other than gather affidavits and medical complaints and what have you, tryin to deal with that; done nothin that we don't usually do, but like I say, it scared em, ·what they had out there in that Big Yard and they knew that Ike and I was out there in the Big Yard and they knew what we was goin to do, which we did basically, but when they took us in and put us in Segregation; as you know, Hank, I've been down that Hole a few times. But when they put me in that Hole that time, I very consciously at times had to push those walls back—from a big open space to a real solitary confinement situation, man, it was just mind shattering. But I made it without too much hassle, I don't think."

Hank: "And Terry is still there?"

Tim: "Yeah, and he's been there about eleven months for no reason."

Hank: "Why won't he come out?"

Tim: "It's not why he won't come out. They will not let him out. He's into that legal work and he's got a couple of dynamite lawsuits."

Hank: "I asked the bulls about him and they said he won't come out."

Tim: "Man, he sent me word a couple of times."

Hank: "Well, the cops are tryin to make it sound like he's in Protective Custody or something."

Tim: "Well, you know, they beat the hell out of him here awhile back. We got charges pending."

A prisoner describes how the hardships in the Big Yard brought out the best in him.

Gary: "Did you get beat up, too, when they took you out?"

Hal: "Oh shit yes. Oh, I got kicked, you know, when I was layin down with my nose in the dirt. I don't know why they didn't cuff me. Now I didn't understand that. I said, 'Man, they're gonna cuff me.' But they just said, 'Keep your hands behind your head.' When I went down I put my hands like this to lay down and when I got down he came along and he said, 'Keep your hands behind there,' and he kicked me. Hey, I still hurt. My damn tailbone right back there."

Gary: "Kicked you right on the tailbone?"

Hal: "Yeah."

Gary: "Dirty lousy bastards. You're in on the big lawsuit, aren't you?"

Hal: "Yeah. Aw, I thought I was dead that night. There was that sonovabitch up on the wall by Nine Tower. What's his name? I saw his name on his name tag. He's a dumb lookin sonovabitch. Big hog-jawed thing. He was up there with a rifle or shotgun. He was just sighting in on us. So I put my hand behind my neck. I said, 'Well, this is good bye.' It's a wonder one of em didn't start shootin."

Gary: "If one of em shot, they all woulda shot."

Hal: "They were firin out there. Shots went off. Aw hell, oh, this is it. It's a hell of a way to end it, isn't it. When I was out in the Yard after they took me out there and took my shirt, my shoes, my socks, just left me with my jeans. That was it. That's why we got so sunburned; we didn't have protection from the sun."

Gary: "How did you get warm when you slept at night? Did you just stay up all night?"

Hal: "No, we snuggled up, man, body heat. Five of us got together."

Gary: "The guy in the middle did alright."

Hal: "Well, since I am this big, where do you think I was? I was on the end."

Gary: "Yeah, like Mama Bear."

Hal: "I put my arm around them and says, 'O.K. At least one side of me's warm.'"

Gary: "Big guy was popular, man."

Hal: "Oh yeah. But there was this one old guy out there."

Gary: "I'm surprised some of them old fellas didn't die. The cold gets to them older guys faster."

Hal: "That's what I was goin to tell you. There was this one old guy sittin out there next to me and, man, he was just shiverin something awful and I said, 'Come on,' and I put my arm around him and he was just a little guy and he fit right in here, you know, under my arm and he was just really shakin. And I got close to him, just as close as I could and he calmed down and quit shakin. This old guy was in his skivvies, skinny."

Gary: "How'd our old boys do? We had a couple."

Hal: "Alright."

Gary: "I can't think of his name now; I think of an old guy that lived on D deck. He was in his sixties."

Hal: "Smith, Yeah, he did alright. I used to take care of him out there. He'd have trouble blowin up his mattress when they finally got the mattresses to us. Well, his mattress was always leakin air out slow and I said, 'Well, here. You can have mine.' Goddam it! All the time I was out there I didn't have a damn mattress to sleep on. I laid right on the ground. Well, I gave him my mattress and I'd go blow it up for him every night and I'd make sure he'd get his medicine, aspirin, or something like that when he needed it. Well, you know, Smith doesn't know how to relate to them or ask them for anything."

Gary: "Aw, hell no. He wouldn't ask them. He'd sit out there and die, probably."

Hal: "Yeah, he would have. People in plane wrecks, when the same kind of things happen, when you're grouped together and you're all sufferin bad experiences and a lot of things happen and people are battlin the elements, you know you have to help the next man in order to help yourself. Seems to be kind of natural, doesn't it."

Gary: "You help those who aren't able to, who aren't quite as able as you are."

Hal: "Well, you learn a lot about yourself. It's not something that you'd want to do voluntarily but when you're forced into it you do learn about other people and you learn about yourself. You get to know them better. You think you do, then it goes back to normal. The very few times when they gave out extra food, if they brought out a pot of chili or something, I'd get a couple cups or I'd get extra coffee, or sometimes they just had bread left and I'd get some extra slices and pass it out."

Several men already in Segregation when the guard was killed, inmates claim, became scapegoats for certain guards who had already been feuding with them. They stated that they were beaten in Segregation, then taken to the Admissions wing and beaten again. Some prisoners witnessed these beatings and tape record-ings were made while the beatings were taking place. H. states that he was witness to the brutalization of one man that took place in the Segregation unit on July 8. In a statement by him, read to the press by B., spokesman for the other men, he described the beat-ing of several men by guards and the sodomizing of one with a police baton. Medical examination verified that this particular inmate had sustained internal injuries as a result of an attack.

"This was on July 2, 1979. At 1:30 PM, Officer R. and Officer T. and one other officer, unknown to this writer took me from Seven Wing, C-8, to the Segregation unit. Officer R. handcuffed my hands behind me and led me to the end of C tier where he kicked my legs out from under me and hit and beat on me while I tried to get back on my feet. I was then dragged down a flight of stairs and out the door where T. took R.'s place holding my wrists as high as he could to allow T. plenty of room to kick and hit me all the way to the Hole. Once in the Hole, L. and G. there took up the beating on me. Sergeant M. saw all of this in the Hole but won't admit it. There's outside witnesses but I can't bring their names out because of court action.

"On July 8, 1979 at 6:30 PM, the Riot Squad came into the Segregation unit and handcuffed B., G., H., and one other un-known person to their cell bars. Not only were they handcuffed but they were stripped naked as well. Then the Riot Squad left and returned about 7:15 p.m., approximately fifteen in force.

"At this time the officers started at B.'s cell and worked their way to H.'s cell, beating and abusing each man in turn for no less than five minutes per man. B. told the officer to stop beating G., at which time Officer T. asked B. if he wanted some, too. T. then had B.'s cell door opened and he and four other officers entered B.'s cell. I had my mirror out, which is a small broken piece of mirror where you can see into another cell or see down the tier, and being only one cell away I heard one of the officers tell B., quote: 'You want to know who's screwing so-and-so's wife.' At this point B. began screaming, and looking into my mirror which I had outside my cell I saw them officers...[The description on this tape of what the prisoner says he saw—the sodomizing with a police baton of a prisoner by a guard—was erased by someone before it was sent to me from the prison.] . . . almost everyone of them [that were beaten] are leaders of the Lifers Club."

Another prisoner describes his impressions:

"They were beaten in Seg and then brought over there handcuffed and rebeaten and thrown into those strip cells. They said [in the newspapers] that prisoners don't cry out and all that stuff. That's true; most of the time they don't, but sometimes, man, they can't help it.

"That stuff down on B tier, the beating of those six men, was the worst shit that I've ever seen in my life, man, and I've been exposed to it for twenty-five years. And I co-signed as an eyewitness. It was done.

"It was a crime, that; ninety percent of the prisoners that are in this institution have never done crimes that were committed by those fourteen officers. They beat those guys in Segregation. They handcuffed them to the bars over there and began beating and harrassing them and everything and it took them seven hours later to move them to Admissions and then when they got them on our tier and got them back in that back room and started beating on them, they went on with batons and leaded gloves. They beat them up considerably and I was an eyewitness to it, fifteen feet away.

"Guys like C., when he went into the wall a couple times, there was blood in there all over the wall. He'd go down, they'd pull him back up by the handcuffs and there was blood on the walls, hair all over where they beat them. We recorded it, you know, as much as we could of it. One of them [guard] was saying, 'No. Don't do that.'

"That was the same time that they had B. inside the strip cell upside down with his handcuffs on him with T. sticking a baton up his ass. That was their whole thing, you know. They had personal things against him cause he had publicity, like one of his charges was rape, so if the bulls read in the newspapers the reports, so what happened in T.'s mind, as small a mind as he is, he's saying, 'Well, he's raped so he's got something coming to him and this is a getback.'

"And they kept telling him, 'This is a getback.' You can hear it on the tape. I remember either G. or H. saying, 'What is this, a getback?' And they said, 'Yeah, it's a getback.' "

The following is an excerpt from a statement made to the Press by F., a past president of Lifers With Hope (Lifers Club).

"What you've got to realize is, you got over 300 people in here doing life for forgery and burglary. And you watch guards take and beat prisoners, jam batons up their ass, and try their damndest to kill them without any repercussions. And then you're expected to sit back and be guarded by these same guards for the next thirteen years. It don't make much sense to me. There's more than just those tapes there.

"It was not a setup as it has been indicated through the newspapers. Christ, you gotta go through three steel doors, three barred grilled doors, and two control cages to have that communication between Segregation and Admissions Wing. O.K., these control cages are manned by guards all the time. It'd be impossible to do that. But there's also other evidence. There's bloodstains on the wall back there by those strip cells. They're probably not there now. But Mr. G., Assistant Director of the Department of Corrections, was on our tier on August 3 and he seemed like he's a pretty fair man, so I told him about these bloodstains and he went back with witnesses and visually inspected and verified them. I have an affidavit to that effect. I've one from Rev. B., one from Dr. T., and one from two counselors. They all verified these bloodstains. I had the tier sweeper take samples of them that I mailed out on the streets and this was sealed and witnessed and has not been opened.

"O.K. The situation in this institution since June 15 is comparable to that of being in a pit with rattlesnakes and no way out. It won't do any good to cut off one or two of the rattles. You have to cut off the head or you'll be bitten and the poison will kill you.

"This is the situation: 1400 prisoners who had no part in the killing of Officer C. The six men in Segregation who were beaten, handcuffed to their cell bars, Maced and rebeaten, then brought to Admissions Wing and rebeaten before being put into illegal strip cells, did not have anything to do with the killing of C. Firing five guards and verbally spanking seven others does not eliminate or rectify the problems that have been created, or the responsibilities for these criminal acts. Some of these crimes were more serious in nature than the crimes that people have committed here who are serving life sentences for. How could you stand to be guarded for ten–fifteen years for forgery or burglary by guards that you have witnessed committing acts of violence, of assault, rape, and intent to murder?"

In part, the overreaction of the guards was caused by years of frustration over a perceived and actual loss of power dating back to the period when Conte instituted radical reforms, the dangers involved in trying to run a *loose* prison and the difficulties of establishing and maintaining authority under such conditions, the sense of alienation and isolation brought about by the guards' perception that the administration was both inconsistent and nonsupportive, the organization of a guards' union led by the more conservative hard-liners who wanted to return to the more repressive system of previous years, an improper selection of guards, many of whom were grossly inadequate in their capacity to deal professionally with their work, insufficient training and lack of job enrichment programs for the guards, the tremendous gap in worldview between guards and prisoners, which contributed to fear and hatred of the prisoners and the failure of the officials to recognize the importance of instituting programs to alleviate this serious problem, the hostility, jealousy, and resentment of some of the guards towards the prisoners, who were often perceived as having privileges that they themselves lacked, as for example, the college program, personal grudges that some of the guards carried toward certain prisoners, strong peer pressures exerted by the more cynical and bitter hard-liner guards long in tenure at the prison, exerted on younger and newer guards, and, very importantly, the corruption of the absolute power the guards held in this situation, which swept them along to such a degree they ignored in many instances orders for restraint and correct procedure from the prison officials.

Words can be used as instruments of war to tyrannize, terrorize, torment, threaten, confuse, subdue, and even conquer others. Evidence that guards were using language in this manner in an attempt to exorcize the power of prisoners is brought out by attorney Bud Gardner in a radio interview on September 20, 1979, regarding events of the *lockdown*.

" . . . I think it was clear from the report of the state·investigators that this was a situation which we can only describe as terrorism. The guards came into the tier [Segregation] where these individuals were handcuffed to the bars and started shouting, screaming insanities and verbal abuse, not only at the individuals that were handcuffed to the bars but to all the other thirty residents of the tier. Those guards who were not directly involved in removing prisoners from their cells were striding up and down the tier making threats to the uninvolved prisoners, and this went on while the prisoners were moved out of the Segregation unit and all the way through the Admissions Tier. The guards were banging on the bars and saying, 'This is the new institution. We're in control. C. lives through us,' and all this kind of thing and, of course, this is a pretty terrorizing situation. And they justified this, according to the state report by claiming this keeps the prisoners off their guard and keeps their minds occupied so that they can't think about resistance. But, of course, in this situation these people were handcuffed and apparently offered no resistance, so it seems to have been a little bit of overkill."[36]

The reality perceived by the guards in this incident reflects not only fear and hatred but also a clear understanding—whether trained or intuited—that language used in such a manner has the power to control reality. But language was not the only means by which the guards threw the prisoners off base. The visual impact their riot gear made upon the men disarmed them, also.

John: "O.K. When we took our first shower during the lockdown, they brought in a tactical squad."

Gene: "I was there."

John: "You were in Admissions?"

Gene: "Yeah."

John: "O.K., well, they come down and these guys were either from Monroe or Shelton, some kind of special squad, and they had these gloves and shields on, and they were roboted up, and they looked straight ahead and they refused to look anybody in the eye or to communicate with anybody and as the door would open they would go into a stance with their long batons, and they were all down, all the way down the tier. Every six feet they had a silon. So after about the eighth or tenth door that opened, the guys just come out and went and took their showers, come back, then they relaxed. This one that was in front of my cell, and he's lookin straight ahead and I'm lookin at him, but he refused to look at me.

"I says, 'What are you, a robot?'

"He wouldn't give no expression or anything. I says, 'Where you from?'

"All they had on was a jumpsuit and boots and everything, and I says, 'Who are you?' I says, 'What the fuck are you, a robot? Are you a human being or what are you, a clone?' I says, and he won't smile and give any indication, so finally I says, 'I've got one question to ask you. Can you hear me? Just nod your head yes or no.'

"And he wouldn't so finally all of a sudden I say, 'Well, fuck, the guy's a clone after all.'

"So all of a sudden he smiles. And then I seen he was alive, you know, far as he could smile, so I figured that he must be human. I thought these guys were silons and they come down with their clubs and they were standing at attention and refused to look or acknowledge anybody. I said, 'Man, all we're takin is showers one at a time,' you know.

"And so they come up behind you and they had two guards behind you that would march you down the tier and they had these guys all along the line to where we're going to take a shower and the showers are wide open and then at the end of the tier you've got about ten other guys standin in front of the showers watchin you while you showered, and I thought, 'Man, what in the hell are we into?' "

After the long *lockdown* the men were released from their cells. Some guards were still carrying grudges, according to the following narratives. A black prisoner speaks first.

"There's only one enemy and they [guards] really hate it when everybody got together in all the lockdowns and demonstrations that we went through which really changed everything in the Joint. I went through all the lockdowns and everything and everyone was side by side when it came to confronting the pigs cause we were all together. They tried to divide us. They tried to make trouble between the black guys and Indian guys. They told us to get the Indians because the Indians caused the lockdown which cancelled out the prison routine, but niggers ain't that stupid. Well, it wasn't a matter of catching on to what they were up to, either. What made it so cold, they act like we cared because the sergeant got killed. Just because they offed that dog, we should care. Their routine wasn't shit. That wasn't nothing and we realized that off the top because they tried this kind of shit before. Most of the prejudice comes mostly from the guards. That's definitely true. See, they start that bullshit. They try to spread rumors especially to keep things stirred up between blacks and whites and other groups. They might tell a black, 'Hey, these whites over here have been calling you niggers and shit.' Or they do stuff like plant things in other people's cells but leave a clue like it might belong to a large group or clique of white guys. Most of those things don't work because there's some pretty good harmony between the races at Walla Walla. It's not like what goes on in places like California."

John: "This is an environment that breeds hate and violence."

Gene: "It's a society, fucked up as it is. It's a society."

John: "Yeah. A dumping ground. They dump all the guys that are convicted of felonies in the state of Washington here at the penitentiary and then expect the guys to live in some type of harmony without any incidents of any type, of violence or any isolated incidents or racial conflicts. They're not even thinkin logically. They're unprofessional. But the hostility between the cons can almost be traced back to anger at the guards."

Gene: "Sure."

John: "You can't come out and start beatin em up, so you can start gettin mad at another race or another group or wing."

Gene: "Yeah, well like they were actually goin around Six Wing tryin to cause trouble with the blacks, you know. 'When we took your stuff, we shook down your cells, that was caused by the Indians and when the lockdown's over, you get em.' Tryin to cause racial conflict. It come out that certain of the guards were agitatin, sayin, 'You know the reason the Joint is where it is.' What they're doin, they're tryin to justify it, you know. 'Get the Indians,' and that kind of threats, tryin to cause racial violence. And it was assured by the leaders of Six Wing [black prisoners] that they have no intention of that, and yet see what they did. Their whole play was to try to turn all the blacks against the Indians."

Throughout all that occurred during the *lockdown* of 1979, only one voice within the prison protested publicly—Father B., the

Catholic chaplain. As Delorme put it, "Even the worst sonovabitches in the Joint love Father B."

Cardozo-Freeman: "Weren't there some good guards who protested what was happening?"

Delorme: "Not out loud. There was only one person that complained. That was Father B. He wrote or talked to newspapers. I don't remember exactly how he complained, but he confirmed questions about guys bein beaten in Segregation and things like that. He made regular rounds down there and he had to check it out all the time, and he said that every time he went down there the guys had bruises and broken noses, shit like that all the time, and he was gettin sick and tired of it, and he made it a point to go down there two or three times a day into Segregation. They couldn't stop a priest, you know, although they did stop him after awhile, but not for long though."

Cardozo-Freeman: "How did they try to stop him?"

Delorme: "Just not let him in Seg. They had to open the doors for him. But it didn't last very long cause there was too much heat. When he made a couple comments [to the press] about what was goin on, they started gettin on his ass then. Then they decided he couldn't go down there anymore cause he was stirrin up trouble and shit like that. He talked to the newspapers and told em what was goin on and said he'd tell it in court, too. He said he was a Christian and he had to say what he saw and they weren't goin to stop him, although they sure tried. They tried to get him busted. They arrested him for having liquor in his car. You know, priests always carry a little bottle of wine. But all the years he's been comin in, all the priests come in have a little bit of wine. Not to use in the prison cause they don't use that in a prison, but they use it in their other parishes, and priests always carry that in their little suitcase. They used that excuse to arrest him one day in the parking lot after he talked to the papers. And then they were shakin him down. When he'd come in they'd stop him on the sidewalk there and make him stand for a shakedown like the rest of the cons and shit like that. But he took it all in his stride.

"The cons admire him. They were happy that he was speakin out. He was the only one that would say anything. Everybody likes him because he's a good man. He's always tryin to help people.

We've had other priests that would tape-record your confessions on Saturdays and shit like that. He doesn't do stuff like that. He come to see me when I had my operation when I was down at the hospital. But there was something going around that everybody signed. Somebody wrote a letter or a petition to Olympia complainin about the treatment Father B. was gettin and everybody signed it. I can't really remember clearly what it was now, but I know it had something to do with that cause he was havin a rough time and, of course, there was cards and people made it a point to go around and tell other people to stop in and see the Father and say 'Hello' just to let him know you cared cause we were afraid that he might fold under the pressure and quit. And at that time everybody was lookin towards him as their only protector in the whole world, really. That's what he was. He was the only person in the whole prison that was on the con's side. He was not on the con's side; he was just on the right side, you know, what he believed in. And he didn't believe in treatin people like that, and he wasn't afraid to say the truth, which is something that you just don't see with people that work in prison. I guess that must rub off on people that work in prisons. They don't tell the truth even when they see something wrong. They value their stupid job so goddam much. Course, they shouldn't have to work under a threat of gettin fired for defending something that's right, but they do. It's a fact. It's a team thing. It's like politics, I suppose. You just don't say anything that will get your side in trouble regardless of whether it's murder or what it is."

Cardozo-Freeman: "How old is Father B.?"

Delorme: "He's close to seventy. Great big man, big shock of white hair. We were his flock. He's an ex-professor, too. He taught in some college somewhere and he's had churches here and there. He likes his job here. It's more meaningful for him. Yeah, he had some pretty sad days but he held his head up and kept on walkin, and everybody was really proud of him. The guys would be willin to die for Father B. They would go an awful long way in his defense. He puts up a good mark for the good side. He's a good model in that respect. We all should have such character. I think he does a lot of good in that part of it. Actually seein a strong person and a rightful person in action, see, and it makes you feel small the way you been livin. Yeah, he has an awful lot of friends.

Don't have to be Catholic to go talk to him and have some help. He'll just sit there and he'll pick up that phone and just call your folks if you are worried about em or something like that, or call the hospital, or whatever needs to be done, see, and that's a really, really big favor to ask in here, you know. It's almost impossible to get a phone call from a caseworker or anybody, so he'll just pick up that phone and do it. And he's always invited to everything. Chicano Club, or whatever we have goin, all the groups. He's always invited to come."

Cardozo-Freeman: "Does he always go by himself among the men?"

Delorme: "Yeah, always. He always walks around the cell blocks and on the tiers. Might come in your house, sit on the bed and have a cup of coffee. Yeah, he's always around, visible and accessible."

Cardozo-Freeman: "He isn't afraid?"

Delorme: "Oh hell no. He laughs at people that are afraid. He laughs at those guards and people that are afraid of people. It just shows that something inside them's wrong. The guys shout clean across the compound at him, 'Hi, Father B. How's it goin, Father?' and give him the ole high sign, the ole raised fist, and he'd give it right back to you. 'Hang in there, Father. Keep up the good fight.' He's a very pleasant guy, always smilin; only couple days I didn't see him smilin. That was when he seen what was goin on. You don't have to worry about him lettin you down or bein afraid. You'd follow a guy like that anywhere."

A CON'S VIEW OF THE BULLS' SITUATION AT WALLA WALLA

Cardozo-Freeman: "In your opinion, why did the guards do this?"

Delorme: "The bad feelings and frustrations was building up through the years, many, many, years in cases of the old time guards that had been here for maybe ten, fifteen, twenty years. There was no exceptions when it came to the night of the riot when people were gettin pissed on and gettin beat up and gettin kicked and smashed around. Everybody jumped into the act. There were lieutenants, captains, they were all hid behind those helmets but we knew who they were. People recognized them. There were also sergeants, young guys, old guys, everybody was there. Young folks, old folks, everybody come; join the guards' Sunday school and have a lot of fun! Anyway there was no exceptions, so the anger, resentment towards us, the hate and bitterness went back a lot of years. It constituted a lot of abuse, verbal abuse, physical abuse, lack of noncommunication between the guards and the cons. The only communication bein a con callin a guard a "dicksmacker,' the guard callin the con an 'asshole' or a 'punk;' that's still goin on. There hasn't been any improvements in the situation and I don't really imagine it's gonna change in the immediate future. So it very definitely took a while building and when the opportunity arose, course, it took extreme circumstances and events to bring it all about and afterwards it was awful difficult.

"There was no personalities excepted in the population. The guards just blinded themselves to whom they were whippin on, even though it was somebody they might get along with every day; so to try to get back to some kind of normal situation afterwards was really hard. The bad feelings still haven't disappeared. There's still sergeants, lieutenants, and other old time guards that sat quietly for years, did their job, took the verbal abuse, and then on one explosive night they busted some heads and did everything they could to vent their anger towards us. Then after that they showed obvious guilt as they walked around the institution or did their job. Or their tone of voice changed; it was quieter. They couldn't look you in the eye. In some cases, guys went to extreme lengths to grant a request even. I would say it was from guilt because prior to that if you asked for something from a certain dog-assed lieutenant, he'd tell you to go fuck yourself. But after that it seemed to be a lot easier to get something out of some of those guys that had taken part in that violence against us. I know it was directly connected to guilt.

"I was pretty surprised and disappointed and depressed to see how people change so much. It was almost like a mob. Just like a riot situation on the street where the ordinary person might not pick up a rock and throw it at the police but in a hysterical or particularly violent moment like that will get involved but it's just not them. I was pretty mad for a long time at a lot of people but I had to figure it out, somehow. I had to rationalize what happened in my own mind. It was a matter of necessity. I couldn't leave; I still had to live there. I still had the pigs guarding me; the same pigs that were tryin to kill people were the same guys now that I was expected to act normal toward. I was expected to go back to normal and not show any outward signs of anger. I mean you just had to. You can't just go on like that. The population realized that. We had a couple months of hate and bitterness and it made everybody get sick to their stomachs, so when it came down to gettin off lockdown, which presented a totally new situation, then it brought everything to a head and the question was, 'Now what's gonna happen? Is it get-back time for the convicts now? Are they gonna come outa that Yard, come out of them wings and start killin guards?' That was the question in everybody's mind. It was the fear of most of us convicts.

"We didn't want it to happen, most of us. We wanted to do our time and let this thing lay somehow and figure it out, and that's why when the legal people helped us in Seattle and they got the class action suits goin, when they got off the ground and everybody was bein interviewed and everybody got a chance to tell their story, what happened to me; what assholes did what to me; what guards did this and what guards did that, and the cons seen it go on paper, on tapes, that really was a lifesaver because the simple action of meeting with some outside people like that who represented a chance to take revenge legally, it really took out a lot of anger. Bein able to sit there and tell what happened, vent your feelings; these people, the lawyers, sat quietly for hours and hours and days and days and listened and wrote and wrote, and I think they played a super major role in calming down the population and preventing further violence after the lockdown was over because then everybody's attention went to the lawsuit. Their energies, their hate, their anger was channeled into efforts to raise money, to be factual, to support this lawsuit, and it took a lot of heat off the cops. Probably saved a lot of lives.

"It's not hard to be able to see the other side of the picture and sympathize or empathize. It takes a certain kind of person, I don't know if it's a desperate person, I don't really understand the character or personality of people that would take a job like that, that can take that kind of treatment from other people. But in any case, I think their actions were illegal. They were very wrong but maybe they were understandable. Not to everybody, of course, but I think if you're doing your time in a prison and you took the position of an observer, you spend your days, your nights, you observe, you watch what's going on, and you're sensitive to attitudes, then I think it's a lot easier to understand things like that. And you can see it building and you can see why and in many cases you feel more anger at your fellow convict for acting the way he's acting toward a certain guard that you know's not that bad a guard, and you know he hasn't got all that bullshit comin; he doesn't deserve to be treated that way. But it's not uncommon at all for the observer-type of convict to be weighin situations daily, seeing these real complications comin up. You're always makin a judgment as you watch—who's right; who's wrong—and it weighs out about fifty-fifty.

"I don't think those guards, guys that come and apply to work in a prison, they're not there to hurt anybody. They don't say, 'I'm gonna drive to the penitentiary and get a job as a guard so I can go and kill somebody,' or, 'I can go thump some heads so I can get back at those thieves, those reptiles, those animals.' I don't believe that. The percentage of men that would take a job like that, for those reasons, I would say is so minute it's not worth lookin into, really. It doesn't take long to sort em out and they really don't last long, unless the administration isn't that sensitive to who they hire and if they're actually in favor of a real tough policy like that, then they'll keep those guys around like that. But even so, other guards won't let it go on because it endangers their lives to have one guard who's extremely *macho*, extremely cruel. They'll find a way to get rid of him. If not, he'll go to a tower because that guy makes their jobs dangerous. Everybody will just get mad at him; he can stir up fifty convicts and make em hate all the guards around so they watch that, too. They don't like it so they'll calm him down and they'll talk to him and if he doesn't change, he'll be out of the institution.

"Those guys come here ninety percent of the time just because they need a job. They probably been out of work for awhile. Most guys I've talked to recently were pretty desperate for work. I've met a lot of new guys, two weeks on the job who haven't even went inside the walls yet. They're in uniform, but they're in classes and training and there's a lot of em that really seriously want to do a good job. They want to be liked. They want to get along with the guys. Course, they have some really funny ideas of what a prison's like so they're in trouble right off the bat. A helluva lot of em come in with ideas about the prison they get off of TV, but I think as a rule people that come to work at Walla Walla start off pretty good. They're not there as do-gooders. They're not there to save lives or make people walk the straight and narrow road but I've never heard anybody say they came there to be a guard because they hated convicts. I had one advantage to talkin to people like that. Most of the young guards that I talked to, talked to me as though I was one of them because they never knew I was a convict. You'd have to work here for awhile to even know I was a convict because I worked in the barbershop and because of the way I was dressed and everything. Most people thought I was a civilian barber so they talked pretty straight with me.

"It's really hard to analyze the feelings of guards that have been here ten or fifteen years because those type of guys are almost, well for a few years of their lives, they're like a person with a split personality cause they have one face in the prison and they have another face outside the prison and as the years go by they begin to merge. When they first start out, they're a real person. A fish bull is a real person. He's not afraid to voice his opinion. He laughs, he jokes, he smokes dope, he drinks, he talks about parties, but after awhile he starts clammin up and he puts this face on and then for several years there he is strictly a guard. Pretty soon, there's no more personal contact; there's no more personal conversation and then it takes quite a few years and they get over that kick and they get tired of it or whatever. Then, I guess, while they work here they really change their personalities; they rebuild their personalities and they become a certain type of person for the rest of their lives. But that's something else. You're always tryin to read the Man; you're always tryin to figure out where his head's at. Is he a liar? Will he tell you 'yes' and do the opposite? Is he phoney? What is he? Is he a sex maniac on the street? Is he a drunk? Does he beat his wife? You wanna know what they're about so you can judge how they'll react to certain situations.

"The old time guards, they're more real. It's easier to deal with em. They kinda got tired of putting on a phoney face, but they get awful callous, too. The prison wears on you. It hardens you to life around you and it works and wears on the guards the same way it works and wears on the convicts. There's no difference and that's just something that has to be when people are dying and people are livin like animals, bein cruel to each other; their attitudes and the way they talk; you have to just get hardened to it, so after years and years you're pretty much alike, except the convict's attitudes remains the same. The old thief usually stays an old thief. He has learned that his side of the fence is here and the guard and his values and attitudes are on the opposite side. It's cop and con, cop and con all the time and it just kind of stays that way."

Cardozo-Freeman: "Could the tension of working under such stress have contributed to the guards blowing up?"

Delorme: "Well, yeah. There's gonna be some bad reactions under those circumstances. I suppose if I was well trained I could hold my temper, though. I don't know what kind of trainin they used to have but it didn't amount to much. And they didn't have guidelines as far as education goes. We've had guards that could barely even write. But no people that had any education past high school, except some of the higher ups and it makes a real difference when it comes to bein able to talk things out or understand where people are; understand the cons, their anger and their resentment and things like that.

"I think they need better educated people, better trained. They need classes. They didn't have classes to sit down and teach these guys. One of the things that the guards need is courses in the psychology of people, like the guys that are in prison, where their anger comes from and what it's really directed at. To teach these people that the insults aren't personal. They're not really personal. That would help a helluva lot. It doesn't make the guard's day any better but they won't build up grudges against the cons like the old crew did. The first chance they got to get back at anybody they did, cause they didn't understand. Them guards were runnin in gangs. They had cliques, some real ignorant people that were just all muscle that were leadin the pack, so when they started actin crazy, the guards that didn't want to get in on that, the violence and things, were scared not to. Just like the convicts; they went along with it or they got beat up their own selves. But I think it's a pretty good example of what happens when the fight gets personal between guards and the people they're guarding, and when the influence comes from guard leaders that have almost the same intelligence as Biker leaders or something. Maybe the other guards listened to em more because they didn't have respect for the lieutenants and the captains in the place. They thought the place was too loose so they started looking to their own peers and it became a real fight.

"It was buildin up for years, too. I don't think this will happen again with a better calibre people that they're tryin to hire. They put limits on em, asked for high school and college graduates. They made em go to class and train a helluva lot longer. Course, even now they got more trainin on how to shoot people than how to help people, so even with the change in attitude, their trainin is still predominately pro-violence. They call it self-protection and riot control. But the convicts know these procedures, too, and they resent it and get mad. They know that guards are out there every day shootin at targets and the way they consider it, is they're just trainin and gettin ready to kill em. They shouldn't concentrate on them bein in a shootin gallery. As long as they can handle a gun. I think there has to be specific areas, like certain tower guards, they're the only ones that have guns, so only when they're workin in the tower would they have to go out and start shootin. I don't think I'd run everybody out thirty–forty at a time every day, shootin at targets. People in the prison can hear those gunshots goin off every day and they know what they're doin.

"I would spend an awful lot of time with classes and try to arrange for guards to have credits for their classes, too, college credits, which might encourage a helluva lot of em to go back to school in their nighttime or whatever, but a lot of sociology and a lot of psychology classes focusing on why people do what they do. Understanding human nature, understanding lower-class people.[37] Course, most of the guards are from the lower class, too. I don't know if you can ever teach country folk to tolerate and understand city folks, the two cultures clash. Course, the country people believe in only what they've been raised with, which makes it awful difficult. Everything is sinful or they don't tolerate minorities, for one thing. That's a problem of people from them kinds of communities. To them, these guys are all Communist. They believe in customs and they grow up in it and most of the guys in prison from the cities are pretty wild and they seem or they appear to not have any values, not have any kind of faith or religion. They really do seem like a bunch of crazy bastards. The guards that are working here that have those kinds of attitudes resent the cons and just say, 'I don't want to understand. I hate them bastards. I'm gonna keep em in here the rest of their lives. I hate them bastards.' They just hate, period. They wish atom bombs would be dropped on all us animals."

Cardozo-Freeman: "But they're afraid, aren't they?"

Delorme: "Yeah, they're afraid. And they do take things personal. An awful lot of guards had the attitude, they were hoping something would happen so they could kill a whole bunch of them bastards. Absolutely no patience or tolerance with minorities. Washington's a bad state with the Indians. Everywhere the Indians have trouble with everybody. The blacks have an awful lot of trouble and so do the Mexicans. Course, that's the minorities.

"If a guard is born and raised in that area of the state and he quit school in the ninth grade, there'd be no chance of changin him. I don't think I'd hire him at all. Course, it's pretty hard to demand college educated people in situations like that. People that are interested in helpin people are not really interested in bein guards. People like that only apply to make a livin and most of em have set a goal not to work over a couple of years or only to work until something better comes along, so they don't seriously get into any kind of commitment even though they go through trainin. Besides, you can't demand educated people unless you can raise the pay."

Cardozo-Freeman: "How could guards be helped not to be so fearful of prisoners?"

Delorme: "Well, they ought to use inmates in the training, guys that can talk for the rest of the crowd, talk with all new guards and maybe with older ones, too. It would be an ongoing type of rap session thing, so they can kick this stuff around and maybe the guys could just flat tell em, like when they scream down the tier and say, 'Open my door, you stinkin asshole!' It don't really mean you're a rotten asshole; it's just something to say. It's not directed at that guy. He don't even know who's the guard out there. You say it because you're locked up. You say it to say it. I don't know, it just comes out that way. But the guard at the door, it shouldn't ruin his fuckin day. I mean, say, 'Oh, that guy hates me,' cause it ain't that way. I think we had so many guys [guards] who took that personal and they were scared.[38]

"I think the attitudes, the hate, the resentment about bein locked up and, well, your living conditions, your attitude in here, the names you call and the shit you throw, it all changes and goes with the way they're keepin you. The less you're treated like a human, the worse you get about that shit. Somehow you have to show the guards in training how that works. It doesn't seem that complicated. They should treat the prisoners pretty much like they like to be treated. It's a long slow process but in time the cons change. The cons gotta know what the attitude is toward them by the administration and by the guards. They have to know what the attitude is before they'll try to change. And they will try to change if you know that the guards are going to be tryin, too. It's almost like a husband and wife fight. They're both fightin and neither wants to stop first. Pride and a lot of little personal emotions are involved in it.

"Course, the attitudes and courtesy and respect, it helps a great deal, but it doesn't do nothin for bein cramped four men in a cell. That always comes back to haunt you every day and every night that you have to go into that thing. Of course, you can't run free. Hell, you committed a crime. But you gotta have some space to live. You gotta have a cell but you should have it by yourself. All those things have to be worked on together.

"They should absolutely use good people who are in prison in the guard training. Good people. I mean it's gotta be people that other people [in prison] respect. I would definitely use them regular in some phase of the trainin program. They could be open to questions by the guards. The new guards wouldn't even know what kind of questions to ask. Number one is to get their fears out in the open and eventually you'd have a catalog of the same questions on the things they don't understand, fear type things they've seen in the movies, stuff they're afraid of, to have that all out in front. I would imagine all the guys would ask the same questions, just like all the cons that go to prison have the same fears and it takes months and months to understand em and work em out. They can't be dealt with in one day. Get past that then maybe they'll listen a little bit, and then you could go from there and that's when you could get into the part about really understanding where all the cussin comes from with the guys that are locked up, and then when you're standin on the end of this tier and opening the cell for somebody and they call you a bunch of motherfuckers or a sack of snakes, you can just, oh, I don't know, you can daydream if you want. You don't have to pay any attention to it. You shouldn't have to. It's not gonna go any further than that. You don't give dirty looks back. You don't wait to pay the guy back by taggin him for some chickenshit little thing. You know that's what happens when the guards take it on a personal level. They also insult back. When they insult the convict, the convict just gets self-righteous as hell. He don't think he's got it comin, you know. How come he's gettin picked on this way? It's bad enough on em gettin locked up.

"And the final analysis there is that when you're locked up, the fact that you're in prison is punishment enough. You don't deserve anything else. That's enough right there. That's how the guys see it. The rotten livin conditions are considered extra added punishment. Bad attitudes with guards, gettin beat up, everything like that is considered extra added punishment that they've added to your sentence that the judge didn't give you. You're goin by the book your own self. Just losin your freedom is punishment. You don't have to be treated like a dog; you don't have to be kicked around. The cons, of course, they gotta learn that they have to treat other people with respect. There are ways if you sat down with people. I wouldn't let the guards tolerate that kind of disrespect. I've always thought they made a big mistake when they just started lettin people call em names and throw stuff at em without doin anything about it. I don't mean beatin em up but they've gotta answer for it somehow.

"What you do in prison is all determined by whether you're goin to have to answer for it or not. If you don't have to worry about going to the Parole Board that year and they're not going to know that you've been an asshole all year, you haven't actually attacked anybody, but you've been callin everybody names and throwin shit; then you'll probably do it. But if you're gonna answer for it, you do put some controls on yourself then. When I first went to Walla Walla people weren't cussin them guards out like that. You would get tagged for it and that was alright. You didn't hear all that shit then. I thought that was right. They should write them up when they get in their face and start callin em names. You've got to answer, man, for what you do. You can't be sittin in prison and not be accountable for everything cause that ain't the way it is outside. Right? Somewhere that trainin has to start, too. The guards have to be accountable for what they do but the cons have to be more accountable for what they do. I don't mean the guy should have extra added time on his sentence. Course, the language does come from anger, from hatred and stuff like that, but it doesn't mean you should be free to scream and holler and act like a baby all the time. Somehow you have to start dealin with that stuff. They don't allow guards to call people names. The important thing is that the guards should understand when it happens, not to take it personally but at the same time they should write tickets for that kind of talk, especially on somebody that just repeatedly does it all the time because it influences other people to do it.[39] You can spot the guys who are really bad about that. If they want to be treated with respect, then they should treat the guards with respect. And it can be that way. Sure it can. And that's just a part of treatin each other like men.

"Respect comes from the cons when a guard is doin a good job, bein professional. You know yourself when we went through all this turmoil, guards that were professional, guards that were tough but fair were respected because they did do their job right.[40] Course guards that were respected were far and few between, but the guys that really are able to handle themselves are respected. I don't mean run in an punch somebody out. I mean handle situations without writing people up unnecessarily and givin em extra time on their sentence or causing em to lose privileges and things like that when it wasn't necessary. That's part of handlin yourself professionally. Breakin up fights, preventing things, bein able to spot situations, know the hot spots, take that upon yourself to learn about those things, not avoid em. A lot of guards learn the hot spots strictly just so they can stay the hell away from it. A good guard learns just exactly what the convict rules are. He not only learns their attitudes and something about human nature, but he learns the rules to do his job by. There are rules and he shouldn't add to that or subtract from that. He should have em memorized by the time he goes inside the walls."

Cardozo-Freeman: "He should know the convict culture?"

Delorme: "Yeah, and they should learn the lingo because they're really crippled for a long time until they do. They don't know what they're hearin and they do take a lot of slang as insults when they're not insults. That's part of not knowing about the cons."

Cardozo-Freeman: "One young guard asked me what *punk* meant."

Delorme: "When you call a young guard a punk, it has the same meaning as it has on the streets—you're young, snotnosed; you don't know anything. You're a punk, yet. But when you call another convict a punk, it means something else. It denotes a whole lot of sexual shit. To be a punk in here ain't too cool. But anyway, it's important the way the guards carry themselves. They can't be fearful all the time. You've gotta be able to look people in the eye and be almost like a referee, but you can't be super unbending. You gotta be able to understand, to listen to a situation, to both sides of it, and if you don't feel capable of making a decision about an argument, go over to the control area and talk to the sergeant or someone about it.

"An argument over a rule shouldn't go very far because the rule's in the book. And we cons, when we break a rule, especially with a newer guard, we'll try every way in the world to reinterpret it, to show that just somehow we stayed inside the guidelines just a little bit. But when you beat em, man, when you can be talking a guy outta shit, lyin to em and shit, particularly because he don't know and he doesn't want to go through all the trouble of runnin over to the goddam control room, even the other guards will laugh at him cause he's being conned. A good guard catches on to these games. You can't be talking people out of everything. The cons don't like people who everytime they turn around they can't make a decision, shit like that. Or they let certain cons get away with stuff and another guy comes along and he gets tagged for doin the same thing. A guy downstairs will say, 'Hey, come on. I've got some magazines.' And the other will say, 'No, I can't come down. M. is workin today.' But then the guy will say, 'At four o'clock some dummy is comin on; then I'll come down.' And then you can do any goddam thing you want to cause they don't know the difference anyway and they're too fuckin scared to stop you, see.

"You [cons] gotta have guidelines. You've gotta know what you can do and what you can't do. Just like out on the streets. You gotta stop at a stop sign. There shouldn't be times when you can run through a stop sign in the Joint and just sayin, 'Oh what the hell, there ain't nobody around.' I'd go through the rule book and throw all the little petty-assed shit that doesn't need to be there, but I'd really make sure I had the right rules that are good for control, that help for the safety of the prison. Some of the rules about movin around the cellblocks to other people's cells on other tiers is good for safety. Those kind of rules, I would be sure they're there to cover people cause that's how people get killed; guys runnin down the tier and jumpin in their cells.

"They've always been terrible about lockin and unlockin doors and I guess that's because of the locking system here at Walla Walla. It's such a fuckin hassle with the locking system that it just becomes easier to leave the goddam door open. If they had a different locking system, it might cut down on the violence. The thing's so damned ancient. It is a real hassle. It's a real arm buster after a few hours, lockin and unlockin doors, crankin the damned tier, and all the guards get tired doin that shit. Pretty soon they just leave it open and they set their own times when they lock all the doors. They say, 'Well, heck, I'll do it every fifteen minutes,' and so your cell door will stay unlocked for fifteen minutes cause he doesn't want to close it every goddam time a door's been left open. It would pay the prison to redo the whole thing. They should have real updated locking systems where a guy don't have to work like he's rowin a damned boat every time he has to open the door.

"Good guards, you can go to em if you got a problem and talk it out and maybe get some suggestions. If they have the power, and they do, to call up and make an appointment with the caseworker when you're not on call, they should do it if you got a problem. Some just absolutely won't do it. There are situations that come up when you need to get over there [to see caseworker], family situations and personal situations. Some of the guys that have been around longer that are fairly decent, at least they'll listen to you. When they're listenin to you and talkin to you, you're keeping it more on a man-to-man basis.[41] They understand, and you just know from talkin to em that they consider you a person with problems and consider your family. They even ask how your family is once in awhile. That acknowledges that you are a human being and you do have other people in your life, and that means a lot to you. A lot of good guards, they'll help you straighten some things out or do what they can to help you in an emergency situation like make a phone call or something. Somewhere along the line they understand. It might not sound very important to them but somewhere along the line they've been told or learned that small situations can be like life and death matters to a guy locked up in prison. They don't laugh it off and tell guys, 'It ain't no big deal; forget it.' They respect that problem and they don't belittle it and they do the best they can, so even if a guy don't solve the problem, it helps.

"I love to see a guard that goes down the tier or works in the wing that will give a guy a minute or two to listen to his problems, and he'll get on the phone because he recognized the importance of a visit, when a guy lost a visit, or he needs a special phone call to keep him from going off, getting mad, maybe hangin himself. He don't need all the rules sayin no phone calls. You need to be able to read a person, what they need, and do it.

"So what am I sayin? Somehow, you have to be able to understand how important little things get to people. And one guy with a big mouth can stir up fifty guys over his problem, get em mad over it, cause he didn't get any kind of an ear down here from the Sarg. He wouldn't clear him over to see his caseworker or something, or if he did see his caseworker, the caseworker didn't have time or didn't recognize what it was about. Those little things are not little things. They're life and death to a guy in prison. And young guards should be capable of doing that, yet at the same time bein careful not to get conned."

ADDENDUM: THE BULLS' POINT OF VIEW

In order to give some balance to the prisoners' interpretations of the events that occurred during the great lockdown of 1979, statements taken from interviews with three guards who participated in the lockdown operations are presented here.

Interview with Sgt. G.

Cardozo-Freeman: "Can you tell me what happened during the lockdown of '79?"

Sgt. G.: "I got in on that about two hours after it started when they tore up Eight Wing. I was there and I never saw any brutality and I was part of getting probably about 200 or more inmates out of Eight Wing. I saw a lot of pushing and a lot of jerking around and this kind of thing, but I saw no beatings. It didn't happen, not even to the Indian guys.

"In some cases there were accidents. For instance, I went down on one of the tiers and there was this Indian guy, a big tall guy. I'm short and I had to lead him back up the front where they was handcuffing them, and I had hold of the back of his shirt, and he simply outran me and I fell down because the water was like this from the wrecked plumbing, the feces and urine and everything in the wing, and, well, some of them fell down, too. I know when I went out with this one Indian guy and was going down the ramp, I had hold of his handcuffs and said, 'O.K., lay down.' And I overestimated my own strength for this guy and he ended up on his head. But it was not deliberate. I felt bad about it but didn't have time to apologize and babysit him, and his neck wasn't broken so I went back and did my job. Now, I'm sure there was a lot of that. People were nervous, scared."

Cardozo-Freeman: "What about the business in the Hole?"

Sgt. G.: "I don't know. I wasn't there. I'll say this, though. Mr. K. and Mr. T. were there and R. was there. I wonder if you met R.?"

Cardozo-Freeman: "I'm going to talk to him."

Sgt. G.: "O.K. I've got a lot of respect for R. He's a rough-edged man but he's an honest man and there's no doubt in my mind that if R. had seen this, even though he was an officer, he wouldn't let a lieutenant get away with it. He has enough strength mentally and physically. He can take it. He could deal with it O.K. And no doubt in my mind, if he had seen that, he would have put a stop to it. It wouldn't have happened. It would have been stopped right now."

Cardozo-Freeman: "Would you say that with the stress they were under, being pushed to the limit with the insulting language and name-calling, which had been going on for so long, and the fears and frustrations of trying to work in such an open facility, and finally the murder of one of the guards by prisoners, that some of the guards might have overreacted to get back at them?"

Sgt. G.: "Yeah. I can see that. Some of them people had taken hostages, harmed the nurses in the hospital; some were pretty darned tough, and the prisoners had been badgering them to the limit, physically and verbally. But I haven't seen it happen."

Cardozo-Freeman: "Would that sort of thing be most likely to happen in the Hole?"

Sgt. G.: "Well, when you go to take a guy to the Hole you expect a fight every time, and you're going to get a fight most of the time. And I tell my guys that once the prisoner's handcuffed, I don't expect him to get hurt. Do whatever you've got to do to take him out if he fights but after that I don't want to see any unnecessary force.

"But basically, it's a holding action. Everybody grabs hold of something and hangs on, is what it amounts to. I got one guy in mind. You had to fight him several times a week and he liked it. He was a masochist. And them guys will get themselves bruised up. But when they let out on you, they're so strong. I've seen a little 130-pound guy with six guys on him and they couldn't control him. That's how strong he was. And he'd get all bruised up. But was that the guards' fault? All they're trying to do is to hang on, see, and, yeah, you have a lot of guys with scrapes and bruises like that."

Interview with Sgt. R.

Sgt. R.: "On the riot of '79, or the riot issue, I was named on that incident in Segregation. I was one of the twelve accused. The allegations were we beat them people up and there were enough of us on that team that night to not allow that, to not allow the brutality and everything else."

Cardozo-Freeman: "Can you explain what happened? We're

talking about the allegation that the guards beat the prisoners in Seg and that one of them was raped with a baton."

Sgt. R.: "As far as 'get-back' the staff didn't go in there to get back at the residents. That's just not our way. They were told to go in and move these people from B tier Segregation to B tier Admissions. I'm not going to say they were handled with kid gloves, but the brutality allegations that come down, you know, that they were beaten with a nightstick and everything else, isn't true. Like I said before, myself and Capt. T. Sgt. M., we taught riot training here at this facility and we taught them the proper use of the baton and stuff like that. You don't use the baton as a club. You lose control. And the nightstick, you can injure people bad that way. And these people were never brutalized, so far as being clubbed like they alleged."

Cardozo-Freeman: "Did the officers use gloves with lead in them?"

Sgt. R.: "Yes. Some of them did. Not all of them. Just some of them. That was one of the protective gloves that were designed that when you had hold of the baton like this here, if anybody hit you on the knuckles like this, you wouldn't get your knuckles busted. That's what they were primarily designed for. They weren't designed for thumping on people or stuff like that. They were called protective gloves and that's what they were designed for."

Cardozo-Freeman: "Some of the prisoners claimed that these leaded gloves were used to hit guys."

Sgt. R.: "Well, like I said in my testimony, I never seen that ... where people thumped on them. I wasn't there the whole time, too, but people that were involved, residents that were involved, they had no broken bones. If we'd beat them with a club like they alleged ... I'd say the biggest part of us were people my size [very big] ... you can take a man's ribs out, or you can take his head off at his shoulders with the power. And it substantiates what they [guards] were saying. One person did come on too strong and he was called down."

Cardozo-Freeman: "Were you there in Seg when they went in and got those guys and moved them to the Admissions wing?"

Sgt. R.: "Yes."

Cardozo-Freeman: "That was where, according to the allegations, that one prisoner was raped with a baton?"

Sgt. R.: "It was in that time frame, yes, the second time. Right."

Cardozo-Freeman: "Isn't it true that a medical examination revealed that something had happened to him?"

Sgt. R.: "The medical staff that testified up there said that he was not sodomized by a nightstick, that in the shuffle there was a possibility that somebody might have kicked him, you know. You're hustling down there and there's feet and arms and elbows and everything else. Mr. H. is noted for his karate. He's a karate expert, you know, and he assumed that stance when they went in to get him. He went down like this here and all you had to do was to get in close to him and get him down and he's putting up a pretty good struggle."

Cardozo-Freeman: "Wasn't he handcuffed at this point?"

Sgt. R.: "No. When he was brought out he wasn't handcuffed and he was putting up such a struggle, and I think they brought him out on the tier and cuffed him, then we got him up for transport."

Cardozo-Freeman: "There was another charge made that some of the prisoners were handcuffed to the bars and then beaten."

Sgt. R.: "That's some of the allegations that they used to prove negligence up there in Spokane. They were cuffed to the bars first time around. Second time around we went and transported them. We uncuffed them and, of course, moved them."

Cardozo-Freeman: "Why did you cuff them to the bars? To hold them while you went in to get the other prisoners?"

Sgt. R.: "For control. They cuffed them to the bars the first time for the control factor, then they went back to the shift lieutenant who knew where the superintendent was and asked him, 'What do we do with them now? Do we take the restraints off and leave them there, or do we move them, or what?' It appears they said, 'Well, we'll move them down to B tier Admissions.'"

Cardozo-Freeman: "Another allegation that was made was that some of the men who were in the riot squad had been drinking when they came on duty."

Sgt. R.: "No."

Cardozo-Freeman: "One of the officers I interviewed told me

that. That they had to rush in as many men as they could and that some of the men were off duty and had been down at a local bar drinking and, therefore, came on duty under the influence of alcohol."

Sgt. R.: "No one was at a bar when we called them. No. I know I had people over from the coast visiting me. It was on the weekend, and I called one person myself who just lives around the corner from me. He was on the riot team at the time the other men came in on duty that night. They hadn't been drinking. It's a farce, I can tell you."

Cardozo-Freeman: "What about the anger the officers must have felt over the death of one of their own men? In some instances, couldn't there have been some men who wanted to get back at the prisoners because of what happened?"

Sgt. R.: "There's no doubt in my mind that is is probably true — the anger, frustration and hostility towards the residents in general."

Interview with Sergeant D.

Sgt. D.: "Mr. K. was on the wall and T. was at the cage area of Segregation. O.K., then he had his other officers and they had the riot squad down on the tier and there was a lot of smoke on the tier and everything else. Lt. T. at the time ordered the residents out of the cells [Segregation] and moved them back into Admissions 'cause they have more strip cells in there. Supposedly, this is what H. said, that they brutalized him. All of a sudden we didn't do a good job, we officers here. The lieutenant was demoted to sergeant and the press blew it way out of proportion. But a doctor's report said that H. had not really been brutalized but, you know, close to it, but not with a nightstick. And H., the way I understand it, didn't claim to be brutalized until two days later, and all of a sudden he says they did it to him when they were moving him. They just brutalized him. From the way I understood that, we had to use nightsticks to get them to move, but like the doctor's own report said, it was not a nightstick that brutalized him. They think he was raped in the cell 'cause they were put in a strip cell, three men per cell."

Interview with Officer M.

Cardozo-Freeman: "Were you inside when all this happened?"

Officer M.: "I just happened to be on my day off. Some of the officers that they say were involved I've known them for years before I ever came to work here and I know they wouldn't do something like they say. For example, they said when they tore up Eight Wing they brought the inmates out of the wing . . . on the concrete right along the wall, and they said that the officers were on the wall urinated on them. Well, I remember different things I read about the whole situation. At the time that they were moving them out of Eight Wing into the Yard there was not one of our correctional officers on the walls. So how can our officers be urinating on them when they weren't on the walls?"

Cardozo-Freeman: "The prisoners said that there was a small faction of guards who were very disenchanted with the administration and there were union men and that some of them behaved very unprofessionally."

Officer M.: "Yeah, that was true. There were some things done, I am sure, although personally I don't know firsthand. But I'm sure there were some things done that probably were very unprofessional. As far as allowing it, some of the officers . . . they had called some of the officers from local bars and told them we had trouble, to get up here. Some of those individuals should not have been allowed to come in. But they needed the manpower. That's why they let them in."

REFLECTING MIRRORS

In 1958, Sykes wrote that prisons in the United States were totalitarian regimes that, unlike most such regimes, do not attempt to "capture the emotional and intellectual allegiance of those who are ruled."[42] Most prisons, he pointed out, seek to *control*, not change, the behavior of their captives. When attempts are made to institute reforms that would result in capturing this emotional and intellectual allegiance of prisoners, resistance is so great the attempt ultimately fails. What Sykes wrote in 1958 generally holds true today. Why is this? Because, in general, prisons tend to reflect society's wishes. "The prison," Sykes states, "is an instrument of the state, an organization designed to accomplish the desires of society with respect to the convicted criminal."[43]

For the most part, society has not been interested in reforming the offender so much as keeping him locked up and out of sight. Furthermore, society's views with respect to the treatment of offenders has generally been punitive in the extreme. This has influenced the nature and development of prisons in the United States from the beginning. As Tocqueville wrote in 1833, "While society in the United States gives the example of the most extended liberty, the prisons of the same country offer the spectacle of the most complete despotism."[44]

Like a mirror reflecting society's wishes and views, those assigned to protecting society from lawbreakers carry out the mandate given them. If the reaction of society is harsh, then the possibility is great that those responsible for dealing with prisoners will reflect this in their treatment of their captives. Furthermore, people who are selected to direct and do this work will tend to hold the same harsh views towards offenders, also. Because prisons are so closed off from the rest of society, there is a tendency to resist accepting new ways of approaching treatment of prisoners. Leadership at all levels tends toward doing things the "old" way. Furthermore, the hidden quality of prisons, of being closed to the public view, contributes greatly to the misuse of power against prisoners. The irony is that the solution that has evolved for dealing with offenders—treating them like dangerous waste and dumping them into hidden holes to decontaminate—does not work. Like nuclear and chemical waste, they resurface and are more polluting to society than they were before their decontamination treatment began.

In order to eliminate violent responses to imprisoned men by those given the responsibility of being in charge of them, society must recognize the prisoner's humanity and become more knowledgeable about what is happening and, hence, rid itself of its indifference toward violent treatment of offenders. Viewed from this perspective, the derogatory labels by which prisoners identify guards as "nonhuman" take on an extended meaning that concerns all people in society. Through the use of such metaphors, the men are perhaps conveying the following message: "We call you nonhuman when you treat us unjustly because, reflecting society's attitudes and beliefs, you refuse to accept us as fellow human beings. But what you do to us, ultimately, you do to yourselves and to all of society, since all men are connected. You cannot take away our humanity without losing your own."

Despite the cruelty, irrationality and inhumanity revealed in some of the narratives presented, there is also another side of the story also revealed that reflects one of the most important traditional values in the United States—the desire for justice for all people. Although it is true that brutality and cynicism exists among some who work with prisoners, many other fine and dedicated men, reflecting this great tradition of justice for all, carry out their dangerous, difficult, and thankless task of guarding prisoners day after day, never once forgetting that their charges are *men*. Prisoners recognize this and reveal their appreciation through their language. Those guards who acknowledge the humanity of prisoners are called *good people*. In the prisoner's view, it takes a man to recognize another man and to give him the respect that he is due simply because he is a man. Under such circumstances, justice reigns and power is never misused.

NOTES

[1]Erdman B. Palmore, " 'Ethnophaulism's' and Ethnocentrism," *American Journal of Sociology*, Vol. 67 (1962), pp. 442–445.

[2]*Dictionary of American Slang*, p. 71.

[3]John S. Farmer and W. E. Henley, *Slang and Its Analogues*, 1890, Vol. 1, p. 365.

[4]In use since before 1926. *Dictionary of American Slang*, p. 106.

[5]In use since before 1907. *Ibid.*, p. 194.

[6]In use since before 1915. *Ibid.*, p. 244.

[7]*Ibid.*, p. 591.

[8]The term appears in the 1785 publication of Francis Grose's *Classical Dictionary of the Vulgar Tongue*. Reported in *Slang and Its Analogues*, Vol. 5, p. 194.

[9]Presumably, "pig" and "China" were connected because of the importance of the animal in Chinese diet and culture. *Grunter* for policeman is also reported in use in London before 1820. *Slang and Its Analogues*, Vol. 3, p. 228.

[10]*Slang and Its Analogues*, Vol. 2, p. 300. *Cagne* or *Caigne* in Old French signified dog and was a term identifying "the archers and watch" before the time of the modern *gendarmerie*. Vol. 1, pp. 148–149.

[11]Goon, identifying a strong-arm thug was used in the fourteenth century by Chaucer. *Dictionary of American Slang*, p. 233.

[12]*Ibid.*, p. 123.

[13]*Cop*, meaning to seize or snatch (or steal) is associated with the Latin *cap-io*, to seize or snatch; also with the Gypsy *kap* or *cap*, to take; and with the Yiddish *cop*, a hand or palm. *Cop* with these meanings is used in the prison. *Slang and Its Analogues*, Vol. 2, pp. 178–179.

[14]From *Guard! Society's Professional Prisoner,* by Robert J. Wicks, p. 4. Copyright © 1980 by Gulf Publishing Company, Houston, Texas. All rights reserved. Used with permission.

[15]*Ibid.*, pp. 6–8.

[16]*Ibid.* On August 13, 1979, during the *lockdown* at WSP after a guard was killed by two inmates, guards were accused of terrorizing prisoners. The union leader and spokesman for the guards made this statement on a radio broadcast: "We went in there and did a job. The Superintendent and Assistant Superintendent of Custody gave us kill orders. Otherwise we went in there with shotguns and we was ordered if there was people out of their cells in the tunnels, we were to kill. Fortunately, there was nobody out of their cells or in the tunnels. We started moving the [prisoners] cells. We met force with force. We have been taught that when we move people, move them quick. We were locked in the wing. There was a chant going on, 'Kill,' and you can imagine 350 people doing time taking up a chant of 'Kill.' We went in there and moved them. I wouldn't be surprised if a few glasses got broke. I don't know what the administration . . . you don't move people, you don't meet force with force without some bruises. As far as brutality charges, nobody has ever explained to me what is brutality. We did our job. We did it fine. The administration patted us on the back, bought us breakfast, and now all of a sudden, we're the villains. But the administration was sitting there watching us up on the walls, watching us bring those people out of Eight Wing. If there was brutality going on, them being our boss, why didn't they come down and tell us or instruct us or did something instead of waiting until it was all over with, then come in and try to kick us in the butt for it."

[17]*The Society of Captives*, p. 33.

[18]*Employees' Manual for Men's Correctional Institutions*, Published by The State of Washington, Department of Social and Health Services, Office of Personnel and Training, n.d.

[19]See Richard E. Farmer, "Cynicism: a Factor in Corrections Work," *Journal of Criminal Justice (New York)*, Vol. 5, no. 3 (1977), pp. 237–246.

[20]"Given the importance of the snitch system, those who controlled it — the authorities — had enormous leverage. They could create distrust, fear, hatred and violence of inmate against inmate. They could direct efforts against selected individuals and thus try to prevent leaders from emerging. Of course, for this to work, the normal prison existence had to be so menacing that the promise of protection was worth almost anything — a promise which also went up in smoke in the Santa Fe riots." Jerry Mandel, "The Santa Fe Prison Riots," *Agenda: A Journal of Hispanic Issues*, Vol. 10, no. 3 (1980), pp. 4–10.

[21]"I'd say about a quarter of the officers working here shouldn't be here. That's my personal feeling. Some of these guys we hire have got more or as much felony records and assaults and beefs as these poor suckers in here. The state law says we can hire a felon. I think it's seven years. Say if you had a felony in Oregon or California and he's been clean for seven years, you can use him here as a guard. We got to hire him. Now that's a corrupting influence. We know that some of our staff are packing drugs into our institution. It's just a matter of setting them up." [Interview with Sgt. P., Walla Walla, June, 1982.] "But what makes it so bad is you take a young officer that hasn't had much experience with life and is steered wrong and before you know it, that officer is packing in here and really innocent and doesn't realize what's happening. And a man that will pack drugs in here will pack guns in here. He has no choice. They'll threaten to tell on him if he doesn't do it." [Interview with Sgt. H. Walla Walla, June, 1982.]

[22]"The first day on my job I walked in [behind the walls] and I asked the officer what I was supposed to do and he handed me the keys and said, 'I don't know. I've only been here five minutes myself. Ask a convict.' And I had a ring of keys and I knew one thing I learned in training was key control. You don't let convicts have the keys, so I hung on to the keys. I finally went in and the convicts told me . . . you've got to trust somebody . . . and he told me which keys to use. And oftentimes when I tried to do something, not just that day, but later on, an inmate would say, 'No, that's bullshit.' And I knew it was about procedure that I was trying to do. And he'd go see somebody and before you know it, I'd be told, 'Hey, you do like you're told.' In other words, the convicts were telling me how to do my job. And the convicts had total control . . . I guess that's what it amounts to. They just virtually had control of everything. They couldn't walk out the gate but that was about the only restriction inside here." [Interview with Sgt. G., Walla Walla, June, 1982.]

[23]"A lot of times I like to rap with them to find out their real feelings. I have found out some of their inner feelings. They're not like I had them pictured. A lot of people will say, 'Well, how do you know that that was their true inner feelings? What makes you think that they weren't just playing games?' I don't take what they say on one occasion as being the truth. I have to observe them and talk with them over a period of time before I make a decision on an individual. We have one individual, a black man. I've got to admit to a certain degree I am prejudiced. A racial person must, to me, prove themselves. I don't care what race they are — black, Indian, whatever, but if they can prove they are worthy of my respect, I'll respect them. I worked in the military with all kinds of people, all different races. But this man, I've talked with him and he's asked my opinion. I found out his wife is a flower grower. She likes raising flowers and he wanted to get some flowers for her for Mothers Day and I said, 'What are you planning on doing?' And he says, 'Well, I thought cut flowers.' And I says, 'Why cut flowers?' So, you know, that was the start of things and I says, 'Well, you know, green flowers would last a whole lot longer and if she likes taking care of plants, this would give her a plant to take care of and every time she looked at it, it would give her something to remember you by.' And he says, 'You know, you're right.' He says, 'Well, what kind would you get?'

And I says, 'I would need to know something about her house, as far as the light is concerned.' And we got to talking and we must have talked for an hour and a half. That was just the start of it. And now I've found out, he volunteered what he's in here for. And I found out, oh man, when he's around other inmates, he's different. He's got to put on a face, he says. 'I've got to. I got to live with these guys.' Hey, I realize that. I realize every one of these guys do and they've got to make themselves look strong and all that. But he seems like a very tender person. He wants to do his time. He's got two more years to do. He's been in here eight. He wants to do his time and he wants to get the heck out of here." [Interview with Officer P., Walla Walla, June, 1982.]

[24]*Dictionary of American Slang*, p. 608.

[25]Iona and Peter Opie, *The Lore and Language of School Children* (London: Oxford University Press, 1967), pp. 320–322.

[26]*Dictionary of American Slang*, p. 607.

[27]*Ibid.*

[28]*Ibid.*

[29]Tut is identified as "Tutnee or Tutnese" in *DAS*, p. 608.

[30]H. L. Mencken, *The American Language*. Fourth Edition. Abridged and Annotated by Raven I. McDavid, Jr., with the Assistance of David W. Maurer (New York: Alfred A. Knopf, 1963), p. 731.

[31]*Alfalfa* is "Pelf Latin;" *Ceazarney* is "Carnese;" and *Bong-Song* is "Ong" in *DAS*. *Agini* and *Elephant* are not identified in *DAS*.

[32]"I think the worst thing about working here is when they're being assaultive toward us. You approach a man and you tell him, 'O.K. You've got to go to Segregation because of . . . whatever. Put your hands behind your back, please.' And he hauls off and swings at you or becomes extremely verbally abusive to you. And we can't say anything back to him, and that gets very, very frustrating. A fellow is human to want to come back on him. All you can do is write them up for an infraction if they're verbally abusive. And my feelings on verbal abuse is that, at least at this institution, it should be a major infraction. It should be made a serious thing rather than a minor thing. I think that would be the first step toward doing something. Verbal abuse can be so important because you can't enforce [against] it, so they stand there and cuss you out. And the younger guys say, 'Hey, they do it so why can't I?' While I don't disagree that it lets off steam and may cut down on the possibility of physical violence, I think that if its done in front of a lot of other inmates, it causes problems. See, it agitates us, especially when you're in here only trying to do your job. It causes a lot of stress. [Interview with Sgt. T., Walla Walla, June, 1982.]

[33]"The thing is, the associate or the superintendent will say one thing and the one that is putting it out . . . say the shift lieutenant or shift sergeant, or the sergeant that is going down on the wings, will say something else, and it's his own interpretation. It isn't coming from the top. It's not the way the superintendent said it. The sergeant or lieutenant is giving his own interpretation." [Interview with Sgt. F., Walla Walla, June, 1982.]

[34]"The worst thing a guard can do, the absolutely worst thing an officer can do in here is to bum beef a guy, treat him unfairly. Bum beef is saying that he did something he didn't do. It happens. I think people say, 'I don't like you and because of the way things are, there's no way I can get back at you and the only way is to bum beef you. . . . ' If you bum beef a guy you're never going to have any communication with him again. It's like calling a black a 'nigger.' Once you do that you'll never ever be able to talk to him. That's the same way with bum beefing." [Interview with Sgt. H., Walla Walla, June, 1982.]

[35]"I made a personal vow that if at all possible when C. got killed, I was going to help make a prison out of this place, and I've had a little something to do with it and we all have, those of us who stayed, especially when them forty people walked off right after this brutality thing. That bunch, the 'dirty dozen', that bunch of guards quit. Well, some of them were good men who had been led down the garden path; they were given bad information, and they were just trying to do their buddy a favor by saying, 'Yeah, I'll go along with it.' But they shouldn't have done it. Some of them, I'm glad are gone, though. I already had a job lined up in another state because I couldn't stand working with them, but when them guys walked out I decided to stay, because a lot of them guys were my problem. They were a brutal bunch of garbage. They eliminated themselves." [Interview with Sgt. T., Walla Walla, June, 1982.]

[36]Quoted from an interview: "In the Crowd," Hal Sherlock, Moderator, Radio Station KRAB, Seattle, Washington, September 20, 1979.

[37]"Before new officers go inside the walls, in the first place I would prepare them mentally. I'd give them race relations training. I would make them understand that everybody is prejudiced about something, but be able to deal with that. I'd give them as much of this training as money and time would allow on human relations training because I think that's where it's all at." [Interview with Sgt. H., Walla Walla, June, 1982.]

[38]"These people in here think I'm crazy. Some of these suckers say, 'You no good so-and-so.' I've never been called so many 'mothers' in my life! They just keep on going and I say . . . you know, it just blows their mind . . . I say, 'Well, thank you. That's the nicest thing you've said all day.' And they go along and shut up and, you know, they say, 'That sucker is crazier than I am.' They know they can't get your goat and they don't do it anymore." [Interview with Sgt. P., Walla Walla, June, 1982.]

[39]"Peer pressure, strictly peer pressure. You can take a guy down, say you're out here in the quadrangle some place and he's going to call you names and fight you every foot of the way 'cause it's strictly peer pressure. He's got to put on a show. And you get him over here in the hospital or somewhere, or you take these people out, you transport them to a funeral or something and they're altogether different people. It's strictly a front in here for their peers. It's a matter of survival. When no one's around they treat you courteously like you treat them." [Interview with Sgt. P., Walla Walla, June, 1982.]

[40]"My philosophy working inside here has paid off. It's to treat individuals in

here like I like to be treated and most of the time it works. When you tell a guy you're going to do something, follow up. Do it. Don't try to lie to these people. Don't try to pacify them or anything else 'cause they're cons and they don't like to be conned. Be truthful with them and say, 'Well, I'll do this for you and I'll get back to you.' Make sure you get back to them and tell them. You could be a hard man in here and everything else like that as long as you're honest and fair. They can deal with that. And they respect that." [Interview with Sgt. P., Walla Walla, June, 1982.]

[41]"A lot of times if you listen to a guy, let him say to you what he wants to say, let him, if he raises hell with you or anything else. Nine times out of ten, he's said what he's wanted to say and he can go off and he'll leave everybody else alone. He won't get on the staff and he won't get on another resident. You know, all they need is somebody to listen to them. All you can do is sit there and listen to them and make a comment, 'Yes, O.K.,' or whatever else there is. In a lot of cases that's all that's needed to calm them down." [Interview with Sgt. P., Walla Walla, June, 1982.]

[42]*Society of Captives*, p. 38.

[43]*Ibid.*, p. 13.

[44]*On the Penitentiary System in the United States and its Application in France* (Philadelphia: Carey, Lea, and Blanchard, 1833), p. 47. An experiment conducted at Stanford University, in which students played at being guards and prisoners in a pretend prison set up in the basement of a campus building, had to be halted because 'guards' began to behave sadistically toward 'prisoners.' The 'prisoners' were profoundly affected by the experiment, manifesting psychological problems such as depression. One of the implications of this experiment is that prisons are so authoritarian that guards inevitably become repressive and misuse their power over prisoners. C. Haney, C. Banks and P. Zimbardo, "Interpersonal Dynamics in a Simulated Prison," *International Journal of Criminology and Penology*, (1973), pp. 69–97.

Chapter 7

OUR LADIES

Much that a man experiences in prison reminds him that he is regarded as an outcast, not only by prison officials and corrections personnel but by society as well. He is preoccupied with affronts to his personal dignity and integrity by guards, staff, or by official policies. How he responds to this treatment is revealed in many of the narratives presented in this study. Nothing saddens or hurts him more, however, than affronts and insults by prison personnel aimed at the women and children in his life. His frustration and anger about his overall circumstance is greatly intensified when this occurs because he is unable to do anything to stop it, and because he is convinced that such actions are deliberate and calculated ways of further punishment.

The prisoner refers to his family and those whom he loves as his *people*. Although this may not seem unusual—after all, they are people—in prison this label carries a special meaning. Throughout history, cultural groups or clans have identified themselves as "the People" to differentiate themselves from others regarded by them as outsiders, revealing a centering on one's own kind, a common sharing of language and worldview, a "belongingness." This is what the prisoner means when he refers to those who are a part of him as his *people*. This identifying label is also sometimes used to refer to the entire population, which reveals the prisoner's sense of his own group, or belongingness in another context.

A TITLE FOR A WOMAN LOVED

A very special member of the prisoner's *people* is his wife or sweetheart; his *Lady*. Sometimes he affectionately calls her his *Old Lady*, a nonderogatory label for one's wife, which has been in use since before 1871, based on the earlier term, *Old Woman*.[1] The

327

term, *Lady*, bears a special significance; a *Lady* is a woman loved: therefore, one of exalted and very special status. This is the meaning the term holds for the prisoner who truly loves his wife or sweetheart. Separated from her, she becomes idealized in his mind. He longs to be with her again, to be comforted by her. In prison, he dreams of changing his life for her and looks to her for inspiration to do this. Although in the past these thoughts were not a part of him, now that she is gone they are, and intensely so. When he remembers her, it is always the best of what she meant for him, only more so.[2]

In some respects, the prisoner's view of his *Lady* is reminiscent of a tradition in Western civilization dating back many, many centuries involving a blending of the Madonna, the mother of Christ to whom one turned to for nurture and inspiration and guidance for changing one's life, with the lady or *liege* of Courtly Love (a tradition that evolved in the eleventh century in the south of France) for whose love a man sought to perfect himself.[3] For the prisoner, nothing is more perfect, more beautiful, than the woman he loves (and who loves him) from whom he has been separated. Locked behind granite walls away from all womanliness, his memories of her—her love, the sound of her voice, and her capacity to comfort, inspire, and please—are all that he can think of. Although in reality, perhaps, she may not be all of these things, in his mind's eye she is now, particularly if their relationship is one of mutual love. For this reason, she possesses the capacity now that he is in prison to help him change his life for the better.[4]

GUILT BY ASSOCIATION

The mistreatment of the *Ladies* of the men by prison personnel is one of the greatest causes of unhappiness and unrest in the prison. In the eyes of the men, the prison authorities' attitudes and behavior towards their *Ladies* reflects the view that they hold of them—like their husbands, sweethearts, or sons, the *Ladies* are regarded as criminals and therefore deserve the same treatment as their men.

"Our Ladies are hated for being what they are—our Ladies. The administration wars against our people, it seems to me and everybody else in here.

"The general attitude of the prison personnel is that there isn't a decent sonovabitch inside the walls as far as they are concerned, so it just follows that a woman that would marry a person like us would have to be a low-life, and probably a criminal herself, so the treatment our Ladies get, it follows right along with that attitude. And believe me, it causes one helluva lot of tension, a lot of anger.

"Every day there's some kind of a beef in the Visiting Room. Somebody gets the visit cut off or something like that. We have a lot of beefs with the staff in the Visiting Room. Seven days a week somebody's having a hassle with one of the women guards. But the hassles start out in front when the Ladies come in.

"First they come into the Joint and they have to have their cars shaken down and they have to have their purse shaken down. Every now and then—seems like once a week—one of the Ladies will manage to forget a roach in the ashtray or she may have some booze, or some kind of pills in her purse which she can't explain and she ends up gettin arrested.

"In some cases the woman is actually packin some drugs and she's not too slick so she gets busted out there. They put the irons on her. They'll call the city police. The city police will come up and haul her carcass off to jail.

"Course, you can imagine what effect this will have on the inmate—just like throwin a rock into still water—the anger and hate ripple out and it goes through the entire population, and even though I may not know the man and will not know the Lady, when I hear about it, I'll be mad as hell, myself. And it adds up. Whatever anger there is, it just adds to it and it doesn't go away. It stays there and it builds.

"I think this visiting thing—I don't think, *I know*—that this visiting thing contributes every day of the week to the tension inside the walls, because every day of the week several people come out of that Visiting Room steaming with news of more harrassment by the guards, disrespectfulness towards our people, which we're all concerned about because we all have visitors and so even if I only have a visit a couple times a year, I'm still tuned right into what's happening in that Visiting Room all the time.

"I'm lookin ahead to what my Lady's goin to have to go through, what kind of hassles I'm goin to have to go through when I get out there, so I'm real concerned. These things that happen to other people affect me, too, so that's why I'll get mad as the next guy, or the guy it's happening to.

"It's not just the shakedowns and the arrests when they come in. It's so damned many complaints from our Ladies about whoever is at the visiting desk where they sign in. They're lucky if they get past there without a real hassle.

"Sometimes the person doesn't have their ID with them and they might not let them in. So we have a Lady sittin out there bawlin and screamin cause she came several hundred miles to see her husband and all of a sudden for want of her driver's license she'll be turned away. If she's smart or if she can keep her self under control, she can get around this. She shouldn't be treated this way in the first place but if she doesn't create too much hassle out there and if there is somebody on duty that can approve the visit—and I think as a rule there probably is, the Shift Lieutenant, or caseworker if it's during the week—he can clear this up. All he has to do is say, 'Let her in,' and she'll get in. But that's a real problem and it makes our people mad. And this happens quite often.

"In some cases, it's our people's fault. Some people will drive over here completely ignorant of the rules and regulations concerning visiting and they'll attempt to get in, or they may be drunk, you see, so it balances out. I mean, the staff isn't always wrong.

"The matter of respect towards the Ladies also becomes a problem cause maybe she will exaggerate, and maybe she won't, but regardless, if she gets in, then she'll tell her husband about it and he'll bring the news inside. 'Such and such did this and this to my Old Lady and she's a dirty dog and we want her out of the Visiting Room.' And pretty soon the next thing you've got fifty guys demanding that this woman guard be taken out of the Visiting Room away from visitors and it can snowball and they usually take it to the RC.

"There have been many, many late night meetings in the RC about complaints on the actions of the Visiting Room personnel or guards. And it's constant. It doesn't go away."

UNDESERVED PUNISHMENT

Women who carry drugs into the prison to pass on to their men are distinctly in the minority. Prison policy for discouraging this, however, makes no attempt to distinguish between the guilty and innocent, consequently all the women may be subjected to the humiliation of a body search when they come to visit their husbands, sweethearts, or sons. Such a policy discourages the women from visiting their men and may contribute to the breaking up of a relationship between a prisoner and his *Lady*.[5]

"They have a procedure here, I'm not positive when it started out but God, it has been the source of more trouble, complaints. It's a constant hassle, and that is the body searches of our Ladies — anal and vaginal searches and under the breast.

"Aw, it's a real, real humiliating procedure. If you can imagine yourself havin to go through that when you come here to see me. You'd have to make a decision: would you allow it or would you forego the visit? And you probably wouldn't visit or wouldn't visit for quite a while.

"So every time one of our Ladies is subjected to this body search, the howls of rage go up in here. They'll start screamin then. And it happens pretty regular and it's even worse if you've never been busted for narcotics and you're not on their 'hot list' as they call it, the hot list for drug trafficking, so there's no apparent reason for your wife bein searched that way.

"A few of the guys, maybe one in fifty, probably their Old Lady is bringin in dope and that's how he's supportin her, you see. She brings in weed and he sells it and sends her the money. But we all take a beatin on it.

"According to the newspapers, everybody is up to it. So all the Ladies get shook down and treated real bad out there; just rude, you know. [News of this happening] spreads all over the tiers and it's something we can't do nothin about. We complain about it but that's all we can do. You see what that creates?

"Our people come up here expectin to be treated that way so when they get here their faces aren't smilin and they're defensive and hostile, and that makes the guys feel the same way. And you get what you give out. This hostility and anger just extends clean out to the front gate now. I mean, it isn't just inside [the walls] here anymore.

"I think how our people are treated has a lot to do with the morale in here. I've seen the whole Joint just about blow up, stay mad a whole week or more over something that happened in the Visiting Room with somebody else's wife or their families. They've been humiliated out there or something like that. A guy's mom is sixty years old and they make her hike her dress up to make sure she's got panties on to visit him. And they'll take our Ladies into the rooms and give them the ole shakedown.

"They do that to our Ladies and a guy gets upset. Some of the women won't go through it. They just lose it and go home. Then the guy won't have a visit and when he finds out why, everybody's mad because that can happen to their Ladies, too. Their people are going to be subjected to stuff like that.

"A lot of people tell their people to stay away from here cause they don't want em put through that. 'I'm not havin my mom getting shook down, havin em feel her breasts to see that she hasn't got something taped underneath.'

"It doesn't make any difference that women guards do the shakin down. It's the fact that it's done. Shakin down your purse is alright, but not that other garbage. Or they should pick and choose who they search. I mean, they got a hot list. They know who passes dope and who don't so that random bullshit is dead action. There should be a lot of discretion on that but it happens because of that attitude they have towards the convicts' families.

"They've got the convicts' families in the same bag that we are. If you're in here and you're bad, then your family must be bad, so they treat them that way. They treat them like they're under arrest. They order them around and are snotty when they answer questions. And some of the women get snappy right back, of course. But then we go back again to where it started in the first place. The prison personnel started being hostile like that so our people expect it when they come here and they get it, so they give it back sometimes, but they try to hold it in because if they don't they're endangering their chances of seein us. So they have to suffer; they have to take it.

"You get real upset when you come out for a visit and your Lady's cryin and has been treated that way. Sometimes you spend the first two hours of your visit tryin to calm her down from cryin. The first thing she does when you step out there is just start bawlin and you don't know why. You've got no idea, but sure enough, they've pulled her aside and given her the treatment and she never has done nothin in her life so you're upset when you come back in here. 'You can do it to me; you can shake me down all you want, but leave my people alone! Leave my Lady alone!' And they've been told that and in those exact terms, too. 'Leave our people alone and do whatever you want to me when they go.' So it creates a helluva lot of tension in here.

"It was nice havin a visit, but you'll probably spend the rest of the week, maybe more, bein mad about it, tryin to have something done about it, which is always a waste of time. And you write letters that complain and you try to see the Superintendent about it and you go see whatever officials want to talk and they say, 'Well, we have to do this.' And they give all their little reasons why they do this. Technically, they can use those excuses so they do. But what they're doing is an attack on us. We know why they do it and consider it as an attack on us that's done deliberately by the administration, the guards, and looked at that way by us cause it isn't done with any real fairness.

"If this guy's been caught with dope a few times, they got to nail his Old Lady every time she comes in. We agree with that. Fine and dandy; if she's been wantin to take those chances she can also take the skin searches. But not our Ladies. My mother, my wife, or whatever. I've never asked them to bring dope in; wouldn't let them. So there's no reason for them to have to get pulled aside and searched like that.

"They [guards and officials] know who's coming to visit. 'Well, this Lady is comin to see Delorme. He doesn't mess with any dope. He ain't never been busted. Shake her purse down and let her go on in.' That's all it should be. Not that other bullshit. But my Lady's subject to that the same as the rest of them.

"It's a policy they've been doin: punish everybody for the sins of a few. It's a constant complaint and what it finally comes down to is the administration tells you, 'Oh, fuck you guys. We're going to do it.' They'll talk about it for awhile but finally it'll come down to that. 'That's the way it's gonna be; like it or lump it, one of the two.'

"That's the attitude they give us so it goes from there and so things start happening in here. The attitudes. The bulls start gettin cussed out more. They get shit thrown at em more. The women guards start gettin cussed out, where before they got on O.K. with the guys. But they gotta take the beef then because they work in the Visiting Room even though they don't shake down the Ladies. That's done by another woman guard out front who's a dog, and you can't never cuss at her cause she's out there. The women guards that you can get at are in here and they have to take that from the guys who are so mad about what happens.

"This is the process that's been going on and it's all to blame for where we're at right now. The way they treat our families is part of the process, part of their general attitude, this war thing that they talk about that they perpetuated. They had to start it in the first place.

"It's a big beef for us. We can't go out the gate and protect our people from them so we lay around our cell, madder than a sonovabitch. You just stay mad for days over stuff like that after a visit and you get other people mad around you by tellin em what happened and they get mad cause they're gonna have a visit and can expect the same treatment. And they stay mad."

Society's solution for punishing felons contributes not only to the dissolution of families but to the emotional, psychological, and economic suffering of wives and children. Donald P. Schneller's study of prisoners' families reveals that the hardships most deeply and consistently felt by wives after economic hardships are sexual and emotional. In many ways, prisoners' wives share the punishments inflicted upon their husbands.[6]

Hank: "Did you say there was a couple fights out in the Visiting Room today?"

Bob: "Pretty close. Arguments. Serious arguments. They caught a couple of guys holding their wives in certain ways. The guy in the monitor room said the guy had his hand up her dress in back. The cop couldn't see. He said, 'You can't hold your Old Lady like that.' He knew what he was doing but he couldn't see it. But so what? After all, it's his Old Lady. What do you think he's gonna do? Stay away from her or what? That's his Old Lady, you know."

Hank: "Do you make out with your Old Lady in the Visiting Room?"

Bob: "Naw, I wouldn't do that in front of everybody. I wouldn't do that, disgrace my lady. It's not me I care about; it's her. But some guys do that, though. If they didn't, they wouldn't put the heat on the rest of them guys."

Ruth Shonle Cavan and Eugene S. Zemans point out that unlike many nations, the United States ignores the marital rights of prisoners and their wives. "In the United States a . . . point of view . . . usually neglected . . . is the human and civil right of an adult to marry and have children. Sometimes this right is thought of as a sacred right and obligation. This neglected point of view is implicit in the practices of certain other countries."[7]

Delorme: "While we're in the Visiting Room, ideally you'd like to get in there and be left alone for whatever time you have to visit. But they keep walkin to the door and starin at us or walkin up and telling me, 'Move your chair over here' or 'You can't touch her' or something like that. But that's what they just constantly do.

"They just roam around that Visiting Room and you get close together so you can talk cause everybody's talkin and it's just a roar when you first go in there, so naturally you huddle up. You're damn near talkin in each other's ear half the time, man. Here they'll come, just constantly roamin around, tap you on the shoulder. 'You have to move away from her.' 'You can't hold her like that.' 'You can't lean on him.' Oh, for chrissake, man! By the end of the visit if you ain't mad, feeling picked on!

"I don't know; somebody tells em to do that so they do. Some of em do it less than others. That's another discretion thing cause some of the women guards, there are two of em there that don't bother you. They'll just keep leavin the room just for that reason— so you can do what you want to do. Nobody just lays on the floor. They're pretty sneaky, but she doesn't come around and bother you. She goes off at two o'clock so at least while she's on duty you know you got until two o'clock to reach over and hold your wife or whatever. You know, it's just nice to do that. Don't have to do anything else.

"But that's considered by the guys as another attack, a personal attact at the convicts in general. It's another way to say, 'Here, you sons-a-bitches. Take this.' Everything is being considered this way now. It's a part of the attack on us.

"Now she can go home cryin or she can go home feelin good for a day or two, and you'll come back in and feel good, glad that she came, or you can dread the next visit. Tell her not to come no more if she can't handle it. Try to toughen her up a little bit.

"You do a lot of talkin out there. A lot of talkin tryin to tell her, 'Don't worry' and 'Be tough,' this and that, and 'This is why it happens' and 'I know they're treatin you just like me but you're married to me so you gotta expect that.' Might work for awhile but more often than not, they can't understand it. So it'll probably ruin things for you."

Cardozo-Freeman: "You mean break up the marriage?"

Delorme: "Yeah. They finally take the kids and say, 'I can't take it no more. I didn't do anything wrong.' You know, get that attitude. Say, 'I'm mad at you when I'm home. I get lonely. I cry. I'm grouchy with the kids. I can't get down here cause it costs too much money.' When that kind of conversation starts, kiss her good-bye. You're usually ready for it by the time that she's got the guts to bring it out."[8]

The violence that goes on in the prison frightens and worries the wives, sweethearts, and mothers of the prisoners. Not only do they fear for the lives of their men, they are apprehensive about their own safety and that of their children when they come for a visit. The men also fear for the safety of their families.

Bob: "Gettin into my wife's feelings; my wife thinks it's bad here and it really is, you know, and you try to play it down. You tell her, 'Well, it's not that bad. I stay out of it. I don't hang around with the guys that get in trouble. The guys I do hang around with are pretty mellow guys. They've got their influence in here but it's in a positive way.' But shit, my wife was scared to death when she came up here for the first time cause that was just after the lockdown. Couple days after that was when that guy got killed and things were really hittin the fan then."

Alec: "She's scared for her own safety, too. I know my mom didn't want to come here."

Bob: "Sure. Just bein in the Visiting Room."

Alec: "My mom said, 'I don't know what's going to happen.' "

Bob: "The Visiting Room, the same dings that are in here go out to the Visiting Room. They might go off out there and try stabbin somebody or doing something, you know, takin hostages. Shit, you know they're out there close to that front gate."

Alec: "Yeah. They've done it a couple times. You never know what's goin to happen."

Bob: "If somebody escaped out of the Visiting Room, they might want to take a couple hostages with em. A baby. Christ, man! My wife brings my baby out here! I think about that. I'm watchin my back out in the Visiting Room just like I'm watchin my back in here. Even more so — my wife and kids are there."

Alec: "Yeah. A married couple come up to visit me. It wasn't fifteen minutes after they'd walked in and two of the inmates broke into a fight and that was the last time they ever come up to visit me."

Bob: "Yeah. They [officials] figure if they can't protect their own bulls, they're not goin to protect our people if they come here visiting. Either that or they won't protect our people cause they act like they don't give a shit. The only thing they give a shit about is tellin you to keep your hands out of your Old Lady's dress."

Alec: "You say your Old Lady was scared out in the Visiting Room about that?"

Bob: "Well, she's nervous. I don't think she's really scared; just apprehensive."

The foreboding reception awaiting the *Ladies* when they visit begins for some even before they reach the prison. Some prisoners report that guards off duty sometimes approach their wives insultingly on the street in the town of Walla Walla. One beautiful young woman who has been visiting her husband every day for the past five years told me that certain guards whistle at her when they see her walking on the street.

John: "She says when she comes to the Joint she gets out in the parkin lot and walks up to the gate there and all of a sudden she starts gettin nauseated and gets the fear factor comin inside the Joint. And it's with her comin right up here on the hill. And they're harrassin her downtown. My Lady has personally been harrassed by V.M. That bull came up and said something smart to her, that he knows she's my Old Lady."

Tim: "So they got the guards that are harrassing our people down town. They get harrassed when they come inside here which, you know, is known by everybody. And when they come to visit, to get in, they delay them. Custody has gone overboard with harrassment."

John: "Violence in here goes up and down with how they treat our people. There are more fuckin assaults, more murders, more tension; there's more everything because that happens. It affects everybody emotionally because they're messin with somebody's family. They can mess with us, fuck with us bad physically and mentally, but when they start messin with our Ladies, our people who are the people that we love and that we have strong feelins for, then that goes into a whole different area."

Tim: "That's what people go to war for, you know, to fight for their country. Well, in here we're fighting for our families."

PRETENDING

There is an unstated agreement honored by all the couples and families in the crowded visiting room—every couple or family pretends that only they are there. Even the children honor this agreement. Everyone wears blinders in an effort to create privacy in the midst of an uncomfortable, monitored public situation. Families and couples seem oblivious to what is going on around them, intent only on their own situation.

"I guess I can run down a typical visit for you. Some days are better than others. I only have a couple visits during the year, maybe three if the money's right. My Old Lady will bring my eight-year-old daughter along during the summer and Christmas.

"When my daughter is here I have to cool it with the love stuff. My kid always manages to plunk herself down between us anyway, so what the hell. On these days I hug my kid a lot, can't get enough of her, really. I try to put a lot of love into these short visits. That's all I can do as her dad.

"We don't talk about much, just play around. She will tell me all her little secrets and the things she does at school, all in a rush when we first see each other. She is shy with me for awhile. But that goes away in an hour or so.

"It's strange the way we can be so private in the middle of everyone. Our people always have trouble at first with all the people talking at once. Eventually, they learn to adapt and shut out everyone else, the same way we learn to do it inside the walls. We huddle in a corner as if we were alone on a desert island.

"I always keep my daughter close to me, and taught her not to look around at others, not to ever stare, and mind her manners. She is a very well mannered little girl, a real little Lady, and I am very proud of her.

"Sometimes I get sad when I think about how fast she is growing. When you see a kid twice a year at that age, you can *watch* them grow. When this feeling hits me, I just reach out and hug her some more; it [the feeling] never shows.

"When my Lady comes alone, it's different. She gets ignored when my kid is here, but she has my complete attention when she is alone. She will take a room in town so she can visit two full days.

"We are close and spend these moments touching and talking softly. We can't make love in the Visiting Room. I won't say 'can't' because we could, but she is pretty modest and really can't get that loose even if she tried. Besides, I don't have that kind of nerve, either. I'd become super conscious of the others around me—little kids, grandmothers, and so on, so it's a little hard to get down in front of everyone.

"We try to express all the love we have in our touch, through our eyes, and with many hours of talking. Hopefully it will somehow sustain us until the next letter, the next visit. We don't speak of the lonely hours or the frustration of being apart and without sex to express our love.

"The prison has a name for our emotions—'lewdness.' Our display of love and tenderness is strictly forbidden. We chance losing our visits for ninety days if the guard spots us, but I really don't care because it will be much more than ninety days before my Lady can save enough money for a return visit."

For three days I sat with Delorme in the Visiting Room of the Minimum Security Building, which is located outside the walls of the prison, pretending I was one of the *Ladies* in an effort to understand what the women and their men and children were experiencing. Throughout that time the male guards stared intently at the couples from behind a counter, presumably trying to discourage explicit lovemaking. They made no attempt, however, to come into the room. They left the men and their families strictly alone. Only the eagle eye was evident, which I found disconcerting. I observed the rudeness with which one guard treated a prisoner when he asked for folding chairs, since all available seats were taken. The guard told him to find his own chair, turned and disappeared into the office behind the counter. The prisoner was outraged because his wife, carrying a small baby in her arms, had no place to sit down.

No women guards are on duty in the Minimum Security Building. I counted seventy people the first day I was there, including the prisoners. Where children were involved, and there were many, the atmosphere was festive and bustling. Families played cards or dominoes; watched television, and "picnicked." Children referred to guards as "pigs," not unkindly, but because for them this is their name. Delorme pointed out that the close and constant visibility of the guards, authority figures, causes many of the children to be ever watchful of their actions and the whereabouts of the nearest guard, lest their fathers be taken out of the Visiting Room because of some minor infraction. Wives *are doing time* right along side of their prisoner husbands. Many resent it, fold under the pressure, and leave their husbands. "Even at home the conversations and thoughts of the wives always turn to events on 'the Hill'." Wives of *lifers* call themselves *lifers* and refer to each other as *long* or *short timers*, just the way the men inside the walls do. Many of the men in the prison come from the poorest economic strata of society and their wives and children reflected this poverty. Traveling across the Cascade Mountains is a great expense for these families. Everywhere families were busily cramming six months of living into a few hours. "Family life," Delorme states, "is conducted in a corner of the room during visits. A full day's visiting will run the gauntlet of emotions—love, anger, rejection [very temporary], sadness, happiness, laughter, tears, scolding and loving the child, nap time, teaching time. This is a much speeded up version of a week's routine in the home and all takes place during the course of a day-long visit." Some couples in the Visiting Room were extremely imaginative in their attempts at getting close to one another. Other couples quietly held each other for long periods of time, saying nothing, as though trying to store up enough love to sustain each during the long separation to come. They seemed surrounded with a bittersweet aura. A few women wept in their husbands' (or sweethearts') arms. One scene was reminiscent of the Nativity (this was December, 1980)—a plain looking young mother with a sad face, her blond hair pulled tightly back and fastened at the nape of her neck, held her tiny baby nursing at her breast, while the young father, holding a blanket shielding them, gazed at the child. Later this young mother told me that it was very difficult for a prisoner's wife to find work downtown. This couple had met at the prison and married the first time he was released; she had been a chapel volunteer at the prison. Both told me they spend a great deal of time "dreaming" of how things were going to be when he is released from prison. Apparently many couples dream about their future.

"It's a strange thing, but we do a lot of trippin together in the Visiting Room. We daydream together and we talk about it. We both fantasize about life.

"We're going to do this and we'll do that and 'I'll get you this, honey' 'I'll get you that.' But in the back of each of our minds we know that that's not the way life is. But maybe it's easier for us like that, I guess.

"It's nice for two people to daydream. Sometimes, even if the woman is logical and down-to-earth, she just kind of gives in to the mood, starts dreaming and tripping with us, rather than be mean and say, 'No. That's not the way it is. It's not the way life is. We never have had anything and we're never going to have anything.' Chasing rainbows. It doesn't take long to rub off on your Lady and we can smile and laugh and play. Guys in prison daydream a lot, too.

"I don't think that I ever remember doing any of the things that I've talked about with my Lady. Even the simple things like traveling around a little bit and seeing the country, or even seeing the state, as far as that goes. Nothing ever comes true. But it sure is fun to talk about it.

"So we go into our little world in the Visiting Room and even our world is unreal, but it's great. It helps you to get through a pretty bad time and I just know that she, well, I don't know, but maybe she carries these daydreams with her. Who can say? I've never asked."

Each evening at nine o'clock a bus pulled up to the front of the Minimum Security Building to carry the prisoners' *people* back to their cars. I boarded the bus for the three days I pretended I was one of the *Ladies*. Each evening I saw women weeping. A young mother with two small children wept as she explained to me on the bus that she could only visit her husband every six months because she could not afford to come the great distance across the mountains. She told me she wanted to stay and visit with him the next day (Sunday) but had no money to stay overnight, so she had to drive back across the mountains that night (a five-hour drive) with her two small children, a grueling trip for a tired and sad young mother. "They [officials] just don't care about the children. They just don't care how it hurts my children," she wept, while I thought of how it was hurting her. Another young mother, a Mexican *Lady* who spoke no English, tried to comfort her two weeping children. "*Dile poppy*, bye bye. *Dile poppy*, bye bye." "Say good-bye to daddy." No one spoke as the bus carried the *Ladies* and their little children to their cars.

A LADY'S INFLUENCE

Some men manage to meet women and begin and continue love affairs with them while in prison. Some even manage to marry them as, for example, the young prisoner mentioned above. Although some of these men are not sincere, indeed, a few use women to help get themselves out of prison and then abandon them,[9] many of these men truly care for their *Ladies* and their behavior changes for the better in prison because of this newfound love relationship. As a general rule, men who have wives or sweethearts who love them and stick by them tend to do their time quietly, without causing problems for themselves or others.

"The guys who have regular visits from their people, their Ladies, don't have a lot of trouble in here. They see their Ladies once a week even if there isn't any sex. But if you love your Lady, you love everything about her. You love even to smell her, just be close to her; that's all.

"And those who see their Ladies are more content, and they don't have violence; they live from visit to visit and their mind is up out of this garbage in here. They're more in contact with something that's real, something that's pretty and soft. The problems they are thinking about are her problems with gas and rent. It gives them something to think about, something real instead of this funny stuff in here. They look forward to visits.

"Guys whose wives live across the mountains visit for weekends. The Ladies are weekending. That's what they call it. They come on Friday and they stay and leave on Sunday night so they can visit.

"Some people have their wives move downtown and they visit twelve half-days a month. They have a special visiting contract, they call it. The men sign a contract agreeing not to visit except in the nighttime, or one half of the day, like in the mornings and at night, so they can have a full day if they want. That way it leaves a little bit of room for the people that come from out of town.

"The people who have visits regular, it's almost a club, I swear. They have things that they talk about that's pertaining to things that happen in the Visiting Room. They know the officers by name. They laugh and joke with the female officers. She [guard] comes to know the regulars by name; she gets to know their business; knows their wives.

"I've often noticed that the female guards will get involved in things. That's good. It fits right in there.

"But like I say, these guys are always up out of it. They have ongoing problems that go from week to week, plans and schemes; that's what they're always thinking about. They're out there all day several days a week. Their minds go home with their Old Ladies, really. They try to keep their thoughts on the streets."

For a period of time up until 1978, the prisoners were allowed to invite their families and friends into the prison to be with them for monthly celebrations that were sponsored by the individual clubs. The men worked diligently planning each monthly festivity. The prisoners' clubs were filled with wives, sweethearts, mothers, children, and friends during these celebrations. Over this entire period no incidents of violence ever occurred. The men always responded responsibly to this privilege. This tradition was discontinued in part because guards were both disapproving and resentful. They argued that allowing such privileges to the prisoners made their work doubly hazardous and furthered the drug trafficking problem in the prison. The officials dismantled this program along with many others when the lockdown of 1979 took place.

"Our club was happy when we were havin Pow Wows, but they took all that away. A lot of people were comin in from Yakima and the Umatillas and they'd wear their Indian outfits. The girls would wear the shawls and the guys would wear their bells. All the cons in the Joint would watch when our people came in cause they looked good.

"We'd meet em as they came in and take em up to our club. You weren't supposed to let anyone in under sixteen but B.R. and D.V. let us bring little kids in, too. And we'd dance and we'd talk and we'd pay to get some snacks for em and some pop. We'd do this once a month and we'd have this to look forward to.

"You see, after one of our meetings was over we'd just start plannin for the next time and that would keep your mind occupied on positive things. We'd be plannin, savin our money, and cleanin up the place. The guys were proud of the club. They were always shinin the floor. I got kind of known as crabby about it bein dirty and I was always on their ass about cleanin it. I'd work on it and the guys would help.

"So because there was gonna be women in the Joint, it reminds you of something that you really want. It's something that's important to you. Well, it kind of reminds you that you're more valuable maybe than you think to somebody else. If you don't have the sense to care about yourself, maybe somewhere along the line your wife reminds you that she cares. Seein her reminds you."

A Chicano prisoner, one of the *good people* about whom Delorme spoke in a previous chapter, talks about the influence his wife and child have had on him.

"Do you know when I really took a look at myself, Gene. When I started changing? This is my fourth time in the penitentiary, too, man.

"I'm a baker. I can walk the streets and get a job anywhere. I've been in therapy, been to schools and everything but the only thing that has really helped me is some meaning came into my life outside of myself.

"The system, the whole system takes away a person's self-worth and that's where true meaning is for an individual. Meaning came to me outside of myself; it came from my wife and from my daughter.

"Everytime I started doing something wrong, I'd say to myself, 'This ain't right. It's not right for them.' Or like I would punch somebody in the jaw. Before, I would take that as socially acceptable to myself. It was part of me. I felt it was good. But then when I would do it, I would say. 'Man, what would my daughter and wife think if they could see me punching this guy in the fucking jaw, making the blood come out of his nose or something?'

"This is when I started seeing things like that as being animalistic. I started sayin to myself then, 'I want to be proud of what I do, man.' I don't want to ever be ashamed to tell my wife and daughter, 'Hey, this is me.' I want to be able to tell them, 'Hey, that's my husband.' 'That's my dad.' I don't want them to see me punchin on someone. That would have a bad psychological effect on my daughter and my Old Lady.

"And at the same time when I found meaning outside myself it made me go off inside myself to stop and look and think, 'Well, who am I? What am I doing?'

"I want to be a good provider when I get out. I was out there one time and I didn't provide good, man. I ended up coming back to the penitentiary even though I was with it when I was out. To me, that's what hurt me the most. It's just leavin them out there and putting them through all the pain that they have.

"And what got me lookin at the system more and seeing the system from a different light is the fact they would give me the big bitch, me, being married and having a wife and daughter. Classify me as a habitual criminal and give me a life sentence. That's like sentencing my wife and daughter to life.

"From that I started looking at the other prisoners, their wives and daughters, their families and I stopped and looked at it and I said, 'Well, they ain't punishing me. They're punishing them. If they wanted to punish me, they'd make me pay some kind of restitution, pay money or whatever it would take.'

If a guy passes a bum check; if he's got a wife or kid out there, or if he's got a dope habit and he's gotta go caper to support that habit; if it's his weekly check if he's trying to work, he's got a problem. Dig? But you can't get a man like that and throw him in prison. It's like throwing gas on a fire. It don't even help him, man. All it does is to blow it up more, burns everybody around him — the family, his Lady and children.

"But if they really wanted to help that man, what they would do was get him in to some kind of meaningful drug program. I mean a program that really works."

Delorme's *Lady* is nine years old. She accepts her father's situation because she has never known him to be in any other. As both grow older, his efforts at changing his life become surer and surer.

"I had a visit yesterday. My daughter was over. A friend of mine brought her. They drove across the mountains to see me. It was a good day, a good day. She's growing fast, as all kids do.

"I guess when they get to be nine years old they really start sprouting. She's nine now. A little blonde just like her mother. She's getting clothes conscious, making record collections. You know all kids do. All the girls, of course, start a little earlier. Their interests are quite different. It's tough on me cause I can't keep up. I kind of fall behind on those things.

"I tend to keep thinking back a few years and keep in my mind's eye that she's still a baby, of course, so I think our conversation probably isn't what it should be, the father-daughter conversation. That worries me a little bit but it'll come along; it'll work itself out. If she has to talk about anything, serious questions, you know, I just ask her if she's got anything she wants to tell me and she says, 'No.' So we get back to nothing.

"Anyway, it's been kind of a real strong relationship between me and that kid. Being back in here so many times, I miss her for a while and she's what, a couple months old? And I leave. When I come back, she's two years old. I leave her for a few months and come here and I go back and she's four years old and I'm with her for a while and we have fun; we get super tight and I get busted and I come back here and I get out and she's six years old, seven years old. Oh God. It's just kind of impossible to keep up with the growing pains, or whatever you want to call them, the stages in her life.

"Even though we've all been through it, I still fall behind in that area cause I don't understand the stages that a kid goes through that good. Only that I sit back when I'm thinking about her and my thoughts are, 'I wonder what she's thinking about me?' Things like that. What's important to her? I know, probably, what's real important to her.

"I especially worry about what she thinks of me and I don't suppose that she could ever understand the why's and whereof's of my situation—why I'm always gone. And that's what I've been waiting to try to answer when she asks, but she didn't ask. She accepts these visits as 'That's our day' and that's it. She doesn't seem sad. She's a little shy when we get started off. But thank the Lord for even two visits a year. Could be worse. Could be like some people and be on the outs with my ex-wife or something like that and then it'd be a problem to ever see her. But in my case my ex-wife cooperates every way she can and agrees that it's best for now that we should see more of each other. So she encourages my daughter to write, sends me her grades, and makes it convenient for W. to pick her up and bring her over and I really appreciate that fact. It means a lot to me now.

"This morning I made a phone call to see if my daughter got home safe. We had a storm here yesterday while I was having my visit. They had to drive back across the mountains and they didn't have snow tires or anything so I kind of worried about that all night. I called and everybody was safe and sound and back in their little homes. Kind of took a load off my mind."

FOR LACK OF A LADY

For many men in prison there is no *Lady* (or family), no one to love or love them. These men suffer greatly from lack of emotional nourishment and commitment. If they have any "family" at all, it is the other prisoners. Men without wives, sweethearts, or families, research shows, have greater difficulty changing their lives for the better when they leave the prison. A great percentage of them are recidivists.[10] Some men, and there are a considerable number, prefer to remain imprisoned, as this is the only home that they have. Since there is no reason to do otherwise, their tendency is to identify completely with the prison culture.

Delorme: "Jimmy is an alcoholic as I told you before. He just says he doesn't care. He doesn't talk much, spends all his time in the Hole or Segregation. He only gets out once in awhile. Don't stay out long, about a week is his limit."

Cardozo-Freeman: "Does he have anybody who visits him?"

Delorme: "No. The only people he knows is his cousin; she's married and lives in Canada."

"I always wished I could find him a girl friend. I tried but he don't stay out of the Hole long enough, you know. If he had somebody that he cared for it would change everything for him in here. It would.

"You should see how he'd dress up when C. would come to see me back when we were allowed to bring our people inside the walls. God damn! Nobody in the Joint knew him; they couldn't believe it! He came out with the nicest suit on. I mean a regular suit and a shirt and tie and new shoes. God, that couldn't be Jimmy! I'm telling you, it was knocking people out around the Joint when he walked over to say hello to C. and me.

"He's usually a pigpen and he's usually drunk or getting arrested for getting drunk. He's going downhill fast with that arthritis he's had since he was a kid.

"But he's a good little guy, really a good little guy except that he gets into so goddam much trouble with his drinking.

"He could have been out of here a year ago but he says, 'I don't care. I don't have no place to go.' If only he could be different on the street, except I don't think he ever could. He's a real ole drunk on the streets.

"He uses that arthritis as an excuse and it's a good excuse as far as I'm concerned, too, cause he is gonna be crippled in a matter of a few years."

Cardozo-Freeman: "And there's nothing in here that he's interested in?"

Delorme: "The only thing he ever stuck with was school, typewriter repair. He likes to work. He's a genius, an electronic genius, man.

"When I asked him if there was any kind of film he'd like to see when I was ordering films from Seattle—we had this little film program going—he gave me a list of films. I couldn't read the goddam thing! They were all radar, X-ray, electronic typewriters and things like that.

"He's got books I can't even read. When he gets in the Hole I send him down one of his books. Plus I always include some AA literature; he knows that's a joke.

"I like to listen to him talk about things like electronics. He tries to explain things to me. He sits around, fixes my wires, my typewriter all the time, takes it apart and has it all over the place. I can't figure out if he's ever going to get it back together, but he does and it works fine, looks good, all clean and nice. He's kept that old typewriter going for a couple of years.

"But he doesn't care, I guess. Course, I care. I babysat him until I couldn't do it no more.

"But I understand him, you know. He doesn't want out right now. That's understandable I suppose in a way. He won't leave the Joint. They threw him out to the Building [MSB] and he came back in voluntarily. He got lonesome so he came back in and he says that he don't care nothing about gettin out because he don't have anybody waitin for him. Maybe he's just coverin up. I don't know."

Although this following young *first timer* in prison refuses to allow his mother to visit him because he is ashamed of his circumstance and wishes to spare her more suffering, he reveals that he longs to see her. Without outside contacts, the danger of this young man becoming a recidivist are greatly intensified.

Bud: "I've never had a visit here in my life."

John: "You haven't had any here?"

Bud: "My family isn't in this state, number one."

John: "Oh, you have relatives in Philadelphia."

Bud: "No. My mom moved out. She's down in Florida now with my sister. My brother's in the army. He's back in New Jersey."

John: "You're an orphan out here."

Bud: "Yeah. Holding down the state all by myself. Doing a good job of it, too. I could have had people visit me if I was in Monroe, which is twenty-thirty miles from Bellevue. I could have had people from the church coming out, a lot of my friends, but they sure as hell don't want to spend the price of a motel and the gasoline that it costs to come over here, you know, blow the whole weekend just to come over and see one person. So I get a lot of inferiority from people who are going out and having visitors all the time."

John: "Yeah, I was wondering if it bothered you."

Bud: "It also bothers me from the aspect that if I ever come up with parole, they're gonna say, 'Nobody gives a shit about him. They never come and see him or anything else.'"

John: "But it's not really a problem for a guy whose people are out of state. It's people that do have a lot of family and they don't get a visit or letters. Then they begin to wonder because they figure you need somebody out there. The more people you've got, they can look at your records and see you've got close contact, then they know you've got a little bit of help out there. But they wouldn't want to hold you up on that."

Bud: "I've got support but they don't come down and see me."

John: "You've got some church friends and stuff and that's good as gold, so you could bring that up and maybe you should be thinking about gettin in contact with those people now, a letter once a month or something like that to let them know you're thinkin about them."

Bud: "Letters, I mean I average receiving between ten–fifteen letters a week and I write just as many."

John: "With the price of gas it's reasonable to not have people come this far. I used to get a lot of visits and I don't have very many any more because they're too expensive."

Bud: "Well, I've heard there's a church around here where ..."

John: "You'd be a good candidate for the one-on-one program. Have you asked about that?"

Bud: "Maybe that's what I'm thinking."

John: "They probably come from Seattle and Tacoma, church people. They're all Christian people. Most of them are business people and they take you on and you're assigned a couple and they come and visit you and most of the time they send you packages in the mail and things like that."

Bud: "Mail wouldn't bother me but I wouldn't like people spending money on me."

John: "But these people, they know in advance when you're expected to get out. They either give you a place to live, help you get a place to live, help you get a job if they can't hire you at their own business, and they're willing to do that. And you know in front if you're on the list of one-to-one sponsors that's what they're going to do. And if you don't have relatives in this state, then you're a fine candidate for that program."

Bud: "Well I've got relatives in this state but they don't consider me a relative. Who do I find out the information for that from?"

John: "Either ask some of the guys around here or ask your caseworker about it cause I don't know who's running it right now."

Bud: "Well, it'd be nice to have a visit once a month or once a year, or on Christmas or something like that. But I don't know if I could ask anybody to come in to this place to see me."

John: "Why? Because of the funny things that are going on out there?"

Bud: "I thought about it. I don't know. Prison is not an environment for entertaining, you know. It's a disgrace being in prison. I'm not proud of it. My mom she wanted to come up and visit me over the Christmas holiday and I said, 'Well, you can come up and you can try to get in but I will not send you a visiting form and I will not sign one.' And I have it down with my counselor. It's understood that unless it is a dire emergency I want no family, relatives, in here unless I requested it."

John: "You are a heartless fellow. You're cold, man; you're cold. You shouldn't do that to your mother."

Bud: "In other words this way she won't feel as though she's deserting me, you know. She won't feel as though she has to come up to see me."

John: "Well, what would that have been, a good-bye visit? Was she already in Florida when she wanted to come?"

Bud: "Yeah."

John: "She must have some bucks. You live in the city's fancy, fancy neighborhood so she must not be hurtin too much."

Bud: "I don't know. She came down to the county jail to visit me there and it put her out seeing me behind bars, and I mean, it'd be a better visiting situation here cause I can touch her. She can see me, besides, not through snot-filled glass, you know."

John: "Does she bawl?"

Bud: "Oh yeah. She's very sentimental. All of us are. Even I am."

John: "She probably wouldn't cry here cause she'd see you more relaxed."

Bud: "I like it much better when I can sneak in on the phone and give her a call, send her a tape, and hear her voice or something like that. She'll probably be gone before I'm released anyway. That bugs the hell out of me."

John: "Why? Is she sick?"

Bud: "She's sixty-seven years old. She's got a lot of kidney and liver problems. She's got degenerative arthritis. So if I'm going to do five or ten years I seriously doubt if she'll be around when I get out. I hope she is, you know."

John: "Maybe that's on her mind, too, you know. All the more reason to spend a day or two with her."

Bud: "Well, I'm going to try to have her remember me the way she remembered me on the streets."

John: "You should let her make a decision like that. Mother love is awful strong. You mean an awful lot to her."

Bud: "Well, if she would have called me and said, 'I really want to come up and see you,' then I would allow it. I don't want her to feel as though I thought she deserted me because she can't afford to come up to see me or she can't take the time or something like that. I don't want her to feel obligated to come up and see me. If I really knew she wanted to do it on her own for her own reasons, not because she thinks I want her to, then that's different."

John: "Then you don't just flat out refuse her; you should leave it open."

Bud: "No, if she comes up here and she was visiting some friends or her sister or brother in the Seattle area and they want to drive over for the weekend, that would be different, but for her to fly up from Florida just to come up to visit me, no way in hell. I don't see that and I don't think she'd get that much of a psychological benefit from here. She's got my sister and a couple of grandkids down there for her. She's got family around right down there so she's not alone."

LOSS OF A LADY

Men are devastated when a woman they love leaves them. Wolfram Rieger, who worked for two years as prison psychiatrist at the Federal Penitentiary in Lewisburg, Pennsylvania, found that "the most common precipitator of an emotional crisis [of prisoners demanding psychiatric crisis intervention] was the termination of a relationship by a wife or girlfriend." The men manifested all the symptoms of an acute depressive reaction, suffering from "severe hopelessness, a strong sense of helplessness, defeat and frustration." In a study he conducted at the prison of fifty-eight suicide attempts, those that were most serious were precipitated by the recent loss of a loved one through divorce or death. He writes that he was moved by "the enormous human suffering" brought about by the dissolution of a marriage or a long-standing relationship with a woman.[11]

"The guys worry all the time about their wives not being faithful, especially when they first come in [to the prison]. That family that you probably have been ignoring, the kids probably haven't seen their dad twice out of the week, all of a sudden they become all important. Everything else is taken away from you and what's left is your family and you. So all of a sudden, they're the whole world and you suddenly realize how much they mean to you and here you are in here and they're out there and that's all you can think about. Everything else is gone and that's one thing you try to hang on to.

"When you're in Shelton you don't make decisions because you don't know how much time you're gonna get yet. You hope they won't give you too much time. Then you hope it won't sound too bad to her when you tell her, 'I've got five or six years.' When you tell her you generally say, 'Aw, I only got three years,' but you figure you got three years to work on the rest [of the three years] if you have to tell her you got more. And if she hangs on for that long, if she hangs on for a year, she'll probably hang on for the rest of the time."

One experienced *old timer* gives some friendly advice to a young *fish* trying to spare him heartache should his wife desert him while he serves his sentence.

Joe: "When I first got here and I hadn't seen my Lady in a couple months, that was kind of a shaky experience for me. I was used to being around her for the last four and a half years, and when I did finally see her I was afraid to hug and kiss her. I just didn't know whether I had the right to. And I don't know, it's just a weird goddam feeling; I felt like an alien coming into a different planet. It was just weird! I got back into that feeling of being close but then it's a cold sonovabitch feeling when you know you've gotta go and she's gotta go and it's gone again."

Gene: "Sure, a woman is half a life. They just chop you off in half a life, half a human being. A woman and a man is one person, really, and when they take that woman away, boy, that's a cold life. You're feelin cold and when you go out there to the Visiting Room you take those cold feelings with you unless the night before you trip about it. Really trip about it and get your feelings loose and be ready for the emotions because when your Old Lady's finally here, she's in front of you, then those feelings you've hidden come up. They're good feelings, real good feelings. They're not bad feelings, you gotta remember that. They're the best things you got in life, bein able to be compassionate towards people and bein able to love another person. That's the best part of you. But those feelings are still wrapped up cause you gotta keep a cover on em in here. But it's good to see her.

"Like I say, the ice starts melting after you're there a while and you keep lookin at her, keep lookin, and everything's so different about her from what you're used to in here. Her eyes are soft. There's no hate in her eyes. There ain't no sneakiness in her eyes and she ain't lookin for dope. Everything is so completely opposite from what you're used to seein and dealin with. Yeah, and something else — it's tough to leave her but be thankful for them hours you get together though because that keeps you in contact with what life's all about, and a woman, I think, is what life's all about."

Joe: "I feel lucky in one respect to still have her, you know, cause she's gone through a lotta bullshit with me, and for me to still have her is amazing, if I really sit down and think about it. And that's what I think is going to help me when I get out, too. Maybe I shouldn't have those expectations."

Gene: "Well, you haven't been here long enough to where you start sortin things out, but eventually when you're here a while you're going to take all your marbles out of one basket. You've got to."

Joe: "Oh yeah, I understand."

Gene: "She's awful important and it's going to be great and a lot of expectations you've got there, but you've got to put a little safety back there for yourself just in case. Keep something there for Joe, then you can make it in any event. Protect yourself just in case."

Joe: "Yeah, cause if it doesn't work out then I don't lose."

Gene: "Yeah, cause there she is and here you are and your immediate goal is to get back to her. But out there is a big ole basketful of there, the whole world to pick from. So you keep lookin back at this and just get your whole mind in order so you can start plannin for eventualities so that it doesn't fuck with you all that much."

Joe: "If me and my Lady broke up now, it would hurt. I'd be awful down but I wouldn't try to hide it. I wouldn't sit here in the cell and say, 'Fuck her,' cause that ain't true. I don't feel that way about her. Like you say, it's better for her and all that shit. Yeah, that's true, too, and I'll still feel bad but I'll cope with it. And it's not out of coldness. It's not.

"It's just like you say, I'm lucky. As long as we're together it's just luck cause I can't see no real reason other than maybe I don't understand love that much. With her it's love. But that's not having a real high regard for myself, either.

"I say to myself, 'What's there to love?' you know, but if that's the way it is, then that's cool cause it helps me. I've got somebody to write to, someone to keep me in touch and all that. But I'd really have to try and look at other people and other things I could do without her. But I hate to and I often wonder if it's because of the security she offers me.

"And on the other hand, there's things that I want to do for her, that I've never done for her. I've had all my chances but I ain't made her happy. It's always been take from her. Her give to me but I've never given up anything and I'd like to do something for her. Just take her somewhere or do something with her, buy her something; I don't care what.

"What would make her happy would be for me to stay out of trouble. What's making her happy now is I'm getting an education and when I hated school so fucking much! You wouldn't believe how much I hated school a few years ago. But not now."

Although a man may say he understands his wife's behavior and doesn't expect her to remain faithful to him during his imprisonment, he is deeply hurt if this occurs. Other prisoners try to lighten the seriousness of this potential hazard through joking and teasing.

Delorme: "You walk up to a guy and ask, 'You got any dirty pictures of your wife?' And the other guy says, 'No. I don't have anything like that.' And you tell him, 'Wanna buy some?' and you reach in your pocket real quick. That's a standard little joke on em, especially if you know a guy that really, really does hard time over his wife. It's just teasing him."

Cardozo-Freeman: "Where did this Joe-the-Grinder come from?"

Delorme: "I don't know. Used to be a prisoner that would get out of here an go look up someone else's wife. He's a guy who knows who's in the Joint and he goes to see that lovely Lady and tells her how her husband's doing and by morning he's still telling her. Probably by the next week he's wearin your clothes and drivin your car. That's Joe-the-Grinder."

Cardozo-Freeman: "Does that really happen?"

Delorme: "Yeah. It really happens. Joe-the-Grinder is usually somebody you knew in the Joint and probably was your friend. That's who that guy is. You laugh about it. It's a joke but it really happens sometimes. You tease the guys about it.

" 'So what are you worrying about it for? Joe-the-Grinder's takin care of your wife. Probably got your clothes by now. Probably wrecked your car.'

" 'Aw, she wouldn't do that.'

" 'They all do it, dum-dum.'

"But it's for their own good. You do it in a teasing way. You keep doin it because some day they'll snap to where *it's* at, that that really can happen. It ain't because she's a bad girl but that she's a human being. It's hard for people to accept that, but it's part of accepting something you can't change."

PROTECTING LOVE

Keeping in touch with one's family is very important for the prisoner. "The positive feelings he has because of his family's love are probably the only means he has of justifying his life to himself. The idea that his family will be waiting for him after he is released gives him hope for the future. The loss of his relationship with his family would leave a prisoner without any significant attachments with the outside world and cause him to lose positive feelings about himself."[12] Unfortunately, keeping one's *Lady* while serving a prison sentence can be a difficult and worrisome feat.

"Many people live from visit to visit, live from letter to letter, and do a lot of phoning in between. This is pretty common and in some cases there's even jokes about it because some guys seem to go to breakfast, go to the phone room; go to dinner, go back to the phone room; go to supper, spend the evening at the phone room.

"These guys are lucky, of course. The Old Ladies probably live downtown, otherwise they could never afford a phone bill like that.

"The people that live over on the coast generally will limit their phone calls to one a week. Even that gets pretty expensive. Four calls a month is a pretty high price for most of our people.

"Of course, our Ladies try to say, 'Oh, don't phone me, but I get worried about it.' They worry and it hurts them.

"You get a hundred dollar phone bill every month and we're not talkin about people with dough. We're talkin about people on welfare. Women that are workin their butts off waitin on tables, workin in canneries, you see. They're not pullin down those big bucks, and the kind of wages they're makin sure as hell don't indicate a hundred dollar a month phone bill.

"So they will try and if we're lucky we may have some kind of offering come in here, small as it may be. And we may be able to contribute to paying for the phone a little bit to keep it goin.

"We'd all like to call more than once a week. We use that to tell each other, 'I love you and take care of yourself' and 'What's happening?' and 'Are you havin problems?' and 'What can I do?' and 'I'll write' and 'When are you comin down to see me?' and maybe talk about ongoing problems and say 'Hi' to the kids. And you feel good. More than anything else, you feel good when you leave the phone. That feeling can carry on for hours, take you through the rest of the evening.

"Sometimes I myself have went to the phone room at night after supper or in the afternoon and expected to get a call through. Couldn't reach anybody. Somehow things aren't the same the rest of the day. Seems like a little wind went out of your sails or something. It's probably real selfish. I don't know how you look at it but I don't know, our feelings are bruised so damned easy so we're not tough. We're definitely not too tough. Not when a phone call can kick the pins out from under you.

"But all this is aimed at holding on to that wife, these visits, these letters, these phone calls. They all say the same thing: 'I love you, honey.' 'Please wait for me.' 'I'll be home.' 'We'll be O.K.' 'Gonna get through this.' 'You'll have to be tougher.' 'Gotta be strong.' And 'Daddy will be home soon.'

"And you keep tellin them this and the months drag out and the years go by and you just hope and you pray. You write your letters and she tries, of course. She tries.

"Since the advent of the telephone in this prison, it's like a new invention, and the elimination of the separating table between visitors, families have been able to draw closer together. Problems are discussed and solved during visits and on the phone. The wife may cry and the children can tell of their new adventures in first grade, so the relationship and family ties can grow, in a crippled sort of way. The bond connecting is love, the chain holding all this together, and delivering the message on the phone. So any interruption in this flow of communication can be devastating to both inmate and family.

"The connection between inmate violence, or a general bad attitude within the prisoner and trouble at home, has never been emphasized, nor has this area been looked at as the source of much of the unrest and tension behind the walls. It has been my experience after many years inside this prison that violence, tension, riots, suicides are all closely connected with the interaction between prisoner and family."

In research conducted in Great Britain, Alice Crosthwaite points out that "many wives feel that their husbands have an easy time in prison, with no responsibilities and no worries and that it is they, the wives, who really serve the sentences."[13]

Tim: "She tries to find ways to counter that loneliness and frustration that she feels, the anger that she often has over me when she's at home and she's having a terrible time with the kids or something. And she'll get damned mad at me because I should be there and from what they've told me, I get cussed out quite a bit at home. 'He ought to be here to take care of these kids, blah, blah, blah.' But it's understandable. It goes away, I guess, her anger. And I got that coming."

Gene: "We all do. We're just sittin in here and we're just kickin back. We create a problem if we haven't got any. Although it's tough doing time, it's tough being in a damned cell, I really don't think it's as tough as her tryin to live without self-respect when she's on welfare, strugglin along to feed those kids, gettin up in the mornings with em, gettin em off to school, and fight with em and love em and keep the home together while you're gone, put a roof over their heads, clothes on their backs."

Tim: "That's tough. Now we're talking tough, you goddam right."

Gene: "There's a helluva lot of us in here that haven't been able to handle that chore in life. We marry women, we have children and we just can't seem to follow up on it. I'm a little guilty of that myself. More than a little bit. Quite a bit."

There is a price that must be paid for protecting one's feelings while in prison, and families suffer as a result. Feelings of love and compassion for others are deeply buried for reasons of self-preservation in prison. Unfortunately, getting in touch with them again becomes very difficult.

Gene: "You keep that protection up, that wall that you built, that emotional insulation from hurt, or feeling hurt, you know, not letting anyone get to you. And you know you've got that and it gets stronger every day that you're here, just thicker and thicker. If it would just go away when you get a visit or when you get out and you could give your kid a hug, give your little kid a hug, and your Old Lady, give her a kiss. But they'll feel nothin but a coldness from you. They'll feel coldly isolated and they won't know how to talk to you about it. They won't know how to deal with it and the subject really won't come up cause they really won't know how to explain it. And you gotta start now, man. Is it there? Am I doin that, man? I'm bein nice to em but it ain't that, man. There's that feeling, you know, which I haven't been able to describe but I'm gettin hip to it by just studying and analyzing myself."

Hank: "I know what you're talking about cause that's the way I used to act toward my Old Lady."

Gene: "But a guy does have trouble bein able to give love. I mean really give love. You're not soft, anymore. You're in a culture that doesn't have feelings. There's no value in emotions. Emotions is a dirty word in here, to be compassionate or tender, those things are useless in here. But they're a part of bein a human being, the part that you have to hide. You have to consciously cover up that you feel bad cause this guy got killed. You can't express that, man. You gotta hide it. That's gotta make some scars, man. That's hard on your psyche, man, to do that.

"It ain't easy for people, believe me. You get to the point where things get so bad that you learn how to control your own emotions, wrap em up and put em in mothballs. You can't play with em like that, man. It's a risk. But if you try you can lay back in your bunk and cry. If you try hard enough you can reach down just like sortin through a box. I can, man. I really can.

"I picture it in my mind. A bunch of spools of thread, you know what I mean? And I got em and I know what they are and I can pick that one. That's my daughter and if I sit here by myself and nobody's in the house I can start toying with that. That thread is my daughter. It's the binding thing between us. I can start pullin that out in my mind's eye, pullin it out, pullin it out, thinkin about her and I start to get a lump in my chest. My feelings start a lump in my chest, man.

"A couple times a year I get to see her and I start thinking about my feelings for her and my bein gone so much; what does she feel? And what have I done to her? And this and that and build it up and wham! Unless I consciously reach down and touch them feelings, they'll never pop up with me and then they don't bother me.

"Same way with my Old Lady. She's in that box. When I know she's going to come and visit me, that whole week that I know she's going to come I got to pull them feelings up to be half tender with her, otherwise, I just sit there and visit with her like she's just a friend, a buddy. You know what I mean? That just comes from years of bein in here."

Hank: "Man, that ain't normal."

FOR LACK OF LOVE

"Family ties, whatever focus they may take—wife-husband, mother-son, father-children—all take on a significance that is out of proportion to the actual street relationship. This continues throughout the prisoner's stay in confinement. His every waking moment can be adversely affected by a simple quarrel on the phone with his Old Lady.

"Every man's nightmare is a death in the family. A death in a family is a tragedy on the streets, also; however, this time of grief is multiplied for both the prisoner and his family because of restrictions imposed by this particular prison.

"I recently experienced the pain and anger connected with the death of my father. I was pretty fucking mad because of all the changes they put me through when I asked to attend the funeral. It was a real mind-fuck!

"First off, I had to do a lot of sniveling to get permission to go. They do allow a guy to go to deathbed visits and funerals. In fact, they give you one choice—you can take your pick of the two. If you choose to see your mother and father while they are still alive and kicking, then you sign away the right to attend their funeral. That's right—sign the paper saying, 'I won't ask to go to the funeral.' That really sucks!

"Anyway, when my Dad passed away I went straight to my caseworker and asked if I could go. Several months before, my brother and I had made a trip to see him in the hospital in Tacoma. So believe me, it was really a fight to get someone to approve this second trip. It was approved, and I was due to leave at five in the morning.

"I felt pretty bad, but from the time I got the news of my father's death, I never had a minute alone. I had to choke it all down and never shed a tear. I cried inside and that hurts even more.

"When I got up the next morning, I packed up my medicine bag and eagle feather. I also had a nice Indian prayer to say at the church. They cracked my door and I headed for Control. That's like an all-night pig station; it is always open for business. I'm gettin mad just talking about this.

"I was escorted to the Visiting Room to wait for the two guards assigned to be escorts. After a few minutes they came into the Visiting Room with their arms full of chains.

" 'What the hell are these for?' I asked.

"They had cuffs, a waist chain, and leg shackles.

" 'You'll have to wear these while you're away from the Joint.'

"I said, 'You mean every minute? You going to leave them on in church in front of my family and friends?'

" 'Every minute,' he says.

"I had to make a hard decision. I could see my mother and family, especially my little daughter, watching these two sloppily dressed goons lead me into the church and graveyard. You can't even get in and out of the car with all that shit wrapped around you, not without help anyway. It really wasn't hard to decide what to do.

"I said, 'Take me back to my cell and cram those chains in your ass.'

"It took a long, long time to cool down, *months*. My attitude was bad. Anytime I had to talk to a guard or the administration, I would freeze up thinking they each had a part in it. I built the whole trip around the chain into a conspiracy against me!"

This narrative of Delorme's shows how a tragedy in a prisoner's family and the prison's lack of compassion and understanding for a prisoner's feelings can profoundly affect his state of mind. Interrupting the prisoner's line of communication with his family can be shattering. It need not be a death in the family, as Delorme points out.

"It needn't be a death to blow the day, week, or month. The prisoner becomes depressed, nervous, and very irritable during these moments. Life in the house is interrupted for his cellies. His temper becomes short and there is a very real chance that violence may erupt between either he and a cellmate or some other con on the Breezeway who is not ready for any shit from anyone.

"There is a saying in this prison that is used just for these men.

When they start to tell someone about the trouble at home, they have a fifty-fifty chance of hearing, 'Here's a dime. Go call someone that gives a fuck.' This saying is a sure bet to end all conversations of this nature."

THE WEAPON OF LOVE

The clues to the prisoners' worldview in this chapter are revealed in the language he uses to identify those whom he loves. He insists that those who are an extension of him—his *Lady*, his *people*—be accorded the same dignified treatment that he asks for himself. The labels *Lady* and *people* signal this message: in order to impress upon others his personal worth, he bestows upon his family titles that "ennoble" or elevate them—*Lady*, a title of nobility and courtesy and *people*, a title of dignity and exclusivity. "She is my *Lady*. Don't treat my *Lady* discourteously. My *Lady* is very special to me, very important for my survival in here. She reminds me of everything that is good in me; she gives me hope. If there is a possibility that I can change, it will be for her and because of her. And please treat my *people* with respect. Understand that I love them, and that what happens to them can profoundly affect me and how I behave in here."

Love is a central idea in this chapter. Should society—and prison officials, who can only do what society allows—recognize the power and rehabilitative qualities inherent in its many forms, love would make a formidable "weapon" for prisoner reform. Society seems unwilling to extend love to imprisoned men (and women); instead, those who break the laws of society become outcasts. Because society withdraws love, it denies a prisoner his self-respect so that he comes to believe he is worthless; instead of loving himself, he hates himself and turns that self-hatred outward harming others in the process. Society forbids the prisoner to lie in love with his *Lady*; forbids him the natural and human right (some would say God given right) to be loved and comforted by a helpmate. Games of humiliation and divide and conquer are sometimes played by those in charge of the prisoner, to such an extent that he is often driven to turn on his fellow prisoners, forgetting that they are his brothers. And, finally, society denies the prisoner the fair and just treatment that it extends to animals in zoos: he is thrown into a crowded cage with other men in a space so small he cannot protect his private self or spirit. These are but a few examples of society's withdrawal of love from the prisoner.[14]

Over and over the narratives reveal the preoccupation with personal dignity that the prisoner has. He is not willing to give up on this. No matter what happens to him he insists that dignity must be a part of his stance. No injustice or no affront ever convinces him to capitulate. Like Sisyphus he persists, demanding that others recognize that he is a man and, therefore, entitled to being treated as one. His very insistence proves his manliness. He will not be bowed; he will not be intimidated; his spirit will not be broken. Affronts to his personal worth as a human being will continue to be met first by outcries of angry protest and then, if ignored, he will add to his language actions that dramatically and violently demonstrate his hurt and outrage. A man can only stand so much; beyond a certain threshold he can go no further. And yet, in this instance there is something more: the prisoner comes close to begging when he cries out in anguish, "Do what you want to me, but leave my Lady, my people, alone!" Here is something different in his response to indignity, a vulnerability, an Achilles heel. He cannot stand to have those he loves mistreated by prison personnel, therefore, he is willing to accept his captor's conditions in order to spare his *Lady*. This is the closest he comes to capitulating to his "enemy."

The humanity of the prisoner comes into sharper focus when his family is considered. The realization that he loves and is loved and that his ties to and concern for his family connect him to the normal world are threads of hope leading to the possibility of positive change in him that cannot be underestimated. It is a tremendously valuable resource for helping him. The fact that the prisoner's family is overlooked or given little consideration in his rehabilitation is further evidence that society's attitude reveals that a man in prison lacks all the dimensions that define him as a human being.

NOTES

[1]*Dictionary of American Slang,* p. 363.

[2]David Showalter and Charlotte Williams Jones, "Marital and Family Counseling in Prisons," *Social Work,* Vol. 25 (1980), p. 225.

[3]C. S. Lewis, *The Allegory of Love* (New York: Oxford University Press, 1958), p. 4; and Dorothy Sayers, *The Comedy of Dante Alighieri the Florentine,* Cantica II: *Purgatory* (Baltimore: Penguin Books, 1962), pp. 9–71. No man (and poet) better reflects the influence of this synthesis of the heavenly Madonna with the earthly mistress than Dante with his beloved Beatrice, the "God-bearing vessel" from whom he was separated in early life and whose influence on him both in his life and poetry was so profound. Because of his love for Beatrice, Dante achieved a tremendous intellectual and spiritual growth in his personal life, and in his poetry escaped from Hell, transforming himself from a sinner into someone worthy of her companionship in Paradise. See *The Comedy of Dante Alighiere the Florentine,* Cantica II: *Purgatory,* pp. 24–44.

[4]S. C. Cobean and P. W., Power, "The Role of the Family in the Rehabilitation of the Offender," *International Journal of Offender Therapy and Comparative Criminology,* Vol. 22, No. 1 (1978), pp. 28–38. The importance of using families to help rehabilitate prisoners is supported in the following research: Aaron Bindman, "Why Does Rehabilitation Fail?", *International Journal of Offender Therapy and Comparative Criminology,* Vol. 17, No. 3 (1973), pp. 309–324; Barry S. Brown and John D. Spevacek, "Work Release in Community and Institutional Settings," *Correction Psychiatry,* Vol. 17, No. 3 (1971), pp. 35–42; Bob Martin, "The Massachusetts Correctional System: Treatment as an Ideology for Control," *Crime and Social Justice,* Fall–Winter (1976), pp. 49–57; and R. A. Washbrook, "The Homeless Offender: An English Study of 200 Cases," *International Journal of Offender Therapy and Comparative Criminology,* Vol. 19, No. 3(1975), pp. 270–274; and Pauline Morris, *Prisoners and Their Families* (London: George Allen and Unwin, Ltd., 1965).

[5]Most of the narratives in this chapter were collected before the *lockdown* of 1979 and reflect some policies and procedures that were discontinued or modified since that time. In particular, the body searches to which all women were randomly subjected, described in this narrative, were halted through legal proceedings brought about by irate prisoners. Today, 1980, a woman coming into the prison cannot be searched in this manner without a court order obtained by prison officials.

[6]Donald P. Schneller, *The Prisoner's Family* (San Francisco: R and R Research Associates, 1976), p. 77.

[7]"Marital Relationships of Prisoners in Twenty-Eight Countries," *Journal of Criminal Law, Criminology and Police Science,* Vol. 49, No. 1 (1958), pp. 133–139. South American, Asian, and Scandinavian countries, as well as Canada and Russia, have programs for prisoners that allow them furloughs or conjugal visits.

See John Conrad, *Crime and Its Correction* (Berkeley: University of California Press, 1967), pp. 59–171. Mexico is one of the countries that allows conjugal visits, not only for wives, but for sweethearts. In a letter of March, 1981, David W. Maurer wrote to me of his knowledge of Lecumberría Prison in Mexico where he conducted research in the late 1930s: "While Lecumberría Prison is not at all typical of other Mexican prisons, its policies are far in advance of those in the U.S. and most of Europe. In this prison it is recognized that (1) men and women must have a normal sex life, (2) that in this process, the dignity of both parties must be respected, and (3) that prostitutes should be rigorously excluded. This policy applies to both men and women in the Federal prison. Conjugal visits are permitted once or twice a week and the women line up at the prison gates in the early evening. Everything from Indian women with papooses on their backs to women in high fashion dress, obviously from the upper middle class, can be seen there. Either wives or sweethearts are allowed in. The women stay all night and leave about 7 A.M. Of course, they can bring in food and other supplies. There is very little search for contraband. As the women enter and leave the prison, it is an impressive sight, for a woman must love a man a great deal to sleep with him in prison. All guards stand at attention with their hats in their hands, showing the women total respect and courtesy. Any man who makes a cat-call or disrespectful remark is dealt with by the convicts and guards alike. Lecumberría was, at the time I was there, the only good prison in Mexico, but it was remarkable in its treatment of convicts. At that time, there was also something of this spirit in certain prisons in Denmark and Sweden, and I spent some time in Lecumberría with Jacques Monnard (a hard-core criminal) who had killed Leon Trotsky. He told me that the Russian prisons were even more humane, but I suspect that he had never heard of the Gulag Archipelago." See also David W. Maurer, *Memoirs of an Argot Hunter* (in press), Chapter entitled, "Durance Vile." Quoted with permission of the author.

[8]Laura J. Bakker, Barbara A. Morris, and Laura M. Janus conclude that "marriage seems to be the relationship most vulnerable to deterioration during imprisonment [that] 25 percent fewer wives of first term prisoners were still visiting after three years." "Hidden Victims of Crime," *Social Work*, Vol. 23 (1978), p. 144.

[9]Wolfam Rieger, "A Proposal for a Trial of Family Therapy and Conjugal Visits in Prison," *American Journal of Orthopsychiatry*, Vol. 43, No. 1 (1973), p. 118.

[10]In a study conducted in 1956, Daniel Glaser found that 71 percent of parolees with family ties were successful on parole, as compared to 50 percent of those without family ties. *The Effectiveness of a Prison and Parole System* (New York: Bobbs-Merrill Co., 1969), p. 366. Similarly, in 1976, Norman Holt and Donald Miller found that "only 50 percent of the 'no contact' inmates completed their first year on parole without being arrested, while 70 percent of those with three visitors were 'arrest free' during this period." *Exploration in Inmate-Family Relationships* (Sacramento, Calif.: Research Division, California Department of Corrections, 1976), p. 26.

[11]"A Proposal for a Trial of Family Therapy and Conjugal Visits," *American Journal of Orthopsychiatry,* Vol. 43, No. 1 (1973), p. 188.

[12]David Showalter and Charlotte Williams Jones, "Marital and Family Counseling in Prison," *Social Work,* Vol. 25 (1980), p. 225.

[13]"Punishment for Whom? The Prisoner or His Wife?" *International Journal of Offender Therapy and Comparative Criminology,* Vol. 19, No. 3 (1975), pp. 275–284.

[14]Yet love is irrepressible, despite this denial, and it appears even in a maximum security prison. Throughout this book examples of love's irrepressibility are clearly evident.

Chapter 8

A PUNK IN THE BUNK

And God said, it is not right that man should be alone; I will create for him a help mate. . . . "[Genesis II] And God created woman — out of man!

M. A. K. Halliday applies the term "anti-language" to the language of prison subcultures and the criminal underworld. Both groups, he states, are "anti-societies." "An anti-society is a society that is set up within another society as a conscious alternative to it. It is a mode of resistance, which may take the form either of passive symbiosis or of active hostility and even destruction."[1] Such antisocieties generate antilanguages, which define "an alternative social reality."[2] This social reality "appears as a distorted reflection of the structure of the particular society from which it derives."[3] The language spoken (antilanguage) is "a counter-reality, set up in opposition to some established norm. . . . Social meaning will be seen as oppositions: values will be defined by what they are not, like time and space in the Looking Glass world (where one lives backwards, and things get further away the more one walks toward them)."[4]

In no area of prison life does the social reality of prisons appear so clearly to be a "distorted reflection" of the established norms of society as in the area of sex. Everything seems reversed, upside down. Men are women; a *turn out* is a debut, a coming-out party celebrating the arrival of "womanhood." Deprived of the presence of women, prisoners respond to the awfulness of their condition metaphorically, both in language and behavior. Parody, irony, and burlesque are mixed with horror and grim humor as the men describe or act out their situation. Worldview is inverted.

369

PUNKS, WOLVES, AND QUEENS

Although all men do not attempt to compensate for the loss of women through homosexual experience while in prison,[5] some men in prison attempt to compensate by creating sex roles that are parodies of sex roles in society, in particular the female role. When members of one sex in a prison are deprived of the company of the opposite sex, they attempt to fill this void.[6] Take men away from women and they will create women out of men, almost in parody of Genesis II.

Duane: "Got to have a punk in the bunk to take care of the house. A punk in the bunk is like a crack in the shack. Yeah, they wash your clothes, they clean the house, make your bed, wipe you off, wash your back, or you wash their back."

Pete: "Goddam near a punk in every bunk in this joint, man. I'm surprised when I find out about a guy cause there's plenty that don't swish around here, and you'd never guess they played the game til you catch em or somebody else tells you, 'Oh, man, that guy's fuckin so-an-so.' "

Hank: "People think that there's one in every house. The streets think you can't walk through this joint without not dealing with em and that's kinda ridiculous. Like guys will come in here, straight johns, and start screwing one of these punks, then they write their Old Ladies and say, 'I can't help it. That's Joint routine.' You know that's crazy. That's not Joint routine. That's not a common thing in here. In fact, I doubt if twenty percent of the population do one or the other."

If men come into the prison already having made the free choice to play the role of women before they entered, they are known as true *queens*. Their situation may be similar to that of Sandy, a transvestite, whose problems center on being one of a few "women" in a male population of about 1400 and whose favors are, as a consequence, in high demand. If not enough true *queens* exist in the population then new "females" are created, or "fashioned," out of the existing male population. Young men or boys new to the prison who are "cute or small"[7] are generally chosen to be *turned out*; that is, fashioned into women through verbal seduction, verbal threat of violence, or homosexual rape. These men-turned-women are not regarded as *queens* but rather as *punks*, or pseudo-homosexuals. Many are *turned out* against their will, generally out of fear of being killed or hurt.

Pete: "Well, I really don't know what to say about the fruitcakes in here. I guess I should say there's not that many ripoffs like there used to be in the old days. Not that many forceable rapes, you know. Guys jumpin off in somebody's path and rippin em off."

Duane: "That saying, 'Shit on my dick or blood on my blade," used to be kind of a standing joke in here but that's just about the way you run it down. It still happens occasionally but it's not a common occurrence, although the fear is still there."

Pete: "The kids that come over here are still scared shitless. That's what they expect to happen to em. They don't beat em up that much, though. When a new guy goes into a cell they probably hit on him. They might end up fuckin him. It happens but I don't see no new guys comin out beat up."

Duane: "There was one kid who came in here last year. I knew what was goin to happen to him, man. He was just a pale, skinny white kid with curly hair. Sure enough, man, a few days later he was walkin down the tier askin to suck people's dicks. Guys were makin him do that and chargin for it. He went in with so-and-so and those guys, and they all fucked him that night, made him suck their dicks, and the next day they came around with him runnin him in the cells. Man, everybody fucked him. They did that to him for a couple of weeks. He finally checked into PC, but he waited, you know. He's over in PC now. He didn't give no resistance to em. He was scared shitless when he come in here. When they said, 'Start suckin,' he went right to his knees."

Pete: "What probably happened to him was he probably went to the wrong people when he came off the Chain. He went into the wrong cell and they started fuckin with him and finally they decided to just take him on cause he was small. But that wouldn't have necessarily happened to him in every cell."

Generally, other men regard *punks* with contempt because "they lack the courage to save their manhood."[8] Paradoxically, even if a young man puts up a battle initially only to be overpowered in a gang rape, the prison population still regards him with contempt in the way that some men regard women who have been raped as being spoiled or contaminated. *Punks* are second only to *stool pigeons* on the bottom of the hierarchy of this prison. A *punk* is thought of as "weak as a woman" and, hence, reviled.

Al: "A Joint punk hasn't any class simply because he's a Joint punk. He is weak, gutless, a piece of shit and all the other names that go along with sell-out of your manhood."

Paul: "I can't get upset about their problems."

Al: "Some of em say, 'Aw, the hell with it. What's an asshole, anyway? I'll shut her back up when I go back out onto the streets, go back to my wife and kids. Be a wife while in here,' or whatever."

Paul: "I think they're probably just insecure weaklings. I don't think they even rationalize. I think they just found a way to keep from gettin hurt, man."

Al: "Yeah, I guess they're just told to drop it and that's it, man. Goes down on him and the fucker just starts suckin. The guy makes a snap decision—black eye or suckin a dick and down on his knees he goes. Once he's done it, what the hell, why not?"

According to Delorme, certain personalities are more likely to be singled out for initiation into "womanhood." His description in this narrative implies that these young men are like "meek maidens," frightened and unsure of themselves.

"I have often wondered about what makes some people get singled out for treatment. I can walk down a line of new men and put my finger on the weak ones.

"I used to have a job of meeting the Chain when it came in on Wednesdays. There was always some I felt sorry for because I knew what kind of people they were. I can talk to some little guy and know right off the bat that he's pussy. It's a lot of things, mostly strength of character, the strength of their personality.

"Some people can just give off a vibration of Good People. They are friendly and talk easy. They smile and can laugh at themselves. They seem healthy is the best description. Another description is that they have the personality of a normal size person. They look you in the eye.

"There is the small guy personality that really sucks. They talk loud, make threats, start fights and are generally just plain assholes because they are small. They can generally get along, too.

"These two small types are able to move into the population

and get along very well. The little asshole will go with the rest of the would-be tough guys and spend most of his time causing trouble around the Joint. He is demanding as hell and thinks the guards are here to follow his orders. The other will make friends very easy. He isn't a threat to anyone. But he also is generally such a pleasant or funny little guy that even the wolves would rather enjoy his company than bother him. These Good People are protected by the population. It isn't a threat by any special group. It's an implied threat.

"Sometimes you talk to these new guys and they look away, or look at the floor. They are nervous as cats. They may talk too loud or too much, or they talk too low. Sometimes, maybe because I'm friendly and at ease with them, one will just sort of move to me and hang by my elbow. He hangs on to everything I say and seems like I'm there to protect him or something. That guy is in trouble unless he backs off.[9] I'll generally pull his coat, explain, but if he's too scared he won't be able to think right for days. These guys are like lambs going to slaughter in some cases. I try hard to put these new people at ease before they go to the cells. I play down all the stories and tell them to just be themselves. I lie some in that I say that no one is out to get them because they're new. Of course, some guys are at ease and fall right in.

"It would be wrong to say that every guy that comes through the gate is attacked if he is small or cute. It just doesn't work that way at all. The people that do these things seem to be able to spot something in a person that tells them to go to work on them. This is like singling out the weak or lame in a herd and running them down even though there are smaller animals in the herd. Of course, it isn't hard to see the character defects in a man if you talk to him for awhile, but some of these people use a lot of psychology in their conquest and more guys are talked into giving it up than are actually forced."[10]

Strength of personality takes the place of physical strength in some instances and serves both to win the admiration of the population as well as ward off attack from *wolves*.

Duane: "Look at Little Man Johnson. He's the smallest man in the Joint and no one's fuckin him. If he had to get up on a box to punch you in the nose, he'd do that. He wasn't no bigger than a

fuckin minute when he first come in here. Loudest little sonovabitch in the Joint. He was a pretty little blonde boy."

Gene: "Yeah, he'd stand up for himself, man. People probably
protected him like a pet around here when he first come in."

Duane: "He stood up for himself around here."

Gene: "I think he was seventeen when he came to Walla Walla."

Gang rapes are, in part, a reflection of displaced hatred and
desire for revenge against society and everything in it which the
men regard as unjust and repressive. This inmate, in another part
of his narrative, bitterly denounces society, which he states severely and unjustly punished him for using drugs. "I never wanted
to hurt anybody. All I wanted was to feel good and they threw me
in prison." Today he is a tough and ruthless *wolf* preying on new
men who come in on the *Chain*. He describes his technique in this
narrative. The victim of this attack ended up on the Third Floor,
the psychiatric unit of the prison.

Cal: "One night they move a guy in my cell. There was me and
my two friends livin in a cell in Seven Wing and they moved the
guy in. I knew he was weak. I'd known him from Chehalis on up
but I didn't know if he was a homosexual.

"So, you know, we're talkin about it and I'm talkin to my cell
partners, 'Well, what do you think? Do you think we should bum
this guy for a fuck?' And they said, 'Well, it's your cell. Whatever
you want to do.' What they were really sayin was, 'Yeah, you bum
him for a fuck and we'll bum him if he'll go.' That's what it
amounted to.

"I didn't really know the guy; I didn't want to come right out
and ask him so I wrote him a note and I was layin on the bottom
bunk. I'd already talked it over with these two other guys and we
were just kids and it was kind of a joke. It was something to do
more than anything else, really.

"So I wrote the guy a note and I handed him the note and I
waited around three or four minutes and it said, 'A cop on a fuck
and if it's O.K., let me know.' He writes and it says, 'Yeah, if you
want to.'

"This is really funny. So we jumps up and we get to talkin, man,
and they say, 'You're not gonna fuck him on my bed,' and I said,
'You're not gonna fuck him on my bed, either.' We got goin back

and forth about how we were gonna fuck this guy and we'd heard stories about how you just cut a hole in the blanket, you know, big enough to get your dick through and you just lay it over and fuck him with the blanket. Finally, I said, 'No. Hell, if I'm gonna fuck him, we'll just fuck him on the bed. To hell with the blanket.' So the guy gets down and he was like . . . he wasn't really a homosexual. He was just weak. I mean, I think he probably liked it but it was a pain."

Gene: "Was he ugly, too, like the other guy?"

Cal: "Yeah, he was another ugly one. He was scared, too."

Gene: "If he'd said, 'No,' would you take it anyway?"

Cal: "I guess he must have thought so. Anyway, I get down there and I nail the guy, and the other two cell partners nail him and I went back for seconds. I was terrible. So the next night we come in for count and he isn't there for count and we found out he had checked in to the Third Floor. And that was the end of him. I never seen him again."

Wolves and *pimps* (*daddies*) vociferously deny that they are homosexuals and brag that they *pitch* but do not *catch*. They define homosexuality only in terms of the female role.[11] These men force themselves upon the new and inexperienced men who come in off the *Chain*.[12] They employ every tactic a "wolf" outside the prison would use to seduce a real woman. The prison *wolf*, however, unlike his counterpart beyond the walls, resorts to rape if seduction or threat efforts fail. Some of these men come into the prison with records of rape against real women, giving rise to the hypothesis that the *wolf* in prison is more intent on violence against the weak than on achieving sexual gratification.[13] Studies show that rape against women also follows this violence-intent pattern. Delorme is speaking.

"You're right about the wolves. They get pretty mad if they are called 'queer.' I notice that, also. Most of the guys I know who are active inside the prison at this game I wouldn't care to know on the streets. The one daddy I told you about is a rapist. He has lost count of all the women he has raped. I know of several others who are rapists on the streets and play the queens in here.[14] These guys are all sick. Just offhand, I can't think of any pimps or wolves that would be known as homosexuals. Another thing; these wolves are the nicest people if you are physically strong and on their level; otherwise you are not human and should be kicked around. The weak people were born to be their victims."

This *wolf* openly admits that violence against the weak and the desire for power over others were important reasons for his sexual attacks.

"After I was here a while I started fuckin punks. I used my prick as a weapon is what I done, man. It was more or less a conquest, you know. I seen myself as a certain kind of guy and I had to get in on it. [the game] That was part of it—knocking off the ole broads. I just didn't give a fuck. I'd strike out for homosexual experiences. I'd fuck anybody that pulled down his pants. Just anything, man, to get away from the frustrations and tensions.

"I talked a little shit at first and then because I thought it was the thing to do, I did it, more or less out of wanting to be accepted because before, the thought of fuckin a man had never even appealed to me, but I did it out of acceptance because it seemed like all the heavies around the penitentiary fucked punks. Another thing; I was naive then. A lot of em talked about it that probably never did it. But it was a big joke and things like that.

"I had a job workin in the kitchen makin three dollars a day. That was real status, man. I had tight rolls and a punk and I was uptown. That's the way it was. Oh yeah, and bonaroo clothes. The clothes had to be bonaroo.

"So I got me a fruiter and he was an ugly motherfucker. He was terrible, man, but I felt like, you know, I guess I felt like I had somebody under my control. I made him stay away from me. I met him in the movie. Well, you know, I liked it. Part of me wants to block that out, now that I think about it. I fucked probably once or twice a week; got so I did it every time I got a chance. It got good to me. I really liked it."

Common belief among strictly heterosexual men in the prison is that men who use *punks* eventually become *punks*, although *wolves* vociferously deny this.

Gene: "We have a sayin here, 'If you pitch, you're eventually gonna catch.'"

Duane: "Pitch and catch is the same thing as top and bottom."

Gene: "When you're pitchin it means you're doin the male shot.

If you're catchin, you're the broad. Well, in here we call it pitchin and catchin, and the thing is it seems that all the Joint daddies, the big time pimps and wolves after a while, they always end up catchin. They always end up bein a little gay themselves."

Duane: "If you're pitchin, you're fuckin one of the punks. But we say if you're doin that, if you come out of the closet enough to fuck another man, then eventually you're goin to do the other. He's goin to be fuckin you, too. So you'll be flip-floppin. That's what you call that, flip-floppin."

The following narrative of a former *daddy* gives some insight into why some men may choose to remain *punks* once they have been *turned out* in this prison, although it is important to remember that once initiation takes place, it is nearly impossible to be anything else. Notice that in this man's statement on *pitching and catching*, he does not consider himself a homosexual.

"There's been a couple of individuals that I've seen come in to the institution who weren't accepted by many people, who weren't gettin much attention, and that was their way of getting the attention that they wanted, or of being accepted by someone instead of being a complete outcast.

"Having lived with one guy that was bisexual in the institution, I know for a fact that that guy sought male attention while here because he was lonely. That was his way of reaching out to other people, to make him feel like he was O.K., to be accepted. The guy was a super lonely person. He celled with me for a while when we were over in Six Wing before I even had any idea of what his real trip was. Until he drove on me one day and said, 'Hey,' you know, 'take care of your problems here, man.' I'd been here for a while and my frustration level was pretty high and I was about ready for anything at that particular point. And so I had dealings with him for a while. He just wanted affection more than anything, you know, attention.

"One of the reasons I got out of the game, why I chose not to participate in that particular thing was because 'what goes 'round, comes 'round,' with that particular thing. So it wasn't my thing because when everybody knows your business, the Man knows your business, too, and it's not one of those things you want to be made public. I didn't, and at that time if you got caught up in any kind of homosexuality, the institution would write a letter home and I sure didn't want my wife getting a letter saying, 'Your husband was caught in a compromising situation,' and they ain't saying if you're pitching or catching."

Interviews with the inmates point out that the *queens* look, think, dress, and act like women; some even sit like women. The *queens* seek affection from the men and play up to them in the same way that real women do. Delorme points out that "they like to be kissed and get a hug every now and then, the same way you do, I suppose."

"Candy is a big tall white broad just as skinny as a rail and looks like a woman, but a straight up and down woman. Got nice cheeks, though; she's got nice cheeks. We check her out goin into the shower. Ain't got a feather on her is all I can say. Some of em wear bikinis when they go in to the shower, little bikini panties so you can't see their stuff. They all get back in a steaming corner, get to washin and scrubbin up and taken care of business.

"I swear to God, sometimes you see a broad walkin in the wing with panty hose on and a short skirt . . . it's a helluva sight, I'll tell you, and she has better legs than those goddam women case-workers that was walkin around here."

"Girl watching" is a humorous tradition carried on by many of the heterosexual men in the prison.

Tim: "I think after you're here a while, they all start lookin good. I was standin out there in the Breezeway this morning checkin Candy out carryin her needlepoint around."

Gene: "I checked her out at breakfast. I was checkin those hips out. Looked pretty fine. Yeah, she's got hips like a woman."

Tim: "When I came back in 1976 and I saw Candy, I thought, 'Jeez, what have they got, women runnin around inside here now? I never saw any women around here before.' "

Some *queens* are treasured by the population for their feminine demeanor. Delorme explains.

"We have another little queen in here. She has a lot of class and a steady lover. People, including me, are just naturally protective towards her. The guards beat her up real bad and people were more upset about that than their own lumps and bruises. She is like a little lady — quiet and shy, friendly, cute — all you could ask for in a queen. She is never called a punk ... well, the guys who just have a thing against these people will call them punks, cocksucker, all the typical redneck terms. Most of the guards hate the queens."

Queens, whose status is considerably higher than *punks,* fall into two categories that correspond very much to the traditional belief in the free world that only two kinds of women exist—good and bad. In this narrative Delorme contrasts the differences in *queen* behavior.

"Sandy has class and in describing the way she acts and dresses and conducts herself, I think you will see what class is all about in prison. First, if she came walking down the tier right now and my cell door was open I couldn't talk her into dropping in for a quick freebie; nor could I scare her into it. She has a man and she wants to be faithful just like his wife. That's one form of class.

"Sandy is proud of her looks and takes care of herself like any self-respecting woman would. She dresses as well as she can. She isn't too gaudy with the makeup. Most of the time she wears the normal clothes like pants and top, but on what I call her cute day, she puts on more feminine clothes, maybe even a skirt and pantyhose. Ain't bad, either. This seems to be the pattern for all the queens. Sandy is all part of the class thing, wouldn't be caught dead in work boots or dirty clothes. When we look at a queen for the first time, we either say she has class or she's a dog. So the idea of class comes from personal appearance as well as personal conduct or character.

"A lot of queens [who are dogs] have extremely dirty mouths, and some of the twisted shit that comes out of their mouths is even hard for the average convict to take. They are also just plain obscene at times and like to make gestures like grinding their ass if they catch you looking at them, or running their tongues around in their mouths in a suggestive way. Somehow the word got around over the years that this wasn't all that cool and if a bitch has any class at all, she won't do it."

Dogs are *queens* who by being disloyal to their *daddies* bring about violence or threat of violence in homosexual relationships in the prison. Again, similarity with the stereotypical image of the "bad" woman in conventional society and the consequences of her behavior are unmistakable. Infidelity and duplicity bring about gossip from the prison community, loss of face for the *daddy*, and an end to the relationship. Delorme continues:

"Prisoners have killed and been killed over queens. But it isn't like I decide to go out and just take a queen away from someone by killing the daddy. What generally happens is the bitch has started to flirt and she may even fall in love with some guy. They will sneak around the Joint just like some wife out on the make in the real world and her new boyfriend will meet her in some secret place like the back room of one of the clubs or down in the movie. The movie is dangerous because her other daddy will have friends who will snitch her off. And this will go on until a fight comes up. What will happen first is that she will get a good ass kicking and she better straighten her act up and fast or she will land in the hospital.

"The daddy, who will also be the pimp, has to make a decision because the whole Joint will be laughing at him and he'll be out of business if he can't handle this one bitch. If he doesn't make a strong move one way or the other, the bitch will just up and move out of the cell and in with her new lover. Or she might kick her pimp's ass and move him out of his own cell. This happens every now and then.

"Becky recently beat up her old man and he is now in protective custody. People around here didn't like him, anyway, and he was due for a challenge because Becky is sort of a fox as queens go. She also likes to be popular and have other friends and her old man was too crazy behind her fine little ass. He wouldn't even let her sell any pussy. That's crazy, or would you call it love? In any case, she solved the problem in the only way she could and saved his miserable life doing it because the wolves were out to down him for good."

A *queen* who is regarded as a *dog* may be compared to a loose woman in conventional society. She betrays her man and causes trouble by creating jealousies, which may break out into violence, whereas a *classy queen* may be compared to a good woman in free society. She is faithful to her man, is careful of her conduct and personal appearance, takes good care of her man and his *house*, and recognizes her obligation to make her man happy.

Sandy explains how she feels about her relationship with her man.

"I stay very faithful to him. I'm going to respect and go by his code, cause that's the thing in the house, to go by your man's code. My job is to keep his house clean and to make him happy, which I don't mind cause I'm in love with the guy and he loves me. There ain't nothin we wouldn't do for each other. So as far as stayin loyal, I stay very loyal."

There are differences between *wolves, pimps,* and *daddies.* A *daddy* often becomes genuinely attached to his *kid,* whereas a *wolf* does not. The *pimp,* on the other hand, is a businessman. Delorme explains:

"A wolf, as a rule, isn't interested in a relationship with a punk or a queen. He just wants to make sure he gets some of the action, pussy. Also, and probably most important, they prey on the newer men, sort of like getting a cherry or virgin. A wolf can also become a regular daddy. It does happen but it doesn't last long. He also likes money or dope and will make a deal for his punk at any time.

"The daddies generally get very attached to their kid and will get violent to protect them. Neither daddies or wolves are to be classified with the pimp who is in the business strictly for the bucks. The daddy with his kid, generally some mousey-looking little punk who couldn't make it on his own for a minute, will be the couple who have set up housekeeping. Of course, all the queens call their pimps 'daddy' but it doesn't mean the same thing.

"Pimps are out for the bucks and, of course, it is a status symbol for blacks, just like on the streets. Daddies or jockers generally don't share their little sweethearts but now and then if they get in a bind, the kid will be put out to cop a few joints, give head or sell his shitter, until they have some money.

"The wolf doesn't give a fuck about anything or anyone but his own pleasure. Basically, it's the same with the other two but not to the same extent. The wolf could care less about keeping a punk if some dope comes along. 'Go for what you know.' If he has busted a nut in the punk he is ready for some better action on the Breezeway."

The technique a *wolf* uses in wooing a *kid* is masterful and shows great insight into human psychology. *Wolves* parody traditional man-woman courtship patterns in conventional society. Delorme points out the difference between a *kid* and a "small cute guy."

"The thing about the small cute guys shouldn't present any problems for you to understand. It really boils down to a guy being either a punk or not a punk. You can't hide a weakness like that in here. Any homosexual tendencies, latent, will be spotted and rooted out by someone.

"Can't say that I don't know how it's done because I do. Just the same way you nurture a girl. It isn't obvious at all. Even the kid doesn't know what is going on. He thinks he has a super friend and the wolf will play on this and may take months before he makes a move. The final move may be with the use of dope or get the kid drunk, and that night the 'friend' will end up taking him off. Once it's done, the wolf, or friend, will promise not to tell a soul what went down that night.

"Of course, the kid has been broken in so there is no use trying to back up, so there is no use trying. The reasoning and logic could make a nun drop her panties, if they wear them. The real trouble starts if a kid tries to stay straight even after he gave it up. Then he will get his little ass slapped around. Sometimes that's all it takes, or some threats of violence and gang rape. The last item will generally make a good punk out of him.

"You have to treat the kid like a real little man while at the same time you are playing on and drawing out the woman instincts in him. The whole thing takes so many different forms. It's hard to believe sometimes that a kid doesn't actually know what is going on. The thing that lulls him is his belief that since he didn't get beat up and raped the first week, he might be safe. And his new-found friend hasn't even hinted at anything sexual or teased him about his looks. In fact, the friend will profess his hatred for homosexuals and other 'wolves.' Everyone else in the Joint knows and watches like a father waiting for a baby to be born. Can you get the picture now?

"It's so subtle most of the time. At least it used to be. This place did get a little crazy over the last few years and some of the art went out of the game. Peer pressure regulates this game. Once some form of sanity returns to this population and they begin to frown on the caveman shit again, then the finesse will come back into play. It's similar to wartime. Some armies go into a town and while they are there all the women are raped. When things are more settled and order is restored, then the romances start and the courting as a means to the same end; just takes a little longer, that's all.

"O.K., I'm talking about young men with obvious feminine characteristics. Not so obvious to you, of course. Usually very quiet and sort of shy. This shows that they are unsure of themselves and are mixed up and afraid, probably because they are latent homosexuals and it is bothering them now. The younger men — under twenty-five — are generally still mixed up and still haven't dealt with their problem. It's even better for the wolf if the kid has been raised by only a mother because a mother tends to hold back the manhood in a youngster for as long as she can, and so the sexual identity is still a problem. These emotions can be worked like clay.

"These kids, because of the sexual thing, actually enjoy attention and compliments. They don't mind being called pretty or cute, and as long as everyone is careful not to spook him, he will begin to flirt, giggle, and *be* cute. The rest just falls into place, and we have a class punk.

"Now the other small cute guys, they are really not worth all the hassle for the wolf if it is obvious that they have their shit together and their pants on right. They are comfortable around the rest of the men and fit right in. They are rowdy or just plain normal. They don't drop their eyes or get nervous, except in a humorous sort of way. Some big bruiser might tease him, which doesn't bother him, or make a playful grab at him. Probably he will yell and duck around a table and call the guy a big ape or big cunt, and threaten to tear his head off.

"This type could be forced, but probably only once. And he might stick a knife in your back later because he will know how to take care of himself. Of course, he might just go crazy, or he might kill himself. Also, the person who forced him will not be looked on too favorably by the friends this little guy has made. I say 'little guy' and not 'kid' because that's what people will call him or refer to him as, if they don't know his name. He will be respected by all, and that will show, the respect. If I could put these two types side by side for you, it would be very clear."

AFFECTIONATE RELATIONSHIPS

Relationships sometimes occur in the prison that look very much like genuine love relationships, many of which are of long duration. These couples are devoted to each other and tend to keep to themselves, living like conventional married people in the free world. These relationships serve positive emotional, psychological, and social functions, helping the men survive their prison experience with a minimum of psychic scarring. Few heterosexual men in the prison, unless in constant touch with devoted and faithful wives on the outside, have such emotional security.

"There is a difference in the homosexual relationships that do develop between two people where the tie is love, or a super-strong friendship bordering on love. And yes, they do set up housekeeping that could be said to simulate a home-style condition minus the kids. This happens quite often and for the most part these couples are left strictly alone to live the way they want to live. They are generally very quiet and are inseparable as they travel about the institution. Companionship and protection is what they give to each other. They will hustle all the small things that are considered luxuries and they share everything like a small family or married couple. And often they do get married. This will include a reception and cake.

"The last wedding I went to in here was several years ago. Artie was the bride and John was the groom. Both were weight lifters and that's how they met and so they started living together. They worked in the kitchen and I worked there, too.

"We used to make pruno every weekend and about thirty of us would always get down and get drunk. So one day these two sprung the news on us. They said, 'Man, we think we'll get married.' What they were hinting was, 'Why don't you guys give us a party?' So it went from there.

"The following weekend after most of the workers in the kitchen were gone, we stayed behind and brought out the ole cake and the booze and the ice and the food and we started having a regular little party. There wasn't any ceremony, no prayers or anything like that, but even the cops were in on it, a couple of Old Timers. They showed their good will by watching over us. The high point of the wedding was that Arty didn't want to drink too much because she had to go lift weights, but John said, 'Aw hell, I don't want to leave.' So she stomped off in a huff and left the groom behind. He ended up in the Hole—he got caught weaving down to his cell—and in the doghouse with her."

Columbus B. Hopper, a civilized voice advocating conjugal visits for married men in prison, believes that sexual problems in prison result from a "failure of the authorities to understand sex," that the needs of prison inmates are more emotional than biological. The men, he states, suffer from deprivation of affection. It is the lack of this important and natural need that makes prison inmates so vulnerable to homosexual experience in prison, since "homosexuality . . . gives testimony to the fact that humans can meet their emotional needs with persons of the same sex." Although conjugal visits (or furloughs) do not help unmarried inmates, he believes that such policies would allow all men to retain an outlook that is "normal in perspective."[15]

PIMPING AND HUSTLING IN PRISON

Some *queens hustle*; that is, play the part of prostitutes in the prison. Most of these are *pimped*—owned by *daddies* who send them out into the population to earn money. This activity, of course, parallels what happens on the streets in the free world with real women. Although male prostitution is a growing phenomenon in the free world, the model for prostitution and pimping in this prison is a parody of the female prostitute-male pimp tradition in conventional society. Like the girls on the street in the free world, the *girls* who operate without *pimps* in the prison often are in greater danger of violence than those who are owned.

"All the hustling in here is done the same way. Either the girls are loners or else they are hooked with a daddy. The loners really take their chances. They are constantly subject to being ripped off one way or another. They are always in danger of being raped or beaten and forced to go with someone. It is always the loners that end up getting killed when someone falls in love and the kid shines him on."

The *girls* work very hard for their *pimps* but seem to receive little in return for their labor.

"There's a lot of singles runnin around the wing. They usually got daddies somewhere. They're like them street hoes. They're not really on their own. They got daddies and they do make the bucks. Candy is one. Sherry is another. They all got names like that. They do a lot of business in the cell blocks and the dive off into your cell for a price and give you a head job or whatever you want and you pay em off and they shoot off down the line and then they hit someone else, see. And they just do that all day and in the evening. They make the bucks and then they give the bucks to their daddies. He buys em what they need and he gives em dough so they always got money."

Some prisons separate known homosexuals from the rest of the population as officials believe that these "women" are troublemakers. This prison does not. Some heterosexuals despise the homosexuals, but in general, the prison population is more tolerant of true *queens* than the prison guards.

"Pimping is a safe business in prison. The girls are respected that work for a pimp and behave themselves; they're not sluts. If they do screw around, they get their butts kicked. They flirt but just to get business.

"The cops allow the pimps and whores to operate in the open in here. They will let them in and out of the cells and turn their heads. They also turn away from the bad stuff like rape and assault.

"Rape on a man has the very same or worse affect than on a woman. Even if the man is a homosexual, gays are people, too, no matter how strange they are. They have the same feelings as we do; they hurt and even have pride and self-respect of a sort. If they are assaulted and raped, they have nothing and may very well commit suicide or go insane. It's very sad. I see the girls that are with the better pimps as much more secure and happier people, with their little purses and fancy hairdo's. They don't hang their heads or lower their eyes."

Generally, the pattern in the prison follows the free world pattern—most of the *pimps* are black and keep white *girls* in their *stables*. The following narrative describes an unusual situation in this prison—a white *pimp* with black *girls*.

"Hustlin a whore in here is no different than on the streets. You do your job as a good pimp and they will do their job as a good whore and make the bucks.

"There was this dude named Harry. His girls are gone now. He had two bitches over there, both black bitches, but he thought he was King Shit, I'm tellin ya. Harry talked more shit than the law allowed about his bitches. He'd say, 'Man, I got some bitches! My hoes get out and make the dough, make the dough.' His ole rag-tag broads he had, they weren't worth two cents, for chrissake. You couldn't sell them sonovabitches for a coke. I guess they hustled around a little bit. They give up a lot of head, you know, but I don't know . . . as hoes go, they weren't worth a bag of snakes. They looked like a bag of snakes! Both them bitches were ugly!

"Anyway, he was proud of em, you know. And I know he put em out on the streets during the day. They hustled the wings and I didn't see em out there in population that much; mostly hustled in Six Wing. And he run em out, man. He kicked em out of the house. And he works, see. He works at the Engineering Department bringin home the bacon so he had plenty of money to keep them hoes in zuzus and wham-whams. That's assorted sundries and candies and stuff.

"He was good to em; give em a place to live. He was one of them weirdos. He was a white dude about fifty years old. Very strange to see a white dude livin with blacks in here.

"So he had his ole harem over there in Six Wing and he put them hoes to work during the day. They scuffled around. As long as they were bringin home the bucks they can stay, but if the broad fucks off and gets lazy and fat; if she doesn't want to get out and get down, well then he hands her a yellow slip. You either kick her ass, get her to straighten her act up or run her ass off, or sell her to somebody that can handle her."

The most famous *pimp* in the prison is Tall Tim, a living legend. Tall Tim actually supplies *girls* to *pimps* and does little or no *pimping* himself. He is a type of white-slaver, since he deals only in white *girls*.

"You always see Tall Tim at the movies. See, everybody goes to the movies, gettin all ready, man, and the flicks start and you always gotta check Tall Tim sittin there. He sits pretty tall in the saddle.

"He's a big black dude, fancy dresser and he's always got these little white broads sittin with him. Everybody will walk by, check em out and he sits there like a king, you know, big rooster in a barnyard. Just be smilin, bowin, talkin shit. You know what I mean? He's got his suit on and a little Stetson hat, man. Boy, he'd be dressin down for a motherfucker—that's what he'd say. And he'd come on down to the ole movie, man, and he'd bring his hoes with him. Looks like he just left his Cadillac parked at the curb or some damn thing, and he'd strut his stuff around there for a while, man, and then sit down. In a couple of weeks he'd have a couple of new ones. He'd done sold those. Sell em for a hundred bucks a piece or some damn thing, depending on what they looked like.

"He makes the bucks by gettin em prepped and ready and sellin em for hard cash instead of gettin out hustlin. They learn how to dress and they learn how to act, and they learn how to make the dough, and by the time he's ready to sell em, they're worth a few bucks.

Very high prices have been paid by one man to own another in this prison. Stories circulate about this. Some say, for example, that as high as five hundred dollars has been paid for a particularly attractive *girl* to Tall Tim. In prison, Tall Tim reveals his entrepreneurial talents as a middleman supplying *girls* to *Joint pimps. Pimping* is not only carried on by individuals, but by certain clubs who buy a *girl* and put her to work not only sexually, serving the needs of the members of the club and selling herself to others at their bidding, but also keeping house for club members.

Bill: "For instance, take Tall Tim. Tall Tim paid two hundred bucks for that punk. Tall Tim is one of the pimps we're talkin about. Big black dude."

Gene: "Yeah, must stand about six foot four and weigh 280–290 pounds."

Bill: "He's always got a couple white ladies with him, Joint ladies."

Gene: "He went and paid one of the clubs here something like three hundred dollars for a punk. Anyway, it's just like white slavery going on here for a while. And people are still doin it. People are still paying money for a punk. I mean, rather than just have em sell any pussy, you can own it!"

Bill: They made a lot of money for some club or organization at one time or another for a while. Sandy, for example. I know for a fact they used to have a thriving business going over in the so-and-so club when she first came in."

Gene: "Yeah, if you had five dollar scrip, you could go over and get satisfied."

Sandy tells about what has happened to her since she has been in prison. Although asked about her tenure with Tall Tim, she declined to talk much about her experience with him.

"I realize how young I was, man, and how cute, and I knew I was goin to come here. I've always been a queen cause that's the way my parents raised me,[16] but I knew that just coming here I'd have to give in, come out of the closet, or go to PC.

"I didn't have nobody. I didn't have no people here. I came here, I got in a cell with some other guy. He and me was hooked up together. That night I came out to chow and I was up in the library and there was a little guy that tried to put a jacket on me. And we went down to the club and he told the president there that I was a problem as Sandy. And I told him, 'If there's a problem, it's what you're creatin.' And all this time he's goin around tellin em bum stuff about me and I wanted to do something about it.

"But I realized the fact that ladies don't go around and start stuff, you know. So I had to hang on to my moral code, be a lady, which I always have been. If people hit on me, then I ain't got no choice but to hit em back to protect myself. As far as fightin and violence, that ain't me, really. I'm supposed to keep passive and be like a lady. I always have tried to keep that moral code. But bein in a penitentiary, it's kinda hard.

"Every day you got people that cap on you, call you all kinds of sluts, homosexuals. I mean just every name you could think of verbally in the book. But there are times that it gets to you so bad that you gotta let it loose some place sooner or later. You're here . . . what can you do? You ain't got no other dessert but to hit somebody, you know, to get rid of your anger.

"When I went to Shelton I stayed under cover cause at that time I was only seventeen, my first conviction, second degree burglary. I got three years for it and I'd heard stories of the tank, which you're probably aware of. You hear stories about the penitentiary, you know. If you go there you're goin to be poked and punked off and maybe be killed or beat up because of what you are, so that's why I stayed under cover.

"I knew ahead of time that I was goin to come here, that I wasn't goin to have no alternative but to be what I really was. I came here wearin tight pants cause I knew I was goin to have to give it up to somebody.

"Well, naturally, I didn't like the idea of being pimped off and all that stuff. But O.K.; when the guy was gettin short, he sold me to somebody for two hundred dollars. No. I take that back—three hundred dollars. Well, if he'd a waited for a little bit longer, he'd a got five hundred bucks cause the guy was fixin to offer five hundred.

"As I was sayin, I was sold to this guy and that was a mental mind trip. The guy was black and I'm kind of a racial person since I come from Texas and it's very racial down there compared to this state. And there was a little mind play to take the guy for his money. Well, when I went there I was supposed to work my way back to make the guy really argue with me and make him want to get rid of me so they'd take him for the money. O.K. So we took him for the money.

"He had another queen. I couldn't stand living with another queen cause a man can't have two ladies. That's totally out of whack, you know. Well, naturally, me and her was always arguing and bickering cause I couldn't stand her.

"The guy was goin out to MSB and so he sold me to another black guy. Well, this guy, man, I finally got tired of his shit. He didn't want me to pimp and go to school. The idea was that the guy was black, you know. I couldn't stand it, man. He'd try to run my life and tell me what to eat and what not to eat; what to do and what not to do, and I got tired of that shit and I finally told the man, 'I might be a queen, but I'm callin you out now cause I'm tired of your shit. The only way you're goin to stop me is to stab me and by the time you get that knife out of your sheath, you're a goner cause I'll down your ass.' And I had one of the clubs backin me up. Well, he wasn't goin to let me out of the house, so I used my head a little bit—used finesse. But anyways, finally he let me go the pill-line. Well, I never came back, you know.

"I normally don't mess with narcotics but I was so tense and uptight I had to get away from reality at the time so I smoked a couple of nickels of weed. Well, naturally, that made me feel a little more at ease.

"I moved into the club. I made it clear that I was only goin to be there temporary. Finally, another offer came up to me. I really liked this guy . . . I liked his looks. You know, just attractive, and I moved in with him and I've been there about two years now and I don't think I'd ever move from there. I know I wouldn't move.

"My man is the one that calls the shots in the house. Nobody else does it. We got two other guys in there that kinda wear half-pants and half-skirts cause they're not ladies. They don't wear panties, you know. They're just bisexuals. And so as far as the lady that's in the house, I'm the only one that's there. And he calls . . . the man calls the shots."

Delorme points out that the need to feel safe in a hostile environment is the most important of the *queen's* needs in prison, and that everything she does while in prison is meant to assure that safety. Perhaps Sandy's attitude toward herself as a woman appears ultraconservative when compared to contemporary attitudes among many real women in the world, particularly women of the middle class. Like countless real women in history, however, Sandy believes her duty is to be passive and obey her man's code and to keep her man satisfied and happy because what she receives in return — security in a hostile environment — is worth the sacrifice of personal independence and freedom. Many women in society have made similar accommodations with their men, and for the same reasons. Like some real women, however, Sandy, who is obviously spirited and proud, can only stand so much unjust male domination. When power is abusive, Sandy rebels. Although space does not permit more of her personal narrative, she tells us that she has suffered much physical abuse from many of the men in the prison, including the guards, and often defends herself by fighting back. She has been in the Hole twenty-two times. Presumably, other *queens* and *punks* have similar attitudes and experiences. Although they may not all be as spirited as Sandy, survival is uppermost in their minds and determines their particular behavior. Sandy's narrative reveals her great pride in trying to live up to her code as a true lady and she laments her perilous situation in part because it causes her to sometimes set aside her "femininity" in order to protect herself both emotionally and physically. Pride in her feminine behavior may relate to a positive function she and those like her serve for some of the heterosexual prisoners.

HETEROSEXUAL ATTITUDES

Many heterosexual men are tolerant of and even enjoy the *classy queens'* presence and have made efforts to protect them, as well as would-be *punks* from the *wolves.*

Gene: "I ain't got nothin against the girls. Most people don't. They do what they want to do. They don't bother anybody. If they do bother somebody, then they get in trouble. But they're real strange and that's just them, you know. They got to live with themselves and that's a helluva way to have to be. But who's to say what in the hell is right for who? And I think the opinion in here is you're pretty much free to be what you want to be, I guess, other than to be a stool pigeon."

Duane: "The kids that get beat up and fucked, man, it doesn't seem like we hear about them anymore."

Gene: "Well, it quit happenin because the RC got hold of a couple guys that did that. That kinda cooled it because there's enough [punks] in here without beatin up the new kids and rapin em. If a guy don't want to be a punk, he shouldn't be a punk. That was kinda firm in here for a long time and it sorta came back. If he was weak enough where he could be talked out of it, that was fine and dandy. Even threatened out of it, that was fine and dandy. But if the sonovabitch wanted to fight and all four cell partners jumped him and fucked him, then them guys are in trouble. Morals of a sort. Nothing wrong with Joint justice. That, I really approve of."

Duane: "Guy might be able to fight his ass off with one guy but not everybody. That doesn't make him no fuckin punk, and that's dead action."

Gene: "I think that last time that happened . . . I'm not positive what happened to those guys but I know there was some fuckin bloody heads around here. The kid went to PC. He's still over there. Nothin would have happened to him but he was straight, you know, and when they did that to him, he didn't want to face anybody. Course, he felt threatened by them after what happened to him."

Several of the taped conversations collected reveal the men's good natured banter about the real *queens*, particularly the more feminine ones. They talk about how foxy Betty or Janie is, what nice legs Tootsie has, how cute Baby looked one morning coming down the tier in her new blouse, or how neat Mimi looked going to the *carwash* in her negligee. And they joke and laugh about the *dogs*, whom they describe as looking like prizefighters in women's garb, obviously neither pretty nor feminine-looking. In a more serious manner, they talk about their wives and sweethearts in the free world and how they miss the sound of their voices or the smell of their perfume. The need for the presence of women in their midst is so desperate these men accept the *queen* in part because she brings through make-believe a feminine dimension of life into the prison. In women's prisons an attempt is also made to create male in the midst of female. The women imprisoned long for masculinity in their midst in the same way that imprisoned men yearn to be close to femininity. Prison upsets the plan of nature so an attempt, albeit pathetic, grotesque, or horrifying, is made to compensate for this great and tragic loss.

A "WOMENS" PROTEST MOVEMENT

Further similarities between "women" in prison and women in the world beyond the walls manifest in various ways. In addition to being housewives, that is, keeping their men's cells clean, some take in laundry and wash clothes for a quarter a piece, while others have sewing machines and do tailoring. And sometimes the *girls* get tired of having to do this work for the men. Sandy states in this narrative how she hated being owned by a club that *pimped* her and forced her to keep house for them.

"What I didn't like about the club was that they was always sayin, 'Sandy, do this. Do that. Sandy, wash this. Sew that.' I just got tired of their shit, man, and I told em, 'I ain't nobody's fool, you know. Now I don't mind doin to an extent but I don't like bein used and I'm bein used.' "

The women's movement in the United States, which evolved because of grievances against unfair male domination, is paralleled in the prison by a "women's movement" that grew out of a similar mistreatment by men. During the summer of 1977, several near-violent incidents occurred as a result of Tall Tim's methods of buying and selling *girls*. Once he received money for the sale of a *girl*, he ordered her to move back in with him. He did this several times, placing the *girls* in greater physical danger than himself. These actions coincided with the arrival of several *queens* from Seattle who belonged to a politically radical group called the George Jackson Brigade. In response to this problem, the group immediately set about organizing all the *queens* into a club called Men Against Sexism, MAS. The *queens'* main complaints centered around their being bought and sold. They also wanted the freedom to pick their own *daddies* and to keep the money they earned from *hustling*. Before the creation of MAS, the *queens* had been helpless against their enslavement, but as a group recognized by the prison administration, they were able to unite against a common enemy. MAS was disbanded by the officials in 1980.

The women's movement in the United States has often pointed accusingly at the Book of Genesis in the *Old Testament*. Genesis states that because Eve was the first to disobey God and because she urged Adam into disobedience against God, woman must be punished by being subservient to man. K. M. Rogers writes that "this story justified the subjection of women both explicitly and implicitly . . . and provided divinely inspired 'proof' of their natural depravity and inability to control their impulses . . . [and that] the influence of the story of the Fall on the Judeo-Christian tradition can hardly be overemphasized."[17] This influence has throughout the centuries encouraged some men to deprecate and revile women and consider them as objects to be used and abused, as unworthy of being on the same level with them. Certainly, many of the narratives presented here reveal a parody of this attitude on the part of some of the men in the prison towards the make-believe women who live in the population. They are seduced, raped, beaten, forced to please men, often in degrading ways and against their will, assigned the usual drudgeries real women have always been assigned, which most men have disdained doing, and they are reviled and gossiped about, particularly if they are considered unattractive or "bad" women. Only three positive things can be noted about the "women's" situation: most of the men are tolerant towards them provided they are not troublesome, *classy bitches* are protected by the population if they are particularly popular or *foxy*, and the prettiest and most feminine serve as pathetic reminders for some of the men of the normal masculine-feminine dimension in the world beyond the prison.

SORROWS MULTIPLIED

Some men who have become *punks* experience more than a hell on earth in prison in their efforts at survival. Their self-respect gone, they move from day to day being shamed and rebuffed. The following narrative points out that this *punk* has participated in his own degradation and humiliation in his pathetic efforts for affection and acceptance. Reduced to an untouchable, his story is tragicomic.

"This broad was called Big Mamoo and this guy was so ugly. That bitch was so ugly she couldn't even get a goddam daddy! That sucker ran around . . . she had to pay the motherfucker. That S.O.B. was ugly. I mean ugly! And she give up a lot of head, you know. She didn't really make money off it. She was always movin from cell to cell and the guys would keep her in their cell for a little while, just long enough to clean their house, then they'd kick her out.

"What was really funny was that one time I was at work in the kitchen, me and my brother, and this guy come runnin over to the kitchen all in a panic where I was and he said, 'Man, you guys are in trouble. Big Mamoo done moved in your house.' I said, 'Bullshit. Get outa town.' He says, 'No, I'm serious, man. You better check it out before she gets all her shit moved in.'

"I knew she'd been movin around from cell to cell tryin to find a place and me and Jimmy had two empty bunks in our house. I didn't believe him but I went back anyway.

"Big Mamoo was a white dude. He was about forty years old. He was one of them guys . . . he looked like someone who escaped out of Buchenwald or someplace. He had a really heavy beard. He could shave two or three times a day and he'd still have five o'clock

shadow. I mean, not something you'd want to kiss. You know what
I mean? And he wore whites that were always funky from the
kitchen. He was a hard workin bastard.

"And I went back to my house back in Seven Wing, truckin
down the tier. Everybody's laughin. Even the sergeant's laughin,
'Ho, ho, ho. I like your new cell partner a lot.' Then it dawned on
me, man. There must be some truth to what this guy was sayin to
me. I lived on F deck. That's the top tier, the third tier up and I
hustled on down to my house. Christ! There's that sonovabitch
and he was sittin on the shitter back of the house just coolin it. Me
and Jimmy had the funkiest goddam house in the wing and already our house was cleaned up. Man, our beds were made,
everything was all nice and spic and span and the guy was sittin
back there sweatin. That meant there was hard work involved.

"Boy, I was mad! I was burnin up and I says, 'What the hell you
think you're doin? Who in the hell told you you could move into
my house?' and he says real pitiful . . . the sonovabitch was bigger
than me; he outweighed me, and he was just sittin back there and
he says, 'I didn't have any place to move to. Please let me stay and
I'll keep house for you and I'll do this and I'll do that.' I says, 'Man,
you gotta get outa this house.' I says, 'I'm goin back to the kitchen
and if you don't have your shit outa here by the time me and
Jimmy get home, we're goin to throw all your shit over the tier,
and you, too.'

"And then I went back to the kitchen and talked to Jimmy. I told
him, 'But the house is clean.' And Jimmy said, 'Get that sonovabitch
outta our house!' And I was thinkin how neat it would be to always
have a spic and span house and maybe a headjob once in awhile.
Course, I didn't play that shit. I still don't, but I was tempted. But
this sucker was too ugly. You know what I mean?

"So anyway, we had to hold firm on that one. That's the only
time, man. If it would have been anybody else, they coulda stayed.
But not Big Mamoo.

"We came back . . . well . . . I was soft hearted, see. That's why I
told him, 'If you ain't gone by the time we come back . . . ' But hell,
we wasn't supposed to come back for four or five hours. I didn't
have the heart to really kick him right out then. I figured I'd go
over and counsel on him, but Jimmy didn't want to talk about it.

He busted on back to the cell, throwed that big ugly guy outta the fuckin house. She went truckin on down the tier with her bags and baggage, hoofin on out. That was the closest I ever came to bein a daddy.

"Aw shit. Big Mamoo was the movinest hoe in the Joint. The movinest hoe. Everybody only let her stay just long enough to clean the house up a couple of days, give everybody a headjob. No, most of em didn't even use her, man; she'd give you a nightmare! She stunk, she snored, but she cleaned good house. She washed all your laundry. But that was just so she'd have a place to live."

Delorme's comments that follow reveal the contempt the general population feels toward these men who have chosen this manner of accommodation to prison existence.

"Big Mamoo was what is commonly just called a Joint punk. He did what he did just to get by til he got out. No respect for himself. He didn't take care of himself. He didn't do nothing and that's the way guys like that are treated. The population calls them dogs and punks and pushes them around. Treats them like dirt. They're not a man. They're nothing. Not queens, you know.

"There's a lot of special classifications for those guys. They're the ones that have the toughest go as far as that game goes. They bring it on themselves. It's just their own weakness in them to operate like that. They never stand up for themselves. I guess you can just slap them and take things away from them and they take off running. But they're back for action the next day. Somehow they slip and slide and duck and dodge and tuck their tails between their legs at the proper time and they get by. They're survivors. That's the way they pick to make it in here. It's a tough go but it works for them.

"How they live with it, I don't know. It don't bother them much when they get out, I guess. If they meet somebody from the Joint; if they're married and have a family or something, that would be a helluva thing to think about. Probably gives them a reason to stay out cause that old punk ain't been in for several years, so maybe that was the incentive for him to stay out—not having to go back to that and act like that. Who knows?"

And there is a darker, more horrifying side of what happens to those young men whose minds cannot tolerate what they experience when they are forcibly changed from men into women. Delorme talks about his friend who was devastated by such an experience.

"I was telling you about Billy, a friend of mine. Like I said, he was handling the teasing real well at the reformatory, but he was transferred to the state penitentiary. Anyway, he was about twenty-two at the time. I came here shortly after that.

"Billy was already getting moody by the time I got here. Some of the guys were hitting on him pretty regular. He didn't know how to handle it because he knew this type of teasing was serious. He wasn't big enough to make any threats and he didn't want to kill anybody, so he would just sort of hang his head and try to walk away, or if he was in a group he would blush. Either of these moves is bad.

"Eventually, someone—probably those that wanted him—put a jacket on him, saying he was taking it in the ass. So all of a sudden he had a reputation as a punk. People that he thought were his friends started to shine him on. Others started to call him a bitch, or even worse, stare at him and grin or leer.

"I hung in here, of course. I tried to tell him to act normal and quit pouting. He could have toughed it out and the rumor eventually would stop. But he got worse and he was assaulted somewhere along the line. I didn't run around with him so I didn't always know what was going on with him. All of a sudden he ended up on the Third floor.

"When he was raped he went into a slump and started sort of walking with his head down and talking to himself. He quit taking care of himself and became the Joint's Pig Pen like in the Peanuts cartoon. Maybe he tried to find some safety in the other world of insanity. I really don't know. But I do know that there are people in here that only act crazy to make others stay away from them and for the most part it will work. But it won't work if you're a cute young man. A crazy young man is only more defenseless to those who make this their way of life in here.

"So Billy was used by different guys for awhile until he finally ended up on the nutward for good. By this time the convict attendants in the hospital were all using him daily while the free people turned their heads.

"Billy's maximum sentence expired finally, but he stayed on the Third Floor. He aged twenty years before he left here. Billy started out with a three-year sentence and ended up doing more than ten years flat without ever being given a day more than the original three years by the Parole Board. His life was over, his mind was gone, and we can only guess at the hate and resentment that his family has to live with, having their son's life destroyed by this experience."

Thousands of young men in jails and prisons throughout the United States experience this horror each year. Although most somehow resist retreating into madness, they never recover from the psychic damage done to them. It is a paradox that the public is so outraged when men rape women. The demand is that such offenders be sent to prison, yet the rape of men by men in prisons and jails provokes no outcry. Unless a man dies or is killed while in prison or jail, he eventually is released, returning to the streets armed with deep fury and hatred against the society that allowed this to happen to him. How these men make society pay for its cruelty and insensitivity is yet to be documented. This prisoner, without realizing it, reveals that he suffered such an experience years ago.

"And there's things that could be done for a fella instead of just lettin him just sit here gettin madder and madder and then goin and gettin back at the fucker for doin this; you know, ruinin my life. And the kids, the people that you rape and get those sexual things goin, that causes a lot of anger and the only ones that you're goin to pay back is the public cause you won't be able to make a move in the prison cause you'll get killed. So you just take this fuck in the ass. But somebody's goin to pay for it someday. Lots of em out there [in society] are goin to lose their lives, or they're goin to lose their property, and the reason will be that that kid lost his manhood and his self-respect and he didn't have to. I never wanted to let go of my anger. I thought it would sustain me, you know. I thought . . . well, I can't be that bad . . . be a punk."

The language and behavior surrounding prison sex reveals a worldview that is a distortion of normal societal norms. The antisociety slaps society in the face in its response to the deprivation that society imposes upon it. Clearly, prisoners satirize and show contempt for the norms of the dominant culture that devises, diabolically it seems, the forms punishment takes in this and other prisons in the United States. Halliday states that "an anti-language is a metaphor for everyday language," that the anti-language is, "in terms of Levi-Strauss' distinction between metaphor and metonymy, metonymic to society." The antisociety is, in its structure, "a metaphor for society in the same way the anti-language is a metaphor for the language."[18] Prisoner worldview bitterly and harshly condemns society in its counterreality. Stripped of his dignity and self-respect, removed from all that is natural, the feminine dimension obliterated, the prisoner responds in his awful pain and deprivation with a grim, mocking, and twisted parody of what reality actually is. The metaphor of the *punk* is a distortion of the organizing principle of the American economic system. The prisoner is presenting through the metaphor what Daniel Bell calls a "Coney Island mirror caricaturing the morals and manners of society."[19] From this perspective, rape (exploitation) of *punks* in a prison is a metaphor reflecting the exploitation (rape) of human beings and natural resources evident in some aspects of the American economic system.

The supreme act of power of the state is to reduce a prisoner to impotence, to take away his sense of manhood and self-respect. This, very importantly, includes removing him from everyone and everything that reminds him that he is a man. The state "screws" the prisoner; he, in turn, does the same to his fellow prisoners. The supreme act of power for a prisoner is to reduce another prisoner to the status of a woman. In turn, the supreme act of humiliation is to be reduced to the status of a woman. *Punks* become the living metaphor of the "big rape." They are the scapegoats at the very bottom of the pit of hell designed by the state. The prisoner who screws his neighbor simply imitates, albeit distortedly, his "betters" in free society; after all, he has learned by observing them. Everyone profits but the *punk*.

A *punk* suffers the most hellish existence of all the damned in prison. He suffers invective, vilification and humiliation, regardless of whether or not he resisted initiation into "womanhood." Why? Manhood is paramount in the minds of the prisoners because the state has removed it from them; therefore, they turn in *fear* against the *punk* because he represents the final blow to manhood—he has been womanized. To be reduced to impotence is horrible but to be made into a woman is beyond horror.

Why don't prisoners put a stop to rape in jails and prisons? They could if they wanted to. The tradition of turning men into women continues because it serves a very important function: it is a metaphorical act, a statement or message about the condition of imprisoned men. Society denies that a man in prison has the need for women in the way that men have in free society. In doing this, society deprives him of one of the most important ways he has of defining his manliness. But the prisoner *is* a man. In Genesis, God decrees that man should not live without a help mate—woman. Why is the prisoner excluded? In prison, God's decree is overridden, so in a Godless place the prisoner plays God: he creates his own woman—out of man. Torn from God's presence, the prisoner becomes a demon, populating his hellish universe with a mocking imitation of God's creation—woman.

NOTES

[1]M. A. K. Halliday, "Anti-Languages," *American Anthropologist*, vol. 78 (1976), p. 570.

[2]"Anti-Languages," p. 572.

[3]"Anti-Languages," p. 573.

[4]"Anti-Languages," p. 576.

[5]Edward Sagarin, "Prison Homosexuality and Its Effect on Post-Prison Behavior," *Psychiatry*, vol. 39 (1976), p. 245.

[6]For information on what happens in women's prisons, see Esther Heffernan, *Making It in Prison* (New York: Wiley-Interscience Press, 1972); and Rose Giallombardo, *The Social World of Imprisoned Girls* (New York: John Wiley and Sons, 1974).

[7]Alan J. Davis, "Sexual Assault in the Philadelphia Prison System," *Trans-Action*, vol. 6 (1968), pp. 8–16. In 1968, Alan J. Davis, then Chief Assistant District Attorney of Philadelphia, was appointed by Judge Alexander F. Barbieri to supervise a three-month investigation conducted jointly by the Philadelphia District Attorney's office and the Police Department on sexual assaults in the Philadelphia prison system. The 103-page report revealed that, "nearly every slightly-built young man committed by the courts [was] sexually approached within a day or two after his admission to prison, and that many of these young men [were] repeatedly raped by groups of inmates." Others, because of the threat of gang rape found protection through a "homosexual relationship with an individual tormentor." The report conservatively estimated that 2000 assaults had

occurred in the prison system in a twenty-six month period. Of this estimated number, only ninety-six inmates reported the assaults to the prison authorities but only sixty-four of these assaults were reported on prison records, and only forty of those reported resulted in punishment by the authorities. The investigation revealed that guards in the Philadelphia prison system refused to show concern or take responsibility for preventing rapes. "One victim screamed for over an hour while he was being raped in his cell; the block guard ignored the screams and laughed at the victim when the rape was over." All quotes reprinted by permission of the publisher.

[8]He has what Erving Goffman calls a "spoiled identity." Erving Goffman, *Stigma* (New York: Prentice-Hall, 1963).

[9]"Sexual Assault in the Philadelphia Prison System," pp. 14–15. Data collected in the investigation of the Philadelphia prison system on the victims and aggressors revealed that on the average that the "aggressor tended to be older, heavier, taller, and more serious offenders," and that "both victims and aggressors tended to be younger than the average inmate." Victims looked younger and less athletic for their age, were better looking and less physically coordinated. Violent assaultive felonies were noticeably common among the aggressors; that is, rape, weapons offenses, robbery and aggravated robbery, and assault with intent to kill. Victims' offenses were generally less serious offenses such as violating parole, delinquency, car thefts, and AWOL from the armed forces.

[10]*Wolves* ingratiate themselves with the new men, offering to help them out in those first few days in order to entice them into sexual submission.

[11]"Sexual Assault in the Philadelphia Prison System," p. 15. "We were struck by the fact that the typical sexual aggressor does not consider himself to be a homosexual, or even to have engaged in homosexual acts. This seems to be based on his startlingly primitive view of sexual relationships, one that defines as male whichever partner is aggressive and as homosexual whichever partner is passive." Virgil L. Williams and Mary Fish, *Convicts, Codes, and Contraband* (Cambridge, Mass.: Ballinger Publishing Company, 1974), p. 59. Williams and Fish report that pseudohomosexual activities on the part of *wolves* is believed by the men to be an acceptable response to their deprivation and claim that prison populations accept and even respect sexual aggressors but that *queens* and *punks* are stigmatized; particularly *punks*. The heterosexual men at the Washington State Penitentiary do not respect *wolves* in their midst and recognize that they are a constant source of violence and unrest within the population.

[12]Delorme speaks about a *wolf* who hovered over him when he first came into the prison. "When I was a lot younger and new here I had an older guy that was in love with me. The asshole scared me by lurking around all the time. I used to be friends with him until I saw what he was up to. He was crazy. I sure as hell never gave him any reason to think I was queer or ready to turn over. But that sort of thing happens all the time. He even threatened people around me and thought everyone was after me. That's the way people get killed. He could have very easily killed me because he was insanely jealous. He did eventually kill some kid in

here. It still gives me the creeps. Like I said, I was planning on killing him or paying someone to do it for me for a hundred bucks. That was just because I was scared myself. But the very same situation happens to both straight people like me and gays. It's generally the older cons who have been in several joints. This place is a playground for them, with hundreds of very young pretty kids running around. All the wolves have a ball. It's a picnic, thanks to the courts and the prison system in this state. I would like to see their sons spend a couple weeks in here."

[13]"Sexual Assault in the Philadelphia Prison System," pp. 15–16. "A primary goal of the sexual aggressor, it is clear, is the conquest and degradation of his victim. We repeatedly found that aggressors used such language as 'Fuck or fight;' 'We're going to take your manhood;' 'You'll have to give up some face,' and 'We're going to make a girl out of you.' Some of the assaults were reminiscent of the custom in some ancient societies of castrating or buggering a defeated victim.... Another primary goal of many of the aggressors, it appears, is to retain membership in the groups led by militant sexual aggressors. This is particularly true of some of the participants in gang rapes. Lacking identification with such groups, as many of the aggressors know, they themselves would become victims."

[14]"Sexual Assault in the Philadelphia Prison System," p. 15. Davis's investigation revealed that a disproportionate number of aggressors were blacks who attacked whites. Based on the 129 documented assaults, it was found that 15 percent (20) were white against white; 29 percent (37) were black against black; and 56 percent (72) were black against white; no whites attacked blacks. There is evidence that other minorities besides blacks turn on whites in prison when they outnumber them. See *Agenda: A Journal of Hispanic Issues*, vol. 10, no. 3 (1980) and Anthony Scacco, *Rape in Prison* (Springfield, Ill.: Charles C Thomas, 1975).

[15]Columbus B. Hopper, "Sexual Adjustment in Prisons," *Police*, vol. 15 (1971), pp. 75–76. In conversations with some inmates at Walla Walla I learned that they agree with Hopper. Such a policy, they said, would help them feel that their humanity has not been completely stripped from them.

[16]Sandy states elsewhere that her parents raised her to be a girl and that her earliest memories are of being dressed and treated as a girl by her parents.

[17]*The Troublesome Helpmate: A History of Misogyny in Literature* (Seattle: University of Washington Press, 1966), p. 4. See also Vern L. Bullough, *The Subordinate Sex* (New York: Penguin Books, Inc., 1974), and Eva Figes, *Patriarchal Attitudes* (Greenwich, Conn.: A Fawcett Premier Book, 1970).

[18]"Anti-Languages," p. 578.

[19]Daniel Bell, *End of Ideology* (New York: Free Press, 1960), p. 128.

Chapter 9

THE GREAT ESCAPE

Ordinarily, time and space are conceptualized in the human mind not as danger but rather as something infinite. Both are viewed as intangible concepts impossible to experience in the physical sense. For the prisoner, however, time and space hold another dimension. Trapped by others against his will in an enclosed, sharply defined, and restrictive space for a particular period of time, his mind, troubled by the dangers to its well-being, devises ways of escaping the boundaries of this artificially imposed temporal-spatial restriction. The unnaturalness of this experience plays a significant role in the formulation of his prisoner worldview. To be sure, all humanity is bounded by the limitations that time and space impose, but these boundaries are fixed in nature. For this reason, they are not ordinarily viewed as repressive or dangerous but rather as natural: man is *free* to move within the time and space that nature has set for him; but the prisoner, who once enjoyed this natural freedom, no longer has it. He lives as a captive within an artificial universe whose temporal-spatial laws are distorted struggling to adjust his spirit to this sharply enclosed universe that operates in a manner so contrary to the human condition.[1] The problems created by this unnatural environment threaten his psychological well-being, consequently he seeks ways to overcome his predicament. Like Houdini, he tries to escape his spatial and temporal chains by *going over the wall*. Unlike Houdini, however, his escape is not a physical one but rather psychological: the *great escape* is a retreat into the mind. In *Asylums*, Goffman identifies the *great escape* as "spiritual leave-taking," a "special kind of absenteeism, a defaulting not from prescribed activity but from prescribed being."[2] There are many ways by which the prisoner accomplishes this escape or "spiritual leave-taking." Some of these ways are healthy; others are not. Either way, the *great escape* is one of the psychological aspects of *doing time*; in the prisoner's worldview, it is the metaphor for psychological survival.

APOLOGY FOR THE GREAT ESCAPE

Protecting one's inner self is as important in prison as protecting one's physical life, since so many situations threaten the psychological well-being of the prisoner. Daily, for example, he must contend with the stress of living close to death and violence. Every minute of the waking day and night, the prisoner is forced to keep his mind in a state of readiness in order to flee the dangers that may invade his mind. This is difficult since it places a serious drain on his psychological resources. At every turn he must contend with the restrictions imposed, not only upon his physical being but upon his interior self as well, since psychological space is denied him. Forced to live with fellow prisoners rat-like in a crowded cage, he is never allowed solitude, something vitally necessary for refueling the mind if one is to sustain enough psychic energy to contend with psychological stress. The prisoner has no peace, quiet, or serenity, no way of stepping back away from it all except to retreat into the mind. The blows his mind receives when he views the murder of a fellow prisoner stun him and send his spirit reeling, seeking escape from the shock and pain. The prisoner who has managed to hold on to his humanity in the midst of this unnatural universe feels these experiences deeply. Memories are seared into his mind that cannot be erased; memories of violent death's ugliness and of helpless men crying out to him whom he is unable to help. He is trapped within the moment and space of these inescapable occurrences. To save himself he must flee. To survive psychologically he closes his mind off from the horror and pain of it all and retreats: he makes the *great escape*. Unless a man has buried his humanity so deeply he no longer feels—and this is what has happened to those who murder their brothers while in prison—he suffers from the regret he feels for not being able to come to the aid of a fellow human being. At night, locked in his cell, he may be plagued by memories of what he has seen and heard. His dreams may be nightmares, reenactments of the horrors he has witnessed during his waking hours.

"What are we escaping from while we're doing these things, you might ask? Well, we're escaping from murder, assault, rape, hustling, homosexuality, insanity, phony friendships, empty conversations, boredom, and I guess mostly the coldness, the real coldness of it all. That is prison. You try not to see, hear, or you ignore these things.

"It is possible to give your eye, mind, and body a break from the ugliness, stress, and tension that we're with seven days a week, fifty-two weeks a year, year after year after year. So I think I've said it before, too. I don't want to see this stuff. I don't want to hear it. I don't want to know about these things. The best way to do that is to make yourself scarce. Get up out of it. Slip and slide around it. Duck and dodge it all day. The old saying, which is changed in here with just one addition, that fits here or any prison is, 'See no evil, hear no evil, speak no evil, and evil will not touch you, hopefully.' Doesn't always work. You try.

"One good reason why you want to escape is you want a place to go. You want a place to be away from the evil, bloodshed, violence, murder. Like hearing a man beg and cry, scream while he's being stabbed sixty-five times. Seeing a man have his throat cut while two others stab him in the back. This guy doesn't scream. This guy makes a wheezing, bubbling sound cause his throat's cut. He gasps. It's a terrible sound. The blood foams up and comes out in a fountain. He's wide-eyed. The eyes are glazed. He's terrified cause he knows he's dead. Looks around for help and you back away just like everybody else. This is what you're escaping from. This is the thing that you're taking yourself away from. You don't forget these things. You never will. You never forget these things when you've seen them, when you've heard the sounds and you've watched the man die and you haven't done anything about it. You don't forget. You can't forget you didn't help. Aw, the hell with it!

"And if you're in your cell at nighttime sometimes, it doesn't happen all the time; when it happens—rape—it's generally a real pitiful whimpering, begging sound. Some young guy being gang-raped and beaten, probably spit on, probably being kicked around, cries for help. You can hear his scream to be all of a sudden muffled because someone is holding his hand over his mouth. Other guys in the cell keep watch up and down the tier with a mirror, probably a shaving mirror, and they use it like a rear view mirror, stick it out the bars and watch. Tell the other guys to hurry up so they can have their turn. So this happens at night and you can't get away from that.

"About all you can do is turn your radio up, put your earphones on if you've got them. And if you've got a brand new cell partner, if he's a fish, there's a real look that comes on his face. He'll be wide-eyed and start looking around, start asking questions and you tell him, 'Aw, it ain't nothing. Forget about it.' But he won't forget, either. He's scared, wondering if they're going to do that to him, I guess. You don't forget that, either.

"Those are the things that you can avoid during the daytime if you try, if you've got places to go, because it also happens in the daylight. Doesn't make any difference. You don't need darkness to fuck a punk; you don't need darkness to kill a man.

"There's a strange thing I've noticed about a man that's murdered. Very often the man that's being murdered will tell his attackers, 'You're killing me!' My brother, Broncho; that's what somebody that was witness said Broncho hollered at the guys that were stabbing him: 'You're killing me!' A young guy, twenty-two years old, that was killed on the tier below me once, they stabbed him sixty-five times. And he cried and screamed every time they stabbed him, and that's what he kept saying, 'You're murdering me! You're murdering me!' And he prayed and screamed for his mother, screamed for the cops, begged them not to kill him, but they killed him. In a frenzy they killed him. Went completely insane. They were covered with blood from head to foot when they came out of that cell. Three of them. They weren't charged. They weren't convicted. They were caught but they put them in Segregation for a while then let all three of them go and they killed somebody else again.

"But if you're in your club or if you're having your visit, or if you're over making a phone call, or you're over playing music in the club, or you're out playing baseball, you won't be in your cell and you won't hear those cries and screams. You won't have nightmares. You'll hear it second hand. You won't hear it at night. You won't think about it five years after it's happened. I still hear that guy crying. That's what you escape from.

"And it does something to you. That's the terrible thing. If you witness it or if you're close to it, it does something to you inside that you have to fight. I don't know how many years you have to fight it. I don't know! I can't describe this, to let a man die. Somehow, you've got to convince yourself there's nothing you can do. That's not your nature, you know, to let things like that go on.

"So it's tough but somehow you get past it. Somehow you put it inside and you keep on going and you just hope and pray that you won't be in the vicinity when it happens, so you won't see it again. And if you're not doing anything the first time that happens to you, I'm pretty sure that you will start looking for things to do to take you out of the area. Like I lived in Eight Wing, so things like that, if they were going to happen, would probably happen in Eight Wing. When things were bad, I found reasons to stay out of my cell until late at night, because after nine o'clock at night everybody is locked up and chances are very slim that anything will happen like that. Maybe somebody will get raped; maybe a lot of people will get fucked, but that's not the same as being murdered.

"I think you can understand the reasons for escape. I wonder if you could see what I'm trying to tell you here. It's important to find a way to avoid these things. And you remember this now and maybe work on it in your mind and maybe expand on it yourself because that's the same way it affected me, which is very deeply.

"It's important that you use the different forms of escapism, not so much because you're afraid of it happening to you, but it's important that you don't see these things. It's important that you don't have to touch it mentally, because that damages. It hurts. It isn't so much that they're afraid that somebody is going to come and jump on you. In some cases you know pretty damn sure nobody is going to come jump on you, but I don't give a goddam how big we are, how strong we think we are; when it happens and when you see it, you're not ready for it. It happens suddenly. Sometimes you're walking around like a goddam dummy and you haven't got everything buttoned up. I'm talking about your emotions and your feelings. So it goes in deep [what you saw]. Then you have another psychological problem that you have to work out, as if you didn't have enough already.

"So that's a pretty important aspect of escaping. That's protect-

ing yourself, protecting your mental health. That's just as important as protecting your physical self. You could go on if you see
this; if you're healthy it shouldn't affect your life. Only it'll affect
you inside your mind personally. It affects you in those quiet
moments, you see, until you've accepted and explained, rational-
ized everything to yourself.

"I expect it's the same thing with the veterans from the different
wars. They've seen a lot. The only Vietnam veterans in here that
you hear really telling stories or talking about it are full of
bullshit most of the time. But you got normal, healthy young men
that went, they actually experienced, they killed, they saw death;
they were close to death; it touched them. It was all around them.
These guys in here don't talk about it. They don't want to think
about it. They don't want these images coming back into their
mind. It's only the bullshitters who were over there and didn't do
anything. Then you get stories from them all day long.

"And the guys who really experienced death in war, just as it
bothers them, they become quieter. It changes them. Their personality becomes introspective. It's not that they're thinking
about these things. I don't know what they're thinking about.
Maybe the quietness indicates that there is a battle for control
going on inside. Maybe it takes a little bit more than subconscious
effort to hold these things down, hold these pictures away from
them, these memories, so that a little bit more of energy and a
little bit more of extra effort is necessary. It takes a little bit more
of concentration, so it pulls you away from your outward approach
to people and makes you a little more reflective. It just seems that
way, anyway. You pull kind of within yourself and that can handi-
cap you. It's a real danger. I think I can handle it; I'm sure I can
handle it."

TRIPPING

The simplest and perhaps most common way of escaping the
hazards of the spatial-temporal restrictions that the prisoner experiences is through *tripping*; that is, escaping on the magic carpet of
fantasy.[3] As long as a man recognizes the demarcation lines between reality and fantasy, his psychological game is not dangerous

to him and may even be a healthy way of helping him to cope with his situation.

Joe: "I daydream about gettin out. And you just go every step through what you'd like to do. I just go through the future."

Gary: "I trip about going to college. But I don't know what the college looks like so I have to kind of invent it. I have my room all fixed up. Have the colors on the walls. I have pictures and I have everything together. I've got my typewriter and I know what color it is. I've even fantasized about people gettin mad at me for typin too late at night and stuff like that, how I'll deal with it. I even see the clothes I'm gonna wear. See my classrooms; I hope they're not as big as some are. And I trip about a car and goin out and doin this and that and seein people I know. And fishin a lot. And you get further and further into it. I've always wanted to go on one of those charter boats but I never have. Isn't that funny? I've never been on the ocean and I've lived there half of my life."

Joe: "You trip about things that make you feel good. If you think about prison that brings you down fast. So you try to forget it as fast as you can. If you're married you might trip about your wife. Or your girlfriend or about girls."

Gary: "I think tripping about things that are outside lessens the importance of things in here. And if you let things in here get important, that's where you get some guys who might want to kill. Or you get involved in these schemes and all that bullshit might become too important to you."

SNAPPING TO WHERE YOU'RE AT

Men recently arrived in the prison sometimes refuse to acknowledge that they are there. Although they are not mentally disturbed, their refusal to adapt themselves to their situation causes them and those around them considerable trouble. This condition is not so much a form of escapism as it is a case of never having arrived. These men refuse to accept that there are new spatial-temporal conditions to which they must adapt. It may take two to three years for some men to acknowledge their predicament. Other prisoners waste no time trying to get these men to *snap to where they're at.*

Gene: "We're talkin about escapism in prison. You know it's not possible to live totally in a dream world twenty-four hours a day unless, of course, you're crazy. And really, that's not what prison is. Your friends and your cell partners, they'll make it pretty clear just exactly where you are all the time. Brutally clear. Actually, it's a kindness on their part. In fact, everybody's doin it for the same reason I am. You can see a man that's goin off into a fantasy trip, escapism. When you see he's doin it too much, you have to be a little unkind, I suppose it is. Snap him to where he's at. You remind him again and again. 'You're in prison, man! You'd better get your shit together.' "

Pete: "Sometimes it takes you two or three years to snap to where you're at. The more you drink, the more you use dope, the longer it takes you to snap to where you're at, as they say. 'You're in prison, idiot. You might say you know it but you don't act like it.' "

Gene: "The thing about some people is that they rush around like they're waitin for a bus or something. They're doin this and they're doin that with everything. Their letters, the way they dress, the way they just go hang out. It's like they expect a call over the speaker anytime tellin em to get their stuff together, it's time to go, and they go on like that.

"A person like that, you don't like to be around em too much because they make you nervous. They're rushin around. They all do. They're just kinda blindin themselves. You gotta slow down. They have to do this and have to do that. They don't accept the rules. They don't accept guards; they don't accept their position in here. They still want to do what they want. And they take a long time to change. Some people take more than two or three years. They have a rough go."

Pete: "Once in awhile you drop a lug on em. If you've got one of those guys in your cell he'll irritate you. He'll be talkin about his Old Lady or talkin about clothes or doin this or that and say, 'Oh man, the guard gave this to me' or 'The guard told me this,' and you'll tell him, 'Oh man, you're in prison. Why don't you wake up?' And that's about all you can think of to say to the guy because his whole attitude is not right and he makes your time kind of rough because you don't have answers for him. He'll ask questions a lot but he won't accept the answers you tell him. You can't give him the right answers."

Gene: "I've had guys in my house like that drive me right up the wall. And then I've wondered, 'Man, maybe there's something wrong with me. Maybe I've just been here too long.' But this guy, man, he's driving me crazy. He's goin crazy about his wife. Pissed off cause the guard won't run down there and do what he wants. And he can't get out; the gates aren't set to his time schedule. Nothin works the way he wants. Everything has to be what he wants and so about the only thing a guy like me can tell him is, 'Well, the guard is just doin his job and that's the way the rules are.' But he don't want to hear that shit.

"Those guys are runnin around chasin their tails. Those are the guys that eventually go to drugs and drinkin. Eventually, they will end up as dopers and boozers because they can't handle the Joint. They can't snap to where they're at. Every time they sober up they're back into that bag so they never leave themselves room to really look around and do anything right."

MADNESS AS THE GREAT ESCAPE

Madness in prison represents the psychological escape that becomes permanent, a protective journey from which the prisoner may never return. The leap over the wall his mind takes is so great that he remains absent from the prison throughout his entire stay. Some men, who are genuinely disturbed and withdrawn while in prison, give up their madness when they return to the free world. Although viewed as an unhealthy accommodation, this adjustment to prison existence is actually a psychic lifesaver and may, after all, be the most appropriate response to life in a mad universe. There are some men who so admire those who make this adaptation that they themselves feign madness as a protective device for coping with the dangers and stress of prison (and jail) existence.

Gene: "The mental cases in prison have all committed some type of crime. The state can't throw people in prison just because they're bugs. Those who come in crazy probably did caper while he was in the same condition."

Hank: "Quite often some guys get busted then crack up in the jails. 'They want to play but don't want to pay.' Some guys are not really nuts but know and use all the symptoms so they can be put in single cells in the county jails. It is a hassle for some people in the bigger tanks because of the large percentage of rapes and beatings of the weaker white guys."

Gene: "The guys who try to fake a nut bag are tryin to have an excuse for their crime, also hopin the judge will send em to either a state hospital for observation and commitment, or they will earmark em for the Third Floor at Walla Walla. The Third Floor is appealing because they never have contact with the population, plus if they wait a year and then make rapid progress, they can make a play for the gate and not do so much time.

"I suspect that the increase in mental cases walkin around in prison is directly connected to the budget cuts and treatment cutbacks in our large hospitals. The way things are goin now the nuts will make up half the population in here within five years. Our state hospital used to hold several thousand. Now they haven't even got a thousand. So where are all the patients?"

Hank: "At one time a few years ago it was suggested by some of the cons to the Superintendent that all of the nuts in here wear yellow shirts. The regular cons try to keep up on just who is or isn't a nut. These guys are identified and have a hard time tryin to find places to live."

Gene: "They created a special tier for some in the Admissions Building. The real extreme psychotics are segregated and are generally kept on Third Floor. Some are kept in Segregation if they are dangerous or have already killed somebody. As a general rule, they are outwardly ignored but closely watched by everyone. That might sound contrary but I think you know what I mean.

"You asked who are these people? They're no one special except for their illness. A new mental health unit, so they say, has been built at Monroe, but from the reports and the pictures I've seen, it is just a new super-maximum security unit with complete isolation for each man. The cells are larger because each is equipped with a shower so that a guy can't even come out for a shower."

Hank: "The kind of insanity that seems to prevail in here is obvious. The pressure, the stress, the tension comin at you from every direction day and night; the mental energy and effort that you expend tryin to put that shield over you, that isolation."

Gene: "I'll say this about it—I possess three masks. A smile mask, a clam mask, and a diplomatic mask. I wear them well, but the older I get, the more difficult it is to wear them for more than a very short time. You understand? It gets so tiresome, God! And we get a little extra burst of strength each day. I don't know where some get it but I pray I don't let it fall down around my ankles, which it has done. And in this way we can cope.

"But some guys are not so healthy and you see what you might call a transient form of paranoid schizophrenia and it settles over some guys and they withdraw. They don't talk anymore."

Hank: "They talk to themselves and they slink around, slip and slide around the institution."

Gene: "They're all in their little worlds, the paranoid ones. It can be awful irritating sometimes when they stare at you cause you don't know what's behind those funny eyes they got. So they think you're plannin to kill em or plottin against em or you're a Commie or what, you know. You wonder what's goin on in their minds then."

Hank: "You have to stay loose around em cause they're so goddamed loose that they may attack you because they've built this big paranoid trip about you and you don't even know it."

Gene: "So it is transient because it goes away when they get out of here. The pressure is off em; it lifts like a lid. They leave the institution and they're able to function. They're able to go home and be fairly normal. They'll be a little more nervous than they were before. I've seen that happen again and again and again to people, includin myself, where the pressure got so great that the mind withdrew. We went into that dreamworld and we escaped. Just as if we went over the wall, we escaped."

SNIFFING

The men who escape by inhaling chemicals like carbon tetrachloride run the risk of becoming so completely disoriented that they behave as though they are suffering some form of mental illness. Delorme, who spent a considerable amount of time when he was younger using this method of *going over the wall*, describes exactly where his *great escape* took him.

"I got started at Monroe inhaling the fumes from different chemicals like carbon tetrachloride and things like that. I continued that little game over here and hit er a pretty heavy lick a couple years. The effect on me was I ended up on the mental ward for a couple months here pretty screwed up in my head from that stuff and I guess I'll never read the jacket on it, I mean their diagnosis of what happened, but they had a bogus diagnosis — chronic schizophrenia — and that's not the case at all.

"More than anything else, all it was was a poisoning; overloaded the system with the chemicals. The high on that stuff comes from lack of oxygen, really. But in any case, I ran around here hearin voices, seein things, and just generally gettin more and more run down from constantly fightin it, so I did end up on Third Floor, the booby hatch or ding ward. My friends got me up there for a good reason. They were concerned for my welfare so they tricked me, got me there, checked me in. I sort of twiddled my fingers and talked to myself up there with the rest of the nuts. One day, luckily, it just sort of went away; I got slowly back in control.

"My description of what was happenin to me at the time was my mind was like a three-dimensional crossword puzzle and all the parts normally would be together, but in this case all the parts become disconnected so that at any given time there was dozens of things goin on at the same time in my mind. There was voices and images from without and images and voices from within. Hallucinations, bells, whispering, ghosts, everything at once all day. And at night I was talkin to the Grandfathers, the Elders. As I saw them they were like Elders. They were wise men and they wore robes and I could see them and they were tryin to help me and I had been tryin to talk to em anyway. And I had several terrifically vivid things happen to me.

"One time I was layin on my bed and it looked like the walls of the cellblock exploded all of a sudden. I sat up real quick on my bed and this great big golden eagle — and he was shinin like he was made out of gold — he flew in. He came in just streakin. He just hit me in the chest with both his feet and he took my heart out and flew away. I thought I was going to die. But I didn't. It was kind of a pretty moving experience. So vivid.

"When you're sniffin, what it does, it just puts your mind in a state of hypnosis and that's why people talkin to you and different sounds create suggestions. Your mind visualizes what they're sayin and what the sound is. It'll create a picture to go with a specific sound like a bell or something. I may hear a bell ringin and when I'm sniffin, just that fast, I'll see it. I'll actually be there just like I was transported somewhere. I may be all of a sudden walkin out of school, out the doorway because of the sound of that bell and this little trip may last ten seconds and then something else will happen.

"We used to have a lot of fun doin that. We'd sniff until everybody's mind and face looked blank and they knew when they were ready. Then we'd take turns readin a story out of a book or something while the other three guys in the cell listened. And they listened with their eyes closed and they'd be laughin and gigglin and all the time I'd be readin the story they'd be visualizing three different things; three different stories in their minds would make up the pictures as I went along.

"When we understood how this worked more, we were able to play with it and kind of ad lib. But there's a lot of forces you need to understand. You need to be able to pull your mind out of it if something is beginning to happen that you don't like. You need to be able to understand it immediately and not only explain it to yourself but to hold yourself back and break all contact with it, and that's not possible when you're in a state of mind that chemicals put you in.

"So anyway, it was a pretty rough go. It was real tough in the mental hospital, mostly because I was afraid. I wasn't afraid of people around me; I was afraid of insanity. I have always been afraid of insanity. I think I fear it more than death. But I spent a couple of months on the mental ward. I cried, I hollered, I bitched, I screamed, I was afraid. I was afraid of what was happenin because I was rational enough to understand and see insanity for what it was and I lost track of time.

"My first thought was had I been up there for twenty years or had I just come up there? I couldn't see the difference. But eventually my system kind of flushed itself out and my nerves got better and I was able to start seein things in their proper perspective a little better and I worked myself out of there.

"I was on my best behavior when I did an interview with the

doctor. I knew I really had to get it up for this. It took all the strength I had to hold the whole thing together. Just like holdin a whole bunch of ropes together and not lettin em get away. That's what I had to do with the pieces of my mind, the fragments that were floatin. I pulled em all together just long enough for that interview with the doctor so that I made a pretty good impression on him so, I guess, he put down that I had a case of nerves. But when I was in interviewin with him, my little faces and things were peekin out of his desk at me and voices were whisperin smart aleck answers to me, but I just ignored em all and put em back like they were little pets that were irritatin me and I didn't want anybody to see em. I just pretended I didn't see em, pretended they weren't there, but when I got out of that office, boy, I just exploded! I was dingier than a shithouse mouse the rest of the day.

"A couple months and I was out of there and I was back on the track. Course, during that time my friends, my brother and all of them, they sent me notes; they sent me cigarettes and they'd come up and visit me and they reassured me and that helped a lot.

"The mental health tier was just a tier over in the Admissions Building. It was put over there when they had a lot of room. Now they don't have a lot so it's in the hospital. They called it Self Recovery and it holds twenty-two or so people, single cells.

"They used to take the least violent of the nuts, the ones that were able to at least feed themselves and wander around and not get into too much trouble on the tier, because they didn't let you out here in the population. The infamous Dr. H. used to run that program in conjunction with the Third Floor program he had goin. Third Floor was the number one booby hatch, so he had both programs and we had some psychiatric nurses down there, supposedly.

"And we had some ladies from somebody's auxiliary or something from downtown. Christian ladies. They seemed to enjoy comin up once or twice a week and teachin us how to make plastic grapes, plastic apples, plastic bananas; show you how to paint by numbers.

"Oh, the little ladies; I love em! They had more tricks for a fella, I'm tellin you. They were alright, though; they were doin what they could do. But they were funny to a lot of us. Here we are, an ole bunch of rowdy hoodlums and the ladies got us all sittin around a big table fingerpaintin and got clay in our hair and plastic all over everything. They had us makin some of the goddamndest projects, I swear to God! Aw shit, a little therapy. You know what I mean?

"But they worked with us where we all sat in circles and I wish I had a tape recorder for some of those conversations. I'm tellin you; you get ten–twenty nuts sittin in a circle tryin to have a conversation and you really got something out of the ordinary, I'll tell you. And they usually had some young sweetheart from one of the universities around here kind of stirrin the whole thing. Half the people would be in love with her. And we had a TV set we watched.

"I'll tell you the big trick they had was keepin everybody on Thorazine. They give you Thorazine three–four times a day and that was guaranteed to keep everybody quiet, in line, and just kind of shufflin around like zombies. I took my share of Thorazine, then after a week or so I started hidin it because I couldn't handle it anymore. When you take Thorazine you can't even think and I had a visit one day and I had just taken my medication. Oh my God; it was a terrible visit! My mind was just completely blank all day. Every time W. would ask me a question, I'd have to mull it over a little bit and she'd have to repeat it over two–three times to get through to me so that was the end of that. I never took anymore. So I was on the sneak.

"I'd hold it in my mouth until I turned around and got out of sight, then I'd spit it out and generally I would give my Thorazine to some guy who I thought really needed it. I made sure to give him mine to go along with his cause we did have some pretty rowdy sonovabitches. That was one way to calm em down. They thought they were gettin big dope, so they'd take it. And that put em out for the count, boy.

"Anyway, they used to let me leave there and go up to the Indian club just about any time I wanted to go. I did kind of cure that sniffin down there a little bit. I was able to pull all the pieces together and get back on the ole track again. I mean some things are pretty tough on your mind. If the chemicals are that strong, they will build up and blow your mind apart like a firecracker. It's nothin permanent. I'm not feelin any ill effects from it these days. I feel pretty together.

"I went to forestry camp after I came through that experience in the bughouse. Once I got that cleared up I went to Washugal Honor Camp, which is about two–three hundred miles away from here. It's in western Washington. It's in the mountains; beautiful country over there about twenty–thirty miles from Vancouver. And the camps, they're a lot nicer than here. They're like logging camps except they have barracks they've made for permanent residence. They used to have dormitories where about seventy guys slept. No radios or TV and things like that.

"When you work in the woods you have a lot of different crews goin a lot of different ways each morning to work. And I got out there away from this penitentiary where there were beautiful trees and the beautiful blue river that ran right by the camp, all the green grass, and if you can believe this, I'm tellin you there were deer! Four–five–six at a time would walk right up on the grounds to the camp and walk right up to you and eat out of your hand! I'd never seen anything like that and I was really flabbergasted the first time I seen it.

"The guy told me, 'Here, offer them this. Hold out your hand; put this little hard piece of candy in your hand.' And man, I'd seen em comin across the highway. They jumped over the fence there, about eight of em that time. Fairly good-sized deer and they walked right up to us. Just walked right up! Christ, I didn't know if they was goin to attack us; if they was goin to bite me; if they had teeth or what they were about. But I held my hand out with the candy in it and this lady deer, I mean doe, she walked right up and took the candy right out of my hand. But I never forgot that.

"And we had two–three little baby deer, little fawns, that we'd find. When the crews were out workin they'd bring em back to camp if they'd find em abandoned or their mothers had got shot or something like that, and we'd raise em there at the camp. And somebody would take care of em like a pet dog, feedin em with baby bottles. They were really a lot of fun. A fawn is fun to watch. I laughed so hard; when they'd go runnin across the field, they'd bounce like kangaroos. They like to run, boy, just run and run and run and then they'd come back when you're sleepin and you wake up and there's a little baby deer lickin your hand. They like to lick the salt off your hands. Or they're layin on your bed when you come back from work. There's pet squirrels in the camp. Pet raccoons. It's really something else.

"Can you believe it, Chiquita, when I first went there I didn't like it? I was tryin to come back? I went to the office about two days after I'd been there and I requested transfer back to the penitentiary. I'd never been so goddam lonesome in my life cause it was so quiet. I felt like I was out on the Mojave Desert. Oh, for chrissake; that's where I am now! But I mean bein in here for so long got me so damned used to bein in a crowded cell and just elbow to elbow with the guys all day long in the dining hall. There's hundreds of guys in the dining hall. Noise, noise, all the time, you know, so that's why when I got out to that forestry camp I thought it was the end of the world. I swear to God, I damn near cried, I was so lonely. I was homesick for in here! That's unbelievable! I told my partner, I says, 'Listen, man, I can't handle it. I've got to get out of here. I'm a city boy. I ain't used to all this bullshit.'

"I hadn't seen nothin yet, you see; you gotta remember that. I hadn't seen all those deer and the beautiful sky at nighttime with no smoke, no smog. You're up in the mountains about four–five thousand feet. It's higher than the cities. But I wanted to go back. I said, 'Oh man, I miss my brother. I miss my friends. I don't give a shit if it is the penitentiary, I want to go back anyway.' And to me, camp was just another penitentiary. Besides it was so goddam quiet and I couldn't see no possibility of any excitement. No riots, no fights or anything.

"And my buddy said, 'Listen, do this; give yourself two weeks, man. Two weeks, that's all I'm askin. If you still want to go back, to hell with it; I'll go back with you.'

"So I says, 'O.K. Two weeks and not a day more and then I'm gettin the hell out of here.'

"Shit, two weeks later they couldn't drag me out of there with a truck. I had adjusted. I got a fishin pole; I started fishin. I started seein the animals. I opened my eyes and I started seein things in the woods. I think the Indian really came out in me then cause I loved it up there. God, it was so nice. Sure, it was still part of the prison system but the pressure wasn't there. No pressure.

"Eventually, after you'd be there quite a while, you're back to your smart aleck ways, then you start bitchin about little tiny rules and things like that, but there's no comparison, for chrissake!

"The night sky used to really knock me out. I used to sit out on the stairs on the back porch of the dormitory and I'd take my coffee and go out there when it was dark and lean back and just stare at the sky for hours. I just couldn't get over it. The one thing that would make me kind of sad and that's the night sky if it's pretty and clear. I get homesick because I think that proves to me that we're not from this earth, really. I think our home is way, way out somewhere in the sky."

THE BOOZER'S TRIP

The steady supply of prison brewed alcohol guarantees for many men a constant vehicle for *going over the wall*. Some men who were not heavy drinkers before their imprisonment became alcoholics while in the prison. Many alternate drinking with drugs as an escape technique. A considerable amount of enthusiasm and ingenuity accompanies the making and *stashing* of this popular clandestine beverage. Hidden "stills," some of them "on the hoof," seems so numerous as to be everywhere under the noses of the guards. Considering the odor this brew is supposed to emit, one wonders whether the guards suffer olfactory handicaps or are charitably turning their heads and purposely smelling the air from a different direction in order to allow the prisoners their escape.

"Boozing is another big form of escape. We have a lot of drunks in here, a lot of fellas that have turned alcoholics. It is possible to stay drunk all the time. Really, all it takes is a little effort. Put one batch up, drink it, party, pour the other one off. It takes a little work to keep it goin, but there are drinkers in here who are hard core enough and determined enough that they will do this.

"The common drink is homemade pruno[4] that is made everywhere at anytime out of anything. And there are pruno stashes all over the Joint. They're buried in holes or hid in closets. They're hid in ventilators. They're in laundry buckets. They're up in vents; behind toilets. They're in mattresses. They're hangin in clothes that are hangin up from the ceiling.

"A pruno stash is a place where you stash a plastic bag or bucket and let it sit three days without gettin busted. They used to go to pretty elaborate hidin places but they just started gettin a little loose so they started makin it in the houses again, so that Eight Wing in particular used to smell like a damned tavern half the time. But they make a lot in Six Wing, too. Used to make a lot of booze in the Coke Shack; in the clubs. The industries always has a stash goin all the time. They make gallons and gallons out there.

"It's transported around the institution in hot water bottles and there's little plastic buckets. Nobody is carryin a bucketful of pruno around, but they will carry a couple of hot water bottles and they tie a string around it and they tie it over their necks and it's under their coat, two hot water bottles full of booze under their arms so they'll carry it around that way.

"Pruno stashes; this cell is big enough to stash at least a gallon or more. You can use plastic bags cause they can be fitted into all these little areas. And you put your potatoes and fruit, yeast, sugar; you can put all that garbage together and that's what you get back. If you were makin it just with potatoes, you put three potatoes in a gallon of water.

"I'll tell you how I made some for Jimmy. I used oranges. I put about ten oranges in lukewarm water. I didn't have any yeast so I put two or three slices of bread in it and I put sugar in. Then it took five or six days. It fermented then it turned the sugar to alcohol. The fruit hurries it up. It gets rotten or something so the whole mess gets as strong as cheap wine and tastes just horrible.

"If you make it in your cell you have to be careful because they can smell it, so you take a little plastic tube and if you've got a wash bucket or an empty five gallon paint bucket, which they let you have to wash your clothes, or a gallon jug, you can put that hose in it and you cap the top with rags and then you either run it into another can or jug with water in it. Then the bubbles, the smell, goes in the water. Bubbles come up clear. Or you can run it up into your vent so it doesn't smell.

"In the summertime you can make it outside or in the auditorium during a movie. The only time we go to the movie is on Wednesday and Friday nights. You can go to the movie on Friday night and take all your makins with you and pack all your sugar and everything and your bags and take it to the movie cause they don't shake that place down because we're never there. So you make it on Friday night and come back Wednesday night and it's already done. If you buy it, it costs seven bucks a gallon.

"I made pruno for Jimmy cause I thought it would be a good present for him and I gave it to him. I took a little sip to see if it tasted right and it did, so then I surprised him. He didn't have a radio or anything down in his cell. He lives above my tier. So anyway I had these milk cartons and I filled about six or seven of em and I hooked em all together with a string like a train and I told him, 'Pass your line down. I got something for you.' He thought it might be a tape or something cause I used to pass him tapes, so when he passed his line down I hooked em on and told him to start pullin on it. Stuck em out on the tier and up they went. He kept pullin on the line. 'What the hell is that?' he says. Pulled it in and he opened one and I heard him let out a scream. He was really happy.

"It's just a line you pass stuff with from one house to another. Maybe some old timers call it something different. We just say, 'Pass your line.' In this prison we don't use it as much as in tighter prisons but now [on lockdown, 1979] we are startin to use it, so probably a name will come forth.

"You can get a runner so you don't have to use the line to get things around. We're usin runners now. A runner is some con who's out and you say, 'Will you take this down to so and so?' So some of these things will come back as the prison gets tighter.

"But now it's just 'Throw your string or your line down.' And you get good at it. You've got a crack under your door, maybe only that big. You got to fire that thing through that crack. If you're in cells like this, facin each other, you have to rebound it like a pool table to get something somewhere. You can't go like this in a solid door. But if I wanted to get a line down that way I'd have to bounce it off that wall to keep it goin. You throw it against the far wall and it ricochets. But in jails your far wall is usually a lot closer. It's pretty far away here. You use something round that will roll, or you use something flat like metal; you know how metal slides. You really give it a whip. You got forever to keep tryin so if it takes you twenty tries to get it, what the hell. If you get it half way, the guy will meet you."

THE DOPER'S TRIP

One of the most common forms of escape in the prison is through drugs. Many men acknowledge that drugs help them to survive their prison experience. One prisoner states, "I'm into drugs in here cause I like the feeling of not feeling." According to the men, marijuana is so widely used as to be almost the norm.[5] Many men believe the officials recognize that marijuana use helps tranquilize the men and for that reason allow its use. Whether or not this is so, many men make their *great escape* by using marijuana and hard drugs. Drugs are one of the major causes of murders among the prisoners; first, because it is so expensive and, second, because some drug dealers in the prison are *burn artists*.

Gene: "There's so many ways that we find to use to escape in here. We dive into drugs. Get em anyway we can from the streets. Try to talk the hospital out of something. Probably the best you're gonna come up with is tranquilizers."

Tim: "They have drugs comin in constantly from the streets. Visitors might bring em in. The women might carry a balloon of heroin in her snatch, sneak past all the searches, get it in, then it completes its journey from the Visiting Room inside the Joint up somebody's kiester."

Gene: "A kiester stash is dope up a guy's rectum. They still get by in spite of anal searches if you got it pushed up there far enough. So there's a constant supply. If they get busted they go to something else."

Tim: "There's plenty of guards that will do it, bring it in."

Gene: "Like I told you the money is good."

Tim: "There's a lot of money in here. The Joint's always got a lot of white money, thousands in here floatin around. One person sometimes gets busted with a couple thousand dollars, so you can imagine how much is spread around the rest of the institution."

Gene: "Dopers are a pain in the ass, but that's their trip and they interfere in a lot of different ways. They try to keep on their own a little bit just because they kind of flock together. They don't flock together for protection; they flock together because they pass dope. One knows and the others don't know who had a visit that day, so if the guy is a doper they just track him down to see what he got. They start in the morning and they don't end until two or three. Every day if they're not dopin they're lookin. It's the same exact routine that we do on the streets.

"Most of the dopers in here were dopers on the streets. If you were a dope addict on the streets you can't stand yourself, mostly. You see then, if you're not loaded, you get drunk cause you don't like bein sober very long. Dope addicts on the streets use booze, too, like they do in prison to keep from thinkin about where they're at. If you sober up for awhile then a couple hours is about all you can handle and you say, 'To hell with it.' You don't like the way you feel towards everything."

Tim: "I've been into dope pretty heavy. That's the way I felt and mostly it was I couldn't stand myself. I felt rotten when I was off it, really rotten. You're just tryin to get away from feelin. I couldn't settle down anywhere and be happy with anything. But you don't give yourself a chance so it's suicide. I wished I'd died a lot of times and I O.D.'d two or three times but I'd wake up. Tough."

Gene: "Dopers will sell everything they have for dope. They try to talk you out of everything you got. They're tradin for dope all the time in here. Tradin and tradin and tradin and tryin to talk their wives and girlfriends into bringin in dope."

"The majority of em don't work or they don't go to school. They usually keep their time free. If they're in school, it's damn near as bad as on the streets. If something comes up they'll leave in the middle of the class. Keep runnin back and forth to do this and that. Even though it's a prison it's there, the dope, so their life revolves around dope and they're not really interested in shapin up their lives. Anything else is just maybe some little half-assed program just so they can have something for the Parole Board to say, 'Yeah, he went to school.' But there's no effort or anything so that's their lives all day long. That's their great escape. They're just constantly talkin about it; if they haven't got it, they're talkin about where to get it.

"Most of the violence in here, as I've said before, seems to be connected to drugs because it's so goddam valuable. People kill each other over drugs. They just put everything in it. You can't rip off a guy's dope, for chrissake! You can have his wife or you can have his kids but you can't have his dope. That's death, man.

"If the guy's got burnt, if he's spent a hundred bucks, he gave some guy a hundred bucks' worth for half a spoon of smack and he don't get loaded, there's gonna be a fight. Probably somebody is gonna get killed over it. That much money, you know. But as far as dope goes, they're goin to get stabbed or hurt over twenty bucks' worth, too, because of the deliberateness of the burn."

Tim: "Nobody likes a burn artist. A burn artist is someone that takes and sells you something that isn't marijuana, or takes aspirin and shaves it down and makes it look like Dilaudid. He's a burn artist if he gets some smack and he cuts it down, steps on it so damned much you couldn't get loaded if you wanted to."

SEGREGATION AND THE HOLE AS AN ESCAPE

Being locked in a single cell in isolation and away from friends who provide emotional support is, for some men, preferable to contending with the psychological stress of trying to survive in the general population. One prisoner achieves this particular escape through another escape—pruno. Apparently, alcohol is not a sufficient enough protection for his sensitive spirit. Like tornado warnings, his growing nervousness and tension signal to him that it is time to escape to the "cellar" (Segregation) to await the calming of the great storm within. There are other men in the prison like this who find release from the tensions and stress of the prison through this spatial-temporal isolation.

"You know, even Seg and the Hole can be a form of escape. I really think it is in Jimmy's case. He didn't seem to be able to handle the pressure too well out there in the population. About two weeks seemed to be his limit.

"He'd come out of Seg then he'd go to the Hole. He'd do ten days in the Hole and then he'd come out of there and they'd give him thirty days in Segregation. So generally, he'd do his thirty days, then when he came back to the wing we would talk and laugh; we'd talk about plans and things like that.

"He'd have plans about goin back to school; doin this and that and he'd write a few letters, then after about one week you could watch him goin down hill; start gettin nervous; start gettin irritable; start turnin up drunk again and pretty quick, darn it, they'd shake

his house down; they'd catch him again. He just spent all his time
hustlin dope, sellin weed, hustlin weed, tryin to get loaded. So if
he wasn't drunk he was loaded; one of the two. Two-three weeks at
the most and he'd be back in the Hole.

"And there's many guys down there like Jimmy. I accused him of
it and he denied it. I said, 'You like Segregation, don't you. You
can't make it out here. It's too much for you, isn't it. Too heavy,
man. You can't handle it, fella; you gotta go down, duck and sit in
that damned place and get fed all day long, gettin waited on like a
goddam baby. You can't come out of your cell so you don't have to
worry about gettin in fights. You don't have to worry about doin
anything. You don't have to clean your house because you don't
have anything.'

"He'd say, 'Oh no. I don't like it down there. I hate it down
there.'

"It's obvious he don't hate it down there. I hate it down there so
I never go down there.

"So there's fellas in Segregation that are down there for years
and years. They just can't make it out here. They don't wanna
make it out here. They can't. They come out and they act tough
and they're all huffy and loud but they're scared to death. So it's
just a matter of time, a very short time, and they'll be right back in
Segregation. So there's a form of escape. It's very real."

This *great escape* is achieved by retreating into the deepest
recesses of the inferno. It is a physical move further into the
depths of hell in order to free the mind of its chains. Perhaps there
is irony in this—seeking greater spatial restrictions of the physical
self to gain freedom (and safety) for the mind. In hell, it seems,
one may actually go on a retreat. Perhaps this is not ironic but
smart—when one is in the midst of pandemonium, one finds a
hole in it and hides. For Jimmy and others like him who choose
this form of the *great escape*, spiritual leave-taking is not leaping
over the wall but rather jumping into an abyss.

THE SIDEWAYS TRIP

The *great escape* that ends forever a man's experience within the
twisted confines of the prison universe is suicide. Suzanne Charle

states that more suicides occur in jails and lockups than in state and federal prisons. Nevertheless, suicides, which are considered to be epidemic in jails, are also on the increase in prisons across the nation.[6]

"Suicide in prison is one of the easier events to understand. I often wonder just how many men give serious thoughts to ending it all by doing a sideways trip. I know I have, and I also remember that once I began to seriously consider giving up the fight, my depression became all the worse. It is truly a vicious circle and it isn't easy to get hold of long enough to start some reasonable thinking. It is a hard way to get out of the Joint. It's a hard way to get out of anything.

"Suicide is regular around here and really isn't thought about except by those planning to take the final plunge. Friends of mine who have snuffed themselves always surprise me. It isn't easy to guess who will or will not kill themselves.[7]

"Some guys never even make it to the prison because they can't handle the pressure of the county jails. Shelton is bad and generally, I would guess, if a man were going to cut his wrists or hang himself from the bars it would happen during the first few weeks there.

"Generally, the bars or the reality of prison isn't the real factor. The men who give up have very deep emotional problems. If they don't know it before they get here it won't be long til it comes out in a rush.

"We simplify suicide in prison and simply say to each other. 'He must have been a weak bastard,' even if we have the brains to realize that it is never that simple. Many men are driven to death by a constant pressure from those around them. They may be punks or maybe they did something on the streets and must pay for it once they get to the Joint and have to face their old friends or enemies. Sexual attacks can be such a traumatic occurrence that a man will feel so completely degraded he will *want* to die rather than look at himself or others.

"Who can pin down all the reasons that cause a man to kill himself? There are no concrete reasons. Many men are Joint punks, cocksuckers, dings, rats, crazies, cop-lovers—all those things that cause others to reject them.

"Life can be pretty unbearable on a daily basis, yet men manage to live, to survive, in spite of rejection, kicks in the ass, name-calling, abuse of every sort from everyone. They live to get out. Somewhere inside they manage to cover and protect their soul til that gate swings open for them.

"When someone I know dies, I always begin to think back through a few days just trying to remember some strange action that might have been a sign. I guess there is always the fear that it could happen to me if my friends begin to die.

"The stress and anxiety is never ending. After a few years behind bars we can't even escape in sleep. Our dreams become restricted and prison invades that one sacred place we would like to keep free—our spirit. So the stress becomes a twenty-four hour monster.

"Somehow a man has to know the dangers and understand this aspect of prison. For some it is a shock and they never are able to cope. I wonder how they deal with the real world? It is possible to bury one's head in a bottle of alcohol or a good hit of dope outside. It is another form of suicide but it isn't so sudden. Of course, it is also possible to drink yourself into a daze in the Joint, and many men do just that.

"I suppose I should mention some of the forms of suicide. Cutting the wrists is a popular method. Cutting one's throat isn't unusual. Hanging, with a braided bed sheet tied to the bars, is probably the number one method. Poison is not often used except by accident. Example: the strong cleaning fluids and industrial wood strippers and industrial glues that many of us use to get high on. It is put on a rag, sock, or towel and inhaled.

"The Hole and Segregation cells are depressing enough to drive many men to take their lives in order to escape. For some it would appear to be the only way to get out. After years of living in the cramped confines of a segregation cell with no hope of getting out, it is easy to see why a man would prefer death.

"It would be very clear to you if you could really know what life is like in a segregation cell. You're segregated from society when you go to a prison but all prisons maintain their own small prison within the walls so that complete isolation can be achieved. For some, I would have to admit, there is no other way they can be held."

SCHOOL AND CLUBS AS AN ESCAPE

Some of the escapes over the wall are healthy attempts to deal with the psychological stress of prison life. Working (available for a fortunate minority only), participating in the college or vocational programs, or devoting time most of the day to club activities are some examples of ways the men have of manipulating their time-space restrictions to counter and control the stress and tension of their imprisonment. If a man can occupy his time productively in an area in the prison where he is relatively safe from dangers inherent in this compressed universe, he lessens considerably threats to his psychological, as well as physical, well-being. Such escapes also help to counter the boredom or monotony that often accompanies prison existence.

Gene: "For me and three-four hundred other men, education is a very positive and a very real method of getting up out of it. Gettin up out of it—what would you compare that to?"

Tim: "A herd is milling around about all day long; anything can happen."

Gene: "Trouble could jump off any minute out here in Peoples Park, the Yard, the rec areas where the TV's and phone room are, or the Breezeway."

Tim: "Guys are just millin around all day long; they just constantly wander from one area to another; just constantly moving and this is where things jump off—the fights, the threats, the knifings."

Gene: "Our brother, Broncho, was killed in the phone room over there. Others are killed on the Breezeway. So if you can find something to do all day, you can get the hell up out of that, out of the ugliness, brutality, assaults, rip-offs, rapes, wolves, danger of bein shot accidentally by a tower guard, the racial fights and arguments out there."

Tim: "You've got to get yourself up out of that somehow, escape it, because if you hang out in places like that you start thinking like those people and their little petty squabbles, the little petty hustles around the Joint. They're pitiful, but that can easily become your objective for the day."

Gene: "Education, I think, is the major great escape and it is a great escape for many guys."

Tim· "Our education department has a total involvement of about 500 or more men and that includes the vocational school, so this is eight-nine hours we can disappear. We can get into a positive learning atmosphere where people are doing things other than talk about the Joint. And it's nice and it holds over."

Gene: "It stays with you til the next mornin, really, cause you go away from the school and you have assignments and you have homework to do."

Tim: "You feel good about a test if you did good on it, a paper that you got good comments on that you didn't know you could do in the first place. So you leave the school and you pretty much have the rest of the evening scheduled. You may not even have time to go out and mess around in the Yard or spend too much time over in the TV room, but that's alright; you're escaping."

Gene: "Club activities could take up all day, too. You could spend from mornin til night. It's possible to go up to the club about eight o'clock in the mornin and stay there the rest of the day. Come out for chow; come out for a visitor or phone call and stay up there until nine o'clock at night, which is lockup time. You go back to the house also for four o'clock count. There's a phone in the club so that if you're lookin for somebody to visit or call you, they can call the club and let us know, so a guy can go take care of business, come right back again, which many of em do. All the clubs are like that."

Tim: "The men sit around and play dominoes or cards all day. There's a lot of card tables in the clubs. They have radios goin and they play tapes all day. Others play pinochle. Sometimes there's a hot little poker game goin over in the corner. Some men are doin homework."

Gene: "There's no fights goin on. There's a ping pong table and a TV set. No fighting, no bickering, no arguing going on. So that's a real form of escape for many of the men. We can keep our heads out of all the trouble, arguments, assaults, brutalities, and evil and ugliness of the Joint by staying up there most of the day. In the final analysis, just about every little side road we take, every activity we choose to take part in, every club we join, our radios, our TV sets, our letters home, our phone calls, our visits; they're all designed to do the same thing and that's to take our minds away from where we're at, what we've seen, what we've heard. To pull up out of it for awhile and relax. Above all, relax; give our minds a break."

RELIGION AS THE GREAT ESCAPE

Some men at Walla Walla who ordinarily would not be religious in the free world turn to religion as a psychological survival tactic. Clemmer, although recognizing that religion was important in the lives of some of the men at the New Jersey State Prison, was of the opinion that the majority of the men were "religiously insincere."[8] Delorme believes that many men in prison who are sincerely religious have an easier time enduring the pains of imprisonment. The Black Muslims are a good example of this.

Black Muslims at Walla Walla hold strictly to their religious beliefs. A dedicated and disciplined group, their religious stance — nonviolence — has contributed greatly to stability within the prison. Recognized as a respected group within the prison population, they are identified by their neatness, seriousness of purpose, and composure and dignity. Aziz, a Muslim prisoner, describes the contribution the religion of Islam makes in helping men grow and find strength in the midst of prison life.[9]

"With the Name Allah, most gracious, most merciful. Character-ized by its unity, respect for the elderly, and compassion with the young offender, the Islamic Community is indeed very unique. Under these stressful conditions, only Allah [God] knows what is in the hearts and minds of the men who embrace the religion of Al-Islam.

"The sincere person accepts Al-Islam, the Way of Life, because he believes in the One Allah [God] and that Prophet Muhammad is the messenger of Allah. This religion appeals to a man's sense of reasoning and offers good sound principles, identity, and dignity.

"Self-control and orderly conduct are essential ingredients for establishing and spreading sound and high morals within this prison. The sincere Muslim shouldn't be within the categories of punks, breezeway bums, snitchers, or bible pushers. Survival for the Muslim within this unnatural environment is much more dif-

ficult than for the hustlers slippin' and slidin', snitchers constantly
looking over his shoulder like a hoot owl, or the doper looking for
an outfit or a hit of dope. A true Muslim must put his righteousness
on front street every day. Sometimes he is laughed at or thought of
as stupid because he objects to smoking, abusive language, smut,
drugs, or refraining from the very things which led to his incarceration.

"Once a week, three Muslim brothers are designated to greet
the Chain's new arrivals to invite them to the Islamic orientation
classes. Since the assignment officer, who assigns the new inmate
to his cell, doesn't consider the inmate's race, age, or religious
preference, finding suitable housing is imperative, or the poor
guy would probably get beaten up, stabbed, or thrown out of the
cell. Therefore, the first objective of the orientation class is to
attend to the physical needs, such as finding suitable housing.
Muslims also offer sound advice for survival in this unnatural
environment such as the people to avoid and borrowing things
that might create nonnegotiable debts. Real estate is a very lucrative business within these walls. The Islamic Community had
their fair share of purchasing cells and reserving them for the
God-fearing inmates.

"There are inmates who convert to the Muslim life-style because it may offer them protection, religious privileges afforded to
the Muslims, or even a pork-free meal. A true Muslim is not one
to be overpowered by debt, fear, or oppression. We seek refuge in
Allah and not in administrative protection. We are instructed to
solve our problems through reasoning, diplomacy, and intelligence.
Anyway, for whatever reason a person may accept Al-Islam, we
welcome them without suspicion or discrimination.

"The majority of Muslims are respected throughout the prison
because we would take a weakling of a man's mind, with the
teachings of Al-Islam, transform his mind into a dignified strong
leader. In the course of a few weeks you would see him preoccupied with constructive ideas and serious pursuits. Those Muslims
who were able to translate their faith into action and rise above the
petty harassment of officers or inmates would become outstanding
leaders within the prison population. But, on the other hand, it
was difficult for some of the new converts to stand upright and

speak out with authority on various issues which violated the convicts' code and/or were gross violations of prisoners rights. That takes a great deal of courage.

"Our obligation as Muslims are to reassure the individual that Allah is God and the author of all energies. Allah has absolute power over all things and makes the final decision in all matters. Because many inmates have such lengthy sentences, they become insensitive and want to give up on life. They may feel that because their chances for release are so remote that there is no need to improve their character or conduct.

"We try to encourage them to come into the light of truth and out of their ignorant ways of suicidal and homosexual tendencies. We should never accept the labels 'convicts' or 'subhumans,' because Allah has blessed each of us with a resilient spirit, which can rise up at any time. We encourage them to never become disheartened because of outrageous maximum sentences, but to study the law books and resurrect themselves with the use of the pen, and then one day, when the door of this prison coffin is opened, visible scratches on the door will give evidence of those countless humans that have been buried alive. The public will then become concerned and investigate this graveyard and the criminal justice system who allows warehousing of human beings.

"On Saturday, visiting Imams [ministers] are permitted to teach and lend support to our moral development and spiritual growth. The Islamic program offered at the Washington State Prison consists of Prayer, Orientation, and Arabic languages classes. We have Jumah [congregation] Prayer on Friday. During Jumah Prayer, occasionally our community would be invaded by provocateurs who professed to be Muslims or desired a change in their lives. Since truth clearly stands out from falsehood, it was not our intention to expose anyone based on suspicion, but as the Resident Imam or Minister taught from the lectern, anyone within hearing distance who may have evil inclinations or a mind filled with lies or weak ideas would become very uncomfortable. The person would eventually leave or submit to truth.

The Islamic Community was never overly concerned about external opposition or internal disputes. The Holy Qur'an [Koran; the Bible for the Muslim and mankind] served as our guide which helped settle all our affairs. The word *Muslim* denotes *peacemaker*. As Muslims, we shouldn't be the aggressor in actions or words.

"Once we took direct aggressive action against a Breezeway hustler. He had been accused of abusing a new arrival who had just accepted Al-Islam. This hustler had a record of strong-arming the weak. Several very strong Muslim brothers sought out this individual. When they found him, he was armed and hiding in his club area. He pleaded with us and swore that he was completely innocent of all allegations. Had it not been for one from among our group who was knowledgeable of the Holy Qur'an, the hustler would have been severely injured. As it turned out, the new convict admitted that his account was exaggerated. The lesson learned was—to rely on the Qur'an in all matters. Allah says, 'O ye who Believe, if an unrighteous man brings you news, *look carefully* into it lest you harm a people in ignorance, then be sorry for what you do' (Chapter 49, Verse 6—H.Q.). This and many more isolated incidents were nothing more than a test of one's mettle, to serve as an example, and to strengthen the community as a whole.

"Either through apathy or lack of regards for safeguards, basic constitutional rights were either denied to the inmates or not allowed by the administration at the Washington State Penitentiary. Before and after the lockdown of 1979, one of the biggest problems facing our community was our right to religious assembly and worship. The 1979 lockdown brought changes within the administration. The new institutional policy was to disband groups or organizations formed and operated by inmates.

"The Muslims here have to constantly remind the prison officials that the Islamic Community is *not* a club or organization but rather a religious body. Our Community is universally accepted and legally sanctioned by the constitution of the State of Washington and the United States Constitution. These laws are reinforced by a long line of Supreme Court landmark decisions. It does not seem proper for the prison administration to disband this religious body if they recognize these authorities.

"Confiscating religious materials from inmates, depriving our religious community of an adequate place to worship, are acts of this prison administration, as well as withholding typewriters, filing cabinets and, in general, giving us the run around when we request a place to worship or study. This may sound a bit far-fetched but it happened and is still happening. We Muslims have no regular room to come together for the daily prayers enjoined on us by the Holy Qur'an."[10]

Delorme describes the role religion plays for the native American prisoner at Walla Walla:

"It's an escape mentally and physically, at least for a short while, because the Sweatlodge is located in the prison where they haven't a lot of traffic and where you don't usually hang around. Most of the guys that take part in the Sweatlodge, for the majority it really is the only time they've ever paid any attention to their own religion. Goin to a sweat, as they call it, takes time. On the outside [free world] I don't really think anybody allows themselves to slow down that much. But in prison there ain't nothin else to do so you can go ahead and sweat for a couple hours. For ninety percent of the guys who sweat in the prison, they wouldn't do it outside. It's supposed to give you some rules to live by and some try to live by the rules. It has a calming effect on those that use it. Even more so for the guys who try to follow the ways of the Sweatlodge. Indian religion says you're not supposed to run around killin people or bein mean. It's like the Ten Commandments.

"I used to get pretty irritated with some of the young guys — I suppose they got something out of it — because that was the only actual thing they would do was go to the Sweatlodge. But they didn't live by the ways [of the religion] the rest of the day. They did things they shouldn't do. When we first got the Sweatlodge it was hoped that by practicing and learning what the Sweatlodge was all about it would have a calming effect on guys that were drinkin and sniffin and fightin, but just like every other religion, people went to church on Sunday and act crazy the rest of the week.

"As an escape at least it occupies hours of every day. I don't take part in the Sweatlodge but I have noticed that for some guys it has an effect. It does give them something to believe in, something to study. I'd have to say it does give them strength and show them ways to deal with prison. In some cases, they'll almost accept suffering, almost as if it was something special. Like: 'We've been gettin killed for 200 years and there's no way to escape it except to be a man,' and almost wish for it in a way. It's like in battle you hold your head up higher the harder you're hit. So it does give strength to them in those respects.

"I've known some guys that have not been able to cope with the everyday stress but when they took up their religion and really got into it, and I mean Protestant and Catholic, too, they made it in prison even though they may have dropped it when they got out. I believe that religion in prison, ridiculed or not, has saved a lot of lives.

"Our religion is not different. The little Sweatlodge is actually a chapel. It's beautiful to the guys although it looks funny and it's raggedy. The guys will die for it and, obviously, they have died for it. It's beautiful, the little ground it stands on. To them it represents Indian history as far back as they can remember. It's a temple, a gateway, for all our ancestors that gather there to watch over them, the spirits of the Grandfathers. And the guys believe that. It helps those of us who even don't like to get into a little tiny space like that. Just knowing the Sweatlodge's there helps."

KICKING BACK AS THE GREAT ESCAPE

When the prisoner is in an area of the prison where he is most likely to feel safe, he is able to lift himself momentarily up and *over the wall*, forget the dangers and boredom of the prison, and share with others whom he trusts conversation, coffee, cigarettes, or food. Although these moments may occur in his club or in the education area, for example, they are most likely to occur while he is in his *house*. It is during these moments that he can *kick back*, relax, make the *great escape*, and forget, for the moment at least, the awful aspects of life in prison. In addition to relaxing by himself or with his friends, he is also able to read or study, listen to music, or watch television. Many of the conversations that appear throughout this book were made while the men were *kicking back* in their cells. The following is a description of life lived in the *house*, the one place in the prison where a man is best able to relax and drop his guard.

Cardozo-Freeman: "How many guys in your cell?"

Delorme: "Four. One has to get up at eight because he goes to the Coke Shack and works. I'm up so I usually wake him up. In the morning is a good time to do schoolwork. Everybody wakes up gradually after I'm up."

Cardozo-Freeman: "Do you talk?"

Delorme: "No. There's never a word said [in the morning]. It might be hard to imagine but with four guys in a cell we might be two days and not a word said to each other. You do what you're doin, ask a question, or 'You got a match?' That's it. No conversation. Other times we can't shut up. But the mornings like that the whole wing is real quiet. Everybody is still snoozing so the TV's are all low and the radios are on. They're on low. Like I say, I'm the only one awake listenin to news shows like Good Morning America. Then you have books and you have coffee. Somebody might bring you something to eat if they feel like it, or if you catch em walkin by and they got a lump under their arm you know they got some donuts or something.

"I can sit on my bunk and touch that bunk across from me with my feet really stretched out a little bit. In the middle of the cell we have a low table with legs cut down and with wheels on it because we're lazy. That way we can pull the TV over with our foot and turn it off and on and push it away again and you never have to get up. And it's also stacked full of books and papers, mostly from school. We got two-three tables in the house like this. We use those to stack stuff on. Just the TV table has wheels on it. And there's a toilet in the back of the house and there's a sink back there, a medicine cabinet with a mirror. Those you can buy. You order em from Wards or somewhere. There's four electric outlets, two on each side of the house and you can have extension cords. You kinda weave those through your bedsprings so they are out of our way.

"Some cells are painted fairly good. Some of em are really junky. We have pictures all over the walls. I got family pictures on my wall. I got W.'s picture on the wall; nobody elses. It's too hard to sit and look at play-girls all over the wall. I don't know how guys can live like that sometimes. Some cells, the entire wall, entire ceilings, down the back will be nothin but girls. The guys paper the walls with girls. Even the bottom of the top bunk. Everywhere they look, where their eyes go, there's pictures of girls. I guess it's to remind em of women."

Cardozo-Freeman: "Do you cook in your *house?*"

Delorme: "Yeah. Cookin is the best part of the place. It really tastes good. There's only a few ways to cook stuff. Cooking never was a hassle but beatin them guards in the kitchen out of the staginis, steaks, was. For a guy to rip off a stagini, you have to be about half slick. Slick or stupid, I don't know which now. But there's a bit of slick to it.

"My brother used to work in the butcher shop so he could get at those steaks all the time. Sometimes when things were really bad, a guy might even take some ole baloney out of that sucker. But we didn't like to take baloney if we could help it. Stagini steazakes. Stagini on the ragini. Tenderloin staginis, sirloin steazakes, porterhouse stagini steazakes [Agini and Ceazarny codes]. Shit. Be livin high on the hog. High on the hog. Go in from work, fix up a couple lumps of steaks; that's what you call it when you gotta take something out; it's called a 'lump.' Probably that name just came cause that's what it is, a lump in your pants or a lump under your arm.

"You gotta wrap the steaks up real good cause they'll leak blood or leak water. Don't like them frozen ones but sometimes you have to take frozen ones out. Certain guards shake down a certain way. There's a side door where all those kitchen workers come in and go out so when you're goin out, the pig'll be over there shakin down a line of people, so what you do is go kick back in the corner with a couple cups of coffee and you just check the guy out for awhile and see how he shakes down. Older guys that are kinda fat and lazy, they never hit you below the knee. Most of em don't even hit you below the waist when they're pat searchin so if you see that, you go back in the clothing room and you get some string and you take the steak, it's in the butcher paper, which is a waxed paper, you wrap it around your ankle and tie it with a string and you tie on as much as you can onto your legs, as much as you can carry outta there. You wear kinda baggy pants. Then when he shakes you down, he shakes your belt down, shakes your waist down, shakes you down under the arms and you ain't got nothin; you'll be clean so you just kinda boogy on outta there, man. But your ankles be like Alley Oops'.

"And you get on back to the house and pull out the ole stash and then tuck it away in the corner somewhere and then at night you make sure you bring in some extra rolls of toilet paper and you take the toilet paper and make donuts. That's what they call it—donuts. You take toilet paper and roll it round and round and round your hand, but you do it real loose. You gotta visualize that now, real loose. The purpose of that is so there's air inside the toilet paper because if it's tight, it just smolders. There won't be no flame. You take two-three dozen turns around your hand with the toilet paper and it's fat, so you take it and double it in half and you make a roll with it. It looks like a large donut. And you make up about a dozen of em cause each steak takes about five or six, dependin how big you make em.

"And then at nighttime after lockup you fix the kitchen up. Our kitchen was the toilet. You either use that or use cardboard cause those toilets in the wing, you can always smell em. They always stink. No matter how clean you make it there's still a gas sort of that comes up out of the sewer and it doesn't smell too hot. But anyway you can use that for the stove. You take a pan or something that's fireproof and then your stove itself is either a metal dustpan or another pie pan. Whenever I talk about plates I'm talkin about pie pans that we used to steal out of the bakery. Then you use one pie pan to put your toilet paper in and set em on fire and then you pull the curtains across [curtains are put up by the men for privacy while in their 'bathroom'] and one guy cooks while the other guys keep jiggers down the tier with the mirror and you keep watchin both ways with the mirror.

"As soon as it's cool, we take the steaks from their hidin place and spread em on top of the table. They're usually filleted tenderloins. They're about as big as a book and you lay em out on the table and salt and pepper em real good; might even sprinkle a little butter on em. Then I get a coat hanger and kinda bend it and make an oval on one end so that you can lay your steak on there without it fallin through. Usually your steak's kinda drapin over the edge. Your hand really gets hot so you wrap it with a cloth or you wear some ole cotton gloves, and then as soon as my partner tells me it's cool on the tier, ain't no magini on the tagini, then I torch the ole toilet paper roll and put the first steak on and I sit there and hold it, just like roastin marshmallows. And I get a big flame goin, see, and it even gets better after you get goin cause the grease of the steaks starts drippin down on the toilet roll and keeps it burnin a long time, like a candle or can of Sterno. Anyway, it keeps it burnin so when one side is nice and cooked real good, you flip it over and give the other side a lick. Man, it tastes good! Boy, I'll tell you! Mmmm Mmmm. Then you cook the steaks one at a time.

"And where's the smoke goin, you say? Well, right up behind the toilet there's a small vent cut in the wall and it travels up through the ceiling somewhere, up into heaven or whatever. It's one of those things you never know where they go to, they just go. It's a flue and it's always suckin air out. You can feel the air suckin through. So what we do is just cook real close to it so it'll smoke right up in it. Sometimes we used to make cardboard hoods right up over it so as to direct the smoke a little bit better cause that was about a half-assed serious beef sometimes when you'd be cookin. So you just get goin, cook four steaks and cook a big pile of toast.

"If we're really hungry, we might bring in some eggs. Course, me, ole Hog Jaws, I always have to pack me in some 'taters and some eggs. So I'm the last to cook for cause mine takes awhile. I cook me some fried potatoes. I even scramble eggs cause that's the fastest. About all you need is to get your pan nice and hot, put some butter in it and scramble seven-eight eggs, cook up two-three potatoes, have about four pieces toast, have a steak, and then two or three nice hot peppers, cup of coffee, settle down to some serious greasin, serious greasin. Whew! Oh man, that be good. I'm tellin you! So that's how we cook with them toilet paper rolls.

"If you're too lazy to steal some staginis you can always just take bread back cause good ole toast and butter is always good. We always got a jar of jam in the house. We can buy jam legit at the store so we always got jam. They also sell cans of chili, pork and beans, Vienna sausages, things like that. If you're cookin a can of store bought chili then you just crack the top and you sit it in some hot water and put your stinger in there and then you just keep your water boilin and that's how you cook canned stuff.

"We used to make homemade stingers before they made these little ole stingers legal and that's just an ole radio cord or an ole lamp cord and then on the very end of it you hook one wire to two razor blades. Then you take the two razor blades and bring em very close together and insert a couple pieces of wood in between to keep em from touchin each other. If they're too far away from each other they don't work. If they're too close together they short everything out. So you probably have a sixty-fourth of an inch between em and then you take thread and you wrap it around in a couple spots to hold it steady, then you drop it in your cold water, plug it into the wall and buzzzz. It makes noise and it boils water, man, really boils that water. Boils eggs that way; boils coffee that way, water for canned goods. Anything that has to be fried, cook it with toilet paper rolls.

"Boy, we'd steal a lot, man, out of that kitchen, that night crew. Damn, we were rippin it off! I worked in the bakery so I'd always mix lumps of cocoa and give em to a lot of people. What I'd do is take the regular cocoa and I'd mix powdered milk and sugar with it and then you got a good mixture. Just dump in some hot water and stir it up. That was our drink we stole out of the kitchen.

"Just regular ole routine, too, gettin past the guards. New guards are a pain in the ass, so when a new guard's on, what you do when you bring your lumps out, you always make it a point to leave early cause during mainline chow everybody's goin out the front door and you don't get shook down. You go out and come back or take your lumps out and give em to a friend and he'd pack em out and then you'd pick it up from him later. But when the right guards were on, it didn't make a fuck so we'd just slide on out the side door when he was on, man, and it wasn't shit. Like I say, we'd sit over in the corner and watch how he shakes down and then we'd get his routine down pat. A lot of guards don't like to feel around your crotch; they get embarrassed, I guess, so when you see the guard's like that and he's just pattin guys' pockets, he's stayin away from the guy's crotch, then you go in the back room and whatever you steal, you make sure you slip it down the front of you cause he won't touch there. Down in front and around the ankles was the best go cause after awhile even them fish bulls get so damned lazy they won't reach all the way down. All they do is pat.

"And then there's a lot of old time guards, they just knew everybody was packin. The fact of the matter is they even hate the shakedown so what they did was they pat you everywhere they knew that you probably wasn't carryin nothin. A guy'd go out of there, boy, big ole lumps stickin out all over him. Down his socks, down his waist, down behind him; he'd come up to the guard, the guard would pat his arms on the outside, pat down his waist just a little bit on the edges cause he knows he ain't got nothin on the side; he's got it all tucked back, and say, 'Go ahead.' And away he'd go—loaded.

"They used to give you ten fuckin days for packin a damned sandwich. I'm talkin about ten days in the motherfuckin growler! Down in the Hole. Shit. The slammer for the lousy sandwich! That was in C.S.S.'s days. Back when him and M. were here. Boy, you really had to be about half slick then. There was that Lt. T. and this little creepy sergeant they used to call Bug Eyes, and another bull. Them three had a fuckin trick. The lousy motherfuckers, they'd test you if they caught you with a bunch of fuckin lumps. I got busted one night with a lump of cookies. It pissed me off. Man, I ain't into cookies at all, you know what I mean? So I'm bringin out about a dozen motherfuckin cookies for this asshole. It was big ole dried peanut butter cookies, the worst fuckin kind of cookies in the goddam world. And so I tell him, 'Yeah, I'll bring you some cookies, man.' Of all the goddam days to be tryin to sneak out of the kitchen with a lump of cookies and I ran into Bug Eyes. He'd been in the kitchen so fuckin long, man, he's got everybody made. You come roarin outta that kitchen and start headin for that door. You can't stop and turn around cause he knows you're packin em, so he'll go around and get you.

"So here I am comin around the corner and I know what I'm doin. I'm headin for the wing thinkin I'm about half goddam slick with this lump of cookies down my pants and Bug Eyes is standin there, so he pats me down and finds the fuckin cookies, man. He's · got a grin on his face, too, dirty little sonovabitch. Takes me over to the table, sits me down at the table. He says, 'O.K., start eatin. If you don't eat em, then you get tagged. If you eat em all I'll let you go.' Goddam! I says, 'O.K. I'll eat em,' I says. I didn't want to go to the fuckin growler for ten days. So I'm goin over and get some milk and he says, 'No. Unhunh. You sit down and eat those fuckin cookies and you ain't havin no coffee; you ain't havin no milk.' Oh, goddam! I knowed I was in trouble. So I sat there and ate those fuckin cookies. I like to died; I was hurtin, man! It's alright if you like cookies, I guess, but jeez, I detest cookies! I ain't been able to eat a cookie since. If I get cookies in my packages, man, I give em away or sell em.

"Anyway, I've got a regular iron that I use in here to cook with. Not a steam iron; a regular iron. Once in awhile I used to make toast on it. Turn it upside down, it makes toast. If I feel like it I get some cheese and I make toasted cheese sandwiches. That's a good little stove. Easy to clean. Some guys got hot plates. I've only seen a couple real hot plates but I've seen a lot of homemade hot plates. You can find one of them old heaters and take the heatin element out of it and just bring that in and hook it up to a light cord and you make your own hot plate. Once in awhile you run into a toaster. In Eight Wing we had a four piece toaster so we used to cook steaks in our toaster, too, cause you just crank it down. It didn't pop up so it was always on until you unplugged it. We'd just set a pie pan over on top of it. All the heat comes up and makes a little stove out of it. That was a little bit fancier than buildin a fire.

"Everybody doesn't cook. A lot of people just don't do it cause they don't want to get a tag for it. In the wings, maybe half the cells on one tier have one time or another cooked something up. There's just a few that cook all the time like we used to.

"So anyway, we have a kitchen in our house, we have a bathroom, then we have a library where the books are. If there's a book over there, that's the library and if there's a jar of coffee over there then that's where the kitchen's at. If you move the jar of coffee over there, it's the kitchen over there. Some cells have things built around their sink. A lot of guys build em to stack together, or they build em in wall to wall, and when they shakedown, they [guards] tear everything out and throw it over the tier. They start over again.

"You start by comin into a room like this and you steal all that wood and you run out of here with it. You steal this table, take the legs off if you have to and run it back to Eight Wing. Whatever you can get. That's where I got my typewriter. That's where I got everything. If they leave the door open in here, we'll take the TV; we'll take the typewriters, the coffee machine. They all end up in Eight Wing. Mostly Eight Wing does that. It's funny. I've hauled planks in there so big I almost had to have help with em. The cops just turned the other way. And I'll be up there just bangin and sawin and hammerin and finally get something built. A shelf or a table or something. Then you keep hittin the hospital for bed boards. That's a good place to get wood cause they'll keep sendin over these big bed boards for your back. They make beautiful shelves. They don't seem to keep track of em so you're good for a bed board once every two–three weeks. Tell em you have back trouble.

"Anyhow, it's pretty quiet in our house. There isn't any real loud music comin out of the house except when I'm not there. We have the TV, then we have my radio and tape deck. I should say, 'had' cause they took it all in the shakedown. Anyway, we have plenty of entertainment-type things. We have lots of books cause Steve and I especially, we do a lot of readin, a lot of studyin. Most of his books are on his headboard on the end. It's built a little different so that it'll hold more junk. You load it up with books. Some guys have pictures on their head boards. Some head boards are nice and neat; some aren't. Most school people's head boards aren't too neat but you know where everything is.

"I have books from one end to the other on mine. I read, I watch TV. Never do one or the other; I do both at the same time. We kick back in there. You say, 'What are you goin to do, man?' He says, 'Aw I don't know. Think I'll just go in and kick back awhile.' If he's goin to do that he's gonna write letters and he's gonna watch TV and listen to the radio or talk to his cellies.

"Sonovabitches kept me up until after three last night. Gossip, boy, do we gossip. Like a bunch of ole hens or something. We gossip even in our barber shop, which we call the Hen's Nest. We talk about girls. If two other guys are talkin side by side in their houses they'll talk for two or three hours sometimes.

"Late last night there was some good music on and I heard Steve—he's kind of a poet—he starts sayin, 'Man, the street is loaded with single bitches. Two o'clock in the morning on Sunset Strip . . .'

"And I heard Bruce next to him say, 'Wait a minute. Wait a minute. O.K.'"

"You just kinda get all set up close to the bars so you can listen, see. Steve just starts takin off and everybody listened. And Bruce is always tellin jokes. But he kinda likes to listen to Steve talk about girls. And Steve starts paintin a picture like a movie, you know. And Bruce says, 'Wait a minute now' and gets his radio all set up with the music for background and sits down. Just out of the blue he started talkin about how the streets is loaded with single bitches and it was about two o'clock in the mornin and everything was gettin ready to jump on Sunset Strip. Bruce knows a story is comin on. Then they talked awhile about all those single girls down there in California and how easy it was to score, and then they talked about dope for awhile and music, then California in general. Pretty soon Bruce came in with a few of his funny jokes again. Then they were quiet for a long time with the music blastin away. I just kinda sit down and giggle two or three cells away. I was tryin to read all this stuff and I kept hearin em. You can't ignore a joke. I listen, too, when they start talkin about things. The jokes were kinda funny last night."

Cardozo-Freeman: "Do any of the men keep animals or birds as pets?"

Delorme: "There used to be cats in here. Last summer there was a couple ole broken down cats that lived inside the Joint. There was another that lived in Eight Wing. Most of the guys hated that cat. Somebody was goin to end up killin him anyway. He'd give you a heart attack and shit like that. I used to hate that cat. I used to wish that I'd throw the sonovabitch over the tier or something cause he was a big cat and he was a snotty bastard and he wasn't friendly at all. The only reason he'd hang around was if you'd feed him and people didn't like that. The chumps that used to feed him every day bring him raw kidneys and something out of the kitchen.

"He hung around their cell all the time, but you see what he'd do, he'd roam around and that's why people didn't like him. He'd just scare the shit out of people. He'd make you have a heart attack, see. I'd be laying there readin late at night and not expectin anything, just kickin back, and he'd just step right through the bars and when he walked he held his tail way up in the air and just out of the corner of my eye something would move. Just scare the hell out of you. Or he'd wake you up. He'd be wanderin around when everybody was snoozin at two or three in the mornin, man, that sonovabitch would jump up on your bed. He's bad for the ole ticker.

"The Lifers had a bunch of goldfish but they bushwhacked the goldfish pond and put poison in it. They put something in it that killed the goldfish. When they was gone they was gone, I guess. Everybody thought the guards did it cause they knew everybody liked the fish. That's why nobody wastes time with animals in here. Maybe, I suppose, because you don't waste your time with something you're gonna lose anyway. The cops are gonna take it away from you.

"Sometimes I've seen birds fly around inside the wing. They come through open windows. But nobody pays any attention to em. They land in front of you when you're on the sidewalk. You gotta walk around em or you gotta sometimes kick at em to make em get the hell outta the way. Fat little pigeon birds, sparrows, little jail birds. Years back when I was here there was a guy that caught one of those owls and he used to wander around with that owl on his shoulder all the time. He had it pretty well trained. It would come to him. Guys used to feed the jail birds, the stupid little fat swallows around here but nobody really pays any attention to em now. Don't even get fed anymore. No animals here but us chickens."

Cardozo-Freeman: "What are the men most likely to talk about when they are *kicking back?*"

Delorme: "The typical conversation between convicts isn't about stealin and it isn't about killin people, or it isn't about hurtin people. It's not about rippin off someone. It's about women. It's about our families. It's about our kids. It's about movies. It's about sports. You see? It's about things like that, mostly. Laughin, jokin, diggin each other, and rankin on each other. And of course, we talk about our gripes sometimes and what's goin on in here. And where I'm at [Admissions Tier] we try to help each other. Like Jerry, he's always with us. He's got a deep voice. Well, he's crippled and he's in a wheelchair so we pretty much take care of him. He got shot to pieces by police a few years back, which crippled him, and he's a little shaky around tape decks but he'll get used to my tape recorder, so I think you'll hear him once in awhile. We tease him a lot. We take his wheelchair away from him and have drag races up and down the tier and we force him to exercise and make him walk around with his cane and get him to exercise on the tier to strengthen him up a little bit. He's happy. He has a pretty distinctive voice. Can't talk good. That shooting affected his talking like a stroke does some people. He talks slow. Has a hard time forming words."

Kicking back images the dropping of one's psychological armor and relaxing comfortably. Having a pleasant time while in hell is possible if one is within a particularly safe niche and surrounded by others who one knows are not threats to the self. Under such circumstances the prisoner can forget, momentarily at least, the negative aspects of his existential situation and concentrate on those inner resources within the self or collaborate with trusted others, to make the *great escape*, thus creating a spatial-temporal sanctuary where anxieties and fears ordinarily experienced can be laid to rest. *Kicking back* is a positive way of *killing time*; a way of giving the mind a temporary rest from the stresses and tensions of prison survival. The following are examples of conversations which were taped while the men were *kicking back* in their *houses*.

A conversation about eating cats:

Lefty: "Did Mussie tack his little hide up on the wall?"

Joe: "It was Leo's cat."

Lefty: "Leo would get mad. Leo will kill over that cat."

Joe: "Oh, he was mad. He says my ole brother shouldn't be gettin mad over a cat. He said the cat was good, though."

Lefty: "Good for what?"

Joe: "I ain't never ate any cat."

Lefty: "Good for catchin mice but I don't even think them suckers were catchin mice."

Joe: "I've been invited to people's houses when they stew cat."

Lefty: "Have you?"

Joe: "But I'd never go cause I didn't like the thought. Glad it wasn't my cat. I don't know, that's probably what happened to my cat, probably why they invited me."

Father B. is sometimes the subject of conversation. A folk hero among the men, stories about him flourish:

Hal: "Father B. and we were having this memorial for Handy, you know, that little convict that died last week?"

Steve: "Was he that real ole geezer?"

Hal: "Yeah. You know, he's been in and out of all kinds of penitentiaries. Been in this one a long time. He was an ole hustler, dope addict, and Father B. got close to him in his last couple months that he was in the hospital. So we had this little service for him over in the Chapel and I said a few words about the Gospel. Couple other guys said a few things. I didn't even really know the guy. They needed somebody to read. Anyway, Father B. was talkin about stuff on him and he said when he was in the hospital he asked the guy if he wanted to be baptized and he told him, 'Aw fuck it, Father.' Everybody broke up."

Steve: "Yeah, Father B. is kind of a jolly looking guy anyway."

Hal: "Kinda looks like one of the Apostles."

About *dings*, pretended madness, and other subjects:

Joe: "Who's Speedy down there talkin with the last hour?"

Mike: "Number seven [cell]."

Joe: "The ding?"

Mike: "Yeah. He still is."

Bill: "Yeah."

Joe: "He's still givin him the what-for, huh?"

Mike: "Yeah, he still is."

Bill: "Hey, Speedy is one helluva guy. He's cleanin the guy's house out, you know. You know what he did? The guy, they wanted him to clean his house. They wanted Clark or Barnes to store his stuff and they went and got him a locker. O.K. They got the locker, got his clothes and everything in it. The guy took the locker out and put it in the day room. So those guys brought it back and put it in his house again and said, 'Now you have to use this.' So everything's O.K. and the last time, he's draggin his feet right up to it and when he goes to lunch and comes back, no footlocker. Where the hell is it? He took his footlocker and took it down the tier to the big dumper out there. So they had to go out and get his footlocker again."

Joe: "That's the one that just moved in the other day?"

Bill: "No. He's been here quite awhile."

Joe: "What does he look like? Is he an old guy?"

Mike: "No. He's a young guy."

Bill: "Yeah, he's about my age."

Joe: "They'll turn us all into psychiatric nurses. I ain't havin nothin to do with young guys anymore. I did that for awhile, too. Most of em are dingy just to get by in here, you know, so nobody will fuck with em."

Bill: "It's comfortable to them in that they're not involved."

Joe: "Yeah. It's a method of not accepting any kind of responsibility for anything."

Bill: "Well, there are those that pretend but there's quite a few in here that are really sick, physical and mental."

Joe: "No, I'm not talkin about them. That type, you're pretty much able to pinpoint em. There's a couple of blacks that do it, too. You can tell when you listen to em callin home. There's no craziness when they call home. I mean it disappears. They get back into regular conversation."

Mike: "Wait til he starts talkin about albino ardvaarks and the sex life of the purple armadillo."

Bill: "Something crazy, man. Especially the sunburned armadillos they used at Armageddon. They were braised sunburned armadillos they used at Armageddon. They were sent in there to ravish the town and they went down."

Joe: "The dings are real important in here. A ding's a ding."

Bill: "That's right."

Joe: "We sure get our share of em. We got one between me and you. Got one couple next to you."

Mike: "No, just one."

Bill: "Unless you count Speedy."

Joe: "One sniffer."

Mike: "We do."

Joe: "Yeah, what's his name, the long-haired kid with glasses?"

Bill: "Oh yeah, he's always hittin on me to bring over some typewriter repair fluid."

Mike: "I know who you mean."

Joe: "That stuff is ferocious to your mental and physical being."

Bill: "It's a killer."

Joe: "I know. I did it, man, for years. He got his box [locker] back in the house?"

Speedy: "Yeah. He had his box over there. Garbage, that's where it went."

Joe: "Did Jerry go get it?"

Speedy: "No, he went up and got it."

Joe: "I don't know, brother; she's a pretty tough life."

Speedy: "Ain't it a tough life?"

Joe: "What'd you do, glue his box to the floor?"

Speedy: "No, just put all his stuff back in it and got all them dirty towels and all those sheets out of it."

Joe: "Are they just out layin around on his floor?"

Speedy: "He had all his personal stuff in the big box."

Joe: "I hadn't noticed."

Speedy: "It was gettin to stinkin."

Joe: "Pretty close to you guys."

Speedy: "I know he's going to do the same thing again."

Bill: "They got it down there now?"

Joe: "What is this thing with the footlocker? He doesn't like it? Does he think there's something hidden in it?"

Speedy: "I think he wants control over whatever he's tryin to do. Footlocker doesn't give him that kind of control. He feels he has to contain whatever that big glob of clothes has or something."

Joe: "He's got to kick it a couple of times now and then. Well, he should be on Third Floor, I guess. Speedy, you can have him. Make him your personal ward."

Speedy: "Ugh. Give him to Jerry."

Jerry: "Nope. No way."

Speedy: "You ought to hear that guy's conversation."

Joe: "That crazy guy?"

Speedy: "Yeah."

Jerry: "He's too far away."

Speedy: "His German accent is really, really bad. He comes out with some weird things. Talks about atomic bombs and butchering people and black marketeers and minorities."

Joe: "Do you live next to him? Can you get him on tape?"

Speedy: "I can get him on tape."

Joe: "Get talkin to him about his opinion of the prison, how a ding gets by the daily fuckin routine of a ding, man. Bells start ringin when he wakes up in the morning and don't quit until the next day. Bugs are after him, and all that shit."

Mike: "Oh hey, we were talkin about mental illness, the myth of mental illness up in the Social Problems class and I raised my hand and I say, 'You know, I have half a mind to do one helluva good article on schizophrenia.' "

Joe: "What about the other half?"

Mike: "The teacher looked at me. Some of the conversations that we have, you must admit that those that are in earshot sometimes wonder. We talk about some weird things. Rolfings. I told them the other day. We got into a big deal about rolfings. Well, it's a kind of massage, you know. We was talking about it and I told them, I said, 'Did you know that rolfing your groin can cause blindness?' "

Bill: "And insanity. How about the dendrophids?"

Mike: "Those are the people that have an outstanding love for keyrings."

Joe: "For what?"

Mike: "For keyrings. Yeah, that's what a dendro is. Yeah, they love dating keyrings."

Joe: "Pretty perverse thing."

Bill: "If you've got to date a keyring, I don't know; to each his own. I prefer women myself."

Mike: "Dendrophilia is a perverse condition which rarely strikes an individual. The first case history of a dendrophiliac is a German psychologist or something."

On playing jokes on the guards:

Toby: "Was you there when me and Bobby faked that fuckin beef and stamped a tee shirt with my number on it, blood all over it, sprinkled blood from the kitchen all the way past the patrol to the high school?"

Tim: "Oh yeah. Pig's blood?"

Toby: "Yeah. They went and got it."

Tim: "Yeah, I remember that. I was layin in some other wing."

Hank: "Kinda looked gross."

Tim: "Slimy."

Toby: "Big drops of blood all along the Breezeway. There was another one. One time, man, we put somebody on the stretcher over in the kitchen. Tied his head with a big bandage, blood drippin from the motherfucker, and we run up and got em to clear his cell, to take this guy to the hospital. It was close to chow time and we wanted to beat that rush so we're whippin about ninety miles an hour and we get over by the fuckin gates and stopped, let the guy off and prop the stretcher up and go on our way."

On plans to help get along with one another better:

Brian: "Yeah, I was thinking exactly the same thing the other day and we can do that. We should do that pretty quick. Let everybody know where our heads are at and we'll say, 'O.K., listen. Let's do this. Just be different from everybody else in the fuckin Joint and don't judge a guy because you don't like the way he combs his hair.' "

Jerry: "Or just the way he walks."

Brian: "Yeah. Don't judge him for that. Let's look out for each other a little bit and say 'Hello' and try to be real people, man to man. Things really will change. There's some guys that are quiet by nature. Some have a lot of mental pressure on em. Even that'll help these mental cases. They see everybody's not out to get em and they'll start comin out of their shell and we'll probably see more normal people. Prison is a bad situation."

Jerry: "If they would just sit down in a group, go and just talk and get to know each other."

Brian: "I'd like to do that, yeah."

Jerry: "So would I."

Brian: "I would love to do that."

Speedy: "There might be people down here that don't want to do that. Don't want anybody to get close, friendly with em, or get close to em."

Brian: "Well, yeah, and they should say so, too. And we can accept that and that's fine and dandy, too. We can probably get us a tier meeting. Guys like you and I and Speedy and Pat. Just make sure we kinda talk to everybody and let em know that, too."

Speedy: "Yeah. I think that would be a real good idea."

Brian: "Well, you'd see a helluva relaxed atmosphere. Don't you think it is here anyway? [Admissions Tier]"

Jerry: "Yeah."

Speedy: "It's movin in that direction."

Jerry: "You don't have to worry about somebody coming and stealing nothing if you leave it sitting on the table or anything like that."

Brian: "Yeah. Well I feel that way, too. Should be that way."

Speedy: "I mean you've got to live with each other in here. Why should you steal from each other? I mean if I've got something and you want it and I've got enough of it all you gotta do is ask."

Brian: "Yeah. That's part of it, too, loaning things to em if you got it."

Speedy: "If a guy needs shampoo and soap and things, if a guy needs some stuff like that, don't have to know me for ten years to ask me for something."

Jerry: "Lot of people don't see it that way though. They're closed in on themselves and they have a tendency towards that thing that everybody is out to get them and they don't want to borrow nothing from nobody cause they feel like they're in debt to them and they've got to pay them back."

Speedy: "They'd be owin."

Brian: "Yeah and that puts a guy through changes, too, cause he's always wonderin, 'Is this guy gonna drive on me today for what I borrowed from him? Or is he gonna stab me cause I didn't pay it back to him?' So then you got people that take advantage of that, too."

Or remembering past events in the prison:

Duane: "Was you here when S. killed that guy? I was in there with Larry, Tanks, me, and this other guy called Obie. Next door was Sam L. and it really was something else. This guy was movin in and all of a sudden I'm in there one day and I seen this guy movin his shit into Sam's cell and the next thing I know, man, the guy drew a knife on his partner over on E deck. And at that time I couldn't picture myself going around E deck into somebody else's cell cause I didn't have that authorization.

"Apparently, the beef was over some missin cigarettes cause both of em were barbers at that time, so this other kid pulled a knife on S. So he tried to cut S. up and so they got in a fight. So S. took the knife away from him and started stickin him and so the cops came up and they took the guy and put him on a stretcher and started runnin him to the hospital. And so S. got a little bit more mad every time he thought about it and S. ran downstairs out the gate and still had the knife in his hand and started stabbin the guy while the cops had him on the gurney. He stabbed him so many times that he upset the guy once off the cart and the cart flipped over, and he broke the knife in the guy in front of the Control Room and he still wasn't satisfied so he started beatin on the guy with his fists until finally more officers came and jerked S. aside and took him inside Big Red.

"And he didn't go to trial for it or nothing. He just got a couple years' flop out of it for killin that guy. Oscar Hocks lived beside me. We used to call him Oscar Hocks cause he passed out socks from Boston. He tried to pull a bulldog trip in the cell."

Stew: "He tried to turn him out?"

Duane: "Yeah."

Stew: "Was he a white guy or a black guy?"

Duane: "Bossin him around and shit like that. Anyway, remember Blackie? Louisiana Blackie? I was in my cell and about a week later, Blackie died. I'm sittin there in the house and Blackie's tier man, so he comes over and bullshits with me. We're drinkin coffee and so he's goin over to get me a couple of books to read and I'm waitin and waitin. It's about nine o'clock in the morning, too, and so he goes all the way across F deck, back down the wing and he comes up on the long side of E deck. I think he was in cell three or four on E deck, and so I'm sittin there waitin, man, waitin and waitin, and finally it was about 10:30, man, and a guy comes along. I says, 'Hey, man, you seen Blackie?' He said, 'Man, didn't you hear?' I says, 'Hear what?' 'Blackie's dead.' I says, 'What?' 'He had a heart attack. He got halfway in his cell and he died.' And man, I was madder than hell. I was concerned about them books.

"These other guys went and ripped off Blackie's mattress. Some guys went and ripped off his store, took his candy, coffee, and cookies and other gourmet delights."

Stew: "As soon as he had a heart attack?"

Duane: "Yeah, as soon as he was dead. They pulled his mattress out from under him, got his watch."

Stew: "Shit."

Duane: "Shoes."

Stew: "Vultures; huh."

Duane: "Yeah. Stripped him off, ripped him off and I'm there waitin, man, waitin for Blackie to come back with that shit for me. I'd only been here in Walla Walla two weeks, man. A killin and two stabbings. One before I got here. One after I was here about a week. It just didn't seem possible that people would die that fast. And then I get to thinkin, I told you tonight that this place is probably the closest thing to a natural jungle in the world, with survival of the fittest is what it's about. You gotta be tough to survive in this place."

Stew: "It isn't just anybody that can come into prison all their goddam life and stay sane."

OUT THE GATE

The final *great escape* comes when the prisoner actually leaves the prison after having served his sentence or been paroled. For some, this *great escape* is only temporary; they are returned to the prison for violating their parole[11] or committing another crime. The psychological adjustment of moving from a distorted and constricted spatial-temporal universe into the free world is profound. A man carries with him into this greater and freer time-space dimension the burden of his negative self-image, the fear that he cannot adjust, and that he will be reviled and unforgiven by society. Many are ambivalent about *squaring up*.

Steve: "Would it be slicker to stay out? We can stay out. What do you think is ahead? I don't think I'm slick enough to get out and continue to try to steal, see. You been doin that all your life so with a little bit of effort you could keep on doin it and probably not come back. How come we don't learn how? So I'd rather stay here instead of tryin to sweat it. I've tried and tried. I've tried to walk the fence. I've tried and tried. I wish I could."

Duane: "You've never tried."

Steve: "No, not for long."

Duane: "You're like me. You get out there, you go to school, you do anything you can to stay out there but you're gamin, Jack. I know I'm gamin. At least I can face up to the fact that I'm gamin. I went to business school, I'm gamin."

Steve: "I didn't go to no school when I got out there."

Duane: "But you did, you took that job at O.J.T."

Steve: "Oh yeah."

Duane: "But you were never really interested in it. If you was interested in it you would have stayed right there and did it, you see. Your head is like mine in a way. You want to get out and you want to be lackadaisical and procrastinate, to try to rejuvenate the good feelings that you used to have. You wanna feel em for awhile, so you procrastinate to do something that would be beneficial to you. You sit back like I did and say, 'I'll just get drunk today. Go out and get loaded or go check this broad out, you know, or see what's happening first and then do it tomorrow.'"

Steve: "I just asked you if you want to."

Duane: "I don't know."

Steve: "We can't forecast the future either."

Duane: "I look at it this way. Right now I don't have very many veins left in my body that I can use anyway. The ones I've got that I can use to get loaded on are damn near inaccessible to me, so I'm to the fact I have to swallow it. I have to horn it or skin it and I don't like horning. I don't like skin popping and there's the possibility that maybe I do want to quit. Really can't say."[12]

Steve: "If you do, it ain't goin to be nothin this joint or any other prison did."

Duane: "It will be because I fuckin have to. I want to."

Steve: "Won't be because of programs in here or because you're scared of the penitentiary."

Duane: "I don't think anybody is scared of the penitentiary once they've been there."

Steve: "They're scared to start with. I know that."

Duane: "I mean they talk about the death sentence. The death sentence doesn't deter anything because you still got people stacked up on death rows. But I don't believe I actually think about squaring up, I actually think about gettin a job, I actually think about the future.

"I think about my kid. O.K. I dream about my kid and it's actually the first thing I've ever really had in my life, that means to say that was my own. I hate to think about when my daughter gets about thirteen–fifteen years old and she says, 'Say, Dad, what have you done for a livin?' A dope thief, a thief, an armed robber, a convict, a conniver, you know. What the hell will I say? So it's time, you know. It's time that you better stop as well as me and think of that stinkin hole card we got. That hole card is only good for so long, Jack, and after so long the damn thing wears out, man. Sweat deteriorates it.

"You know I think I'm a hustler. I'm pretty damn good but

pretty damn good isn't good enough anymore. Not in this sophisticated age. Jeez, how many people we know who blowed a good
score? They're still up here. Maybe they're not here on the good
scoring beef but on a petty chickenshit scoring beef. But you know
and I know that we got a little bit of sack. We know whatever we
have to do. We might not think too good at times. At desperate
times we might revert, fall back to what we know the best. I
suppose it would just be like if we were starvin in the mountains,
man, and we had 'No Huntin' signs up and we got a gun with
plenty of ammunition. We're goin to have to kill something to eat,
Jack, or else we're dyin."

Steve: "You know, once a drunk always a drunk and once a thief
always a thief."

Duane: "I think that's stereotypin. I don't think it's possible.
The same as sayin once a smoker always a smoker."

Steve: "Well, you can square up. If you have a business of your
own and one of those big houses and kids. But you won't feel good
about your past, really. You know, the good ole fuckin days. That
ain't gonna go away from you."

Duane: "I tell you what I think. I think if you and me stop and
think of what you might be missin, if you do square, you'd be real
successful, you'd think, 'Man, look at Sonny. Got that fuckin drug
store.' Somebody held it up and you get to thinkin, 'Jeez, I wonder
how much narcotics. Wonder how much geez they got. I bet
they're loaded like dogs.' I think about that.

"I dream about makin a sensation, a big stinkin sting or one of
them scores where you say, 'One big score, man, and that's it.' A
big scorer; that's me, Jack. I think about it when I get out of here. I
think about.... aw Jeez, man, you know what I'm thinkin about
right now? I'm thinkin about transportation. Thinkin about the
type of car to get which would be most inconspicuous. When you
start thinkin like that, man, you know what you're thinkin. You're
thinkin about doin it to a poison shop.

"You're thinkin, 'Man, if I could just get one score to put me on
my feet I'd just get out.' That's what you're really thinkin. A score
to get you by with until you get on your feet, man, to get a job or
position. That's what I think. Just one job, man. Just one good one
to keep me from goin out and hustlin every day. Then you start

thinkin, 'Now what kind of a job could that be? Well, maybe there's a pharmacy that's got some D's that's easy, that I can get and fast.' You know, be nothin. And you get desperate. That's what does it. And I don't know if I'm goin to do it when I get out again or not. I'm hopin it will change. Maybe if I make enough money while I'm in here, you know what I mean? Maybe I can get enough money to save so I can get out with a little poke. Better than forty dollars and a ticket to Tacoma. That's death, you know."

Steve: "Yeah."

Duane: "Maybe if I made enough money while I was in here something might be done. I'm tired of bein bounced around like a handball. I'm sure tired, Steve. I think everybody in here's tired just sittin in here and wastin away, gettin fat, sloppy, bitter. We're all tired of tryin to live the same existence."

In addition to the economic and social handicaps a man faces when he goes *out the gate*, he experiences psychological problems that are common to those who have become institutionalized. Ex-convicts, like former mental patients, tend to behave in ways that are regarded as out of place in the free world. Their institutionalization conditions them to what Goffman refers to as "situational improprieties."[13] The contrast between life in prison and in the free world is so great that the men are often overwhelmed by it, particularly during the first weeks after they have been released. The rules and folkways of the free world confuse and sometimes threaten them, tearing down their self-confidence, which to begin with is very fragile. One glaring fact emerges: a man's prison experience does not prepare him to cope with life in the free world. The distorted techniques he must learn in order to survive in prison become so strongly imprinted on his mind that when he is released into the free world, he goes forth chained psychologically to his prison experience. The internalization of distorted prison ways and worldview serve as invisible shackles from which he has great difficulty freeing himself. As a consequence, he moves into the free world still a prisoner.

Will: "You know, the funny part about it is that surviving in here, it doesn't make you any better at getting along on the streets through thick and thin and all that shit. You say, 'Hey, man, I made it through the fuckin penitentiary. I can slip and slide through anything now.' You get out there and you can't slip and slide through the fuckin phone bill, you know what I mean? It don't work that way. Your same tricks, they don't work out there. You can't shank people. You can't beat people up and you can't intimidate em. Every fuckin thing you try to do, they call the cops. That ain't against the law in here but it's against the law out there. You can't push people around. You can't even threaten to kill somebody out there. That's assault."

Hank: "You can't gorilla the motherfucker. You can't give em that wolf ticket, man. They won't go for it. They just open their mouth and scream, 'Police.' It's weird."

Will: "Yeah, back to the fuckin Joint. 'Man, I'll kill that sonovabitch!' 'You can't kill me. I won't stand for it! You can't do this. You know who I am, you sonovabitch?' "

Hank: " 'I'll call the police. I'll call the police.' God, that used to drive me up the fuckin wall cause those little dinky sonovabitches was gettin in my fuckin face in a tavern, a bartender tellin me to get out or some fuckin thing. 'You motherfucker, I'll kill you. I'll kill you!' The fuckin punk goes to the phone and you want to tear his head off."

Will: "All this bein slick shit in here ain't worth a shit out there. It don't work on the Old Lady. It don't work on your mother. It don't work on the welfare. You plan on stirrin up the world with them people and they don't give you no check, no money. Don't work on the parole officers. And there you stand, man. What do I do now? Whatcha gonna do out there, huh? I ain't got no fuckin job. Got no money. Can't bulldog the fuckin foreman or nothin. Even if I got a job it's goin to be a week or two before I get any money. And what do you do for clothes?

"If you're lucky you got people to help you. But a lot of guys ain't got no people to help em. And they ain't learned shit by bein in here. Number one that I can see, you're goin to lose all the motivation you got. All the confidence has got to go out the window. The only thing you got left is a little self-respect, but you can't eat self-respect. But you gotta have a little self-respect somewhere along the line and you gotta have a little self-confidence, which goes with it. That's important to find a job.

"Us long-term cons, when we get out of here, we can't even give change right. You can't even order a coke right. You stand there with the stinkin waitress and it looks like you're a fuckin dummy cause you're tryin to count these strange coins in your hand and you get down with it and they're in a fuckin hurry and then they start gettin uppity at you cause they gotta give you a couple minutes and you look like you're a retard or something."

Hank: "I got problems with makin change, all those little things. It takes a long time to adjust out there."

Will: "Takes you twenty minutes to get up nerve to cross the street. You can't judge how fast them cars are comin and then you got the fuckin light that says 'Go' and you don't go for that shit cause it'll probably change back too fast and you'll find yourself in the street. You're standin there screamin. So I used to take off runnin across the fuckin street; the car would be way down the street, too, and I'd leave my Old Lady back on the other curb across the street waitin for the 4,000 pound fuckin automobiles to stop on a dime. Not me, Jack. I'm goin to cross the motherfuckin street talkin big shit on the other side like I done won a battle.

"Even after I was out awhile, man, I used to embarrass my Ole Lady, she said, if I hesitated and take long and start lookin around and all this shit. And me, man, I'd fly across the street. And even when I give it a helluva try, we'd still be in the middle of the street. If a car comes around the corner or down the street, man, I'll break and run. Gotta get to safety quick. I look up and down that street so hard that my neck would hurt. That and makin change and orderin things in a restaurant was a pain in the ass. I couldn't do it."

Hank: "Or like gettin off on the wrong floor of the elevator. Rather than get back on, I'd walk up ten flights, or the elevator door would open and there would be more than two–three people in there and I just shook my head like I wasn't waitin for it and I'd walk up the stairs."

Will: "The people, the crowds, man, I couldn't deal with em. Just a matter of adjusting. And yet we're crowded in here. But we're all wearin the same kind of clothes, you know. With people out of a cell, barefooted with your clothes torn up, nobody gives you even a second glance.

"But when you're on the streets and you're tryin to do everything right, which includes tryin to dress right, and already you feel ten years behind and you don't know if you got the right kind of pants on or shirt, and you're lookin at everybody, at the way they're dressed. Course, nowadays you're lucky cause everybody looks trampy anyway. But even so, if you got clean clothes on or new clothes, you still feel like a sore thumb standin in the middle of a crowd, man. I do. It's a pain in the ass."

Hank: "John was tellin me when he got out he was sayin he'd look around and he'd think everybody was lookin at him and he had this feeling everybody would think, 'Boy, that motherfucker's a con right there.' It was just a total feeling of paranoia. They probably didn't know him for jackshit. They didn't know if he was a convict or a cop."

Will: "I tell you one thing that didn't help me much; was this nice lookin little chick. I kinda had a crush on her. She worked at the studio I was workin in. Nobody knew I was from the Joint except the boss. I took her to lunch several times. She was a pretty blonde and she started laughin at me one day, man. We were sittin there talkin. We were at Woolworths, at that little counter, and I says, 'What's up? You're always laughin at me.'

"She says, 'Aw, it's so cute the way you talk.'

"I says, 'What do you mean? The way I talk?'

"She says, 'You say things I never heard for years. It's kinda strange.'

"Man, I really froze up on that broad. There was no reason to but I just froze up on her rather than try and explain myself. It just made me so fuckin self-conscious. I went on a silent trip for six months. I didn't want to ask her, 'Well what did I say?'

"So it just fits right into how you feel, anyway. It took me months to get up enough nerve to even ask her to go to lunch with me anyway. I felt inferior or something, anyway. The only reason I didn't approach her in the first place was I didn't have any good conversation. How do you get in a conversation? 'Where did you go to school?' or 'What kind of work do you do?' All you got is this ole blank spot where the prison was.

"I spent three months tryin to get my answers together before I asked her out to lunch again in case she tried to trap me somewhere. I had my army history and my jobs, school and everything, pet names and dogs and kids. If she hit me with that shit it just turned me upside down. It's funny."

Joe: "I can see how you feel. I've only been out of circulation here not too long and I feel strange right now. I wonder how the fuck I'd do right now if I got out in the street."

Hank: "I don't operate too good around these women who come in here. It took me quite awhile for me and C. to get together.

"The first time she was into the club, like she asked me, 'How come you never talk to me? You look at me a lot.'

"I said, 'Well, all the lookin is I was scared of you cause I don't know what the hell to say to a broad anymore. I figured you don't want to talk to me anyway, an ole convict. I don't know what the hell to say to you. I don't know what really to talk about. So talk about my life? That's just a bum trip. That ain't nothin.'"

Will: "Actually, it's hard to meet a woman once you're out there. You end up goin after somebody you feel is on your level, and what's your level? You end up goin to a fuckin tavern lookin for some dummy in a bar that ain't goin to have the smarts to ask nothin, you know. She ain't got no conversation."

Hank: "Just take a beer in her hand, take her home and go to bed and you don't have to worry about no intelligence or anything like that."

Will: "That ain't right. When you get outta here, unless you plot against it and try to keep your head above water, they don't have to put you down. You put yourself down. You meet all them expectations, man. You're this and you're that. You're no good. You're lowlife. You're unworthy. No morals. All that bullshit, man. That's the kind of shit that's in the air surrounding you all the time."

Hank: "That's what this Joint will do to you bit by bit."

Will: "You accept it as true and you build that. You build your character that way, which is no character at all, which is obvious as hell to people out there by the way you act. You hang your head. You don't talk.

"A nice lookin chick comes in, there's no way you'd say anything to her because she's not on your level. She's this and that. There's different classes and you can't socialize cause these people they're a better class. Or they look like they got dough and they talk about things I don't know nothin about. I only know about stealin. I don't know anything about gardens and workin and goin to parties and this and that. So there's a whole world you eliminate right there. Stay away from em. And that's probably where all that fun is.

"You could fit in if you tried. They'll accept you, you know. Square johns ain't that bad, see. But a guy doesn't give himself a chance, man, and if you shut yourself out, boy, you're in big trouble. You'll get outta here and be a lonely sonovabitch. You're a loner."

The best intentions of *squaring up* often fail because of the stress of trying to adapt to the ways and demands of the free world. Irwin describes in great detail the problems that newly released men face. He compares the men to puppets tied to strings that are controlled not only by their parole officers but by their economic, social, and psychological handicaps.[14] Often the stress of the "puppet dance" causes a man to feel so yanked and pulled that he gives up, collapses, reverts to his old ways, and finds himself behind the walls of the prison again. For some the stress of trying to succeed in the free world is so great they are actually relieved when they are returned to the twisted spatial-temporal confines of the prison universe. Their spirits, having been confined for so many years, have adapted to this distorted and constricted mode of existence. They can no longer adjust to the world beyond the walls of the prison.

Russ: "I don't know what it is. Everybody doesn't take it the same way. Some guys seem to have more freedom in here than they feel they have on the streets. They get along better in here. They're happier. I see some guys I know personally, man. They're always in a foul mood at home. When I see em in Tacoma they don't laugh and they don't joke like they do in here."

Jim: "Well, them guys are institutionalized."

John: "Well, Hap's that way. Hap's a real clown in here. Dog Eyes. He's a clown, man. He has lots of friends. Makes everybody laugh. Man, he's always jokin. He never takes nothin serious. Well, man, on the streets he's always mad about something. Hardly ever smiles and shit, you know."

Russ: "You really don't have any direction out there. You can go for so many years without having any goals and direction."

John: "Out there if you really haven't time to set any goals then you're already in a situation where it's not so unusual for you to commit a crime or hurt someone, and then if you don't got no direction then it's difficult to handle them responsibilities. I know that personally. And in here you don't got them responsibilities. They take that away from you. So you can't make it out there."

Ironically, the prison experience ends in the same way it begins — in chains. This time, however, the chains are psychological rather than physical restraints. Although a man may become very adept at making the *great escape* while in prison, his efforts at coping psychologically with the dangers inherent in the restrictions of his prison universe are responsible, in part, for shackling him in his attempts to deal with life in the freer spatial-temporal world beyond the walls of the prison, particularly if he has spent many years in prison. Delorme explains:

"It would seem that a man who can make his way through this type of system would be able to make it anywhere. Not so. You give up too much, let go of too many values and lose sight of the real world. To pick it all back up and reverse the process is to rebuild your mind. With no help, it is a monumental job and few of us even understand what has happened to us, let alone figured out the psychological tricks for a workable healing process."

The psychological barriers that a prisoner must build in order to protect his spirit while he is in prison are not easily dismantled. Adaptation to life in prison is not suitable for adaptation to life in free society. Prisoner worldview is too specialized, too narrow and the uses of space and time far too different. Every dimension must be altered if adaptation to the free world is to succeed.[15] Unfortunately, beyond the prison's work-release program, which is helpful, there are few "decompression chambers" or "debriefing sessions," few ways of easing the long-term prisoner's transition; consequently, the culture shock experienced when moving from one worldview into another may be great. Once out of prison, a man may discover that psychologically he is still a prisoner chained to his former universe, unable to break loose.

NOTES

[1]Although it is true that men in submarines or spaceships, for example, suffer from the stress of close confinement, there are important differences. To begin with, the men are not being punished; they are there of their own free will;

they are carefully trained for their ordeal, and finally, and perhaps most importantly, they are not surrounded constantly by others sharing their restricted environment who may be extremely dangerous to their psychological and physical well-being.

[2]*Asylums,* p. 188.

[3]Clemmer refers to this prison activity as "reverie" or "reverie plus." See *The Prison Community*, pp. 244–247.

[4]The men in Clemmer's study referred to their prison brewed alcohol as "potato brandy." *The Prison Community,* p. 243.

[5]Nalder reported that "marijuana is so popular that several prisoners readily told the note-taking visitor that they smoke weed. . . . " *Seattle Post-Intelligencer,* November 20, 1978.

[6]"Suicide in Cellblocks," *Corrections Magazine,* August (1981) pp. 6–16.

[7]Nalder reported that records at Walla Walla revealed that twelve men had committed suicide since January, 1972. *Seattle Post-Intelligencer,* November 20, 1978. (Several prisoners I spoke to believed that the suicide rate was much higher than this, however.)

[8]Clemmer classified church as "leisure activity" because the men in the prison were not required to attend services, and because many of the prisoners, he reported, saw church to be more entertainment than religion. He also stated that prisoners looked upon church-going inmates as being "the intellectually dull, the emotional, the provincial, and the aged." *The Prison Community,* p. 234.

[9]Malcolm X describes in his autobiography how his religious beliefs, acquired while in prison, helped turn him away from a life of crime. Malcolm Little, *The Autobiography of Malcolm X* (New York: Grove Press, 1965)

[10]"A recent example of harrassment was last Friday [Sept. 10, 1982] when we needed a room for our religious services. At the control room we requested to use the old visiting room, which had been previously used in lieu of the Chapel. The control room sergeant told us that we were out of luck this week because the place was being used to accommodate the overflow of visitors. The fact that we needed an alternate meeting site seemed to come as a complete surprise. The control room sergeant instructed us to stand in the area adjacent to the control room while some alternate site for our services was discussed inside.

"The other officers emerged from the control room and asked who we were and what we wanted. Our explanation did not satisfy them so they ordered us in a preemptory manner of disdain to clear the area. The brothers took exception to the officers' manner and informed them that we had been instructed to stand there by the control room sergeant. The officers pressed the sergeant who responded by throwing up both hands and saying he didn't care where we stood. The sergeant never assumed responsibility for directing us where to stand. This situation had *all* of the potential for developing into something *very serious.*"

[11]Guards and prisoners at Walla Walla point out that reasons for returning to the prison for parole violations are extremely punitive and contribute greatly to the large numbers of recidivists there. Nalder wrote, "Too many men are being

sent back for parole violations for things so minor as buying a car without permission, guards and prisoners complained. (At least one example of a car buyer was found.)" *Seattle Post-Intelligencer,* November 19, 1978.

[12]*Horning* dope is sniffing it; *geez* is dope; *D's* are Dilaudid, a strong pain killer used as dope; *do it to a poison shop* is robbing a drugstore (for dope). Delorme explains that "Duane's conversation about his lack of veins means that through the years he has 'burned out' most of his large veins which are used to shoot dope [main-lining]."

[13]*Asylums,* p. 305.

[14]*The Felon,* pp. 107–204.

[15]At Walla Walla, men who are soon to be released are transferred from behind the walls of the prison to the Minimum Security Building and are allowed monthly furloughs home, an effort on the part of prison authorities to help the men adjust to the difficult transition. Half-way houses are maintained also by the state. According to Delorme, however, not everyone who should takes advantage of this program. He believes that "older long-term cons benefit the most from work-release and half-way house programs."

Chapter 10

CON-LINGO

"When I first set foot in a county jail the language changed from light-weight street slang to heavy jailhouse slang and prison slang. Mixed in with it was an assortment of what I would describe as grunts, wheezes, and reverse Russian. The language of a prison is hard to learn, but once you have been set down in the middle of it and know you're here to stay, it becomes second nature to make use of the jargon. One of the first words you will hear is 'drum' [cell], 'Where are you drumming?' 'Tank' is another word for the larger multibodied cells. These are some of the simple slang terms for parts of the jail. 'Getting busted' and 'stuck off on the shelf' for a couple weeks to a few years is a sure way to learn the language, and the ways of the prison.

"Some of the squares that hit the growler are so super straight that they can't grasp the meaning of any of the language and so they will wander around in a daze for weeks, and all the time they ask stupid questions and have that idiot look about them. Some people are actually shocked that the guards would kick them off in the ass or call them a name, or refuse to let them make the phone call that they have always heard was their right. These are the people that have a rough time in county jails and they never seem to learn anything. They can't hide or blend in with the other cons because they wouldn't know how, and their language will always give them away. Even if a man does pick up a few words, and say that he does learn to use them in the proper context, his tone of voice or the way he uses the slang words will still put him on the spot and he will front himself off as the tank dummy. Of course, the roles will be reversed on the street if these same men meet in the square john's home situation. Then they will look cross-eyed at him and say, 'What the fuck is this?' Well, maybe they won't say it just that way, but you know what I mean.

"Anyone who has ever watched 'Police Story' or 'Kojack' on the boob-tube has heard a lot of the current terms used in the county jails. In this respect they are fairly accurate. The jail is full of the street slang, which is associated with being rousted by the pigs, and being bum beefed for no apparent reason: 'riding a beef,' 'copping a plea,' 'dealing with the cuter' [prosecutor], 'hanging tough,' 'walk' [get released], 'bull-pen' or 'tank' [drum tank], 'back-row' [hole], 'make the croaker' [talk the doctor out of some pills]. People generally use the term 'speed' or 'crank,' rather than 'uppers' for drugs. County jail slang comes from the cons or other regular thieves that are sitting on the shelf waiting to 'catch a chain' or 'hit the bricks.' If some piece of language comes in off the street that is catchy and has the proper meaning then it will stay in the jail. The same holds true in the prisons.

"The name, secret language [Agini, Ceazarney, etc.], as applied to the prison, is a daily con-lingo that is used all over the prison and is learned the same at the ABCs in grade school. It has a reason for its existence and is really put together for a special reason. Prison language can be invented or put together for use by two people or a hundred. Over a period of years some of the more popular con languages are used in bits and pieces by everyone.

"People in the prison are very sensitive to words, voice tone, posture, loudness or softness of voice. They read between the lines and look for hidden meanings in what is being said. So words are chosen carefully for the most part."

Con-lingo is slang. The *Oxford Dictionary* defines slang as "language of a highly colloquial type, considered as below the level of standard and educated speech, and consisting either of new words or of current words employed in some special sense." Maurer points out that the boundaries separating true slang from argot and cant (from the Latin, *cantus:* sing) are becoming blurred; there is constant movement from one category to the other.[1] Flexner and Wentworth define cant, jargon, and argot as those aspects of language out of which come slang: "*Cant* is the conventional, familiar idiom used and generally understood only by members of a specific occupation, trade, profession, sect, class, age group, interest group, or other subculture of our culture. *Jargon* is the technical or even secret vocabulary of such a sub-group; jargon is 'shoptalk.' *Argot* is both the cant and jargon of any professional criminal group."[2]

The cant and jargon spoken by prisoners includes the argot of professional criminals but is not wholly composed of it; therefore, it cannot rightly be identified as such. It is, instead, a close relative of argot, containing in addition to criminal cant and jargon other aspects that grow out of the unique and particular environment that is the prison. Prisoners readily identify their language as *con-lingo*, recognizing that their speech is unique to them. *Con-lingo* is composed of slang brought in from the outside, criminal argot, including the language of drug addiction also brought in from the free world, terms unique to prison life in general, and words and expressions that relate to a particular prison. Specifically, *con-lingo* at the Washington State Penitentiary is a combination of street terms from the urban centers of Seattle and Tacoma, black vernacular, the language of the drug culture and counterculture, criminal argot mostly from the West Coast, terms commonly found in prisons across the country, and language unique to this particular prison.

A comparison of the *con-lingo* in this study with that collected at Walla Walla by Robert A. Freeman in the 1950s reveals certain differences. The 1950s glossary contains many words and expressions that deal with crimes common during Prohibition and the Great Depression. Terms about the rackets of the mobster, pickpocket lingo, and safe-cracking terms, for example—all the domain of Maurer's research and expertise—are common, as are hobo terms, which occur in great profusion. Drug lingo, although present, is not strikingly so, and no linguistic influence of blacks appears at all; both are strongly evident in the *corpus* presented in this study. Approximately 400 of the thousand or more terms in the 1950s glossary are still in use in the prison (drug expressions, criminal argot, and general expressions relating to this prison and prison life in general).

The prisoners up through the 1950s were very different from those of the 1960s and 1970s. Their language reveals another time, another prisoner who committed crimes that were often different from those of the later decades, and another society outside the walls of the prison. But there are similarities between the old and new folk speech—the preoccupation with sex, for example, and the imaginative poetic imagery that is so pervasive.

The lingo of both eras is filled with figurative language, particularly metaphor. Humorous understatement (litotes) and irony are also pervasive. An example of poetic language, rhyming slang— the invention of British Cockneys (and Irish, according to Julian Franklyn),[3] which was adopted by London thieves and carried by them as convicted felons to Britain's penal colony in Australia where it was brought to the west coast of the United States by British, Australian, and American underworld people who plied their trade in Shanghai, Australia, and San Francisco, is a delightfully witty and whimsical "play" lingo spoken at Walla Walla, particularly by *old timers* who date back to the early 1960s or before. As a prison lingo, rhyming slang—prisoners refer to it as "Australian rhyming slang"—is found by and large only in western prisons. Many examples found in the 1950s glossary are still in use.

The language of both eras is earthy, imaginative, colorful, irreverent, and ironic. The lingo of the 1960s and 1970s differs from the earlier argot in that it is often "cool," sometimes vituperative, also violent. Violent imagery is particularly noticeable. In both lingos the tendency to play down serious situations or concerns through humorous and euphemistic disparagement is a strong characteristic. The function of this, as James Hargan observed in the 1930s, is to lessen the seriousness or awfulness of reality in order to make it bearable.[4]

Both lingos are, as Halliday points out, antilanguages reflecting the biases of antisocieties. Both reveal the creativity and verbal facility of prisoners and people of the underworld. A stereotype of convicts, particularly of the older eras, is that they are not very bright; the legacy of their lingo reveals that this is definitely not so. Perhaps the lingo of the 1960s and 1970s is more sophisticated and may reflect a better educated prisoner, but both lingos reveal verbally facile and imaginative poetic prisoners who enjoy playing creatively with words.

The lingo of the later decades does not appear to reflect the world-weary cynicism so much as does the language of the 1950s. Perhaps this is because the prisoner of the later era is younger than his counterpart of the past. Certainly he is less polished as a criminal and this, too, shows up in the general lack of technical terms for his crimes, except for the *lingos* of the *hustler* and *booster*, occupations common to drug addicts. Generally, the new prisoner does not look upon his criminality as a profession to take pride in, as did many of the old thieves who inhabited the prison during and before the 1950s. But then, this may reflect the general lack of pride in work well done said to prevail today in society as a whole. Perhaps the prisoner is less polished as a criminal because he may be a drug addict, and therefore, his crimes are committed in haste with little thought, planning, or skill, since what is uppermost in his mind is his next *fix*.

A great number of crimes committed by men who were serving sentences before and during the time of this study were drug-related. A glance at the Glossary will reveal how important the argot of the drug culture is in the prison. This preoccupation with drugs by such a large number of men contributes in important ways to worldview; for example, although not conclusive, a comparison of the number of terms and expressions in the prison relating to drugs to those having to do with sex reveals a greater number of words for drugs and drug use. The language of prisoners in the 1930s as presented in Clemmer's study of Menard and the language in the Glossary compiled by Freeman at Walla Walla in the 1950s reveal an overwhelming preoccupation with sex; whereas, this study suggests that prisoners of the later decades prefer drugs to sex. If this is so, a dramatic change in prisoner worldview has taken place.

The influence of black vernacular is strongly evident in the Glossary. Black terms and expressions are commonly adopted and used by most groups in the prison. Blacks comprise approximately one-fourth of the population, and in all likelihood, their language will continue to influence the development of the prison *lingo*. Addiction to drugs has been widespread among blacks, as Maurer points out, and this accounts for "the widespread tendency of the argot of the black addict to proliferate all aspects of the drug subculture. An extension of this is seen in the tendency of the dominant culture to borrow heavily from the phraseology of the ghetto."[5]

A glance at the Glossary will reveal much about the life and

concerns of the prisoner. Where particular emphasis is placed on
a concept or situation, many alternative terms tend to develop
around it. This signals important preoccupations or values and,
therefore, reveals much about prisoner worldview.[6] Good examples of this are terms or expressions dealing with ways to be killed
in the prison: *burn, bury, dust, hit, ice, off, plant, snuff, stick, take
(someone) out, waste, wipe (someone) out.* Undoubtedly, many other
terms exist that were not collected, as the preoccupation with
being killed while in this prison is overwhelming. Time, the way a
prisoner serves his sentence, is another example. As with "kill,"
all the expressions for "time" used in the prison were not collected:
hard time, easy time, flat time, big time, dead time, heavy time, cell time,
and so on. One final example concerns the crime a man commits:
*beef, murder beef, drug beef, robbery beef, new beef, old beef, bum beef,
cold beef, sex beef, chickenshit beef, sales beef.* One can assume that
among the most important aspects the language reveals about the
prisoner's worldview are his preoccupation with the crime he
committed, the way he serves his sentence, and whether or not he
will survive his prison experience.

What Maurer says about professional criminals and the development of their language can be applied to drug culture and
counterculture people and their languages. Legitimate society is
hostile, not only to professional criminals but to those who commit street crimes, take drugs, or drop out. As a consequence, these
groups experience social and economic ostracism. In order to
protect themselves from the pressures of legitimate society, as
expressed through law, they have formed counter organizations.
These counter groups, because of their resistance efforts, are tightly
organized and, therefore, extremely powerful in their influence
over their own. Part of their power comes from the closeness that
develops, because each group shares the same stigma, habits, and
security problems. This strength manifests itself in beliefs, values,
customs, mannerisms, and particularly in the language each uses.
"Speech patterns reflect the behavior patterns of the group, as
well as the traditions and group's subculture, insofar as this rudi-
mentary culture differentiates the criminal group from legitimate
society.... To a greater or lesser degree the language of the group
is semi secret; it is in effect, a union card for it is difficult for an

outsider to know and use the argot like a professional. The argots are the keys to behavior patterns as well as the techniques used by the counter culture."[7]

Maurer points out that "subcultures and specialized linguistic phenomena seem to arise spontaneously and simultaneously; language seems to lie at the heart of their cultural genesis. They develop against the background of a dominant culture already highly sophisticated in handling symbols, and this tends to shape the subcultures into entities of special symbolism, all of which tends to nurture a heightened sense of group identity." Repression produces language development for purposes of unity. The more intense the persecution, the greater the generation of language. Indeed, Maurer points out that if societal pressure ceases the language and subculture atrophies. "It appears that, without some of these pressures, subcultures become abortive or tend to atrophy. There must be a threat from the dominant culture . . . and this threat intensifies the internal pressures already at work. The language indigenous to the subculture tends to intensify the attitudes, values and technology which characterizes the group. The development of techniques, especially those which may be a threat to the dominant culture, may be disapproved or suppressed, which excites increased linguistic activity, usually accompanied by an intensification of internal cohesive forces and an increased emphasis on secrecy."[8]

Language development in the prison (itself a counterculture or antisociety) occurs in the same way and for the same reasons. The repression by guards and officials (who represent the repression of the dominant culture) creates new language among prisoners in their attempts to strengthen unity to counteract the threat from without. "The more intense the persecution, the greater the generation of language." New language is generated also to convey and intensify "attitudes, values and technology which characterizes the group." For example, in response to the repressive incidents that occurred during the great *lockdown* of 1979, new names emerged for the riot squad—*silons, robots,* and *clones*—and for areas of the prison that were altered presumably for security purposes by officials—when it was paved over, *Peoples Park* became *Peoples Parking Lot.*[9]

In further describing how language shapes and in turn is shaped by culture, Maurer states that the special language of the group tends to pull those in the subculture toward greater homogeneity. "Through it, group identity is further developed, and, as the subculture becomes stronger, it tends to pull away from the dominant culture, becoming more aware of itself as its communication system becomes more versatile. It comes to believe what it hears, and is more positive in what it says. The behavior pattern shapes itself ever closer to what the group says it is and what its acts prove it to be."[10]

Finally, in describing the characteristics of the argot used by narcotic addicts (so much of which appears in this study), Maurer writes that the language vividly reflects the life-style of the addict: "...the ecstasy of narcotics, the necessity for escape from the world of reality, the compensatory effect of drugs upon the inadequate personality, the constant preoccupation with the needle as a symbol, the eventual exclusion of all other motives for living and the complete preoccupation with the necessity for securing drugs. There is also the ever present evidence of the substitution of drugs for sexual activity."[11]

Much of what the prisoner thinks and feels is revealed in this study of his language and culture—what he values; what he rejects; what he believes about himself, his family, his peers, society, and those representatives of society who are his keepers; what his attitudes and beliefs are; what he hopes and fears; in short, his worldview. It is hoped that this presentation of the system of values that lies beneath patterns of behavior as revealed through language will help bridge the vast abyss of misunderstanding that exists between those who imprison and those who are imprisoned.

NOTES

[1]*The American Language*, p. 703.

[2]*Dictionary of American Slang*, preface, vi.

[3]For the origin and characteristics of rhyming slang, see Julian Franklyn, *Dictionary of Rhyming Slang*, Second Edition (London: Routledge and Kegan Paul, 1975). For rhyming slang's journey to the west coast of the U.S., see David W. Maurer with Sidney J. Baker, "Australian Rhyming Slang in the American

Underworld," *American Speech,* Vol. 19 (1944), pp. 183–195. For rhyming slang found at Walla Walla up through the 1950s, see Inez Cardozo-Freeman, "Rhyming Slang in a Western Prison," *Western Folklore,* Vol. XXXVII (October, 1978), pp. 296–305.

⁴James Hargan, "The Psychology of Prison Language" *The Journal of Abnormal and Social Psychology,* Vol. XXX (1935–1936), pp. 359–365.

⁵David W. Maurer, *Language of the Underworld* Collected and Edited by Allan W. Futrell and Charles B. Wordell (Lexington: The University Press of Kentucky, 1981), p. 277.

⁶Halliday calls this "over-lexicalization," the "provision [in the language] of a large number of alternatives for important concepts of the counter culture." Although "over-lexicalization" appears to hold ethnocentric bias, what Halliday means—that these word clusters signal important values and attitudes—is important. Halliday is quoted in Roger Fowler, "Anti-Language in Fiction," *Style,* Vol. XIII, (1979), No. 3, pp. 259–277.

⁷*Language of the Underworld,* pp. 259–260.

⁸*Ibid.,* pp. 264–265.

⁹A new name for *Lifers Park* emerged during the 1979 *lockdown:* " . . . a small square of green known as Lifers Park was now, after being paved over, referred to as 'Spalding's Slab." *Who Rules the Joint?,* p. 110.

¹⁰*Language of the Underworld,* p. 265.

¹¹*Ibid.,* p. 273.

Appendix A

GLOSSARY OF SLANG AND ARGOT TERMS

Most, but not all, of the *con-lingo* collected during the time of this study (June 1978–December 1980) is included in this glossary. In no way does it represent all such language spoken at Walla Walla during that time. Included here also are many of those terms in the 1950s' collection that were still in use through December 1980. Undoubtedly, many new words have been added and some deleted since that time since language is dynamic and, therefore, constantly changing.

The purpose of the glossary is to assist the reader in understanding the vocabulary. The citations included are for the interest of the reader and are not meant to suggest any definitive etymology. Some terms not indigenous to prisons are included because they play an important part in the construction of the prisoner's worldview.

For the reader's information, the citations refer to the following dictionaries or glossaries of slang and argot: *BJA: Black Jargon in America*, by David Claerbout, 1972; *DAS: Dictionary of American Slang*, 2nd. ed., by Harold Wentworth and Stewart Flexner, 1975; *DSA: A Dictionary of Slang and Its Analogues*, 7 Vols., Compiled and Edited by John S. Farmer and W. E. Henley, 1890–1904; *DSUE: A Dictionary of Slang and Unconventional English*, by Eric Partridge, 1961; *LU: Language of the Underworld*, by David W. Maurer, 1981; *LB: Lexicon Balatronicum: A Dictionary of Buckish Slang, University Wit and Pickpocket Eloquence*, Compiled by Frances Grose, 1811; and *WWCL: Walla Walla Con-Lingo*, Compiled by Robert A. Freeman, 1954–1958.

A-DECK. Solitary confinement. Also *back row, growler, hole, slammer.*

ACAPULCO GOLD. Marijuana. *LU.*

ACE-IN-THE-HOLE. A one year prison term. "What did you get?" "They gimme an ace." *WWCL.*

ACID HEAD. A user of LSD. *LU.*

ACTION. 1. Selling narcotics. 2. Anything having to do with illegal activities. *LU.*

AGINI. One of the secret languages used in the prison. Also *Alfalfa, Bong-Song, Ceazarney, Elephant, Tut.*

ALFALFA. One of several secret codes used. See *Agini.*

ANGEL DUST. 1. Marijuana powdered or chopped for inhaling or smoking. 2. Heroin, cocaine, and morphine powdered and mixed for inhalation or injection. *LU.*

APES. Tough or troublesome prisoners.

ARTHUR DUFFY. To run away. "To take it on the Arthur Duffy." *WWCL.* Also *hit the road; take a mope; take it on the lam; to split,* etc.

ASK FOR COTTON. To ask for the filtering cotton used previously by another drug addict in order to extract what residue is left for a very small shot or *hit.* Implies that the second user of the cotton is out of drugs. *LU.*

ASSHOLE. A derogatory (or affectionate) term for a fellow prisoner or a guard.

ATTITUDE, HAVE AN ATTITUDE. To be aloof, uncooperative or hostile. *LU.*

BABYSITTING. A temporary helping hand extended to new prisoners by other *cons.* "I used to babysit on the new fish when they came in on Wednesday."

BACK FENCE. Gossip. "Tell me some good back fence."

BACK ROW. Solitary confinement. "The pigs took Bill to the back row for fighting." Also *A–Deck, growler, hole, shelf, slammer.*

BACK YARD. Gossip. See *back fence.*

BACK-ME-UPS. Friends who you can count on in a fight. "I got a beef with the Bikers later; are you guys going to give me some back-me-ups?" Also *back my play.*

BACK MY PLAY. See *back-me-ups.*

BAD. Very good. *BJA. LU.*

BAG. 1. A stereotyping category used by classification personnel or prisoners in determining who and what a person is. For example, *nut-bag*. "Someone has determined that you may be unstable so you are officially, or unofficially, put into a 'nut-bag' category." Also *jacket*. 2. A quantity of drugs packaged in small amounts. "Who's got the bag?" *LU*. Also *dope bag, balloon*.

BAG IT. To put something aside, forget it. "All you try to do when you get out of the Joint is to bag it for awhile."

BALLOON. A quantity of drugs wrapped in paper or cellophane, but usually in a rubber balloon. *LU*. Similar to *bag*.

BANKERS HOURS. To get a conventional job. *WWCL*. Also *eight-to-five, square up*.

BEAN. A benzedrine (amphetamine) capsule or tablet. *LU*. Also *benny, whites, blancas (Mexican term)*.

BEAT. To outwit or cheat someone in the prison through actions or language. "I know my way around here; who can or can't be beat." *LU*.

BEEF. 1. A charge for the commission of a crime. *LU*. 2. A crime. Also *bum beef, chickenshit beef, cold beef, drug beef, heavy beef, murder beef, new beef, old beef, robbery beef, sales beef, sex beef*. 3. A fight. 4. To complain, argue, protest. "What's your beef, man?" [*LB*: 1811.]

BEES AND HONEY. Money. Rhyming slang. *WWCL*.

BELLY BURGLAR. "The guy who heads up the cooking, whoever makes out the menu." *WWCL*. Also *belly robber*.

BENNY. Benzedrine (amphetamine) capsules or tablets. *LU*. Also *bean, blancas, whites*.

BIBLEBACKS. Prisoners who are religious, many of whom are viewed as insincere. "Biblebacks are guys who hang around the chapel all the time."

BIG MUDDY. Prison gravy. *WWCL*.

BIG RED. The segregation unit, which includes solitary confinement, segregation, and death row.

BIG SHOT. "Inmate leader, or anybody that's known by more than three people." [*WWCL*: A notorious criminal or leader of a mob.]

BIG TIME. 1. A long prison sentence. 2. Serving a sentence in an adult institution. "You're lucky, boy, this is a reformatory; if you don't cool your shit, you'll see what the big time is all about." *WWCL*.

BIG WHEEL. "A Joint politician, a hustler, a suck-ass. Jonathan Alt is a big wheel in the library." *WWCL*. Same as *big shot*.

BIKER CLUB. The Washington State Penitentiary Motorcycle Association (WSPMA).

BILL. One hundred dollars white money. [*WWCL*: Money.]

BIM, BIMBO. Ding or turkey. [*WWCL*: A girl].

BING. A hit or shot of dope, a jolt of narcotics. *WWCL; LU*.

BING IN THE WING. A hypodermic shot of narcotics in the arm. *WWCL*.

BIT. A term in prison. To do a small bit is to serve a short sentence. *WWCL; LU*.

BITCH. 1. A prison female (homosexual). 2. To complain.

BITCH (THE). To be classified as a habitual criminal by the state. Shortened form of Habitch. "A guy is rousted for three or four beefs, then the state bitches you." *LU*.

BITCH AND HOLLER. 1. Dollar. Rhyming slang. *LU*. 2. A common expression for complaining, or expressing dissatisfaction in the prison.

BLACK CLUB. Black Prisoners Forum Unlimited (BPFU). One of the important clubs in the prison.

BLADE. A knife or other sharp-edged weapon. Also *my (or your) shit, shank, shiv, sticker*.

BLANCAS. Benzedrine tablets (Mexican term). *LU*.

BLANKET ASSES. Derogatory name for native American prisoners.

BLAST. 1. A shot of dope. 2. A shoot out. *WWCL; LU*.

BLASTED. To be under the influence of drugs. *LU*. Similar to *fucked up, loaded, stoned, zonked*.

BLOOD ALLEY. A dangerous walkway located between Four, Five, and Six Wings where killings and knifings often occurred.

BLOT OUT. To kill. *WWCL; LU.*

BLOTTER OUTER. An assassin.

BLOW. 1. To lose or destroy. "We blew the tape we were making." [*DSUE:* To cause to disappear; spend, waste. c. 1850.] 2. To erupt suddenly into violence (the prison population). "The Joint's going to blow anytime now."

BLOW OVER. To allow time for a tense situation in prison to pass. "Why can't they just lay low and let it blow over?"

BLOW SMOKE. 1. To boast; brag. 2. To lie. "Aw, don't pay any attention to him; he's just blowing smoke."

BLUES. Morphine.

BOAT AND OAR. Whore. Rhyming slang. *WWCL; LU.*

BOGUS. Anything false; counterfeit. "Jim sold me some bogus dope yesterday." *LU;* e.g. *bogus beef, bogus check, bogus dope, bogus food, bogus job,* etc.

BOLTS AND NUTS. Insane. *WWCL.*

BONAROO. 1. Anything good, desirable, or attractive. "John's got a bonaroo old lady." 2. Well cared-for clothes worn in prison. "That's a bonaroo coat you've got there." *LU.*

BONG-SONG. One of the secret lingos used in the prison. Also *Agini, Alfalfa, Ceazarney, Elephant, Tut.*

BONNIE FAIR. Hair. Rhyming slang. *WWCL.*

BONNIE RUE. Bonaroo. Rhyming slang. *WWCL.*

BOO-COO. Plenty. "We have boo-coo weed in here." *WWCL.*

BOOST. To shoplift. A term used by a professional, one who makes a living by shoplifting. *LU.*

BOOSTER. A professional shoplifter; not an amateur. "Dewey ain't home; he's out working [boosting]." *LU.*

BOOZE. Prison term for alcohol. [*DSA:* To booze: to drink heavily; to tipple; to guzzle. An old term employed as early as 1300.] Also *pruno.*

BOOZER. 1. A prison alcoholic. 2. One who drinks alcohol. Also *juicer.*

BOZO. A dummy, a turkey. [*WWCL:* An unimportant fellow.]

BOZY. Someone domineering, arrogant, overbearing, etc. *WWCL.*

BRACELETS. Handcuffs, shackles. *WWCL.*

BREAD SNATCHERS. An affectionate term describing a prisoner's children or the children of his friends. "Who's taking care of your bread snatchers while you're in here?" [*DSUE:* Bread-snapper—a child: Glasgow lower class, c. 1880.] Also *crumb snatchers, mice, rugrats.*

BREAK, TO MAKE A BREAK. To escape. *WWCL.* Also *to book, to split.*

BREEZEWAY. The "skid row" of the prison.

BREEZEWAY BANDITS. Inmates who rob other inmates on the *Breezeway.*

BREEZEWAY BUM. A prisoner who begs (bums) for such items as cigarettes, money, drugs, or candy, on the Breezeway. Similar to *Breezeway ding.* "I'm really getting tired of supplying smokes to that Breezeway bum every day." Also *Breezeway roamer.*

BREEZEWAY DING. An eccentric prisoner who spends most of his time on the *Breezeway.*

BREEZEWAY ROAMER. Similar to *Breezeway bum.*

BRO. 1. A close friend or relative. 2. Also used by the ethnic groups when identifying one of their own members in the prison. "One of my bro's is coming in on the chain today." Also *brother.*

BROAD. A homosexual who plays the female role in the prison.

BROTHER. Same as *bro. BJA.*

BROTHERS AND SISTERS. Whiskers. Rhyming slang. *WWCL.*

BROWN. Mexican heroin. Also *Mexican brown, shit, skag, stuff, smack.*

BRUNSER. Anus. *WWCL.*

BU-FU. Slang term for the BPFU (Black Prisoners Forum Unlimited). Used by nonblack prisoners.

BUCK. A homosexual. "John would like to borrow a couple of bucks to take home for the evening."

BULL. A prison guard. [*DAS:* 1893] Also *cop, dog, goon, gooner, hog, pig, robot, silon, the heat, the man.*

BULLET. "Where you have drugstore bandits, you're referring to narcotic suppositories, like Dilaudid or opium suppositories."

BULLETPROOF TOAST. A Joint special consisting of slightly dunked and fried bread. (French toast?) *WWCL.*

BULLDOG. To coerce; "bully." "The stronger clubs are able to bulldog the smaller ones into going along with their crazy shit." Also *gorilla.*

BUM. 1. Bad. [*DSUE:* Inferior, bad, dishonest. c. 1880.] 2. To beg. "Let's put the bum on Paul for some smokes."

BUM BEEF. A conviction on a trumped-up charge. "They railroaded Jimmy on this bum beef charge." *LU.* Also *bum rap.*

BUM PAY. Anyone who doesn't pay his debts in prison. "Look out for Bill; he's a bum pay."

BUM RAP. See *bum beef.*

BUM STUFF (SHIT). Inferior narcotics or marijuana.

BUM'S RUSH. To dismiss; to be ejected bodily. *WWCL.* Also *root out.*

BUNCO. "Any caper designed to clip a mark via confidence, and involving trickery." *WWCL.* Also *finesse.*

BUNDLE. A narcotics term, especially in Tacoma. A bundle would be a *good score* of narcotics out of a hospital or drugstore. [*WWCL:* A role of money garnered from capering, etc.]; *LU.*

BUNK. Inferior drugs. "That bag of weed I bought was pure bunk."

BURGLAR COP. 1. An officer of the law who accepts bribes from crooks. 2. One who actually capers. *WWCL; LU.* Also *bunco man,* *confidence man,* one who is *on the take, shakedown artist.*

BURIED DEEP. Someone who does a long term in the *hole.* "Bury you in Siberia; bury you so deep they gotta pipe sunlight to ya." [*WWCL:* To be sentenced to a long prison term.] *LU.*

BURN. 1. To kill someone. Also *bury, bushwack, dust, hit, ice, off, plant, snuff, stick, take (someone) out, waste, wipe (someone) out.* 2. To cheat, swindle. [*DSUE:* c. 1700.]; *BJA.* 3. To sell inferior or fake drugs.

BURN ARTIST. 1. A drug dealer who sells bad or fake drugs. "He's a burn artist if he gets some aspirin, cuts it down and makes it look like Dilaudid." 2. Anyone who cheats or steals from someone.

BURY. 1. To kill someone. Also *blot out, burn, bushwhack, dust, hit, File 13, give (someone) the business, ice, knock off, muck out, off, plant, rub out, snuff, stick, take (someone) out, waste, wipe (someone) out.* 2. To give someone a long prison sentence. *WWCL; LU.*

BUSH PAROLE. To hide (in the bushes) when one escapes from prison. *WWCL.* See *Parole dust.*

BUSHWHACK. 1. To assault. 2. To kill someone. Also *burn, bury, dust, hit, ice, off, plant, snuff, stick, take (someone) out, waste, wipe (someone) out.*

BUSINESS. A hypodermic needle and plunger. *WWCL.* Also *fix, factory, Ike and Mike,* etc.

BUST A NUT. To have an orgasm.

BUSTED. To be arrested. "We got busted in our cells smoking weed." *LU; BJA.* Also *popped.*

C. 1. Cocaine. 2. A hundred dollar bill. *WWCL; LU.*

C.I.'d. To be officially identified as criminally insane. "Pete was C.I.'d by that headshrinker."

CAGE. The control room in Segregation. [*DSA:* A minor kind of prison. 1500.]

CAKE AND WINE. Dine (on bread and water). Rhyming slang. *WWCL.*

CAKES. The buttocks.

CALL SOMEONE OUT. To challenge someone to fight. "I'm going over and call that bastard out, so we can get this shit settled once and for all."

CANDY. Anything good. "In baseball when you get a nice pitch, that's candy, a sweet one."

CAP, CAPPING. A friendly way of exchanging insults. "Your girl friend is so ugly that she wears two bags on her head in case one falls off." Also *play the dozens*, a black tradition, and *ranking*.

CAPER. 1. A theft. "We got a good drugstore caper lined up in Tacoma tonight." [*DSA.* 1867.] 2. To steal. "He's gotta go caper tonight to support his dope habit." *WWCL.*

CARWASH. The shower in Eight Wing.

CEAZARNEY (CARNEY). One of several secret lingos used in the prison. Also *Alfalfa, Agini, Bong-song, Elephant, Tut.*

CELL TIME. The hours spent in the cell. "I'll be doing lots of cell time this weekend so I can get some letters written."

CELLIES. Cellmates.

CHAIN. The bus that transports maximum security prisoners from one institution to another.

CHARLIE ROUSERS. Trousers. Rhyming slang. *WWCL.*

CHEESE AND KISSES. Missus, Mrs. Rhyming slang. *LU.*

CHICANO CLUB. The United Chicanos (UC). One of the important ethnic clubs in the prison.

CHICKENSHIT BEEF. A charge for a minor or insignificant crime, such as stealing sandwiches from the kitchen.

CHRONIC. A chronic offender. "That's what I'm marked as, a chronic offender, a repeater." *WWCL.*

CHUCK. A term used to describe poor quality food, such as prison chuck. *WWCL.*

CHUMP. A person who can be cheated out of his money or drugs. "That chump was really taken for a ride last night." [*LU*: A victim. Not as derogatory as *sucker.*]

CITY. Any city jail. *WWCL.*

CLASS. 1. Term applied to homosexuals who have a high standing in the prison because of their behavior and looks. 2. "Applies to others in the prison who may dress, walk, talk and live in a 'classy' fashion."

CLASS-A DRUGS. Narcotics obtained from a drugstore or hospital pharmacy. Considered by drug addicts as "Class A", the best dope available.

CLEAN THE BOOKS. To cause a suspect to cop out to unsolved crimes, via promises, threats, etc., in order to show an efficiently run police department. "You might as well clean the books; we got a hundred burglaries anyway; go for it all." *WWCL.*

CLIPPED. 1. To be flat broke. 2. To swindle, or to be swindled. *WWCL.*

CLONES. The prison riot squad. Also *robots, silons.*

CLOWN. A mark; a turkey. "There's a lot of clowns in here." [*WWCL:* An officer of the law.]

COASTING. 1. Serving an easy prison term. 2. The euphoria experienced after taking drugs. *LU.* Also *grooving, tripping.*

COKE. Cocaine. "Only a free coke could keep me from hitting the wall." [*DSUE:* c. 1910.]

COLD BEEF. A gruesome crime, like murder. A cold-blooded crime.

COLD STORAGE. 1. Any place of incarceration. *WWCL.* 2. "Cold storage is someone in a plastic bag — dead."

COLD TURKEY RAP. A criminal charge based on indisputable eye witness testimony. *WWCL.*

COME DOWN. 1. To withdraw from drugs or alcohol. *LU.* 2. Also applies to situations that take place. "The street people of the sixties saw the police brutality and the action coming down."

COMMIE. Anything that is foreign, "unAmerican." Tortillas are commie food, for example.

CON. 1. A convict (convicted felon). [*DAS:* c. 1917.] 2. To be deceived by prisoners (convicts). "Other guards will laugh at him cause he's been conned." *LU.*

CON-LINGO. Prison argot and slang.

CON-MAN. One who relieves others of their possessions in prison through the use of fast talk and tricks.

CONNECT. One who supplies drugs to others for resale or use. "Just about everyone who uses hard drugs either has, or is working to get his connect going." *LU.*

CONTRACT. An agreement between a moneylender (or drug dealer) and another inmate to collect money owed him. "The dealers run contracts on guys for bum pay on dope."

CON-WISE. An inmate who has learned how to talk and act in ways that impress gullible officials of the prison. Implies insincerity on the part of the prisoner. "John didn't get any action from the Parole Board because they think he is con-wise."

COOL. 1. A situation in control. "If things don't look too cool, you don't have to stay in your cell." 2. In control of one's emotions, aloof, detached. "Man, that guy's cool; nothing bugs him." *LU; BJA.*

COOL IT BACK. To calm down under pressure. "I try to cool it back cause when that happens my defense goes." Also *hang tough.*

COOL OFF. To calm down; to slow things down. "To cool it, to back off, to play off; to take it easy and let things straighten themselves out." *WWCL.*

COOLER. Segregation or the hole. "Sit there in the cooler for awhile." *LU;* [*WWCL:* Any place of incarceration.]

COP. 1. A policeman or prison guard. 2. To buy drugs for someone. "Everyone is either trying to cop dope or sell it." *LU.* 3. To obtain something. [*DSUE:* Catch, capture. c. 1700.] 4. To steal. [*DSA:* 1864.]

COP A FIX. To obtain a ration of drugs. *LU.*

COP A JOINT. To obtain sex.

COP A PLEA. To admit to a criminal charge. To plead guilty. "When I go to court today I think I'll cop a plea to burglary II." Also *make the cop. WWCL; LU.*

COP A SLAVE. To get a job. *WWCL; LU.*

COP A SNEAK. To get away by running or walking rapidly. *WWCL; LU.*

COP OUT. 1. To plead guilty. 2. To quit. 3. To retreat from reality. *WWCL; LU.*

COPPER. Policeman or guard. [*DAS:* 1848.]

COPS AND ROBBERS. The "game" played between criminals and the criminal justice system.

COUGH-UP. 1. To give up information; to squeal under pressure. *WWCL.* 2. "Sometimes it means you come up short on dope, like they might put the pressure on you and you cough up the dope."

COUNT TIME. The regular check-up period in which all prisoners return to their cells in order to be counted. "Got to cut this game short now because it's count time."

COUNTY. Any county jail. *WWCL.*

COUNTRY CLUB. A name that applies to federal minimum security prisons, or any prison where rules are lax and time is easy. Applied by some to W.S.P. during the 1970s.

COVER. A hideout. "To cop a sneak on somebody around here, you gotta have somebody cover for you on the end of the tier; and when you're in the kitchen you have somebody cover for you when you steal a sandwich." *WWCL.*

COWBOYS. Prisoners at Walla Walla who come from the small towns and rural areas of the state.

COWS AND KISSES. Missus. Rhyming slang. *WWCL.*

CRACK. To open the door. "They cracked my door and I headed for Control."

A CRACK IN THE SHACK. An expression referring to homosexuals in cells. A variation of "a punk in the bunk." "What's happening in there?" "We got us a crack in the shack, man. Want to get down?"

CRANK. Narcotics that stimulate (amphetamines). "Don will be back pretty soon. We gave him the money to get some crank on the Breezeway." Also *speed.*

TO CRANK UP. To get motivated; stimulated. "I don't know how in hell to get him cranked up on the streets but he's a good hustler inside the walls."

CRASH, CRASHING. To crash a door means to kick it in. To crash a door (or break a window) and dash into a drugstore or other place in order to steal. "Been out crashing them poison shop [drug store] doors again, huh?" *WWCL. LU.* As opposed to *creeping.* See also *hit and run.*

CRAZIES. Dings, nuts. A "crazy" person. "Man, I never seen no joint with so fucking many crazies running around!"

CREEP, CREEPING. A stealthy method of entering a house or business establishment in order to steal. "Let's see if we can pull a creep on Rexall Drugs when they close tonight." *LU.* As opposed to *crashing.*

CREEP OFF (SOMEONE'S) PAD. To steal property from someone's cell. Also *creep the pad and beat you for your stash.*

CREEP THE PAD AND BEAT YOU FOR YOUR STASH. To sneak into someone's cell and steal their property. Also *creep off (someone's) pad.*

CREEP THIEF. A sneak thief. *LU.*

CREEPER. A sneak thief. "Someone who finesses a pharmacist behind a drug store counter for drugs. The creeper does the diving. You do the creeping, but you have a diver that goes with you. The diver goes behind the counter and gets the narcotics and the creeper does the pulling. The puller pulls the clerk's and the pharmacist's attention away from what the diver is doing." *WWCL; LU.*

CREEPERS. Soft-soled shoes worn by burglars. *WWCL; LU.*

CROAK. To die. *WWCL.*

CROAKER. A physician or surgeon. *WWCL; LU.*

CUSH. 1. "A buffer; something that separates you from the law." 2. Money. *WWCL; LU.*

CUT. 1. To adulterate drugs, usually with milk sugar. *LU.* 2. Assault with a knife or other edged weapon. "One of our brothers cut a Chicano last week."

CUT ME SOME SLACK. Give me a break. *BJA.*

CUT (SOMEONE) LOOSE. 1. To exclude someone from what is going on (the *action*). 2. To let go, release. *LU.*

CUT THE Z's. To sleep. Also *Z's.*

CUT OUT. To leave a place. *LU.*

CUTOR. Prosecutor. *WWCL; LU.*

D's. Dilaudid. An artificial pain killer, very potent, much valued by addicts.

DADDY. A homosexual who plays the male role. "Who's your daddy today, bitch?" [*DAS:* c. 1912.] Also *jock, jocker, old man, wolf.*

DAY-CARE CENTER. Describes the atmosphere of the prison when the ratio of younger cons increases. "They run around the Joint like kids in a day-care center."

DEAD ACTION. 1. A negatively viewed situation. "To make a move like that is dead action, cause they can nail your shit before the guard can open the door." 2. Conditions in the prison. For example, attending church would be extremely dead action.

DEAD TIME. Serving one's sentence where nothing is happening. County jails are considered dead time. The reception center is dead time. "Man, that Shelton is dead time to the max, no visits, no phone, no mail, no yard-out, no movies."

DEAL WITH THE CUTER. An expression that applies exclusively to the method of plea bargaining with the prosecutor for a lesser charge. "I decided to deal with the cuter and go for a possession charge rather than hold out and get hit with a sales beef."

DEALER. Anyone who buys and sells drugs in the prison. *LU.*

DEEP FREEZE. In solitary confinement.

DEX. Dexedrine (amphetamine). *LU.*

DI. Dilaudid. See *D's.*

DICK-SMACKER. A derogatory term for guards. "Hey, you stupid dick-smacker, get down here and open this door."

DIG A GRAVE. Shave. Rhyming slang. *WWCL.*

DING. 1. An inmate who behaves erratically or who is insane. "That ding ain't wrapped too tight, so watch out for him." 2. A label used with affection or hostility, depending on the situation and people involved.

DINGBAT. A variation of *ding.*

DINGIER THAN A SHITHOUSE MOUSE. To be extremely psychotic or mentally incapacitated to a point where one cannot function normally. "Watch out for that dude, he's dingier than a shithouse mouse."

DINGIES. Variation of *ding.* [*LU: Dingies* are bums or hobos, who practice minor con games. *Ding* has evolved from this term.]

DINGING OUT. 1. Behaving erratically. 2. Conversing in a senseless and rapid manner. Both produced by the use of stimulant narcotics. "The dopers will be rapping and dinging out on speed all night long."

DING WARD. The psychiatric unit of the prison. "You'll cool your shit after they throw your ass in the ding ward for a few months." Also *booby hatch, bug house, nuthouse, Third Floor.*

DIP. A pickpocket. *WWCL; LU.*

DIVE. To make a move, go somewhere, do something. "Let's dive off into the chow hall and pig out for awhile."

DIVER. A sneak thief. [*WWCL:* A pickpocket.] LU. See *creeper.*

DO A HITCH. To serve a prison term. *WWCL.*

DO TIME. To serve a prison sentence. See *big time, cell time, dead time, easy time, flat time, hard time, short time.*

DOG. 1. A derisive name for guards. "Don't even bother asking him; he's a stone dog." 2. An unattractive homosexual.

DONUTS. Toilet paper fashioned into donut-shaped rolls by many turns around the hand. These are used like coals for cooking food stolen from the kitchen. "I'll get the meat ready while you guys make some donuts."

DOPE. Drugs. [*DSUE:* c. 1890.]

DOO-BE. A marijuana cigarette. "Roll us up a couple doo-bies real quick." Also *hit, joint, number.*

DOPE BAG. See *bag.*

DOPE FIEND. Narcotics addict. *LU.* Also *doper.*

DOPER. Narcotics addict. "All the dopers in the Joint would gladly spend all their dough to stay loaded." *LU.* (In this prison the term is loosely applied to anyone who uses dope.)

DOT AND DASH. Mustache. Rhyming slang. *WWCL.*

DOWN. 1. To kill someone. "Hal was out to down him for good." Also *burn, bury, dust, hit, ice, off, plant, snuff, stick, take (someone) out, waste, wipe (someone) out.*

TO BE DOWNED BY THE PAROLE BOARD. An expression used when the Parole Board refuses to reduce a man's sentence. "Man, they downed Jimmy cause they didn't believe his story."

DOWNERS. Tranquilizers, depressant drugs, barbiturates. "Don't think I'll play ball tonite. I took a couple downers so I'll just kick back for the rest of the night." *LU.* See *uppers.*

DO YOUR OWN TIME (OR TRIP). To mind your business in prison. "Don't be worrying about me, man, you just do your own time and I'll do mine." Also *pull your own time (or trip).*

DRESSING DOWN FOR A MOTHERFUCKER. To dress up for a special occasion. A black expression. Emphasis is on "down." "Big man be dressing down for a motherfucker tonight cause he's got two new hoe's [whores] to sport around."

TO DRIVE ON SOMEONE. To confront someone. To "get in someone's face." "He was in his house alone when three cons drove on him and told him to give up his shit. [dope]."

DROP. The delivery of drugs (already paid for) at a specific time and place. "My old lady will make the drop tonight and we'll have the shit by midnight." *LU.*

DROP IT. To bring a person down with a blow. Similar to a *Sunday punch.* "I want him to remember it; just drop it. Tell him it's from me."

DROP THE COUNT. To miss the daily count that is done by the guards to see if anyone has escaped.

DRUGSTORE DOPE. Class A narcotics—from morphine to codeine—sold only by prescription in drugstores. Considered by addicts as the only safe drugs to use, but not the strongest.

DRUM. A jail or prison cell. "Where are you drumming?"

DUCK AND DODGE. 1. To avoid trouble or violence. 2. To avoid the law when on the streets. "I duck and dodge in here so I can keep out of trouble." *LU.*

DUDE. A man. A common street term often used in the prison. "J.T.'s a real cool dude." *BJA.*

DUMDUMS. Demerol®.

DUMMY. Someone in the prison who is regarded as slow, dimwitted, stupid. "The cops are no dummies; they see what's happening and that brings the heat."

DUMP TRUCK. A court appointed attorney who likes to plea bargain or make trade-offs with the prosecutor. "My dump truck wants me to cop a second degree burglary. Fuck him!"

DUST. To kill someone. "If a guy burns you for some dope once, dust him so he can't beat you twice." Also *burn, bury, bushwhack, down, hit, ice, off, plant, snuff, stick, take (someone) out, waste, wipe (someone) out.*

EASY TIME. The opposite of *hard time.* One who is able to serve a sentence relatively trouble-free. One who remains cheerful or calm throughout the experience.

EIGHT-TO-FIVE. To give up criminal activities and get a job. Also *pack a bucket, square up.*

ELEPHANT. One of several secret lingos used in the prison. Also *Agini, Alfalfa, Bong-Song, Ceazarney, Tut.*

END OF THE ROAD. Walla Walla.

FACE. Oral sex. *WWCL.* Also *French, head, head job, skull,* etc.

FACTORY. A hypodermic needle and syringe. "Have you got a factory I can use to do some dope?" *LU.* Also *fit, horse and wagon, Ike and Mike, outfit, rig.*

FALL IN. 1. To enter into the prison with little or no preparation. "The fish just fall in here off the chain and are on their own." 2. To come upon something by surprise.

FANNY BLAIR. Hair. Rhyming slang. *WWCL.*

FAST ON THE TRIGGER. To be short-tempered. "You can't be fast on the trigger in this place; you gotta stay cool."

FEATHERS. Body hair. "We check her out going to the shower; she ain't got a feather on her."

FIELDS OF WHEAT. Street. Rhyming slang. *WWCL; LU.*

FILE 13. 1. To be killed. 2. To die.

FINESSING GAME. Using language to cheat someone.

FINGER. To identify someone to the guards, police, or others. "The guy came out of the chow hall and the punk fingered him." *WWCL; LU.*

FINK. An informer. *LU.* Also *rat, stool pigeon, snitch.*

FIRST TIMER. Someone who is serving a prison sentence for the first time. Also *first time loser.*

FIRST TIME LOSER. Same as *first timer.*

FISH. New inmates. *LU.* Also *new fish.*

FISH AND SHRIMP. Pimp. Rhyming slang. *WWCL; LU.*

FISH AND SOUP. Suit. Rhyming slang. *WWCL.*

FISH BULL. A young and inexperienced guard. "Wait until a fish bull comes on duty then we can make a move."

FISH TANK. A holding cell for new inmates entering the system. "They will be taking us to the fish tank at Shelton on Tuesday."

FIT. A hypodermic needle and syringe. "I need a fit to shoot some dope." *LU.* Also *factory, horse and wagon, Ike and Mike, outfit, rig.*

FIX A RAP. To make favorable arrangements through bribery or influence on a criminal charge. *WWCL; LU.* Also *square a rap.*

FLASH. The euphoric feeling experienced after injecting narcotics. *LU.*

FLATTEN OUT. To finish a prison sentence. "Man I only got to flatten out six years in prison and I'll be out."

FLAT TIME. To do a prison sentence with no parole. Five-on-five is receiving a five year sentence and doing five year's time. "I did five-on-five flat time so now they ain't got no hold on me."

FLAT TIRE. A term used to identify someone in the prison who either has one leg or a foot injury that causes him to limp.

FLEAS AND ANTS. Pants. Rhyming slang. *WWCL.*

FLIP-FLOP. An expression for describing a homosexual relationship in the prison in which both partners play both roles. Also *pitch and catch, top and bottom.*

FLOATER. 1. A dead body in the water. 2. An order to leave town or the state. *WWCL.*

FLOATER'S PAROLE. A parole that permits the parolee to go where he pleases without the usual supervision. *WWCL.*

FLOP. Extra time added on to a prisoner's sentence because of bad conduct. "Joe got a couple year's flop."

TO FLY A KITE. To pass a letter or note to someone in prison. "Don't shout it, send me a kite." *LU.*

FLUTE. Penis. "Brutus coccus; ole tricky dick; boner; so many terms." *WWCL.*

FLUTE PLAYER. A homosexual. *WWCL.* Also *girl, sissy, skin flute player,* etc. *WWCL.*

FLY LIGHT. "To take a mope; split, to bag it; to truck; to hook it. That's all traveling with no luggage. We will have to fly light upon release." *WWCL.*

FLY RIGHT. To conduct oneself properly, to behave. "Straighten up, and fly right, sucker." *WWCL.*

FOUR F's. "Find 'em, feel 'em, fuck 'em, and forget 'em." [*WWCL:* Find 'em, flop 'em, frig 'em, and forget 'em.]

FOX, FOXY. A sexy prison female. "Tina is a pretty foxy young thing when she cleans herself up." *BJA*.

FREAK. A narcotics user who enjoys playing with the needle. *LU*. Also *needle freak*.

FREAK OUT. To act irrationally. "These guys were all freaked out on joy-juice." *LU*.

FREAKY. Something weird, bizarre. *LU*.

FREEZE, FREEZE ON. To refuse to acknowledge a person. Similar to *shine (someone) on*. *LU*.

FRENCH. Oral sex. *WWCL; LU*. Also *face, head job, skull,* etc.

TO FRONT. To give someone drugs to sell and to pay for them after they are sold. "I let somebody else front the dope for me." *WWCL; LU*.

FRONT (SOMEONE) OFF. To make known a fact that another person wants to conceal. "Man, you really screwed me up when you fronted me off like that."

FRONT STREET. 1. To become visible, known, in prison. 2. To put oneself in a dangerous situation.

FRUIT, FRUITER. A prison homosexual. *LU*. [*LB*: Fruit vine. A woman's private parts, i.e. that has flowers every month and bears fruit in nine. 1811.] Also *fruitcake*.

FRUITCAKE. A prison homosexual. Also *fruit, fruiter*.

FUCKED, FUCKED UP. Under the influence of narcotics, alcohol or a combination of alcohol combined with barbiturates or amphetamines. *LU*. Also *blasted, loaded, stoned, zonked*.

FUNKY. 1. A term used to describe anything pleasurable in the prison, especially music. (The soul quality in black music.) 2. Anything attractive. "Donny sure wears some funky clothes." 3. Anything dirty, stinky, dusty; altogether, not nice. [*DSA*: A powerful stink. 1690.]

FUNNY MONEY. Counterfeit money.

GAFFEL. To arrest. "The pig gaffeled me up and took me to the growler." *LU*.

THE GAME. Living by a set of unwritten rules known to all in a particular culture, in this case, prison. "For us it's cops and robbers, dealing, stealing, hustling, sex, and so on. This term also applies when we are out on the streets." [*DSUE*: Preceded by *the*, means thieving among thieves. 1812.] *BJA.* Also *play.*

GAMING. 1. Playing the "game." See *game.* 2. To be insincere. "I'm gaming, Jack, when I say I'm going to square up." [*DSA*: A trick. 1854.]

GAMING AND CAPERING. Stealing.

GAY AND FRISKY. Whiskey. Rhyming slang. *WWCL; LU.*

GEAR. A homosexual. *LU.*

GEEZ. 1. Drugs. "She's strung out and depends on her pimp to supply her with geez." *LU.* 2. An injection of drugs. *LU.*

GEORGE. Everything is satisfactory. "That's George, man." *WWCL; LU.*

GESTAPO. Prison guards.

GET BACKS. Revenge in prison. "Those guys got some get-backs coming for what they done to Johnny last week."

GET DOWN. 1. To do something. Generally involves sex, fighting, sports, drugs, partying. "The wolves want to get down with the kid and turn him out." *BJA.*

GET IN ON THE ACTION. To be part of whatever is going on in prison — dope, sex, and so on. Similar to *pick up on the action.*

GET IN SOMEONE'S FACE. To challenge; to annoy; to start trouble. To get in someone's face is to stand up and challenge, or call someone out — curse, accuse, or threaten them. "I think I'll go over to the kitchen and get in that guy's face because of what he said about my old lady."

GET IT ON. To fight. "The Indians said to the Mexicans, 'Let's get it it on now!'" *BJA.*

GET OFF ON. 1. To feel the pleasurable effect of drugs or any enjoyable experience. "We got this nut who gets off on acting like this for awhile and nobody knows what he's doing." *LU.*

GET ON SOMEONE'S CASE. To reprimand; to nag; to scold. "I'll get on John's case to see if I can get him to go into action." *BJA*.

GET ON THE LINE. To communicate with fellow prisoners in solitary confinement by shouting into the toilet after water has been removed from it. See *phone, open line.*

GET SHORT. To come to the end of a prison sentence; to run out of "time." "I'm getting so short I don't have time to read a book."

GET SOMETHING: GIVE SOMETHING. A prison expression meaning you get back what you give.

GETTING UP OFF A LITTLE INFO. "Doing some lightweight informing, which is different from regular *snitching*. Saying something unintentionally to friendly guards, or to the administration that puts the heat on a wing, or causes a shakedown or something like that."

GIRLS. Homosexuals who play the female role in the prison. See *queen.*

GITGO. From the beginning. "I knew from the gitgo that this caper would turn out to be a bogus operation."

GIVE HEAD. To perform oral sex. *LU.*

GIVE IT UP. To relinquish possession of something. Applies in two situations in the prison: 1. As a sexual expression, to give up sex to another. "You better give it up." 2. To give information (or an object) to someone.

GIVE SOMEONE THE BUSINESS. To kill.

GIVING UP BACKS. Being initiated into homosexual practices. *LU.*

GLADIATOR SCHOOL. A violent prison. "Lompoc [a correctional facility in California] is known as a gladiator school because of the intense racial and gang warfare which goes on there."

GLOM. To steal; to grab hold of. *LU.*

GO DOWN. The way things happen. As applied to jails or prisons, it refers to the experiences of the men while they are there. "The things that go down in the city and county jails [rapes and beatings] are frustrating and dehumanizing."

GO FOR BROKE. To commit suicide. Also *go the dutch route, hari-kari, knock yourself, sideways trip.*

GO FOR WHAT YOU KNOW. To do something if you think you know what you are doing.

GO HALFERS. To split the rent on a cell or to split payment on a drug purchase.

GO THE DUTCH ROUTE. To commit suicide. *WWCL.* Also *go for broke, hari-kari, knock yourself, sideways trip.*

GO TO BAT. 1. To go to trial. 2. To face the issue. *WWCL.*

GOD FORBID. Kid. Rhyming slang. *WWCL; LU.*

GONE TO KOREA. Gonorrhea. Rhyming slang. *WWCL.*

GOOD PEOPLE. 1. An *old timer* who has a positive influence in the prison. *WWCL.* 2. Someone who is liked. *WWCL;* [*LU:* This is an expression from the professional underworld dating back to before the 1900s. In the 1930s, professional criminals who retired were called "good people."]

GOOD TIME. The amount of time granted, and deducted from an inmate's sentence, for good behavior. *WWCL; LU.*

GOOF-BALL. A narcotic that causes dullness, quiets the nerves, induces sleep. *WWCL; LU.* Also barbiturates, *goofer, sleeper, yellow jacket.*

GOOFERS. Barbiturates. "You'd think guys in here would respond more to downers like goofers or trackwisers like Valium®." *LU.*

GO OFF. 1. To become violent. 2. To lose control. "Those dings might go off in the visiting room and try stabbing somebody."

GOON SQUAD. A derogatory term for riot squad. "The guard ran back to the desk and summoned the ole goon squad." Also *gooners, goons.*

GO OVER THE WALL. To escape. To climb over the wall.

GOOSING THE POPULATION. An expression used when the prisoners believe that the guards are harrassing them. "Them pigs are steadily goosing the population."

GORILLA. To bully or threaten someone. "You can't gorilla the motherfuckers cause they scream for the cops." [*LU*: A hoodlum or thug.] Similar to *wolf ticket*.

GORILLA WING. Eight Wing, which has the reputation of being the most troublesome wing in the prison.

GO STRAIGHT. To quit all criminal behavior and activities. To live by the rules of the majority culture.

GRASS. Marijuana. *LU*. Also *pot, shit, weed*.

GREASER. A slang term used in the prison to describe Mexican prisoners.

GREASING. Eating. "I think I'll go over to the chow hall and do some serious greasing."

GROOVING. The euphoria experienced after taking drugs. *LU*. Also *coasting, tripping*.

GROWLER. 1. Solitary confinement. "The goons drug me off to the growler just for ripping off a sandwich." Also *A-deck, back row, hole, slammer, shelf*. 2. Prison toilet. Also *crapper, groaner, rapper, shitter*.

GRUNION. Money. "Man, I ain't got a grunion on me; I'm flat-assed broke."

GUN BEEF. 1. A complaint charging one with a crime in which a gun was used. "A gun beef is a mandatory sentence—five or seven years." *WWCL*. 2. "Getting captured with a horse and buggy in the joint." (using hypodermic needle and syringe.)

GYPSY PACE. Face. Rhyming slang. *WWCL*.

H. Heroin. *LU*. Also *horse, Mexican brown, shit, skag, smack, stuff*, etc.

HABIT. A physical and emotional dependence on drugs. "Some dope fiends manage to keep habits going in here." *LU*.

HALF A C. Fifty dollars. *WWCL*.

HAMMER AND SAW. Jaw. Rhyming slang. *WWCL*.

HAMMER AND TACK. Back. Rhyming slang. *WWCL*.

HANDY DAN. Man. Rhyming slang. *WWCL*.

HANG IT UP. 1. To stop doing something. "Think I'll hang it up for awhile." 2. To give up using drugs.

HANG TOUGH. 1. To not crack under police pressure. 2. To wait a moment or two. 3. To take things easy. *LU.*

HANGING PAPER. Passing, or attempting to pass counterfeit money or bad checks. *WWCL; LU.*

HANK AND FRANK. Bank. Rhyming slang. "Gotta ease on down to the Hank and Frank to make a withdrawal." *LU.*

HARD CASE. An uncooperative or difficult prisoner. "I don't think they'll take the dope outa here cause it mellows out a lot of their hard cases."

HARD TIME. A prisoner unable or unwilling to adjust to the normal prison routine will do *hard time.* A prisoner who remains overly concerned about his outside ties (i.e. wife, children) or one who is being harassed or threatened by others will do *hard time.* Doing hard time is not limited to first-timers. "I sure hope Bill gets his visit soon, he is really doing hard time this week."

HARDWARE. Weapons of any kind. *WWCL.*

HARI-KARI. To commit suicide. Also *go for broke, go the dutch route, knock yourself, sideways trip.*

HARNESS BULL. A uniformed policeman. *WWCL; LU.*

HARVARD AND YALE. Jail. Rhyming slang. *WWCL.*

HASSLE. Trouble or harassment, particularly from guards. "The cops won't hassle you if you know how to slip and slide." *LU.*

HAUL. The loot, booty, or plunder taken. *WWCL.*

HAVE THE DROP ON. To have an adversary covered; to be in an advantageous position. *WWCL.*

HEAD JOB. Oral sex. *LU.* Also *face, French, head, skull,* etc.

HEART AND LUNG. Tongue. Rhyming slang. *WWCL.*

HEAT. 1. The guards (or police). "If you gotta talk to your connect, do it someplace where the heat ain't gonna see you." *WWCL; LU.* 2. Pressure applied by the police or guards. "Man, those pigs were really putting the heat on us." *WWCL; LU.*

HEAVY. 1. A prisoner who has gained a reputation for being dangerous, or who has enough money and influence to hire muscle (tough prisoners) to give them power. *WWCL; LU.* 2. Something important or serious. *BJA.* 3. Any major caper, such as murder, armed robbery, and so on. *WWCL.*

HEAVY BEEF. A charge for a serious crime such as murder or armed robbery.

HEAVY DOPE. Heroin. All Class A narcotics. "The Bikers used to control the heavy dope in here."

HEAVY LICK. To be treated harshly or sternly. For example, when a prisoner is expecting an eighteen-month sentence, but the Parole board gives him five years. "When I went before the Parole Board they hit me a heavy lick."

HEAVY TIME. A long sentence.

HEEL. To arm with a pistol or other weapon. *WWCL.*

HEEL AND TOE. Go. Rhyming slang. *WWCL.*

HEEL AND TOE MAN. One who steals in a sneak thief manner. "I'm talking about a good thief, a heel and toe man, a guy that's a good booster." *LU.* Also *booster, creeper, till tapper.*

HEELER. A sneak-thief. "We know some Indians in here who are probably the best heelers on the west coast." *WWCL.*

HEIST. A forcible stopping and robbing of a person. A *hijack.* *WWCL; LU.*

HEIST MAN. One who specializes in stickups and robberies. *WWCL; LU.* Also *hijacker, stickup artist.*

HIGH. 1. The maximum euphoria experienced by those who take drugs by mouth. *LU.* 2. The euphoria experienced by use of drugs, alcohol or "sniffing glue" in the prison. "All they live for in here is getting high." Also *loaded, stoned, tripping, zonked.*

HIGH ROLLER. One who gambles for high stakes, particularly at craps. *WWCL.*

HIJACK. To steal from forcefully. "They slammed you up against the wall; man, it was big hijack time all the way in here." *WWCL.*

HIT. 1. A marijuana cigarette. Also *doo-be, joint, number.* 2. The taking of a drug whether in pill form or by injection. *LU.* 3. To kill. Also *burn, bury, bushwhack, dust, ice, off, plant, snuff, stick, take (someone) out, waste, wipe (someone) out.* 3. To steal. *LU.*

HIT AND RUN. Same as *crash.*

HIT ON. 1. To make a proposition, especially sexual. "One of these guys hit on me and said, 'You better give it up!'" *LU.* 2. To beg for something from someone. "Those Breezeway bums are always hitting on you for some weed." *LU.* 3. To discuss or talk about something. "We're not talking much; just hittin on this and that."

HIT THE BRICKS. To be released from prison or jail. *WWCL.* Also *hit the streets, on the streets, on the bricks.*

HIT THE GROWLER. 1. To land in jail. 2. To be put in the *hole* (solitary confinement). 3. To sit on the toilet.

HIT THE KIP. To go to bed. *WWCL; LU.*

HIT THE STREETS. To be released from prison or jail. Also *hit the bricks, on the streets, on the bricks.*

HIT THE WALL. To escape from prison.

HOG PEN. The control room where guards are stationed. "Just saw four guys going into the hog pen with cuffs on, what's up?" Also *pig station.*

HOLD. A detainer, placed on a prisoner who is about to be released, charging him with an offense for which he has yet to answer. *WWCL.*

HOLD COURT. To shoot it out with the law. *WWCL.*

HOLD OUT. To keep out as a part of the take from a caper. *WWCL.*

HOLD OVER. Temporary imprisonment enroute to the Joint. *WWCL.*

HOLD YOUR MUD. To keep yourself under control emotionally. "You either go down fighting or you hold your mud."

HOLDING THE BAG. To be in possession of drugs. "All the creeps come out of the woodwork to hustle you when you're holding the bag."

HOLDING HEAVY. To be well supplied with money or narcotics.

"In Tacoma, holding heavy means you got a big stash of narcotics." *WWCL*.

HOLE. Solitary confinement. [*DSA*: A cell, hell. 1540.]

HOLE–CARD. A secret back-up; an "ace-in-the-hole."

HOME, HOME BOY, HOMIE. Someone from the same neighborhood or street gang. Similar to *brother, bro*.

HONEST JOHN. One who works for a living. *WWCL*. Also *hoosier, square john*.

HOOF IT ON DOWN. To walk away. [*DSUE*: Hoof it. To go on foot. c. 1700.]

HOOKED. 1. To be addicted to drugs. 2. To be addicted to a pastime or occupation. "Hustlers are hooked on that game they play." 3. To be connected to something. "We just make it a point to be in the other side of the Joint when we're not hooked up to the shit that's coming down [trouble]."

HOOKED UP TOGETHER. A close homosexual relationship in the prison.

HOOKER. 1. A thief. 2. A prison prostitute. Also *bitch, whore, working girl*.

HOOK IT ON DOWN. To walk rapidly.

HOOK UP. A drug connection.

HOOP PEDDLER. A prison prostitute. *WWCL*.

HORN IT. To sniff cocaine or heroin. [*WWCL*: nose] *LU*. [*DSA*: Horn. The nose. 1823.] Also *sniff, snort*.

HORSE. 1. Heroin. *LU*. 2. Someone who brings contraband (especially drugs) into the prison. Also *mule, pack horse, pack mule, pipeline*.

HORSE AND BUGGY. A hypodermic needle and syringe for narcotics use. See *horse and wagon*.

HORSE AND WAGON. A hypodermic needle and syringe. Also *factory, fit, Ike and Mike, outfit, rig*.

HOSE. Copulation. "Hose that chump down." *WWCL*.

HOT. 1. Wanted by the law. *LU.* 2. Stolen or illegal merchandise. *WWCL; LU.*

HOT PAPER. Spurious checks, bonds, paper money, etc. *WWCL; LU.*

HOUDINI. To escape. *WWCL.* Also *break and run, heelin' tough, take a mope, to hit it, to split, to hit the wall.*

HOUSE. A prison cell.

HOW STRONG ARE YOU? How much money are you holding? *WWCL.*

HUMMER. A fake arrest (by guards) in order to search a prisoner's cell. "I was busted on a hummer." *LU.*

HUSTLE. 1. The ways in which an addict supports his habit in the prison. 2. "Refers to scrounging up anything in here from a sandwich to a blowjob." [*LU*: To obtain money by illegal means such as pimping, con games, prostitution, or other rackets commonly worked by addicts.] 3. To work on illegal enterprises. [*DSUE*: One who works energetically and impatiently on unscrupulous endeavors. 1886.]

HUSTLER. 1. A thief; one who lives without working (in the conventional sense). 2. A prostitute. *WWCL; LU.*

I SUPPOSE. Nose. Rhyming slang. *WWCL.*

ICE. To kill. Also *burn, bury, bushwhack, dust, hit, off, plant, snuff, stick, take (someone) out, waste, wipe (someone) out.*

IDIOT STICK. A shovel, mop, hoe, etc. *WWCL.*

IF YOU PITCH IN HERE, EVENTUALLY, YOU'RE GOING TO CATCH. An expression meaning if a man plays the male role in a homosexual relation in prison, eventually he will trade places with his partner and assume the female role.

IKE AND MIKE. Spike (hypodermic needle). Rhyming slang. "Pass me the Ike and Mike so I can do this thing."

IN A TIGHT. In trouble; in need of assistance; in a jam. *WWCL.*

IN THE AIR. Don't know; undecided. *WWCL.*

IN THE KNOW. One who has gained inside information. *WWCL.*

INDIAN CLUB. Confederated Indian Tribes (CIT). Native American prisoner organization.

INDIAN RESERVATION. E Deck in Eight Wing, or wherever there are several cells close together that hold Indian prisoners.

IN FRONT. At or from the beginning. "And you know in front when you're supposed to walk."

INMATE. One who follows the rules, who toe's the line, is friendly with guards; as opposed to *real con*. "He sure as hell ain't no convict; he's a stinkin inmate and that's that."

THE INSIDE. To have information, to know what is happening. A shortened term for "the inside story." "I'll get you the inside of what's up." [*DSUE*: Secret intimate trustworthy information. c. 1880.]

IN THE O-ZONE. To experience the effect of LSD or amphetamines. "When we say he's in the O-zone, we mean the ding done blew his brain on acid or speed."

IRISH LASHES. Glasses. Rhyming slang. *WWCL.*

IRONS. Handcuffs. "She gets busted and they put the irons on her."

THE ISLAND. The federal penitentiary, located at McNeil Island in the State of Washington. *WWCL.*

IVORY BANDS. Hands. Rhyming slang. *WWCL.*

IVORY REEF. Teeth. Rhyming slang. *WWCL.*

J.P. Justice of the peace. *WWCL.*

JACK. Money. *WWCL; LU.*

JACK AND JILL. Till. Rhyming slang. *WWCL; LU.*

JACK HORNER. Corner. Rhyming slang. *WWCL.*

JACK MOHOFFEY. Coffee. Rhyming slang. *WWCL.*

JACK-RABBIT PAROLE. To escape from prison. To run like a jack-rabbit. *WWCL.*

JACK-ROLL. A caper in which the mark is assaulted; to strong-arm. *WWCL; LU.*

JACK SCRATCH. Match. Rhyming slang. *WWCL.*

JACKET. 1. A stereotyping category often used by classification personnel or prisoners in deciding who and what you are. *WWCL.* [*DSA*: (American thieves'). To denote; to point out. 1859.] Also *bag.* 2. An official record kept on each prisoner. *WWCL.*

JAILBAIT. Girls who are under the legal age of consent. *WWCL.*

JAILBIRDS. 1. Birds that fly into the prison. 2. Prisoners. [*DSA*: A prisoner. 1603.]

JAILING IT. Serving an easy prison sentence. Also *easy time.*

JAM SOMEONE UP. To pressure someone. "The Bikers have really got me jammed up tight over that lousy sawbuck I owe."

JAMOKE. Coffee. *WWCL.*

JANOSCO. The penis. *WWCL.* Also *hose, flute, snake,* etc.

JAYCEE'S. A prison self-help group.

JIGGER MAN. One who acts as a lookout and gives a signal when the bulls are coming. *WWCL.* Also *outside man, point-man.*

JIGGERS. 1. An exclamation of warning that a guard is coming by someone standing watch while accomplices violate prison rules. "Jiggers! Here comes the cop!" 2. To keep watch. "One guy keeps jiggers down the tier with a mirror while the rest are ripping off [raping] the fish." [*DSA*: A doorkeeper; a *screw*; a jailer or turn-key. 1749.]

JIM MAGEE. Key. Rhyming slang. *WWCL.*

JIMMY BRACKEN. Stop crackin' (don't talk). Rhyming slang. *WWCL.*

JIMMY BRIT. Take a shit. Rhyming slang. *WWCL.*

JIMMY DALT. Salt. Rhyming slang. *WWCL.*

JIMMY HOPE. Soap. Rhyming slang. *WWCL.*

JOB. A specific caper, as in, "Let's go pull a job." *WWCL.*

JOCK, JOCKER. A homosexual who plays the male role in prison. *WWCL.* [*DSA: Jockum,* the penis. 1567. Also *Jock,* to copulate. 1690.] Also *daddy, wolf.*

JOE GOSS. Boss. Rhyming slang. *WWCL; LU*

JOE HOKE. Smoke. Rhyming slang. *WWCL.*

JOE THE GRINDER. A cad who moves in when the husband or boyfriend is in prison. *WWCL.*

JOINT. 1. A marijuana cigarette. "Come into the house and smoke a joint." *LU.* Also *doo-be, hit, number.* 2. The Washington State Penitentiary. *LU.* 3. Penis. *LU.*

JOINT HABIT. Drug addiction in the prison. "A Joint habit is 99 percent psychological."

JOINT LADY. A prisoner who plays the female sexual role.

JOINT POLITICIAN. A prisoner who connects himself to the political game of the prison. One who enjoys the limelight and dealing with the prison administration.

JOINT SCRIP. See *scrip.*

JOINT TOUGH GUY. A prison bully. "Joint tough guys hold muscle power, but they're not really jumpin on people."

JOLT. 1. A term served in prison. *WWCL; LU.* 2. An injection (shot) of narcotics into the vein or the skin. *WWCL; LU.*

JONES. A large drug habit. "I've got a heavy Jones going." *LU.*

JOY JUICE. Carbon tetrachloride, or 201, a very strong chemical inhaled by some inmates to get high. "These guys were all freaked out on joy juice." *BJA.* Also *moon juice, sniffings.*

JUG. Jail. *WWCL; LU.*

JUICE. Any intoxicating beverage. *WWCL; LU.*

JUMP. 1. To attack someone. "Sometimes the guys jump the new fish when they first come in." 2. To go into action. "I'll lay around for thirty days then jump out and get a job." 3. To begin. "Trouble could jump off any minute out here in the Breezeway."

JUMP BEHIND COUNTERS AND GRAB A DRAWER IN A POISON SHOP. To reach behind, or sneak behind a drug store counter and steal the entire stock of Class A narcotics stored there.

JUNK. All forms of narcotics. *WWCL; LU.*

JUNKIE. A narcotics addict. "Junkies are dyed-in-the-wool dope fiends." *WWCL; LU.*

JUST BECAUSE YOU'RE PARANOID DOESN'T MEAN SOME-ONE ISN'T AFTER YOU. A common expression that reflects conditions in the prison.

KANGAROO COURT. A prison hearing where the verdict has already been agreed upon prior to the testimony of the defendant. "I don't want to go into that Kangaroo Court. Might just as well go straight to the slammer and save some time." *WWCL.*

KANGAROOED. One who has been subjected to a kangaroo court. *WWCL; LU.*

KICK OVER. To take; rob, etc. "So we kick over this joint." *WWCL.*

KICKING BACK. To relax in the prison. "Man, I'm burned out on the Yard. Think I'll go in and kick back for a few hours."

KICKING IN POISON SHOPS. Robbing drug stores for narcotics.

KID. 1. An immature, small, young prisoner. "Leave the kid alone; he doesn't know what's going on around here." *WWCL.* [*DSA*: A young thief. 1823.] 2. When preceeded by *my, his,* or *your* implies a homosexual. "Hey, Jake, where's your kid at today, you ole sex prevert. Did you sell him already?" *WWCL.* (A *kid* is always seduced by a *wolf.*)

KIESTER. The buttocks. *WWCL; LU.*

KIESTER STASH. Drugs deposited inside the rectum (in a rubber balloon). "Jim is going to kiester stash the stuff while he's in the visiting room." *LU.*

KINKY. Dishonest. "I've got a kinky job to pull tonight." *WWCL.*

KIP. A bed. *WWCL; LU.*

KITE. A letter or note to someone in the prison. *WWCL; LU.* Also *fly a kite.*

KLINK. Jail. *WWCL.*

KNIFE BEEF. A fight with a knife.

KNOCK ME DEAD. Bread. Rhyming slang. *WWCL.*

KNOCK OFF. 1. To rob. 2. To arrest. 3. To kill. *WWCL; LU.* Also *knock over.*

KNOCK OVER. To rob or burglarize.

KNOCK YOURSELF. To commit suicide. Also *go the dutch route, hari-kari, sideways trip.*

KNOWLEDGE BOX. A school house. *WWCL.*

LADY. A woman on the outside who has special significance to a prisoner. "My lady will be up to visit over the weekend."

LADY FROM BRISTOL. Pistol. Rhyming slang.

LARK. A caper. *WWCL.*

LATCH. To grab, hold, seize, etc. "Latch on to me, man." *WWCL.*

LAUGHING ACADEMY. The psychiatric unit of the penitentiary. *WWCL.*

LAY LOW. 1. To hide from the law. 2. To avoid confrontations with guards. "Why can't they just lay low until the heat is off?"

LEAN AND FAT. Hat. Rhyming slang. *WWCL.*

LEAN AND LINGER. Finger. Rhyming slang. *WWCL.*

LEGIT. That which is authorized by law; legal. "I'm going strictly legit when I get out of here." *WWCL; LU.*

LET IT SLIDE. To allow some statement or action that could start an argument or fight pass without saying or doing anything about it.

LID. A commercial measure of marijuana equal to approximately one ounce or fifty cigarettes. "Out of a lid of grass, I make about four hundred dollars." *LU.*

LIE DEAD. To sit tight; to stay out of sight. [*WWCL:* To feign death.]

LIFERS. 1. Prisoners doing a life sentence. 2. Lifers With Hope—prestigious club in the prison.

LIFERS PARK. A small enclosure with a garden and fish pond maintained by the lifers.

LIFT. To steal. *WWCL.*

LIGHT-WEIGHT NOTHING. A small drug habit. *LU.*

LITTLE AFRICA. Six Wing, where most of the black prisoners live. Also *Watusiland.*

LITTLE GUY. Same as *little man.*

LITTLE MAN. A small, young prisoner, recognized by the population as someone who is very manly and therefore cannot or should not be made into a *punk.* Also *little guy.*

LIVE. A good situation, or some kind of action taking place that is worth attending; as opposed to *dead action.* "Hey, Don, I hear the movie tonight is really live; want to hit it?"

LIVE ONE. One who is easily cheated. *WWCL; LU.* Also *mark, sucker.*

LIVER AND LUNG. Tongue. Rhyming slang. *WWCL.*

LOADED. To be under the influence of drugs. "Dopers in here want to get high just as quick as possible, and for as long as possible, and as loaded as possible. This is what they value, respect, love, and lust for." *LU.* Also *blasted, fucked up, zonked, stoned.*

LOCKDOWN. To lock prisoners up during times of danger. "We had a lockdown today because somebody got stabbed on the Breezeway. We gotta stay in twenty-four hours a day during a lockdown." Compare to *lockup.*

LOCKUP. To lock prisoners in their cells as a routine matter. "It's too late to go anywhere tonight because it is almost time for lockup." Compare to *lockdown.*

LONER. A prisoner who does not associate with others. "Loners, particularly new guys who don't know their way around here, are in danger of getting bushwhacked."

LONG CON. 1. A prisoner serving a long sentence. 2. A confidence game that may require weeks of preparation before the sucker is ready for clipping. *WWCL.* Also a *tall con.*

LONG TIMER. One who has served, or has to serve, a long sentence in prison. *WWCL.*

LOOK AT THE GATE. Applies to someone who is soon to be released from prison. "They give some of those guys so much time that they can't even look at the gate and they mix em with guys who are lookin at the gate. That causes problems, man."

LOOSE. 1. A prisoner who behaves erratically. "Joe is loose, see. He ain't wrapped too tight, so watch him." 2. Insane. "We got guys in here who are insane. They're not dings, we call em loose." 3. Describes lax conditions that sometimes exist in the prison.

LOUSE. An informer. *WWCL.*

LOW LIFE. A prisoner who is disliked, generally because he robs cells or sells inferior or fake drugs.

LOW PROFILING. One who does their time quietly, unobtrusively.

LUMP. Packages of food hidden on the body and smuggled from the kitchen into the cells. [*DAS*: A package of food. c. 1936.]

LUMP (ONE'S) MELON. To be hit on the head. "Did you see that ding! He sneaked up and lumped my melon for no reason. Shit, there ought to be a law."

LUSH HOUND. An alcoholic. *WWCL.*

LUSHER. 1. One who robs or rolls drunks. 2. A chronic alcoholic. *WWCL.*

M. Morphine. *WWCL.*

M.S.B. The Minimum Security Building, which is located outside the walls of the main institution.

MAGIC WAND. The police baton carried by guards when they go inside the walls to break up a disturbance. "The goon squad comes right behind with their magic wands to lump your melon."

MAINLINE. 1. An expression that means it is time to eat in the "chow hall." "Let's hit it, Don; they just called mainline." *WWCL.* See *shortline.* 2. To inject drugs into a vein. *WWCL; LU.*

MAKE A PERSON. To identify; to put the finger on. *WWCL; LU.*

MAKE A PLAY FOR THE GATE. Programming one's activities in order to obtain an early release from prison. "Bikers are strange, no visible efforts at playing for the gate like a sane person would do."

MAKE BOOK. To leave. "We're going to make book as soon as we're through here; we're taking off, leaving the area."

MAKE THE COP. To plead guilty. "They make all kinds of deals with people to make the cop, to lower the charges in order to further up the system, so everybody don't get a jury trial and it doesn't plug up the system."

MAKE THE CROAKER. To talk the doctor out of drugs. "I'm going to try to make the croaker for some quarter grains [morphine]."

THE MAN. Any person in authority. "If the man comes up on the tier, you yell out." *LU; BJA.*

MARK. 1. A victim, or intended victim. 2. A place designated to be robbed. *LU.*

MAX. 1. The maximum time to which one is sentenced by a judge. 2. To go all the way; to take it as far as it will go. *WWCL.* See *to the max.*

MEET. A meeting. "We have to go to a meet after this." *WWCL; LU.*

MELLOW. Pleasant, peaceful. Refers both to the men and the prison. "The Joint is pretty mellow now that they shipped those apes out of here." "I hang around with guys who are pretty mellow; they stay out of trouble." *BJA.*

MELON. A person's head. *WWCL.*

MERRY OLD SOUL. Hole. Rhyming slang. *WWCL.*

MESSED WITH. To be harassed. "He comes here, gets messed with, and checks into P.C."

MEXICAN BROWN. Mexican heroin. Also *brown, shit, skag, smack, stuff.*

MILK AND CREAM. Dream. Rhyming slang. *WWCL.*

MIND-FUCK. To have an experience that is emotionally upsetting. "The trip [visit] with my old lady turned out to be a total mind-fuck."

MIND BUSTER. Something irritating, fantastic, shocking. Also *mind trip.*

MIND TRIP. "Anything that rattles you or is interesting enough to make you stare at it or be emotionally affected by it." Also *mind buster.*

MISBEHAVE. Shave. Rhyming slang. *WWCL.*

MISBEHAVE AND AN OCEAN WAVE. Shave and a massage. Rhyming slang. *WWCL.*

MOB. An organization or gang of crooks. *WWCL; LU.*

MONNIKER. A person's name or nickname. *WWCL; LU.*

MOON JUICE. Same as *joy juice.* "Man, that joy juice will really send you to the moon."

MOP AND PAIL. Jail. Rhyming slang. *WWCL.*

MORPH. Morphine.

MOTHER AND DAUGHTER. Water. Rhyming slang. *WWCL.*

MOTHERFUCKER. A much used expression denoting many situations or things. "I'm going to get out of this motherfucker [prison]."

MOXIE. Patient courage under affliction; fortitude; guts. *WWCL.* Also *sack.*

MUCK OUT. To kill.

MUSCLE. Tough prisoners who can be hired for protection. "Senior Citizens hire muscle to protect them."

NAB. 1. To arrest. 2. To seize or catch suddenly. *WWCL; LU.*

NAIL. 1. To seize someone; to apprehend; arrest. "The cops nailed his shit." *WWCL.* [*DSUE:* To catch or get hold of, or secure. 1760.] 2. To commit a homosexual act. "Anyway, I get down there and nail the guy, and the other two cell partners nail him and I went back for seconds."

NAIL YOUR SHIT. To attack someone. "He'll nail your shit before you can get out of the way."

NEAR AND FAR. Bar. Rhyming slang. *WWCL.*

NEEDLE FREAK. An addict who enjoys playing with the needle. *LU.*

NICKEL, NICKEL BAG. A pinch of marijuana wrapped up in a little triangle (torn off from the corner of an envelope) is called a nickel. It makes about two joints. A package of marijuana that sells for $5.00 is called a nickel bag, regardless of the amount. In the 1960s, a nickel bag was about the size of two small matchboxes. The size of the bag in this prison is an indication of the inflation process and the high cost of drugs in the prison. *LU.* Also *nickel of weed.*

NICKEL OF WEED. Marijuana. About two joints. *LU.* See *nickel.*

NICK-NACKERS. 1. "Nick-nackers are guys who will take any kind of dope; they're thrill seekers." 2. People who take drugs only on weekends: *part-time dopers* or *week-enders.*

NINE WING. The prison cemetery located behind the prison hog farm.

NOODLE GAZER. Someone who stares at others in the shower. *LU.*

NORTH AND SOUTH. Mouth. Rhyming slang. *WWCL.*

NUMBER. A marijuana cigarette. "Let's go do a number." Also *doo-be, hit, joint.*

NUT, NUTTY. Insane. "They make jokes about him and stuff; say he's a nut." [*DSA*: Off one's nut. Crazy. 1876.]

NUT BAG. To have mental problems. "Were you still having problems on the streets with that nut bag?"

NUT DOCTOR. Prison psychiatrist. Also *bug doctor.*

THE NUT WARD. Psychiatric unit of the prison hospital. Also *booby hatch, ding ward, third floor,* etc.

O.D. An overdose of narcotics. "It's awful hard to O.D. on drug store dope." *LU.*

OFF. To kill. "They were gonna take the guards hostage that night and off the guys who killed their brothers." Also *burn, bury, bushwhack, dust, hit, ice, plant, snuff, stick, take (someone) out, waste, wipe (someone) out.*

OFFENSE IS THE BEST DEFENSE. An expression commonly used in prison.

OFF THE WALL. To abruptly change the subject of a conversation. *LU; BJA.*

OH MY CATARRH. Cigar. Rhyming slang. *WWCL.*

OH MY DEAR. Tier. Rhyming slang. Bottles and stoppers, Oh my dear means cops on the tier.

OLD BLACK JOE. Toc. Rhyming slang. *WWCL*

OLD LADY. A prisoner's wife or sweetheart. *BJA.* [*DAS:* A wife, especially one's own wife. Based on the earlier "old woman." Not considered derogatory. 1871.]

OLD MAN. Prison lover or pimp. "Big John's her new old man." Also *daddy.*

OLD TIMERS. Men who have been in prison for several years.

OLE TRICKY DICK. Penis. Also *bone, brutus coccus, flute,* etc.

ON THE BRICKS. Out of prison or jail. *LU.* Also *hit the bricks, hit the streets, on the street.*

ON THE BOOST. To engage in shoplifting. *WWCL; LU.*

ON THE DODGE. Avoiding contact with the law. *WWCL; LU.*

ON THE DUMMY. To refuse to give up information to guards or prison officials. *LU.*

ON THE ERIE. To eavesdrop. *LU.*

ON THE GRIND. A job. *WWCL.*

ON THE HEAVY. To be on a strong drug habit. *WWCL.*

ON THE MUSCLE. To make one's way by sheer brawn; a real toughie. *WWCL.*

ON THE PROWL. 1. On the watch for; as for an easy touch. 2. Capering. 3. Looking around, as for pleasure. *WWCL.*

ON THE SHELF. To be in solitary confinement.

ON THE SNEAK. Anyone who moves about stealthily. "Pig's on the sneak on A-Deck!" *LU.*

ON THE STREETS. Out of prison or jail. *LU.* Also *hit the bricks, hit the streets, on the bricks.*

ONE WAY. Selfish; inconsiderate. "He's really one way about it, man." *WWCL.*

ONE-WAY TICKET. An execution. *WWCL.*

ONES AND TWOS. Shoes. Rhyming slang. *WWCL; LU.*

OPEN LINE. Refers to the "telephone system" in Segregation. See *phone.*

OREGON BOOTS. Leg irons. *WWCL.* Probably evolved from "Rindquist boots," the term for leg irons used at Bukota, Washington, where the first penitentiary was built.

OSCAR HOCKS. Socks. Rhyming slang. *LU.*

OUT FRONT. To be honest, frank. "I have been pretty out front with you about this whole deal."

OUT THE BACK DOOR. To escape from prison. Also *go over the wall.*

OUTFIT. Hypodermic needle and syringe. "As soon as the outfit is put back in its secret stash, they're on the move again." *WWCL; LU.* Also *factory, fit, horse and wagon, Ike and Mike, rig.*

OUTSIDE MAN. A look-out who stands point, as during a caper. *WWCL; LU.* Also *jiggerman, point man.*

P.C. Protective custody. "He checks into P.C. because those guys have threatened to off him."

P.O. A probation or parole officer. *LU.*

PACK. 1. To transport drugs or other contraband into the prison. "If a pig decides to earn some extra cash by packing, he'll bring in weed." Also *pack horse, pack mule, pipeline.* 2. To carry a weapon. "The Chicanos have their warriors, too; but we never know which of their group is packing."

PACK HORSE. One who brings drugs or other contraband into the prison. Also *horse, mule, pack mule, pipeline.*

PACK MULE. See *pack horse.*

PACK A BUCKET. To get a conventional job. Also *bankers hours, eight-to-five, gig, square-up.*

PAD. A prison cell. Also *drum, house.*

PAPER. Checks, stocks, bonds, etc. *WWCL; LU.*

PAPER HANGER. Someone who steals through forgery, passing bad checks or stolen credit cards (fraud). [*DSUE*: c. 1925.]

PAROLE DUST. Fog in which a prisoner hides when he goes over the wall. Similar to *bush parole.*

PARTNERS. Two men who are good friends or who caper together.

"My partner will be up on the next chain." *WWCL.*

PASSER. One who passes or attempts to pass rubber checks, counterfeit, etc. *WWCL.*

PAT SEARCH. A superficial examination of a prisoner by guards searching for contraband. *LU*

PEEL. To hit in the head with a pipe or other weapon. "That con sneaked up on him and peeled his head."

PEEPERS. Eyes. *WWCL.*

PEN AND INK. In the pink. Rhyming slang. *WWCL.*

PEOPLE. 1. Prisoner's family. "When will your people be here to see you?" 2. Prisoners. *BJA.* 3. A term used to indicate that one is reliable and trustworthy. *WWCL; LU.*

PEOPLES PARK. A recreation area located between Seven Wing and Big Red. The name was changed to *peoples parking lot* when Superintendent James Spalding had it paved over after the lockdown of 1979.

PEOPLES PARKING LOT. Peoples Park renamed. See *Peoples Park.*

PERSUADER. Any weapon with which to put on pressure, such as a club, sap, gun, shiv, etc. *WWCL; LU.*

PHONE. The system of water pipes through which prisoners in Segregation can talk back and forth by removing the water from the toilet bowl and shouting into the opening. See *getting on the line, open line.*

PICK UP ON THE ACTION. 1. "To tune in on what's going on in the prison." 2. "To get some dope." "To pick up on the action is to 'score' with whatever is going on." Similar to *get in on the action.*

PICK YOUR BEST SHOT. To take the right action at the right time in prison. Also *play your best hand, take your best licks.*

PIECED OFF. To cut pieces from an ounce of narcotics such as morphine, cocaine, or heroin. One ounce is one piece; one-half ounce is one-half piece; and so on. *LU.*

PIG. A derogatory term for any person in authority, especially a guard or police officer. *WWCL: BJA:* [*LB*: A police officer. A China Street pig; a Bow Street officer. 1785.]

PIG OUT. To overeat. "Let's dive into the chow hall and pig out for awhile."

PIG STATION. The control room where guards are stationed. "I headed for Control; that's an all-night pig station." Also *pig pen*.

PIGS' LATIN. Prisoners refer to the secret language (codes) sometimes used by guards as "pigs' Latin."

PIGEON. An informer. *WWCL; LU.* Also *fink, rat, ratfink, stoolie, stool pigeon.*

PIMP. A prison procurer of *queens* and *punks.* [*DSA*: To procure. c. 1696.] *BJA.*

PINS. Legs. "Joe got his pins knocked out from under him when Toby punched his lights out."

PIPE. To inject narcotics into a vein. "I think I'll pipe this one."

PIPELINE. 1. Someone from the outside who brings in drugs or other contraband. "If you got a good horse or pipeline you can get the dope in." Also *horse, mule, pack horse, pack mule.* 2. The slang term for the vein into which narcotics are injected. 3. To inject narcotics directly into a vein. Also *pipe.*

PIPE WRENCH. To open a door by the use of a small pipe wrench in order to commit a robbery. "We used to pipe wrench doors for color TV sets and fast little burglary trips."

PIT STOP. Coming back in on a short-term parole violation, six months to a year in duration.

PITCH AND CATCH. An expression describing sex in prison. "Pitching is the male shot; if you're catching, you're the broad." *WWCL.* Also *flip flopping, top and bottom.*

PITCH AND PINE. Shine (a black). Rhyming slang. *WWCL.*

PLANT. To kill. Also *burn, bury, bushwhack, dust, hit, ice, off, snuff, stick, take (someone) out, waste, wipe (someone) out.*

PLATES OF MEAT. Feet. Rhyming slang. *WWCL; LU.*

PLAY. 1. A man's method of operating once out of prison. What a member of the underworld does to make a living. *LU.* 2. A prisoner's method of operation (making a living) while in prison. Also *game, hustle.*

PLAY OFF. To cool things down.

PLAY FOR THE GATE. To adjust your conduct so that you can compile a record as a model prisoner and be paroled sooner.

PLAY THE DOZENS. To exchange insults in a friendly way. "Your old lady's picture is in the dictionary next to ugly." A black tradition enjoyed and played by all groups in the prison. Also *capping, ranking.*

PLAY THE QUEENS. To engage in homosexual activities with "female" prisoners. [*DSA*: Play the quean means play the whore. c. 1696.]

PLAY YOUR BEST HAND. To take the right action at the right time when in prison or committing a crime. "In order to stay out of the Joint, we have to change our game and play our best hand." Also *pick your best shots, take your best licks.*

PLOW THE DEEP. Sleep. Rhyming slang. *WWCL; LU.*

POINT MAN. A look-out employed by criminals engaged in capering; a jigger man. *WWCL; LU.* Also *outside man.*

POISON. Drugs. *LU.*

POISON SHOP. A drug store or hospital that has narcotics. Poison means the opiate drugs and cocaine. *Doing it to a poison shop* means robbing a drug store for narcotics.

POKE. 1. "A poke is a small stash of money hid somewhere." [*LU*: A pickpocket term for wallet. *DSA*: c. 1696.] 2. To rape. "I was poked and punked off when I first got to the Joint." [*DSA*: To copulate. c. 1709.]

POP. 1. To swallow drugs in pill form. 2. To inject drugs into a vein. *LU.* Also *mainline, pipeline.*

POP OFF. 1. To make an impertinent remark. 2. To fly into an uncontrolled rage. "I'm fast on the trigger. I pop off, then drop back to everybody's level cause I don't want to argue."

POPPED. To be arrested. Also *busted.*

POT AND PAN. Can. Rhyming slang. *WWCL; LU.*

POT OF GLUE. Jew. Rhyming slang. *WWCL; LU.*

POTHEAD. Someone who smokes marijuana. "Most of the potheads in here learned to smoke in school before they ever came into the Joint." *LU.*

PRIDE AND JOY. Boy. Rhyming slang. *WWCL; LU.*

PRIME THE MARK. To set someone up to be cheated. "Agini is street hustler's talk for priming the mark." *LU.*

PRUNO. Prison-made alcohol. Also *booze.*

PULL A CREEP. To leave quietly. *WCCL.*

PULL A CREEP JOB. To hit somebody (steal) when they can't see you. "Anytime you snatch something when there's people guarding it and you get away with it, that's a creep." *LU.*

PULL (ONE'S) COAT. To make someone aware of the situation. To explain. "I'll generally pull his coat but if he's too scared he won't be able to think."

PULL YOUR OWN TIME. To mind your own business. "You're gonna have to learn to start pulling your own time for a change." Also *do your own time (trip), pull your own trip.*

PULL YOUR OWN TRIP. Same as *do your own time.*

PULLER. A sneak thief. See *creeper.*

PUNCH (SOMEONE) OUT. To hit someone. "You can shoo a ding away or give him a shove, but you don't punch him out."

PUNCH (SOMEONE'S) LIGHTS OUT. 1. To give someone a black eye. 2. To knock someone out.

PUNK. Someone who plays the female role (initially not by choice) in a homosexual relationship in prison. *WWCL;* [*DSA*: A harlot. c. 1575; *LU*: "Punks are different from queens. They're penitentiary made."] *BJA.*

PUNK IN A BUNK. An expression commonly used referring to prison sex relationships. "Got to have a punk in the bunk to take care of the house." Also a *crack in the shack.*

PUSHER. A dope dealer. *WWCL; LU.*

PUSHING DAISIES. To die.

PUT A JACKET (ON SOMEONE). To start a rumor about a person that he is either a snitch or a homosexual. This is usually done in anger or for spite. "I really don't think that guy is a fruit; someone just put a jacket on him." [*DSA: Jacket,* American thieves' term. To denote; to point out. 1859.]

PUT IN THE MIDDLE. 1. To maneuver an individual into a position where he cannot turn informer. 2. To put another person on the spot. "I can't do it man; you put me right in the middle." *WWCL.*

PUT LUMPS AND BUMPS (ON SOMEONE). To use a hypodermic needle and syringe.

PUT ON THE DUMMY. A situation where no one raps to an individual, usually because of some shady deal, or stool activities. *WWCL; LU.*

PUT THE ARM ON. 1. To strong-arm someone. *WWCL.* 2. To arrest someone. *WWCL; LU.* Also *roust.*

PUT THE BITE ON. 1. To borrow. 2. To extort. *WWCL.* [*LU:* To try to borrow money.]

PUT THE HEAT ON. To pressure, or interrogate. *LU.*

Q. San Quentin prison. *WWCL.*

QUACK. To fool someone. To make a "duck" out of someone. "You duck! You really got quacked." A friendly expression.

QUEEN. A homosexual who plays the female role by choice. *WWCL:* [*DSA:* Quean (or Queen). A slut, hussy, or strumpet. To *play the Quean* means to play the whore. c. 1696.] Also *bitch, cunt, fruit, fruiter, fruitcake, gear, girl, Joint lady, pussy, queer, rooter, slut,* and countless other expressions.

QUEER. A prison homosexual. [*DSA: Queer-bird:* A jailbird, a convict. 1560. Queer: criminal, base, counterfeit. 1696.] Also *fruit, fruiter, fruitcake, punk, queen* and many other negative terms.

R.C.W.'s. Revised Code of Washington (law books containing the revised laws of the state). Prisoners have access to these books in the prison law library.

R.T. The rescue trainee, a prisoner, who works in the hospital and acts as a first-aid medic.

RACKED UP. 1. Placed in solitary for an infraction of rules. 2. Arrested. *WWCL.*

RACKET. A criminal *hustle* in the prison. "The Bikers were into the dope racket for awhile." *WWCL; LU.*

RAGGEDY. Tattered and torn, shabby. *BJA.*

RAGS. Clothing. *WWCL; LU.*

RANKING. A friendly way of exchanging insults. A black tradition enjoyed by all groups in the prison. *LU.* Also *capping, playing the dozens.*

RAP. Talk. *WWCL; LU.*

RAPPING AND DINGING OUT. An expression used to describe those who talk and act in an irrational manner usually as a result of taking stimulant drugs. "The dopers will be rapping and dinging out on speed all night long, tonight."

RAPO. A prisoner serving a sentence for rape. "Guys in here hate rapos. It's a disgusting crime and guys who commit it are creeps."

RAT. 1. A prison informer. 2. To inform. *WWCL; LU.* Also *fink, snitch, stoolie, stool pigeon.*

RAT AND MOUSE. House. Rhyming slang. *WWCL.*

RATPACK. To gang up on one person and beat them up. "Them Bikers will ratpack their own kind."

RATTLE AND JAR. Car. Rhyming slang. *WWCL; LU.*

REAL CON. Real cons distinguish themselves from inmates. Real cons do their time more professionally and have a higher status in the prison. They tend to follow the convict code. "If you're a real con; you won't snitch if you see some dude get wasted."

REAL ESTATE BUSINESS. Owning, renting, and buying *houses* (cells) in the prison. "The pigs are going to start cracking down on the real estate business because some of the new guys are sleeping in the hospital just because they can't afford to buy a cell."

RED HOT. 1. Wanted bodily by the police. 2. Recently stolen merchandise. *WWCL.*

REHASH. To try something again; to repeat.

REPEATER. A recidivist. "We're just old repeaters flying back and forth in here off the streets just to say 'hello.' " *WCCL.*

RETARD. A name used to identify someone who has irritated another or who has done something foolish. Usually a friendly term. "You fucking retard, quit fooling around and let's go."

RIDE A BEEF. To take the blame for a crime committed by another person. "My old lady ended up in Purdy (woman's prison) because she rode a beef for Dennis."

RIDE IT OUT. To endure or get through a difficult situation. Also *tough it out.*

RIG. A syringe and hypodermic needle. "I need to borrow a rig to do some dope." *LU.* Also *factory, fit, horse and wagon, Ike and Mike, outfit.*

RIGHTEOUS. 1. Something wonderful. 2. Something intensive, "very." "Man, that dope was righteous!" *LU.*

RIP OFF. 1. To rape someone. "All you hear about this joint is people killin each other, rippin off the youngsters. . . . " 2. To steal from someone. "It isn't cool to let people know you're holding the bag [drugs], since someone will rip you off." *LU; BJA.*

ROACH. The end of a marijuana cigarette. "Save all the roaches so we can squeeze a joint later." *LU.*

ROAD GAME. "Burglary is my road game. Anything that you do; that's your road game." [*WWCL*: The gambling game at which one is most adept.]

ROARING OAR. Door. Rhyming slang. *WWCL.*

ROBOTS. A derogatory term for the prison riot squad. Also *goons, gooners, goon squad, silons.*

(THE) ROCK. Alcatraz. *WWCL.*

ROCK PILE. "Any kind of a job you've got is a rock pile." *WWCL.*

ROLL. To rob someone. "Moe rolled the lush." *WWCL.*

ROLL ME IN THE GUTTER. Butter. Rhyming slang. *WWCL.*

ROOT. 1. The penis. 2. To eat ravenously. 3. To go out and look around or look for something. 4. To work at any of the various capers in order to make a dishonest living. *WWCL; LU.*

ROOT AROUND. To root or dig out. Sometimes used when referring to guards as *pigs.* "Those pigs are rootin around the tiers now."

ROOT OUT. To be ejected forcibly. Also *bum's rush.*

ROOT AND TOOTER. Fruiter (homosexual). Rhyming slang. *WWCL.*

ROOTER. A homosexual who plays the female role in the prison. "Rooters always carry purses around in here."

ROPE DANCE. Execution by hanging. *WWCL.*

ROSCOE. A pistol. *WWCL.*

ROSES RED. Bed. Rhyming slang. *WWCL; LU.*

ROUST. 1. To arrest. 2. To strong-arm a person. "The pig's gonna try to roust me, man." *WWCL; LU.*

ROYAL D'AMOUR. Floor. Rhyming slang. *WWCL.*

RUB OUT. To kill. *WWCL.*

RUN IT DOWN. To tell a story. To give someone information about something. To explain. "You don't have to run it down to me; I already know what's going on." *LU.*

RUN MONEY. Your cash roll put away for later use.

RUNNER. A prisoner who delivers messages for both guards and prisoners. Although paid for his work, runners have been known to deliver contraband from one wing to another, as for instance hypodermic needles and syringes for drug users. *WWCL.*

RUNNING SOMETHING DOWN. Explaining something. *BJA.*

SACK. A term that refers to the size of a man's testicles which, symbolically, is connected to the amount of courage he has. "The guy might be stupid to fight that bunch, but you gotta admit he does have some sack!"

SALT. 1. To bury, as in prison. 2. To get rid of. *WWCL.*

SALTY. 1. Hostile, unpleasant. "Just because I took his girl friend, he's salty about it." [*WWCL:* briny.] 2. Knowledgeable. "A professional robber is salty; he knows what he's doing." *WWCL.*

SAME-O, SAME-O. An expression meaning "everything's the same as it was before."

SAND. Sugar. "Nobody better put any sand in my jamoke [coffee]." *WWCL.*

SAWBONES. One who practices surgery. *WWCL.* Also *bones.*

SCORE. 1. A single theft, or the proceeds of a theft. *WWCL; LU.* 2. To complete a theft. *WWCL; LU.* 3. To obtain something of value — sex, drugs, alcohol, clothes, and so on in prison. *WWCL.* 4. To purchase drugs. [*DSUE:* The gaining of a point or points in a game. c. 1840. To succeed. 1880.] *LU.* Also *cop dope.*

SCREAM. 1. To complain in the prison. "He's always screaming about some damn thing." Also *bitch, snivel.* 2. To run, or walk rapidly. "Man there must be some action going on; I just seen the goons go screaming towards the Yard."

SCRIP, JOINT SCRIP. Prison "money." $7.00 scrip is $5.00 U.S. currency. [*DSUE:* A small piece of paper. c. 1615.]

SECOND STORY MAN. A burglar who robs homes. *WWCL.*

SEE MY SIS. Take a piss. Rhyming slang.

SEG. The segregation unit in the prison.

SELL HIS SHITTER. What a *punk* or *queen* does for a living.

SELL ONE OUT. To betray. *WWCL.*

SENIOR CITIZENS. Older men in the prison. Also *seniors, old timers.*

SENT UP. Sentenced to prison. *WWCL.*

SET UP. The description and prearranged plan for a caper. *WWCL.*

SEWER. The injection of narcotics in a large vein. "Guess I'll throw one in the sewer." *WWCL; LU.*

SHAKEDOWN. A search by guards of prison cells for contraband. *WWCL; LU.*

SHAKEDOWN ARTIST. One who extorts or blackmails. *WWCL; LU.*

SHAM. To pretend; counterfeit. "To sham someone is to feed them a line of bullshit." *WWCL.*

SHANK. A knife or other sharp edged weapon. *LU.* Also *blade, my (or your) shit, shiv, sticker.*

SHECKELS. Money. [*DSUE:* c. 1870. From Shekel, the most important Hebrew silver coin.] Also *doubloon, coin, scratch.*

SHELF. Solitary confinement. "I spent ten days on the shelf for packin a shank." Also *A-deck, back row, growler, hole, slammer.*

SHILL. A decoy; an accomplice. *WWCL; LU.*

SHINE (HIM) ON. To ignore someone. "The guy's a ding; shine him on." *LU.*

SHIP OF JUNK. A shipment of narcotics. *WWCL.*

SHIT. 1. Marijuana or heroin. "Do you know anybody who's got some shit?" *LU.* 2. A name for a thing or an action. A word with countless meanings: "He'll nail your shit [attack you] before you can get out of your house and call for help." "He talks big shit [boasts] but he ain't done shit [anything]." We got our shit [we're organized] together." "When the shit comes down [trouble], it'll be their necks; not ours." "Let's get the shit on now [let's fight]." And so on.

SHIT ON MY DICK, OR BLOOD ON MY BLADE. A challenge, which in prison lingo means, "Either I fuck you or I kill you; take your choice."

SHIV, CHIV. A knife or other sharp weapon in prison. [*DAS: Chive:* A knife, especially considered as a weapon. 1674. *DSA:* Thieves' language (gypsy). 1725.]

SHOOT THE MOON. To go the limit. *WWCL.*

SHOOTING GALLERY. "Someone's house [cell] where everyone goes to shoot dope."

SHOOT THE SHOT. To make a move. To take some action. "The wolves are always waiting like vultures when some new kid comes in to shoot the shot."

SHORT CON. 1. A prisoner serving a short sentence; a short-timer. 2. Any sort of confidence game that does not require an elaborate buildup. *WWCL; LU.*

SHORT DECK. Not all there mentally; about thirty cents on the dollar. *WWCL.*

SHORT HUSTLE. To cheat someone out of something. [*LU:* From *short-con*, a confidence game played for the amount of money carried on the person of a victim. Commonly played on the streets by drug addicts.]

SHORT TIME. A small amount of time left to serve on a sentence. *WWCL.*

SHORTLINE. Eating time for prison kitchen workers. Precedes *mainline*, when the rest of the prison population comes to the dining hall to eat. See *mainline. WWCL.*

SHORT TIMER. One who serves a brief sentence or has served the majority of his sentence and is now close to being paroled.

SHOVEL AND BROOM. Room. Rhyming slang. *WWCL.*

SHUCKING AND JIVING. Clowning, lying, pretending. *BJA.*

SHUT THE ACTION DOWN. To cease activities, whether legal or illegal. "Since that murder, nobody's dealing [selling drugs], man. Everybody's shut the action down." Similar to a *low profile.*

SIBERIA. The hole. *WWCL.*

SICKO. 1. A person who behaves grossly. "That sicko bit some guy's ear off before he killed him." 2. A mentally ill prisoner. "They ought to put him on third floor with the rest of the sickos." 3. Someone who hangs out around the hospital.

SIDEWAYS TRIP. A prison suicide. "We've had quite a few sideways trips recently." Also *go for broke, go the dutch route, hari-kari, knock yourself.*

SING. 1. To confess. 2. To inform. *WWCL.*

SINGLE O. 1. One who capers alone. 2. Someone who does something by himself. "If I shot some dope without sharing, I'd be single-o'ing." [*WWCL:* A male, and particularly a homosexual.]

SINK. A term that applies to new men (fish) entering the prison who do not survive the experience, i.e. who become psychotic or commit suicide.

SIT ON THE JOINT. An expression that describes how guards discover illegal activities carried on by prisoners. "All the cops have to do is sit on the Joint [sit/stand somewhere] and watch certain areas where drugs are sold to find out who's doing what."

SKAG. Heroin. *LU.* Also *brown, Mexican brown, shit, smack, white, white dope.*

SKIN IT. To shoot narcotics directly into the fatty part of the arm. "I don't think I'll pipe this one cause my veins are all used up; I'll skin it." *LU.* Also *skin pop.*

SKIN POP. An injection of narcotics beneath the skin. *LU.* Also *skin it.*

SKIP AND HOP. An expression that denotes a lack of seriousness on the part of some prisoners in serving their prison sentence. "Those guys skip and hop in here, play games, find things to do."

SLACK. To go easy on someone. To give someone a break. "We don't cut them no slack if they say they're Christian." "Give me some slack."

SLAMMER. Solitary confinement. Also *A-deck, back row, growler, hole, shelf.*

SLAP. To get even with someone. "I pray for a good tunnel escape just to slap it in their face."

SLICK. 1. Clever, swift. "She's packin drugs and she's not too slick so she gets busted." *WWCL; LU.* 2. An underhanded person. *WWCL.*

SLIDE. To walk. To move or go somewhere. Denotes a relaxed slow pace. [*DSUE:* To decamp. Before 1859. To move stealthily. 1899.] *BJA.*

SLIP AND SLIDE. 1. An expression that describes how prison hustlers ply their trade on the Breezeway. 2. To avoid danger or trouble in the prison.

SLAT AND LATH. Bath. Rhyming slang.

SLEEPER. A narcotic that quiets the nerves, induces sleep, causes dullness. A *downer. WWCL.* Also *goofer, goof ball, yellow jacket.*

SMACK. Heroin. "Joint smack is made from street heroin." *LU; BJA.* Also *brown dope, Mexican brown, shit, white dope* (European or Chinese heroin).

SMOOTH A RAP. To bribe or influence authorities in order to make favorable arrangements on a criminal charge. Also *fix a rap, square a rap.*

SNAP TO WHERE YOU'RE AT. To come to the realization that you are in prison.

SNIFF. To inhale narcotics or chemicals, such as carbon tetrachloride. *LU.*

SNIFFINGS. Carbon tetrachloride, or 201, a very strong chemical (used in the furniture factory to remove paint), which is stolen and used by some men to get high. Placed on rags and inhaled. "They found another tube of that sniffings in my house." Also *joy juice, moon juice.*

SNITCH. A prison informer. [*DSA:* Thieves' cant. To inform. c. 1812.] Also *fink, rat, stoolie, stool pigeon, nark.*

SNITCH KITE. A note by a pigeon to an officer informing on another. *WWCL; LU.*

SNITCH (SOMEONE) OFF. To betray someone. "The bastard went to the man and snitched me off."

SNIVEL. A prisoner term for complaining, whining, pouting. [*DSA:* To complain. 1440.]

SNORT. To inhale heroin or cocaine. *LU.* Also *horn, sniff.*

SNOW. Cocaine. *WWCL; LU.*

SNUFF. To kill someone. Also *burn, bury, bushwhack, dust, hit, ice, off, plant, snuff, stick, take (someone) out, waste, wipe (someone) out.*

SOCKED AWAY. In solitary confinement.

SOD BUSTER. A sodomist. *WWCL.*

SOLID CONVICT. A loyal, dependable prisoner; one whose loyalties are with the group; a prisoner who can be trusted not to give out information. *WWCL.*

SONG AND DANCE. Pants. Rhyming slang. *WWCL; LU.*

SONGS AND SIGHS. Thighs. Rhyming slang. *WWCL.*

SORROWFUL TALE. Jail. Rhyming slang. *WWCL.*

SPACED (OUT). To experience the effects of a drug. "Might as well forget talking to Fred; he is really spaced out today." *LU.* Also *in the O-zone, spacey.*

SPACEMEN. Users of LSD. "Spacemen are acid heads in here."

SPACEY. 1. A person who is scatter-brained or a little dingy. "He's so fucking spacey that I don't know what he's talking about half the time." 2. Experiencing the effect of LSD or amphetamines. Variation of *spaced.*

SPANISH GUITAR. Cigar. Rhyming slang. *WWCL; LU.*

SPEED. Methedrine, a stimulant drug. *LU.* Also *crank.*

SPEED FREAK. A user of methedrine.

SPEEDBALL. Narcotic. "Something like an amphetamine mixed with heroin." *WWCL; LU.*

SPEEDER. A narcotic, usually a mixture such as cocaine and morphine. *WWCL.*

SPLIT. To leave abruptly. "You just split, man; hit the road and didn't come back for count." *LU.*

SQUARE, SQUARE JOHN. 1. A member of the dominant (or majority) culture; a law abiding citizen. *LU; BJA.* 2. A member of the dominant culture who has been sent to prison. *LU.* [*DSA: Keep square.* Lead a straight life. 1604.]

SQUARE A RAP. To make favorable arrangements via influence, bribery, etc. on a criminal charge. *WWCL.* Also *fix, smooth.*

SQUARE UP. 1. To give up criminal activities and earn a living within the law. "I think I'll try to square up this time so I can stay out for awhile." [*DSUE:* To pay a debt. 1862.] 2. To give up narcotics. *LU.*

SQUEAL. To inform. *WWCL; LU.*

SQUEALER. An informer. *WWCL.*

SQUEEZE. To extort; to put on the pressure. *WWCL.*

STAGINI. The agini term for steak. Agini is one of several secret codes used by some of the men.

STALL. An accomplice; a decoy. *WWCL; LU.*

STAND PAT. 1. To plead "not guilty." 2. To refuse to implicate others. 3. To refuse to change one's story or testimony. *WWCL.*

STAND POINT. To act as a lookout. *WWCL; LU.* Also *jigger man, point man.*

STASH. 1. A concealed plant of narcotics. *LU.* 2. A concealed plant of prison alcohol (*pruno*). *WWCL.* 3. A hiding place for contraband, such as weapons; anything hidden away. *WWCL.* 4. To conceal or hide something; to set aside. *WWCL.* [*DSA:* To set aside. To *stow it.* 1785.]

STEADY TRIP. 1. "A long-term hangup—like a girl friend." 2. "Any preoccupation or activity that lasts for months." "Hey, John, that girl you're seeing has kind of turned into a steady trip, right?"

STELAZINE SHUFFLE. The peculiar gait or shuffle that a prisoner assumes after taking Stelazine, which is caused by the effects of the drug on the nervous system and muscles. Also *Thorazine shuffle.*

STEP, STEP ON. To cut street heroin with milk sugar. "Two-step dope is bad; three-step dope is worse."

STICK. To kill someone. Also *bury, burn, bushwhack, dust, hit, ice, off, plant, snuff, take (someone) out, waste, wipe (someone) out.*

STICK-UP ARTIST. One who specializes in holdups and robberies. *WWCL.* Also *heist man, hijacker.*

STING. 1. A successful thieving act. 2. To cheat. [*DSUE:* To rob, to cheat. c. 1812.]

STINGER. A prison-made water heater (for coffee).

STONE. Total, complete, one-hundred percent. "How you do your time in here is important, the difference between becoming a stone criminal or getting out of here a half decent person." *LU.*

STONED. Under the influence of narcotics. *LU.* Also *blasted, fucked, fucked up, loaded, zonked.*

STOOL. An informer. *WWCL; LU.* Also *rat, rat fink, stoolie, stool pigeon.*

STOOL PIGEON. A prison informer. "We ask the cops if they brought over any stool pigeons." *WWCL; LU.* Also *fink, rat, stoolie.*

STRAIGHT PEOPLE. 1. Heterosexuals. 2. Good (honest) people.

STRAIGHTEN UP YOUR HAND. To get your affairs in order; to reorganize or change your actions. "You had better straighten up your hand before you get your ass burned good."

STREET PEOPLE. The "new" prisoner. Applies to the majority of prisoners occupying the prison since the early 1960s. "Street people bring new games in when they come in here—drugs, language, attitude, clothes, and all that's current in the street culture. Street people differ radically from the old con in the prison before the sixties." [*LU:* Groups on many urban streets who beg, sing, and idle. They are often *hippies,* q.v. runaways and traffickers in narcotics and other contraband.]

THE STREETS. 1. The free world. Beyond the prison walls. *WWCL.* 2. That area of the free world where drugs and other underworld activities occur. *WWCL.*

STRETCH. 1. A prison term. 2. To hang. *WWCL.*

STRIDES. A pair of pants. *WWCL.*

STRIPES-A-PLENTY. A Joint spider. A large brown spider (in the prison) with white horizontal stripes across it's back.

STRONG-ARM ARTIST. A thief who specializes in muggings or any caper where physical force is employed. *WWCL; LU.*

STRUNG OUT. To be addicted to a narcotic. "The pimps keep them street broads strung out on dope." *LU; BJA.*

STUFF. Heroin. *LU.* Also *brown dope, Mexican brown, shit, skag, smack, white, white dope.*

SUCKER. A victim or potential victim. *WWCL.* [*DAS:* A person

easily deceived or cheated; an easy victim, a dupe. Before 1900.]
Also *chump*.

SUNDAY PUNCH. "A blow which comes from your blind side so
you generally never know what hit you—fist, club, knife, etc."

(A) SWEET ONE. Anything good. *WWCL*.

SWIM. To survive in the prison. Applies to new men (*fish*).

SWISH. To act, walk, or gesture as a homosexual in the prison.
"They don't swish around here and you'd never guess they played
the game."

SYDNEY HARBOR. Barber. Rhyming slang. *WWCL; LU*.

THE SYSTEM. 1. The prison. 2. The criminal justice system of
the state. "It's a copout to go along with the system; it's like saying
the system is right and you're wrong."

TAG. An infraction slip given by guards for rule-breaking. "The
pig tagged me for carrying a shank."

TAKE. To rob; to victimize. "They were trying to figure out which
one of these marks they were going to take." *LU*.

TAKE A FALL. 1. To be arrested. 2. To be convicted of a felony.
WWCL; LU.

TAKE A RAP. To receive a jail or prison sentence. *WWCL; LU*.

TAKE IT ON THE HEEL AND TOE. To leave hurriedly. *WWCL*.
Also *take a mope*.

TAKE IT ON THE MOPE. To leave hurriedly; to escape. *WWCL;
LU*. Also *take it on the heel and toe*.

TAKE THE RAP. To plead guilty. *WWCL; LU*.

TAKE (SOMEONE) OUT. To kill someone. Also *bury, burn, bushwhack, dust, hit, ice, off, plant, snuff, waste, wipe (someone) out*.

TAKE YOUR BEST LICKS. To take the right action at the right
time. Also *play your best hand, pick your best shots*.

TALK PLENTY SHIT. To boast, to brag. Black expression.

TALL CON. A prisoner serving a long sentence. *WWCL*. Also *long
con*.

TANK. A county jail term for a large cell holding at least a dozen men. "Rapes are frequent in the tank." *WWCL.*

TAP THE ROOTERS. To use homosexuals in the prison. "I don't tap the rooters in here; I get by somehow without women."

TEMPERATURE. The mood of the overall prison population; the state of morale. The overall feeling or atmosphere within the prison. The term is also used by prison officials. "What's the temperature in here; is it going to blow?" Similar in meaning to *vibrations.*

TEN-PERCENTER. 1. "A person who spots the mark, points it out, sets it up and you go do it and give them ten percent of the money or ten percent of the whole take." *WWCL; LU.* 2. The percentage of men in the prison who are violent. "They're [legislature] talking about a 400 bed facility to really segregate the ten percenters from the non-violent prisoners."

THEY WANT TO PLAY BUT DON'T WANT TO PAY. An expression that applies to prisoners who are angry because they are being punished for their crime. "They want to steal but don't want to pay for it once arrested, implying that they don't know the game of cops and robbers." See *win some, lose some; tit for tat.* Variation: "You want to play; don't cry when you've got to pay."

THIRD FLOOR. The psychiatric unit of the prison. Also *booby hatch, bug house, ding ward, nut house.*

THORAZINE SHUFFLE. Same as Stelazine shuffle.

TICKLE AND SCRATCH. Match. Rhyming slang. *WWCL.*

TIGHT. 1. Conditions in the prison when rules are strictly enforced or when there is a *lockdown.* 2. To be close friends with someone. *LU; BJA*

TIGHTEN (ONE'S) GAME. To be careful while breaking prison rules. "When I have a lot of heat on me I tighten my game so I won't be caught."

TIGHT ROLLS. Custom-made cigarettes, as opposed to hand-rolled. "I had tight rolls and a punk and I was uptown."

TILL TAPPER. One who steals from cash registers. *LU.* Also *heel* *and toe man.*

TIME. A sentence served by a prisoner. There are many expressions for *doing time: big time, cell time, dead time, easy time, flat time, hard time, heavy time, short time.*

TIT FOR TAT. 1. An expression that acknowledges that if a man is apprehended in the commission of a crime, he realizes that he will have to pay the price. Understanding what the stakes are in the "game" of *cops and robbers.* 2. What you give, you get back.

TO THE MAX. To the limit. *BJA.*

TOP. To execute by hanging. *WWCL.*

TOP AND BOTTOM. An expression describing sex in prison. *WWCL.* Also *flip-flop, pitch and catch.*

TORCH. To set fire to someone's house (cell). "When they torched that ding's cell, it was hotter than hell in here."

TOUGH IT OUT. To put up with a difficult situation until it is over. "Tough it out for a day, then if things get too rough for you, let's talk about it, but don't check into P.C." Also *ride it out.*

TOWN CLOWN. Sheriff or constable. *WWCL; LU.*

TRANKS. Tranquilizers.

TRICK BAG. The place in which those who are victimized find themselves. "When I first come in here, the bulls were into that old trick bag game." *LU.*

TRIM. To swindle. *WWCL; LU.*

TRIP. 1. The experience of taking hallucinogens. "I was a real sniffer; anything for a trip." *LU.* 2. To fantasize. 3. To make conversation. "He can't even trip, you know. Got nothing to say."

TRIPPING. The euphoric feeling experienced following the use of drugs. Man, we were really tripping last night!" *LU.* Also *coasting, grooving.*

TROT. An expression describing how guards (*pigs*) walk. "The pig comes trottin down the tier after me."

TUMBLE AND TRIPS. Lips. Rhyming slang. *WWCL.*

TURKEY. 1. A bundle or cheap suitcase. *WWCL.* 2. A *dummy* or *sucker.*

TURN (SOMEONE) OUT. To turn a man into a "woman" in the prison. "The wolves want to get down with the kid and turn him out." [*LU: Turn out.* To initiate someone into the rackets of the underworld; to start a novice out with a grifter job (crooked gambling). Before 1900. *BJA:* "To initiate a beginner to the scene — drugs or whatever else is fashionable."]

TURN OVER. To sell or trade something in the prison. "They get a little excitement seeing what they can turn over on the Breezeway."

TUT. One of several secret lingos used in the prison. Also *Agini, Alfalfa, Bong-song, Ceazarney, Elephant.*

TWIST AND TWIRL. Girl. Rhyming slang. *WWCL; LU.*

TWO BY FOUR. Door. Rhyming slang. *WWCL; LU.*

UNDER THE GUNS. An expression used by the prisoners on those occasions when riots or possibilities of riots occur and guards stand on the walls aiming guns down on them. "I won't put any Indians out under the guns without some rational plan for change."

UNCLES AND AUNTS. Pants. Rhyming slang. *WWCL.*

UPPERS. Stimulant drugs, such as amphetamines. *LU.*

UPPERS AND LOWERS. Molars (teeth). Rhyming slang. *WWCL.*

UPTOWN. To be stylish. To be in the "big time"; to be living well and associating with all the right people. "I had tight rolls and a punk, and I was uptown."

USER. A drug addict. *WWCL; LU.*

VATOS LOCOS. Chicanos in the prison who have grown up in the barrios of large cities in the Southwest. "Vatos locos in here know their way around; they know how to play the game."

VIBRATIONS. An expression denoting the mood, stance, or attitude of the prison population at any given time. The state of morale, which can be good or bad. "With those kinds of vibrations going around now, somebody's going to get knifed in the next day or two." Similar in meaning to *temperature.*

VIOLATE. To violate one's parole (parole violation). "What you going to do, man, violate me for buying a lousy car?"

VIOLATOR. A recidivist. "A violator is a guy who knows his way around the joint cause he's been here before."

WAKE UP HIT. An expression for drugs taken or used in the morning. "You save a portion of the dope so you can have some in the morning, like a cup of coffee." *LU.*

WALK. To be released from jail or prison. "When 8:00 AM rolls around tomorrow I'm going to walk."

WALKER. A term for a prisoner who cannot settle down in his cell. "There's nothing worse than sharing your house with a walker — back and forth, back and forth."

WALKING PAPERS. The official papers authorizing release from prison. "One day they'll come to you and say, 'Here's your walking papers.'" Similar to *walk.*

WALK THAT WALK AND TALK THAT TALK. An expression meaning that a prisoner knows how to impress the officials. "It means being con-wise, knowing what to say and when to say it. I played that game at Monroe. I walked that walk and talked that talk."

WALK THE FENCE. To play both sides, legal and illegal, when out of prison.

WALLA WALLA. The Washington State Penitentiary. A common expression, not only for the prisoners, but for the people of the state.

THE WALLS. The Washington State Penitentiary. A term used by the men when they are either on the streets or doing time in another institution. "Every Wednesday the chain heads for the Walls." (Refers to both the walls surrounding the prison, and the name of the town, Walla Walla, where the prison is located.)

WAR. Outbreaks of violence between clubs. "All our wars start behind two people."

WAR CLUBS. Police nightsticks or batons used by guards.

WARPED IN THE HEAD. To be insane, unstable. "Those dings are warped in the head."

WARRIORS. Men in the prison who volunteer to carry weapons and protect their own particular club or group.

WASTE. To kill someone. "They're going to get themselves wasted by being caught up in a beef in here." Also *burn, bury, bushwhack, dust, hit, ice, off, plant, snuff, take (someone) out, wipe (someone) out.*

WATCH YOUR BACK. To protect oneself from attack in the prison. "I'm watching my back out in the visiting room just like I'm watching my back in here."

WATUSILAND. Six Wing, where most of the black prisoners live. Also *little Africa.*

THE WEAKER THE PIGEON, THE STRONGER THE HAWK. A common expression used in the prison.

WEED. Marijuana. *LU.* Also *grass, pot, shit,* etc.

WEEPING WILLOW. Pillow. Rhyming slang. *WWCL; LU.*

WHAT GOES 'ROUND: COMES 'ROUND. A commonly used expression meaning: "You eventually have to pay for what you do to others in here."

WHATS GOING DOWN? What's happening? *BJA.*

WHEELMAN. The man behind the wheel of a get-away car. *WWCL.*

WHIP ALL THE WAY OUT. To lose control of oneself. "I couldn't deal with that baby bottle treatment on third floor; I'd of whipped all the way out on that one."

WHIRL AND TWIRL. Girl. Rhyming slang. *LU.*

WHITE. Chinese or French heroin. Also *skag, shit, smack, stuff, white dope.*

WHITE DOPE. Chinese or French heroin. Also *skag, shit, smack, stuff, white.*

WHITE MONEY. Real currency or money; as opposed to scrip. "$7.50 scrip is worth $5.00 white money in the Joint." *WWCL.*

WHITES. Benzedrine (amphetamine) capsules or tablets. *LU.* Also *bean, benny, blancas.*

WHORE. A prison prostitute.

WIN SOME, LOSE SOME. An expression used which acknowledges what happens when one plays the game of *cops and robbers.*
Also *tit for tat.*

WING BULL. A guard who is in charge of a cell block, or wing.
WWCL.

WIPE (SOMEONE) OUT. 1. To kill. 2. To injure. "We heard they
broke his hands with a hammer; really wiped him out." Also *burn,
bury, bushwhack, dust, hit, ice, off, plant, snuff, stick, take (someone) out,
waste.*

WIRED. To be tense, upset. Refers to the prison or the men.
"There's been a murder in the joint and people are fuckin wired
tonight. Everybody thinks we're getting locked down."

WIRED IN. To have important connections. *WWCL; LU.*

WOLF. The aggressor in a homosexual situation. "If a wolf wants a
kid, he'll try and talk him out of it. If that don't do, he'll slap him
around or rape him." *WWCL.* [*DAS:* 1917.] 2. A prisoner who is
physically aggressive; a troublemaker; a bully. *WWCL.*

WOLF TICKET. A threat or threatening attitude used to frighten
someone into doing something. "You can't give em the ole wolf
ticket cause they won't always go for it." Similar to *gorilla.*

WORK. Hustling (stealing) for a living. *WWCL; LU.*

WORK ON YOUR HEAD. An expression for psychological therapy.
"We ain't got no shrinks at the joint to work on your head."

WORK OVER. To do bodily harm. *WWCL.*

WORKING GIRL. A prison prostitute.

WORKING STIFF. Someone who works at honest labor; a square
john, etc. *WWCL.*

YAHOOS. "These are guys in prison who are squares, cowboys,
farmers; guys who are not wise to prison or city ways. Naive."

YARD. 1. One hundred dollars. 2. An outside recreation area
within the walls of the prison. A large area of grass located at the

back of the prison that contains ball diamonds and handball courts. *WWCL.*

YARD-OUT. To exercise in the "yard." Prison or jail expression.

YELLOW JACKET. A narcotic that quiets the nerves, induces sleep, causes dullness. *WWCL.* Also *goofer, goof ball, sleeper.*

YELLOW SLIP. A yellow interview sheet used to get a cell change.

YES-MAN. A term that applies to some members of the Resident Council who are considered ineffective and will only agree with the prison administration, rather than argue a point.

YOUNGSTERS. Younger inmates, generally those under twenty-five years of age.

YOUR GAME IS UP. To die. "When the stretcher comes to pick up your carcass, that means your game is up."

ZONKED. Under the influence of narcotics. "The next step is Third Floor and they're zonked full of that dangerous drug." Also *fucked, fucked up, loaded, stoned.*

ZU-ZUS AND WHAM-WHAMS. A prison name for candy, pop, chewing gum, and so on.

Appendix B

AUTOBIOGRAPHY OF A PRISONER:
EUGENE DELORME—THE EARLY YEARS

I was born in Marty, South Dakota. It's not really a town, I guess. It's a mission, an Indian mission, and my mother ... well, for chrissake! Now I never thought of it that way—another institution ... I was born in an institution! Holy catfish! My mother, she grew up in a mission school because her folks died when my mother and her sister were kind of young; they were teenagers. They're still together all these years. My mom's taken care of her sister, Ruby, cause she's blind. I didn't live in the Dakotas very long because I got pneumonia two times running so the doctor said they better get my ass away from that kind of climate or I probably wouldn't make it. So anyway, they moved out of there, came straight through to Aberdeen [Washington]. I was about a year old then. Aberdeen is a little town on the coast here, fishing and lumber. It's an old town and it's just depressing as hell to even look at.

We spent our childhood in Aberdeen. Even now, it's a small place, only about twenty-five to thirty-five thousand people live there. I don't remember a real lot from those days. What did we do? We played. There was white kids all around us who we didn't always get along with and it wasn't personality because we were probably too young then, but just because we was Indian. We got attacked by the white settlers around us there and it's a anti-Indian town, anyway, as is every town, I guess. But I never felt comfortable around white people, white kids. Even now it bothers me. I've got a little more pride in myself now, in my race and my heritage. I sit here and trip back about grade school days and how my brother and I fought our way through that period of life. We literally fought our way through it. In the old days we battled all the neighborhood kids. They bumped our heads with rocks every time we was goin home from school, or we got bushwhacked, gettin called names. I think back to those days and it makes me uncomfortable, probably because I felt so uncomfortable alone, especially in school, the first and second grade. I tried to squeeze as far back in the room as I could. I dreaded recesses. I dreaded school. It was a nightmare when the damn teacher would single me out to read or do anything because when everybody would look at me, I just felt dirty, I guess. I was told that; even the adults down there, maybe everywhere, they just don't mind callin a little kid a "dirty little siwash" [savage], "dirty little blanket-ass," "Why do we let them goddam Indians in here?" or something like that in the stores and the taverns when I'd go lookin for my dad, or in restaurants. I guess I was awful uncomfortable around white kids because that's all they got down there is white kids in school and I don't even remember ever meetin any other Indian kids. There was a high school, a junior high school and a rotten-assed Catholic school that we all went to and they were all on the same street. I sure hated that Catholic school. We started third grade in that school. We went to the first and second grade in the raggedy-muffin part of town. By the time we got in school, my dad was already drinkin pretty heavy. He was always at the tavern. I remember him and my mom fightin a lot. My mom took over the job of makin money and bringin the food home. We were five or six years old and when the little business she had at home folded—we had this two story house and in the basement my dad and mom built a little shop to make crabpots, they would finish the crabpots. They employed five or six people. This guy down in Westport, he had crab boats and he'd take the crabpots. And we was makin pretty good money doin that. Then the business folded up. It was hurt by a guy that went into the line pretty heavy.

My brother and I, even at that age, we just did what we wanted and what we wanted to do was just play when we wasn't in school. There are lots and lots of canneries and logging companies and lumber mills down there and our biggest thrill used to be to break into the offices or the lunchrooms when they were closed on Sundays and runnin around in them. It was kind of a kick bein where you wasn't supposed to be, I guess. Of course, we also come up with something to eat, too, every now and then. We were just kind a like the mice in the place. We had our own special holes in the buildings that we could squeeze through, so as the mice would be comin through, we'd be comin through, too. We'd run around in there and play and finally we'd get tired and go home.

We didn't hang around the park or play baseball or things like that. We just never did. It was a habit we got into because, my brother and I, we avoided groups of kids like the plague. We just had each other as company and the hell with everybody else in the world cause any time we got around a group of kids they always ended up stompin us, anyway, you know, because we was Indians. And I think their parents taught em that. "You see an Indian, beat him up." Or, "if you see an Indian, a dirty little Indian, bonk him on the head with something." Goddam it! I'm not dirty and never was! I used to think I was, though. I used to feel that way around other people. I never enjoyed the company of other kids or did any of the things that they did because it was like suicide to walk into the city park. Even at recess at school it was a cold whippin. Recess at school, I ended up standing with the girls or something cause I couldn't get into any games. Couldn't get any ball to play with. Somebody would take it. If it wasn't the kids, the teacher would come and take the damn thing away from me and give it to them. So we just had to putter through those years and I don't remember anything really fun about bein a kid. I was in a hurry to grow up so I could pay back some of those bastards. They picked on me; they picked on my mom; they picked on everybody in my family, it seemed like to me. The cops were always beatin up my dad when he was drunk. I was determined to survive long enough to get big enough to do something to em all. That's what I wanted to do. Of course, I never did. Maybe I'm just lucky that I never did but I was always on the verge for a long time. The potential for violence was always there. Definitely.

Catholic school was the worst. Them nuns, boy, whippin. If they weren't doin it, the priest was. I don't remember how I acted but I know I probably acted like I was deaf and dumb, cause I'd never talk. I stood quiet all the time. I'd stay by myself all the time. At recess I'd either try to stay in the room or go sit on the front steps of the school until the bell would ring, then go back in and that's what I remember. When school was over, I'd run home. I had to run home because this older kid everyday he'd ride by me on his bicycle and he'd either hit me with a belt or a stick or a rock. He'd spit on the sidewalk and tell me to "lick it up, Delorme." He'd call me all kinds of rotten Indian names. It was his game. Every day he always used to do that. He was big; he was too big for me. I was scared of the punk, you know. My mom used to come and meet me at school once in awhile. She worked at the cannery and so she couldn't come too often. Give me a little protection, you know. Listen to me . . . cryin like a baby!

We had a couple of white kids who were poor slobs and lived in the old Junky Jones houses like we did. There was this one real estate guy who owned every rundown junky house he could find and they called him "Junky Jones." So that used to be a target for the other kids, too. They'd say, "Ha, ha, ha. You live in a Junky Jones house. You live in a Junky Jones house." I never did figure out if this guy was real or not but I knew I lived in a Junky Jones house. It wasn't the best place in town, I'll admit that, but it was a roof over the old head, you know what I mean?

Well, some of the white kids that lived in Junky Jones houses lived pretty close to us so we started runnin around with a couple of brothers and we formed this little gang, and I remember things started gettin a little better then. By then there was four or five of us, but we was ready for anything, then. We went around lookin for the little chumps to beat up. Boy, I'll tell you . . . that was right down my alley, too. I had a lot of bones to pick with a lot of people. So when I was old enough to know what a goddam stick was for, I sure as hell jumped at the chance of using it and gettin back at a few sonovabitches.

So we got off into a regular little gang called the "Night Owls." We'd sneak out of the house . . . well, me and Donny didn't have to sneak out. We'd go out of the house, cause they didn't pay no attention whatsoever. My mother was involved takin care of Ruby, my blind aunt, and my younger brother who was a baby then and my sister and my dad, who was a full-blown drunk, a wino. So I mean they didn't really miss me and Donny. It was better; it was easier on them that we were able to take care of ourselves and hustle our own food over at our friends' house. We'd eat there, we'd eat here, and we'd steal food or we'd break into a restaurant. So we had stashes all over town. We'd bring a lot of food home, too. We'd bring gunny sacks with canned goods and meat home and it was party time. We might come trippin in ... hell, me and my bro might come trippin in around midnight or one o'clock in the mornin and if we'd bring some food with us, by God, everybody would get out of bed and eat. I think I told you before ... we was like Robin Hood stealin from the rich to feed the poor. In our case, it was our family cause after my dad started drinkin and quit bringin home any money it was strictly up to my mom, and women didn't make so much. They were lucky if they got a minimum wage then. My mom's worked all her life; she's still workin and she ain't never made more than minimum wages. I don't think they had any minimum wages in those days cause she didn't make a helluva lot of money. She worked at a restaurant; that was her best job. But one day she didn't go to work because she had a car wreck, collided with a jeep head-on and that put her in a hospital for a couple of months. Crushed her chest, so it was rough for a time then.

My family was used to scrapin. My old Ruby, she could make a meal out of anything. Give her a handful of flour, boy, and a little bit of salt and she'd come up with something for us to eat, that's for sure. My dad would shoot some seagulls and we'd eat them seagulls. He didn't have no gun; he'd shoot them suckers with a sling shot. He made a sling shot out of plywood and then he'd shoot em with these steel ballbearings. Knock them babies right out of the air. But he used to trick em. He'd sprinkle breadcrumbs or something out back, then he had this little hole cut in the wall of the house and he'd hide in there with his slingshot, see. And when one of them big old dumb birds would come and land on there and start peckin at that bread, he'd knock them babies over. That's our Indian chicken, you know. We never ate any of the dogs in the neighborhood, but I know that they probably thought about it. You know what I mean? We never had a dog; we always had a cat, but I'll tell you one thing; before these four kids would starve, that old cat would go into the stewpot, you goddam right. But we had a little something to eat every day. I don't remember goin a day without eatin, even if it was just plain biscuits, baking powder biscuits, or fried potatoes. That was what it was most of the time. We'd have gravy on them baking powder biscuits. That was pretty standard fare around our house, and I still like it. My favorite food is still hamburger gravy and toast, or hamburger gravy and biscuits and fried potatoes. I love em. I love eggs, too. For awhile we had some chickens. Well we was fat, then, when we had those chickens cause we had eggs. We didn't kill the chickens to eat em unless worse got to worse, then we rubbed out everything and ate it.

When we crossed the bridge to the other part of town things got worse; that's when times were toughest. Pickins weren't so good. My mom worked at a cannery then for awhile and my brother and I, we had been picked up quite often by the police and threatened with foster homes and this and that, and it never did scare us much. They used to say, "Aw, you're gonna end up in Walla Walla," you know, "Walla Walla State Penitentiary," things like that. I never believed em, but it hit pretty hard, I'll tell you, and it's pretty clear today right now, too. I firmly believe that that had a lot to do with my eventually meeting their expectations, because at that age, of course, when adults tell you that, especially the chief of police or other policemen that you're goin to the penitentiary, then something's goin to click in your mind and that's goin to be your ultimate goal, regardless of whether you know it or not. I won't get into the psychology of the thing but I was very aware of it and I'm fightin it even now.

We stole, we went on to bigger things, my brother and I. Like I said, we had our little gang and we ran around and did a lot of crazy things. You can get pretty crazy at that age. We burglarized everything in town, I think. I don't think there was a store in town we didn't get into. We stole bicycles constantly. We even stole a car now and then. Seven or eight of us dingy kids would jump in a car and away we'd go. God, the driver would have to be sittin on a pillow, which was generally me. Couldn't even reach the foot pedals hardly, but we'd go screamin down them highways, full speed ahead. Cops would be chasin us. One time they chased us for a long ways. Boy, they fired a couple shots in the trunk of the car before they finally got us pulled over and they looked in the car and seen all these dingy kids. There wasn't one of us that was over ten years old. They chased us about ten miles in an old Chevrolet we stole. We didn't even know who was shootin at us. We knew the sirens were blowin and we were goin to give em a run for their money, man. "Step on it, boys!" Al Capone and his mob. They dragged us all screamin and kickin out of the car, took us by the ear to the old police station and we spent a couple days in the juvenile hall over that, but we got out. We went home. We made the paper on that one. We had our pictures in the paper, all those dumb lookin kids in the paper.

I guess I was ten years old before I started stealin bigger things like the cars, breakin into buildings, schools, causin a helluva lot more damage. A lot more damage. People started gettin a little bit more serious. My brother and I have always been inseparable. At the time we ran around with a couple other brothers, white kids. Like I say, this was a small town. It's close to two rivers, close to the ocean. Those two rivers don't really close the town in but it cuts right through the town and so there's a lot of fishing boats. We used to steal a lot of stuff off the boats. That got us in a lot of trouble, you know. We got picked up dozens of times prowlin around at nighttime inside a building or some damned thing. But we always got to go home. My mom would always be down snivelin and cryin. Course, in that size town they know the police department pretty good, damn near everybody in it. We used to live pretty close to the police chief, so we kind of had an in there, you know. We used to go down to his house a lot. He'd give us a ride in the car once in awhile and stuff. So anyhow, they knew the family. They had picked up my dad so many times for bein drunk or beatin my mom up that I imagine they didn't even keep count anymore. Most of the time they'd just take him and let him go somewhere down the street someplace and tell him not to go home until he sobered up, or stay away from the house until the next morning.

So anyway, my mom worked hard trying to take care of us, so I expect that had a lot to do with the things that happened to Donny and I. Even so, I don't ever remember any kind of discipline from my mother. Each time we'd get arrested like that she'd just be happy that we'd get home. And she'd say, "Boy, you guys are lucky this time." But that was all. More than anything she was just happy that we'd be headin back home again after a long day at the old police station.

So it went on, never really changed our ways because we didn't have anything else to do. We didn't make it much further than the fourth grade in Aberdeen because they finally got tired of us and arrested us on burglaries. We left a trail of candy bars about three miles, candy bar wrappers from this cannery we had broken into. We stole all the candy bars out of all the machines so they just followed the trail of wrappers on down to the river bank and snatched us up. That time things didn't come out too good. They give my mother a choice—they would either put us in a foster home or she could send us off to Schmawah, which was an Indian school in Oregon out of Salem about six or seven miles. So she said, "Well, I'll send the boys off to the old school." She'd been talkin about doin it for several months, that maybe that would help. So that helped make a decision there and the welfare bought us each some duds. Bought us each a box to put our clothes in and some new coats and things and we was off runnin.

I forget where they got the car to take us down there but we got down there, anyway. The family took us down and they went back to Aberdeen. That was tough. Tough! Oh, ho, ho, I do remember that! Sonovabitch! Yeah, that was a rough go. I wasn't happy at all. That was the first time we'd ever been away from home and we knew we weren't gonna go home for awhile. We never did get along with other kids anyway, and this whole school was kids. Gosh, it seemed like thousands of em, at least a couple thousand. But we were loners. I remember there was a lot of cryin and bad feelings the first day or two, so about the third day my brother and I packed our stuff and out the window we went. We said, "Well, we'll just start truckin, man. We'll go across here and through a couple fields and down a couple roads and should see Washington over the next rise." So we hit the road about the crack of dawn. We never knew we had more than 150 miles to go. Needless to say, we didn't make it; the State Patrol picked us up and took us back.

So we was there and eventually we got used to it. It was a lot of discipline. I remember a lot of countin, a lot of standin, walkin in file lines, and a lot of fights. Course, that was an Indian school and I had to be the only kid in the goddam school that had light hair. I had real light hair when I was younger and my brother Donny, he was a normal-lookin Indian, you know, dark hair, dark eyes. I had to have blonde hair and green eyes. I still have and Indians are a pretty goddam prejudice people, anyway. But eventually, we got to like the place and we got into the routine of things in the new school.

We came back to Aberdeen in 1953. My dad, of course, he was still off into the wine bottle. My family was livin in a haunted house. My dad went to the penitentiary that year. He and a couple friends broke into a warehouse and stole a bunch of beer. So they packed his ass off to Walla Walla here in 1953. He got out in 1955, so actually he did less than two years. He got one to fifteen years, and he only did about a year and a half.

But the haunted house that we was livin in, it was our last house in Aberdeen. My mom said, "I'm packin everybody up and movin to the big city, Tacoma." And we went. I was almost a teenager by then; I was 12 years old. Needless to say, we didn't like Tacoma either, and we were all set to leave when we got there. We lived in a housing project. We was on welfare, of course, and I was ready to start seventh grade. Donny and I, we cooled back for just a short while, then we started up all over again. As soon as we cased the town, we started adventuring around lookin for something to get into. Didn't take us very long to find something. My brother was first. He got busted breakin into a store. He went to Chehalis at Greenhill, which is a state training school. When he headed there he was twelve years old so, course, it was only a matter of time and I went several months later. I was thirteen. They got me for breakin into a truck and stealin cigarettes. I don't remember if I smoked or not. I don't think so, but everybody in my family did, so another kid and I broke into a big semi and took a case of cigarettes. We got arrested for that. It wasn't my first arrest in Tacoma. We had some trouble but I can't remember what we was arrested for. But we had been arrested several times. But this time we went to Chehalis. So that was my first gig there. It was alright, I guess. Wasn't too far from home. Anyways my folks could get down there and old mom, you could always depend on her to come and visit. I stayed down to the state training school, Greenhill, for the better part of a year that time and I escaped. I escaped several times while I was there. I was involved in just everything you could be involved in that wasn't right. Settin fires, breakin windows, just generally raisin hell, you know. Otherwise, I could a got out of there in ninety days. I could a been home but I stretched it out. Didn't look like they were goin to let me go so just about every eighty days when I was sure they wasn't goin to let me go, I'd just let myself go. I'd boogie on out. Away I'd go. Get arrested. Got in a lot of trouble in those escapes. Got in an awful lot of trouble because ... I don't know ... you just get a little bit wilder. You just feel, "I can do any goddam thing I want to cause it just doesn't make any difference." And I was pretty much up on the law concerning juveniles, I'll tell you that. I was pretty much aware of the limits of the law, so I knew that they couldn't do a helluva lot to me. So all the burglaries and robberies that I pulled, I knew they wasn't goin to do anything to me other than send me back to the trainin school once I got caught. So I went pretty wild.

When I got kicked out of Chehalis, I went back out to a gang I had been runnin with and we did a lot of fightin and we did a lot of stealin. I quit school in the seventh grade, as did most of the others. We called ourselves the "Rebels" and that's what we was. By that time we seldom went home. I think I'd turned seventeen. We used to go home to sleep once in awhile over at each other's houses and eat, but we all lived on the lower east side of Tacoma. It's a ghetto. Maybe not as bad as the big cities but all in all lots of people there was on welfare. All the people we associated with was Indians. They lived down there because they were close to the river where they do all the fishin. And the big Indian hospital was there. It's not a hospital now but it was then. Cascadia. Well, these guys that I ran with in this gang, we was really committed to each other. About as committed as you could be at that time, so we were really just like one. All we did was live for kicks. I never even started the eighth grade. They tried to get me into some kind of school in Chehalis but that didn't work out. I was into a school building and I was there one week. I viewed that school building as a means of escape one day and I got out of there and got away. So they never invited me to try the school again. I never did finish much schoolin. The rest of the guys all quit, too. We'd all been in jail. Everyone of us been in jail numerous times for drunkin fightin or some kind of burglary. Mostly fightin.

In the summer of 1957, we were goin to dances. I used to have a car cause I was always stealin cars. I'd go to Seattle or someplace and steal me up a car and bring it back. Change the plates and drive it for a month. Didn't get caught that often. In fact, didn't get caught for that. So it worked out. So we had a car we all kicked around in and we went to all the dances. Go in the parkin lot and take our beer with us. We smoked and we drank. The only thing we didn't do was shoot dope, none of us. It wasn't because we wouldn't but because they really weren't doin that then. There wasn't that much around. We didn't pull off any kind of organized capers or anything. We just lived from day to day on whatever we could bum. Bus come by, we'd even bum money from the bus passengers.

We used to terrorize the buses so much that they decided to just eliminate that damn bus stop and went right on by. Just makin it a generally pretty rotten neighborhood, thanks to our efforts. And if we couldn't get anything there, we'd move up the hill. There was gangs at McKinley; there was gangs at Sixth Avenue. There was gangs all over. But we were a little bit more serious in that we were more dangerous than the normal gang because we didn't just fistfight. We'd take a shot at a dude and we'd cut him up. A lot of other guys didn't really get off into that much violence as we did, so when we did come around to somebody else's neighborhood, it generally remained pretty quiet, until we left cause when we came, we came prepared. Baseball bats, knives, guns and we'd come up and break into places and leave with some kind of money and go back down to our little hideaway. We made a lot of trouble that summer but we didn't go to jail too much. We did go to jail for drunken fightin at restaurants and different places. They'd snatch us for doin some damned thing. We'd have parties and the cops would always end up comin and draggin us off. But we'd always get out in two or three days.

Then late in 1957, they had a dance at the Red Mill. In those days, taverns closed generally at 12 o'clock and this dance would go on until two or three in the morning. By the time everybody came out to that dance they were drunk, and they'd come from several towns around. We spent more time out in the parkin lot than we did inside at the dance. We had our cars back in a sort of circle. We all stayed kind of off in a corner in the back of the parkin lot. Staked our claim. We had our women, we had our booze. Anybody that came near that we didn't know was subject to attack. One night we had a helluva fight goin out there. We had a fight with some guys from Sumner, a helluva battle. There was about twenty or thirty of us. We recruited others that wanted to get down and fight with us. I was carrying a sword. It was longer than my leg. Somewhere along the line I took that sword out and I hit a guy with it and about that time the cops stepped around the corner so I dropped it and I ran and kind of got lost in the crowd, but he kept his eye on me and he snatched me up and handcuffed me to a tree. He couldn't think of anything else to do with me cause my partners were following along and throwin stuff at him and givin him a bad time. He called for reinforcements and some state patrol showed up, county guys and stuff. It wasn't a half hour and we had a full-scale riot goin. Destroyed at least seven cars. Kicked all the windows out. A lot of injuries on both sides and, goddam, I never could get loose from that tree. They caught my brother and two other friends of mine and they didn't have them for long because the rest of the fellas took em back away.

So anyway they got me out of there and put my ass into a police car, took me out through a little back road, got me into Tacoma under escort, and took me to the county jail. I was seventeen. Of course, they knocked the shit out of you first. Took me into this little back room and they said, "How old are you?" And I told em, "Well, I'm seventeen." And the cop knocked me down and he said, "You look eighteen to me." So he commenced to kick the shit out of me. They never asked me no questions. They just kicked the shit out of me cause they were a little hostile. A couple of their boys got scuffled there in the hassle and I was the only one they had they could get back at and they charged me with inciting to riot, first degree assault, everything they could think of. Anyway, the assault charge was the only one I was worried about because it carries a mandatory sentence and a mandatory isn't that good to get. A normal sentence you could get five years for burglary and you get a third off, so you do three. If you get a five year mandatory sentence, you do five years. You can't even get a third off. You get that for violent beefs, assaults and armed robbery. Anything with a weapon.

But they needed a witness in order to convict me. So I went to court for inciting a riot but they really couldn't stick that on me, so I only ended up stayin eight days in jail for bein drunk and a minor. I was handcuffed to a tree so I hadn't hit no cops or nothin so they couldn't charge me. Took me eight days to heal. Took me longer than that to heal from the beatin them cops gave me and I think that had a lot to do with them not pressin charges cause when I went to court my mother and them were screamin about the cuts and bruises all over my face. Both my eyes were black, my nose was all smashed, my lips were all smashed. My teeth were knocked loose, my ribs were kicked in. That was all by the cops in Tacoma. County Sheriff did that, so my mom was screamin about that, demandin an investigation and the judge asked me about it and the cops were in the court, too. They were more than a little worried. When it happened, they were pretty excited, same as we was, so I told the judge, "Well, it happened out there at the dance. Some goddam drunks came up and hit me with a bat. Beat me up." I didn't rat on the cops and so I think that was the main reason they didn't press the charges. They didn't bother me after that. The fact of the matter is they started sayin "hello" and started gettin pretty friendly that day in court. I took the heat off them sonovabitches. If I'd told the judge, I'd probably had about a half dozen of em for assaultin a minor, but I figured you live in that town, you know; there's no use startin that. It's all a game and that was just my loss. That was it, I lost. That's part of the game. Someday my day would come. I always thought of it that way. I'd have fantasies about blowin cops away but that kind of went away. I'm not mad at anyone in particular. I've had cops save my life. I've had cops save my brother's life, so it balances out eventually. You just kind of keep track of it. I keep track. I keep score, and I can't say that even bein in prison I've been beat that much. The only beatings I've suffered in prison is by guards that work here or worked at Monroe.

BIBLIOGRAPHY

Abbott, Jack Henry. *In the Belly of the Beast.* New York: Random House, 1981.

Abrahams, Roger. "Joking: The Training of the Man of Words in Talking Broad." In Thomas Kockman, ed., *Rappin' and Stylin' Out*, pp. 215–240. Urbana: University of Illinois Press, 1972.

Abrahams, Roger D. and Troike, Rudolph C. *Language and Cultural Diversity in American Education.* Englewood Cliffs, N.J.: Prentice-Hall, Inc., 1972.

Alighieri, Dante. *The Inferno.* Translated by John Ciardi. New York: The New American Library, 1954.

————. *Purgatory.* Translated by Dorothy Sayers. Baltimore: Penguin Books, 1962.

Allport, Gordon. *The Nature of Prejudice.* Garden City, New York: Doubleday & Company, 1958.

American Friends Service Committee. *Struggle for Justice: A Report on Crime and Punishment in America.* New York: Hill and Wang. 1971.

Arnold, David O. *The Sociology of Subculture.* Berkeley: Glendessary Press, 1970.

Babcock, Barbara, ed. *The Reversible World.* Ithaca, N.Y.: Cornell University Press, 1972.

Bakker, Laura J., Morris, Barbara A., and Janus, Laura M. "Hidden Victims of Crime." *Social Work, 23* (1978): 144.

Barak (Glantz), Israel Leonard. "Punishment to Protection: Solitary Confinement in the Washington State Penitentiary, 1966–1975." Unpublished Ph.D. dissertation, The Ohio State University, 1978.

Bartollas, Clemens, Miller, Stuart J., and Dinitz, Simon. *Juvenile Victimization: Institutional Paradox.* Beverley Hills: Sage Publications, 1976.

Bauman, Richard, and Scherzer, eds. *Explorations in the Ethnography of Speaking.* Cambridge, England: Cambridge University Press, 1974.

Beaumont, Gustave de and Tocqueville, Alexis de. *On the Penitentiary System in the United States and Its Application to France.* Carbondale, Ill.: Southern Illinois University Press, 1964.

Beck, Robert. *Pimp: The Story of My Life.* Los Angeles, Holloway House, 1969.

Becker, Howard S. *Outsiders: Studies in the Sociology of Deviance.* New York: The Free Press, 1973.

Behan, Brendan. *Borstal Boy.* New York: Knopf, 1959.

Berne, Eric. *Games People Play.* New York: Grove Press, Inc., 1964.

Bernstein, Basil. *Class, Codes and Control: Theoretical Studies Toward a Sociology of Language.* Vol. 1. London: Routledge & Kegan Paul, 1971.

_____. *Class, Codes and Control: Applied Studies Toward a Sociology of Language.* Vol. 2. London: Routledge & Kegan Paul, 1973.

Bindman, Aaron. "Why Does Rehabilitation Fail?" *International Journal of Offender Therapy and Comparative Criminology, 17* (1973): 309–324.

Black, Max. *The Labyrinth of Language.* New York: Frederick A. Praeger, 1968.

Bluestone, Harvey, O'Malley, Edward P., and Connell, Sydney. "Homosexuality in Prison." *Journal of Social Therapy, 12* (January, 1966): 12–34.

Boroff, David. "A Study of Reformatory Argot." *American Speech, 26* (October, 1951): 190–195.

Bowker, Lee H. *Prison Subcultures.* Lexington, Mass.: Lexington Books, D.C. Heath and Company, 1977.

Bradbury, Malcolm, Heading, Bruay, and Hollis, Martin. "The Man and the Mask: A Discussion of Role Theory." In Jackson, J. A., ed. *Role.* London: Cambridge University Press, 1972.

Braly, Malcolm. *On the Yard.* Boston: Little, Brown and Company, 1967.

Bronstein, Alvin J. "Reform Without Change: The Future of Prisoners' Rights." *Civil Liberties Review, 4* (September–October, 1977): 27–45.

Brown, Barry S. and Spevacek, John D. "Work Release in Community and Institutional Settings." *Correction Psychiatry, 17* (1971): 35–42.

Brown, Claude. *Manchild in the Promised Land.* New York: Macmillan, 1965.

_____. "The Language of Soul." In Kochman, Thomas, ed. *Rappin' and Stylin' Out,* pp. 134–139. Urbana: University of Illinois Press, 1972.

Brown, H. Rap. "Street Talk." In Kochman, Thomas, ed. *Rappin' and Stylin' Out,* pp. 205–208. Urbana: University of Illinois Press, 1972.

Brown, Richard H. *A Poetic for Sociology: Toward a Logic of Discovery for the Human Sciences.* Cambridge, England: Cambridge University Press, 1977.

Bullough, Vern L. *The Subordinate Sex.* New York: Penguin Books, 1974.

Burke, Kenneth. *The Philosophy of Literary Form.* New York: Vintage Press, 1957.

Burns, Henry, Jr. "A Miniature Totalitarian State: Maximum Security Prison." *Canadian Journal of Corrections, 9* (July, 1969): 153–164.

Burroughs, William. *Junkie.* New York: Ace Books, 1953.

Cardozo-Freeman, Inez. "Rhyming Slang in a Western Prison." *Western Folklore, 37* (October, 1978): 296–305.

Caron, Roger. *Go-Boy!* Ontario, Canada: Thomas Nelson & Sons, 1978.

Carroll, James L. "Status Within Prison: Toward an Operational Definition." *Correctional Psychologists, 4* (September–October, 1970): 49–56.

Carroll, John B., ed. *Language, Thought and Reality: Selected Writings of Benjamin Lee Whorf.* Cambridge, Mass.: The Technology Press of M.I.T. and New York: Wiley & Sons, 1965.

Carroll, Leo. *Hacks, Blacks and Cons.* Lexington, Mass.: Lexington Books, D. C. Heath and Company, 1974.

Cavan, Ruth Shonle and Zemans, Eugene S. "Marital Relationships of Prisoners in Twenty-Eight Countries." *Journal of Criminal Law, Criminology and Police Science, 49* (1958): 133–139.

Cervantes Saavedra, Miguel de. *The Adventures of Don Quxiote*. Translated by J. M. Cohen. New York: Penguin Books, 1976.

Chaneles, Sol. *The Open Prison*. New York: The Dial Press, 1973.

Charle, Suzanne. "Suicide in Cellblocks." *Corrections Magazine* (August, 1981): 6–16.

Chase, Stuart. *The Tyranny of Words*. New York: Harcourt, Brace, 1938.

Cheska, Alyce Taylor. "Theoretical Contributions to the Study of Play." In Salter, Michael A., ed. *Play; Anthropological Perspectives*, West Point, N.Y.: Leisure Press, 1978.

Claerbout, David. *Black Jargon in America*. Grand Rapids, Michigan: William B. Eerdmans Publishing Company, 1972.

Clark, Kenneth B. *Dark Ghetto*. New York: Harper and Row, 1965.

Cleaver, Eldridge. *Soul on Ice*. New York: McGraw-Hill, 1968.

Clemmer, Donald. *The Prison Community*. New York: Rinehart, 1958.

Cobean, S. C. and Power, P. W. "The Role of the Family in the Rehabilitation of the Offender." *International Journal of Offender Therapy and Comparative Criminology, 22* (1978): 28–38.

Cohen, Albert K., Cole, George F., and Bailey, Robert G., eds. *Prison Violence*. Lexington, Mass.: Lexington Books, D. C. Heath and Company, 1976.

Conrad, John. *Crime and Its Correction*. Berkeley: University of California Press, 1967.

Conrad, John and Dinitz, Simon. *The Prison Within a Prison: Discipline at the Impasse*. Final Report of the National Isolated Prisoner Seminar, Washington, D.C.: The National Institute of Corrections (March 1978).

––––––. "Position Paper on the Isolated Prisoner," Columbus, Ohio: Academy for Contemporary Problems, 1977.

Cressey, Donald R., ed. *The Prison*. New York: Holt, Rinehart and Winston, 1961.

––––––. "Adult Felons in Prison." In Lloyd E. Ohlin, ed., *Prisoners in America*, pp. 117–150. Englewood Cliffs, N.J.

Crosthwaite, Alice. "Punishment for Whom? The Prisoner or His Wife?" *International Journal of Offender Therapy and Comparative Criminology, 19* (1975): 275–284.

Csekszentmehalyi, Mihalyi. *Beyond Boredom and Anxiety*. San Francisco: Jossey-Bass Publishers, 1975.

Davidson, Theodore. *Chicano Prisoners: The Key to San Quentin*: Case Studies in Cultural Anthropology. New York: Holt, Rinehart and Winston, 1974.

Davis, Alan J. "Sexual Assaults in the Philadelphia Prison System and Sheriff's Vans." *Trans-Action, 6* (December, 1968): 9–17.

Denenberg, R. V. "Profile: Washington." *Corrections Magazine, 1* (November–December, 1974): 31–44.

Divons, Kenneth and West, Larry M. "Prison or Slavery." *The Black Scholar* (October, 1971): 6–12.

Duffey, Clinton and Jennings, Jean. *The San Quentin Story*. Westport, Conn.: Greenwood Press, 1968.

Dundes, Alan, ed. *Mother Wit From the Laughing Barrel*. Englewood, N.J.: Prentice-

Hall, 1973.

Elli, Frank. *The Riot.* New York: Coward-McCann, 1967.

Erickson, Gladys. *Ragen of Joliet.* New York: Dutton, 1957.

Ericksson, Torsten. *The Reformers: An Historical Survey of Prisoner Experiments in the Treatment of Criminals.* New York: Elsevier, 1976.

Estrin, Herman and Mehus, Donald V. *The American Language in the 70s.* San Francisco: Boyd & Fraser Publishing Company, 1974.

Farmer, John S. and Henley, W. E. *Slang and Its Analogues.* 7 Volumes. London, 1890–1904.

Farmer, Richard E. "Cynicism: A Factor in Corrections Work." *Journal of Criminal Justice (New York), 5* (1977): 237–246.

Figes, Eva. *Patriarchal Attitudes.* Greenwich, Conn.: Fawcett Premier Book, 1970.

Flexner, Stewart and Wentworth, Harold. *Dictionary of American Slang.* New York: Thomas Y. Crowell, 1975.

Fanon, Frantz. *The Wretched of the Earth.* New York: Grove Press, 1963.

Foucault, Michel. *Discipline and Punish: The Birth of the Prison.* New York: Pantheon Books, 1977.

Fowler, Roger. "Anti-Language in Fiction." *Style, 13* (1979): 259–277.

Fowler, Roger, Hodge, Bob, Kress, Gunther, and Trew, Tony. *Language and Control.* London: Routledge & Kegan Paul, 1979.

Fox, Vernon. *Violence Behind Bars.* Westport, Conn.: Greenwood Press, 1956.

Freire, Paolo. *Pedagogy of the Oppressed.* Translated by Myra Bergman Ramos. New York: Seabury Press, 1968.

Freud, Sigmund. *Beyond the Pleasure Principle.* New York: Liveright Publishing Corporation, 1950.

Gagnon, John H. and Simon, William. "The Social Meaning of Prison Homosexuality." *Federal Probation, 32* (1968): 23–29.

Garfinkel, Harold. *Studies in Ethnomethodology.* Englewood Cliffs: Prentice-Hall, 1967.

Giallombardo, Rose. *Society of Women.* New York: John Wiley, 1966.

———. *The Social World of Imprisoned Girls.* New York, John Wiley & Sons, 1974.

Giglioli, Pier Paolo, ed. *Language and Social Context: Selected Readings.* New York: Penguin Books, 1979.

Glaser, Daniel. *The Effectiveness of a Prison and Parole System.* New York: Bobbs-Merrill Company, 1969.

Goffman, Erving. *Asylums.* New York: Anchor Books, 1961.

———. *Encounters.* Indianapolis, Indiana: Bobbs-Merrill Company, 1961.

———. *The Presentation of Self in Everyday Life.* Garden City, N.Y.: Doubleday Anchor Books, 1959.

———. *Stigma: Notes on the Management of Spoiled Identity.* Englewood Cliffs, N.J.: Prentice-Hall, 1965.

———. *Strategic Interaction.* Philadelphia: University of Pennsylvania Press, 1969.

Goldin, Hyman, ed. *Dictionary of American Underworld Lingo.* New York: Twayne Publishers, Inc., 1950.

Grayzel, John Aron. "The Functions of Play and the Play Motif at a State Penitentiary." In Michael A. Salter, ed. *Play: Anthropological Perspectives*, pp. 94–103. West Point, N.Y.: Leisure Press, 1978.

Griswold, H. Jack, Misenheimer, Mike, Powers, Art, and Tromanhauser, Ed. *An Eye for an Eye*. New York: Holt, Rinehart and Winston, 1970.

Grose, Francis. *A Classical Dictionary of the Vulgar Tongue*. Edited by Eric Partridge. London: The Alcuin Press, 1931.

Gumperz, John J. and Hymes, Dell. *Directions in Sociolinguistics*. New York: Holt, Rinehart and Winston, 1972.

Hall, Edward T. *The Hidden Dimension*. New York: Anchor Books, 1969.

_____. *The Silent Language*. Westport, Conn.: Greenwood Press, 1980.

Halliday, M. A. K. "Anti-Languages." *American Anthropologist*, 78 (September, 1976): 570–584.

Haney, C., Banks, C., and Zimbardo, P. "Interpersonal Dynamics in a Simulated Prison." *International Journal of Criminology and Penology*, 1973.

Hayden, Marie Gladys. "Terms of Disparagement in American Dialect." *Dialect Notes*, 4 (1915): 194–223.

Heffernan, Esther. *Making It in Prison*. New York: John Wiley, 1972.

Hertzler, Joyce O. *A Sociology of Language*. New York: Random House, 1965.

Hoffman, Ethan. *Concrete Mama: Prison Profiles from Walla Walla*. Text by John McCoy; photographs by Ethan Hoffman. Columbia: University of Missouri Press, 1981.

Hoijer, Harry, ed. *Language in Culture*. Chicago: University of Chicago Press, 1954.

Holt, Norman and Miller, Donald. *Exploration in Inmate – Family Relationships*. Sacramento: California Department of Corrections. Research Division, 1976.

Hopper, Columbus. "Sexual Adjustment in Prison." *Police*, 15 (1971) :75–76.

Hudson, Julius. "The Hustling Ethic." In Thomas Kochman, ed. *Rappin' and Stylin' Out*. pp. 410–424. Urbana: University of Illinois Press, 1972.

Huffman, Arthur V. "Problems Precipitated by Homosexual Approaches on Youthful First Offenders." *Journal of Social Therapy*, 7 (1961): 170–181.

Huizinga, Johan. *Homo Ludens: A Study of the Play Element in Culture*. Boston: Beacon Press, 1950.

Hymes, Dell. *Foundations in Sociolinguistics: An Ethnographic Approach*. Philadelphia: University of Pennsylvania Press, 1974.

Irwin, Godfrey, ed. *American Tramp and Underworld Slang*. New York: Sears Publishing Company, Inc., n.d.

Irwin, John. *The Felon*. Englewood Cliffs, N.J.: Prentice-Hall, 1970.

_____. *Prisons in Turmoil*. Boston: Little, Brown and Company, 1980.

Irwin, John and Cressey, Donald R. "Thieves, Convicts and the Inmate Culture." *Social Problems*, X (Fall, 1963): 142–55.

Iverson, William. "A Short History of Swearing." *Playboy*, 8 (September, 1961): 101.

Jackson, Bruce. *In the Life: Versions of the Criminal Experience*. New York: Holt, Rinehart and Winston, 1972.

———. "Prison Folklore." *Journal of American Folklore*, LXXVII: 310 (October–December, 1965): 317–329.

———. *A Thief's Primer*. Toronto, Ontario: Collier, Macmillan Company, Ltd., 1969.

Jackson. George. *Soledad Brothers*. New York: Bantam Books, 1970.

Jacobs, James B. *Stateville: The Penitentiary in Mass Society*. Chicago: The University of Chicago Press, 1977.

Jacobs, James B. and Retsky, Harold G. "Prison Guards." *Urban Life, 4* (1975): 5–29.

Johnson, Burges. *The Lost Art of Profanity*. New York: Bobbs-Merrill, 1948.

Johnson, Falk. "The History of Some 'Dirty' Words," *American Mercury, 71* (November, 1950): 538–545.

Kantrowitz, Nathan. "The Vocabulary of Race Relations in Prisons." *Publications of the American Dialect Society, 51* (1969): 23–24.

Kilpatrick, James. *The Smut Peddlers*. Garden City, N.Y.: Doubleday, 1960.

Klein, Nicholas. "Hobo Lingo." *American Speech, 1* (1926): 650–653.

Knight, Etheridge. *Black Voices from Prison*. New York: Pathfinder Press, 1970.

Kochman, Thomas, ed. *Rappin' and Stylin' Out*. Urbana: University of Illinois Press, 1972.

Kress, Gunther and Hodge, Robert. *Language as Ideology*. London: Routledge and Kegan Paul, 1979.

LaBarre, Weston. "Obscenity: An Anthropological Appraisal." *Law and Contemporary Problems, 20* (Autumn, 1955): 535–543.

Labov, William. "Rules for Ritual Insults." In Thomas Kochman, ed. *Rappin' and Stylin' Out*, pp. 265–314. Urbana: University of Illinois Press, 1972.

Lancy, David F. and Tindall, B. Allan, eds. *The Anthropological Study of Play: Problems and Prospects*. Cornwall, New York: Leisure Press, 1976.

Leech, Kenneth. *Youth Quake: The Growth of a Counter-Culture Through Two Decades*. Totowa, N.J.: Littlefield, Adams & Co., 1977.

Lewis, C. S. *The Allegory of Love*. New York: Oxford University Press, 1958.

Lewis, Orlando F. *The Development of American Prisons and Prison Customs, 1776–1845*. Montclair, N.J.: Patterson Smith, 1967.

Lewis, Roger. *Outlaws of America: The Underground Press and Its Context*. Middlesex, England: Penguin Books Ltd., 1972.

Lexicon Balatronicum: A Dictionary of Buckish Slang, University Wit, and Pickpocket Eloquence. (Compiled originally by Captain Frances Grose. London: C. Choppell, 1811.) Unabridged from the original edition with a foreword by Robert Cromie. Northfield, Illinois: Digest Books, 1971.

Liston, Robert A. *The Edge of Madness*. New York: Franklin Watts, Inc. 1972.

MacNamara. Donal E. J. and Sagarin, Edward. *Perspectives on Corrections*. New York: Thomas Y. Crowell Company, 1971.

Major. Clarence. *Dictionary of Afro-American Slang*. New York: International Publishers, 1970.

Malcolm X. *The Autobiography of Malcolm X*. New York: Grove Press, 1964.

Mandel, Jerry. "The Santa Fe Prison Riots." *Agenda: A Journal of Hispanic Issues, 10* (1980): 4–10.

Martin, Bob. "The Massachusetts Correctional System: Treatment as an Ideology for Control." *Crime and Social Justice* (1976): 49–57.

Maryland, James. "Shoe-shine on 63rd." In Thomas Kockman, ed. *Rappin' and Stylin' Out*, pp. 209–214. Urbana: University of Illinois Press, 1972.

Mathiesen, Thomas. *The Politics of Abolition*. Oslo, Norway: M. Robertson, 1974.

May, Rollo. *Power and Innocence: A Search for the Sources of Violence*. New York: W. W. Norton, 1972.

Maurer, David W. *The American Confidence Man*. Springfield, Ill.: Charles C Thomas, 1973.

———. "The Argot of the Confidence Man." *American Speech, 15* (April, 1940): 115–123.

———. "The Argot of Forgery." *American Speech, 16* (December, 1941): 243–250.

———. "The Argot of Pickpockets." In *Language of the Underworld*, pp. 234–256. Lexington: University of Kentucky Press, 1981.

———. "The Argot of the Three-Shell Game." *American Speech, 22* (October, 1947): 161–170.

———. "The Argot of the Underworld." In *Language of the Underworld*, pp. 37–58. Lexington: University of Kentucky Press, 1981.

———. "The Argot of the Underworld Narcotic Addict." *Language of the Underworld*, pp. 83–110. Lexington: University of Kentucky Press, 1981.

———. "The Australian Element in American Criminal Argots." In *Language of the Underworld*, pp. 141–155. Lexington: University of Kentucky Press, 1981.

———. *The Big Con: The Story of the American Confidence Man and the Confidence Game*. New York: New American Library, 1963.

———. "Circus and Carnival Argot." In *Language of the Underworld*, pp. 24–36. Lexington: University of Kentucky Press, 1981.

———. "The Laying of the Note or You *Can* Cheat an Honest Man." In M. Estellie Smith, ed., *Studies in Linguistics*, pp. 324–343. The Hague, Netherlands: Mouton & Company, 1972.

———. *Language of the Underworld*. Collected and edited by Allan W. Futrell and Charles B. Wordell. Lexington: University of Kentucky Press, 1981.

———. "The Lingo of the Good-People." *American Speech, 10* (1935): 10–23.

———. "The Lingo of the Jug-Heavy." In *Language of the Underworld*, pp. 59–67. Lexington: University of Kentucky Press, 1981.

———. "Marijuana Users and Their Lingo." In *Language of the Underworld*, pp. 156–161. Lexington: University of Kentucky Press, 1981.

———. *Narcotics and Narcotics Addiction*. Springfield, Ill.: Charles C Thomas, 1973.

———. "The Nature of the Confidence Games." *Encyclopedia Americana*, 1968.

———. "The Nature of Slang." *The Encyclopedia Britannica*, 1973.

———. "Prostitutes and Criminal Argots." *American Journal of Sociology, 44* (January, 1939): 546–550.

_____. *Whiz Mob: A Correlation of the Argot of Professional Pickpockets with Their Behavior*. New Haven: College and University Press, 1964.

Mayer, J. P. *Alexis de Tocqueville: A Biographical Study in Political Science*. Gloucester, Mass.: Peter Smith, 1966.

Mencken, H. L. *The American Language*, Fourth edition. Abridged and Annotated by Raven I. McDavid, Jr., with the assistance of David W. Maurer, New York: Alfred A. Knopf, 1963.

Menninger, Karl. *The Crime of Punishment*. New York: Viking Press, 1968.

Miller, Walter. "Lower Class Culture as a Generating Milieu of Gang Delinquency." In David O. Arnold, ed., *The Sociology of Subculture*, pp. 54–63. Berkeley: Glendessary Press, 1970.

Milner, Christina. *Black Players: The Secret World of Black Pimps*. New York: Bantam Books, 1973.

Mitford, Jessica. *Kind and Usual Punishment*. New York: Alfred A. Knopf, 1973.

Moore, Joan W. *Homeboys*. Philadelphia: Temple University Press, 1978.

Morris, Pauline. *Prisoners and Their Families*. London: George Allen and Unwin, Ltd., 1965.

Moynahan, J. M. and Stewart, Earle K. *The American Jail*. Chicago: Nelson-Hall, 1980.

Murton, Thomas. *Accomplices to the Crime*. New York: Grove Press, 1969.

Nelson, Victor. *Prison Days and Nights*. Boston: Little, Brown, 1933.

New York State Special Commission on Attica. *Attica*. New York: Bantam Books, 1972.

Opie, Iona and Opie, Peter. *The Lore and Language of School Children*. London: Oxford University Press, 1967.

Palmore, Erdman B. "Ethnophaulism's and Ethnocentrism." *American Journal of Sociology, 67* (1962): 442–445.

Partridge, Eric. *A Dictionary of Slang and Unconventional English*. Sixth Edition. New York: The Macmillan Company, 1967.

_____. *A Dictionary of the Underworld, British and American*. London: Routledge & Kegan Paul, 1950.

_____. *Slang: Today and Yesterday*. New York: Bonanza Books, 1950.

Patterson, H. and Conrad, E. *Scotsboro Boy*. New York: Garden City Press, 1952.

Thomas, Piri. *Down These Mean Streets*. New York: Alfred A. Knopf, 1967.

Ramsey, Bruce and Gettinger, Stephen. "Washington State Seeks a Return to Normalcy." *Corrections Magazine* (June, 1981): 33–37.

Reich, Charles A. *The Greening of America*. New York: Bantam Books, 1971.

Rieger, Wolfram. "A Proposal for a Trial of Family Therapy and Conjugal Visits in Prison." *American Journal of Orthopsychiatry, 43* (1973): 118.

Rogers, K. M. *The Troublesome Helpmate: A History of Misogyny in Literature*, Seattle: University of Washington Press, 1966.

Roth, Loren H. "Territoriality and Homosexuality in a Male Prison Population." *American Journal of Orthopsychiatry, 41* (1971): 510–513.

Rothman, David J. *Conscience and Convenience: The Asylum and Its Alternatives in Progressive America*. Boston: Little, Brown, 1980.

———. *The Discovery of the Asylum: Social Order and Disorder in the Republic*. Boston: Little, Brown, 1971.

Roszak, Theodore. *The Making of a Counter Culture*. Garden City, N.Y.: Anchor Books, 1969.

Rudovsky, David, Bronstein, Alvin J., and Koren, Edward I. *The Rights of Prisoners*. New York: Avon, 1977.

Sagarin, Edward. *The Anatomy of Dirty Words*. New York: Lyle Stuart, 1962.

———, ed. *Deviance and Social Change*. Beverly Hills: Sage Publications, 1977.

———. "Prison Homosexuality and Its Effect on Post-Prison Behavior." *Psychiatry,* 39 (1976):

Salter, Michael A., ed. *Play: Anthropological Perspectives*. West Point, N.Y.: Leisure Press, 1978.

Sapir, Edward. *Language*. New York: Harcourt, Brace, 1949.

———. *Selected Writings in Language, Culture and Personality*. Berkeley: University of California Press, 1951.

Sapir, J. David and Crocker, J. Christopher. *The Social Uses of Metaphor*. Philadelphia: University of Pennsylvania Press, 1977.

Scacco, Anthony M. *Rape in Prison*. Springfield, Ill.: Charles C Thomas, 1975.

Schmidt, J. E. *Narcotics Lingo and Lore*. Springfield, Ill.: Charles C Thomas, 1959.

Schneller, Donald P. *The Prisoner's Family*. San Francisco: R and R Research Associates, 1976.

Schrag, Clarence. "Social Types in a Prison Community." Masters Thesis. University of Washington, 1944.

Sellin, J. Thorsten. *Slavery and the Penal System*. New York, Elsevier, 1976.

Selling, Lowell S. "The Pseudo Family." *American Journal of Sociology,* 37 (September, 1931): 247–253.

Serrill, Michael S., and Katel, Peter. "Anatomy of a Riot: The Facts Behind New Mexico's Bloody Ordeal." *Corrections Magazine* (April, 1980): 7–16, 20–24.

Sheehan, Susan. *A Prison and a Prisoner*. Boston: Houghton Mifflin Company, 1978.

Showalter, David and Williams Jones, Charlotte. "Marital and Family Counseling in Prisons." *Social Work,* 25 (1980): 224–228.

Silberman, Charles. *Criminal Violence, Criminal Justice*. New York: Random House, 1978.

Spradley, James P. and McCurdy, David W. *Conflict and Conformity: Readings in Cultural Anthropology*. Boston: Little, Brown and Company, 1974.

———. *The Cultural Scene: Ethnography in a Complex Society*. Chicago: Science Research Associates, 1972.

Spradley, James P. *You Owe Yourself a Drunk: An Ethnography of Urban Nomads*. Boston: Little, Brown and Company, 1970.

Stastney, Charles and Tyrnauer, Gabrielle. *Who Rules the Joint?* Lexington, Mass.: Lexington Books, D. C. Heath and Company, 1982.

Steadman, John Marcellus. "A Study of Verbal Taboos." *American Speech, 10* (April, 1935): 93–103.

Studt, Elliott, Messinger, Sheldon L., and Wilson, Thomas P. *C-Unit: Search for Community in Prison.* New York: Russell Sage Foundation, 1968.

Sutherland, Edwin, ed. *The Professional Thief.* Chicago: University of Chicago Press, 1937.

Sykes, Gresham M. *A Society of Captives: A Study of a Maximum Security Prison.* Princeton, New Jersey: Princeton University Press, 1958.

Sykes, Gresham M. and Messinger, Sheldon. *Inmate Social System.* Theoretical Studies in Social Organization. Social Science Research Council, 1960.

Szasz, Thomas S. *The Myth of Mental Illness.* New York: Harper & Row, 1974.

Toch, Hans. *Violent Men: An Inquiry into the Psychology of Violence.* Chicago: Aldine, 1969.

Toelken, Barre. *The Dynamics of Folklore.* Boston: Houghton Mifflin, 1979.

Trager, George L. and Smith, Henry L., Jr. *An Outline of English Structure.* Washington, D.C.: American Council of Learned Societies, 1956.

Tyrnauer, Gabrielle, "What Went Wrong at Walla Walla?" *Corrections Magazine* (June, 1981): 37–41.

Tyrnauer, Gabrielle and Stastney, Charles. "The Changing Political Culture of a Total Institution: The Case of Walla Walla." *Prison Journal, 57* (Autumn–Winter, 1977): 43–53.

Vedder, Clyde B. and King, Patricia G. *Problems of Homosexuality in Corrections.* Springfield, Ill.: Charles C Thomas, 1967.

Waddell, Jack O. and Watson, O. Michael. *The American Indian in Urban Society.* Boston: Little, Brown and Company, 1971.

Washbrook, R. A. "The Homeless Offender: An English Study of 200 Cases." *International Journal of Offender Therapy and Comparative Criminology, 19* (1975): 270–274.

Washington State. *Employees' Manual for Mens' Correctional Institutions.* Olympia: Department of Social and Health Services, Office of Personnel and Training, n.d.

———. *Report: An Analysis of Program Needs of Prison Inmates in Washington State.* Olympia: Department of Social and Health Services, April, 1980.

———. *Washington State Penitentiary, Walla Walla, Washington.* Olympia: Department of Institutions, Division of Adult Corrections, n.d.

Weiss, Carl and Friar, David James. *Terror in Prisons: Homosexual Rape and Why Society Condones It.* Indianapolis & New York: Bobbs-Merrill, 1974.

Wepman, Dennis, Newman, Ronald B., and Binderman, Murray B. *The Life: The Lore and Folk Poetry of the Black Hustler.* Philadelphia: University of Pennsylvania Press, 1976.

Westley, William A. "Secrecy and the Police." *Social Forces, 34* (March 1956): 254–257.

———. "Violence and the Police." *American Journal of Sociology, 59* (July, 1953): 34–41.

Whorf, Benjamin Lee. *Language, Thought, and Reality.* New York: John Wiley & Sons, Inc., and Technology Press of M.I.T., 1959.

Wicker, Tom. *A Time to Die.* New York: Ballantine Books, 1975.

Wicks, Robert J. *Guard! Society's Professional Prisoner.* Houston: Gulf Publishing Company, 1980.

Williams, Virgil and Fish, Mary. *Convicts, Codes and Contraband.* Cambridge: Ballinger Publishing Company, 1974.

Wilson, Rob. "The Mentally Ill Offender: A Growing Debate Over the 'Mad and Bad.'" *Corrections Magazine* (December, 1980): 5–17.

Wolfgand, Marvin E., ed. *Prisons: Present and Possible.* Lexington, Mass.: Lexington Books, D. C. Heath and Company, 1979.

Wright, Erik Olin. *The Politics of Punishment.* New York: Harper Row, 1973.

Yee, Ming S. *The Melancholy History of Soledad Prison.* New York: Harper's Magazine Press, 1973.

INDEX